MATERIALS HANDLING

Principles and Practice

MATERIALS HANDLING

Principles and Practice

Theodore H. Allegri, Sr.

CBS Publishers & Distributors Pvt. Ltd.

New Delhi • Bengaluru • Chennai • Kochi • Kolkata • Mumbai
Hyderabad • Uttarakhand • Nagpur • Patna • Pune • Jharkhand

ISBN: 81-239-0840-7

First Indian Edition: 1987
Reprint: 2002, 2004

Published by **Satish Kumar Jain** and produced by **Varun Jain** for
CBS Publishers & Distributors Pvt. Ltd.,
4819/XI Prahlad Street, 24 Ansari Road, Daryaganj, New Delhi - 110002
delhi@cbspd.com, cbspubs@airtelmail.in • www.cbspd.com
Ph.: 23289259, 23266861, 23266867 • Fax: 011-23243014

Corporate Office: 204 FIE, Industrial Area, Patparganj, Delhi - 110 092
Ph: 49344934 • Fax: 011-49344935
E-mail: publishing@cbspd.com • publicity@cbspd.com

Branches:

- ***Bengaluru:*** 2975, 17th Cross, K.R. Road, Bansankari 2nd Stage, Bengaluru - 70 • Ph: +91-80-26771678/79 • Fax: +91-80-26771680 E-mail: cbsbng@gmail.com, bangalore@cbspd.com
- ***Chennai:*** No. 7, Subbaraya Street, Shenoy Nagar, Chennai - 600030 Ph: +91-44-26681266, 26680620 • Fax: +91-44-42032115 E-mail: chennai@cbspd.com
- ***Kochi:*** Ashana House, 39/1904, A.M. Thomas Road, Valanjambalam, Ernakulum, Kochi • Ph: +91-484-4059061-65 Fax: +91-484-4059065 • E-mail: cochin@cbspd.com
- ***Kolkata:*** 6-B, Ground Floor, Rameshwar Shaw Road, Kolkata - 700014 Ph: +91-33-22891126/7/8 • E-mail: kolkata@cbspd.com
- ***Mumbai:*** 83-C, Dr. E. Moses Road, Worli, Mumbai - 400018 Ph: +91-9833017933, 022-24902340/41 • E-mail: mumbai@cbspd.com

Representatives:

- Hyderabad: 0-9885175004
- Patna: 0-9334159340
- Jharkhand: 0-9811541605
- Nagpur: 0-9021734563
- Pune: 0-9623451994
- Uttarakhand: 0-9716462459

Printed at:
J.S. Offset Printers, Delhi (India)

Preface

There is a proliferation of books and printed materials in the technical world today. Much of what is written is of great value and contributes to the advance of our technological society. Many works, however, are so abstruse in their composition that they have appeal or value only to small, select, and elitist groups. This work, however, transcends this limited milieu; it has a broad scope that cuts across the many lines of physical distribution to present the theoretical aspects of the subject in a way that is of basic value to every practitioner of the arts of materials handling and management.

The author's background in the subject field is as broad as the scope of this text. He has been able to draw upon his experiences as an industrial engineer and as a director of the Packaging Division with the Federal Supply Service; as a marketing research manager with Towmotor, forklift truck maker, a subsidiary of Caterpillar Tractor Company; and, as a materials handling manager and manager of physical distribution for the Caterpillar Tractor Company in its world headquarters. Mr. Allegri has conducted seminars in materials handling and materials management and has been a speaker at many of the national conferences of the Materials Handling Institute.

This book is recommended to its readers as a means for advancing understanding of the state of the art of physical distribution and as a means for enhancing the productivity and cost-effectiveness of the materials handling and materials management of their organizations.

Contents

MATERIALS HANDLING

Principles and Practice

Chapter 1
The Systems Concept of Materials Handling

I. INTRODUCTION TO MATERIALS HANDLING

The Industrial Revolution which occurred during the late eighteenth and early nineteenth centuries saw the beginning of the "factory system." This was, generally speaking, the beginning of modern industry as we know it today. It contrasted sharply with the "domestic system," or the system of household industry and the type of family employment that was commonly practiced under the medieval and Renaissance trade guilds. It is not that there were no factories before the Industrial Revolution, since there were many small factories and some fairly large workshops prior to that time. The division or contrast between domestic industry and the factory system lies chiefly in the fact that steam power and machines began to be employed in order to vastly increase manpower and productivity per man-hour of the individual worker.

As the factory system developed, the need for materials handling also developed. This was true in both manufacturing and distribution operations. Thus, factory and warehouse owners and operators began to spend money for labor-saving devices to handle materials.

Although materials handling does not add value to a product, it usually adds a significant element of cost. There are varying estimates as to how much materials handling actually costs; these range from 20% to 35% of the cost of the product. However, there are exceptions to this general rule. For example, in a chemical plant there is very little labor input; most of the materials handling is performed by tanks and pipes and other fixed equipment. In this instance, naturally, there would be very little cost per unit of output. On the other hand, an industry in which there would be fairly significant costs for materials handling is food processing, where each unit of product is handled and inspected many times before it arrives at its final destination, the consumer's platter. Even in these two industry examples, however, the matter of the precise cost of materials handling is relatively vague.

One difficulty in selling materials handling projects to top management is the lack of precise measurements concerning the actual cost of materials handling. The selling of these projects will be discussed in a later chapter; however, for the time being we should realize that one central concern of materials handling engineers is the matter of obtaining the detailed information needed to support their conclusions. This is necessary in order to focus management attention on the problem and convince company decision makers of the need for action.

Many company managers realize that materials handling costs are high but think that most of this cost is inevitable and cannot be easily avoided. Despite the rising costs of indirect labor—that is, materials handling labor—and despite many technological improvements by equipment manufacturers, many companies have failed to accord to materials handling the recognition it deserves. It is the purpose of this text, therefore, to assist its readers in developing the skills they have in this important field in order to communicate the need for their companies to change to the systems approach to materials handling.

II. THE SYSTEMS CONCEPT

Experienced materials handling practitioners know that companies run the gamut from those that have neglected replacing obsolete equipment to those that install the most modern equipment without regard to the question of utilization or payback. If the proper tools are used for systematic analysis of materials handling problems, no system or equipment will be installed without having as one of its basic criteria an adequate monetary payback—all other things being equal. Stated simply, we must avoid extremes, and we must use a method commensurate with the scale of the problem, in order to obtain the *least total cost of materials handling.*

The systems approach to materials handling demands that all elements of the chain of cause and effect be analyzed so we may accomplish our objectives.

Systematic analysis or the systems approach to materials handling demands that our solutions to materials handling problems satisfy certain important conditions, as follows:

1. That they resolve more problems than they create; that they do not transfer the problems into other areas; and that the amount of return on investment adequately justifies the solution.
2. That they not only resolve the immediate problems, but that they take care of the problems for a reasonably long period of time; and that they readily permit expansion, modification, or necessary change without unreasonable cost—in other words, that they will not become obsolete too rapidly.
3. That the solutions are as simple as it is possible to make them; for, if they are simple, acceptance on the part of management and everyone else concerned, *including the operators,* is more palatable and, therefore, more easily and more rapidly achieved.

The best solution to materials handling problems does not usually come very easily. But, it generally comes about by a systematic analysis of pertinent factors; by examining, insofar as it is possible to do so, the total system; and by applying the proper technique or techniques from a broad range of disciplines.

The important consideration is that the technique, or the method, should fit the application and be commensurate in value with the scope of the problem undergoing analysis.

With the proper perspective distilled from all the factors involved, the least total cost of the system can be developed. And, that is the ultimate objective of the systems approach to materials handling.

III. DEFINITION AND SCOPE OF MATERIALS HANDLING

Whenever material is moved in a manufacturing, distribution (warehouse), or office environment, materials handling occurs. Also, in the vast sea, air, and land transportation network, materials handling occurs in the various aspects of preparing merchandise for shipment, in order filling, and in moving materials in and out of carriers, be they private, government, or commercial.

In order to see the various elements of handling in their proper perspective and not to confuse the woods with the trees, we must look at the broad field of materials handling through a systems approach, by examining the layers, or strata, in which handling occurs.

1. In the first layer we have the man or woman handling the individual part, workpiece, or unit.
2. In the second layer we have the room, department, or plant in which handling takes place.
3. In the third layer we have the complete handling system, composed of a chain of events that could very well start with the supplier, or the raw material source, and go through the factory and distribution network to the ultimate consumer and beyond, to waste disposal and recycling of any part of the material or object received by the consumer.

The three layers are indicated in Fig. 1-1. It is necessary to observe each layer very carefully and, by a process of systematic analysis and integration, to combine all three layers so that the broad base of the system may be firmly constructed.

IV. SOME BASIC PRINCIPLES

As mentioned above, materials handling comprises 20% to 35% of the cost of a manufactured product, more often than not; and for agricultural products and foodstuffs, this figure may sometimes be much higher.

Since materials handling is such a large element of cost, the materials handling engineer's primary function is to eliminate or minimize handling. His

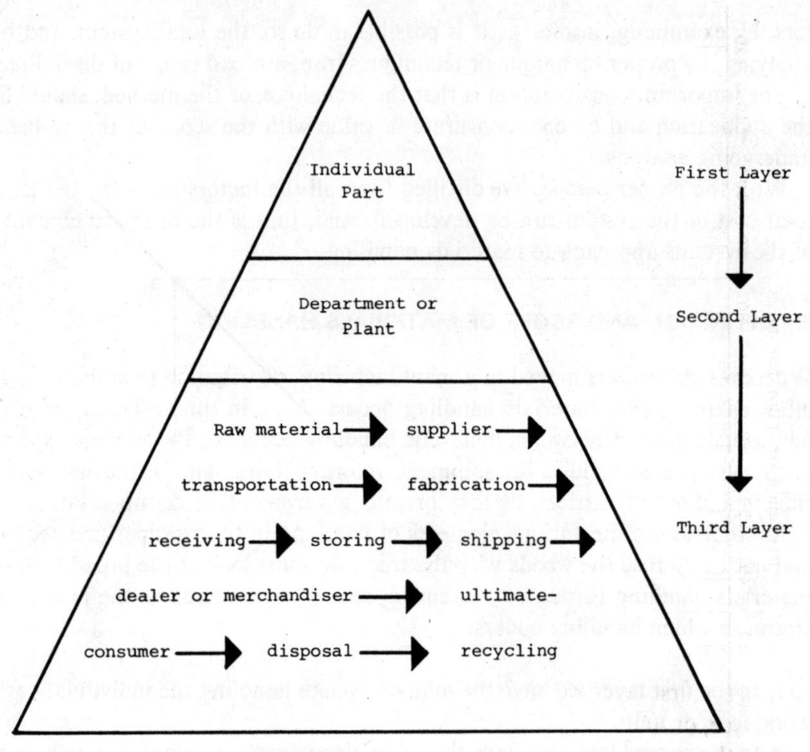

Fig. 1-1. The strata involved in the systems approach to materials handling.

motto could very well be, "The best handling is the least handling!" This, then, becomes one of our targets, and there are many of these targets in every plant. Even when factories and warehouses become fully automatic, we shall still be able to refine systems and programs, and the software and hardware of automatic and computerized installations. But, more about these things in a later chapter. Suffice it to say that since materials handling is concerned with the movement of materials, every movement has to have a *pick-up* and *set-down,* and most of the time there is a *transportation distance* between these two points.

Since the pick-up costs and the set-down costs are relatively fixed, the variable we have to manipulate is the transportation distance between the two points.

Figure 1-2 illustrates the importance of shortening the transportation distance. *As the distance or time factor increases, the cost per unit of product handled increases* (provided all other factors remain the same). For example, the handling in (A) is less expensive than the handling in (B) in Fig. 1-2.

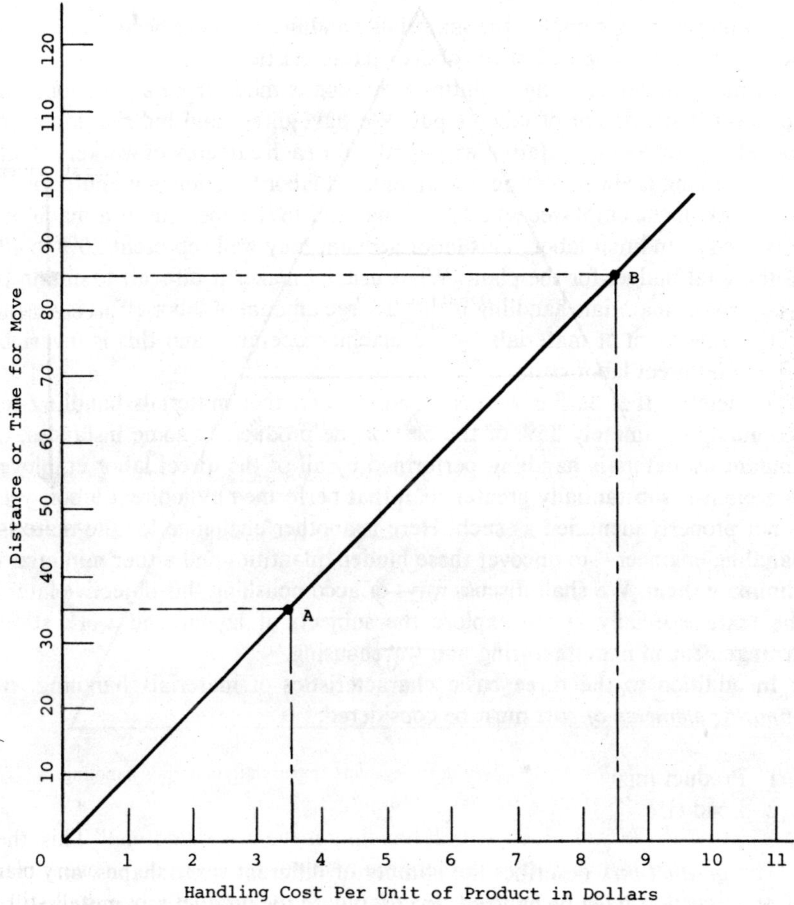

Fig. 1-2. Handling cost versus distance or time.

As we can clearly see from Fig. 1-2, when the cost of picking up materials and setting them down is fixed, the only variable is the distance or time it takes to go from the initial pick-up point to the point of storing, stacking, or depositing the load.

It can be said that there are *three basic characteristics of materials handling:*

1. Picking up the load
2. Transporting the load
3. Setting the load down

No matter how complex the materials handling problem becomes, its basic ingredients are composed of the above characteristics.

In many manufacturing facilities a division is made from a functional and accounting standpoint of labor input. We have direct and indirect labor personnel and, of course, differing wage scales for each category of workers. Materials handling is always considered an indirect labor function in manufacturing. The work of the employee who brings material to the operator at a machine is classified as indirect labor. This labor account may well represent 20% to 40% of the total budget for the plant. What usually makes it difficult to obtain the true costs of materials handling is that a large amount of labor effort is devoted to the movement of materials by the machine operator, and this is invariably hidden in direct labor costs.

Remember that earlier we discussed the fact that materials handling represents approximately 35% of the cost of the product. In some instances, the amount of materials handling performed by all of the direct labor employees in a plant is substantially greater than that performed by indirect labor, yet it is not properly identified as such! Here is another challenge for the materials handling engineer—to uncover these hidden quantities and either minimize or eliminate them. We shall discuss ways of accomplishing this objective later in the text, especially as we explore the subjects of layout and work station arrangement in manufacturing and warehousing.

In addition to the three basic characteristics of materials handling, *two opposing elements of cost* must be considered:

1. Product mix
2. Load size

The *product mix* describes the number of different sizes, shapes, and types of products that must be handled. Invariably, as the product mix increases, the cost of handling increases, because of the difficulty of handling products of several sizes. For example, if steel drums, cartons, and nonuniform pallet loads are received across the same receiving platform, the different methods and type of equipment used to handle these diverse items will add to the complexity and cost of handling. On the other hand, if only cartons of a certain size are handled, then the problem is simplified; and, handling equipment can be standardized, keeping costs per unit handled at a very low level. Thus, we can say that, "Keeping the product mix low keeps handling costs down!"

Load size can increase or decrease handling costs, depending on several factors. For example, as unit load sizes increase, handling costs usually decrease. It is less costly to handle a pallet load of bricks than to use a hod to carry them a few at a time from point to point. It is less costly, also, to transport a pallet load of flour sacks than to handle the sacks of flour individually. Also, it is much more economical, if the scale of the enterprise permits this, to handle the flour in bulk tank cars than to pack the flour in sacks and palletize the sacks. Thus it is a matter of degree; but, generally speaking, as the load size increases, the cost of handling decreases, provided the volume of materials handled justifies the cost of the equipment required to do the handling.

V. THE WHY AND HOW OF HANDLING

Commerce and industry have always thrived on competition. Unfortunately, although the consumer profits from keen competition among members of the business community, some manufacturing, or distribution, or retail merchants disappear from the business scene because they become submarginal producers or succumb to a number of overwhelming inefficiencies. One of the most prevalent inefficiencies is that of poor materials handling practice.

Current periodical literature supplies many examples of good materials handling practice, and new equipment is being invented and produced in relatively large numbers in many parts of the world. If it were just a question of reading the literature and buying new equipment, the world would have very little need for materials handling engineers. But, it is in putting together all the elements of the system that the materials handling engineer makes his largest contribution to the profit picture of any enterprise.

As competition increases in an industry, or from country to country, it is the relative efficiency of the materials handling system that, in the final analysis, helps achieve the objective of the least total cost of handling and gives the competitive edge to an organization.

In manufacturing, machine tool suppliers sell the same high speeds and feeds to your competitior that they sell to you. In warehousing, your competitor can use the same powered industrial trucks or the same high-rise, high-density storage racks or stacker-crane retrieval machine that you do. You have to stay competitive, therefore, by improving your materials handling system, all other factors being equal.

So, after we have eliminated mechanical equipment and mechanization from our equation, there remains the materials handling system. It is by the systems approach, therefore, that we are attempting to do the following:

A. Improve Production Operations

Production effectiveness can be increased by having "The right quantity of material, at the right place, at the right time." It is by eliminating or minimizing machine or operator time that many cost savings may be made, especially since an orderly flow of work through a plant increases the morale and productivity of the work force. By systematizing this flow, in a manner to be described later in the text, the maximum output or through-put may be readily established. In a later chapter also, we shall describe how to minimize or eliminate manual handling or powered industrial truck handling by semi-automatic and/or automatic processing.

B. Improve Indirect to Direct Labor Handling Ratios

There is an upward trend in most industry segments that reflects the growing labor force required to service and maintain increasingly complex equipment, for example, numerical controlled machine tools. There is another upward trend in the size of the labor force required to perform materials handling functions within the plant. One function of the systematic analysis of materials handling problems is to minimize unnecessary labor and make the enterprise more profitable so that the job security of the total work force is enhanced as the company's position is improved relative to a competitor's position.

C. Reduce Damage Due to Materials Handling

In-transit movements, either from suppliers to plant, from plant to plant, or in-plant, have a tendency to increase the level of damage that occurs to the product being handled. Suffice it to say that one of the cornerstones of good materials handling is a solid and well-conceived packaging program. This packaging program should encompass the type of containers, packaging method, identification of product, etc. This subject is discussed later in the text in more detail, since it is vital to successful handling.

Since scrap and rework can be costly, we should make every attempt to prevent such losses by the proper training of materials handlers and by getting good data on the costs of damage due to materials handling. When we know the scope of the problem and the type of damage that has occurred, we can take steps to minimize or eliminate it.

D. Maximize Space Utilization

Factory and warehouse space becomes more costly each year. It is even more costly when viewed from the standpoint of the dislocations and lost time that occur when a move is made or when plant expansion takes place.

In layout planning, therefore, the materials handling engineer should have a direct input into new projects, or for that matter, any project that affects the handling of parts in one way or another.

Materials handling is a vital part of layout planning, but of equal importance is the materials handling interdependency that is found in both production scheduling and inventory control. Somewhat later we shall discuss the materials management concept, and the reader, who is our materials handling practitioner, will see the effect that purchasing has on the materials handling effort.

For the time being, as we are proceeding in a step-by-step manner to develop a broad base for the systems approach to materials handling, it is necessary to have at least a nodding acquaintance with some of the factors that are related to the systems concept.

Therefore, when we talk about maximizing space utilization, we are saying that by discretions exercised by purchasing, and from production schedules that are related to inventory, we can do a much better job of materials handling in utilizing factory and warehouse space.

E. Reduce the Accident Rate and Severity of Injury

The fifth objective has to do with the worker himself, and it is placed last because it is often overlooked. The most important element of any materials handling project is the safety of the worker. Without due regard for this factor the systems concept becomes invalid and worthless. The real professional in this business makes safety his number one concern, always. Expert materials handling practice requires each job involving the movement of materials to become safer every time it is performed, rather than the reverse. In short, good practice should remove all factors that contribute to carelessness and an increase in the accident rate. I need not stress that insurance rates go up, also, in relation to the number of accidents that occur in a plant, and that time lost is not only measured in terms of the worker himself, but in all the detailed reporting that is required of supervisors and plant management. The new OSHA* requirements, also, bring the safety of materials handling practices into sharp focus, and we shall discuss this subject in its proper place as it affects handling.

EXERCISE NO. 1

To the reader: The following statements are of two types: (1) completion and (2) essay. It may be of some value and an enhancement of the learning process for you to attempt to fill in the blank spaces. The answers, of course, are all in the text. Each chapter concludes with statements that require completion, or questions to be answered. Whether or not you wish to spend time on these exercises is your decision. However, it has been found that exercises such as these strengthen one's recall, and in that sense they may be found profitable.

1. The Industrial Revolution began in the late ____________ and early ____________ centuries.

---

*OSHA: the Occupational Safety and Health Administration of the U.S. Department of Labor.

2. The contrast between domestic industry and the factory system lies chiefly in the fact that ____________ power and ____________ began to be employed in order to vastly increase manpower and productivity per man-hour.
3. As the factory system developed, the necessity for ____________ ____________ also developed.
4. Materials handling does not add ____________ to a product, but it is usually a significant element of ____________.
5. There are varying estimates as to how much materials handling actually costs; these range from ____________% to ____________% of the cost of the product.
6. One of the difficulties with selling materials handling projects to top management is the lack of precise ____________ concerning the actual cost of materials handling.
7. Many company managers realize that materials handling costs are high, but they feel that most of this cost is ____________ and cannot be easily ____________.
8. Many companies have failed to accord to materials handling the ____________ it deserves.
9. It is the purpose of this text to assist you in developing those skills you have in this important field in order to ____________ the need for your company to change to the ____________ ____________ ____________ ____________ ____________.
10. The systems approach to materials handling demands that our solutions to materials handling problems be scientifically precise and that they ____________ more problems than they create; that they do not ____________ the problems into other areas; and that the amount of return on investment adequately ____________ the solution.
11. The systems approach to materials handling demands that our solutions to materials handling problems be neat, in that they not only resolve the immediate problems, but that they take care of the problems for a ____________ ____________ period of time; and that they readily permit expansion, modification, or necessary change without ____________ cost.
12. The systems approach to materials handling demands that our solutions to materials handling problems be as simple as it is possible to make them; for, if they are simple, ____________ on the part of management and every one else concerned, including the operators, is more palatable and, therefore, more easily and more ____________ achieved.
13. The important consideration in applying the systems approach to materials handling is that the technique, or the method, should fit the application and be ____________ in value with the scope of the problem undergoing analysis.
14. The least total cost of materials handling is the ultimate objective of the ____________ ____________ to materials handling.
15. Whenever material is moved in a manufacturing, distribution (warehouse), or office environment, ____________ ____________ has occurred.

16. We must look at the broad field of materials handling in the ____________ ____________ by examining the layers, or strata, in which handling occurs.

17. The complete handling system is composed of a chain of events that could very well start with the ____________, or the raw material source, and go through the ____________ and distribution network to the ultimate ____________ and beyond, to waste disposal and recycling of any part of the material or object received by the consumer.

18. Since the pick-up costs and the set-down costs are relatively fixed, the variable we have to manipulate is the ____________ ____________ between the two points.

19. As the distance or time factor increases, the cost per unit of product handled ____________.

20. The three basic characteristics of materials handling are:
1. ____________
2. ____________
3. ____________

21. Two opposing elements of cost are:
1. ____________
2. ____________

22. The ____________ ____________ describes the number of different sizes, shapes, and types of products that must be handled.

23. As unit load sizes increase, handling costs usually ____________.

24. In this first chapter, five objectives of the systems approach to materials handling have been given. In your own words, after each of these objectives, explain what they mean to you:

A. Improve production operations:

____

____

____

____

____

B. Improve indirect to direct labor handling ratios:

____

____

____

____

____

C. Reduce damage due to materials handling:

____

____

____

____

____

D. Maximize space utilization:

E. Reduce the accident rate and severity of injury:

Chapter 2
Unit Load Handling

I. UNIT LOADS AND CONTAINERIZATION

A. Unit Loads

One of the most logical developments to evolve from the art and science of materials handling is the unit load concept—the handling of a quantity designed to be treated as a single mass—which is a simple outcome of mechanically assisted handling. Employing this concept, we can make the statement that, "The larger the mass moved, the lower the unit cost, all other things being equal."

The uniformity of individual items, and their ability to be stacked, or interlocked in a pallet pattern, or to be placed on a skid, also affect the size and effectiveness of a unit load.

There are usually four areas in both manufacturing and distribution where unit loads should be carefully considered: shipping, receiving, in-process handling, and storage.

There are some pitfalls in applying the unit load concept, however, and it would be well to discuss them at this time. In the first place, we should *never* use the unit load concept between successive work stations, unless no satisfactory alternate method is available. The reason is simply that time and energy have to be expended in neatly stacking the material on a pallet or skid load, or putting it into a container; and, subsequently the material requires destacking, or the material must be removed from the container. Whether to apply the unit load concept here also depends on two further considerations: (1) the quantity to be moved, and (2) the time interval between the operations at successive work stations.

If relatively large quantities of material are to be moved between successive operations, consideration should be given to conveyorizing the material between the two work stations. If this is not possible, then it would be well to explore the economic advantage of relocating the production equipment in order to conveyorize this transfer between the two points. Sometimes the product mix may militate against this mechanization, but at least it would pay to evaluate all of the pros and cons before going to the unit load concept or placing the material in containers. Even trays that fit on a skid (or on a conveyor) would be worth evaluating in such a situation.

As noted above, the time interval between successive operations may require that the material be stored for a certain period. If this is the case, then certainly the unit load method would be advantageous. The only problem in using this method would be that the production schedule might have to be rearranged to make successive operations follow in rapid and continuous succession; so the two points involved could include a bridging conveyor, chute, storage silo, mechanical manipulator,* or the like.

B. Containerization

We have been using the term unit load; however, the section heading combined the terms unit load and containerization because to many people they are virtually synonymous. This confusion is the second major pitfall to guard against because containers can be a many-headed monster in any plant operation, and, as we shall see, containers are a special kind of unit load.

By the time the correct container has been developed and/or evaluated, a succession of large purchases may have completely boxed in the company and committed it to a style and type of container that may not permit very much flexibility in handling in-plant, or between plants, and may not readily fit the present major product lines.

In one major corporation over 80 different container styles and sizes were being used. The company had, over the course of years, acquired a number of other, smaller companies. Each successive acquisition brought with it a number of different containers. Finally, because interplant shipping had become a nightmare, a container standardization program was initiated. At last count the company was down to about 40 container configurations and sizes. Fortunately, work is being carried out to reduce this number further.

Thus, there is a definite difference between the terms unit load and containerization. A unit load can be said to be any quantity designed to be picked up, transported, or stored in a single mass. Containerization, on the other hand, has a much broader connotation. Containers range in size from small, manually handled boxes, or trays used at a work station or stored in bins, to the mighty 40-foot-long seavans used in overseas shipping. One may hold ounces of product, whereas the other may carry many tons. In other words, one container may be a unit load, or it may take many containers to build up the load into a readily handled, economical unit.

In our discussions we shall cover the wide range of subjects represented by

*Mechanical manipulator: an industrial robot used to load and unload machines and perform highly repetitive and, generally speaking, unskilled tasks.

both unit loads and containerization. For the present, let us say that the range of container sizes in a plant should depend on both the individual piece parts to be handled and the volumes involved.

C. Container Programs

Some considerations in developing a plant container program are the following:

1. Limit the number of container sizes and configurations based upon the part sizes and volumes.
2. Keep in mind the need for flexibility.
3. Keep in mind the need for increasing inventory turnover.
4. Design the containers for maximum utilization.
5. Properly identify your containers.
6. Place tare weights on containers.
7. Develop purchase specifications for your containers.
8. Inspect containers at least on a sample basis, if not 100%, as they come to your plant from the fabricator.
9. Periodically, count all containers by category, i.e., at least annually.
10. Keep your containers cleaned and painted.
11. Consider color-coding containers by function.
12. Consider arrangements with suppliers and/or customers so that containers may be used for shipping, thereby eliminating or minimizing some of the requirements for packaging.
13. Consider the stacking features of rigid containers, nesting features of others, and, if collapsible containers are used, determine what kind of longevity you expect to obtain before purchasing any large quantity.
14. Wire-mesh containers are self-cleaning and are to be preferred to solid steel containers, especially where noise is a factor; depending on the type of wire-mesh container used, noise levels may be 5 to 15 decibels lower when parts are dropped into the container, compared to solid steel containers.
15. Wire-mesh containers also may be used advantageously for washing parts without removing them from the container.
16. Parts will dry and cool faster using wire-mesh containers rather than solid steel containers.
17. Wire-mesh and solid steel containers are to be preferred over wood, plastic, or corrugated containers for the sake of cleanliness and fire protection.

Illustrations of practical container and unit load applications are presented in Figs. 2-1 through 2-6, whose captions describe both the application and the

A

Fig. 2-1A and B. Corrugated steel tote boxes commonly used in heavy manufacturing; capacities may be 4,000 to 6,000 pounds. Courtesy Powell Pressed Steel Company, Hubbard, Ohio

terminology being used to designate each of the several types included in this chapter.

In addition to the 17 factors (listed above) affecting the design and selection of containers, there are structural and carrier spatial relationships that must be resolved by the materials handling engineer, as described below.

D. Structural Relationships to Be Considered

1. Floor load limits of the building, or storage area. (This is so whether the area is indoors or outdoors. Some soils upon which concrete slabs are

Fig. 2-1. *(continued)*

poured may have very low shear resistance and poor load-bearing capacity; this is mainly the case with alluvial soils, marshy locations, and former river bottom lands—land that in prehistoric times may have been covered with water and has retained many of its former, poor load-carrying characteristics.)

2. Building bay size and column spacing (take center-to-center column spacing and include width of columns).
3. Door sizes, i.e., height and width of entrances.
4. Elevator sizes and capacities, whether the unit load or container is transported by an industrial power truck or other transporting means.

Fig. 2-2. Seavan, 8′ × 8′ × 20′, conforming to the International Standards Organization; note the ISO corner locking fittings for ease in lifting and transporting by rail, sea, or highway. Capacity about 20 tons. Courtesy The Port Authority of New York and New Jersey.

Fig. 2-3. A rigid, noncollapsible heavy-duty, wire-mesh container for the handling, shipping, or storage of heavy castings, forgings, stampings, etc. Capacity about 5,000 pounds. Note drop-front. Courtesy Cargotainer Division of Tri-State Engineering Company, Washington, Pennsylvania.

Fig. 2-4. Another type of lighter duty, rigid wire-mesh, drop-front container. Courtesy Cargotainer Division of Tri-State Engineering Company, Washington, Pennsylvania.

5. Dock ramps and ramps inside the buildings that must be traversed.
6. Stacking heights within the building. In other words, how many tiers can be safely stacked in a given height?
7. Container or unit load stacking heights. That is, can the container be safely stacked upon itself, or must it be placed in tiering racks or storage racks?

E. Carrier Spatial Relationships to Be Considered

Figure 2-7 indicates some of the more common transportation equipment dimensions.

As you can see from the figure, there is a considerable range in both over-the-road carrier and railway car dimensions. To be universally acceptable a

Fig. 2-5A and B. Two types of stacking and knock-down type of tiering racks that help form unit loads.
A. Courtesy of Jarke Corporation, Niles, Illinois.

container or pallet is required to become, at best, a compromise between the in-plant characteristics and the means of transportation.

While unit loads and the transporting means are becoming larger, one of the disadvantages in this period of transition is that enough of the smaller modules remain in the system that it becomes necessary to provide for their use.

F. Objectives of Container Programs

The ultimate objectives of a manufacturing plant's container program are as follows:

B. Courtesy of Tier-Rack Corporation, St. Louis, Missouri.

1. To use the same standard container that has come from the (raw, or purchased finished) material supplier at the first point of use within the plant.
2. To store in-process materials in the same standard container, and transport materials intraplant without rehandling or changing them to a different container.
3. To ship interplant or to the customer in the same standard container.

It is not always possible to use the plant's standard containers in (1) and (3), above. Substitution of knocked-down containers, such as that shown in Fig. 2-

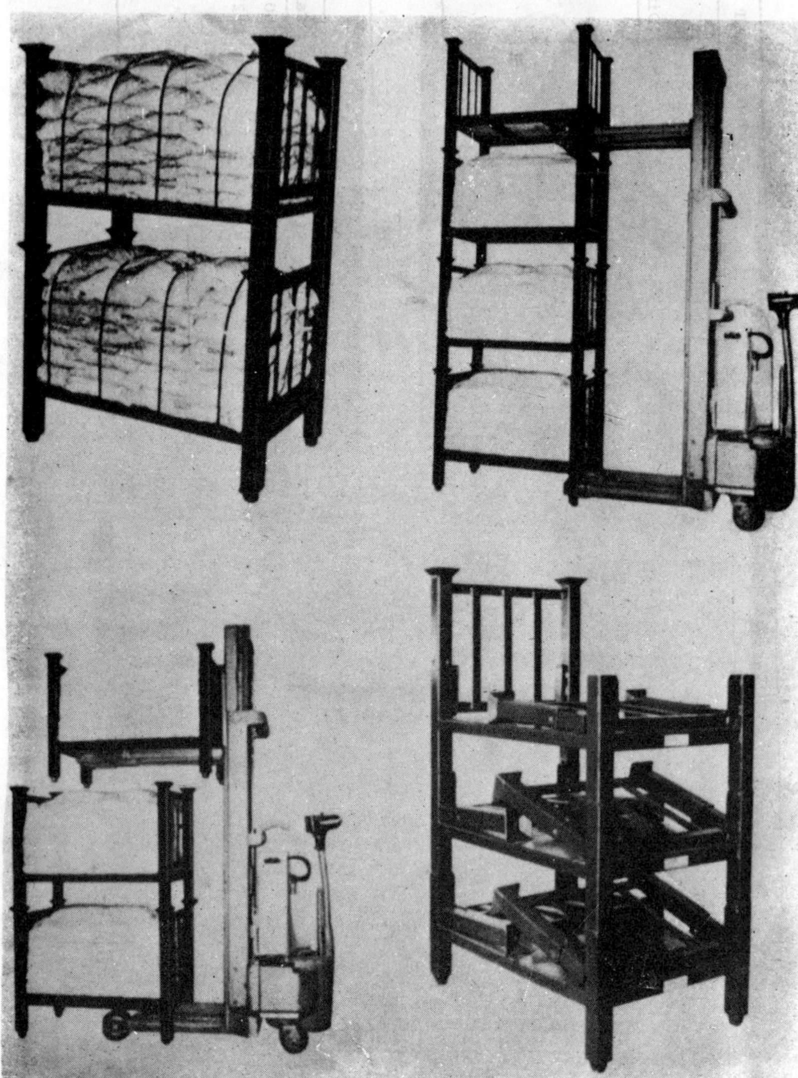

Fig. 2-6. Another type of knock-down, tiering rack. Courtesy, Jarke Corporation, Niles, Illinois.

Truck van dimensions - May vary with manufacturer

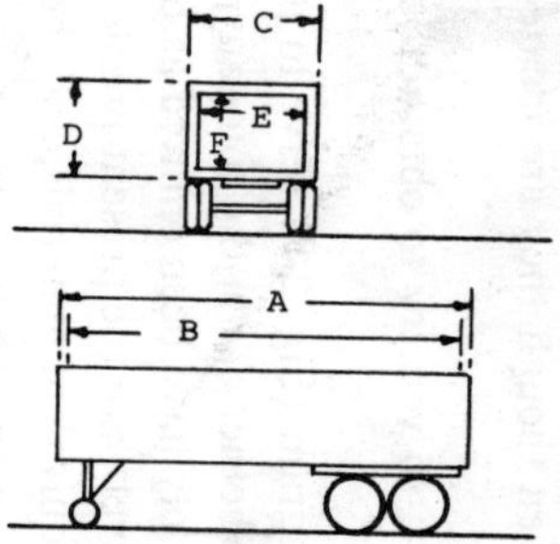

	DRY FREIGHT		REFRIGERATED FREIGHT	
	Approximate Range Available	Most Common Dimensions	Approximate Range Available	Most Common Dimensions
A Nominal Length	26' to 40'	40'	30'6" to 40'	40'
B Inside Length	25'7-5/8" to 39'6"	39'6"	29'8-1/4" to 39'2-1/4"	39'
C Inside Width	88" to 92-1/2"	92"	Up to 90"	90"
D Inside Height	76-3/4" to 106-3/4"	96"	71-7/8" to 101-7/8"	90"
E Door Width	88" to 91"	90"	Up to 90"	90"
F Door Height	71-7/16" to 101-7/16"	91"	67-5/16" to 97-5/16"	86"

Freight car dimensions - Based on cars presently being used, but may vary with age and builder.

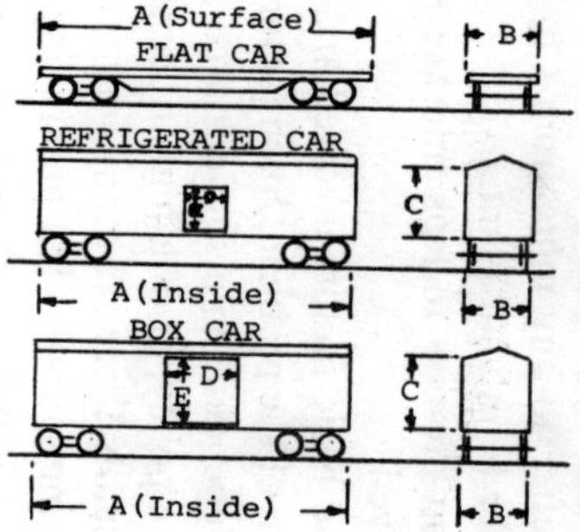

	TYPE OF CAR		
	Box Car	Flat Car	Refrigerated Car
A Inside Length	40'6" to 86'6"	36'0" to 89'0"	33'2-3/4" to 50"
B Inside Width	9'2" to 9'6"	8'4" to 10'6"	8'2-3/4" to 9'2"
C Inside Height	9'6" to 13'2"	-	6'8" to 9'0"
D Door Width	6'0" to 30'0"	-	4'0" to 10'1"
E Door Height	8'9" to 12'9"	-	6'0" to 9'4"

Fig. 2-7. A guide to truck van and freight car dimensions.

Fig. 2-8. Corrugated steel, knocked-down container. Courtesy Eureka Manufacturing Company, Chillicothe, Illinois.

8, will permit the user to return empty containers compacted by at least a four-to-one ratio.

II. THE UNIT LOAD PROBLEM

Consider for a moment the output from two suppliers, "Co. A" and "Co. B." Both have a reliable, well-engineered quality product. You are buying supplies from both companies, but your receiving clerk is complaining of the additional overtime caused by a number of shipments from Co. B. He feels that you would do better to buy more from Co. A, even though they are located 150 miles farther from your plant.

You promise to look into the matter; so you try to obtain all of the facts involved.

The basic factors involved and a diagram (Fig. 2-9) serve to illustrate the extent of the problem. Such factors as whether or not the company will become too dependent on a single source of supply have been omitted as being of corporate policy, or of a higher decision level than the present problem warrants.

Usually there are many sources for equivalent materials, and the problem of selecting suppliers is a purchasing function that should be continually reviewed and evaluated. Thus, our unit load problem should be solved strictly on the

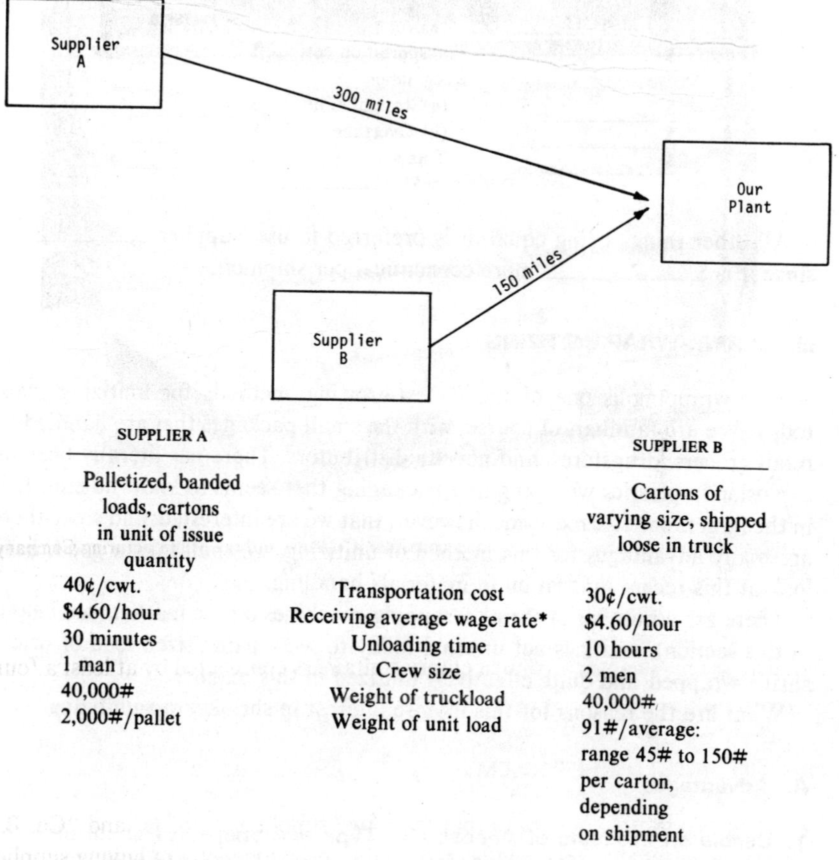

SUPPLIER A		SUPPLIER B
Palletized, banded loads, cartons in unit of issue quantity		Cartons of varying size, shipped loose in truck
40¢/cwt.	Transportation cost	30¢/cwt.
$4.60/hour	Receiving average wage rate*	$4.60/hour
30 minutes	Unloading time	10 hours
1 man	Crew size	2 men
40,000#	Weight of truckload	40,000#
2,000#/pallet	Weight of unit load	91#/average: range 45# to 150# per carton, depending on shipment

*Overtime rate @ $6.90; does not include fringe benefits, but since both crews have same fringes, they have not been included in this problem.

Fig. 2-9. Basic facts of the unit load problem.

basis of economics; that is, what is the best method of handling the incoming material?

A. Questions Concerning the Unit Load Problem

The following questions are based on the unit load problem diagrammed in Fig. 2-9.

SUPPLIER A		SUPPLIER B
$ ________	Transportation cost	$ ________
	Recg. labor	
$ ________	(a)Straight time	$ ________
$ ________	(b) Overtime	$ ________
$ ________	Totals	$ ________
	Difference $ ________	

All other things being equal, it is preferred to use Supplier ________, since it is $________ more economical per shipment.

III. SHRINK-WRAP UNITIZING

Shrink wrapping is one of the fastest-growing methods for unitizing loads today. We are familiar, of course, with the small packages that are handled by retail grocers, drugstores, and novelty distributors. There has literally been an explosion in plastics wrapping and packaging that seems to know no end. It is in the larger, pallet-sized loads, however, that we are interested; and since there are many advantages for this method of unitizing, we shall take a good, hard look at this recent innovation in materials handling.

There are a number of shrink-wrapping machines on the market (see below, in this section), and it is not unusual today to see a pallet-sized load of bricks shrink-wrapped and quite effectively unitized in this manner.

What are the reasons for this intense interest in shrink-wrap unitizing?

A. Advantages

1. Usable on Products of Almost Any Type and Shape. The shrink wrap method is usable on products of almost any type and shape. In fact, if you can place the material on a skid or pallet, the chances are very good that you can shrink-wrap the load. So we can say, "Any product that can be stacked on a pallet can be shrink-wrapped to that pallet."

Some examples of items that can be shrink-wrapped, are:

1. Castings
2. Forgings
3. Fixtures
4. Sheet metal parts
5. Batteries
6. Bricks
7. Grocery items
8. Pharmaceuticals
9. Soft goods

10. Mixed parts of different sizes
11. Oddball-shaped parts

2. Stable Pallet Loads. Pallet load stability is increased through the use of the plastic film, which shrinks to the contour of the load. Thus:

1. The film firms the load.
2. The film anchors the load to the pallet.
3. The load stability of shrink-wrapped pallets can be as high as 35° from the horizontal, as illustrated in Fig. 2-10.
4. Odd-shaped loads are stabilized; the stability of shrink-wrapped pallets extends to normally unstable loads and loads of irregular configuration.

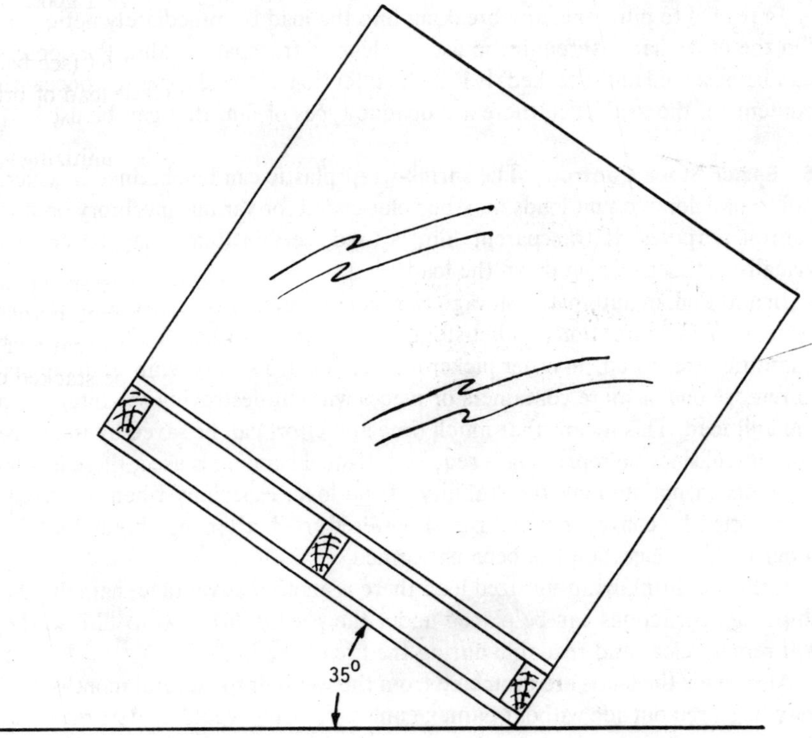

Fig. 2-10. Load stability of shrink-wrapped pallets can be as high as 35°.

3. Protection Against Dust, Dirt, and Moisture. Shrink-wrapped loads virtually ignore the weather for periods as long as two months—indoors and out. The plastic film has the following characteristics:

1. It does not absorb moisture.
2. It does not lose its strength.
3. Loads are virtually dust and dirt-proof.
4. Loads can be shipped in open trucks.
5. Loads can be stored outdoors for a period of time.

4. Protection from Damage and Pilferage. Shrink-wrapped loads reduce damage from spillage because of their increased stability. In addition, there is no steel strapping to damage parts. The wrapping material—that is, the plastic film—will not become loose or fall off. And, if the load settles, it is still tightly held from the sides. Furthermore, depending on the item unitized, the shrink film helps to compact and draw the load together, so that it is more firmly secured to the pallet.

In regard to pilferage, any breaking into the load is immediately noticeable. On the other hand, through the use of clear or transparent film, the contents can be observed and checked. If it is the intention of the shipper to conceal the contents of the load, then there are opaque types of film that can be used.

5. Easier Stock Control. The shrink-wrap plastic can be obtained in several different colors, so unit loads may be color-coded for various inventory or stock control purposes. If transparent film is used, certain items may be checked visually without tearing down the load.

In addition, in automated storage warehouses such as stacker-crane retrieval systems or in conventional pallet-storage rack systems where bulk or unit load quantities are stored, an order picker may cut open a shrink-wrap unitized load to remove one or more containers or pieces without destroying the integrity of the unit load. This means that much time and effort can be saved by the warehouseman, since no repacking is required. If steel banding is used, there is often difficulty in maintaining the stability of the load, especially when it must be transported by conveyor or industrial powered truck after the "break-bulk" or order picking operation has been performed.

With the shrink-wrap unitized load there is another advantage, namely, that shipping instructions can be placed under the plastic shrink-wrap film so they will remain clear and readable during the life of the load.

Also, since the loads are protected from the weather for several months, they may be stored outside without damage unless freezing would be detrimental to the contents. The fact that the shrink-wrap unitized load can be stored outside means that during temporary peak periods when warehouse space may not be immediately available there is no urgent requirement to rent or lease additional warehouse space.

Generally speaking, if a product is stored outside for a relatively long period of time and the product is susceptible to sun damage, opaque plastic films should be used to inhibit ultraviolet penetration.

6. Relatively Low Cost of Packaging Labor and Materials. Packaging material costs for shrink wrapping could be lower than costs using other packaging methods, since the relatively low-cost plastic film may be the only material used besides the pallet. Moreover, labor costs for shrink wrapping may be reduced if semi-automatic or automatic shrink equipment is used. Because of the inherent characteristics of both manual and automatic shrink-wrap packaging equipment, pallet overwrapping doesn't require highly skilled labor. In addition, the lightweight plastic film does not add weight to the load and helps keep load size down to the minimum cubic volume for the material that is unitized. Conventional methods of unitizing, that is, using corrugated containers or steel strapping, usually cost more than the faster, and often more effective, shrink-wrap unitizing using plastic films.

The following exercise indicates the relative cost of steel banding as contrasted to shrink-wrap unitizing:

Cost of steel strapping vs. shrink-wrap (per unit load):

Conventional (steel strap):		
Steel strapping	$1.37	
Corrugated load binder	.75	
Corner protectors	.45	
Labor	3.75	
		$5.32
Shrink wrap:		
Polyethylene film (5-mil)	$3.15	
Labor	.96	
		$4.11
Difference		$1.21

(Note: Equipment costs are not included in the above.)

As you can see from the above exercise, there is some difference in cost between the two methods. Since prices and labor rates do not have a tendency to remain fixed, if a shipper is seriously considering a change in his unitizing methods, then it would be well to recalculate cost savings in terms of current rates and prices.

7. Waste Disposal Problems Minimized. There are currently two major types of plastic shrink-wrap films, polyvinyl chloride (PVC) and polyethylene (PE). The PE film is presently the more popular and cheaper film for unitizing loads, but some bulk, point-of-display merchandise is packaged using PVC, primarily because of the crystal-clear quality of this plastic. However, PVC is more expensive than PE, and the relative efficiencies of the two films are so closely related that a shipper would hardly be justified in using the more expensive PVC.

The PVC film shrinks a little bit faster than PE, but the difference is not enough in unitizing pallet loads of materials to become a cost factor. In terms of disposal, PVC releases toxic chlorides upon burning and so cannot be safely incinerated. PE, on the other hand, can be safely burned or disposed of in a sanitary landfilling operation.

In addition, as far as in-plant disposal is concerned, PE film can be shredded or pelletized with relatively inexpensive equipment. Once this step is accomplished, most film suppliers will pay to obtain the material for recycling. It is estimated that the equipment and labor cost of this method of disposal will be paid for by the amount obtained for the shredded or pelletized material.

B. Equipment and Methods

1. Full Range of Shrink Equipment. There are three modes of shrink-wrap unitizing materials: manual, semi-automatic, and automatic, as discussed in the following paragraphs.

2. Manual Shrink-Wrap Unitizing. There is a "portable heat gun" for manual shrink-wrap unitizing that generates approximately 100,000 BTU's/hr. There are several machines of this type on the market. (See Appendix G of this text for supplier information.)

The portable heat gun can shrink-wrap a load 4′ × 4′ × 4′ in approximately 5 minutes. Care must be taken with this low-production method, since a hole may be melted in the film if the dwell time exceeds a certain limit. A volume of 12 pallet loads an hour would be an upper limit on production for this type of operation; however, it would not require much skill on the part of the operator except for a short, hour-long learning period.

The equipment or gun can be of several types, using either an LP gas cylinder or a gas line. Most bottled gas guns will deliver an air blast of 85 cubic ft./min. at a temperature of 650°F (one foot away) and consume approximately 5 pounds of fuel per hour. Therefore, experimentation or low-production shrink-wrap unitizing may be economically performed using the hand gun (see Fig. 2-11).

Fig. 2-11. A portable hand gun will shrink-wrap a pallet load in 3 to 5 minutes. Courtesy Shrink-fast Company, Tri-State Packaging Supply Corporation, Lorton, Virginia.

3. Semi-automatic Shrink-Wrap Unitizing Machines. One type of semi-automatic machine that is combined with a bag-forming device is shown in Fig. 2-12.

Approximately 20 pallet loads per hour and sometimes a few more than this can be achieved using one operator. A gas-fired heat blower may be incorporated in this design, but radiant heat may be used instead.

4. Automatic Shrink-Wrap Unitizing Machines. There are several types of automatic shrink-wrap unitizing machines, namely:

1. Heat frames (shrink rings)
2. Heat closets
3. Heat tunnels

The shrink ring can be either gas-fired or electric.

An example of an electric heat frame, or what is commonly called a shrink ring, is illustrated in Fig. 2-13.

Fig. 2-12. Semi-automatic bag forming/loading system. Courtesy Weldoron Company, Piscataway, New Jersey.

An example of a bag-forming and heat closet machine is illustrated by Figs. 2-14 and 2-15.

A shrink-wrap unitizing tunnel, which may be gas, electric, or infrared-heated and have a throughput capability of from 30 to 100 pallet loads per hour, is shown in Fig. 2-16.

5. Wrapping the Film. There are several methods for forming and placing the plastic film around the load.

a. *Automatic sleeve forming* produces sleeves around loads up to 96 inches high. Figure 2-17 illustrates the way in which two rolls of film are joined around the load and then the film is heat-sealed in a vertical line, leaving the top and bottom sides of the load free of plastic.

b. *Automatic bag forming* produces gusseted bags around a variety of load sizes. As shown in Fig. 2-18, as the pallet load moves down the conveyor, the plastic sheet, which is folded in half on the roll, is draped about the load and

Fig 2-13. A shrink-ring in action. Courtesy Weldotron Company, Piscataway, New Jersey.

heat-sealed. Then the load moves again into the shrink-wrap heating tunnel at the end of the conveyor. (The heat tunnel portion is not shown in the illustration.)

c. *Vertical bag forming* takes place in Fig. 2-18 where the plastic film in the form of a gusseted tube is draped over the pallet load in such a manner that it is possible either to cut the tube and form a sleeve wrap or to seal the top of the tube to form a bag (Fig. 2-19).

6. Shrink Films. Shrink films are composed of two types of thermoplastic materials, polyethylene (PE) and polyvinyl chloride (PVC), as indicated in the preceding text. The main characteristic of these plastic films is that they are a source of stored shrink energy, and when heated to an approximate temperature of between 300°F and 400°F they have a tendency to return to their original condition, that is, the condition before stretching.

The stored shrink energy is built into the film during its manufacture. Thus, the film is extruded in a plastic state and stretched under controlled conditions of temperature and tension. This is known as the "blown film" method, and if

Fig. 2-14. OSI indexing flow-thru shrink film oven. Courtesy Oven Systems, Inc.

strict control of flow and air pressure is exercised, a certain percentage of stretch can be obtained in both the machine direction (MD) and the transverse direction (TD). Usually there is more shrink permitted in the machine direction, since pallet shrink wrapping requires unbalanced shrinkage in both directions to produce a tight envelope. This is sometimes called a 20–40 shrink, wherein 20% of the shrinkage occurs in the transverse direction and 40% in the machine direction. This controlled process creates a molecular orientation of the plastic that is locked into the film upon cooling. Heating, therefore, produces a rubber-band condition in the surface area of the plastic. Also, the plastic returns to its original gauge, having become thinner upon being stretched.

7. Shrink Film Types. As shown in Fig. 2-20, there are six different types of styles of film that are used in shrink-wrap bag forming.

Polyethylene film, which is the more widely used shrink-wrap unitizing plastic, is available in 2 to 15 mils thickness; however, the 3-mil gauge is most prevalent. In addition to its other characteristics, it has a fairly high tear resis-

Fig. 2-15. OSI manual bagger. Courtesy Oven Systems, Inc.

Fig. 2-16. Signode intermittent motion shrink tunnel. Courtesy Signode.

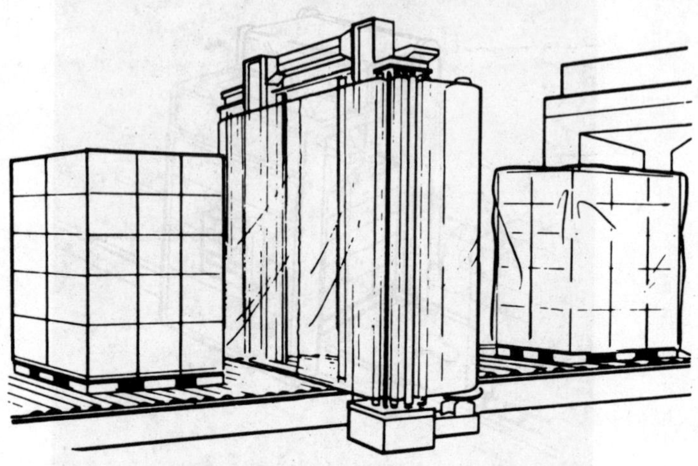

Fig. 2-17. Automatic sleeve-forming machine. Courtesy Signode.

tance. For convenience in calculating film requirements and as a ready reference, a table indicating yield per pound of film is included later in this section (see Table 2-1). For example, a pound of 3-mil or .003 gauge film yields 10,000 square inches of film, or 69.44 square feet, or 7.72 square yards.

For manual bagging operations, the following shrink film types (see Fig. 2-20) may be used with or without automatic shrink-wrap unitizing machines:

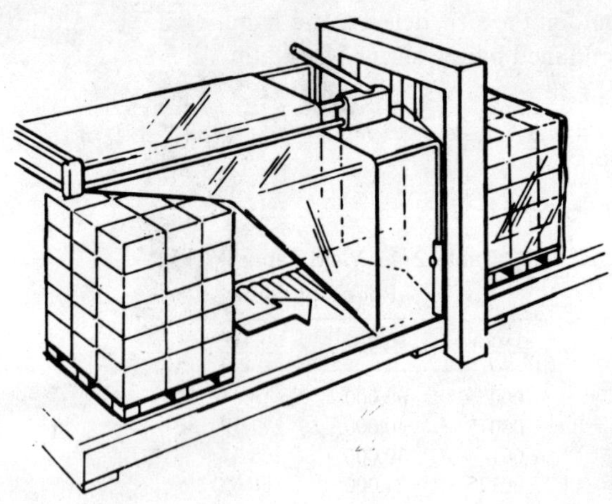

Fig. 2-18. Vertical bag forming. Courtesy Signode.

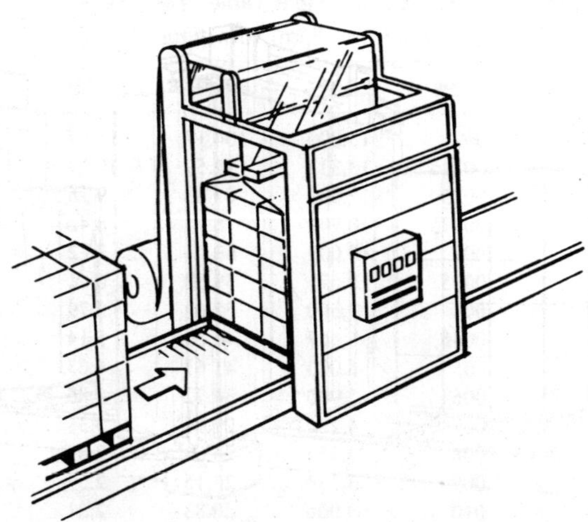

Fig. 2-19. Sealing the top. Courtesy Signode.

Centerfold, rolled and perforated (type 3)
Tubular (type 4)
Gusseted tubular (type 5)
Gusseted, rolled and perforated (type 6)

When one is beginning to experiment with shrink-wrap films, it is well to use a hand gun and try varying thicknesses of film. The film gauge will depend, to a large extent, on the size, density, and handling difficulty of the parts to be stacked and contained by the shrink-wrap film.

8. Yield Table.

Table 2-1. Yield Table (Yield Per Pound of Film).

GAUGE	SQ. IN.	SQ. FT.	SQ. YD.
.0005	60,000	416.67	46.30
.00075	40,000	277.78	30.86
.001	30,000	208.33	23.15
.00125	24,000	166.67	18.52
.0015	20,000	138.89	15.43
.00175	17,143	119.05	13.23

Table 2-1. Yield Table (Yield Per Pound of Film) (*Continued*).

GAUGE	SQ. IN.	SQ. FT.	SQ. YD.
.002	15,000	104.17	11.57
.00225	13,333	92.59	10.29
.0025	12,000	83.33	9.26
.00275	10,909	75.75	8.42
.003	10,000	69.44	7.72
.0035	8,571	59.52	6.61
.004	7,500	52.08	5.79
.0045	6,667	46.29	5.14
.005	6,000	41.67	4.63
.006	5,000	34.72	3.86
.007	4,286	29.76	3.31
.008	3,750	26.04	2.89
.009	3,333	23.15	2.57
.010	3,000	20.83	2.31

IV. STRETCH-WRAP UNITIZING

Stretch wrapping is the newest and most cost-effective method of unitizing pallet loads. While stretch wrapping is relatively new, it is fast becoming one of the most widely used methods of unitization. It has many advantages, the principal ones being that: (1) it reduces in-plant handling costs, (2) it reduces distribution costs, and (3) it reduces damage claims.

A. Advantages

1. It costs less than heat shrink unitizing.
2. It requires significantly less energy.
3. The cost of equipment and installation is less than for heat shrinking.
4. It holds the load together.
5. It requires less floor space than heat shrinking.
6. It can be operated in refrigerated or heat-restricted areas.
7. It requires significantly less film inventory.
8. It can be used with heat-sensitive products.
9. It can be operated on the existing electrical service (i.e., does not require special wiring).

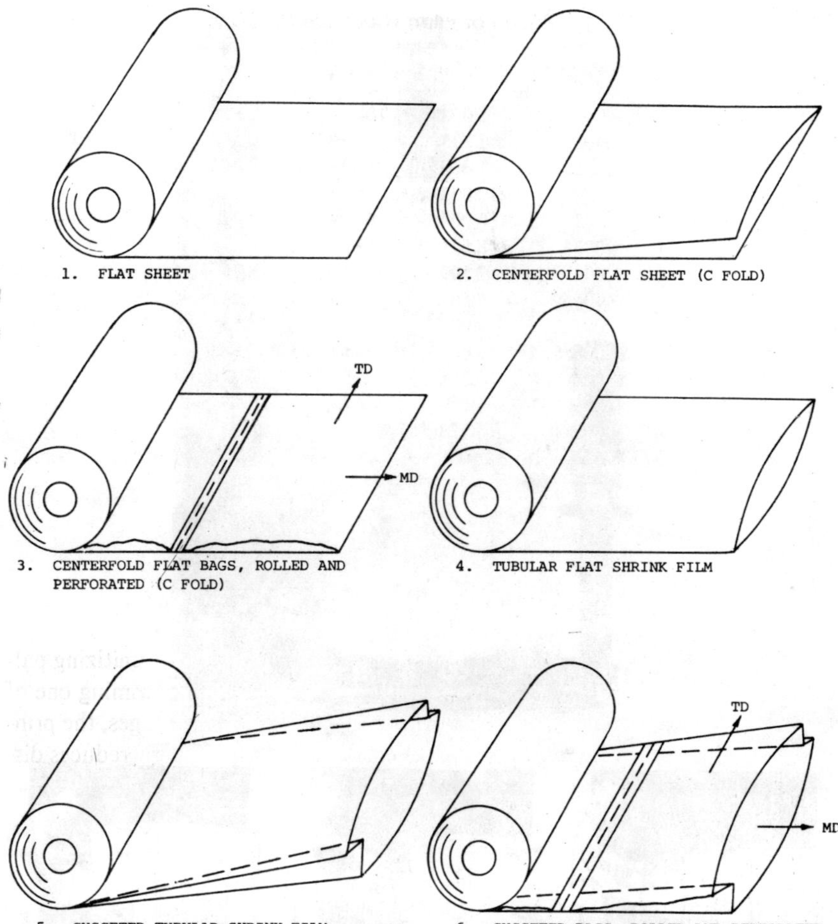

Fig. 2-20. Shrink film types.

B. A Comparison between Shrink and Stretch Wrapping

1. *To unitize only, where the load is held around the girth and no top or bottom protection is required:* Stretch wrapping may be the better way. (See Figs. 2-21, 2-22, 2-23, 2-24, and 2-25 for various types of manual and mechanized stretch-wrapping machines.)

2. *To unitize with top protection (five sides):* When protection for the four sides and the top of the load is required, shrink wrapping is the better way.

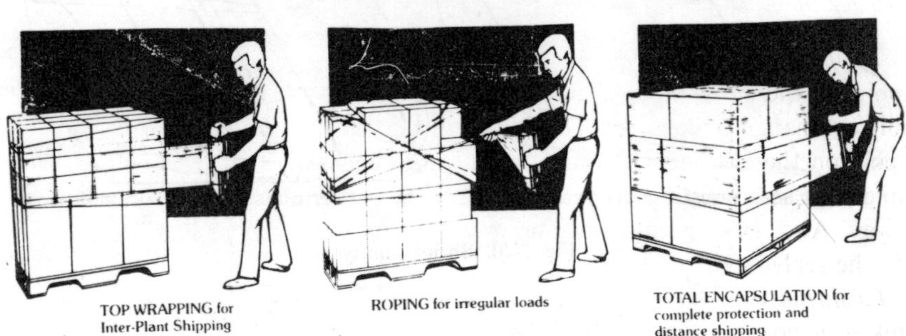

Fig. 2-21. Manual stretch wrapping. Courtesy Presto Products, Appleton, Wisconsin.

The material and labor to cover the top of a stretch-wrapped load with a top sheet of film in order to protect the top are generally not worth it, except when this type of protection is only occasionally required. If protection against water, dust, or pilferage is required, then shrinking is the better way. For dust protection only, stretch would be more economical.

Fig. 2-22. Mechanized pre-stretch wrapping. Courtesy Lantech, Inc., Louisville, Kentucky.

3. *To unitize with top, bottom, and side protection (six sides):* Heat shrink wrapping is the better way, since the bottom side can be protected by a layer of poly overhanging the pallet. The covering bag will shrink over the load, and the poly on the bottom side will adhere to the bag and weld itself tight. A complete air seal is formed that will exclude vermin; foodstuffs can be sealed this way. Also, fresh produce can be protected from oxygen by inert gassing inside the sealed unitized load.

4. *To shrink-wrap boxes or packages:* Standard shrink poly bags when heat-shrunk over boxes, etc., that have themselves been heat-shrunk and wrapped with standard low-density polyethylene film, will stick or weld themselves to the poly bag covering the load. Bundles or bags that have been covered with PVC, polypropylene, polybutylene, or medium- or high-density poly film will not stick. Special anti-stick polyethylene films are available from some bag suppliers at an increased cost.

5. *For outdoor storage:* The heavier-gauge heat shrink film holds up better under the deteriorating effects of direct (ultraviolet) sunlight. Shrink bag manufacturers can add ultraviolet inhibitors (UVI) to the poly during manufacture

Fig. 2-23. Mechanized pre-stretch wrapping from less than 5,000 to 30,000 unit loads per year. Courtesy Lantech, Inc., Louisville, Kentucky.

that will add considerably to outdoor storage life, but at an increase in cost Some stretch films relax and lose their tension at elevated temperatures.

6. *To handle odd-shaped loads:* Shrink film conforms to odd shapes much better than stretch films. The shrink ratio is considerably higher than the stretch ratio, so that the shrink film tends to conform much better to humps and voids in a mixed load where odd-sized packages or objects present a rough terrain to the film. Shrink film shrinks and holds tight in all directions whereas stretch holds mainly in girth (tension).

7. *For heat-sensitive products:* This is rarely a factor requiring consideration however, shrink film when shrunk with high-velocity hot air acts as a barrier to heat penetrating the film; thus, the temperature within the load, or in the outer surface, will rise only a few degrees. When infrared or radiant-heating shrink systems are used, the load temperature will rise slightly higher because of the passage of infrared rays through the shrink film. On the other hand stretch wrapping adds no heat to the load.

Fig. 2-24. Demonstrating "roller-strech" pre-stretch wrapping mechanization. Courtesy Lantech, Inc., Louisville, Kentucky.

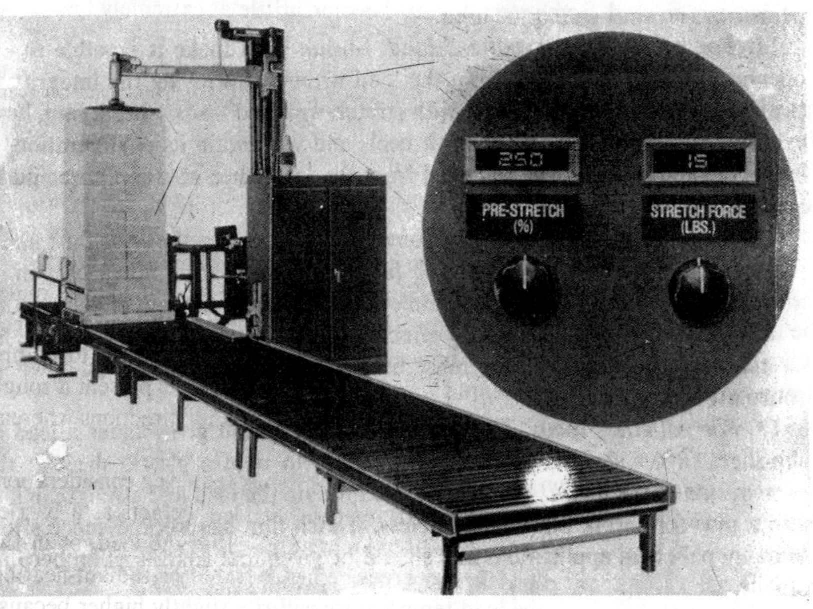

Fig. 2-25. Automatic stretch-wrap system. Courtesy Lantech, Inc., Louisville, Kentucky.

8. *For loads that overhang or are of less than pallet size:* Stretch film is applied under considerable tension in 1 mil (0.001″) thicknesses and can rupture at sharp corners, nor does it easily conform to irregularities in the load makeup. Shrink film will conform to irregularities, is not readily ruptured, will simply tension itself between high and low points, and will hold tight in all directions.

9. *For loads requiring a secure bottom hold on the pallet:* Shrink film is far superior to stretch for this application. Shrink film draws in tight under the pallet and holds in girth and height. The author demonstrated this at one plant by shrink-wrapping a load of engine block castings weighing over 3,000 pounds. The film was 6 mils (0.006″) thick, and after shrinking, a forklift truck with a turnover attachment was able to pick up the load clear of the ground and rotate the entire load of castings bottom-side-up without disturbing the load.

10. *For operation in refrigerated areas:* Stretch film has the edge in this area, since almost no heat is introduced into the refrigerated area. Some successful shrink operations do exist in cold rooms, but this practice is not common. Rotary shrink columns can be used that pass about 6,000 to 10,000 BTU's per load into the cold storage room. Also, through-the-wall heat chambers with air curtains can be used. Some stretch films become brittle at extremely low temperatures and thus cannot be used.

11. *For getting at the unitized load:* Shrink bags make it possible to cut openings to remove product from the load without destroying the integrity of the unit load. This is not possible with stretch-wrapped loads. Shrink film, however, takes a permanent set when it cools and will retain its configuration. If layers of products must be removed from the load, then stretch film could be used.

12. *For pressure-sensitive loads:* Some light loads will collapse or shift under the tension required to apply stretch film wrapping. Shrink film closes in on the load evenly from all directions and even does a slight amount of compacting of a light load without a crushing effect. It does not pull or shift the load. To stretch-wrap, a holding platen must be used along with an up-and-down or convolute wrap cycle.

13. *For palletless loads:* The superior bottom hold it gives under a load or slip-sheet favors shrink wrapping. The ability to weld a plastic sheet at the bottom side of the load to completely encapsulate the load and strengthen it is also a plus for shrink film. Nevertheless, stretch film has worked successfully in many palletless applications and should be given first consideration because of cost.

14. *For short hauls and extra protection:* Many companies stretch-wrap short-haul shipments in closed vans or trailers, but they shrink-wrap loads

requiring extra protection; for example, in export shipping or outdoor storage, or where pilferage deterrence is necessary.

15. *For stretch netting:* Where products must breathe, such as fresh produce, stretch netting may be used. Also, situations in which products are packaged fairly hot and must be unitized rapidly while dissipating heat are good applications for stretch netting. The fabric looks very much like a fishnet, but has a stretching characteristic. The product temperature, if warm, must be in a range that will not melt the plastic netting. Also, this is a very economical method of unitizing light- to medium-weight loads.

V. OTHER METHODS OF UNITIZING

A number of other methods of unitizing loads are used to enhance the stability of the loads in transit or in stacking. Some of these will be discussed in the following paragraphs.

A. Tie Ropes

A quick-tying rope with a special hook is manufactured in filament sizes varying from a fairly heavy twine to a sash-cord or clothesline-weight rope. The tie device is used primarily for in-plant transportation and storage to stabilize loads, usually palletized products in cartons. Also, sometimes when towconveyors haul pallet loads of materials, tie devices are used to keep the loads together. Usually the upper tier of the load is tied horizontally.

B. Rubber Bands

Huge rubber bands about 4 inches wide and 3 to 4 feet long are used in much the same way as the tie ropes described in the preceding paragraph.

C. Filament Tape

Filament tape with a one-sided adhesive coating is used just as the tie ropes and the rubber bands are used. Whereas the tie ropes and rubber bands may be reused, the filament tape is a one-time application. An advantage over tie ropes and rubber bands is that the tape is not stolen by employees or other interested individuals.

D. Glue

For long hauls, palletized or slip-sheet unitized loads, or corrugated or solid fiberboard containers, may have their integrity as a unit load increased by the use of a high-shear, low-tensile glue such as that sold by the H. B. Fuller Company: Type No. 133 Dextrin, or F4764 Resin.

EXERCISE NO. 2

1. A logical outcome of mechanically assisted handling is the __________ load concept.

2. Employing the unit load concept, we can make the statement that, "The larger the __________ moved, the __________ the unit cost, all other things being equal."

3. The uniformity of the __________ items, and their ability to be __________, or interlocked in a pallet __________, or to be placed on a skid, also affect the size and effectiveness of the unit load.

4. Four areas in both manufacturing and distribution where unit loads should be carefully considered, are: (1) __________, (2) __________, (3) __________, and (4) __________.

5. A pitfall that should be avoided in applying the unit load concept is that we should never use the unit load concept between __________ work stations, unless no satisfactory __________ __________ is available.

6. The reason for avoiding the unit load concept between two successive work stations is that __________ and __________ must be expended in stacking the material or placing it into a container from which it must, subsequently, be __________ or __________.

7. Two further considerations in applying the unit load concept are: (1) the __________ __________ moved, and (2) the time __________ __________ the operations at successive work stations.

8. If relatively large quantities of material are to be moved between successive __________, consideration should be given to __________ the material between the two work stations.

9. If it is not possible to __________ the material between successive work stations, then the economic __________ of relocating the production equipment should be explored.

10. Sometimes the product __________ may make it difficult or impossible to use conveyors between successive operations, but at least it would pay to evaluate all of the factors involved before placing material into containers.

11. The time __________ between successive operations may require that we store material for a certain period.

12. If possible and advantageous, the production __________ should be rearranged to make successive operations follow in rapid and __________ succession so that the two work stations may be interconnected by a conveyor, chute, storage silo, manipulator, or the like.

13. A unit load can be said to be any quantity designated to be __________ __________, transported, or __________ in a single mass.

14. In a plant container program, limit the number of container sizes and configurations based upon the __________ __________ and __________.

15. Design containers for maximum ____________.
16. Shrink-wrap unitizing can be used on products of almost any ____________ and ____________.
17. Any product that can be ____________ on a pallet can be shrink-wrapped to that pallet.
18. Some examples of items that can be shrink-wrapped are: ____________, ____________, ____________, ____________, ____________, and ____________.
19. Shrink-wrap unitizing increases the ____________ of a pallet load.
20. Even some odd-shaped loads may be shrink-wrapped. This increases the ____________ of the load.
21. Shrink-wrapping offers protection from dust, dirt, and ____________.
22. Shrink-wrapped loads are protected to a degree from damage and ____________.
23. If shipping instructions must be read under the plastic film, then ____________ plastic should be used.
24. To prevent ultraviolet ray damage, an ____________ plastic shou!d be considered.
25. Polyethylene film may be recycled by first ____________ or ____________.

Chapter 3
The Effects of Flow and Movement on Plant Output

I. WORK FLOW AND MATERIAL MOVEMENT

There are many reasons why it is extremely desirable to optimize the work flow in a plant—whether it be a warehouse, a manufacturing facility, or any other complex organization.

Warehouses, factories, military installations, banks, brokerage houses, hospitals, etc., all have a common requirement: in order to operate most efficiently they require an orderly flow of materials—regardless of the fact that the materials may be orders to be filled, food to be prepared and served, or soiled linen to be cleaned.

A very short time ago, most large mail-order warehouses could only keep pace with the growth of their order-filling requirements by putting more bodies to work. Today, these same, large mail-order houses now employ sortation systems and, in some instances, have even installed computer-operated stacker-crane retrieval systems* in order to improve the control of merchandise moving into and out of storage.

Many hospitals have at least seven people on duty for each patient, and in modern warfare for every soldier in the battlefield there have been as many as seven people behind the front lines in supply support and other operations. Because we are describing large and complex institutions, hospitals on the one hand and armies on the other, we are dealing with very large numbers. If we did not have orderly flows of materials in these instances, there would be utter chaos—besides the wanton loss of life that would result. So the significance of material flow cannot be overlooked by the materials handling practitioner, whatever his or her field of work.

By providing an orderly flow of materials through a system it is possible to avoid one of the common errors of materials handling, namely, back-hauling or the back-tracking of materials. This simply means that once material has

---

*Stacker-crane retrieval system: a highly mechanized high-density, rack storage system for the orderly control of material; the retrieval of the material is accomplished by automatic, semi-automatic, or manual stacker-cranes.

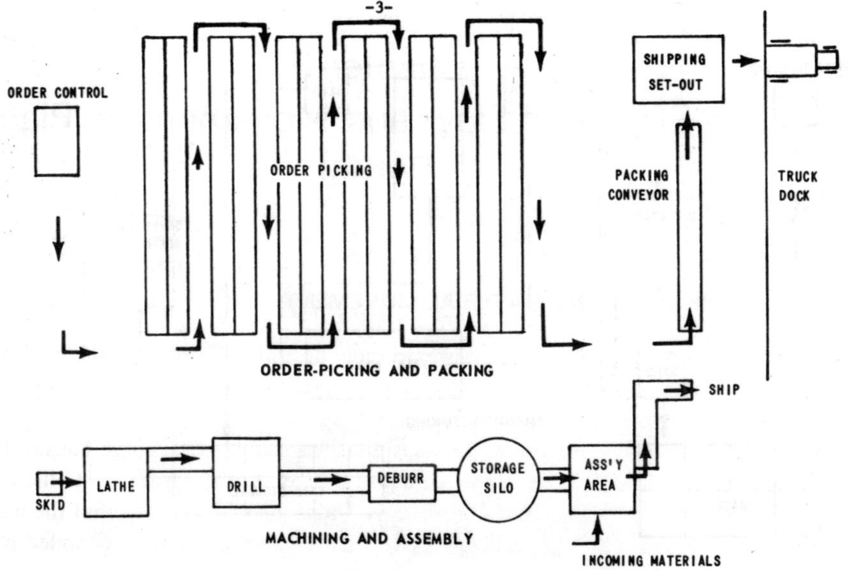

Fig. 3-1. Examples of straight-line flow in a plant.

passsed through an operation it maintains its direction and does not retrace its path. (See Figs. 3–1 and 3–2.)

In every type of facility or organization mentioned above, this one single factor—back-hauling—often causes the collapse of an enterprise, or so confuses its operations that the profitability of the business becomes marginal or disappears entirely.

II. CONDUCTING A PLANT MATERIALS HANDLING SURVEY

A. Introduction and Purpose

You may be wondering why it is that we jump headlong into an area where a great deal of expertise is generally required. And, this assignment—that of conducting a materials handling survey—is generally left to engineering consultants.

The reason that we have plunged into this area is to broaden the scope of the student, materials handling practitioner, or sales engineer. We shall see unfold, in the text of this chapter, many areas that will be developed and dissected more thoroughly in subsequent chapters.

This guide will better enable you to emphasize areas within your own company that may require improvement. In addition, by referring to this text dur-

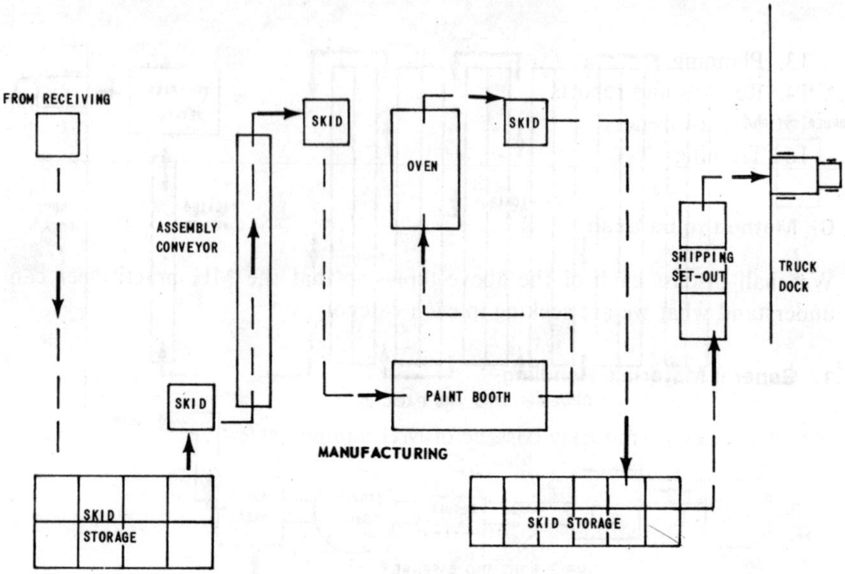

FROM RECEIVING
SKID
ASSEMBLY CONVEYOR
SKID
OVEN
SKID
SHIPPING SET-OUT
TRUCK DOCK
PAINT BOOTH
MANUFACTURING
SKID STORAGE
SKID STORAGE

Fig. 3-2. Example of back-tracking in a plant.

ing your daily activities in materials handling, you may be able to effect necessary improvements that may otherwise have been overlooked.

B. Scope

We shall cover 16 different but related areas in materials handling so that you may immediately take advantage of what you have learned—and by so doing put your knowledge to work. The following areas will be discussed:

1. General materials handling (MH)
2. Manufacturing MH
3. Warehousing MH
4. Packaging MH
5. MH equipment
6. MH manpower utilization
7. Shipping MH
8. Receiving MH
9. Plant layout—general
10. Plant layout—flow of materials
11. Plant layout—space utilization
12. Equipment arrangement and workplace layout

13. Planning
14. Records and reports
15. MH awareness
16. Training

C. Method to be Used

We shall discuss each of the above topics so that the MH practitioner can understand what we are seeking in each category.

1. General Materials Handling

1. Do aisles permit easy passage of MH equipment?
2. Are aisles adequately marked?
3. Are any aisles blocked?
4. Are safe operating speeds of MH equipment practiced?
5. Do intersecting aisles permit easy passage of equipment?
6. Is there interference with MH equipment and walking traffic?
7. Does good houskeeping prevail?
8. What is the condition of floors:

   (a) In working aisles?
   (b) In main aisles?
   (c) Around machinery?

As you can see from the above questions, there is a direct relationship between the orderliness with which work is performed and the flow of work through the plant. In addition, because of the Williams-Steiger Act of 1970, which established the Occupational Safety and Health Administration (OSHA), there are both federal and, in most instances, state regulations that require minimum aisle dimensions, safe in-plant vehicular speeds, and so forth.

Some aisles in your plant may be wide enough to accommodate vehicular traffic, that is, the movement of powered industrial trucks in both directions, but may not have the necessary additional 3 feet for pedestrian traffic that the law requires.

Also, aisles and pedestrian walkways must be adequately marked so that accidents may be prevented.

Floor conditions, also, are among the important factors from a safety standpoint and firm the view of efficient materials movement. Oil spills or shot-blast shot on the floor, loose blocks, and spalling concrete not only cause accidents, but are responsible in some measure for poor morale, low productivity, and product damage.

2. Manufacturing Materials Handling

a. Is the handling of materials by direct labor held to a minimum?
b. Is there an adequate supply of materials at the workplace?
c. Are materials delivered to and removed from the workplace without interruption in the work cycle?
d. Is there good use of mechanical devices for loading and unloading machines?
e. Are waste materials removed from the workplace without interruption in the work cycle?
f. Are departmental in-process storage areas:
   (i) Adequate?
   (ii) Excessive?
g. Are methods employed to load and unload the following systems adequate:
   (i) Washing and cleaning?
   (ii) Painting?
   (iii) Heat treating?
   (iv) Shot blast?
h. Are materials readily accessible to:
   (i) Assemblers?
   (ii) Machine operators?
i. Is there good utilization of racks for storage of materials on the assembly line or in the assembly area?
j. Are subcomponents conveniently and effectively located and arranged in relation to the assembly area?
k. Are containers matched to materials for on-line or assembly-area storage?
l. Are line shortages held to a minimum?

Direct labor in both manufacturing and warehousing should always be used in strictly productive operations. In accounting practice, the movement or transportation of materials in manufacturing is usually considered an indirect labor function. In a warehousing operation the movement or transportation of materials into or out of storage is generally considered a direct labor input, since that is the primary objective or function of the warehouse distribution center.

Now that we have defined our terms, let us take a look first at manufacturing materials handling. The first question (2a, above) indicates our desire to have the direct-labor employee work directly on production-type operations: putting a piece part into a machine, pressing the control buttons of a press or stamping machine, and the like.

If our production worker has to stop his machine because he has run out of parts (2b, above), then he is nonproductive for the amount of time it takes him to locate parts and/or to transport them to his work station. Therefore, having adequate supply of parts at the work station becomes a scheduling problem. The better the scheduling, the greater the production that will be achieved.

In looking at 2c, above, we find that having our production worker continuously employed will also improve production. For example, if a hopper is being filled with piece parts and in order to remove the tub or container we must stop the machine, then we have a production problem that must be resolved. The discharge chute of the machine could be temporarily deflected into another container in a standby position, and so forth, thereby ensuring a continuous and uninterrupted flow of materials.

In 2d, above, it may be seen that press feeding operations of machine loading can sometimes be fairly readily accomplished by using "put-and-take" devices or mechanical manipulators (industrial robots) (described in Chapter 10).

Waste materials (2e) should also be removed from the workplace without having to shut down the operation. This seems to be a fairly obvious need, but it is rather frequently overlooked. Chip removal from cutting tools is often a factor to consider; the removal of dunnage or packaging materials or other waste products should be tackled with a view toward improvement.

In-process storage areas are either excessive or inadequate, depending upon one's point of view. From the plant manager's position in-process storage areas are usually excessive because he is looking at the space as it affects the operations of his profit center. The space costs money, it has to be maintained, it has a requirement for light and heat, etc. Also he would like to see the space used for productive purposes—another machine tool, etc. The superintendent who is running the part over his line feels that he has to have space to put production parts between operations. The materials handling personnel feel that they need more storage space because inventory levels are getting higher—and round and round goes the cycle.

Adequate storage usually means that there is enough space to meet production goals and to maintain stock at levels sufficient for production of required quantities.

The questions raised in 2g are rather tricky because many companies spend considerable sums of money on elaborate and complex systems such as washing or heat-treating yet pay relatively little attention to the manner in which materials are loaded and unloaded from the machines. Carriers on paint lines can sometimes be designed to automatically pick up and discharge the product; tub dumpers and chutes can be used to load and unload some types of heat-treating furnaces, and so forth. The opportunities for mechanizing the types of systems described above should, ordinarily, be considered at the time of purchasing these systems. Usually the cost to convert or modify an installation is a lot higher after a design has been set into concrete, or steel, as the case may be.

The questions raised in 2h will be more thoroughly analyzed in Chapter 10; however, we can anticipate using there the common-sense approach that we are following in this chapter. Valuable time can be saved if we have materials readily available to the operators who are engaged in using them. The same approach should be used for tools, especially portable tools and expendable tool items such as drill bits and the like.

One of the greatest space wasters in a plant is the practice of storing materials only one unit load in height. By examining the question of 2i closely, it is possible to determine exactly how much of a plant's air rights can be used by placing pallet storage racks, or other types of storage racks (tiering racks), in locations that are strategic to the assembly areas.

Also, in assembly operations (2j, above) it is important that subcomponents be located within easy reach of the assembly area. This usually means that the subcomponent itself not only should be stored close to the point of use but in all likelihood should be assembled into its subcomponent unit at a location that is relatively close to the main assembly point. This may not always be possible, but at least this aspect of the assembly operation should be thoroughly explored.

Another significant contribution to improvements in materials handling productivity is made by the matching of containers to materials for on-line or assembly area storage (2k, above). The philosophy of this concept is that the materials should be received from suppliers without repackaging and should proceed directly to the assembly point. Where this is not possible, and the items must be put into storage because of the lot sizes ordered, then the supplier should be attuned to the handling requirements of the plant, at least for all purchased finished materials. If the supplier is properly oriented to the needs of the user, then it should be possible to move the supplier's parts into storage and from storage to the assembly points in the same, supplier's package.

In 2i we are concerned with shortages of parts that must be supplied to the assembly lines. Since work stoppages may result, and at the very least incomplete assemblies must be sidelined until parts are available, we are faced with a very serious problem when shortages occur. It is imperative that a system of controls be instituted so that the proper flow of materials is maintained at all times.

The buck is usually passed to the inventory control people when line shortages occur; however, responsibility does not begin and end in that department. The whole chain of materials movement may begin with the purchasing department, but probably a marketing man or plant manager indicates the "build schedule" to the purchasing department. Perhaps an expediter is also involved, and so on, down to inventory control. In some companies the purchasing agent acts as the inventory control man, production control man, and expediter. The problem then resolves itself into providing a method for obtaining timely and meaningful information concerning quantities. This is especially difficult when the parts to be supplied to the assembly lines are produced in-house. In this instance, the materials handling personnel become very much involved in a "numbers" game.

3. Warehousing Materials Handling

a. Are racks properly designed for pallet and container dimensions?
b. Are rack components standardized?
c. Are there designated locations in the warehouse/stores area for incoming and outgoing materials?
d. Are these staging areas:
   (i) Adequate?
   (ii) Excessive?
e. Is a locator system(s) used for storing materials?
f. Are mislocated materials held to a minimum?
g. Are there written operating procedures for the warehousing functions?
h. Are fixtures stored and located properly?
i. How much attention is given to fixture purging, obsolescence, repair, preservation?
j. Is materials handling equipment effectively used within the warehouse operation?
k. Are special racks used for high-volume parts?
l. Is there effective use made of tote boxes, pallet racks, bins, etc.?

Rack design (3a, above) gained prominence through the extensive work and effort of the Rack Manufacturers Institute.* Their most recent publication "Interim Specification for the Design, Testing and Utilization of Industrial Steel Storage Racks," together with "Supplement No. 1," had an effective date of June 18, 1973.

Federal regulations (OSHA) also have affected many aspects of rack design, as well as provisions of the Uniform Building Code, etc. So if your storage racks are more than 12 feet in height, some rather stringent requirements must be adhered to for your type of installation. We shall discuss this subject in Chapter 6 of the text.

Let us now examine some of the more pertinent design aspects with which the materials handling practitioner must be familiar. In the first place, it is well to consider the possibilities of standardizing pallet storage rack openings so that the greatest number of pallets or containers received may be stored

*Rack Manufacturers' Institute, 1326 Freeport Road, Pittsburgh, Pennsylvania 15238.

without having to be repackaged or removed from one container and put into another, in order to fit into the storage rack opening.

The height of pallet loads and containers is also a major concern. A good principle to follow when ordering storage racks is to err on the side of the largest opening that can be economically purchased.

Where captive pallets and containers are in service, then the layout planner may be able to specify the exact dimensions required to accommodate specific pallet or container sizes, remembering, however, that the power trucker must have at least 2 inches on each side of the pallet in order to place it in the storage opening quickly. In a double opening—that is, where pallet loads are side by side—there would be a total of at least 8 inches of free space between the uprights.

Front-to-back dimensions are also critical. Therefore, if pallet storage racks are placed back to back, a flue space must be maintained that could vary from 6 to 8 inches, depending on local building codes, insurance requirements, and the height of the storage racks. Beyond 25 feet in height another set of conditions will also prevail, as, for example, when interim sprinkler requirements must be met.

In 3b, above, we are concerned with the standardization of rack components such that the racks may be taken down and moved from one location to another as layout changes occur. Another reason for standardization is that by standardizing on specific rack components it is possible to adjust and modify the rack, shelf-bed arrangements to accommodate new products that may be smaller or larger than the former range of sizes.

Of concern in item 3c are the locations for receiving and loading out departmental materials. And, we pursue this question further in 3d, where we should explore the adequacy of staging areas for these incoming and outgoing materials. In a tractor-train operation, for example, sufficient parking space must be provided for trailers, and so forth.

Depending on the size of the warehouse, a locator system (3e) is relatively important. The control of material proceeds in a much more orderly fashion if a system is carefully established to help the order picker locate material. In larger warehouses, personnel changes also create problems that are minimized by an accurate, well-maintained locator system.

Conducting periodic audits to establish the validity of locations is also a necessary part of the warehouse locator system.

If the locator file is maintained as in 3e, then mislocated items (3f) can be held to a minimum.

Written procedures (3g) are a necessary part of any good warehouse operation. The trouble with procedures, however, is that they become obsolete very quickly unless they are reviewed periodically. It is suggested that these procedures be examined critically at least every two years, if not annually.

When we talk about fixtures (3h), we are, generally, addressing ourselves to a warehousing problem in manufacturing rather than in physical distribution. Suffice it to say that one of the main difficulties in production operations is to schedule the repair and maintenance of commonly used fixtures. Some plants waste considerable sums of money by storing fixtures in a haphazard fashion outdoors, or otherwise losing fixtures in a jumble of obsolete parts and other fixtures.

If we pursue the fixture problem (3i) more closely, we should then have a program to purge obsolescent fixtures periodically at a scheduled, predetermined interval; we should repair fixtures which are used at frequent intervals prior to demand for them; we should properly apply preservative coatings to fixtures; and we should identify and locate fixtures accurately in storage.

Regarding item 3j, we could write a book on the subject of the effective utilization of materials handling equipment in the warehousing operation! Since this is a subject for a later chapter, we shall simply say here that one should be as aware as possible of the abuse and misuse of MH equipment, and see that a proper preventive maintenance program is rigorously enforced.

The use of special racks (3k), and the effective use of tote boxes, pallet racks, bins, etc., depend in large part on the industriousness of the warehouse operator, who first makes certain that he has utilized all of his containers properly. If most of the containers are half empty, then it is obvious that a smaller container size, bin, etc., should be used. Use of special racks to store materials also makes good sense if the volume of parts stored is high enough to justify the added cost of purchasing and maintaining the special racks. Special racks for gears, tires, batteries, sofas, armchairs, rugs, sprockets—you name it—make sense only if the volume is sufficient to justify the departure from more conventional handling equipment, or storage aids.

4. Packaging Materials Handling

a. Does the plant have a packaging engineer?
b. Does he effectively perform the in-plant functions of a packaging engineer?
c. Does he communicate with other plant packaging engineers effectively?
d. Is the unit load concept in effect within the materials handling operation?
e. If so, are the unit loads properly designed for use through the entire manufacturing cycle?
f. Have plant packaging and shipping guidelines been established?
g. What percent effectiveness in terms of supplier cooperation has been achieved with these guidelines?
h. Are unit loads identified correctly?

i. Are packaging materials being recycled?
j. How much dunnage is being incinerated, or otherwise disposed of, that could be recycled?
k. Is blocking and bracing of outgoing shipments being performed effectively?
l. Does the packaging take into consideration the unit of issue, and is it possible to obtain modular units?

In the questions 4a, b, and c, above, we are concerned with establishing an effective plant, or company, packaging program. For maximum effectiveness, packaging, like many other aspects of materials management and materials handling, requires a large measure of involvement on the part of many people within a company.

A gauge of the packaging program's effectiveness (4d) is how well the unit load concept is carried out with materials that are shipped from suppliers, or that are handled either in-plant or between plants.

When unit loads are used as an integral part of a company's materials handling system, they should be designed for maximum utility (4e). In other words, they may proceed from storage to any part of the production or assembly areas without being rehandled, or at least the loads can be designed to fit into the various operations without having to be transferred from one container to a different style or size of container, etc.

Regarding question 4f, above, instructions and governing principles for the plant's packaging program should be spelled out in detail so that the process of packaging can be repeated with maximum effectiveness.

When we discuss the effectiveness of supplier cooperation (4g), we are concerned with the application of the guidelines for packaging that have been established by the company.

The correct package or unit load identity (4h) reflects, to some extent, on the way in which suppliers and other departments are responding to regulations or recommendations for proper packaging.

In question 4i, we are concerned with the ecology of packaging. Corrugated board and paper products generally can be recycled. For example, there are knocked-down containers that can be reused, or recycled. When a container no longer serves as a transporatation means, consideration should be given to the recycling of the materials of which the container is composed.

The problems of disposal (4j), have become critical in some industries and in various communities. By determining the "termination characteristics"* of

*Termination characteristic: a phrase coined by the author to indicate the end use or disposal of the packaging materials.

a container or packaging medium, it is possible to anticipate the method of disposal of the packaging material concerned.

As an example, shrink-wrapped unit loads, generally, have reusable skids or pallets, but if not, then the pallet material may be recycled. The polyethylene shrink-wrap film can be pelletized, or shredded for reprocessing.

Outgoing shipments (4k) are under greater control than suppliers' materials, since this type of packaging is performed in-house. We would expect to have fewer problems in this area than in some of the others indicated above. Nevertheless, many companies have a tendency to overpack outgoing shipments so that a great deal of money and expense is needlessly incurred by overdoing the requirements for packaging in the interest of minimizing product damage.

The unit of issue and the modular unit problem (4l) can often be overlooked by busy plant operators. As an example, fasteners and fittings can usually be delivered to assembly line or order-picking stations in unit of issue quantities so that the necessity for counting parts or repackaging is completely eliminated.

There is a great amount of money to be saved when the supplier can pack in unit of issue quantities, but it is difficult sometimes to see the woods for the trees.

5. Materials Handling Equipment

a. Does this facility maintain an up-to-date MH equipment list?
b. If yes, does the listing contain:
   (i) Equipment number?
   (ii) Manufacturer?
   (iii) Year purchased?
   (iv) Equipment specification?
   (v) Area assigned?
   (vi) Probable replacement date?
   (vii) Initial cost?
   (viii) Attachments added?
   (ix) Total dollar value of fleet?
c. How precise are maintenance cost records, and how effectively is cost control practiced? How precise is cost per hour of operation for each vehicle?
d. How well is the scheduled preventive maintenance (PM) program working at this facility?
e. Is the maintenance area(s) adequate?
f. Is *breakdown maintenance* the only or main type of maintenance performed?
g. Is a daily operators checklist required to be completed by each operator?

h. If yes, is a reasonably effective control established to see whether there is compliance?
i. In general, is the proper MH equipment used to perform MH tasks?
j. Is MH equipment standardized throughout the plant?
k. Are hour meters being used effectively?
l. Is MH equipment being properly utilized through the use of hour meter readings?
m. Are material movements planned so that forklift equipment travel is less than 300 feet per carry?
n. Is standby/exchange equipment available?
o. Are standby/exchange units color-coded according to a standard?
p. Are standby/exchange units properly exchanged for PM purposes?
q. Are mobile materials handling equipment units assigned to the operating units by the MH engineer?
r. Are MH equipment replacement studies valid, or are they based upon pumped-up MAPI (Machinery and Allied Products Institute) formulas?
s. Are MH equipment forecasts made sufficiently in advance to avoid fiscal (not forecasted) problems?
t. Are replacement vehicles and equipment tied in with add-on equipment?

In the above questions on materials handling equipment, the preventive-maintenance aspects of a materials handling equipment program are emphasized. Since the subject matter is quite extensive in scope, *the student is asked to indicate the aspects of the above questions that are unfamiliar to him so that he can further study areas that need to be clarified.* If the student is sufficiently familiar with the reasoning and utility of providing answers to the above questions, he may proceed to the next area (6).

6. Materials Handling Manpower Utilization

a. Is there a manning table, or the equivalent, for indirect labor functions in this facility?
b. Is manual handling of materials held to a minimum?
c. Is walking long distance for or with materials held to minimum?
d. Are "put and take" or mechanical manipulators used for machine loading and unloading (or press feeding) operations wherever possible?
e. Do supervisors have control over the assigned labor force?
f. Is there a duplication of activities or assignments?
g. Is the labor force assigned to a particular department or work area in accordance with the work load?
h. How much demurrage has been incurred during the past 12 months?
i. Rate work pace for materials handling in this facility.

In question 6a, above, we are asking the student to compare available manpower with workloads. The remaining questions in this section concern the optimum use to which the work force is applied.

7. Shipping Materials Handling

a. Is dock space adequate for handling materials?
b. Are truck spots, dock plates, levelers, doors, or dock lights adequate?
c. Is shipping space congested, and do queuing problems exist?
d. Are blocking and bracing, and other shipping materials, conveniently located to the shipping floor.
e. Can block and dunnage preparation be performed more economically by a subcontractor or local sheltered workshop?
f. Are there idle employees awaiting job assignments?
g. Are shipping activities performed relatively close to the last operations?
h. In general, if shipping is performed in more than one location at this facility, can physical locations be optimized?

The questions covered in the above list are pertinent to shipping dock activities regardless of the activity or institution. It is true, however, that not all plants have a requirement for the blocking and bracing of outgoing shipments. If we disregard the two questions 4d and 4e, above, the student can be assured of the universality of the above list.

In the following sections, please review all of the questions so that the summary that follows can be readily understood.

8. Receiving Materials Handling

a. Is there the least possible amount of hand unloading of incoming materials?
b. Is proper equipment used to handle incoming materials?
c. Is the space allocated for receiving adequate?
d. Is there more than one major receiving area at this facility? Can receiving locations be optimized?
e. Are there idle employees awaiting job assignments?
f. Are truck spots, dock plates, dock levelers, doors, or dock lights adequate?
g. Is receiving space congested, and do queuing problems exist?
h. Are dunnage and packaging material disposal problems in evidence? Or does the facility have a systematized method for handling trash?

i. Is there much difficulty with supplier packing lists and checking of materials?
j. Are the inspection, quality, and receiving functions properly coordinated?

9. Plant Layout—General

a. What input does the materials handling engineer have in planning new layouts or in revising existing layouts?
b. Is a team approach used by the materials handling engineer and the layout planner and processor in developing new layouts?
c. Are work measurement studies made of existing indirect labor methods before and after method changes are made?
d. Is there a layout detailing storage location plantwide?
e. When was the last survey made indicating how much plant space was dedicated for storage?
   (i) Less than one year ago?
   (ii) Over one year ago?
f. What possibilities exist for adding fixed path* handling equipment?
g. Can layout changes be made to improve work flow?

10. Plant Layout—Flow of Materials

a. Has the flow of materials been planned?
b. Does material flow in a straight line?
c. Can back-hauling of materials be held to a minimum?
d. Are related operations adjacent? If not, have R.O.I.'s** been prepared to determine trade-offs in rearranging equipment?
e. Are aisles adequate to handle the flow of materials?

11. Plant Layout—Space Utilization

a. Is there effective use of available floor space?
b. Is there effective use of available cube?
c. Are outside storage areas effectively used for material storage?
d. Is outside material stored adjacent to the point of use?

---

*Fixed path equipment; conveyors, chutes, elevators.

**R.O.I.: Return on investment study to determine the profitability of capital investment for new equipment. Usually, when machinery is involved, a MAPI formula (of Machinery and Allied Products Institute) is used. We shall discuss R.O.I. in Chapter 16.

e. Is outside storage material adequately protected?
f. How much is spent on rust and corrosion removal?
g. How much scrap, obsolescent material, or spoiled inventory has been generated this past year because of unrotated stock?

12. Equipment Arrangement and Workplace Layout

a. Are machines and equipment arranged for easy delivery of material?
b. Are machines and equipment arranged for maximum operator efficiency?
c. Are machines and equipment arranged to make full use of machine capacity?
d. If conveyors are used, are they at the proper height for the operator?
e. Does the operator have to bend into a container or tub? Or can a tub tilter be used effectively?
f. Can the operation be supplied by a hopper tub? Or chute ?
g. Can special trays or racks improve the efficiency of operations of a particular activity or subsequent operations either in this facility or interplant?
h. Are machines arranged so that over-travel does not extend into aisles or interfere with operators?
i. Are machines and equipment arranged to permit maximum flexibility for production changes?
j. Is the work station arranged to hold the operator's walking to a minimum?
k. Is there adequate sit-down area for materials at the workplace?
l. Are materials placed as close to the operator as is safe? Or, as is practical?
m. Does the location of the supervisor permit overseeing his area?
n. What is the precision of piece counting, and what is its effect on inventory, scheduling, and production control?
o. Is good housekeeping practiced?

13. Planning

a. Is there a materials handling plan?
   (i) Short range?
   (ii) Long range?
b. Is there layout planning?
   (i) Short range?
   (ii) Long range?

c. Do the plans establish goals and priorities utilizing project planning techniques?

14. Records and Reports

a. Are cost reduction savings monitored?
b. Is there a procedure, or form, used for monitoring savings?
c. Are materials handling progress reports required by this plant's management? How often?
d. Is there a listing for total plant space and its allocation by function, viz., manufacturing, storage, maintenance, etc.?
e. Is a monthly, quarterly, or yearly report issued to management indicating the cost of maintaining and operating MH equipment?

15. Materials Handling Awareness

a. Does this plant have a designated materials handling engineer (MHE)?
b. Does he effectively perform the function of a plant MHE?
c. Does the materials handling engineer review all layouts as to their effect on all materials handling activities?
d. Is there integration and coordination (exchange of information) between the materials handling engineer and all other manufacturing engineering functions, materials control, product design, maintenance, production control, inventory control, purchasing, data processing, other physical distribution operations, etc.?
e. Are follow-up audits performed on all materials handling and plant layout projects, and is appropriate corrective action taken when necessary?
f. Is there an awareness of good materials handling practice at all levels of management?
g. Are industrial engineering techniques employed in solving materials handling problems?

16. Training

a. Have materials handling line supervisors received adequate classroom and on-the-job training in the functional responsibilities of their jobs?
b. Have MH equipment operators received sufficient and periodic training in the safe operation of their equipment and job responsibilities?
c. Is there a continuous program of in-house training to improve the overall proficiency of materials handling in the areas of supervisory and other staff personnel?

d. Is there a training program for improving and/or developing the techniques of layout planning?

* * * * * *

In sections 8 through 16, many areas of factory and warehouse operations were covered; these sections, like the proceding sections 1 through 7, have general application to the operating units concerned.

In a brief summation, then, of sections 8 through 16, we would like to call your attention to some outstanding features of each section, as follows:

Section 8: Receiving Materials Handling. Emphasis in this area is on the proper amount of space, tools to work with, and good methods for performing the tasks involved in receiving materials.

Section 9: Plant Layout—General. It is of primary importance in plant layout to obtain sufficient information to approach the layout logically and with understanding. It is especially important to understand the relationship of one department or function to another. It is helpful, as we shall see later, to be able to measure the effectiveness of a department before and after changes are made.

Section 10: Plant Layout—Flow of Materials. The major benefits for the user in planning straight-line flows of materials are that transportation distances are shortened, and that merchandise is not picked up and then set down a number of times unnecessarily. Back-hauling also is to be avoided, since it involves more handling then is absolutely necessary.

Section 11: Plant Layout—Space Utilization. The important element of space utilization is in the use of the cubic content of the facility, or, in other words, making use of the "air rights." Space assignments, permanent locations, and random storage will be discussed later, but the reader can see that many elements of utilization must be considered in order to obtain maximum effectiveness with available space.

Section 12: Equipment Arrangement and Workplace Layout. This section contains questions on a very complex aspect of both manufacturing and warehousing operations. These areas focus attention on arrangement of machines and workplace so that operator fatigue is minimized and the operator is made as effective a part of the arrangement as possible. This means that for every workplace there is at least one best way for performing a task.

Section 13: Planning. This short section is really most important in the overall operation of any business. The planning for materials handling may be involved in or incorporated into a master plan of the organization, or it may stand alone. Whether or not it is part of another planning function, to be most effective over the long haul or in the broad view of the organization, the materials handling group or function should know where it is going and where it plans to be next year, the year after, and in five to ten years. Knowledge of these projected goals saves errors in equipment selection, building occupancy, etc.

Section 14: Records and Reports. This section ties in very well with the preceding section on planning. Consideration of objectives and budgets, together with a periodic review of the facts, helps us to do a better job of planning. Records and reports, if kept to a bare minimum, can serve as indicators of (a) how well we are doing, and (b) where we want to go.

Section 15: Materials Handling Awareness. One of the most difficult tasks for any materials handling engineer or practitioner—and this includes sales engineers and materials handling equipment suppliers—is to obtain proper recognition of the importance of the materials handling function in plant operations. The materials handling engineer has to keep this fire alive in his organization if he expects to succeed in accomplishing his objectives, and the same thing is true of sales personnel, who also depend on the effectiveness of materials handling programs for their livelihood.

Section 16: Training. The use of training and orientation programs is often paid lip service—even in large organizations. There is much greater return in terms of productivity, effectiveness, morale, and the care with which employees handle material if the proper training is achieved. The text you are now reading will enable you as a practitioner to be head and shoulders above your competitor. Your field of view will be larger, you will be able to understand the broader aspects of the manufacturing and warehousing enterprise, and you will be a much more valuable part of the organization.

The purpose of this chapter was to cover a wide range of material and give the reader a preview of some of the later chapters. You have a checklist for undertaking a materials handling survey of your plant at this point; however, it is advisable to wait until you have completed the entire text before you embark on such a venture.

EXERCISE NO. 3

1. Warehouses, factories, military installations, etc., all have a common requirement, and that is, in order to operate most efficiently they require an ______________ ______________ of materials.
2. Most large mail-order houses have kept pace with business growth by mechanizing their operations. Two of these advances are (1)______________ systems, and (2)______________ -______________ retrieval systems.
3. By providing an orderly flow of materials through a system it is possible to avoid one of the common errors of materials handling, and this is ______________-______________ or the______________ -______________ of materials.

4. In order to avoid back-hauling or back-tracking, once material has passed through an operation it should ________ its direction, not ________ its path.
5. Are you aware of instances of back-tracking in your own operation? Most of us (that is, all who are presently engaged in the field of materials handling) constantly fight to keep the flow of materials in a constant direction from the start to the finish of an operation. Can you give an example to illustrate that you understand what is meant by back-hauling or back-tracking?
____
____
6. Working aisles should permit easy passage of materials handling ________.
7. Most aisles in a plant should be ________.
8. Safe operating ________ of MH equipment should be practiced at all times.
9. Intersecting aisles should permit ________ ________ of equipment.
10. Three areas in which the condition of floors is particularly significant, are:
    1. ________________________________
    2. ________________________________
    3. ________________________________
11. The use of direct labor in both manufacturing and warehousing should always be used in strictly ________ operations.
12. The transportation of materials in manufacturing is usually considered an ________ labor function.
13. The transportation of materials in warehousing is usually considered a ________ labor function.
14. If a production worker has to stop his machine because he runs out of parts, then he is ________ for the amount of time it will take him to obtain the parts.
15. In a plant, the better the scheduling, the greater the ________ that will be achieved.
16. Waste materials should be removed from the workplace without having to ________ ________ the operation.
17. In-process storage areas are either ________ or ________, depending upon one's point of view.
18. Many companies spend large sums of money on complex systems for washing, painting, or heat-treating yet pay relatively little attention to the manner in which the ________ are ________ and ________ from the machines.
19. Usually the cost to convert or modify an installation is a lot ________ after the design has been set into concrete or steel.
20. One of the greatest space wasters in a plant is the practice of storing materials only ________ ________ in height.
21. Rack design has gained prominence through the extensive work and effort of the ________ ________ ________.
22. If storage racks are over ________ feet high, they would be governed in part by the Uniform ________ ________.
23. Pallet storage racks should be designed so that the openings will be capable of

handling the greatest number of ____________ or ____________ to be received.

24. The ____________ of pallet loads is also of major concern in designing or ordering storage racks.
25. A good principle to follow when ordering storage racks is to err on the side of the ____________ opening that can be ____________ purchased.
26. If captive pallets or containers are to be stored, then exact ____________ may be used, providing that at least ____________ inches on each side of the pallet are allowed for the power trucker to place the load in the opening.
27. ____________ -to- ____________ dimensions are also critical in designing storage racks.
28. A flue space in back-to-back storage racks is important. Local building codes may indicate a clearance of ____________ to ____________ inches between racks.
29. Depending on the size of the warehouse, a ____________ system is relatively important in order to control materials.
30. Periodic ____________ help establish and maintain the validity of storage locations in a locator system.
31. Packaging requires a large measure of ____________ on the part of many people within a company.
32. A gauge of the packaging program's effectiveness is how well the ____________ ____________ concept is carried out with materials that are shipped from suppliers, or that are handled either in-plant or between plants.
33. When unit loads are used as an integral part of a company's materials handling system, they should be designed for maximum ____________.
34. When containers no longer serve as transportation means, consideration should be given to the ____________ of the materials of which the container is composed.
35. By determining the ____________ of a container or packaging medium, it is possible to anticipate the methods of disposal of the packaging material concerned.

Chapter 4
Receiving, Shipping, and In-Process Handling

I. RECEIVING

In every manufacturing or physical distribution system material flow begins with the receipt of material. In the strictest sense, it may be understood that prior to this time the material had to be purchased, and possibly inspected at the supplier's plant, the material may have been packaged, traffic rates and routing had to be obtained, etc., and all of these activities may have occurred in advance of the receipt of merchandise. We shall not debate this point, since it is the *material movement* that we are primarily concerned with, and the integration of these other factors will be considered when we discuss the subject of materials management.

The principles involved in planning or operating the receiving department are generally the same in either the manufacturing receiving function or the physical distribution (that is, warehousing and storage) operation. For this reason then, we shall examine the internal workings of an efficient, well-planned and organized receiving department.

A. Physical Characteristics of Receiving Activities

The quickness with which material moves from the carrier, across the receiving dock, and out of the receiving department is a measure of its efficiency. Turnaround time or the rapidity with which the receiving department turns over its inventory is the best gauge that can be used to judge this efficiency. Does the material on the receiving floor move out within 4 hours, 24 hours, 3 days, a week? The answer to this question is, generally speaking, an indication of the pace of the overall plant operation.

The same statement can usually be made concerning the shipping department, and it usually follows that if the receiving operation is a good one, the shipping department will usually be up to snuff also, because of the general rivalry and spirit of competition that can be fostered by an alert manager. In fact, it is a very wise and understanding manager who can appeal to this aspect of human nature to get the job done quickly and well.

In Chapter 1 we mentioned that the cost of materials handling amounts to upwards of 35% of the cost of the product in some instances. More often than not, when the distribution network is complex, as it is for many products, the cost of handling may rise to 80% of the cost of the product, or more. Therefore, let us look very closely at the following activities of the receiving function and see how we can attempt to improve on the efficiency of this significant part of the distribution network.

1. Space Utilization. One of the difficulties involved in planning an effective receiving layout is in the product mix of items to be handled, and another difficulty concerns the method of transportation, that is, whether the material arrives by over-the-road carriers, city delivery trucks, rail, or a combination of these transportation methods.

The product mix of items will dictate the type of materials handling equipment to be used, and probably will be the single largest factor in this determination. However, having established the range of sizes and weights of items that are to be handled, we can proceed to the location of doors and truck wells.

The relationship of set-out areas to the carrier and rail doors, and vice versa, will live to haunt an operator if, for example, insufficient space has been provided on the truck dock apron* for a lift truck to back up and make a turn into a set-out area. It is generally better to err on the side of too much space, rather than not enough.

It may be necessary to use an overhead bridge crane situated over the truck well so that flat bed or open vans may be unloaded. In addition, truck dock levelers that are permanently installed as part of the facility are to be preferred over loose dock boards, for two reasons: (1) safety and (2) the fact that they utilize dock space effectively. A loose dock board takes up building space, since to be available at all times it must be kept in an exposed position close to the scene of the action, on the truck dock apron. If material is stacked upon the dock board, then, of course, space is being utilized, but not effectively, and effort is wasted in making it available for use when needed. So this factor of availability becomes a disadvantage of the dock board when we consider the effective use of the receiving area.

There are many types of mechanical and electro-hydraulically operated dock boards; Appendix G indicates several reliable makes, together with many of the other types and styles of equipment required to set up an effective receiving section operation.

2. Intelligent Design of Receiving Space. As indicated above, a certain amount of planning is required in order to achieve the most effective receiving section for the space allocated for this function. It is always better, of course, to decide what space is required first, then put walls around it, rather than to

*Apron: that part of the truck or rail dock between the vehicle and the first set-out area.

try to stretch or compress each part of the operation to fit the available space. Unfortunately, most receiving operations are planned for already existing space, and sometimes the results are not very satisfactory.

In planning receiving space, that is, during the layout stage, it is well to consider what the target turn-around time will be. For example, we have a fairly good idea of how much incoming material will move across the receiving dock each day, on the average. We feel that we can, with a certain crew size, move everything off the receiving floor every four hours. Also, we have projected our business (volume) growth over the coming five years, and we are required to allow for this expansion.

A word of caution, it is much better for a receiving department to be pressed for set-out space than to have too much area. A little back-pressure on the receiving floor is necessary to keep materials moving rapidly.

If material is to be inspected by quality control, then there should be a provision for this type of space. Also, a quality control laboratory, if required for the plant's receiving operation, can be a rather expensive afterthought if not provided in the original plans.

a. Receiving Door Sizes and Dock Height Levels. Over-the-road trucks continue to get bigger (mainly higher), and if these trucks are to enter the building structure, we should see that the door opening is at least 16′0″ high and 12′0″ wide.

If the truck does not enter the building, then of course the height of the opening should be based upon the lowered mast height with overhead guard of the largest piece of lift truck equipment to be used to enter the truck, plus a safety factor of at least one foot. Thus, if the lowered mast height is 83 inches—say 7 feet—the minimum opening height should be 9 feet. Normally, this type of truck door would be 10 feet in height, and a lot of space would be wasted, especially if one wished to box-in the opening with a loading dock seal. The width of the door opening should be at least 8′6″.

Center-to-center distances for all doors and truck spots should be at least 12′0″. This will permit trucks to be backed into their respective truck spots, not easily but adequately, since the driver will be spotting an 8 foot-wide box in a space that has 4 feet of clearance on either side of his truck. The care that must be exercised by a driver in maneuvering his truck in order to back into his truck spot will make up for any difficulty encountered in so doing; that is, the extra care he must use will tend to minimize the number of accidents to docks and adjacent trucks, etc.

A word about truck bed heights, and the great variation that exists between loaded and unloaded truck bed heights. A fully *loaded* truck can be up to a foot lower than its *unloaded* truck bed height. Suffice it to say, however, that the general trend in dock heights is lower. It was not unusual for warehouses and receiving platforms constructed 20 or more years ago to have truck docks at levels approximately 56 inches high. More recently, there has been a tendency to adopt 48 inches as an optimum truck dock height.

Reefer or refrigerated truck beds are generally higher than the over-the-road, unrefrigerated truck, but a 48-inch dock equipped with a dock leveler should be adequate for them.

Of course, if your plant is receiving furniture or drop-frame trucks, then you may have to consider a 32- to 36-inch truck dock height.

In railroading as well as in trucking, there has been a trend to larger cars, both refrigerated and unrefrigerated. Doors have been getting wider, cars have been getting longer, and many specially designed cars are traveling the rails. Whether or not you receive one of the special cars is a factor of your particular business; however, in designing your rail docks you must consider accommodating not only the smaller 40-foot cars with doors 6 feet in width, but the larger cars that are over 85 feet in length, with correspondingly wider doors. (Note: Figure 2-7, in Chapter 2, is a guide to truck van and freight car dimensions. This guide illustrates the large variations in size that have to be considered prior to actual construction of the facility, that is, at the time of layout planning.)

A truck spot should usually be reserved for city delivery trucks, vans, or

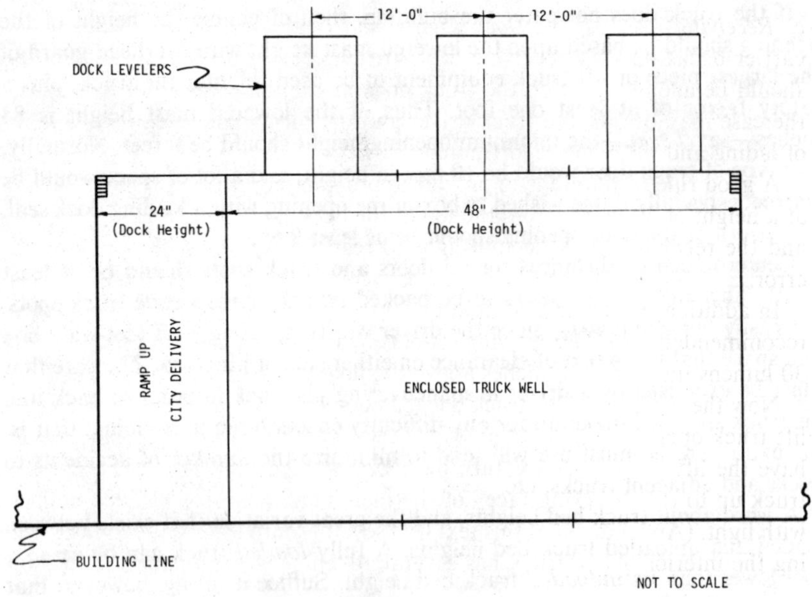

Fig. 4-1. Example of enclosed truck well with provision for city delivery trucks.

panel trucks, either at road level or at most 2 feet high. This can be achieved by the use of a ramp at one side of the dock (see Fig. 4-1).

b. Dock Aprons. We have discussed door sizes, dock heights, and their relationship to the common carrier, the over-the-road truck, and the city delivery vehicle. To make the physical characteristics of the receiving department more efficient, attention must be given to the space on the receiving floor that is directly behind the open door of the truck and lies between the truck and the set-out space of this department. As a rule of thumb, the minimum width of this strip should be the turning radius of the lift truck or other mobile, powered industrial equipment used in unloading the carrier, measured from the edge of the dock board (as the lift truck begins its backward turn), plus 3 feet.

For the sake of giving dimensions that are practical and workable, let us say that you have a 6-foot-long dockboard, and the lift truck has a turning radius of 7 feet; you then add 3 feet, giving an apron width of 16 feet. This would be a minimal dimension. Most of the newer warehouses and plant receiving aprons range from 20 feet wide to considerably wider dimensions. The speed of the unloading operation is greater when there is ample room for a forklift operator to make his backward turn out of the carrier and advance into a set-out area. (We shall discuss towconveyors, etc., and the part they play in receiving operations later in this chapter.)

c. Receiving Area Lights, Dock Lights, and Desk Stanchions. The incoming carrier backs into the receiving bay with his rear cargo door open, and there should be enough light on the truck dock at the dock apron (or rail dock, as the case may be) for the truck driver and the receiving clerk to read the bills of lading and receiving reports, etc.

A good rule of thumb is to provide approximately 30 to 50 lumens* of light at a height of 30 inches from the top of the dock floor. This will give the driver and the receiving clerk enough light to read documents with a minimum of error.

In addition to the strip of light of 30 to 50 lumens on the dock apron, it is recommended that the receiving set-out areas have a light intensity of at least 30 lumens measured 30 inches above the floor.

Now the carrier has his truck backed completely into his truck spot, and the lift truck operator begins to unload the vehicle. At this point it is of value to have the lift truck operator turn on his *dock lights,* so that the inside of the truck up to the "working face" of the merchandise being unloaded is flooded with light. (Appendix G of this text lists several sources for these lights.) Lighting the interior of the truck has several advantages; for example, it enhances

*A lumen, which is a measure of lighting intensity, can be readily tested by a hand-held meter.

the safety of the operation, it tends to minimize damage to the merchandise being unloaded, and it enables the forklift truck driver, or the walkie pallet truck operator, to see the condition of the truck floor so that he will not break through a weak or rotted carrier bed.

Another convenience that speeds the unloading operation is a small desk or stanchion with a flat top, where the receiving clerk may check his invoice, review packing lists, examine the bill of lading, etc. In other words, rather than shuffle papers in his hand, he has a surface on which to write.

d. Enclosed Docks. Earlier in this chapter, we referred to the loading dock seal that boxes-in, or encloses, the opening around the truck door and the frame of the building door. When the magnitude of an operation permits, especially in areas of severe winter weather, an enclosed dock promotes efficiency, especially if the teamwork of a captive fleet and the receiving section are important for a fast turn-around schedule.

If the truck dock is totally enclosed, provision must be made for the elimination of truck exhaust emissions.

Also, the enclosed truck dock should be long enough from the exterior door to the edge of the truck dock to accommodate the largest tractor-trailer combination permitted in your state. Please keep in mind that tractor-truck lengths are increasing, and plan ahead.

The same door sizes mentioned earlier apply to the exterior doors, namely, 16′0″ high and 12′0″ wide. Usually these doors are electric, roll-up types with auxiliary chain-falls that permit raising and lowering the door when power blackouts occur.

Roof trusses of enclosed docks should have sufficient capacity to permit the installation of overhead bridge cranes, where overhead handling of materials from flatbed trucks or open vans is concerned.

e. Chocks and Stands. Up until the time of the Williams-Steiger Act (OSHA), it was considered good practice to place wheel chocks under the rear wheels of a truck at a truck dock. Also, if the box was dropped, that is, if the tractor was removed from the semi (and the box was left at the dock), one and sometimes two wheel jacks, or stands, were placed at the front of the box to keep it from tipping or collapsing as the fork truck operator entered the front end of the box during the unloading cycle. Not only is this good practice today, but OSHA *requires* that the operator do this without exception.

Another plus for a good receiving dock are air-lines that permit truck air-brakes to be hooked-up if the tractor is removed.

f. Towconveyors. In some modern and progressive receiving departments where the volume handled will permit the use of in-floor, drag-chain conveyors, there is a very logical direction for the towconveyor to follow. For example, if the towconveyor services the entire plant, or at the very least the shipping department, it is important that the flow or movement of the towconveyor be from shipping to receiving.

The main reason that this is a fundamental requirement is that pallet-loads of material coming into the shipping department may be offloaded from the towconveyor carts into tbe carriers. Merchandise is taken off these pallets and hand-stacked into the trailer, or van. Then the empty pallets are put back on towconveyor carts for transportation to the receiving department, where they are used to load incoming materials.

If materials are not received loose and unpalletized—that is, if most of the incoming material is palletized—then, of course, other conditions would prevail to determine the flow path of the towconveyor.

Similarly, if a tractor-trailer train is used in the facility, then the above comments would apply with respect to offloading or depalletizing the merchandise and generating a supply of pallets for the receiving function.

In Chapter 9 we shall discuss the pros and cons of the tractor-trailer train versus the towconveyor. At present, we shall continue an overview of the physical characteristics of receiving operations.

3. Unloading and Spotting Carriers. In large warehousing facilities it is sometimes advantageous to spot carriers, especially trucks, at a door that is closest to the point where the material is to be stored. This is especially true where full truckload quantities are concerned. Then a receiving clerk sees to it that security precautions are observed.

a. Trucks. For most ordinary receiving operations that are carried out on a small scale, or for reasons of control of inventory, or to support a manufacturing operation, it is well to consider a single receiving point in the plant. When a plant guardhouse is used, it is usually possible to communicate directly by telephone or intercom with the chief of the receiving department or the dispatcher to find out what truck spot the incoming carrier should occupy. Wherever possible, a procedure should be employed in which the plant security personnel relay to the truck driver a specific spot for his truck. A pay telephone should be installed somewhere on the truck receiving dock for the convenience of carriers. Preferably, this location should not be in the receiving office, but somewhere outside near the receiving truck well.

b. Railcars. As mentioned, railcars are getting larger, and more and more special railcars are now being built in an attempt to compete with truck transportation. Although competition is the obvious reason for these trends, many other factors involved in rail transportation have also influenced them—certainly many beyond the scope of this text.

As we study the railcar method of transporting freight, we find cars that carry 40, 50, or 70 or more tons of merchandise. If several cars are to be received, we can make arrangements with the rail freight office to have the cars spotted for us in a prescribed order. Sometimes this service is very good, especially for good customers and if the railroad team tracks are not too far distant. On occasion, a plant may have sufficient volume to justify the use of a small, donkey engine or a Tracmobile for moving the cars on the plant siding. Cars are usually spotted by the railroad at least once daily, and sometimes twice, depending, of course, on volume. There is sometimes a service charge for extra switching, and this should be held to a minimum.

There are mechanical railcar dock boards; however, it is more common for a steel or magnesium dock board to be placed in the car door by the forklift truck operator.

Reel-type lights are often used on railcar docks, although extendable, wall-mounted lights are sometimes employed to good advantage. All comments concerning truck dock lights certainly apply in this instance.

c. Demurrage. One of the greatest headaches for receiving department management personnel is to incur demurrage* charges for either trucks or railcars. In order to minimize demurrage—notice, I do not say prevent it—it is necessary that there be a proper balance between crew size and the scheduling of incoming shipments. Sometimes it makes more sense to incur demurrage charges than to work a receiving crew overtime. At other times, incurring demurrage costs may be a relatively inexpensive method for providing scarce warehouse space. This depends, of course, on the size of the operation, since a small or medium-size plant may have a temporary need for warehouse space that amounts to only a few days. In fact, some brokers regularly live out of the boxcar as a means of cutting their costs of doing business.

In summary, for most warehousing operations where the main business is warehousing, and even where it is a part of a manufacturing plant, large

---

*Demurrage: the detention of a vessel, freight car, or truck beyond the time originally stipulated in loading or unloading; also, the compensation (penalty) that has to be paid for such delay. The charges vary from coast to coast; however, the present allowances and charges in the central states are as follows:

Rail: The first 24 hours free; next 4 days. @ $30/day; next 4 days. @ $40/day; next 4 days. @ $50/day; etc.
Truck: If the merchandise is at least 80% unitized, the first 2 to 3 hours are free; if the freight is not unitized, then because the shipper pays higher freight rates, he is allowed 6 to 8 hours free; after the grace period the rates are anywhere from $5 to $30 or more per hour, with refrigerated trucks at the high end of the scale.

demurrage charges are usually indicative of an inefficient receiving department.

d. Conveyors and Slug Unloading. In order to increase the efficiency of receiving operations where carriers must be unloaded, some companies have tried using powered telescoping conveyors. Even skate-wheel and gravity roller conveyors, which were first used to manually unload a car or truck, have increased the productivity of this activity. Despite the fact that labor costs—that is, wage rates and fringe benefits—continue to increase, many truckloads and carloads of merchandise are received that are hand-stacked inside the box; and at the receiving end these have to be unloaded manually at great cost.

It would be less expensive in many instances, especially where full truckload quantities are concerned, to palletize the loads or use kraft paper slip-sheets to form unit loads.

In some captive receiving and shipping operations—for example, where a manufacturing plant ships finished goods to its warehousing center in company-owned (leased) trucks—it would probably be profitable to consider slug loading and unloading. Whenever there is a sufficient volume of traffic between the plant and the warehouse, or interplant, we should obtain the accounting department's evaluation of the cost benefits of this method of functioning.

There are several types of slug loading. For example, there is the shuttlebed, in which a walking beam arrangement unloads all the cargo from the truck in minutes. There is also the powered conveyor in the truck floor; it was first used by Kraft Foods in the 1950s, and then a similar version was used by AC Spark Plug Division in Flint, Michigan some years ago.

The above methods have been successfully practiced for many years; however, some interplant shippers have tried them and have become disenchanted when some aspect—most generally of a supervisory nature—has failed. The blame for failure is usually in failing to sell the concept properly, with understanding and patience; and, in communicating wisely and widely so that all who "need to know" are informed. But, let's reserve a discussion of selling materials handling ideas to management for later in the text (Chapter 20).

4. Yard Storage of Receivables. Many types of materials are conveniently and, in some instances, inexpensively stored out-of-doors; for example, lumber, steel, castings, forgings, export packed materials, and items that are included in a wide range of related products.

Therefore, when we discuss the various types of outdoor or yard storage plans, we are talking about those items that are relatively free from damage from the elements for considerable periods of time—months and often years.

On the other hand, for grocery items and soft-goods, stationery, and so on, there is absolutely no economical way, at present, that merchandise may be stored outdoors in its own shipping container, or package.

There are several methods for storing materials and containers in a yard, namely:

1. Block storage
2. Back-to-back storage
3. Sawtooth storage
4. Tiering rack storage
5. Cantilevered rack storage
6. Storage rack storage

In *block storage* (Fig. 4-2) we obtain the highest density, and there is no doubt that this method minimizes storage costs at the expense of added materials handling costs. Even when all of the product or parts are similar, it is very difficult to control the turnover of the stock. When dissimilar parts are stored in the block, then getting at the correct part becomes expensive from the standpoint of labor and machine (powered industrial truck) time, since a number of containers may have to be moved and shifted in order to locate the specific container(s).

Back-to-back storage is somewhat less economical than block storage in terms of its poorer use of available space; however, each column is accessible from an aisle.

Let us consider, for a minute, a few of its disadvantages. (1) If containers are stacked more than one high, there is the problem of tearing down the tier in order to obtain the bottom containers. (2) A great deal of space is wasted in aisles, both main aisles and cross aisles. (3) Aisle widths are dependent upon the aisle dimensions necessary for the largest unit of powered industrial equipment that is to be used; for example, if the aisles have been sized for a side-loading truck, then it would be impossible to use a counterbalanced forklift truck of similar capacity, since the lift truck would require a wider aisle within which to function. (Note: There are several makes of right-angle stacking forklift trucks now on the market, but the largest unit made in the United States has a capacity of only 6,000 pounds; sideloaders, on the other hand, are being produced in 4,000-, 6,000-, and 10,000-pound and larger capacities.)

Back-to-back storage is illustrated in Fig. 4-3.

Sawtooth storage (Fig. 4-4) is very rarely used in outdoor or, for that matter, indoor storage applications. The principal advantage of this type of storage is that a counterbalanced forklift truck may enter the stack and get to every container in an aisle that is only slightly wider than the truck or load. There are obvious disadvantages to this system, since a lift truck must back out of the aisle; and although there is a definite saving in aisle space, the operation becomes relatively slow and awkward.

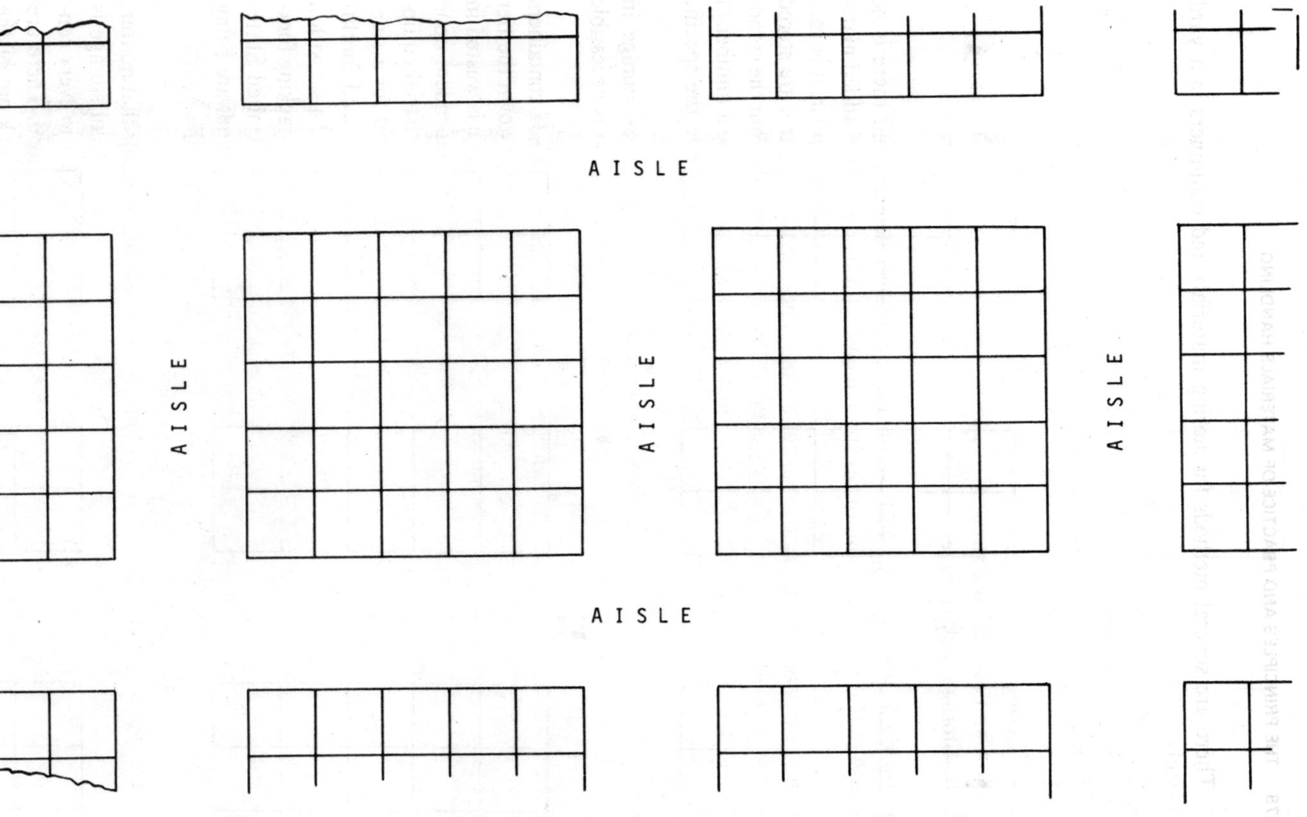

Fig. 4-2. Example of block storage, the economical storage method with high operating costs, especially when material or containers are stacked in two or more tiers.

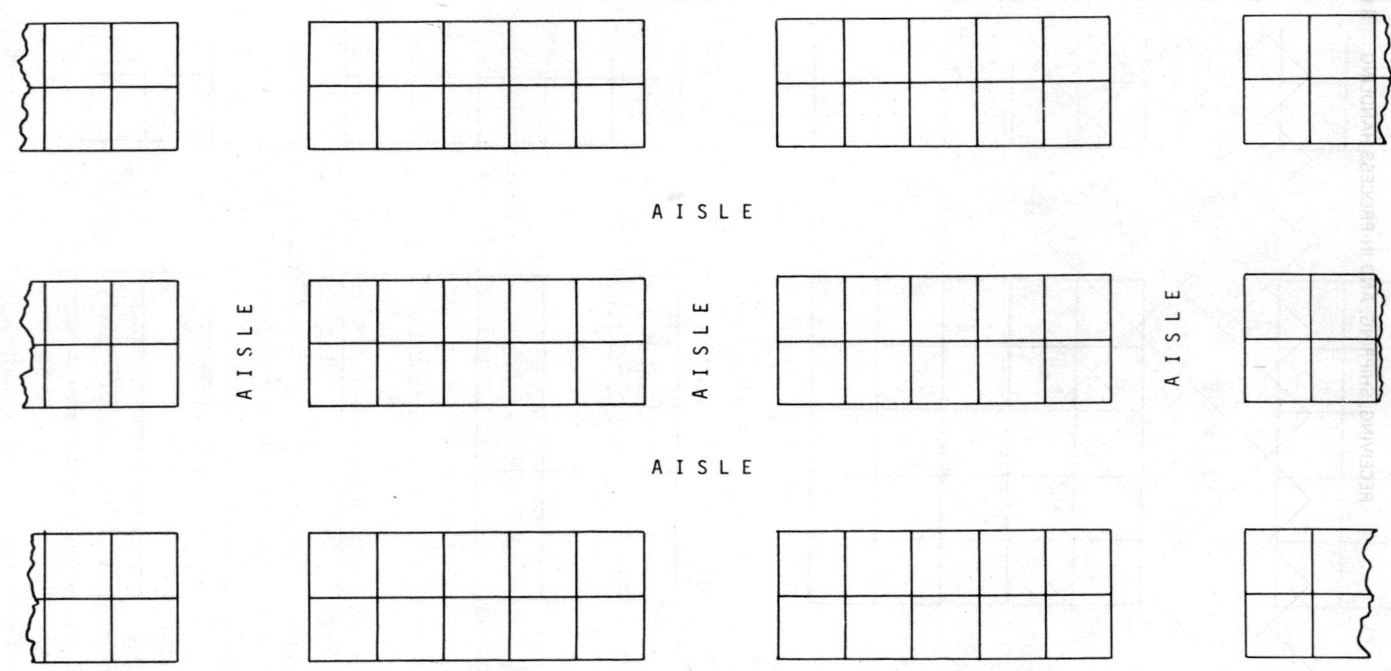

Fig. 4-3. A plan view of back-to-back storage. Notice the amount of floor space required to operate this type of storage yard. This wasted space can vary from 25 to 50% of the total space required.

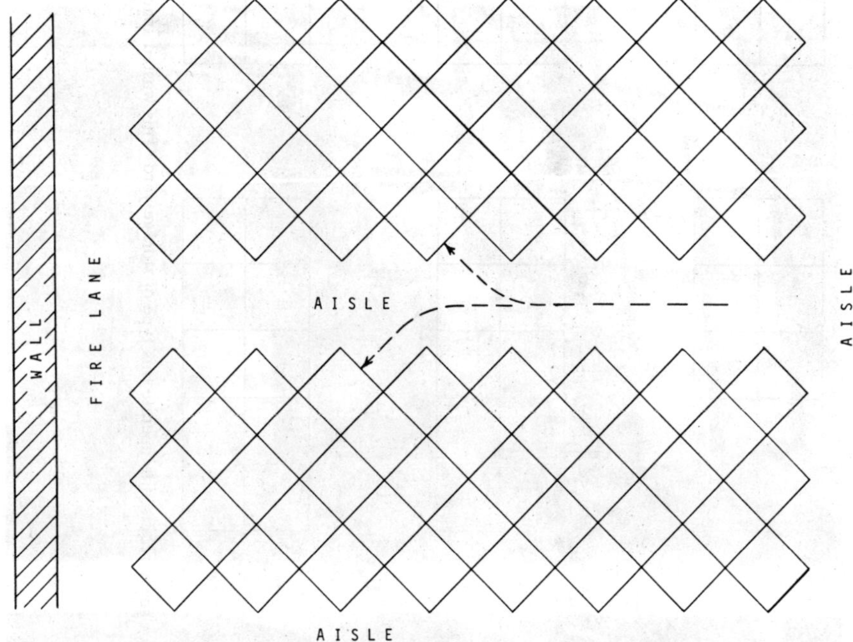

Fig. 4-4. A illustration of the sawtooth storage method showing the somewhat narrower aisles required for this storage method.

Tiering rack storage is just what its name implies—the use of tiering racks for outside (and indoor) storage. The tiering rack becomes, in large measure, just like a pallet storage rack, except with a great deal more mobility and flexibility. The tiering racks can be either the rigid or the knock-down type (see Fig. 4-5).

Cantilevered rack storage has a vast range of potential applications. Cantilevered racks can be used in outdoor yard storage areas for parts, for steel and bar stock storage containers, and the like; or they can be used indoors for the same materials and for such diverse items as furniture and tubing. Most cantilevered racks require lagging to the floor or concrete surface upon which they rest. There is an A-frame type of cantilevered rack that does not require lagging, but it is limited in size and height.

Fig. 4-6 shows the use of the cantilevered rack.

Storage racks or pallet storage racks are usually used back-to-back in indoor applications. Occasionally, they are used to very good advantage for outdoor storage, especially where space is limited and where the instant accessibility of each container, fixture, die, or other material is desirable. (See Fig. 4-7.)

Fig. 4-5. Knock-down tiering racks used for storage. An advantage of the tiering rack is that it can be left in place or taken as a unit with the merchandise directly to the point of use. Courtesy of Jarke Company, Niles, Illinois, and Tier Rack Corporation, St. Louis, Missouri.

Fig. 4-5. *(continued)*

5. Locator Systems. The organization of the physical aspects of the receiving function is extremely critical in that the better organized this department is, the more money it is going to make for the enterprise.

All the methods and equipment discussed so far in this chapter have emphasized the above philosophy. It cannot be overemphasized, since systematic control of all the physical characteristics of receiving demands attention to every detail. One of these important details is *knowing where the merchandise is!*

Thus, all the receiving areas should be plainly marked with floor locations, and all the outdoor storage yards should be clearly marked so that a Kardex, Access, or similar card file can be the locating center for all materials moving into the enterprise.

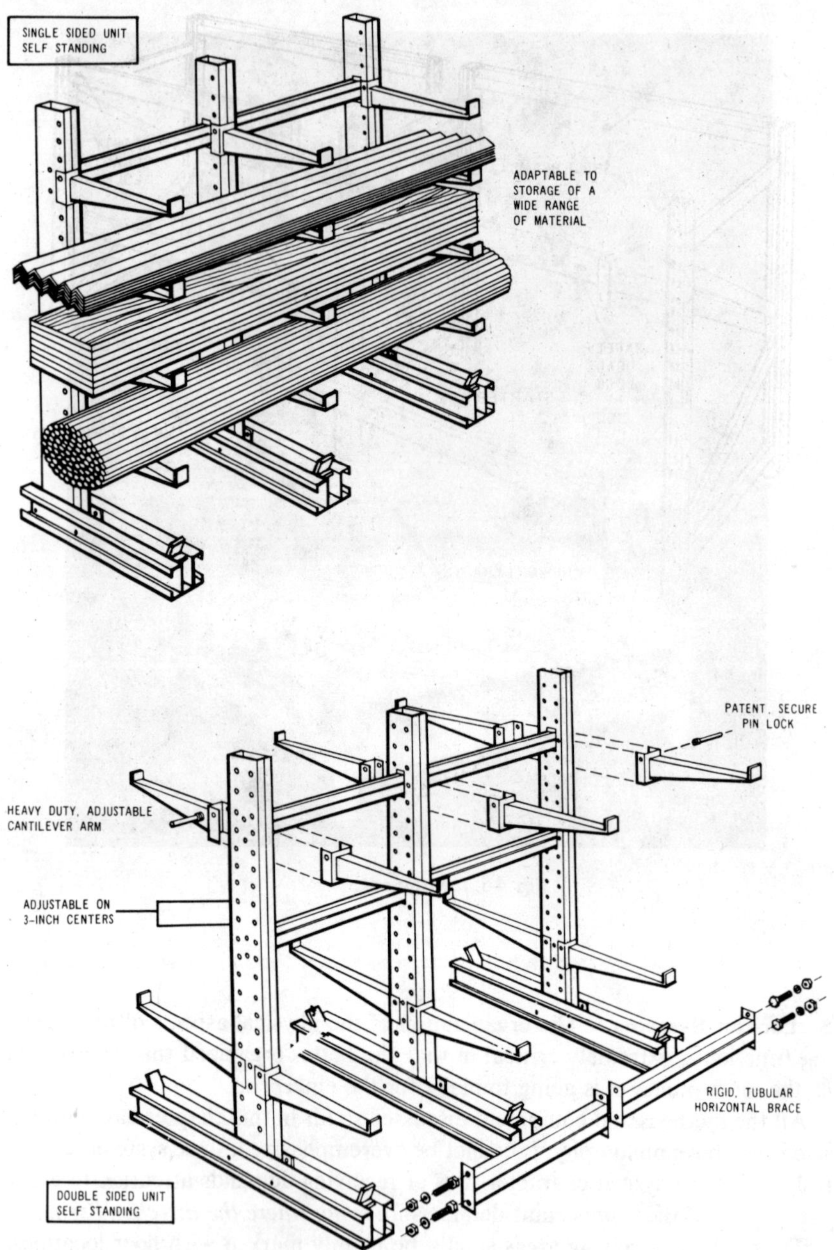

Fig. 4-6. Cantilevered racks in both outdoor and indoor applications.

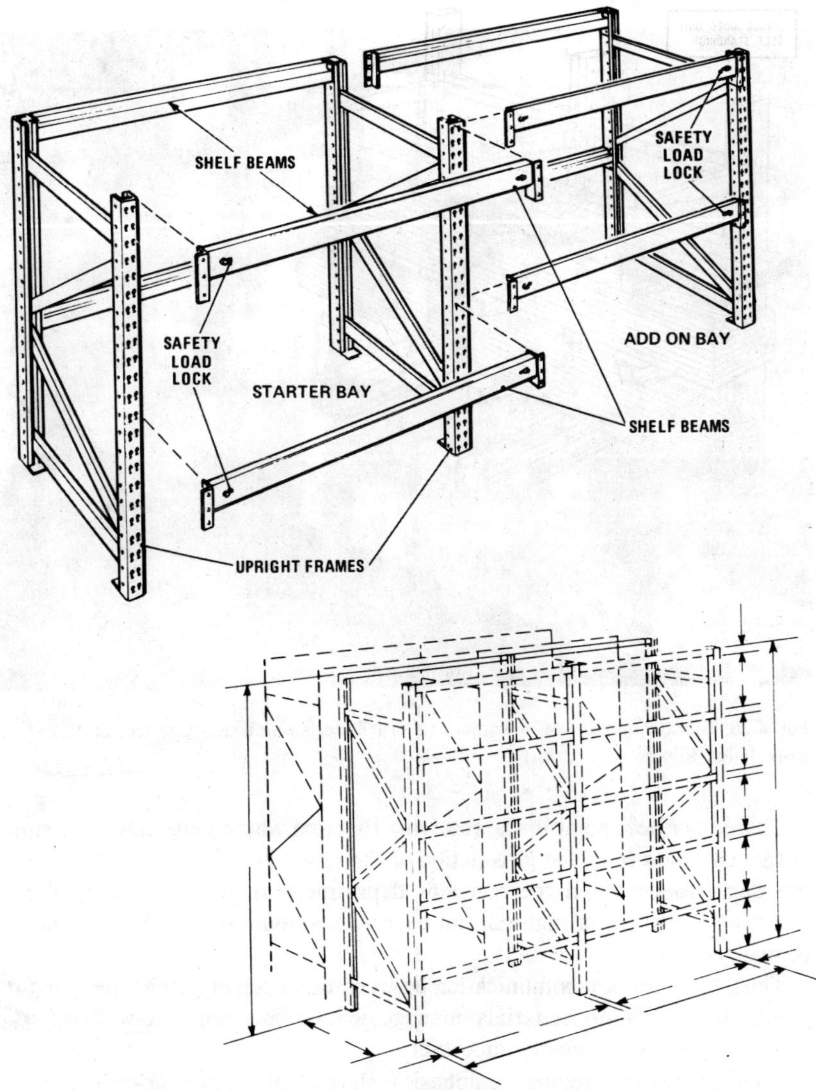

Fig. 4-7a. Elements of a storage rack system.

Fig. 4-7b. Storage rack in use in a wholesale distributor's warehouse. Courtesy of Jarke Company, Niles, Illinois.

There may be a point in the receiving function where materials to be stored in the yard pass from the jurisdiction of the receiving chief to a materials control department; but if the receiving department knows where to send each incoming truckload of material, an enormous amount of double handling can be avoided.

Thus, the lines of communication between the receiving department and the materials control or materials management department, as well as other departments, are extremely important.

Another area that requires emphasis is the expediting of back-ordered materials to the point of use. We shall cover that subject in detail in the next section of this chapter.

B. Receiving, Paperwork and Control

In section A of this chapter we discussed some of the physical characteristics of receiving that support the primary objectives of this function, which are: (1) to identify incoming material; (2) to verify incoming material; and (3) to move this material expeditiously to the point of use or storage within the plant.

Along with these three objectives, there are a number of paper transactions and other clerical functions that provide the control necessary to manage the receiving of materials effectively.

1. Truck and Rail Register. After the incoming truck has been spotted at a convenient dock location, one of the first activities is to record the truck's time of arrival, date, driver's name, trucking company, and bills of lading numbers. This provides a very valuable record, which can help in tracing materials. After the truck has been unloaded, the time the unloading was finished is entered into the log. This comes in handy when demurrage charges must be verified. A very similar but separate register is kept for railcars.

2. Identification of Materials. The receiving and storage of materials requires that materials be easily and quickly identified. Therefore, all incoming receivables should be labeled, or tagged, with legible information even when the data are stenciled or handwritten.

The receiving department must communicate the need for adequate information to accompany all incoming merchandise to the purchasing department, which negotiates these things with the suppliers.

The "adequate" information should consist of:

1. A complete part number.
2. The number of pieces in an individual package or the unit of measure.
3. A purchase order number.
4. Any designation for the latest model or engineering change number.
5. The date the material was packed: month, day, and year.
6. The gross weight of the package in pounds.
7. The supplier's name and address, plus any code name or number indicating what plant (of the supplier) the material came from.

3. Supplier Packing Lists In addition to the proper labeling of every container (or other incoming material) with identification information (section B2, above), the shipper or supplier, as the case may be, must provide a packing list with every shipment.

This supplier packing list specifies what should be received and what to look for. If the list is missing, then there is the possibility that mistakes will be made in verifying the material, especially with respect to quantity.

The information noted above in section B2 is basic to receiving; and, when the material is checked in, not only must each individual container or unit load be marked, but the supplier packing list should contain the total quantity for that specific shipment.

After the receiving checker has verified the load, the supplier's packing list is sent to the receiving office where it can be logged in. The "due-in" board can be adjusted, and accounts payable can be notified.

The "due-in" board can be a graphic display where the number of incoming shipments is not greater than can be readily handled on a visual display board; or the "due-in" information can be kept internally in a computer, with a periodic printout to alert the purchasing expediter and the receiving clerk.

In a computerized system a data terminal operator can place the packing list information directly into an on-line receiving system. The computer will produce a ticket that can be placed on the load; as many tickets as there are loads will be produced automatically once the packing list information has been entered into the computer. Usually, a ticket produced in this manner will indicate where to store the materials, or at what point in the plant the material must be delivered.

The information fed into the computer can then be made available to the accounting and purchasing departments in the form of printed reports.

In manual systems, the same elements that are performed with such speed and precision by the computer must also be documented, and reports must be written, ledgers posted, and so forth. There is a time in every growing company when hand posting is no longer adequate for keeping all of the information received in an orderly fashion. At this point, the computer fills the breach and performs many repetitive clerical tasks more quickly and usually with greater precision than would be possible otherwise.

There are now so many "canned" programs for computers, covering a wide range of applications, that it is a wonder that many companies still insist on re-inventing the wheel and developing their own computer programs, for doing what has been done so many times before. The receiving function, described above, can be used with minor adaptations or program changes by any number of progressive companies to achieve the same simple and straightforward task of receiving merchandise and putting it away!

Computer experts in each company have what they call "exception routines" to handle such things as: (1) *partial incoming receivables,* where only part of the due-in is received; (2) the *hold for inspection* shipment, or partial shipment; (3) the *defective shipment* which either will be returned to the supplier, or will require an adjustment in price to be made; (4) the *damaged-in-transit* shipment, which must be held for further disposition; and, so forth. So the business of our simple and straightforward receiving department takes on all the complexities of a very difficult game of chess. But, despite the number of variations that are encountered, you can still find a very effective packaged program for performing the bulk of the clerical work of the receiving department.

4. Handling Back-Orders. As indicated earlier in this chapter, one objective of the receiving function is to move incoming materials quickly to the point of use or storage within the plant.

Back-orders usually cause problems when they are not spotted quickly on the receiving floor. On the other hand, if someone inadvertently places all of the material into storage rather than sending some of the material to an assembly line or to an order picking operation, there is additional grief. A back-order should be sent directly into shipping, especially if an outgoing order is being held for completion.

Sometimes it is better to send a customer a partial shipment rather than to wait upon a back-order; however, customers have to be trained to accept this occasional lapse in service, and it should not be used without informing the customer beforehand—nor should it happen too often.

Therefore, every receiving operation should make definite provision to flag each due-in so that back-orders can be handled promptly. A computerized receiving system should scan the list of due-ins so that a move ticket indicates the urgency of each back-order as it is received.

5. Hazardous Materials. Each supplier, according to law, has the responsibility of complying with all local, state, and federal laws and regulations that apply to the labeling, shipping, storage, and handling of hazardous materials. A hazardous material is any toxic, corrosive, radioactive, flammable, or explosive substance. In addition, a substance is also considered hazardous if it is packaged in a container considered to be dangerous, as, for example, a pressurized can.

This is another area where the chief of the receiving department should maintain good communications with the purchasing department, and both receiving and purchasing should have a copy of the latest issue of "Hazardous Materials Regulations of the Department of Transportation, Including Specifications for Shipping Containers" (see Appendix A for source).

II. SHIPPING

As noted earlier in this chapter, a friendly rivalry between the receiving and shipping departments can serve a useful purpose in increasing productivity and in lifting morale in the plant.

As part of this rivalry a production scoreboard can be used to good advantage to let employees of both departments know where they stand against some of the targets (objectives) defined by management. Such things as "tons shipped," "line-items shipped," etc., all have a place in managing these departments. Of course, we are using shipping department terminology here, and the appropriate unit of measure should be applied to the receiving department.

One somber note for the management of the shipping department: *Shipping is the one single area in the plant where collusion for theft is most predominant.* Therefore, while we discuss both the physical characteristics of the shipping department and the necessary paperwork and control, it is well to recognize that the systematic organization of this department is absolutely essential to maintain the highest degree of accountability for the material that flows across the shipping floor.

A. Physical Characteristics of Shipping Activities

The shipping department is usually larger than the receiving department in square feet of floor space. One reason for this is that loads must be accumulated to await a carrier, and the materials may move into the shipping department at a relatively slow rate.

In Chapter 5, we shall develop some of the criteria for planning the various departments within a factory and warehouse, including such factors as floor loadings, ceiling heights, and so forth. For the present, we shall assume that we have adequately determined floor loads, and are concerned with the important operating elements of the shipping department.

1. Space Utilization. As we mentioned in our discussion of receiving, the product mix of materials to be handled by the shipping department can be a determining factor in the layout of this department. For example, if a number of small containers are to be merged with larger unit loads, then it may be necessary to provide pallet storage racks or bin shelving at convenient places on the shipping floor.

If boxing or crating is required, then provision should be made to place this relatively dusty operation in some remote, yet well-ventilated, area of the shipping floor. The same thing is true of paint booths and protective-coating activities such as cosmoline and grease (oil) dipping. If possible, all of these activities should be divorced—physically—from the shipping department; it would be better to have the above packaging take place closer to the production operations than in this department. It makes more sense to package a product directly, as a last operation on a fabrication line, than to put it in a temporary container prior to packaging, and then have to remove it from the temporary container—a practice that constitutes double handling. Many companies are, in fact, guilty of such wastefulness.

2. Intelligent Design of Shipping Space. Many of the features referred to in the receiving section of this chapter are applicable to the shipping department. For the moment, let us enumerate them, as follows:

1. Door sizes and dock height levels
2. Dock aprons
3. Overhead lights, dock lights, and desk stanchions
4. Enclosed docks
5. Chocks and stands

Mention was made in the receiving section of dockboards and mechanical and electro-mechanical dock levelers. No modern warehouse is built today without the latter type of dock levelers, nor can the most efficient shipping department be fully effective without these dock levelers.

Aside from the hardware items mentioned above, there is a great need to design the shipping area to provide easy access to it from all parts of the plant. In addition, as loads are built up on the shipping floor, there should be a direct flow of this material to the carrier.

In designing a shipping activity, also, there should be some consideration of future, if not present, conveyorization in order to build up outgoing shipments. The planner and the planning staff have to determine if outgoing volumes will justify tractor-train, driverless tractor, or towconveyor applications, the need for storage racks, and so forth.

3. Loading and Spotting Carriers. While it is important in receiving operations to be able to spot the carriers at a particular truck dock, it is just as important in a shipping function to have the right carrier at or near the outgoing shipment. In the first place, since most carriers are outloaded by forklift truck, this saves travel distance and time; in addition, it eliminates the cross traffic that would occur on the shipping dock if this rule were not adhered to very strictly.

Dock lights, the proper lighting levels* on the shipping floor, a desk for paperwork, all of these things are necessary for the proper loading of a carrier. In addition, the supervisor in this area should make certain that OSHA regulations are followed: wheel chocks, and stands in place and air lines hooked up when the tractor is removed. The work of loading a carrier with pallet loads or containers of one size is not too difficult, but just let the product size, weight, and density vary in the same shipment, and it becomes an art. Truck drivers are sometimes very knowledgeable about this art, and sometimes they are not. Usually assistance can be obtained from a trucking agent; and if the shipper has sufficient volume, the chief of the shipping department may have a trucking agent living on the premises.

Since weight distribution in an over-the-road carrier is very critical, it is best to seek expert advice if there is much difference in the weight of materials being outloaded. This is really not work for an amateur, and a mistake such as putting the heaviest items in the tail end of a truck could prove disastrous.

4. Use of Conveyors, Tractor-Trains, Driverless Tractors, and Towconveyors. A great deal of thought and work have been devoted to attempts to improve the effectiveness of outloading operations in all types of physical distribution and manufacturing enterprises during the past two decades.

*Lighting levels should be at least as high as those described in section I, A2c of this chapter.

Two approaches have been followed in this area of mechanization. The first approach uses the more conventional, and off-the-shelf or commercially available, equipment. The second approach employs a higher degree of mechanization and includes the computer among its components.

We shall examine the first approach in this chapter, and reserve the second approach for Chapter 9.

a. Conveyors. As materials are brought into the shipping department, we have to decide rather quickly where they are to be set-out, so that when the carrier arrives the material can be outloaded without the necessity for carrying out a second order-selection operation. That is usually the reason why most shipping departments store materials one tier high over most of the available shipping floor space, and waste a good deal of the air-rights or cubic content of the facility.

So, there have been shipping departments planned with in-floor conveyors, skate-wheel conveyors, roller conveyors. The in-floor conveyors are powered, whereas the roller conveyors may be powered, controlled by a push button usually from the front or the offloading end, or they may be gravity or nonpowered. Skate-wheel conveyors are usually used with very light loads and are nonpowered, gravity-flow types.

At least one or more conveyor lines in the above systems are used for one carrier. A sign over the conveyor will usually spell out either the name or initials of the carrier, or the destination.

Some of the points to watch for in installing a conveyor system of this type are:

1. Care must be taken that the traffic flow in the department is not hindered.
2. Precautions must be taken that the installation will not prohibit the use of the present type of industrial powered equipment, wherever this is an important factor.
3. If material is stored at random on the conveyors—that is, if it is not scheduled in a last-in, first-out basis in the carrier and placed in the right order on the holding conveyor—then a power trucker has to be able to pick it off the conveyor at any point on the conveyor line.
4. If possible, a locator system should be used to locate materials placed in the set-out area. And, with conveyors in the set-out area the locator system can be very elementary, for example, a pigeon-hole cupboard with each hole representing a conveyor line(s).

b. Tractor-Trains. Tractor-trains can be very versatile and useful for supporting the loading-out function of a shipping department; however, if palletized material is held on the trailer until offloaded into a carrier, a great deal of floor space is wasted. It is much better to use the tractor-train to transport material from other departments within the plant into the shipping area, and to offload the trailers into a set-out area according to the locator system mentioned in the preceding paragraph.

Because of the turn-around space required for a tractor-train installation, it is customary to consider only straight-line runs through the shipping department or, at most, right-angle turns where necessary.

c. Driverless Tractors. Although driverless tractors have been with us for quite some time, at least since World War II, they have been relatively slow in establishing themselves. At the outset, reliability of the guidance system was marginal; lately, these systems have been very much improved. The condition and maintenance of the floors upon which they travel have been deciding factors militating against their effectiveness. Also, the ease with which they can be sabotaged and damaged has limited their universality of application.

But, despite their shortcomings—not the least of which is their relatively high cost—in some ideal applications the driverless tractor has returned a handsome profit to its users. Usually the driverless tractor is effective when it fits into and complements a larger, more complex type of mechanization.

d. Towconveyors. The in-floor, drag-chain conveyor commonly known as a towconveyor is used extensively in large trucking terminals, large warehouses, and large manufacturing shipping departments where vast tonnages are handled daily. The use of a cart with a drop-pin that engages the forged-chain, pusher dog in a track in the floor gives the towconveyor a great deal of versatility, in that it does not require an operator.

In addition, by a series of positions on the front bumper mechanism, the cart may be switched automatically into various predesignated spurs; or by bumping into the car ahead, as in a queue, the cart will lift its pin, thus disengaging the pin from the pusher dog, and will come to a stop by setting its self-contained brakes. When the preceding cart moves on, the drop-pin will again engage the in-floor chain, pusher dog and proceed onward toward its predesignated destination—all by means of the mechanisms incorporated into the design of the system.

The main disadvantages are that mistakes in laying out and installing a towconveyor are exceedingly difficult and costly to rectify, since the track is laid in concrete with much hand labor involved. Many systems today have been justified satisfactorily from the standpoint of their return-on-investment, and one of the leading towconveyor companies has over 400 rather extensive and satisfactory systems to its credit.

From the standpoint of overall cost, a towconveyor installation consisting of motor drives, controllers, sensing units, panel boxes, wiring, etc., may not be as expensive as the several hundred drop-pin carts required to complete the system.

In summary, when comparing the use of tractor-trains, driverless tractors, and towconveyor installations, we find the following applications:

1. Used on large-volume movements only—towconveyors
2. Used on small to moderate movements—driverless tractors
3. Used on both small and large movements—tractor-trains

It is necessary to add, however, that a great deal depends upon the size and complexity of the installation. There are advantages and disadvantages in each system that must be evaluated before the selection of any one type of installation is made.

5. Overhead, Drag-chain Conveyors. Overhead, monorail conveyors with pulling dogs from which warehouse carts may be attached by either a center pole or a chain and dragged along the conveyor route, enjoyed a certain amount of popularity before the in-floor, drag-chain conveyor with all its sophistication (such as spurs to which carts could be switched, indexing means to permit carts to be siderailed at predetermined stops, etc.) started to take over in large numbers. The necessary steel structure, either hanging from the trusses of a plant or placed along the travel path of the conveyor, has definitely limited the application of this type of drag-chain conveyor. Its greatest advantage when compared to an in-floor drag-chain system is that to reroute this type of conveyor after it has been installed is not as costly, usually, as having to reroute an in-floor conveyor. Neither change, however, can be taken lightly because considerable expense is involved in either case.

6. Slug Loading. As indicated above in section I, A3d, whenever a captive truck fleet exists for distribution or interplant movement, serious consideration should be given to the possibility of slug loading.

In slug loading the entire content of the van or carrier is loaded as you would place a clip of cartridges into a gun—all at once, or very nearly so, depending upon the type of slug considered.

Truck beds may be conveyorized, or may have walking beam shuttles to carry freight into and out of the vans. Adaptations of slug types consist of the wire carts on casters used in the softgoods distributing business; and, there are other variations such as the overhead monorails used in the meat packing industry.

7. Locator Systems. In general, when the product mix of materials entering the shipping department is not extensive, or when materials are not usually held for any great length of time, locator systems—other than an overhead designation of carrier or destination—may not be necessary.

In some systems, however,there are many complexities that make a locator system virtually a necessity. This is especially so when there are many small parcels or items involved, and when the documentation required to process the material must be kept in an up-to-date, current manner.

There are many shipping departments that make the finding of material on the shipping floor a second order-picking operation. Not only do these shipping departments become another order-selection type of activity, but because they are so disorganized, they expend an inordinate amount of time and energy in overcoming a fundamental defect of their organization—the lack of an orderly method of handling materials that are presented to the shipping department for processing.

A further complication of a seemingly basic activity occurs when packing and crating must be performed by the shipping department. This operational requirement makes the use of a locator system all the more important.

Thus, when material that comes into shipping is handled, it should be tagged and a location assigned before it is placed in a holding or set-out area. Strict supervisory control should be exercised so that none of the above criteria are violated. Once the procedure is established, it helps to systematize the orderly flow of materials into and out of the shipping department.

Periodically, the shipping department head should verify the accuracy of the locator system by taking a small sample of items that have been posted to either a Kardex, McBee Keysort, IBM, or computerized system, or an Access-type of electro-mechanical locator file.

III. In-Process Handling

A. Introduction

As we continue to develop the thesis of a systems approach to materials handling, we shall see that all of the activities of a plant or multi-plant company must be completely and intelligently integrated in order to obtain the maximum output from the various inputs that are made, chiefly from the capital invested by the entrepreneur (promoter) or the owners (shareholders).

1. Inputs Required. The inputs are, in addition to the dollars invested in the enterprise, as follows:

1. Labor
2. Raw materials
3. Services

4. Utilities
5. Brainpower

Labor inputs are the available manhours purchased from people in the form of factory workers, secretaries, clerical, and supervisory help.

Raw materials take many shapes and sizes, from oil, steel plate, and bar stock to latex and dress goods.

Services are the inputs provided by tax accountants, lawyers, the medical staff, consultants, etc.

Utilities are the gas, electricity, water, and steam that power commercial and industrial enterprises.

Brainpower is the most important input of all the factors involved to derive the output that is the objective of the enterprise: profit. It is naive to think that a business is and was developed to make a widget. There is a tremendous amount of risk that must be taken in order to make a widget for profit; thus we have to concentrate the complete talent of the company on this one overriding concern to remain as profitable as possible, or as necessary.

For the purposes of this section we shall assume a definition of *in-process handling* to be *the movement of materials as they proceed from point to point within the production or order-selection cycle.*

2. The Four Elements of Manufacturing/Production Handling. In the production (fabrication) cycle, raw or purchased finished material is received and then transported to one of four destinations:

1. The material can be held in temporary storage awaiting inspection, pricing, and the like.
2. The material can be placed in short- or long-term storage to be held until needed.
3. The material can be transported directly to the assembly line to become part of the complete product or a subassembly, as is sometimes the case with purchased finished materials.
4. The raw material can proceed to a fabrication line where it may be cut, turned, drilled, and so forth.

B. Handling and Storage as a Percent of Manufacturing Time

It is well known that from 95% to 98% of the time that material is in a manufacturing plant it is either being held in storage or being transported or handled. The remaining 2% to 5% of the time it is being processed by some means or other in order to add value to it.

Thus it is that the manufacturing process is mainly materials handling, which should be given the importance and recognition it justly deserves. It is here that a great deal of the company's profit may be made.

1. Control of In-Process Materials. Control of in-process materials, then, is one of the key elements in our systems approach to materials handling. It is absolutely essential to know (1) how much material is on hand—that is, our *inventory records* must be accurate (or, at least as precise as possible); and we must know, at all times, (2) where the material is to be found.

2. Data Collection. It is necessary, therefore, to install an appropriate data collection system to provide the following information:

1. Production (how many pieces fabricated).
2. The amount of time required to produce the parts.
3. A signal that the last job has been completed, and that new work should be obtained.

The above data may be collected manually as in some small and medium-sized plants, or we can use data terminals and minicomputers that may be actuated by an employee's identification card containing his payroll number encoded in plastic.

3. Data Collection Systems. The range of modern data collection devices and systems is so broad that at least one or more systems and hardware can be found to suit almost every budget.

One method for controlling in-process materials is to place this material in a high-rise, high-density stacker-crane retrieval system and use either a punch card or tape controlling means, or else couple the hardware of the SR (stacker-crane retrieval) with a process-controlling computer. (We shall discuss this aspect of control in greater depth in the next chapter.)

C. Standardization of Containers

In further discussion, however, the four points in section III, A2 above, we should carefully consider the standardization of containers, pallets, etc., used in the in-process handling systems; and, explore all of the methods and devices that can be used to transport in-process parts from point to point in the manufacturing cycle.

1. The Necessity For Review. A quick review of the first three chapters should serve to alert the materials handling practitioner to some of the underlying and basic principles of materials handling, and should help avoid some of the pitfalls in container handling and selection. The future of the materials handling program in your plant may be either endangered or enhanced, depending on how well these principles are applied.

D. Order Selection and Physical Distribution.

In physical distribution facilities the direct labor functions are concerned with four main areas: (a) receiving, (b) shipping, (c) order selection, and, (d) packing.

We shall discuss order selection here, since there is a certain similarity of this function to the in-process handling of the manufacturing activity.

1. The Three Types of Order Selection (Picking) Operations. There are three types of order selection (picking) operations in a typical warehouse:

1. *Bulk*—where loads go in and out of storage in the same container, skid, pallet, or unitized load.
2. *Break-bulk*—where the unit load is broken down, and large parts or individual parts are weighed or counted from the larger unit load.
3. *Bin*—where bulk merchandise is broken down to smaller, individual cartons, or pieces, and usually hand-counted or weight-counted.

2. Control of Inventory. In all of the three types of order picking activities, the amount of control of inventory that is exercised is usually a measure of the effectiveness of the operation. When we discussed in-process handling in manufacturing, we stressed control, and we are again suggesting that the organization of a function (in this case, order picking) requires this element (control) as a basic ingredient, and that it is the foundation of a profitable operation.

3. Order Selection Equipment Requirements. The type of materials handling equipment used in order selection activities has a great deal of influence in determining the productivity of this operation. It is recommended, therefore, that the best possible equipment be employed based upon a satisfactory return on the capital used to acquire the equipment. Also, equipment may be either purchased or leased; or a combination of lease–purchase can be negotiated with most suppliers of industrial powered equipment. In some instances there are advantages inherent in equipment leasing, but one may need the advice of a qualified accountant to make this decision, since corporate taxation practices are involved.

4. Method, Equipment, and Attitude. Generally speaking, a combination of method and equipment that works well in one community may not necessarily produce equally good results in another location. The quality and the general environmental background of employees are often determining factors in achieving various levels of productivity. Despite various regional differences that are found in attitudes and in the way equipment may be either used or abused, it is well to keep employees informed as to changes in methods and equipment.

The department supervisor should be one of the first employees informed when changes in methods or equipment are being considered. Also, if the facility is unionized, the various officials and stewards of the labor group should be involved in the early stages of planning for change. A good deal of labor unrest is created unnecessarily by the gap in communications that exists in some companies. A lack of common courtesy has pervaded some segments of industry to such an extent that a largely antagonistic atmosphere has evolved.

Since management depends upon labor for results, and labor requires the most effective use of managerial talent for continued success, in order for both to perpetuate their mutual business enterprise it is a premise of sound management to communicate information whenever there is a "need to know."

EXERCISE NO. 4

1. In every manufacturing or physical distribution system material flow begins with the ______ ______ ______.
2. The principles involved in planning or operating the receiving department are generally the same in either manufacturing or physical distribution. True ☐ False ☐
3. The quickness with which material moves from the carrier, across the receiving dock, and out of the receiving department is a measure of its ______.
4. Sometimes it is advantageous to foster a spirit of competition between the receiving and shipping departments. True ☐ False ☐
5. One of the difficulties in planning an effective receiving layout is in the ______ ______ of items to be handled.
6. The relationship of set-out areas to the carrier and rail doors is extremely important to the efficiency of a receiving department. True ☐ False ☐
7. We generally use overhead ______ ______ to handle material from flat bed trucks in the truck well when it cannot be handled by forklift trucks.
8. ______ ______ ______ that are permanently installed as part of the facility are to be preferred over loose dock boards.
9. The apron is that part of the truck or rail dock between the vehicle and the first, ______ ______ ______.
10. Truck doors where trucks enter into a building structure should be at least ______ high and ______ wide.
11. Center-to-center distances for all truck spots should be at least ______.

12. Truck bed heights vary considerably, and before establishing the level it is necessary to study the types of trucks that will be using the facility. True ☐ False ☐

13. A rule of thumb for the minimum width of the dock apron is the turning radius of the lift truck used in unloading the carrier, measured from the edge of the dockboard, plus three feet. True ☐ False ☐

14. An efficient truck dock light level should be between ____________ to ______ lumens measured at ____________ inches above the floor.

15. Dock lights that illuminate the working face of the inside of a carrier are a hazard to safety. True ☐ False ☐

16. In certain geographic areas that have severe winters, an enclosed dock promotes the ____________ of the receiving operation.

17. If a truck dock is totally enclosed, provision must be made for the elimination of truck ____________ ____________.

18. An enclosed truck dock should be long enough from the ____________ to the edge of the truck dock to accommodate the largest ____________-____________ combination permitted in the state.

19. Wheel chocks should be placed under the ____________ ____________ of a truck at a truck dock. This is an OSHA requirement. True ☐ False ☐

20. In large warehousing operations it is sometimes advantageous to spot carriers, especially trucks, at a door that is ____________ ____________ ____________ ____________ where the material is to be stored.

21. In order to minimize demurrage it is necessary that there be a proper balance between ____________ ____________ and the scheduling of ____________ shipments.

22. It is sometimes advantageous to incur demurrage charges rather than to work a receiving crew ____________.

23. For most receiving operations, large, monthly demurrage expenses are indicative of an ____________ ____________ ____________.

24. In order to increase the efficiency of receiving operations for unloading carriers some companies have used ____________ ____________ ____________.

25. Even skate-wheel and gravity roller conveyors increase the ____________ of some unloading operations.

26. Slug loading or unloading is used when the entire contents of a truck or van can be loaded or unloaded in a matter of minutes.
True ☐ False ☐

27. Some types of materials that may be stored outside (yard storage) with little or no damage are: ____________, ____________, and ____________.

28. Several methods for storing materials and containers in a yard are:

1. ____________
2. ____________
3. ____________
4. ____________
5. ____________
6. ____________

29. In block storage we must weigh the cost of storage versus the increased cost of ________.

30. Back-to-back storage is somewhat less economical than block storage in terms of its poorer use of available ________.

31. Most cantilevered racks require ________ to the floor or concrete surface upon which they rest.

32. The principal advantage of sawtooth storage is that aisle widths may be made fairly narrow. True ☐ False ☐

33. Tiering racks may be used indoors and outdoors, and in a large measure they are similar to ________ storage racks, except that they have greater mobility.

34. Tiering racks can be either the rigid or the ________ -________ type.

35. Storage racks, or pallet storage racks are usually used ________ -to-________ in indoor applications. They are sometimes used for outdoor storage, especially where ________ is limited and where the ________ accessibility of each container, dies and fixtures, etc., is desirable.

36. Onc of thc important details of managing a receiving department is knowing ________ ________ ________!

37. The receiving area should be plainly marked with ________ ________.

38. All of the outdoor storage areas should also be clearly ________.

39. A Kardex, Access, or similar card file can be the ________ center for all materials moving into the enterprise.

40. The lines of communication between the receiving department and the ________ ________ or materials management department are extremely important.

41. The primary objectives of receiving are:

1. ________
2. ________
3. ________

42. Before incoming materials have been identified, verified, and moved to the point of use within the plant, a truck or rail register should be used to log in these incoming materials. True ☐ False ☐

43. A truck register can assist in tracing materials. True ☐ False ☐

44. The receiving and storage of materials requires that materials be easily and quickly ________.

45. In addition to identifying the materials shipped, a supplier should provide a ________ ________ with every shipment.

46. In a computerized system a data terminal operator can place the ________ ________ information directly into an on-line receiving system.

47. The information fed into the computer can then be made available to the accounting and ________ departments in the form of printed reports.

Computer experts have what they call exception routines to handle such things as *partial incoming receivables,* where only part of a due-in is received. Can you name three other uses for these routines?

48. ________

49. ________

50. ________

51. The shipping department is the single area in the plant where collusion for theft is most predominant. True ☐ False ☐

52. The systematic organization of the shipping department is absolutely essential to maintain the highest degree of __________ for the material that flows across the shipping floor.

53. If a number of small containers are to be mixed or merged with larger unit loads, then it may be necessary to provide __________ __________ or bin shelving at convenient places on the shipping floor.

54. If boxing or crating is required, then provision should be made to place this relatively dusty operation in some remote, yet well-ventilated area of the shipping floor. True ☐ False ☐

55. If possible, packaging should take place close to the production operations rather than in the shipping department. True ☐ False ☐

56. It is better to package a product directly as a last operation on a fabrication line than to put it into a temporary container prior to packaging, then transport it to a packaging operation. True ☐ False ☐

57. In order to be fully effective, a shipping dock should have modern dock levelers. True ☐ False ☐

58. There is a great need to design the shipping area in such a manner that there is easy access to it from all parts of the plant. True ☐ False ☐

59. It is important to be able to spot a carrier at or near a particular set-out area in order to shorten the transportation distance between the carrier and the load. True ☐ False ☐

60. What items does OSHA require for a truck spotted at a truck dock?
1. __________
2. __________
(and sometimes) 3. __________

61. Weight distribution in loading-out a truck is __________ __________.

62. (Always) (Sometimes) (Never) place the heaviest loads in the tail end of a truck. (Cross out the two incorrect choices.)

63. In installing a shipping conveyor system, care must be taken that the traffic flow in the department is not __________.

64. The installation of a shipping conveyor system should make use of existing mobile materials handling equipment where this equipment cannot be replaced. True ☐ False ☐

65. A locator system can be used effectively in the shipping department wherever a large product mix is involved. True ☐ False ☐

66. Because of the turn-around space required for a tractor-train, it is customary to consider only straight-line runs through the shipping department; or, at the most, only right-angle turns. True ☐ False ☐

67. The condition of the warehouse or factory floors has an effect on driverless tractor operations. True ☐ False ☐

68. Mistakes in laying out and installing a towconveyor are exceedingly __________ to rectify.

69. When comparing the use of tractor-trains, driverless tractors, and towconveyor installations, we find the following:
1. Used on large volume movements only: ____________
2. Used on small to moderate movements: ____________
3. Used on both small and large movements: ____________

70. Materials in manufacturing are handled or in storage ____________% of the time; the other ____________% of the time they are being processed or transformed in order to add value to the materials.

71. Control if in-process materials is one of the ____________ elements in our systems approach to materials handling.

72. There are two things we must know about in-process materials: (1) how much is on hand, and (2) where the material is to be found. True ☐ False ☐

73. There are three types of order selection (picking) operations in a typical warehouse; these are:
1. ____________
2. ____________
3. ____________

74. In all three types of order picking operations the amount of ____________ of inventory that is exercised is usually a measure of the effectiveness of the operation.

75. In some instances there are advantages inherent in leasing equipment, but one may need the advice of a qualified ____________ to make this decision.

76. Generally speaking, the combination of method and equipment that works well in one community may not necessarily produce equally good results in another location. True ☐ False ☐

Chapter 5
Factory and Warehouse Layout

I. INTRODUCTION

A. The Relationship of Plant Layout to Materials Handling

The layout of the factory and warehouse is a key element in obtaining the least total cost of materials handling. In Chapter 1, we discussed the systems approach to handling and indicated that an orderly flow of materials through a plant increases the morale and productivity of the labor force.

Also, there are a number of more tangible reasons to improve the effectiveness of layout planning. Factory and warehouse space is becoming more expensive with higher building material, labor, and land costs. In addition, when a layout has to be changed or a plant expansion has to be made, we need to minimize the effects of dislocations of stock and equipment; that is, the transition has to be made quickly from the old layout to the new one, so that a certain level of production is maintained.

A more compelling reason to obtain the best possible layout is that most of the handling operations that are performed in the facility are repeated daily throughout the course of the year. Therefore, if the shortest and most direct manner of handling is not practiced, each increment of wasted time by individuals and equipment builds up quickly to subtract from the total effectiveness (and profit) of the enterprise. Skyrocketing indirect labor costs in warehousing, together with excessive or unnecessary materials-handling equipment wear and maintenance costs, combine to drive profits down.

A poor and ill-conceived plant layout tends to increase the need for in-plant storage space; and the tendency on the part of management is to fight fires rather than to tackle the basic cause of the problem, which is poor planning.

B. When is a Plant Layout Required?

There are several reasons why a plant layout is usually required. A plant layout is understood to mean the drawing on paper of the physical relationships of functions and equipment in a facility. One of the most obvious reasons, of course, for layout planning is that a new enterprise is being started. At this point perhaps only the site has been selected; and if the layout planner and the planning team are fortunate, then none of the building perimeters has been described, nor have foundation drawings been prepared.

A common difficulty with management is that the decision to "go ahead and build" is often delayed to such an extent that the design and construction (D&C) group often prepares drawings and obtains bids on an "estimated" required area.

For example, the D&C people will ask the layout planner how much space he thinks will be needed for the proposed facility. Let us say that the answer is approximately 300,000 square feet. In order to save money, even before final approvals are obtained, the bids will go "out on the street" in order to obtain prices in advance of inflationary cost increases. D&C, architects and engineers (A/E's), using the 300,000 square feet as gospel, lay out a rectangular facility that measures approximately 500 feet by 600 feet with an internal bay size (from centerline to centerline of each column) of 40 feet by 50 feet. The layout planner in the meantime is fitting templates of equipment, conveyors, and so forth to optimize the materials flow of the facility. Several workable layouts are obtained. The green light is given by top management, and the information filters down to the layout planner.

Armed with his approvals for the project, the planner proceeds to show his plans to the D&C group. His best layout occurs in a space 400 feet wide by 750 feet long. A certain solemnity, or silence, engulfs the group. The planner is shown drawing after drawing, site plans, foundation plans, sanitary lines, heating, ventilation, and air-conditioning (HVAC) drawings, etc., and the dimensions are inscribed in concrete and steel—500′ × 600′.

Talk to any number of layout planners, A/E's, and D&C groups in various large companies, and you find the above story repeated time and again. It is obvious that the dedication of each group has militated against their achieving the best possible layouts for proposed projects.

Ideally speaking, a logical sequence of events should precede the actual building phase, in which all of the data collection and layout planning are virtually complete before the site is prepared for the building.

We should also consider the plant expansion layout. The layout planner is fortunate, indeed, when the operations closest to the expanded or proposed expansion are compatible. Sometimes, they are not, as in the following two examples:

Example A. We need to expand the bin picking area of a warehouse that borders a major highway. One side of the facility faces a county service road. There are only two sides of the facility that can be expanded. Unfortunately, the bin area was placed on the highway side next to the shipping and receiving dock, and it is separated from the proposed expansion by a bulk storage area.

Example B. A factory is contemplating a major plant expansion. The side of the plant that offers the best possibility for expansion adjoins some vacant property. Unfortunately, your company does not own this property, and the owner demands an exorbitant price; therefore, expansion in this direction is out of the question. The only available space for expansion requires the removal and relocation of an expensive heat-treating furnace and its conveyors. On the other hand, an alternative solution is to remove and relocate a paint-line conveyor, also expensive, but since it is not as extensive a system as the heat-treat line, it is the lesser of two evils.

The lessons to be learned from this section are to keep lines of communication open from the top of the company on down to the working and planning levels. We have shown that if we anticipate construction details, we place layout planning in a very untenable and defenseless position. Sometimes it may be wise to occur increased building costs in order to obtain the maximum effectiveness of materials movement.

In our two examples, A and B above, we have indicated that good planning and plant layout require that we look into the future and anticipate the necessity for plant expansion whenever we prepare a layout. A misplaced toilet, a locker room with tile walls and showers, a sewer line, drains and downspouts in the wrong location—all spell expensive relocations. And, these are not the least of our worries, as power substations, railroad lines, water towers, fuel tanks, cooling ponds, service roads, etc., can all come back to haunt the planner who lacks the vision to foresee the inevitable.

C. Types of Facilities and Site Planning

1. Facility Planning. Facility planning is one of the most facinating and at the same time frustrating chores facing the planner. From an architectural standpoint, construction materials have increased dramatically to yield hundreds, even thousands, of new choices that are fascinating to contemplate. However, it is frustrating to be confronted with the cost combinations involved in these choices.

The type of facility may be dictated in large part by the type of terrain in suburban or out-country areas; by the neighboring residential communities; by the kind of public image the company desires to reflect; and by the restrictions imposed by local planning and zoning commissions.

In urban communities a multi-storied facility may be prescribed because land values are too high for a single story structure to be built. Then again, in some manufacturing segments of the economy where small electronic units or large appliances are being fabricated, it is desirable to have multi-level component manufacturing, storage, and assembly. A good example of the latter is the new Appliance Park of the General Electric Company in Columbia, Maryland, on the outskirts of Baltimore.

Some companies, on the other hand, are forced into older, multi-storied loft-type buildings in crowded cities where these are the only buildings available, or where these are the only buildings they can afford to lease or purchase. This type of building requires a considerable amount of ingenuity on the part of the layout planner, especially when elevators of limited capacity have to be used to the greatest advantage.

In these multi-storied buildings—usually with low ceiling heights of from 10 to 12 feet on the upper stories, and sometimes as much as 14 to 16 feet on a main entrance or dock level—it is not unusual to have column spacings of only 20′ × 20′. Thus, the relatively inexpensive rental costs of these buildings must be weighed against wasted space, expensive elevator maintenance, down time, and high labor costs.

2. Site Planning. Site planning is usually thought of as a function of the architect, land surveyor, architect-engineer (A/E), developer, and so forth. It is true that preparing contour maps of property is generally a rather specialized area of endeavor. Do not, however, make the mistake of believing that the materials handling practitioner should be divorced from this subject. The truth is that the architect who is preparing the site plan is often influenced more by aesthetics and the lay of the land than by the practical aspects of plant expansion.

For example, a railroad spur cutting across a field may cause a number of problems after a few years, when it impedes the orderly growth of the facility. Thus the materials handling engineer should keep his finger on the pulse of the architect to keep apprised of the situation and to help in decision making. A fire wall inside the building may also cause havoc with the plant layout later on, if it does not do so at the outset. Some insurance underwriters do not like to see too large an area unencumbered with dividing walls; in general, they like to see how a fire can be contained or compartmentalized to prevent its rapid spreading—this despite expensive sprinkler systems, ceiling monitors, or large, suspended fire curtains.

On the other hand, site planning in limited city areas presents rather unusual challenges to both the A/E and the materials handling engineer—How to get trucks into and out of a facility on busy thoroughfares with the least disruption to traffic, and so on. In today's bustling, large cities, offstreet parking is often required, and a number of restrictive ordinances usually confront the layout planner. One of these is a fairly widespread requirement that a three-foot-wide fire aisle be maintianed between storage areas and exterior walls.

These are only a few of the requirements that make site planning an art. Many other factors should be considered in site selection and placement of the facility on the site. First, the land should be large enough in width and depth to accommodate the building desired; second, the site should allow for future expansion; third, the plot of ground should be suitable in soil characteristics for a building to be erected with proper footings without expensive special construction; forth, the area should provide access for rail and truck receiving.

Size and layout arrangement of a warehouse or factory cannot be determined by dollar volume alone. The functions performed within the building must be considered and will directly affect the amount of space required. A warehouse building must fit the individual requirements of the wholesaler involved. A factory must suit the requirements of the manufacturing operations. The following paragraphs point out some key considerations in planning new warehouse or factory construction.

Watch the spacing of columns. Columns should be so arranged as not to interfere with movement and storage of merchandise. Placing columns too close together may restrict space and reduce the effectiveness of handling equipment.

Type of construction may determine the spacing and numbers of columns. However, a lower cost of construction may not be desirable if operations to be performed in the building are restricted. Particular care is advisable in eliminating all column supports with the floor areas. Columns should be enclosed within walls wherever possible.

Consider handling equipment to be used. The type of material handling equipment to be used should be determined and considered in the facility arrangement. If a forklift and pallet system is to be used, doors must be made sufficiently wide and high. Adequate aisle space must be planned for each area as well as for the general floor space in the facility. Ceiling clearance should be adequate to permit stacking of palletized unit loads. Sprinkling systems, ducts, and fan units need to be planned carefully in determining the ceiling height in order that pallets will not strike obstructions when stacked. The size of pallets should be ascertained in advance. Also, the planning of the floor space should be based on the desirable number of pallets to be handled in the processing operations and in the common storage areas.

II. DATA REQUIRED FOR FACTORY AND WAREHOUSE LAYOUT

A great deal of responsibility is vested in the individual or group of individuals performing the plant layout function. Let us discuss this subject as though you were charged with this responsibility.

In order to achieve the best possible layout you must, first, be capable of compromising. At times it will be necessary to weigh an advantage against a disadvantage; so you must become thoroughly familiar with all of the operations performed in the facility to have a firm foundation for decision making.

You cannot afford to accept, complacently, all of the processes, methods, and equipment of your predecessors. Remember, you don't want to repeat their mistakes—that's why you were hired to do this job.

Ask yourself, and the owners, managers, supervisors, and key employees, what is wrong with the present layout?

Next learn what capacity the plant is to be designed for, and determine what growth is required. This latter information most likely would come from marketing information, or the general objectives of the plant management.

The parameters within which you will work will, in general, be the present processing method, and a knowledge of the state of the art or the status of technology in which your plant should operate—now, or at some future time.

To provide this general background in preparation for your analysis or data collection program, you should use all the sources of data available to you, such as information obtainable from a study of the following:

Trade Journals
Trade association information
Equipment manufacturers' information
Similar facilities—your competition's* plants

By doing such preliminary work, the materials handling engineer develops a certain amount of background knowledge that will be useful when the problems of factory and warehouse layout are explored more fully and as the initial phases of layout are begun.

As a starting point for the actual layout, however, we must know a good deal about the quantities and types of materials to be handled, stored, processed, and worked upon in some manner, or another, in our facility.

In Chapter 1, we discussed the philosphy of the systems approach to materials handling, and learned that many of our materials handling problems are incorrectly resolved by being studied in very small segments with little or no regard to the preceding and succeeding stages in the flow of materials. In other words, if we are attempting to obtain the least total cost of materials handling, we must look at the complete range of activities from raw material, or source, to the final destination of the product, whatever it may happen to be.

Becoming familiar with the materials involved in the processing is relevant to an analysis of the problem. If we are dealing with steel plate, we would go directly to the source of its manufacture—the mill, or the steel service center—and determine if its segregation by size, chemical analysis, heat treatment, and the way it is presently packaged is advantageous to our operations. If not, then

*We are not suggesting industrial espionage, but merely suggesting that you should have a fairly good idea of how your competition is performing materials handling.

we should try to have the material properly graded and packaged for our use. Quite often, changes in handling method, or packaging, can benefit the supplier as well as the user, and at no additional cost.

On the other hand, if price increases are demanded by the supplier and he can substantiate the increase, then it behooves us to determine if there is a significant cost benefit to be gained in changing the handling method or the packaging.

In physical distribution operations almost the same approach would apply as indicated for the factory. That is, the materials handling engineer would examine packaging and handling at typical suppliers' plants, and he would then determine if these functions could coexist satisfactorily in the system network he is trying to establish.

A. Commodities and Quantities to be Handled

The scope of the handling function has to be determined before any further work is done; therefore, in planning for the various events (by methodology that we shall discuss in Chapter 18), it is important that sufficient time be allowed for careful review of the types of commodities to be handled and the quantities that must be processed.

For example, this size, shape or configuration, weight, density (if this is important), crushability, stacking or nesting characteristics, and shelf-life are all very important considerations in certain industries. The materials handling engineer must decide which of the many factors involved are necessary in the analysis of the scope of his processing operations and note them, even tabulate and code them, so that they can be examined and manipulated in whatever fashion is most desirable. Once this type of information is properly coded, it may be entered into a computer program if such is found to be desirable, or it may be posted and manipulated manually.

It is important to remember that the scope of the problem usually will determine the tools and equipment to be employed, especially where computers are concerned. When no computer is available, as in some small companies, it is still possible, of course, to purchase computer time and expertise, generally at very reasonable cost.

The quantities of materials to be handled should also be subjected to very intensive analysis. Not only is it important to know the facility input/output quantities, but an analysis should be made of the internal processing or flow of materials within the plant.

A from-to chart, as illustrated in Fig. 5-1, should be completed. A number of important criteria can be established by use of this type of chart. Taking one variable at a time, it is possible to establish the density of moves between departments or activities. It is also possible to obtain numerical densities of the

FROM-T CHART

Location: *Jamestown Plant* Date: *4-1-8* M.H. Engr: *Bill Smith*

Dept. *18* — FROM \ TO	*Unformed Steel*	*De-coiler*	*Shear*	*Blank*	*Brake*	*Storage*	*Weld*	*Chip & Clean*	*Subassembly*	*Storage*	*Assembly*	*Shipping*	Totals
Unformed Steel		3											3
De-coiler			5										5
Shear				8	5		3		1				17
Blank					3	9							12
Brake						3	2						5
Storage							12		4				16
Weld						5		10					15
Chip & Clean						3			6				9
Subassembly						2				4			6
Storage									3		4		7
Assembly												3	3
Totals		3	5	8	8	22	17	10	14	4	4	3	98

Remarks:

Investigate need for additional shear capacity.

Fig. 5-1. From-to chart.

quantity to be moved; for example, number of moves or loads moved, and tonnage handled. Also, by posting other variables it is possible to assign costs between departments, time consumed per total moves per shift, and so forth.

A direct result of such a matrix (or chart) is that the materials handling engineer can use the information obtained from the matrix to portray the data

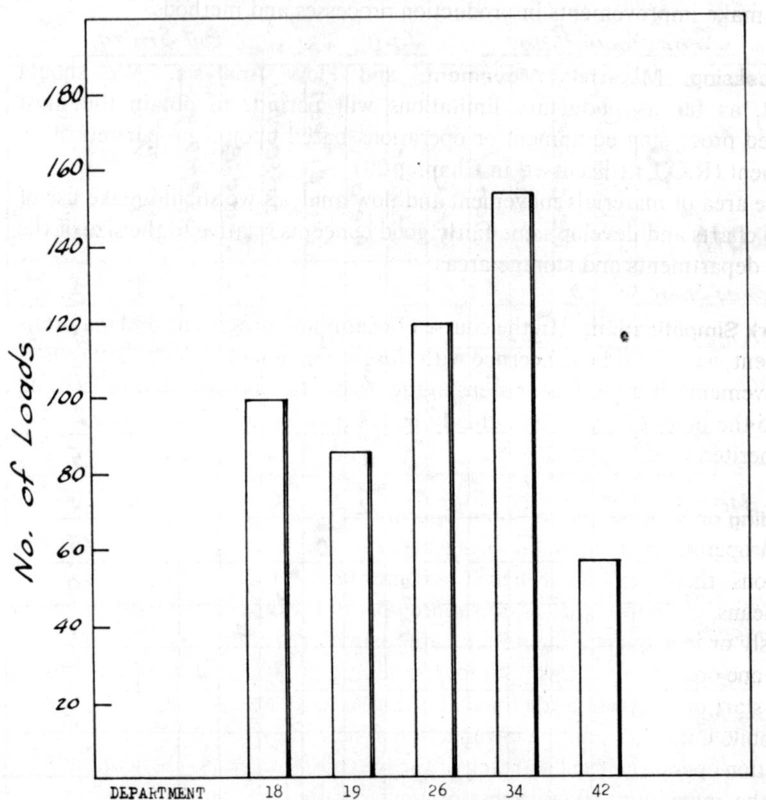

Fig. 5-2. Bar chart using from-to chart data.

graphically. The graphs or displays become very important in presenting this type of information to management to justify plant layout relationships. (See Fig. 5-2, which is an illustration of a bar chart drawn up by means of information supplied by a from-to chart.)

B. Assessment of Improvements in Production Processes and Methods

Assuming that the materials handling engineer has done all of the exploratory work required to obtain information concerning the state of the art, it is important to future plant profits to install equipment and use methods of handling that will keep the plant reasonably ahead of the field. The new plant or expanded facility should not be obsolete before it is occupied! Let's see where we can make improvements in production processes and methods.

1. Processing, Materials Movement, and Flow Analysis. We should attempt, as far as budgetary limitations will permit, to obtain the most advanced processing equipment or operations based upon a proper return on investment (R.O.I.) (discussed in Chapter 20).

In the area of materials movement and flow analysis we should make use of from-to charts and develop some fairly good concepts relative to the size of the various departments and storage areas.

2. Work Simplification. In the course of examining processing and materials movement, we should be concerned with the elimination of unnecessary or useless movements of materials or steps in the production process that do not add value to the product, and may actually be the result of some antiquated function inherited from a predecessor.

3. Adding or Subtracting to Some Operations for Balance. Usually, in production operations of manufacturing and even in some physical distribution operations, there are times when it becomes necessary to "balance the line." This means, of course, that two or more operations that happen either simultaneously or in sequence should take approximately the same amount of time so that one operator is not waiting for the next operator to finish his task before he can start on his own. Such line-balancing activity is quite customary in the automobile industry upon the introduction of new models. In any large-volume production operation, the balancing of the line is extremely important in developing the maximum effectiveness of tools (equipment) and manpower. To obtain maximum output, all other things being equal, it may be necessary to observe each individual process or operation very critically and add some functions and subtract some from each of the separate entitites in the system or line.

4. Use of New Equipment. Sometimes it is possible to use new equipment—for example, to substitute a machine tool with faster speeds and feeds, or to use a powered industrial truck that has a greater capacity, a higher lifting capability, faster traveling or lifting speed, etc., in place of an older piece of equipment—in order to obtain better line balance and to increase the efficiency and productivity of plant operations.

5. Integration of Processing with Materials Handling. As we go through the various steps in processing and attempt to improve the production processes, we should keep in mind that there are materials-handling elements that must be considered. The containers used in an operation may become an important, if not critical, part of subsequent operations. It is well to remember, also, one of the warnings used in an earlier chapter: try to keep material out of containers until the final shipping or consolidation point is reached. Any use of containers during the production process generates unnecessary rehandling and is to be avoided.

Another caveat is not to let the paperwork dictate the handling method. Too often a procedure with its elaborate paperwork structure is inherited or foisted upon an unquestioning materials handling practitioner who discovers too late that he is being led by the nose down a costly primrose path. Decide upon the best materials handling method, and then make the paperwork fit the processing and materials handling.

6. Definite Lines of Travel. As you start your layout work, it is most helpful to remember that there will be many repetitions of the way the material traces its way through the plant during the course of the day, and that this path will be multiplied by the 200 or more work days in a year. The layout planner, then, has to visualize this travel path and provide instructions outlining it as a matter of reference and to form a base for work measurement documentation.

C. Productive Capacity versus Cost

In arranging production equipment in a plant layout, it is well to keep sight of the fact that the higher the productive capacity is for a given floor area, the lower the overhead cost for this production. This means that the fixed costs or burden for each unit of output will decrease as the productive capacity increases. So the challenge for the layout planner is to provide as much production per given square foot of floor area as possible while still maintaining good materials handling practices.

D. Ways to Minimize Materials Handling

As discussed earlier, the best materials handling is the least materials handling. There are several ways to achieve this objective.

1. By Arrangement. By arranging equipment properly in work areas we can make the most effective use of both space and the human factors involved. These human engineering factors are the standing, sitting, reaching, grasping, and lifting characteristics of the human being—the all-important worker who toils at his task eight or so hours daily (minus allowances).

2. By Distance. If the distance between operations is shortened, the time required for performing the task or transporting the part should be shortened. This not only increases the productivity of the operation, but it decreases the wear and tear on transportation equipment.

3. By Line of Flight. If the most direct line of travel is taken, the piece parts or materials are transported more economically and with less damage than they would be with longer routes. Invariably, the mathematical principle that "a straight line is the shortest distance between two points" reduces the amount of materials handling and thus the cost of handling.

E. Efficient Use of Equipment and Labor

A good plant layout makes use of labor and equipment effectively. Some of the ways for accomplishing this are to:

1. Eliminate cramped aisles.
2. Provide enough but not too much storage space between operations.
3. Avoid crowding the space around machines or processing equipment so that the worker does not have enough space to work properly.

F. Ways to Reduce the Amount of Materials In-Process

In attempting the achieve the least total cost of materials handling, we can use what has been called the critical time phasing of materials in process. This means that when we have provided the proper arrangement of equipment and matcrials, in our plant layout, there will be a steady flow of work-in-process throughout the production cycle because we have intergrated the production scheduling with the handling method. By eliminating or, at best, minimizing line imbalance and cushions of work-in-process between successive operations, we can do several things:

1. Provide a steady flow of work throughout the plant.
2. Reduce the total length of time of materials in process.
3. Turn over our inventory much faster, so that capital dollars are not tied up unnecessarily in excess inventory.
4. Be more responsive to schedule and engineering changes.
5. Achieve better utilization of men, machines, and plant space.

G. Proper Safety and Working Conditions

Good plant layout practice requires that the layout planner pay particular attention to both safety and the general working conditions of the plant. "A safe plant to work in" can achieve the psychological effect of increased worker morale. At least, plant management will have provided the proper physical environment for the employees, and thus will have removed one very large subject of complaint in labor—management relationships. Three major safety requirements must be carefully met during the plant layout phase of systems development:

1. The elimination of safety hazards at the work station.
2. The preparation of training materials for workers in the care and correct use of materials handling equipment—one phase of which begins prior to the going on-stream of plant operations.
3. Providing a good working environment.

III. PRINCIPLES OF MATERIALS HANDLING APPLIED TO LAYOUT

If the materials handling engineer will try to keep certain principles in mind when he is working on the plant layout, he will greatly enhance his chances of obtaining a smooth-flowing materials movement system that will produce the least total cost of materials handling.

A. Continuous Flow

Let us examine some of these principles, since processing time and costs are minimized when the product progresses through the various processes in a continuous flow with a minimum of back-tracking, or cross-hauling.

1. Try to avoid batch or lot processing; these procedures should be minimized or eliminated completely.
2. Remember that the slowest process will become the bottleneck.
3. Remember, also, that materials handling is an integral part of processing and should be examined closely in order to improve or eliminate it as an aspect of the process.
4. Try to obtain a direct line of materials flow, wherever possible, and make the routing of materials as automatic as possible.

B. Economy of Operations

The greatest materials handling economy is achieved in a plant when materials are:

1. Moved in direct lines.
2. Moved through a minimum distance.
3. Moved by mechanical, or automatic, means.

C. Balancing Operations

Processing costs are minimized and processing cycle time is reduced when equipment, labor, and materials are applied in a plant layout in a balanced relationship.

1. Sequential operations are in balance when each requires the same or nearly the same amount of time.
2. At each operation there should be balance.
3. Lack of balance causes bottlenecks.
4. The evidence of lack of balance can be seen when the following conditions exist:
   a. Equipment is not fully utilized.
   b. Operations have to wait for materials.
   c. Material backs up at certain operations.
   d. There are a lot of temporary storage locations.

D. Built-In Flexibility

The plant layout should be designed with a degree of flexibility to provide for future growth and change in process and product.

1. Expansion plans should be designed at the time of the initial plant layout.
2. Consider all of the critical operations that could become candidates for expansion, and decide how these units will be provided for in the future.
3. Eliminate or minimize all obstructions in the plant layout that will hinder flexibility; these are:
   a. Obstructed floor areas.
   b. Column spacing that is too close in either direction.
   c. Elevator shafts and pits.
   d. Stair wells.
   e. Toilet facilities and excessively expensive plumbing and sanitation

lines, especially subfloor equipment and heat-treating, etc., in-floor drag-chain conveyors, and the like.

E. Auxiliary Service Requirements

The adequate servicing of the process is contingent upon the availability, in sufficient quantity and quality, of the necessary services and departments required by the process and its personnel. We can divide these services or departments into two groups:

1. Processing. Processing comprises all of the departmental considerations of:

Shipping
Receiving
Storage
Engine or boiler room
Maintenance area
Laboratories and testing

2. Personnel. This category covers all of the services important to employee morale, which contribute, in a very important way, to the over all effectiveness of the entire facility. Personnel services include:

Toilets and washrooms
Drinking fountains
Locker rooms and showers
Dispensary
Cafeteria

F. The Safety Principle

Maximum production is obtained in a plant layout when the potential causes of accidents are reduced to an absolute minimum. The following suggestions are very important:

1. Avoid accidents because accidents and the cause of accidents slow production.
2. Provide sufficient aisle space for both pedestrians and materials handling equipment.
3. Do not crowd equipment and work stations.

4. Provide adequate storage space at equipment without crowding the operator.
5. Provide sufficient room at each piece of equipment to:
   a. Safely adjust the machine.
   b. Make set-ups and change the tooling safely.
   c. Repair the machine.
   d. Inspect the machine.

IV. USE OF TWO-DIMENSIONAL TEMPLATES AND OVERLAYS IN LAYOUT

Plant layout is, as anyone knows who has worked in this area, a combination of science and art. There are, however, some basic approaches to this subject that make the art a little less formidable to the materials handling engineer.

A. Area Allocations for New Facilities

1. Using the from-to chart, and any other data that will indicate the square feet of area each department of the plant will require, we scale on pieces of heavy paper, or tag stock, using ¼ inch to the foot, all of the departmental areas required for the total facility. These areas may be square to begin with.
2. Next, we arrange them in a logical relationship as indicated by our from-to chart and other data. The scaled squares of paper can be arranged as though no walls of the facility exist, for indeed, at this time, they do not!
3. When we are somewhat satisfied with the arrangement, we can lightly tape these pieces to the drawing board using small pieces of masking tape.
4. Next apply a large piece of clear plastic over the entire paste-up. Using grease pencils, trace the flow of the major components and components of piece parts of high dollar value on the plastic.
5. Some additional rearranging of departments or the "blocks of space" may be necessary. Some areas or blocks of space may have to be redrawn (to scale) in rectangular, L-shape, or other designs in order to make the building wall configuration more uniform.

B. Area Allocations for Existing Facilities

Many times it is necessary to plan an operation when the building has been leased or purchased. Therefore, the materials handling engineer must make the departmental requirements fit into existing space. This is usually a very difficult task, and rarely will it be possible to satisfy every requirement 100%. At best, the result is a compromise.

1. The first thing to do is to obtain a floor plan that is accurate and up-to-date as possible. It would be good operating practice to check the drawings on the site to make certain that everything in the building corresponds to the drawings. (I have found that large industrial buildings constructed during World War II and the Korean conflict are not always in accordance with the architect's drawings, simply because wartime priorities did not permit updating these drawings as column bracings were added, or as extra steel was put in place to adjust to larger load-bearing requirements. Such discrepancies can play havoc with a pallet storage rack layout, or a machine placement.) Hopefully, the scale of the architect's drawings is ¼ inch to the foot.
2. While checking on the drawing accuracy, be sure that all columns, posts, interior walls, stairwells, ladders, elevators, doors, windows, railroad tracks, rail docks, truck docks, and roadways are clearly marked.
3. Make the block space templates for each space requirement as indicated in (A-1), above; and arrange them within the confines of the architect's drawing in the most efficient flow pattern attainable.

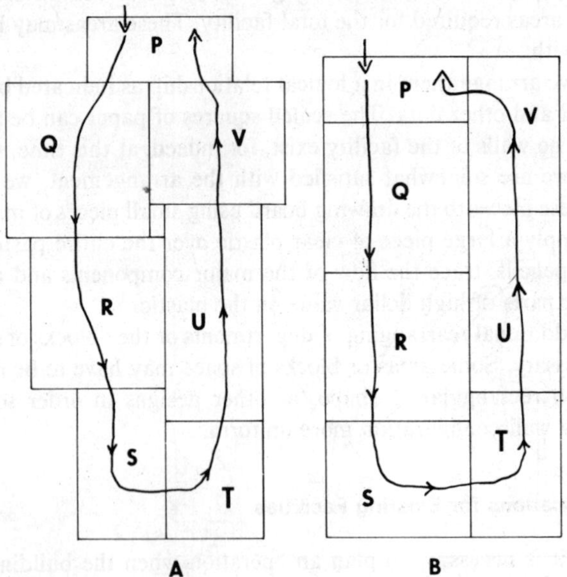

Fig. 5-3. An illustration of the use of paper templates. Each department has been scaled to its approximate requirements and is first arranged in a desirable flow pattern as in A, then adjusted as in B to obtain a workable building configuration.

4. Some cutting and refitting of the space templates may be necessary to adjust the departmental requirements to the space.
5. When the templates have been taped to the drawing, use a plastic overlay to trace the materials movement as in (A-4), above.
6. Some rearranging may be required to achieve optimum flow, but remember it is much easier and less costly to do this with templates on paper than with machines and equipment on the shop floor! Therefore, the more time we spend on doing this task well, the more we shall be repaid for our efforts, by achieving the least total cost of materials handling.

Figure 5-3 illustrates the use of the paper space block templates in arriving at an overall configuration for the new facility. Some variations of this method should be attempted in making a plant layout using existing facilities.

Figure 5-4 shows the use of a clear plastic overlay to trace the flow of mate-

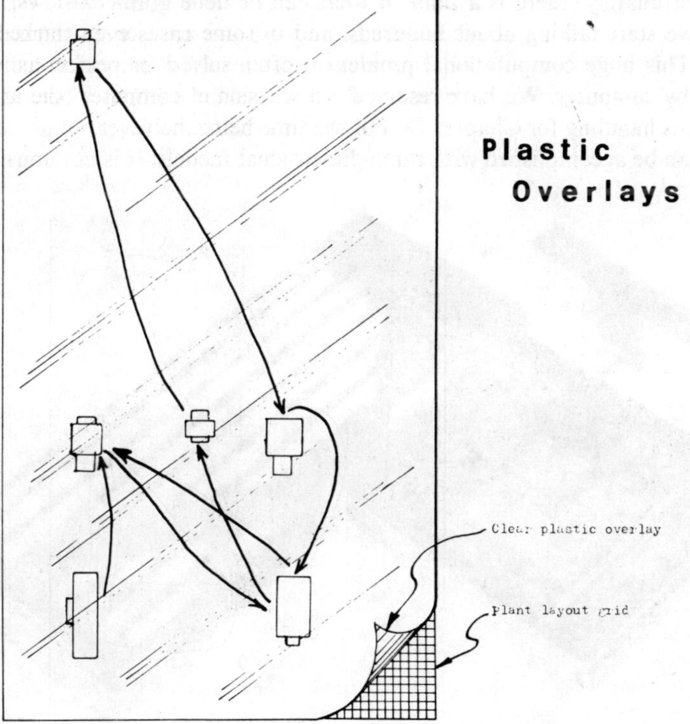

Fig. 5-4. Use of a clear plastic overlay to trace the flow of materials in a plant; a grease pencil can be used to mark the path taken. This method will show what is happening to high-dollar-volume items and materials. Different-colored pencils may be used to graphically demonstrate back-tracking, and will suggest ways to improve the flow of materials.

rials in a proposed plant layout. It is interesting to note that a good deal of information may be revealed, even in existing plants, when a plastic overlay is used to trace the present method of transporting materials within the plant. This method should be used periodically, say every two or three years, to learn what is actually happening to materials movement within the operation, especially when new products are introduced, when old products are made on new or different machines and storage locations are rearranged, etc.

V. USE OF THREE-DIMENSIONAL MODELS IN PLANT LAYOUT

In section IV, above, we discussed two-dimensional templates and layouts that are scaled at ¼ inch to the foot. This type of engineering layout can be made very vivid by color-coding the various blocks of space. Also, the plastic overlay will show flow patterns in more graphic fashion if several different-colored grease pencils are used for the several parts or families of parts.

Unfortunately, there is a limit to what can be done graphically, especially when we start talking about hundreds, and in some cases even thousands of parts. This huge computational problem is often solved, or performed, much better by computer. We have reserved a discussion of computer operations in materials handling for Chapter 18. For the time being, however, let us examine what can be accomplished with three-dimensional models. It is not unusual for

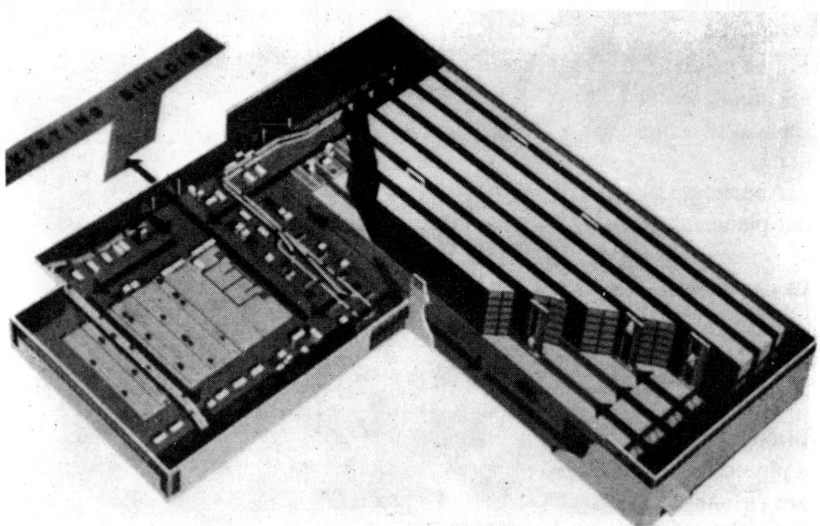

Fig. 5-5. A three-dimensional scale model helps planners visualize the spatial relationships that exist among the several departments, building elements, and equipment. Models like the one shown often help sell management on the need for capital investment.

many of the more complex plant layouts to use both computer simulation techniques (Chapter 18) and three-dimensional models to complement each other.

Figure 5-5 illustrates a three-dimensional model of a high-density storage and order-filling operation used to support an existing manufacturing complex.

A model such as this is very costly—and more complex models often cost $10,000, $20,000, or more. Nevertheless, a number of advantages are gained by modeling; for example, by applying this technique to work station arrangements for physical distribution or machining work centers, it is possible to obtain a very efficient placement of equipment that is directly related to productivity, morale, safety, and other benefits.

A number of highly placed and intelligent management people, for example, sometimes have great difficulty in looking at a two-dimensional drawing and visualizing the operation or spatial arrangement of the layout. Therefore, it is especially important that the materials handling engineer consider having a model made, or making the model himself.

Some homemade models can be very effective in illustrating a machine-line layout, or in showing the spatial relationships in an order-picking, bin area layout. As an example of homemade, built-to-scale, machine tool models, the materials handling engineer or the layout planner can use a short piece of wood dowel-stick glued to a small, rectangular block of wood to represnet a lathe or other machine tool.

Bins and pallet storage racks can be similarly scaled, and can be constucted of small rectangular blocks of wood. A large measure of realism can be obtained through the imaginative design of three-dimensional figures, which can be made to illustrate the layout of the plant, department, work station, or machining center. Also a number of companies sell three-dimensional, scaled replicas of almost every type of machine tool, shelving, storage rack, and the like.

Appendix H contains a list of companies that manufacture supplies for layout planners.

VI. A TYPICAL FACTORY LAYOUT FOR A MACHINE LINE

On the following pages we shall trace the development of a typical machine line layout that is part of a much larger facility in a manufacturing plant.

Figure 5-6 illustrates the way in which a layout is developed. Let's go through the steps, which will be the same for both a manufacturing facility and a physical distribution plant. We should note, however, that although the steps are virtually the same, there may be some slight differences that make a layout for a warehouse or an order-picking operation somewhat easier than that for a manufacturing operation. The main difference is that in most physical distribution facilities you do not find the many hundreds of different types of

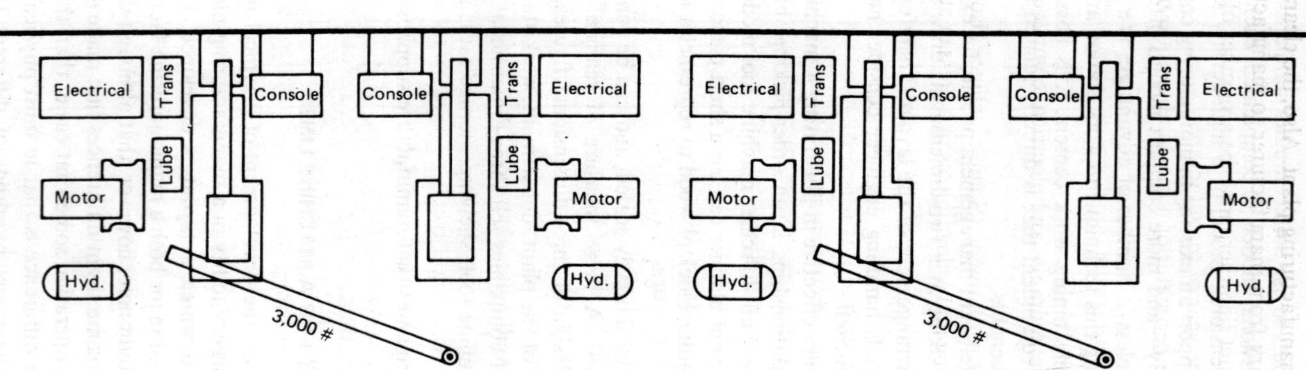

Fig. 5-6. A typical machine line layout showing the machine tools and the supporting equipment, electrical and hydraulic, as well as the overhead jib cranes for hoisting heavy parts into and out of machine fixtures.

machines that are usually found in a manufacturing plant. Also, the clearances required around each machine tool vary from manufacturer to manufacturer, and within each manufacturer's product line there may be a number of variations, depending on the model and the year of manufacture.

The clearances required around the perimeter of a machine tool are necessary to:

1. Service and maintain the machine.
2. Service and maintain some of the hydraulic and electrical components.
3. Change tooling.
4. Bring work to the machine and take it away. (Some machines also have requirements for automatic loading and unloading, as in a press or stamping machine.)

With some of the larger machine tools there is a necessity, also, to make certain that enough overhead clearance is maintained to change tools; for example, in a large, vertical broaching machine the tool must be raised above the highest point of the machine in order to remove it for grinding. The layout planner must become accustomed to working in three dimensions because if he doesn't, he may run into unforeseen difficulties with truss heights and similar obstructions, conduits, utility piping, duct-work, and the like.

From a materials standpoint the layout planner has to decide how he is going to service his line, and, more important, he should know where his material is coming from and where it should go after it has passed through all of the fabrication and inspection operations of his department.

A systems approach to materials handling requires that the layout planner improve the flow of materials through the facility by locating a particular machine line in its optimum location, reducing travel time between the source of the material and the first storage or operation of the line. It is preferable that the first set-down of the material be made in such a manner that the part can be machined or worked upon immediately—for example, setting the part on a conveyor or a tilt-table, etc.—and that back-hauling of materials in the layout be eliminated, or, if this is not possible, that the back-hauling be kept to a bare minimum.

In preparing for the task of drawing-up the sketch of the machine line the layout planner has several choices in terms of the actual drawing materials to be used. For instance, he can use cloth or vellum (tracing paper), depending on whether he requires a long or relatively short shelf-life for his layout. Cloth is not used very much anymore, having been supplanted by mylar. Mylar has the advantage of toughness; it doesn't scratch or become marred very easily, and it makes excellent prints. Also, it can be erased without any ghosting, the erasures being very simply and effectively performed on this plastic surface.

The Dietzgen Corporation mylar, called "Perfect" (cross-sectioned 10 × 10 = 2½ inches), gives ¼ inch to one foot scale, which is recommended for most plant layout work. The "Perfect" mylar serves as the base upon which to place the layout. You will notice that every tenth line is dotted so that the dotted lines are 20 feet apart on the ¼ inch scale. Scale drawings of machine tool outlines (at ¼ inch to the foot) showing various clearances (such as console door, opening swings, jib cranes, hydraulic tanks, etc.) can be placed on mylar by photographic reproduction. A number of different machine tool outlines can be placed on mylar and put in a tray for storage.

When the time comes to place the machine tool outline on the mylar base, it is carefully cut out and mounted on the grid (base) using a 3M double-backed tape made expressly for this purpose. After all of the tools and related equipment, conveyors, etc., have been mounted and the aisles marked, the mylar layout may be printed for a permanent record. Chart-Pak tapes, which are available at any good art and drafting supply shop, can be used on the base to indicate aisles, conveyors, direction of travel, bridge cranes, and the like. Changes can be made to the layout by peeling off the cutouts and the tapes, and relocating or replacing them. (See Fig. 5-6)

VII. A TYPICAL WAREHOUSE LAYOUT

We have discussed the use of cloth, vellum (tracing paper), and mylar bases for layouts. Most warehouse layouts, unlike machine lines, are so rarely changed after their inception that many of the layouts or drawings are made on vellum. After blueprints are made from these layouts, minor changes or revisions can be made very easily using red ink or pencil. Periodically, it may be necessary to update the sketch or drawing, and this may mean tracing the existing portions of the blueprints if the original layouts can no longer be found or traced.

An illustration of the layout of a typical, large warehouse is shown in Fig. 5-7. One of the principal features of this warehouse is a towconveyor system with spurs at convenient locations throughout the facility. There is a towconveyor crossover to eliminate the unnecessary travel of towcarts to the far end of the warehouse. In addition, there are spurs in the shipping and receiving truck wells for the accumulation of orders, and a spur running across the shipping floor to receive empty towcars for dispatch to the receiving floor to await incoming merchandise.

Another objective of good towconveyor installation is to divide the warehouse floor area so that the line or path of the towconveyor is equally accessible to all areas. This is sometimes rather difficult to achieve, especially if the warehouse floor has already been poured, or the facility was initially constructed without a towconveyor.

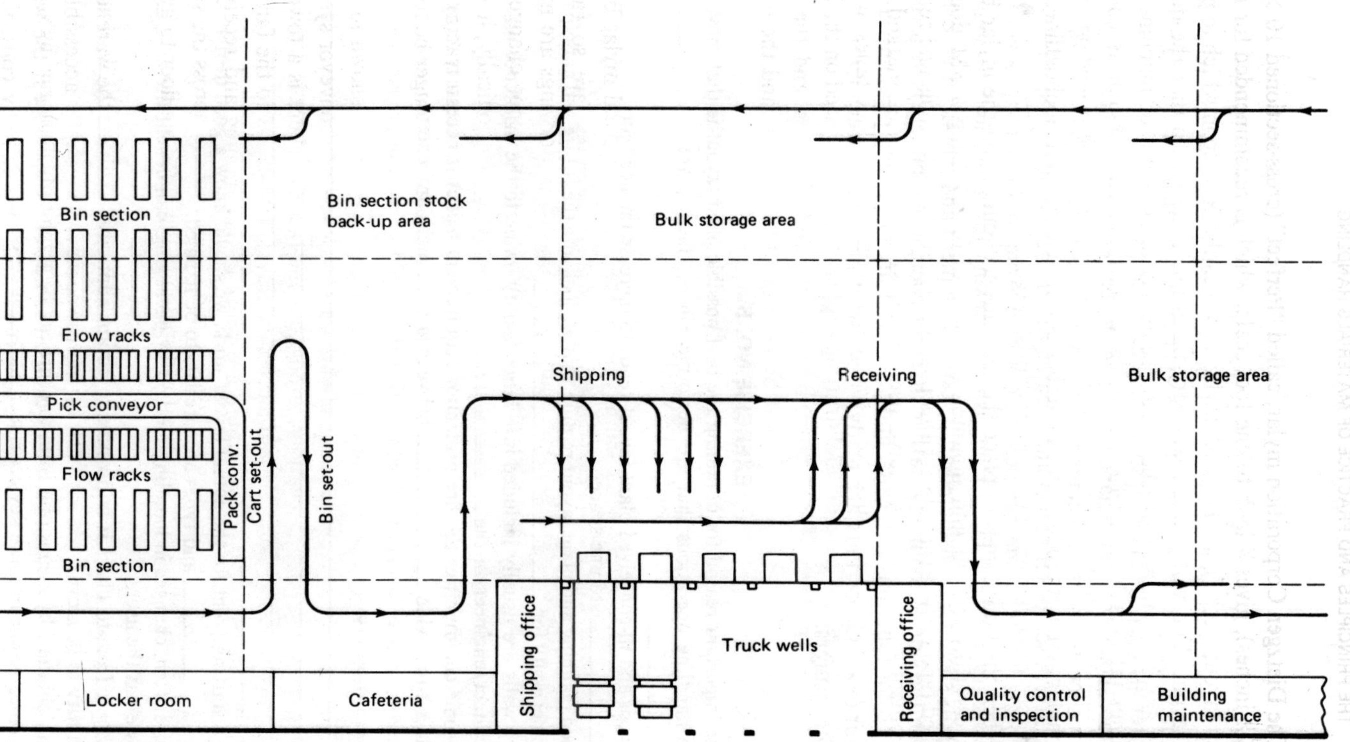

Fig. 5-7. Layout of a portion of a large warehouse with an in-floor towconveyor. Note the spurs on the towconveyor line to service the various departments and areas of the warehouse. Also, notice the receiving and shipping set-out areas, which are also served by the towconveyor.

Service facilities and the inspection and quality control (QC) departments should be readily accessible to the units they serve. For example, the inspection and QC laboratory and office should be reasonably close to the receiving department floor or set-out area. This is so primarily because samples of incoming materials must be taken, inspected, and/or analyzed.

So, too, should the maintenance area and the battery charging area (if there is one) be located near the center of the powered industrial truck population of the facility. Also, locker rooms and a cafeteria (if there is one) should be centrally located. Often a mezzanine area can house some of these nonproductive, but necessary, services. Fire extinguishers, drinking fountains, and personnel (fire) exits should be considered an investment in merit and morale; it is better to err on the side of too many, rather than not enough. Architects have a rule of thumb for fountains and exits, and your local fire protection personnel and the insurance underwriters are ready to advise at any time, especially if they are your insurers.

EXERCISE NO. 5

1. One important reason for obtaining the best possible plant layout is that most of the handling operations that are performed in the facility are ____________ ____________.

2. A poor and ill-conceived plant layout tends to increase the need for ________-____________ storage space.

3. Good planning and plant layout require that we look into the future and anticipate the necessity for ____________ ____________.

4. Fire walls are usually included in a large facility owing to the insistence of the architect/engineer, or the ____________.

5. In some communities the fire protection requirement makes it necessary to provide a 3-foot-wide ____________ between storage areas and exterior walls.

6. Some sources of background information that could be used in preparation for plant layout are:

1. ____________________
2. ____________________
3. ____________________
4. ____________________

7. As a starting point for the actual layout work, we should know a good deal about the ____________ and types of materials to be handled.

8. Quite often, changes in handling method, or packaging, can benefit the ________ as well as the user.

9. Using a from-to chart it is possible to obtain numerical ____________ of the quantity to be moved.

10. Data obtained by means of a from-to chart can be graphically illustrated by various means; one of these devices is a ____________ chart.

11. In the course of examining processing and materials movement we should be concerned with the elimination of ____________ or useless movements of materials which do not add value to the product.

12. Describe in your own words what is meant by "balancing the line."

____

____

____

____

____

____

13. Any use of containers during the production process generates ____________ ____________ and is to be avoided.

14. It is important not to let the paperwork dictate the handling method. True ☐ False ☐

15. In arranging production equipment in a plant, it is well to keep sight of the fact that the higher the production capacity for a given ____________ area, the lower the ____________ cost for this production will become.

16. By aranging equipment properly in work areas we can make the most effective use of both ____________ and the human factors involved.

17. The human engineering factors in work areas are the standing, ____________, ____________, ____________, and ____________ characteristics of the human being.

18. If the distance between operations is shortened, the time interval for performing the task or ____________ ____________ ____________ should become less.

19. By taking the most ____________ line of travel, the piece part or the materials will be transported most economically, and with ____________ ____________.

20. A good plant layout makes use of labor and equipment effectively. Some of the ways for accomplishing are the following:

1. ____

____

2. ____

____

3. ____

____

21. The greatest materials-handling economy is achieved in a plant when materials are:

1. ____
2. ____
3. ____

22. Maximum production is obtained in a plant layout when the potential causes of accidents are ____

____.

23. The clearances required around the perimeter of a machine tool are necessary to:

1. ____

____

2. ____
____
3. ____
____
4. ____
____

24. With some of the larger machine tools it is necessary that sufficient overhead ____________ be maintained to change tools.

25. One objective of a good towconveyor installation is to ____________ the warehouse floor area so that the path of the towconveyor is equally ____________ to all areas.

Chapter 6
Racks, Decking, Pallets, Bins, and Order Picking

I. PALLET STORAGE RACKS

A. Introduction

In the last few years, there have been a number of changes in thinking concerning the application, design, and construction of pallet storage racks.

Probably the greatest impact was made by the federal government at first, and then more recently by the Rack Manufacturers' Institute (RMI), the Uniform Building Code (UBC) standards promulgated by the International Conference of Building Officials, and the National Fire Protection Association (NFPA).

Also, we must not forget the part that the State of California has played in advances in design; and, last but not least, the work done by the American National Standards Institute (ANSI) in providing a means for disseminating information pertaining to standards, which are, in general, comprised of original work and a review of and a collection of the most meaningful work of all of the above groups.

Also, the Office of Safety and Health Administration (OSHA) of the U.S. Department of Labor has the prerogative of using measures from the above sources in instances where safety hazards exist, and will in all probability add a few new regulations. Such a one might well be the ANSI requirement for labeling pallet storage racks with capacity plates indicating rack weight supporting limitations. Whether or not these latest stipulations will be made retroactive for existing rack installations has not been tested in the courts of law, nor has OSHA adopted them, at this time.

OSHA, of course, is concerned about performance (rather than design) that can affect the safety of employees. OSHA has the prerogative, also, of adapting and adopting the ANSI specifications as written in ANSI MH 16.1, or of using strictly functional or performance language in incorporating the standards for racks into federal regulations.

Complicating matters still further in this area of work design is the impact of the California earthquake or seismic standards. (See Fig. 6-1.) The Uniform

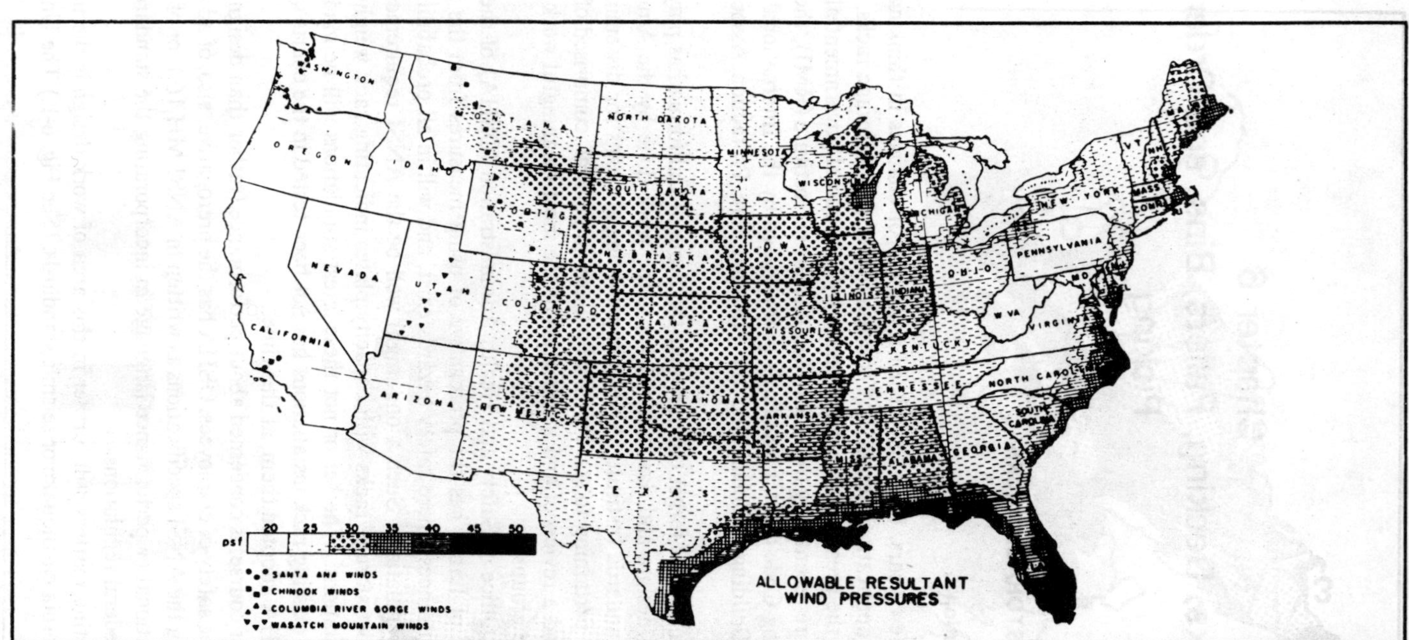

*This UBC reference map gives the Wind Force zones which should be considered when calculating strength requirements for outside racking installations.***

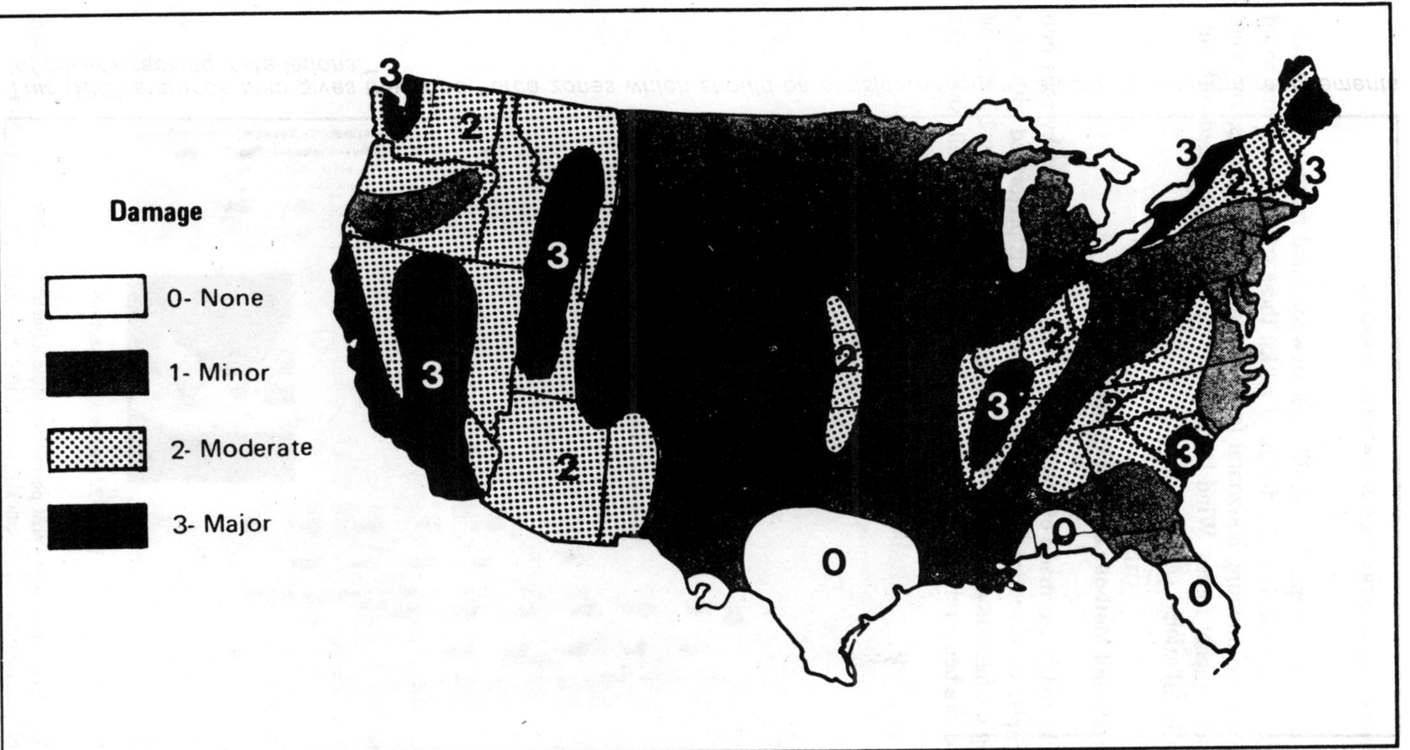

*Calculation formulas for strength requirements under both the UBC and RMI are based on the damage risk zones as shown in the above map the U.S. Coast and Geodetic Survey map issued January 1969.**

Fig. 6-1.

Building Code has adopted the California viewpoint and requires earthquake design provisions built into the design of racks; these specifications are based on design criteria affecting horizontal forces, seismic considerations, and wind loadings and impact forces. Wind loadings are primarily concerned with outdoor rack installations.

B. Materials and Methods of Rack Construction

Most racks today are made of steel strip, which is cold-formed by rolls into fairly complex cross sections. Generally the steel strip is perforated with holes of varying configurations, usually with hole spacing approximately 2 inches on centers before being rolled.* The tube mill or the cold-forming rolls shape the

Fig. 6-2. Storage rack sections.

*This hole spacing on the upright post permits variable adjustment of the shelf beam members, so that each rack opening may be quickly snapped into place at any de. ired shelf level.

Fig. 6-3. Cantilevered racks for pipes and tubes. Courtesy Jarke Corporation, Niles, Illinois.

strip in such a fashion that each fabricator has its own particular cross section, although there are, today, several fabricators that offer similar cross sections, especially for the rack uprights (upright posts). (See Fig. 6-2.)

Although most fabricators of pallet storage racks tend to make their upright post members with fairly rectangular cross sections, two companies, in particular, depart from this general rule. Since Appendix G lists a number of pallet rack manufacturers, all of which are members of the Rack Manufacturers' Institute, we shall not hesitate to mention two different types of racks that are being successfully manufactured today. One is made by the Artco Company, which offers a round, symmetrical column. This Company's upright post consists of an electrically welded, seamed tube used in place of the conventional rectangularly rolled post section of the frame. The other company, Frazier, uses a structural steel I-beam section in its construction. Although these two fabricators use different types of framing members, they still manage to maintain competitive prices in today's market. Also, both of these companies offer cantilever types of racks, as do many of the other RMI member companies. (See Fig. 6-3.)

C. Locking Devices

We have noted that uniform hole spacings in the upright posts permit rapid and easy adjustment of the horizontal shelf beams to the uprights. Although this is true in almost all rack fabricators' components, there are vast differences in the various locking devices, which usually hold the horizontal shelf beams in a fairly rigid position. These "safety load locks," "tapered studs," or "snap-type locks" should be examined very closely because some of them, especially wire or spring types, are extremely dangerous and become safety hazards. Some may be bumped out, or sprung out of place, and leave the loose ends of shelf beams literally hanging in space. (See Fig. 6-4.)

The above types of locking devices are sometimes, mistakenly, used with cantilevered rack arms and present potential safety problems, especially where heavy loads are concerned. In some cases, rubber grommetted safety locks have been used with cantilevered rack arms and have caused accidents, permitting an entire load arm to collapse under a load, or to be bumped out of position by a sideloading fork truck.

D. Shelf Beams

Shelf beams for pallet storage racks also vary considerably in construction and configuration, but they may be categorized in the following ways: (a) one-piece; (b) two-piece; (c) flush, top beam design; (d) step-down ledge design; and (e) structural beam. The first four shelf beams are composed of cold-rolled, formed sections such as are produced on Yoder-type tube mills; the last shelf beam mentioned (e) is a hot-rolled structural I-beam of the type used by The Frazier Company in many installations.

There are still a few companies that provide bolted joints for fastening the ends of their shelf beams to the upright posts of the end frames. However, most pallet storage rack companies now use the slip-joint or hole and stud type of fastening method, and provide a locking device such as mentioned in section (C), above. (Figure 6-5 shows some shelf beam cross sections.)

II. DRIVE-IN AND DRIVE-THROUGH RACKS

Drive-in and drive-through racks have special properties that make their use advantageous in several applications.

To mention a few of the advantages: We would use this type of rack (see Fig. 6-6) when the preservation of the fragility, or the elimination of crushing, of the packaging and its contents is of primary importance, *and* when the materials being stored are similar, in other words, when there is no difference in model number or a characteristic such as serial number, engineering design,

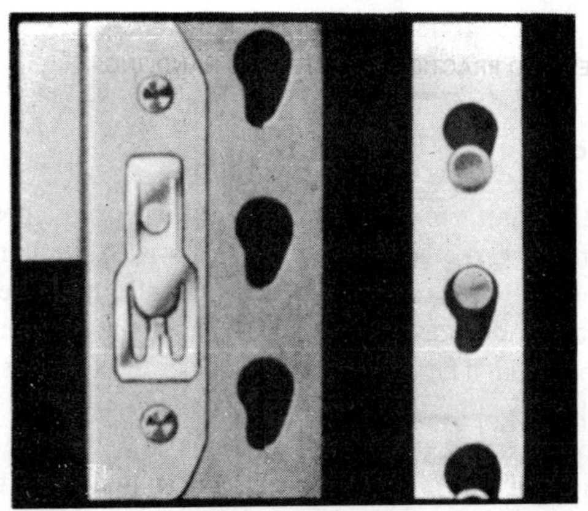

SAFETY SNAP LOCK

SAFETY LOAD LOCK

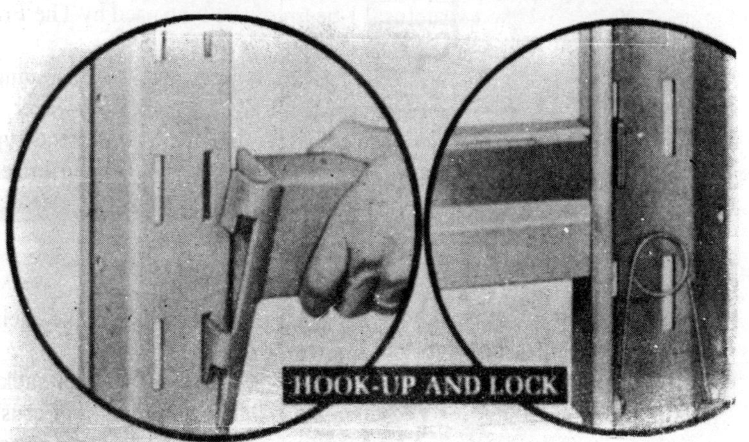

Fig. 6-4. Shelf beam safety locking devices.

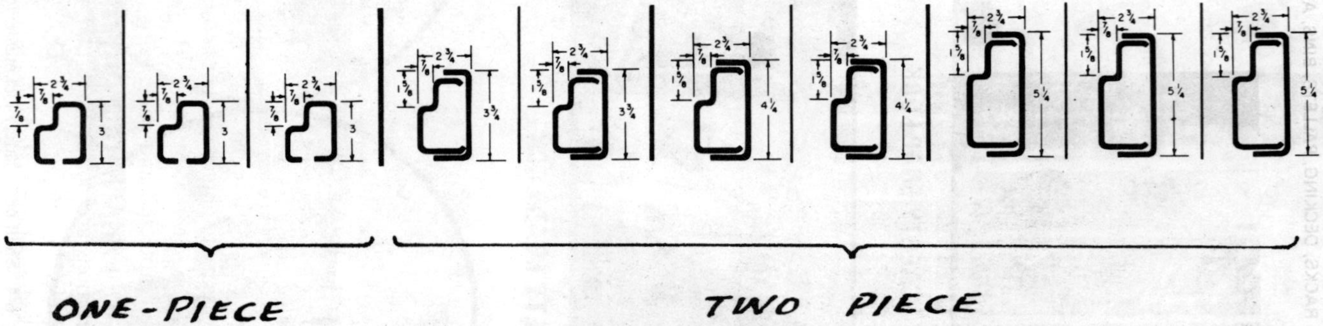

ONE-PIECE

TWO PIECE

Fig. 6-5. Shelf beam cross sections.

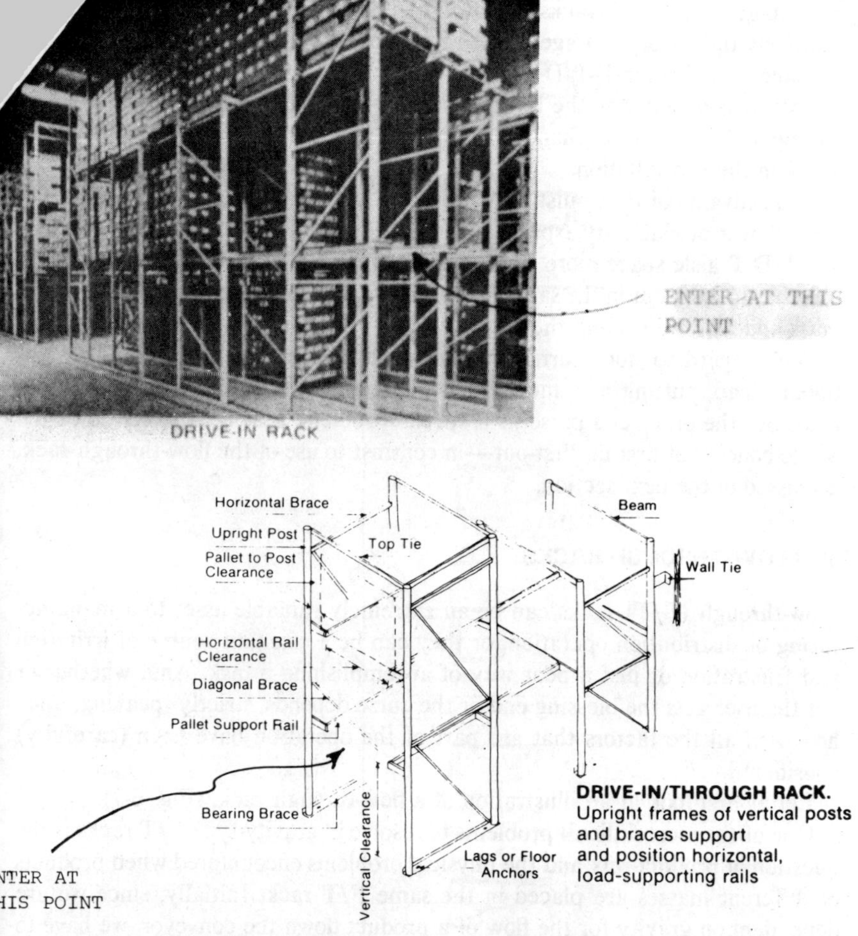

Fig. 6-6. Drive-in and drive-through racks.

etc., that would make it necessary to obtain random access to each load that is stored.

Also, heavy parts, or well-protected and packaged merchandise or parts, may be stored advantageously in the D-I/D-T racks when fast stock turnover or first-in, first-out considerations are not as important, or necessary, as the advantages offered by the racks.

We can improve on block storage methods by using the D-I/D-T racks primarily when we are not concerned with any of the above limitations, and when we do not want each load to be resting its weight on the load below, as would be the case in simple block storage practices (discussed in Chapter 4). Another advantage of D-I/D-T racks is that if the merchandise might be damaged by relatively tight block storage, these racks would tend to minimize that type of damage. Also, since D-I/D-T racks can store a great deal of merchandise almost as compactly as the block storage method, they will give much better storage cube utilization than pallet storage racks, which require greater aisle space in their installation.

A disadvantage that must be considered when installing D-I/D-T racks is their slower productivity aspect; a lift truck operator has to tread his way into a D-I/D-T aisle space more slowly than a wider pallet storage rack aisle, and then has to back out in the same careful manner to avoid damaging the upright posts and load rails along the way.

With regard to stock turnover, since each cantilevered rail contains a stationary load, putting new merchandise in from one end and taking the older loads out the other end presents a special problem; that is, it slows down the whole concept of first-in, first-out—in contrast to use of the flow-through rack, discussed in the next section.

III. FLOW-THROUGH RACKS

Flow-through (F/T) racks can be an extremely valuable asset to a manufacturing or distribution operation, or they can be a constant source of irritation and frustration or just a poor way of accomplishing a task. And, whether or not the user gets the blessing end or the curse depends, strictly speaking, upon how well all the factors that are part of the operation have been (carefully) considered.

Let us first look at an illustration of a flow-through rack. (Fig. 6-7).

One of the most difficult problems to resolve in gravity-type F/T racks is the question of product-mix and the physical problems encountered when products of different masses are placed in the same F/T rack. Initially, since we are dependent on gravity for the flow of a product down the conveyor, we have to adjust the slope of the run to achieve a relatively constant flow of material down the slope. The problem with both roller and skate-wheel types of gravity-flow conveyors is that the pitch can be set perfectly and remain constant with one set of conditions, then vary or deviate from the fundamental conditions through changes that occur in the product-mix, the type of container, the type of pallet or skid, if this is what has been used, and so forth. An F/T conveyor in a rack that has been set to handle a 100-pound load is probably pitched too high to handle a load of 500-pounds, or even some weight slightly higher than the original 100-pound load to which the pitch of the conveyor was adjusted.

Another problem is that the type of container itself may become a source of difficulty. For example, a corrugated container may behave beautifully during

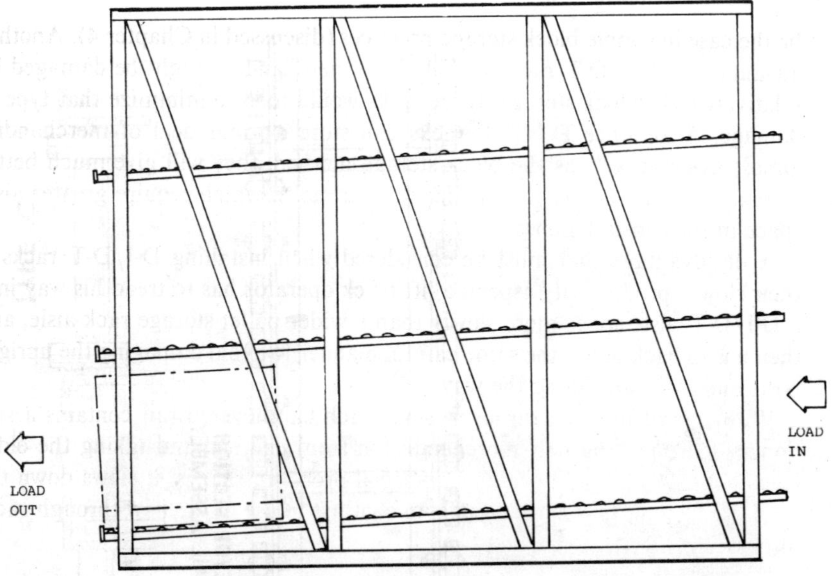

Fig. 6-7. Flow-through rack.

dry weather on a skate-wheel, gravity conveyor; but let the humidity build up during certain seasons of the year, and watch "carton fatigue" begin to take its toll. The carton will hang up on the conveyor and refuse to roll properly, if at all, because damp corrugated board will acquire a permanent set as it stays on the conveyor and will become like putty, or clay, to the indentations of the skate-wheel.

Other problems with gravity-type F/T conveyors involve the construction of rollers, wheels, guide rails, and retarders.

Rollers and wheels, of course, may be sized from the manufacturer's specifications to hold certain weights of loads; that is, in terms of capacity per roll, or per foot of conveyor.

Today there are many types of gravity conveyors on the market besides the conventional steel or aluminum types that have been made for years; for example, different types of plastic materials are used, which may serve our purposes very well. Once we get into higher weights, however, we are forced to use the metallic types.

As an example of poor skate-wheel construction, we should take a look at Fig. 6-8. In these conveyors the type of method of construction has a great deal to do with both conveyor price and performance.

There is one type of plastic on the market that is usually used in single or double strands, placed the length of the conveyor. The manufacturer claims

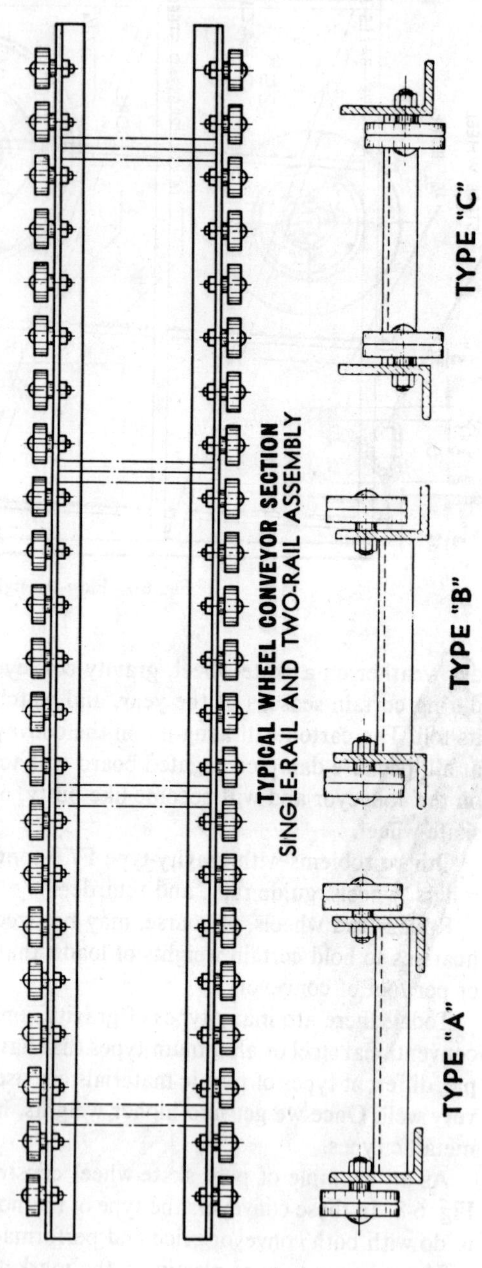

TYPICAL WHEEL CONVEYOR SECTION
SINGLE-RAIL AND TWO-RAIL ASSEMBLY

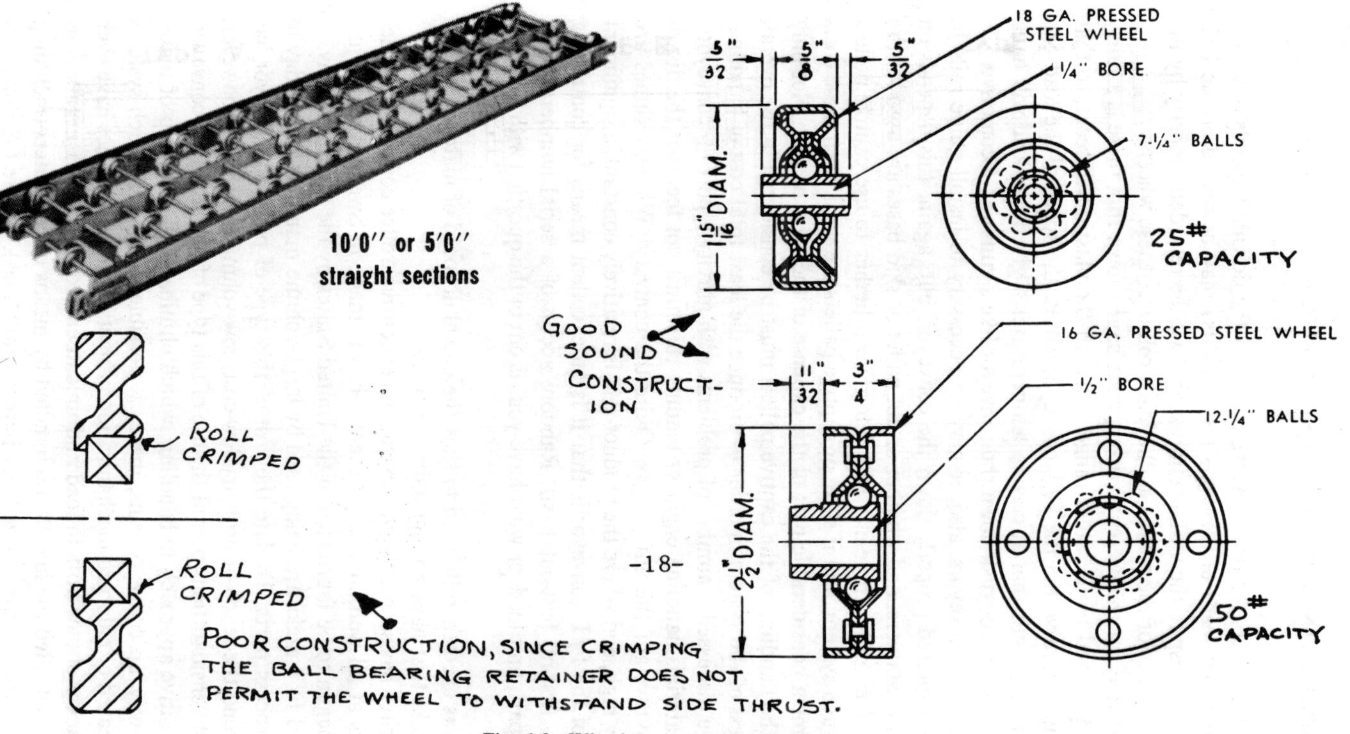

Fig. 6-8. Wheel conveyor construction.

that these plastic-coated wheels serve to retard the downhill speeds of a load to the extent that loads of varying sizes (weights) may be placed on the F/T conveyor and, despite the variance in weight, will be retarded properly by the specific properties of the plastic as the loads roll over these wheels.

Unfortunately, at the present writing, tests have shown that there is a fairly critical and limited temperature range to which the plastic will react, so that as the temperature within the F/T conveyor varies, the speed of the load can vary—with the result that at certain temperatures a given-size load will hang up in the conveyor, or rush down the conveyor like a runaway locomotive.

In some F/T conveyors, also, it may be necessary to install guide rails to keep loads centered properly down the conveyor; but, again, this depends on the type of containers, and whether or not pallet or skid bases are used for the unit loads. Certainly, trade-offs will determine whether to use captive pallets with any such system; and if slave or captive pallets are used, then these costs may become a considerable part of the expense of the total project. Not only that, but the handling of the captive pallets must be considered in the overall effectiveness of the system in order to produce the least total cost of handling.

We have discussed a number of problems with gravity-type F/T conveyors, but the materials handling engineer reading this must not feel that the disadvantages outweight the advantages. Quite the contrary! Where volumes are sufficiently high, and where the product-mix is relatively constant, a significant attribute of the F/T conveyor is that it is an excellent means for controlling stock on a first-in, first-out basis. Random access of a serial numbered container, or part, unit load, or what-have-you, is out of the question with this type of rack.

Retarders are generally used to slow the downhill speed of materials placed in F/T racks that have an unusually steep pitch.

This writer has seen only one, extremely expensive, roller conveyor retarder that works at all well, and until recently it was made in Sweden, having just recently begun to be fabricated in the United States by the same company.

Powered F/T racks are being used by large-volume manufacturers today to store in-process parts. To date the cost of this type of powered conveyor has put it beyond the reach of ordinary low-cost, low-volume operations; however, where cost considerations permit the use of this type of powered F/T conveyor, a more positive approach to handling, which eliminates the hang-up of materials part-way up conveyor runs, makes it possible to integrate such systems with increased or enlarged mechanization projects. Some companies have even placed stacker-cranes at both load and unload ends of these rack installations and have controlled the inventories handled by means of computers (including large-, medium-, and mini-sized computer installations). Figure 6-8 illustrates typical frame and wheel constructions.

IV. POTENTIAL RACK USER REQUIREMENTS; OR, WHAT YOU SHOULD EXPECT FROM RACK SUPPLIERS

Let us assume that you are going to plan for, lay out, and install one of the rack structures described in the preceding pages. If you intend to do a thorough job and plunge into the project with full understanding of the subject, there are five principal sources of information with which you should be familiar. Also, your supplier, if he represents a reputable manufacturer, should be knowledgeable in the code and regulatory areas to ensure your complete confidence in his ability to assist you in your undertaking.

We have already mentioned the following principal sources of rack information:

1. The Rack Manufacturers' Institute (RMI)
2. The National Fire Protection Association (NFPA)
3. Office of Safety and Health Administration (OSHA)
4. Uniform Building Code (UBC)
5. American National Standards Institute (ANSI)

In this discussion we shall concentrate on pallet storage racks, drive-in/drive-through racks, and flow-through racks.

A. The Quality and Type of Steel

The steel used in the above racks should be of structural quality as defined by the specifications of The American Society for Testing and Materials, as listed in the Specification for the Design of Cold-Formed Steel Structural Members in the latest rendering of the American Iron and Steel Institute (AISI), and in the Specification for the Design, Fabrication and Erection of Structural Steel for Buildings in the latest version of the American Institute of Steel Construction (AISC).

If the steels used in your rack specifications are not listed in the above standards, they are not necessarily excluded. They must, however, conform to chemical analysis and mechanical properties or other specifications that establish their structural and physical suitability as indicated in tests performed by either the rack manufacturer or you, as the purchaser. This will in effect prove that the steel will measure up in the same manner and degree as indicated in the AISI and AISC requirements.

B. Drawings and Computations

The local representative of the rack manufacturer should supply you with rack configuration drawings, with all dimensions, and load application computations for every installation that is 12 feet in height, or higher. It is suggested that you, as the purchaser, file these drawings and load application figures, and both the manufacturer and the local representative would be well advised to do the same, since OSHA inspectors may ask to examine these documents. Also, ask the manufacturer to give you certification that his rack installation meets the horizontal load requirements and other design load specifications of the ANSI standards.

C. Labeling Requirements

The Rack Manufacturers' Institute specifications (which may be written into federal law as OSHA regulations at some future date) require that all rack installations display in one or more obvious and apparent locations a permanent-type, rectangular sign of not less than 50 square inches that shall indicate clearly and legibly the maximum permissible unit loads for each shelf of the rack installation.

If the rack installation does not exceed 12 feet in height at the top of the uppermost shelf, and the entire installation does not cover a floor area of more than 3,000 square feet, and it does not contain unit loads of more than 2,500 pounds per shelf and has no double-stacking on the uppermost shelf, then you can disregard the requirements indicated in (B) "Drawings and Computations" and (above) (C) "Labeling Requirements."

D. Rack Anchoring, Bracing, and Vertical Alignment

In all good-quality rack construction the bottom of all upright posts should be supplied with bearing plates. In addition, D-I/D-T and F/T racks (described in the above paragraphs) should be anchored to the floor by anchor bolts or ram-jet bolts* capable of resisting the horizontal shear forces caused by the horizontal and vertical loads transmitted through the rack structure.

Rack installations may not have to be anchored in the above manner if it can be demonstrated that the frictional forces between the bearing plates and the floor are capable of resisting (or overcoming) the horizontal reaction resulting from the rack analysis. It is recommended that this analysis be prepared by a registered professional engineer and properly documented for your files.

On occasion it is necessary to place rack installations where they must be braced against, or to, the building structure. When this situation arises, the horizontal and vertical forces imposed by the rack upon the building must be calculated.

Ram-jet bolts are shot through holes in the bearing plates, directly into the concrete, using a cartridge-type gun.

Before proceeding further, we must define the word "frame" because it has an important meaning to our subject. A frame is composed of upright posts and pallet beams in pallet racks, the rigidly connected members made up of upright posts and top tie-beams, or rail-support beams in D-I/D-T racks, and the cross-braced, or trussed, upright frames.

These frames should be designed for the critical combination of vertical loads in any of the most unfavorable positions, also taking into consideration the horizontal loads and the additional undesirable effects of horizontal sway caused by any looseness of the top tie-beam–to–post connections.

All connections that cannot readily be structurally analyzed should be indicated by testing to withstand the moments of force, shear stresses, and axial forces in combination.

In addition, if the racks are braced against the building, the owner of the building or his agent should be informed of the results of the above calculations and test data.

As to vertical alignment of the rack structure, the user should insist on a maximum tolerance of 1 inch in 10 feet of height. If the rack structure requires more precise vertical alignment because of the method of loading and unloading the racks, then this should be determined in advance of the installation and made a part of the purchase specifications.

D-I/D-T racks also require some special considerations that are not always present in other types of rack structures. For example, it is recommended that top tie-beams always be installed in D-I/D-T racks to ensure the proper degree of stability in the structure.

In Fig. 6-9 two illustrations indicate the ANSI clearance requirements for (a) D-I/D-T racks with pallet guide rails, and (b) D-I/D-T racks without pallet guide rails. The two critical dimensions are ¾ inch and 1 inch respectively (as illustrated).

V. A BRIEF SUMMARY OF ANSI SPECIFICATION REQUIREMENTS

When we take a careful look at the overall ANSI rack specifications, we find that some of the older specifications, carried down to us initially from federal government and military specifications, have been undergoing changes and additions. Let us review them to clarify any misunderstandings.

A. Pallet Shelf Beams

The load on a rack is carried by the beams. The beams are bolted or hooked to the post, thus transferring the load to the post. A beam carries its greatest load when its strongest axis is at 90° to the direction of the load. Essentially,

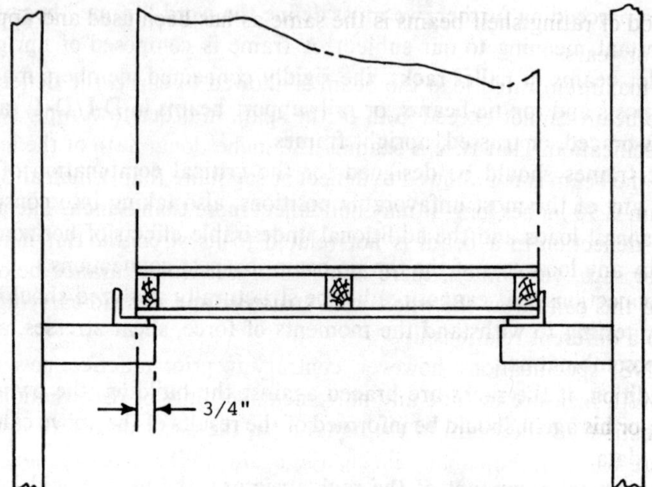

With pallet guides, distance between guide and opposite rail can't be more than pallet width minus ¾".

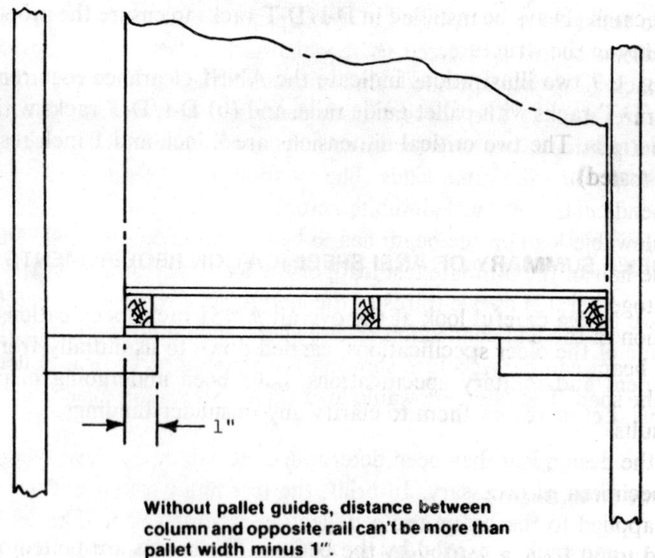

Without pallet guides, distance between column and opposite rail can't be more than pallet width minus 1".

Fig. 6-9. Drive-in/drive-through racks.

this method of rating shelf beams is the same as has been used and applied in industry for years.

At the maximum rated load the beam is allowed to carry, the deflection or sag of the beam cannot exceed $\frac{1}{180}$th of the span, in order to comply with the ANSI specification. That is, if a beam is 180 inches long, $\frac{1}{180}$th of the length is 1 inch; so the beam is not allowed to deflect or sag more than 1 inch altogether. If the beam is 90 inches long, it may not deflect more than ½ inch. The amount of sag or deflection in a beam is not related to its strength. But if a beam deflects, or sags, very much, there is a loss of vertical clearance below that beam, and this can throw the whole rack structure and its load-carrying capability into a different relationship.

The ANSI specifications, however, contrary to prior practice, now require that the $\frac{1}{180}$th measure include any movement, settling, or deformation in the end connections of the beam to the column. In the past, almost all deflection tables were based on how many inches the beam itself would sag, and not on the settling of the end connector—this is new.

If a manufacturer can use the conventional method of calculation found in the AISI and AISC specifications to determine the loads shelf beams can take, he doesn't have to test. But if the shape of the cross section (and we indicated a few of these complex sections earlier in this chapter) does not permit calculation of loads and deflections, the tests outlined in the specifications must be followed.

For the tests, the rack consists of two uprights that are not bolted to the floor, and two beams connected no less than 24 inches from the floor, with front-to-back ties when specified. End connections must be those used in the manufacturer's rack. The specifications described how to load and test the beams in a particular manner for given lengths of time in order to test deflection and to predict allowable loads. The location of test loads along the beam and perpendicular to it must simulate actual loading conditions.

The allowable load on the beam has to be determined in the following way: (1) as one-half of the ultimate test load, or the load the beam can carry before it fails altogether; (2) as two-thirds of the load the beam can carry before there is distortion in the end connection or elsewhere, including rotation; (3) as the load the beam can carry before showing the maximum vertical deflection of $\frac{1}{180}$th of the span. The rated allowable load capacity must be the smallest of the three results.

Once the design load has been determined, an additional test, using a new set of specimens, is necessary. In brief, the test requires that an overload of 10% be applied to the beam and a deflection reading taken. The overload is increased to 50% (or a load equal to 1½ times the design load), and another reading is taken. The residual or permanent deflection of the beam measured at a 10% overload cannot be more than 7.5% of the final deflection measured when the beam was overloaded by 1½ times the design load.

1. Vertical Impact Load Now Required for Beams. An important new requirement for unit load carrying beams is that they must now be designed to include a vertical impact load of 25% of a single load weight when it is placed in the most unfavorable position on the beams. This means that if a pair of beams is designed to support 2,000 pounds (or two 1,000-pound loads) the manufacturer has to allow another 25% of one of these loads (or 250 pounds, 25% of 1,000 pounds) and design the pair of beams to carry a load of 2,250 pounds instead of just 2,000 pounds.

2. Upward Force Resistance. Also, beams must now have support connections that are capable of withstanding an upward force of 1,000 pounds per connection (for instance, from the forks or load on a forklife truck) without failure.

3. Horizontal Loads and Moving Equipment Loads. Horizontal loads must now be evaluated for all racks. See ANSI 8.3.1–8.5.3.

Moving equipment loads must also be considered where applicable. Stacker racks or racks that support moving equipment (wholly or partially) are subject to all the tests for horizontal forces. Also, the manufacturer of moving equipment must provide the rack manufacturer with information on guide locations, as well as maximum forces (and the vectors of these forces) that could be transmitted from moving equipment to racks, plus information on applicable longitudinal and transverse impact factors.

4. Wind Loads. Wind loads must be considered for all outdoor rack installations. These racks must be specifically engineered and installed with consideration of the wind loads that act on the rack, as well as the unit loads. The safety factor against overturning of the rack by wind has to be at least 1.5.

5. Earthquake Loading. Earthquake loading provisions are also given in the specifications, and in these designs the 1½% horizontal force requirement is not applicable. These provisions apply to areas of the country where there are earthquake factors and require that manufacturers meet local or regional codes. See ANSI 8.5 through 8.5.3.

Earlier in this chapter we included the U.S. Coast and Geodetic Survey map indicating seismic zones (Fig. 6-1). This requirement is becoming a very important consideration, which will, no doubt add to the cost of certain rack installations.

6. Overturning. In order to prevent overturning, the height-to-depth ratio of the entire rack shall be six to one, measured to the top of the topmost load, unless the rack is anchored or braced externally. For this particular requirement, see ANSI 8.4, 8.5, and 9.4.

VI. SAFETY RECOMMENDATIONS FOR RACK USERS

In any materials handling operation we are concerned with the safety of our employees and visitors; in addition, a safe, orderly operation is, generally, an efficient operation, and we can minimize damage to products and equipment by making all employees safety conscious. The following recommendations should enable you to obtain the most from your employees in terms of safety to themselves and others, and should lower the cost of operations.

A. Operators and Equipment

Don't permit untrained or noncertified operators to operate your industrial powered trucks; and furthermore, make certain that all lift trucks that must raise their loads, at any time, beyond the operators' eye level are equipped with overhead guards. Also, train your lift truck operators to lift material on and off the shelf beams of the pallet racks—*don't let them drag* materials, pallets, or skids on and off the shelf beams.

B. Minimum Aisles

Aisles for safe and efficient forklift truck operations must be wide enough that the operator can make his passage easily and without danger. Most lift truck manufacturers indicate the turning radius and right-angle stacking widths for forklift trucks; wherever possible, provide an additional margin that will minimize damage to rack structure, the product, the equipment, and, of major importance, the operator! This additional margin in aisle width will pay dividends in increased productivity and faster and safer load movement.

C. Trucks and Pallets

Maintain forklift trucks and pallets in the best possible operating condition. Oversized pallets, or pallets with loose, broken, or missing deckboards, can be dangerous.

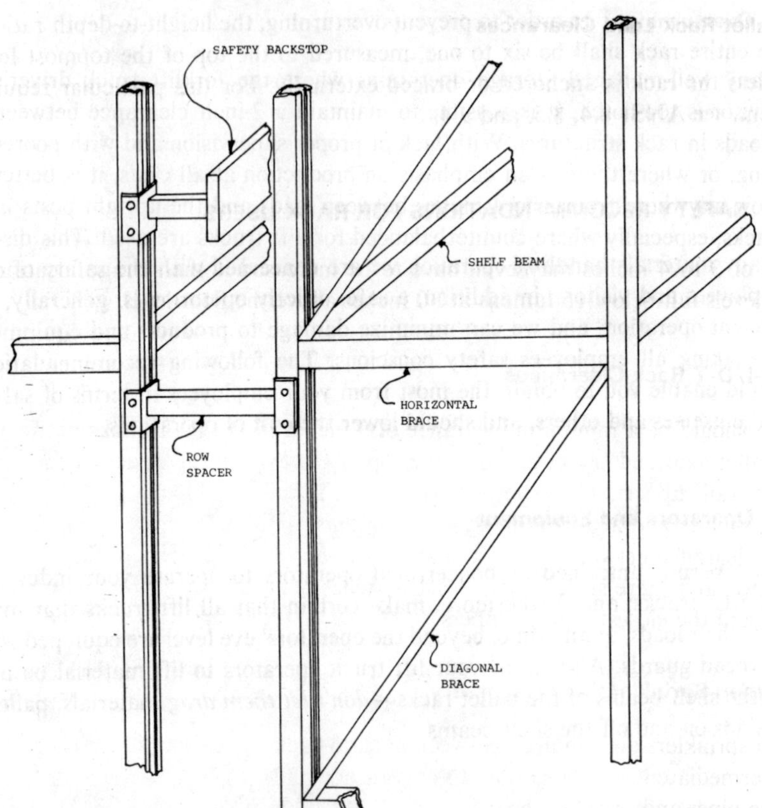

Fig. 6-10. Storage rack with pallet safety backstop.

D. Pallet Safety Backstops

Stops should be placed between pallet storage racks that are back-to-back to prevent unstable loads from being pushed out into the adjacent aisles. Where the storage racks back up into a working area, screenguards should be used on the outermost side so that loads cannot be pushed into working areas where workers and machines may be located.

Figure 6-10 shows a pallet safety backstop.

E. Front-to-Back Members

In certain pallet storage racks use welded front-to-back members in all seismic-rated racks, and especially in racks subject to fork truck bumping, specifically in shelf beams placed over aisles when used to improve storage cube utilization.

F. Pallet Rack Load Clearances

In many well-managed storage operations where the forklift truck driver's supervisor is top-notch, it is possible to maintain a 2-inch clearance between unit loads in rack structures. With lack of proper supervision and with poorer training, or where there is an emphasis on production at all costs, it is better to allow anywhere from 3 to 4 inches between loads and the upright posts in the racks, especially where counterbalanced forklift trucks are used. This distance of 3 to 4 inches may even have to be increased if the storage location light levels fall below 15 lumens at 30 inches above the floor level.

G. D-I/D-T Rack Clearances

There should be a minimum clearance of 3 inches in D-I/D-T racks between the pallet load and the post. From the top of the load to the underside of the rail (or rail support, whichever is lower), there should be a 4-inch clearance on lower shelves and a 6-inch or greater clearance on higher shelves. The minimum clearance between the mast and the rail on either side should be at least 2 inches, and there should be at least 3 inches between any other part of the truck and the closest rack members.

H. When Sprinklers Are Necessary

When sprinklers are required between back-to-back racks at lower levels, that is, intermediate levels, be certain to provide adequate protection and clearance for the pipes and sprinkler heads.

I. Rack Damage Action

It is well, at this point, to quote RMI section 1.4.8, which has been incorporated into the ANSI specification and could soon become part of the OSHA federal law:

> 1.4.8 The bottom portions of those posts which are exposed to collision by forklift trucks or other moving equipment, shall be protected from such collisions by protective devices. If not so protected, the rack structure shall: (1) be designed to maintain its full design load capacity at the usual allowable stresses even if the carrying capacity of an exposed post is reduced by collision damage to one-half that of the undamaged post, or (2) be designed to maintain its full design load capacity at 50% increased allowable stresses even if the damaged exposed post has lost all carrying capacity, or (3) be shown by test to be capable of withstanding collision without collapse even if the damaged exposed post has lost all carrying capacity.

Upon such damage, the pertinent portion of the rack shall be immediately unloaded and the damaged portion adequately repaired or replaced.

VII. CANTILEVERED RACKS

Cantilevered racks have undergone a metamorphosis, or change, over the years—from the simple A frame rack (shown in Fig. 6-11), which is used for pipe, conduit, and bar stock, to the cantilevered rack used with pans (Fig. 6-12), to the cantilevered racks used with various types of stacker-crane and/or sideloader powered industrial trucks (Figs. 6-13 and 6-14).

So, while there is a place in today's smaller operations for the use of cantilevered A-frames that use an overhead jib crane or overhead hoist with chains, chains and slings, and spreader bars, we have come a long way in the use of the cantilevered rack. It has displayed almost endless versatility in the number of imaginative uses being developed for it; furniture, small boats, lumber, and steel plates can be stored on the various types of cantilevered racks presently on the market.

Whatever type of rack you use, remember that aisle spacing and the manner in which the support arms are tied into the uprights are extremely important. Locking devices, as already mentioned should be fail-safe!

Fig. 6-11. A-frame rack.

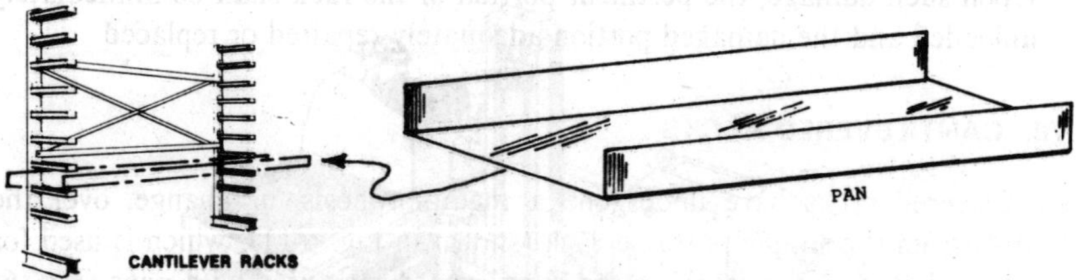

Fig. 6-12. Pan for cantilevered rack.

VIII. RACK-SUPPORTED BUILDINGS

The first rack-supported buildings were erected in Europe, and as well as can be established were constructed in West Germany during its tremendous economic burst during the late 1960s. One such building was reported to be at least 100 feet tall and was equipped with a stacker-crane retrieval system.

The next rack-supported structure reported was at the Ford Motor Company's plant in Degenham, England. This building was 110 feet tall, had Dexion racks, and was also stacker-crane equipped and computer controlled.

The concept of the rack-supported building is not a new one in the United States although we have reason to believe that the concept of using the high-

Fig. 6-13. Man-riding stacker crane removing load from rack opening. Operator is on the far side.

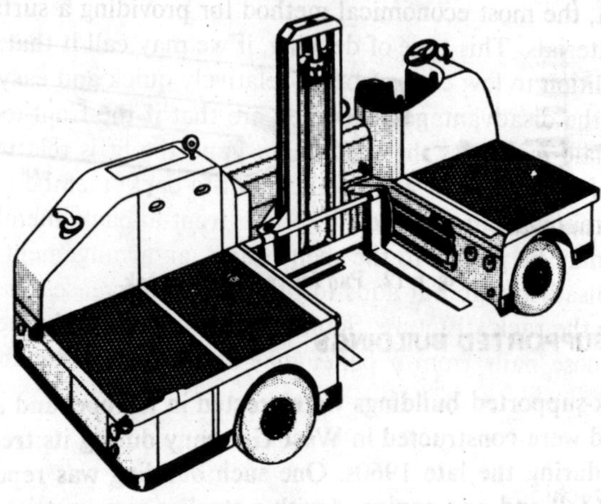

Fig. 6-14. Sideloader truck.

rise, high-density stacker-crane retrieval mechanism as its operating core originated on the other side of the Atlantic.

Other buildings with a lower ceiling height were being advertised a few years ago. At that time they were approximately 30 feet under the truss and were geared to the upper limit of the industrial powered truck.

While there has been no mad stampede by U.S. companies to investigate the merits of the rack-supported, stacker-crane system installation, a few such structures have begun to appear on the American scene.

Ford Motor has at least two, one on the West Coast 65 feet high, and one in Buffalo, New York at about 90 feet. It is believed, however, that the American Cyanimid Company, in Bound Brook, New Jersey, had one of the first stacker-crane retrieval system installations in this country that was constructed as a rack-supported building.

The economics of labor, materials, insurance, land value, and tax structures in the United States have in many instances militated against this type of structure; however, any company that is contemplating a high-rise, high-density, stacker-crane retrieval system with a process control computer to direct the operation should attempt a feasibility study to determine its return on investment before discarding this concept, or neglecting it completely.

IX. RACK DECKING

A. Front-to-Back Members

Many rack installations today rely exclusively upon two front-to-back members placed across a pair of shelf beams for each pallet, or unit load opening. This is, no doubt, the most economical method for providing a surface upon which to place materials. This type of decking, if we may call it that, has the advantage, in addition to low cost, of being relatively quick and easy to install.

Some of the disadvantages, however, are that if the front-to-back members are simply laid in, across the shelf beams, and the fit is relatively loose, there is danger of losing loads, and of the front-to-back members shifting out of place, or dropping out completely. Some front-to-back members may come welded, or may be pinned to the shelf beams, an arrangement that eliminates the above disadvantage but adds to the cost and increases the labor required to assemble the rack structure. Sometimes, also, loose or broken bottom deckboards or loose nails from a pallet may snag or dislocate the front-to-back member.

B. Wood Decking

For a long time, and even in some new, present-day installations, wood deck boards have been set into step-ledge-design shelf beams, where they perform very satisfactorily. The NFPA tests at Natick have shown, however, that fire tends to spread horizontally under the decking and to jump from pallet opening to pallet opening, when wood decking is used and the lumber is set fairly close together or continuously along the shelf beams. Also, the NFPA tests have shown that for certain classes of materials used with wood decking, the fire will jump clear across aisle spaces. The reader is advised to avoid wood decking whenever possible for the above fire protection considerations. (Chapter 7 discusses in greater detail the "Fire Prevention Aspects of Rack Storage.")

C. Wire-Mesh Decking

A great deal of wire-mesh decking has been installed in a number of rack storage structures. Wire-mesh decking is surprisingly strong and goes into place fairly easily; and when a fit becomes difficult, it can be pounded into place readily. Several types of wire-mesh decking are made, fitting almost every type of shelf beam. Wire-mesh decking has good fire protection properties, since it permits sprinklers to wet down through the mesh, in contrast to wood or other types of solid decking. One of the greatest disadvantages of wire-mesh decking is its relative inability to withstand heavy point loading. It does very well when uniform loads are placed upon it, and it can be reinforced with steel channels on its bottom side. However, if point loading occurs—for example, when a skid load of material having four pedestals is placed upon it—25% of the load may be acting upon only one or two welds of the wire-mesh cross bars, and then problems may arise. If light loads are stored, or if loads of the rated capacity of the decking comprise uniform lading of the entire surface (or a large portion of the deck surface), then this problem is not bothersome.

The type of merchandise to be stored has to be of primary concern in selecting any type of rack decking.

D. Solid Steel Decking

Solid steel decking performs as well as solid wood decking. It does not burn, but depending on the class of material contained in the racks, it may tend to spread fire, and it hardly permits the penetration of water from the sprinkler system that is so desirable in fighting rack storage fires. Usually laid in sections across the shelf beams, solid steel decking is relatively expensive although it may be just the right decking for storing dies or fixtures that must slide across its surface during loading and unloading. Solid steel decking is recommended primarily for this type of storage operation.

E. Grate-Type Decking

There are several types of grate decking, most of this material being made directly from steel stair tread or storage mezzanine surfacing. The perforations or slots (openings) in this type of decking aid in water penetration, and it can sustain relatively heavy loads. Its primary disadvantage in most instances stems from its relatively high price, although in some market periods it may be competitive with other rack decking materials.

F. Perforated Steel Decking

A relative newcomer to the market, but a strong competitor, is perforated steel decking. It has all the advantages of wire-mesh decking with none of the disadvantages, since it withstands point loading very well and can be obtained in many different gauges and configurations to suit any type of shelf beam construction. Its perforations, which can be specified as to size and spacing, permit excellent sprinkler water penetration; and because of its competitive pricing, it will be used increasingly.

(See Figs. 6-15 through 6-20 for the types of rack decking described in the above paragraphs.)

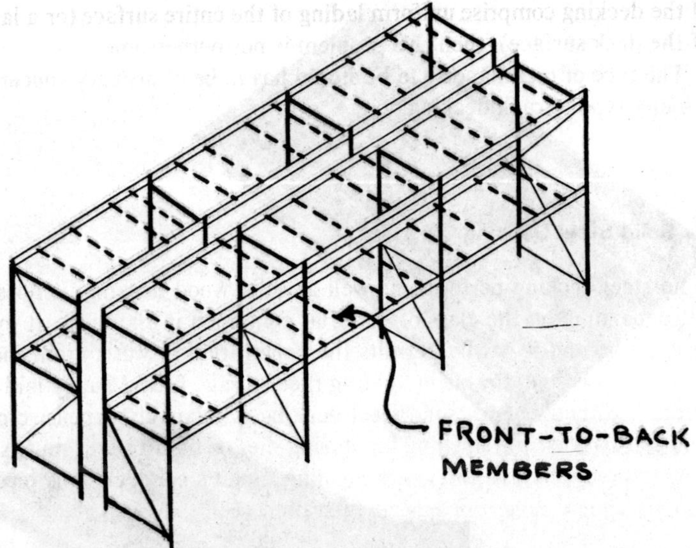

Fig. 6-15. Schematic of storage rack showing front-to-back members.

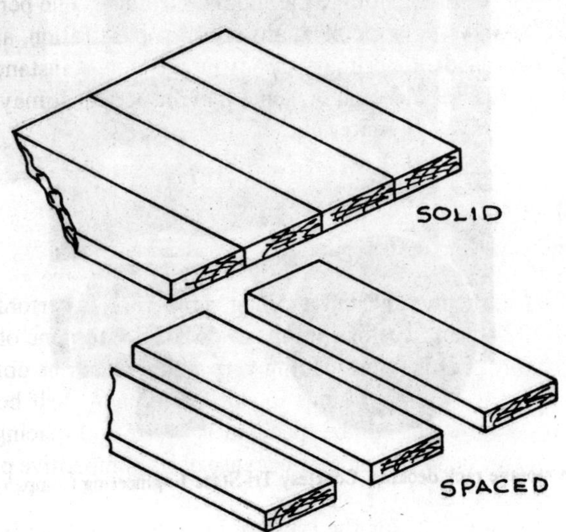

Fig. 6-16. Solid and spaced wood decking.

Fig. 6-17. Wire storage rack decking. Courtesy Tri-State Engineering Company.

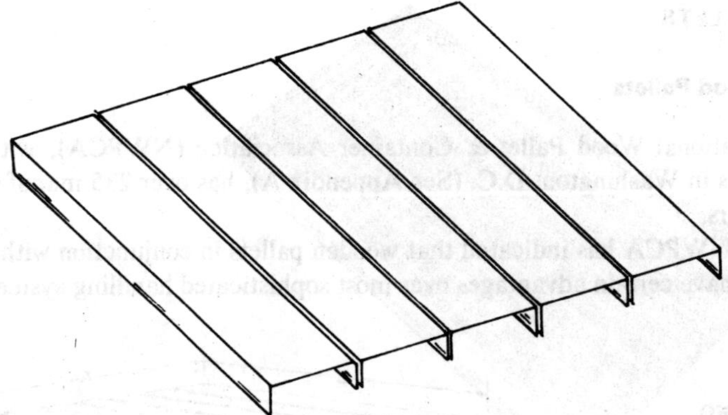

Fig. 6-18. Solid steel decking.

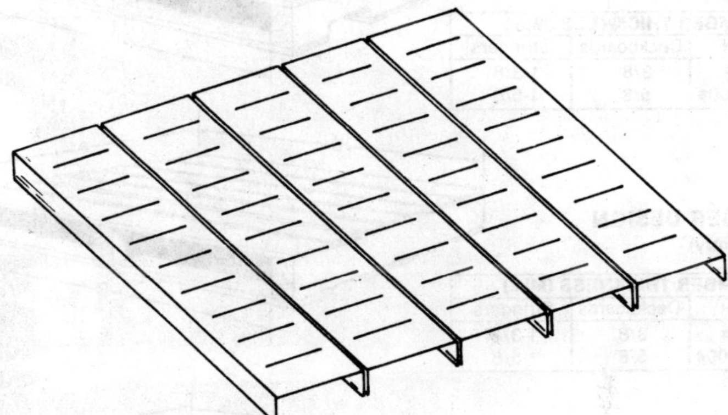

Fig. 6-19. Grate-type decking.

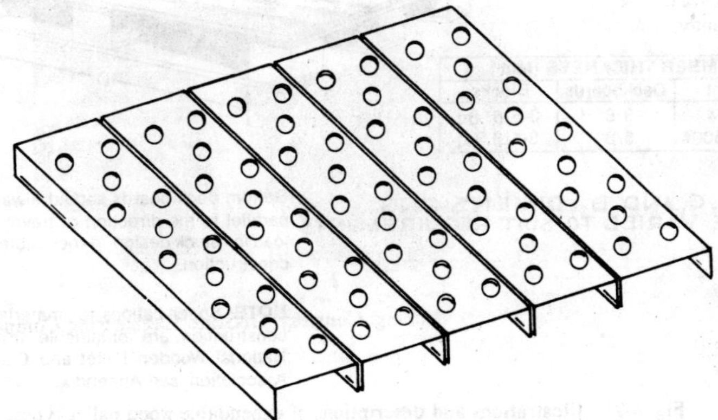

Fig. 6-20. Perforated steel decking.

X. PALLETS

A. Wood Pallets

The National Wood Pallet & Container Association (NWPCA), with headquarters in Washington, D.C. (See Appendix A), has over 235 manufacturing members.

The NWPCA has indicated that wooden pallets in conjunction with forklift trucks have certain advantages over most sophisticated handling systems: they

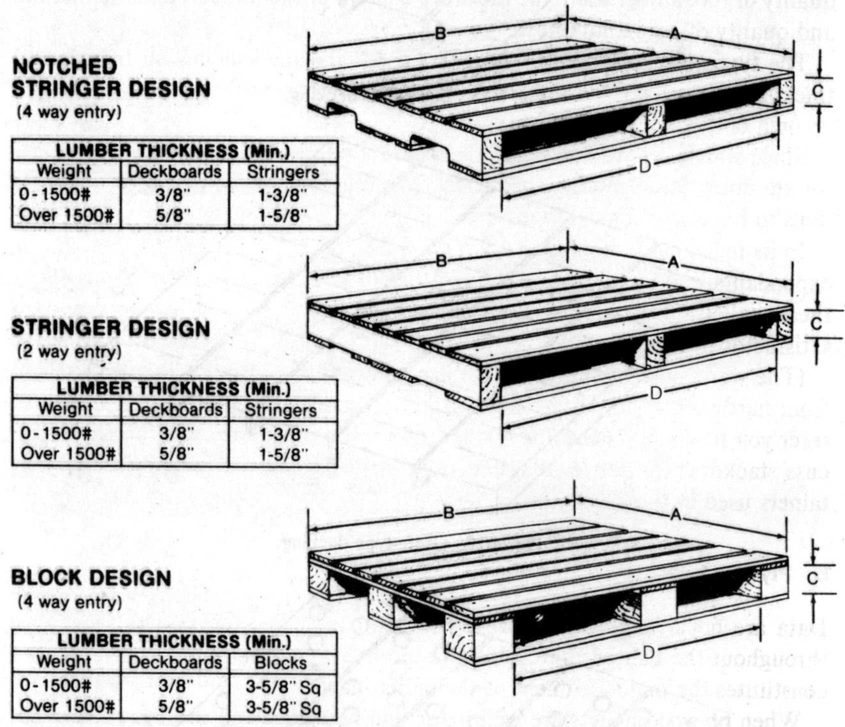

NOTCHED STRINGER DESIGN
(4 way entry)

LUMBER THICKNESS (Min.)		
Weight	Deckboards	Stringers
0-1500#	3/8"	1-3/8"
Over 1500#	5/8"	1-5/8"

STRINGER DESIGN
(2 way entry)

LUMBER THICKNESS (Min.)		
Weight	Deckboards	Stringers
0-1500#	3/8"	1-3/8"
Over 1500#	5/8"	1-5/8"

BLOCK DESIGN
(4 way entry)

LUMBER THICKNESS (Min.)		
Weight	Deckboards	Blocks
0-1500#	3/8"	3-5/8" Sq
Over 1500#	5/8"	3-5/8" Sq

A, B, C, AND D DIMENSIONS MAY BE VARIED TO SUIT REQUIREMENTS

Bottom deck boards should always run parallel to the direction of travel of the load in "block design" expendable pallet construction.

NOTE: Specifications for materials and construction are obtainable from the National Wooden Pallet and Container Association, see Appendix.

Fig. 6-21. Illustrations and descriptions of expendable wood pallet types.

work well; they are of low cost; they are simple; and they are relatively safe to use.

At least 12% of all lumber grown and manufactured in the United States is used in pallet, crate, skid, and box production—certainly an impressive statistic. Since large quantities of materials are moved by rail, truck, sea, and air on these rectangular platforms, we should learn something of the nature and characteristics of the pallet—especially if we purchase materials that arrive at our plants on pallets, or if we have a manufacturing or warehousing type of business that requires the purchase of large quantities of pallets.

Important considerations in the pricing of pallets are the type, grade, and quality of the lumber used, the moisture content of the lumber, and the method and quality of its manufacture.

The type and placement of fasteners used, and the spacing, surfacing, and thickness of deck boards and stringers, all play an important part in the development of a pallet or skid.

Since standards are available for pallet manufacture, it would be advisable for any materials handling practitioner who is responsible for pallet specifications to request technical literature from the NWPCA. (See Appendix A.)

In its technical literature the NWPCA also covers standards for one-way or expendable wood pallets. Great quantities of merchandise are transported on these pallets, and Fig. 6-21 illustrates several types that may be used satisfactorily.

(The warehouse or captive pallet is a heavier type, and is always fabricated from hardwood. There are many variations in size and specifications, and we refer you to the NWPCA for further information. In Chapter 7, when we discuss stacker-crane retrieval systems, we shall cover types of pallets and containers used in these systems.)

B. Plywood Pallets

Data are not available to indicate the number of plywood pallets fabricated throughout the United States, but it is probably only a small fraction of what constitutes the major segment of the pallet market.

When plywood pallets are well made and new, they are excellent means for handling certain types of products for which the spacing between the normal deck boards becomes a problem and a hazard. Two examples are (1) the handling of bagged materials; and (2) the handling of ice cream and frozen foods. Bagged materials have a tendency to tear on standard wood pallets; and when ice cream thaws even temporarily, it forms ridges in the container that are not desirable for the retailing or merchandising of the product. Thus, certain segments of industry have adopted plywood decked pallets, and sometimes even masonite or wood-fiberboard sheets are used to overcome the problems mentioned.

Plywood pallets have a tendency to splinter, and sometimes they become dangerous and hazardous to handle manually over a period of time. Some companies have even tried fiber glass reinforcing of the top decks of plywood pallets to ensure longer life and less splintering. Of course, the original cost of the plywood pallet is usually higher than that of a standard pallet; and when the cost of plastic coating is considered, the return on the investment, even with the slightly longer life span of the coated pallet, is usually inadequate, and is very seldom justified.

C. Corrugated Pallets

One-way or expandable pallets are often made from corrugated board. This material can withstand a normal amount of abuse in transit; however, many suppliers who ship materials in less-than-truckload quantity (LTL) or in less-than-railcar quantity (LCL) find that their greatest damage, using corrugated pallets, occurs in the consolidation terminals of most carriers.

The principal damage occurs in the legs or pedestals of these corrugated containers. Over the years many different configurations of pallet legs have been tried: circular, rectangular, and even plastic and metallic cups have been used.

A new wrinkle in the method of manufacture of expendable corrugated pallets comes from the aircraft industry where a corrugated board is made like a honeycomb; this cellular consistency imparts lightness and strength to the corrugated board.

Stacking corrugated pallet loads with damaged legs (pedestals) is a very frustrating experience, and sometimes creates unstable and extremely unsafe stacks.

If the value of the merchandise to be shipped is relatively high, it would be best for the shipping company's image to use a pallet that can withstand the rigors of present-day transportation much better than the expendable corrugated container. At least the company should engage in a testing program to determine what type of corrugated pallet best suits its requirements and will best satisfy the customer.

If you are on the receiving end, you may have to try some negotiating if your purchasing department is buying strictly according to price.

D. Plastic and Foam Pallets

The U.S. Patent Office probably has hundreds of patents and patent applications covering all sorts of plastic and foam pallets. A number of the comments about corrugated pallets also apply to these plastic types.

One of the only differences is that the plastic pallets, whether they are made of solid plastic or with metal or wood inserts, are getting better all the time. In addition, some of the styrofoam types, which are essentially one-way pallets, do an excellent job of protecting the merchandise in transit.

Warehouse or captive pallets made from these styrofoam pallets can be made to stack well; and in many industries round trips between assembly and manufacturing sources have produced great savings and economies in handling despite high initial costs.

Another type of warehouse pallet that has proved its durability is the high-impact polyethylene pallet. Some of these pallets will outlast a wood pallet at least 3 or 4 to 1, their major disadvantage being their high original cost.

E. Steel Pallets

Certain industries are, of necessity, wedded to steel pallets and skids because they have no other choice. For example, in heat-treating operations or in certain cleaning operations where parts are sprayed with steam, it is impossible to substitute another, more suitable material.

Steel pallets have three major advantages over most pallets in: (1) their durability, (2) their ability to withstand loads that would destroy other types of pallets, and (3) the fact that they are usually repairable despite frequent abuse.

XI. BIN SHELVING

A. Bin Shelving Posts

There are many types of bin shelving on today's market. Almost any small shop with a press brake can make bin shelving, and prices for this type of materials handling equipment can be very competitive for this reason.

Most bin shelving can be classified into three different load types: light, medium, and heavy duty. Another way of classifying bin shelving is by the type of upright post that is used. The upright is important in that it is the main load-carrying component of the shelving. It can be one of four main types, although there are many variations of these basic styles: (1) tubular; (2) structural, or T-section; (3) angle; and (4) beaded type. (See Fig. 6-22 for a description of these basic designs.)

B. Shelves

The shelving steel that most bins are made of is usually 18-gauge material. The most commonly used shelf size is 24 to 36 inches wide, whereas depth

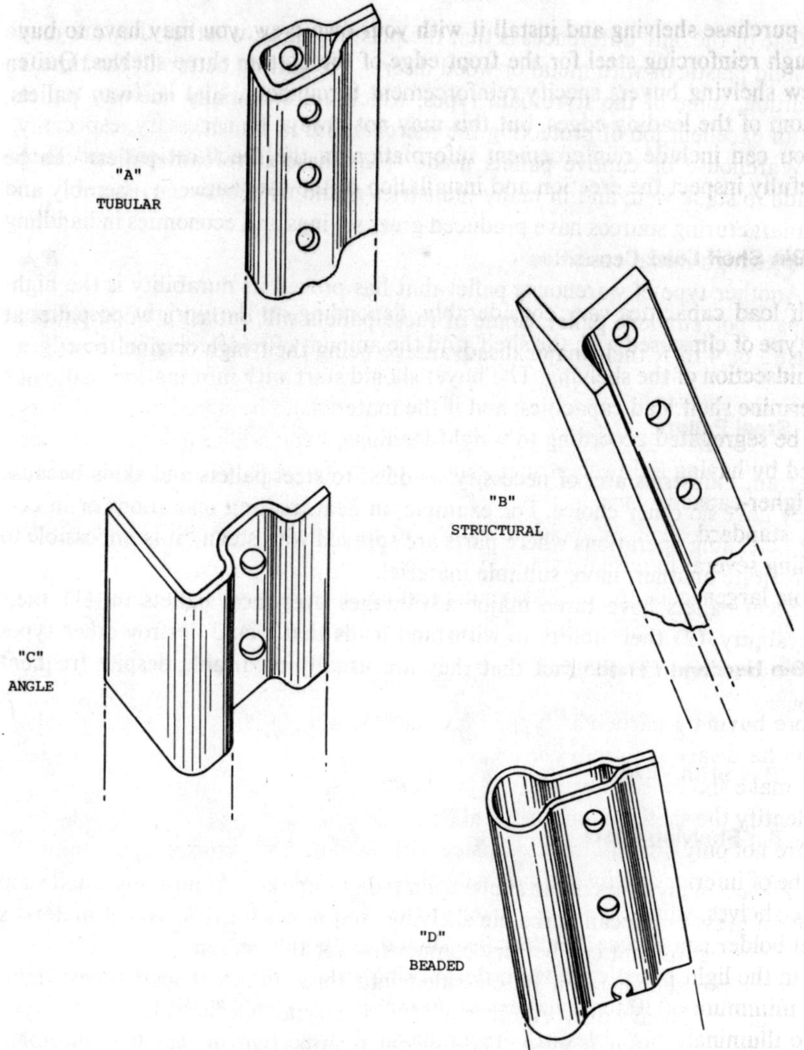

Fig. 6-22. Typical cross sections of bin shelving uprights.

ranges from 12 to 36 inches are not uncommon. The sheet metal gauge of most bins is so light (18-gauge) that it usually pays to have a piece of reinforcing steel placed in the leading edge of the shelf. This piece of insert, which is usually made of 12-gauge material, has the double advantage of increasing shelf load capacity and saving the shelf from bending in the middle, since, invariably, order pickers and stockers will stand on the first two to three shelves. If you purchase shelving and install it with your own crew, you may have to buy enough reinforcing steel for the front edge of the bottom three shelves. Quite a few shelving buyers specify reinforcement throughout, that is, from top to bottom of the leading edges, but this may not always be necessary, especially if you can include reinforcement information in the specifications and then carefully inspect the erection and installation of the shelving.

C. Bin Shelf Load Capacities

Shelf load capacities vary considerably, depending on the upright post type, the type of clips used with the shelf, and the amount of reinforcing on the edges or midsection of the shelving. The buyer should start with information that will determine shelf load capacities; and if the materials to be stored on the shelves can be segregated according to weight loadings, some additional costs may be saved by having lightweight materials in one bin section, and heavy materials in higher-capacity bins.

A standard shelf 24 inches deep by 36 inches wide should be capable of holding several hundred pounds at the very least. Reinforcing the shelves will enable larger loads to be handled, depending on the amount of reinforcement.

D. Bin Hardware and Lights

Before buying a particular type of bin, one should examine carefully the type of bin hardware required. For example, the clips that hold the shelves in place may make shelf assembly extremely difficult. Also, if label holders are required to identify the shelf contents, several potential problems exist. Some label holders are not only difficult to put in place with snap-in fasteners, but the fasteners can be of inferior quality and be easily dislodged. Also, especially on the bottom three shelves, when the order picker or the stocker steps on the shelf, will the label holder come loose? Labels also should be large enough to be clearly visible in the light provided in the order picking aisles. We are speaking normally of a minimum of 30 to 50 lumens at 30 inches above ground level.

To illuminate bin aisles, it is recommended that shielded strip-line fluorescent lighting be used where order picking productivity of a relatively high level is desired. In other words, you would be much better off to depart from the minimal 30 to 50 lumens and provide anywhere from 50 to 100 lumens at 30 inches above ground level. Also, fluorescent lighting fixtures may be supported from the tops of the bins themselves rather than hung from overhead joists.

Although we shall discuss layouts and mezzanine sections later in this chapter, it is well to stress lighting at this point, since it is an important and expensive part of the hardware of bin installation. No bin lighting should be used unless it is shielded; that is, when an order picker or stocker raises his line of

Fig. 6-23 Typical bin shelving arrangement.

sight above the parallel eye level—he should not be looking into the glare of the lighting fixture. Poor order picking productivity, mistakes, and sometimes bad morale are the results of this rather typical mistake in arranging bin lighting. Therefore, lighting fixtures and lighting arrangements are very important in bin shelving installations. (Figure 6-23 illustrates a typical bin shelving section.)

E. Miscellaneous Bin Components

It is possible to obtain shelving with or without partitions, and some bins are arranged in either continuous or discontinuous sections. For example, if, at some later date, you decide to move, or to rearrange your bin installation by moving individual or groups of bin sections, you should make certain at the time when you purchase a particular style of bin that this rearrangement or movement can be accomplished without your unloading the bin shelves and stripping the sections down. Usually it is possible to place forklift truck forks under two 36-inch wide bin sections in such a way that even when back-to-back they may be moved expeditiously, in a group, or at least in a back-to-back unit that is only 36 inches wide. This will depend, of course, on the method of loading and the distance to be traversed. Even full bins, that is, stocked bins, can be sent from one warehouse to another by means of tractor-trailer trucks, or vans.

Also, the upright posts have to be considered in some instances, depending on the type of merchandise to be stored on the bin shelf. For example, some materials can be snagged on T-section posts, and if many items are of textile composition, this might not be the ideal upright post type to use; instead the tubular type would be more suitable.

The heights of some bin shelving components vary from manufacturer to manufacturer, but an industry standard is 7′3″. Higher or lower sections are also available. Therefore, when one is obtaining quotations, it is well to analyze the specifications so that a proper bid evaluation may be made.

In addition, when reviewing the manufacturer's specifications and brochures, it is worth noting whether any mention is made of, or if there are illustrations and dimensions to indicate how the shelf size you have selected may be modified with quarter or half sections, drawers and bin boxes, and so forth. Sometimes if there are a number of small units like fasteners or fittings, it is possible to introduce a rotary stand or two, adjacent to the packing line, to take care of these incidental items.

XII. ORDER PICKING LAYOUT, METHODS, AND EQUIPMENT

A. Introduction

A number of industries are based almost entirely upon order picking. Examples include the following: (1) the wholesale, frozen food distribution business; (2) the pharmaceutical supply house that distributes thousands of products of many different manufacturers, some in such small quantities—a single can of talcum powder or a bar of a special soap—that you sometimes must wonder at their overall profitability; (3) the automotive parts supplier who sells wholesale, but is on a par with the pharmaceutical industry where quantities are concerned; (4) the grocery wholesale distributor who sells his wares to groups of independent grocers and supermarkets, and who used to sell exclusively to the small Mom and Pop grocery store; and (5) a number of rack jobbers who distribute novelties to supermarkets and other businesses. This is not the entire list; I'm sure that you can think of others—the cigar and cigarette vending machine companies, and so on.

So, order picking by and of itself represents a fairly large segment of industry, and when you add to this complement the order picking that is performed by commercial and industrial concerns to satisfy their assembly lines, dealers, distributors, and so forth, you have a vast number of order picking operations, not only in the United States but worldwide.

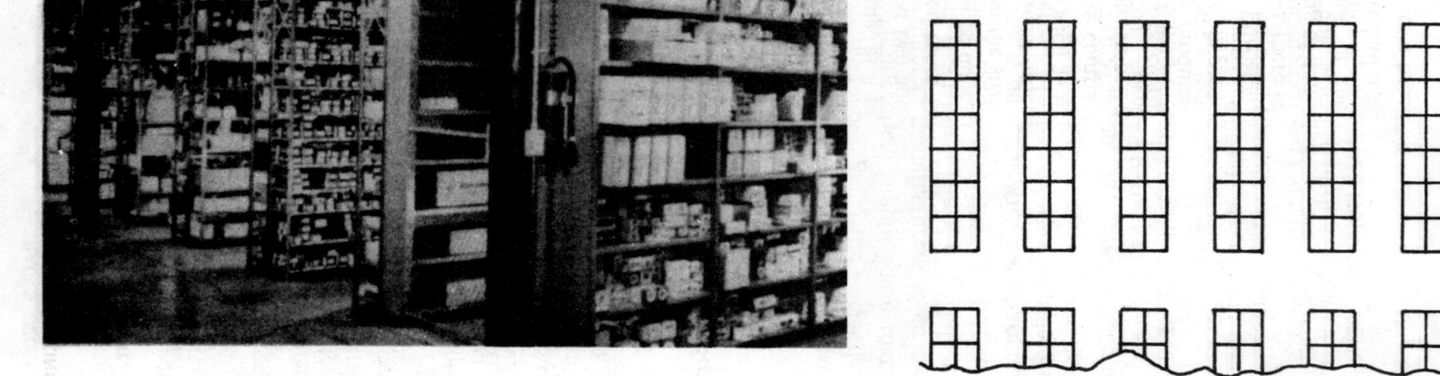

Fig. 6-24. Typical, rectangular bin section (note bulk pallet loads above bins in Fig. 6-23.)

B. Conventional Order Picking Layout, Methods, and Equipment

Let us start with bin shelving, described in the preceding section, and arrange this relatively low-height equipment (7′3″) in a rectangular configuration (see Fig.6-24). If we desire some back-up stock and are not too particular about housekeeping, or the appearance of the bin area, we might store excess stock on top of the bin, in effect adding another bin opening to our unit. At this point we must provide an order picking cart with two or three steps—in other words, a short stepladder.

Now, our original bin section is not very large—let us say, somewhere between 10,000 and 30,000 square feet in area. We have decided on the kind of picking cart—one with a small shelf or writing ledge and maybe only two decks with stationary rear wheels and caster steer front wheels. Our cart is 24 inches wide by 36 to 48 inches long, and it is light in weight, has a steel frame, and is fairly well made in a substantial manner with 3- to 4-inch-diameter wheels of molded rubber. So, we have decided to make our aisles 36 inches wide. We have good lighting, and have arranged our products by zones so that the fastest-moving items are closest to the point of packing.

Our order picker will, no doubt, get his orders on punched cards arranged in picking sequence and will follow a prescribed path through the bin area. In the zones described above, the fastest-moving items should always be located on the middle bin shelves, which is the most convenient location for the order picker.

In stocking the bin shelves, it is suggested that each order picker do his own stocking, at a prearranged time, say the first hour or two in the morning, or the last two hours of his shift, if this is a one-shift operation. Since we haven't allowed room for two carts to pass each other in the picking aisles, stocking should be done at some convenient time, even if a second-shift man has to be used in the stocking operation.

In most order picking operations merchandise usually arrives in bulk quantities, such as unit loads by pallet, skid, large containers, etc. In certain order picking companies or departments, the bulk merchandise is stored in block storage, in pallet storage racks, or in a combination of these methods.

It is especially important if there is any seasonality in order picking departments' products—such as antifreeze in an automotive supply operation, special "deals" in grocery or pharmaceutical supply houses, and the like—to make the space provision for this added volume.

Also, there is the "break-bulk" operation that sometimes precedes the order picking of items and must be integrated into the planning for the orderly organization of the order picking department. Occasionally, a customer may require half a case or more of a certain item. This is not a whole unit load and becomes a break-bulk item, indicating that: (1) some of the unit load may be placed with the customer's order; (2) some of the unit load may be placed in the bin shelving; and (3) some of the unit load may have to remain in the bulk storage area.

The difficulty with having two shifts in the smaller order picking operations is that additional supervision is usually required, which increases the overhead. But, in any event the time for stocking the shelves, which is usually about 25% or less of the total order picking time, has to be geared to the packing and the delivery schedules that must be maintained.

If a captive fleet of delivery vehicles is maintained, and it is possible to get two city deliveries daily, this will, of course, influence the picking, packing, and stocking schedule.

Usually, if the bin-picked items have to be packed, then each order picker can place a number of baskets on his cart. Keeping each order in a separate basket would be ideal, and the picking tickets could go directly with the basket to the packer.

In some companies the order picker picks and packs directly into a carton. The arrangement has many pros and cons. Some companies that have tried this method indicate that the higher carton costs, due to difficulties in sizing the carton to the material picked because the picker usually takes a larger carton to save time, and the lower productivity of the picker do not justify the pick and pack method. Some soft-goods companies, however, use locking-top bin baskets that stack one on top of the other in the transportation vehicle; and this method seems satisfactory, since each store in the system has been allocated a certain number of baskets per delivery.

Thus, there are a number of combinations in system, methods, and equipment. Later in this section we shall discuss ways of putting these all together so that we have a better view of the systems approach to materials handling.

C. The Use of Mezzanines, High Stacking, Flow Racks, and Mini-Retrievers in Order Picking Departments

In the above sections we discussed conventional bins and bin storage order picking. The principal limitation of the conventional methods and layouts is that, usually, head room or ceiling heights permit a better cube utilization of the warehouse space than is made; we can generally go higher than the 7 to 9 feet that we would go ordinarily, under the above circumstances. And, we may not be wasting just the height of the building—we may be wasting floor area as well. So, as we consider the initial investment in a bin order picking department, it is well to consider both the initial plan or layout, and what we will be able to do in the way of future expansion.

Some bin order picking installations go as high as 40 feet, which is the present limitation of the unaided industrial powered truck. Some of these large installations have large numbers of relatively slow-moving parts items, that for some reason management decides to keep on hand and available in order to show an excellent response time to customer requests. Some of these parts may have only one move per month or less; yet because of company policy, or because of manufacturing lead time, they must be kept on hand and available.

The "high-stack," high-density bin order department may use the forklift truck adaptation called an order picker (which is evaluated in Chapter 11). This machine can be further adapted to follow a wire in the floor, like a driverless tractor; and it may be equipped with a CRT or cathode ray tube type of visual display for order picking instructions and inventory control purposes. Also, it may take the operator or order picker from point to storage point at any elevation "simply" (the word is used advisedly) through a complex electronically packaged program derived from a computer. These machines are not cheap, but there are now enough of them in use to demonstrate their effectiveness (for some operations); and a certain degree of reliability inherent in their operation has also been determined.

If we are—in terms of numbers of parts—10,000 to 50,000 in quantity, but do not have over that number so that we would get into combinations of storage methods using stacker-crane retrieval systems or mini-retrievers, or high stacking systems, we should consider a mezzanine type of bin order installation.

All we need is sufficient head room to layer another floor over our existing bin area; or if this is a new venture, we shall be starting with new or acquired space. Ordinarily, lights have to be provided for the lower bin section; this means provide sufficient space to hang the lighting fixtures. Avoid the glare of lights for the order picker as he searches on those top shelves; some type of easily cleaned louvered or egg-crated fluorescent fixture is desirable. Another important specification is the grating for the mezzanine floor. The floor should be rigid without sway when an order picker moves his fully loaded cart down the aisle. Some people cannot take a swaying movement underfoot because of either physical or psychological limitations—opinion varies in these matters.

Here, again, it is advisable to let your working people know what you are planning. Sometimes you meet resistance unless you make your employees feel that they are part of the team.

All the reputable manufacturers of mezzanine equipment are familiar with the OSHA requirements for mezzanines: all exposed edges of the mezzanine must have a railing, and the railing must be 3 ½ feet high. Along the bottom of this exposed edge, also, there has to be at least a 4-inch-high kickplate.

Other OSHA requirements concern the placement of exits and stairwells. Any section of the guardrail that is used to receive pallet loads or unit loads by lift truck on the mezzanine floor must be equipped with chains or other satisfactory means of protecting the mezzanine worker.

Your manufacturer should be prepared to furnish, and you should ask for

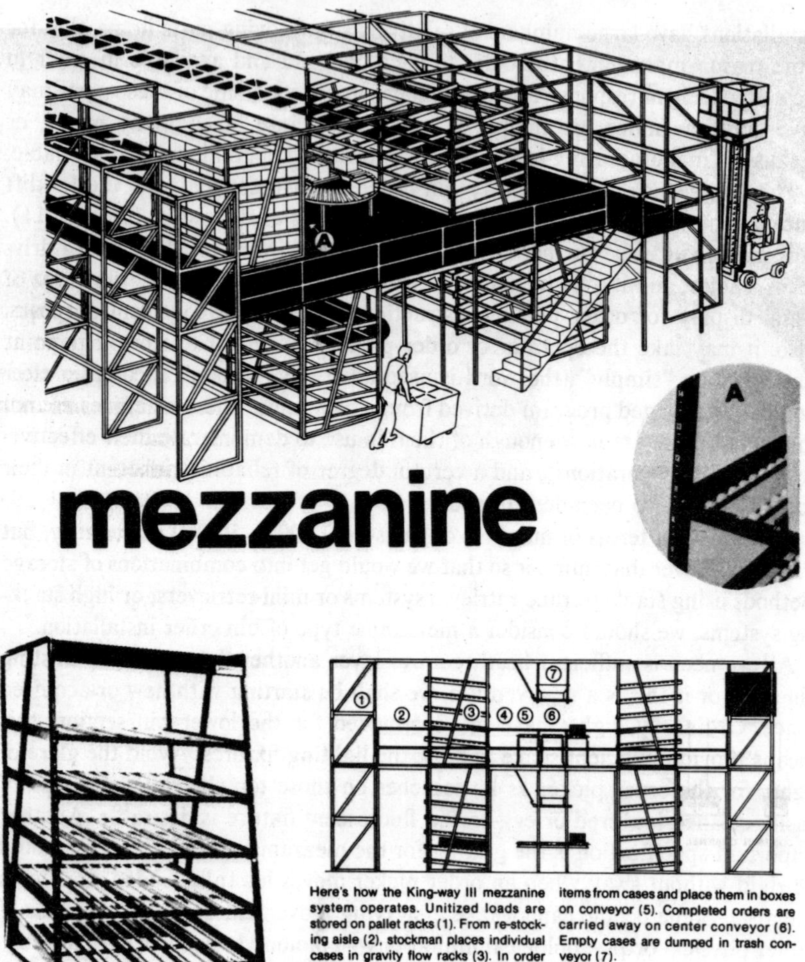

Fig. 6-25 Shelf trucks used in typical bin selection areas.

certification that the mezzanine installation meets all OSHA, state, and local ordinances.

Stocking may be done through the guardrail section, or it may be done, less effectively perhaps, by reversing the conveyor that is used to connect the two levels and by which merchandise is sent down to the packing line. (See Fig. 6-25 for a typical mezzanine installation.) Figure 6-25 shows that pallet storage racks can be used for break-bulk operations, and that by adding a quick-pick

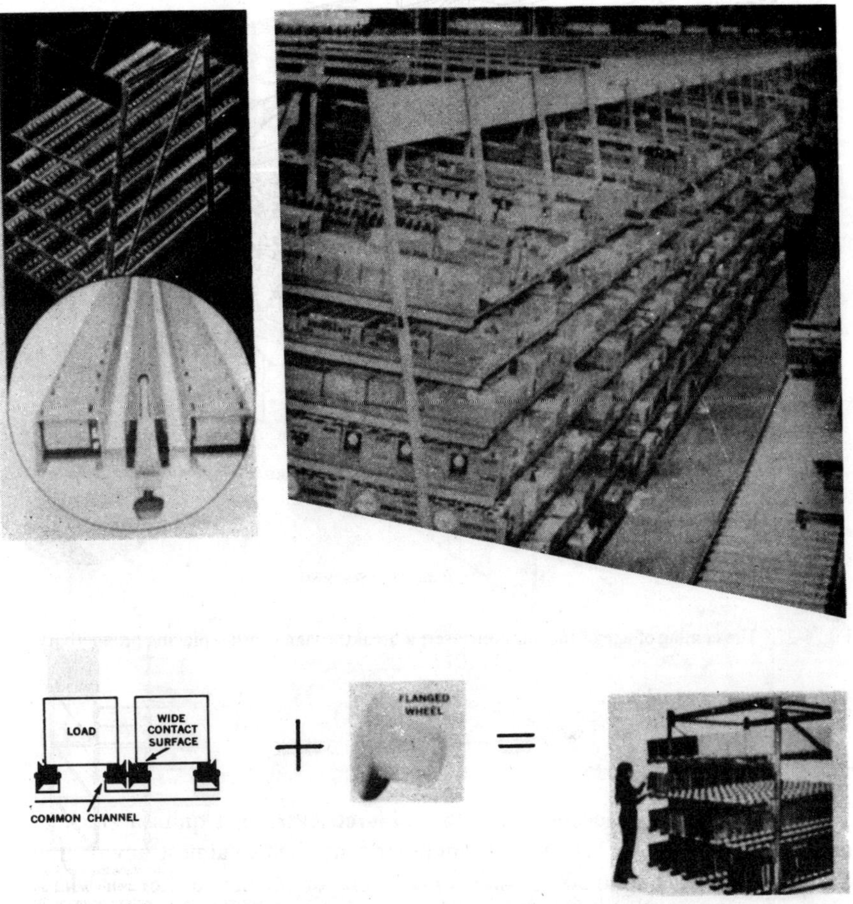

Fig. 6-26. Two types of flow racks.

rack ("flow rack") we can get fast movers taken care of on both decks of the mezzanine.

Flow racks improve order picking productivity by at least 10% to 15% and sometimes more—simply because they provide an increased number of items in the available working space. Figure 6-26 shows a typical flow rack. Some things to watch for in a flow rack are ease of adjustability and erection. Most important of all, does the type of product you have flow properly from the back to the front face of the rack? Because you should stock the rack from the rear, this is an important consideration. Some inexpensive installations (used with certain products) can get by with masonite chutes instead of rollers wheels, or plastic-covered runways, but these are the exceptions rather than the rule.

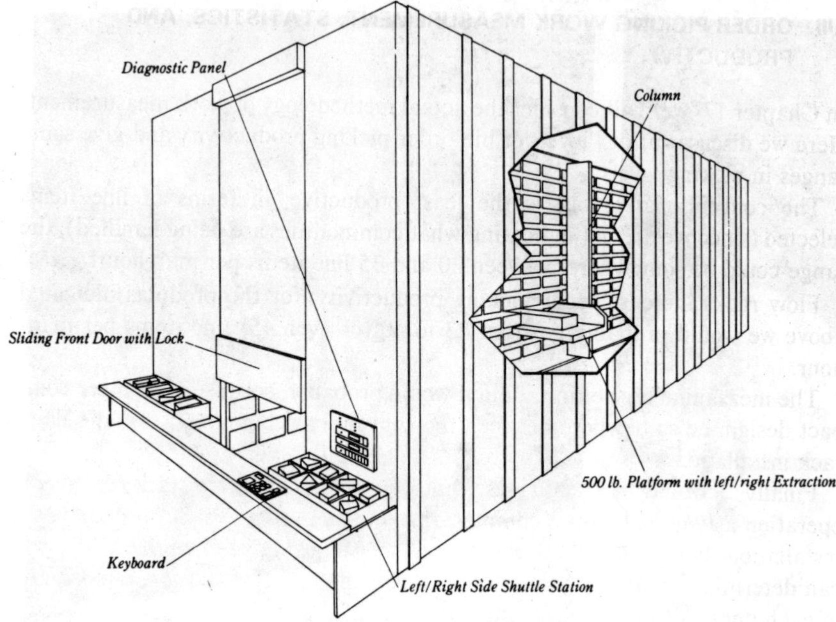

Fig. 6-27. The coming of age of the mini-retriever; a breakthrough in order picking productivity.

Now gaining good acceptance is the mini-retriever—not quite a stacker-crane retrieval system, yet fully as computer-controlled to almost any degree desirable, for loads up to 500 pounds for each bin, or opening, or tier (or whatever you call your retrieval unit).

Some units can perform a "store" command and on the way home perform a "retrieve" command. Depending on the size and complexity of the installation, one operator may be seated between two consoles or units and operate one at a time, alternately. A great deal depends on the commodity handled and the length and height of the storage lane. The reliability of the mini-retriever has sold more units than any other single factor beyond its excellent productivity record for line items selected and its up-time. (See Fig. 6-27).

A console operator may have a conveyor in front of his station and place selected items in baskets to be transported to a packing line. Some operators even do some packaging; but, again, this depends on size, quantity, quality of packing, labeling method, and so forth.

XIII. ORDER PICKING WORK MEASUREMENT, STATISTICS, AND PRODUCTIVITY

In Chapter 17, we shall consider the actual methodology of work measurement. Here we discuss various levels of bin order picking productivity and give some ranges in picking levels.

The conventional layout is the least productive; in terms of line items selected (since we are not indicating what commodities are being handled), the range could be somewhere between 20 and 35 line items per man-hour.

Flow racks increase order picking productivity; for the products indicated above we would probably go from 23 to 40 (or even 45) line items per man-hour.

The mezzanine type of installation would probably, because of its more compact design, be somewhere between the conventional bin layout and the flow-rack installation.

Finally, I would like to suggest that you obtain as many statistics on the operation as you can before commencing your bin order selection department installation. For example, you need a method for sizing your items so that you can determine such characteristics as cube, length, width, height, and weight of each item. Also very important is a listing of the demand frequency of each item by rank; for example, how many calls there are for each item per year, month, week, or day.

Another area not yet mentioned but of great importance is special handling. Do you have any hazardous items that require special handling? Do you have any items of exceptional fragility or value for which you need a separate, enclosed area or locked crib? Also, where will you store your packaging materials? And, how will you dispose of trash? (We shall answer, or rather, propose methods for you to consider for all of these and other questions in subsequent chapters.)

EXERCISE NO. 6

1. Five sources of pallet storage rack information and regulation are:

1. ____________________
2. ____________________
3. ____________________
4. ____________________
5. ____________________

2. Locking devices in pallet storage racks are used to keep the shelf beam in place. ☐True ☐ False

3. Most of the pallet storage racks sold today use bolts as fasteners for their shelf beams. ☐True ☐False

4. Drive-in/drive-through racks are in some respects comparable to block storage of merchandise. ☐True ☐False

5. Flow-through racks can be equipped with either gravity-roll or skate-wheel conveyors. ☐True ☐False

6. Can carton fatigue or carton breakdown become a problem for unpalletized material in flow through racks? ☐Yes ☐No

7. The Rack Manufacturers' Institute in its specifications, which may, in time, become incorporated into OSHA regulations, requires the posting of a rectangular plaque having at least 50 square inches of surface. ☐Yes ☐No

8. The above plaque should state the maximum permissible load to be carried on each shelf of the rack. ☐True ☐False

9. Upright posts of pallet storage racks should have bearing plates. ☐True ☐False

10. A user of pallet storage racks should require that the vertical alignment of the rack should have a maximum tolerance of ____________ inch(es) in 10 feet.

11. At the maximum rated load, of the ANSI specification, it is stated that a pallet storage rack beam is allowed to carry a certain amount of deflection. This deflection of the beam cannot exceed 1/(?) of the span.

12. An important new requirement for unit load carrying beams is that they must now be designed to include a vertical impact load of ____________% of a single load weight when it is placed in the most unfavorable position on the beams.

13. The revised section of the RMI specifications indicates that the bottom portions of those posts that are exposed to collision by forklift trucks or other moving equipment, shall be protected from such collisions by protective devices. ☐True ☐False

14. If the rack is not protected in the manner described above, the rack structure shall be designed to maintain its full design load capacity at the usual allowable stresses even if the carrying capacity of an exposed post is reduced by collision damage to one-half that of the undamaged post. ☐True ☐False

15. When exposed uprights of a pallet storage rack have been badly damaged by collision, should you repair or replace the damaged section immediately? ☐Yes ☐No

16. Wire-mesh and perforated steel decking permit water from overhead sprinkler systems to do a better job of putting out fires. ☐True ☐False

17. Wood pallets, skids, and boxes account for about 12% of all the lumber used in the United States. ☐True ☐False

18. Wood decking helps spread storage rack fires vertically. ☐True ☐False

19. Plywood pallets account for a major portion of all pallets used in industry. ☐True ☐False

20. One of the problems encountered with corrugated pallets is in the pedestals. ☐True ☐False

21. The main load-carrying component of bin shelving is the ____________.

22. Bin shelving is usually of light-gauge steel, and the most common sizes range from 12 to 36 inches deep by 36 inches in width. ☐True ☐False

23. Bin shelving may, usually, be reinforced by adding an insert to the leading edge and in the rear edge. ☐True ☐False

24. Bin lighting is very important and should be at least ______ to ______ lumens at 30 inches above the floor.

25. (1) Some of a unit load in a "break-bulk" operation may be placed with the customer's order, (2) some of the unit load may be placed in the bin shelving, and (3) some of the unit load ______.

26. Two factors to consider in laying out a bin order picking department are: (a) the initial plan or layout, and (2) what we will be able to do ______.

27. An order picker can be used in bin stacks ______ feet high.

28. Mezzanine floors should be as ______ as possible without much sway or deflection.

29. OSHA requirements for mezzanines and stairways must be observed when considering such an installation. ☐True ☐False

30. Flow rack productivity is usually somewhat less than in a conventional bin layout. ☐True ☐False

Chapter 7
High-Density Storage, Fire Prevention, and Nonpermanent Structures

I. HIGH-RISE, HIGH-DENSITY STORAGE

A. Introduction

Although there are many types of high-rise, high-density (H-R, H-D) storage systems in use today, there is some confusion as to exactly what is meant by the term H-R, H-D storage. For the purposes of this text we shall include in this term any rack system over 20 feet high that is serviced by a piece of MH equipment that is not a counterbalanced, forklift truck.

There are many installations, today, of computer-controlled stacker-crane, retrieval systems. In fact over 600 aisles of some form of stacker-crane retrieval have been installed in the United States alone. Not all of these installations are completely computer-controlled; a number use a keyboard and punched card (Hollerith card) type of input. We shall discuss the computer-controlled and card-controlled stackers later in the text, but for the time being let us remember that in considering a *system* we must consider a number of different, sometimes seemingly unrelated factors.

B. The Several Aspects of a Systems Approach

One of the first things to determine when we are contemplating a high-rise, high-density installation is the area it will occupy; we may call this consideration the *location* factor. It should be readily accessible to all of the subareas it serves, and it should not hamper or in any way block access to other working or production areas.

Another important question is the *cost* factor. Will the space that is utilized be several times more densely populated than the previous storage space? Will this increased usage justify the installation labor, equipment, and material cost of the new unit? If production space is being consumed by the present storage method, how valuable will it be if converted into H-R, H-D storage? If manufacturing space is presently costing $60 or more per square foot, will there be a cost avoidance by returning valuable facility space back to more productive use?

Also, we must consider the routing of materials into and out of the area—the *flow* factor. When contemplating a particular area we should try to envision the path that materials must take to arrive at their destinations without resorting to round-about ways of traveling. Then, let us consider the necessity for load set-out areas and their possible locations. Will we have enough space to place and take away loads without creating bottlenecks or blocked passages?

The next important consideration is the *time* factor. When will it be necessary to begin the installation, and when will we need to occupy it? How long will the erection and installation take? Depending on the size of the installation, it may be necessary to make a Gantt chart showing each event in the planning and layout. A typical Gantt chart might resemble the illustration shown in Fig. 7-1.

Then we have to consider the *equipment* factor. Shall we use sideloading trucks, turret or rotating mast trucks, or rack-type, stand-up riders, or stacker-cranes? As part of the cost factor we have to consider what will be our best return-on-investment (R.O.I.) for each piece of equipment. It would be helpful also to know something about the maintenance and repair costs of each piece of equipment. Sometimes the initial price is only the tip of the iceberg as far as equipment costs are concerned, and it is not unusual for maintenance costs for sideloader trucks to run as high as 20% of the cost of the truck per year. For example, a $25,000 sideloader could require $5,000 in maintenance expense annually.

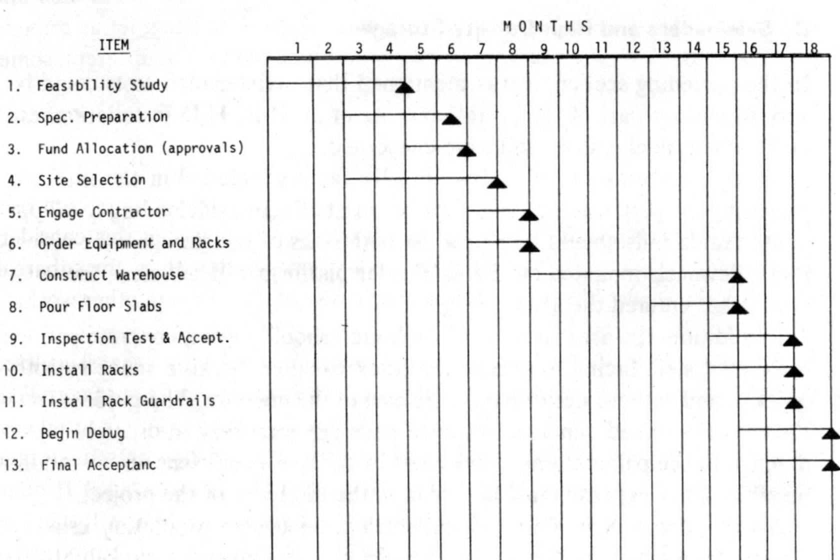

Fig. 7-1. Gantt chart of a typical high-rise, high-density storage installation.

The next consideration for H-R, H-D storage concerns the volume, or through-put, of the installation: the *through-put* factor. The through-put determines such things as cycle times for the installation, number of openings, and the height and length of aisles. Also, shall we have to break-bulk, that is, pick from full or unit loads? Or, shall we be handling only full loads in and full loads out?

Last, but not least, we must consider the labor required to operate our H-R, H-D installation, the *labor* factor. (Perhaps, we should have started this discussion with this factor.) As soon as is possible after the planning stage, when a layout or a mock-up of the area is available, we should have a meeting of the employees in whose area changes will have to be made. In other words, make every attempt to involve and inform the employees so that they can see and understand the important aspects of the new installation and are not surprised as the project develops. In this way a healthy morale can be achieved. There is no system so poor that dedicated employees cannot make it work; on the other hand, there is no system so perfect that a disgruntled employee cannot sabotage it, or make it less effective.

Another facet of the labor factor is the importance of having organized labor, in the form of the union, by our side when we are attempting a new installation. It would certainly be advisable to keep the union representatives a informed, and up-to-date, as any one of our other employees.

C. Sideloaders and High-Density Storage

In the preceding section, it was mentioned that maintenance costs could be a very significant part of the overall expense of an H-R, H-D installation, especially where sideloading trucks are concerned.

Other considerations, of course, involve factors included in the method of preparing the pallet storage racks for the most effective sideloading truck operation. Guide rails should be placed on both sides of the storage rack aisles so that sidewheels mounted on the sideloader platform will self-steer the vehicle once it has entered the aisle.

In addition, the area in front of each rack should have a concrete pad with a rounded steel facing to permit the truck to enter the aisle space smoothly, quickly, and without hesitation on the part of the operator. The guide rails and the steel-reinforced concrete entrance pads are necessary in order to prevent damage to the pallet storage racks and to achieve as efficient an operation as possible. Their expense must be added to the total cost of the project.

Another component of a rapid and efficient sideloader installation, especially if there are a number of tiers in each pallet row, is a push-button, height-selection unit. The height selector places the forks at a level that is preadjusted for each rack opening. The operator centers his truck in front of the load opening

STACKING 30 FT. HIGH from 5½-ft. aisles is no problem with Raymond's Hi-Loader. It handles 4000-lb. loads, travels 5 mph, lifts at 45 FPM. Features three-stage mast, 36-volt power.

DOUBLE-REACH® SIDELOADER Travels sideways in narrow aisles, stacks 30 feet high. Mast assembly rolls out to edge of truck bed, and forks extend an extra 36 to 54 inches into second row. 36-volt power. 2000-lb. capacity.

Entrance pads or guides

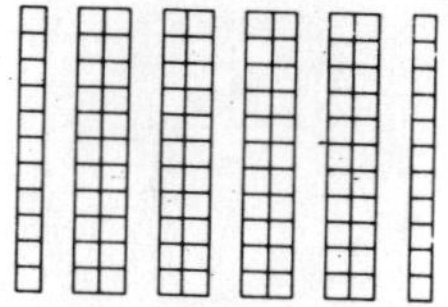

Deep-Reach and Double-Reach trucks eliminate 2 aisles of every 5 required in normal rack storage.

Guardrails as guides

Fig. 7-2. Sideloader rack installation showing guide rails and entrance pads.

and pushes a button labeled with the tier opening, for example, five. The forks will rise automatically to this prescribed tier height. Then, all the operator has to do is advance the forks into the load, and retract the load from the opening. The higher the rack installation, the more important height-selector devices can become. They make a safer operation, and relieve some of the fatigue that accompanies an operator working in aisles with 30-foot-high racks. Figure 7-2 illustrates some of the finer points in sideloader rack installations.

CAPACITY CHART

CAPACITY IN POUNDS
2000
1500
24" L.C.
154
164
174
184
Maximum Fork Height (Inches)

Load center in inches from front face of forks. Specific capacities will be shown on truck nameplate, and capacities based on weight. Capacities shown are computed with upright in vertical position.

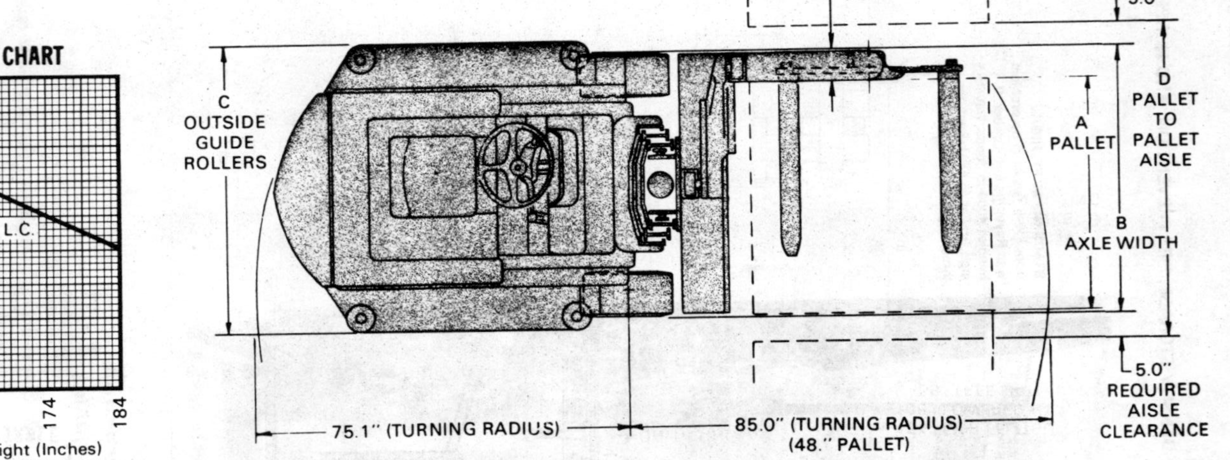

UPRIGHT DIMENSION TABLE

FULL FREE LIFT TRIPLE STAGE		
MFH	OVERALL HT. LOWERED	FREE LIFT
130"	98"	47"
139"	101"	50"
145"	103"	52"
154"	106"	55"
160"	108"	57"
169"	111"	60"
175"	113"	62"
184"	116"	65"

Preferred standard heights.
For overall height raised, add 50.5" to maximum fork height. Other lift heights are available.

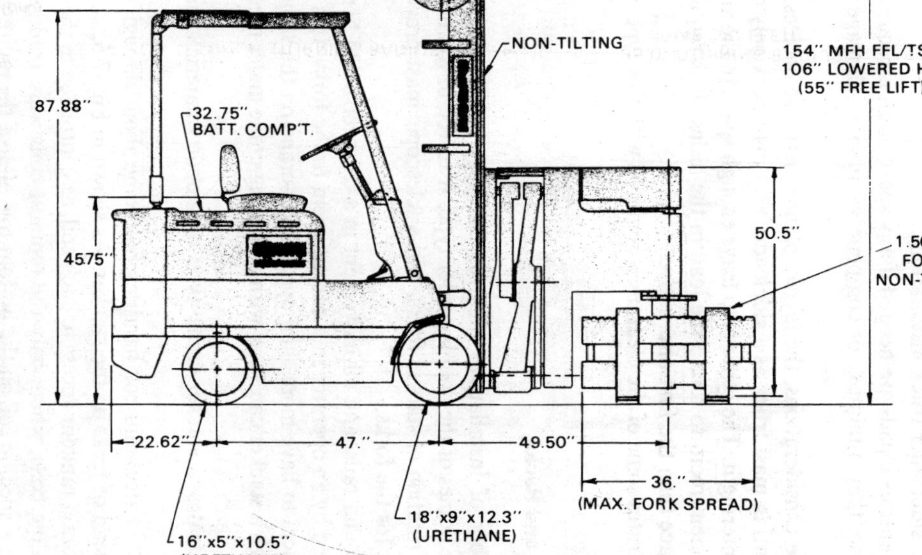

FFL/TSU UPRIGHT SPEEDS (FPM)				
VOLTS	LIFTING SPEED		LOWERING SPEED	
	LOADED	EMPTY	LOADED	EMPTY
36	53	80	70	60
48	76	102	70	60

Pallet Length	A	40"	48"
Axle Width	B	50"	53.5"
Outside Guide Rollers	C	55.5"	60"
Pallet To Pallet Aisle	D	56"	64"

Fig. 7-3. Clearances required by a typical, rotating mast truck.

D. Turret or Rotating Mast Trucks and High-Density Storage

Many elements in the use of turret or rotating mast trucks are the same as those described for sideloader truck installations.

Guide rails and entrance pads are needed if any speed at all is required from the installation; also, they minimize, or completely eliminate, damage to storage rack uprights.

Regarding space considerations, the layout planner has two choices. One is to consider the rotating mast truck as a sideloader that may work only one side of the aisle after entering it. The other is to leave enough space in the aisle that the truck has sufficient room to rotate the load in the aisles. This requires significantly more space than the first alternative.

Figure 7-3 illustrates some of the clearances required with this type of rotating mast truck.

E. Bridge Cranes and Racks

There are a number of installations all over the world where stackers are mounted on bridge cranes of the double-girder type. A turret, or rotating head, provides the 360° rotation of stacker forks, and a telescopic mast provides the vertical movement for the forks.

There are no ground rails, and all movement in a transverse and horizontal manner is controlled by an operator in a cab adjacent to the forks. It is seldom advisable or practical to have more than one stacker-crane on the same set of craneways, although a stacker can work with a hoisting crane under these same conditions.

Figure 7-4 illustrates a stacker-crane type of mobile, materials handling equipment.

An improvement in steel-mill coil handling has come about through the use of a coil prong instead of forks on the stacker. As shown in Fig. 7-5, coil racks provide a way to obtain random access to each coil, as contrasted to the former method of pyramiding coils, where only the topmost coils were readily accessible, and to obtain a specific coil on the bottom row almost the entire pile had to be rearranged. The initial cost of the coil racks and coil prong was easily amortized in this steel mill through increased efficiency and a dramatically improved response to customer orders.

F. Converting Bridge Cranes

Usually double-girder bridge cranes may be converted to stacker-crane use by adding a telescopic mast, forks or prong, and a cab for the operator. The original stacker-crane unit was developed from just such a piece of equipment.

Fig. 7-4. Bridge crane with stacker.

It is well to consider, however, the effects of placing a stacker-crane on an existing overhead bridge crane. If the bridge crane originally had a capacity of 25 tons, it would have to be downgraded to about 18 tons, having given up 7 tons or approximately 25% of its capacity to the additional equipment consisting of rotating turret, telescoping mast, operator's cab, etc.

Despite the loss in capacity, wherever this loss can be safely incurred, there are many practical applications for this type of conversion. For example, steel plate and barstock, which are stored in cantilever racks, are very effectively handled in this manner. In new installations, consideration for plate and barstock handling would ordinarily be given to this type of installation.

We can summarize this discussion by saying that any long, hard-to-handle item could probably be handled more easily with a stacker-crane (converted,

Fig. 7-5. The use of coil prong and racks to expedite coii handling in a steel mill.

bridge-type). However, it is captive to the area served by its overhead bridge crane.

G. Stacker-Crane Retrieval Systems

No single piece of equipment has done more to bring the subject of materials handling to the attention of top management than the stacker-crane retrieval (S/C) system.

For one thing, such systems are extremely expensive and require a great deal of justification to a board of directors. An installation may sell for $500,000 or it may cost over $20,000,000—and there is a broad range between these two extremes. Despite the cost, however, stacker-crane retrieval systems are getting quite a play these days, with a number of systems on the drawing board and in the erection stage all over the United States. As mentioned earlier, there are over 600 aisles thus equipped nationwide. If we assume an average installation with 5 aisles, this would be 120 systems installed; the range is anywhere from one stacker-crane to over 20 stackers in each installation.

While some advertisements indicate that a stacker-crane module can be obtained off-the-shelf, this is not usually possible because a large amount of engineering goes into each installation to fit the module to the buyer's criteria. For example, changes in rack opening width, height, and depth, number of openings, type of information required from the system, building column spacing, etc., all go to make the hardware and the software relatively unique.

When a system is relatively complex requiring complete computer control, it does not become a standard, off-the-shelf commodity that need only be plugged in. Far from it! From concept stage to production usually requires anywhere from two to three years, and sometimes more. Although some companies have met fairly stringent time frames of 24 to 30 months from concept to acceptance, when a large system is involved, the time frames naturally stretch out to even three to five years.

One of the main arguments of proponents of the stacker-crane retrieval system is that it provides control. The reason, or the argument used, is that the area is off limits to anyone but the machine. Even when you have a man-aboard S/C, which has a cab and manual controls, you will hear this argument.

It is also argued, probably correctly, that as the S/C equipment becomes more sophisticated—that is, as it ascends from (1) push-button control, to (2) card reader, to (3) computer control—actual control becomes more and more precise.

In the initial stages of development in the S/C equipment field, it would be very worthwhile, even imperative, to discuss the subject with a materials handling engineer who has taken his company through the struggle of an S/C installation.

There are two principal areas of application for S/C systems: in the physical distribution warehouse for storage and order picking, and in manufacturing either for warehousing of purchased finished materials or for in-process parts. A strong trend beginning to develop is in the manufacturing area for handling in-process parts.

Most warehousing and manufacturing enterprises devote 25% or more of their usable space to aisles and pedestrian walkways. At least half of this wasted area and certainly a good percentage of the air-rights (cube utilization) can be utilized with a properly designed S/C system.

Attempts have been made, also, to categorize S/C systems by height. Thus, we shall consider any system under 30 feet as not being high-rise storage, but it certainly could be high-density—although this term is only relative to the storage practices used. For example, an extensive system only 40% occupied by materials is certainly not a high-density system in terms of practice.

Any system over 30 feet high is considered high-rise storage because this happens to be the *present,* practical limitation of the forklift truck. And, another delineating characteristic is that while both mobile and fixed-path equipment can be used in the low (under 30 feet high) systems, only fixed-path equipment can be used in the truly high-rise system from 30 feet to over 100 feet high.

Almost all high-rise S/C systems are usually composed of these five parts, which must be completely integrated in order for the installation to succeed:

1. Storage racks
2. Conveyors, or the front end
3. Stacker-cranes
4. Computers (hardware)
5. Software package

In any extensive system the storage racks can account for the largest single item of expenditure besides the site preparation and building construction costs. Usually, about a third of the cost of a system is spent on the racks, one-quarter on conveyors, one-quarter on the stacker-cranes, and the remainder is distributed between computer hardware and software.

The high-rise, high-density storage system concept has had a marked effect on warehouse structures, primarily regarding ceiling heights. Up until the early 1960s almost all warehouses were constructed with about 22 to 25 feet of clearance under the trusses. There were a few cold-storage and captive warehouses belonging to food processors that had truss heights (below-the-truss clearance) of about 30 feet, where either frozen case goods or canned case goods were high-stacked in block storage fashion.

Today, up to a dozen buildings each year are constructed with ceiling heights of up to 70 feet, most of them in the 40- to 60-foot range. The extremely high building (from 70 to over 100 feet) is still a rarity; only four of this type have been constructed in the United States, and about a dozen in other countries, where land costs are, generally, much higher than in the United States.

Some of the high-rise, high-density storage buildings have been of the rack-supported type, mentioned in Chapter 6. This building design, in which the storage racks support the roof and the sides, has been very slow to win acceptance or establish a trend in the United States, despite its popularity abroad.

Mobile materials handling equipment—lift trucks—can be used only in the systems that are 30 feet high. There are a few order picking trucks, however, that can service 40-foot-high racks. At these elevated heights the picking speed slows down, and unit costs go up. It is better to consider stacker-cranes in place of mobile equipment if costs can be made to show an adequate return on investment. Also, the advantage of using mobile rather than fixed-path equipment in this instance is that the mobile units can go in and out of any of the rack aisles to a work station, assembly line, shipping area, etc., whereas most of the stacker-cranes are confined to an aisle, unless a transfer device is available. If a transfer car is available, then one stacker-crane may service several aisles, but no more.

One stacker-crane manufacturer has designed a stacker to work in an aisle as a "captive" crane; however, this crane can also move out of the aisle into the main areas of the plant and then return to the stacker-crane aisle. So far, sales of this type of stacker have not been impressive, although in a number of applications this dual capability may be important. One reason why there has been no rush to acquire these units may be reluctance to use a $50,000 (or higher-priced) piece of equipment to transport a load that a $15,000 piece of equipment (forklift truck) can move better.

1. Some Advantages and Disadvantages of AS/RS Systems. Let us examine some of the advantages and disadvantages of automatic storage/retrieval systems, or what are commonly called AS/RS systems.

a. Advantages

1. *Greater Space Utilization.* We have indicated in the above paragraphs that there is a greater utilization of both floor area and air-rights (cube utilization) if we can go higher and, also, eliminate much of the aisle space that is normally wasted in every type of plant.

2. *Improved Cyclic Rate.* Because stacker-cranes can travel in aisles where there are no impediments, obstructions, pedestrians, other vehicles, etc., horizontal traveling and vertical lifting speeds have been maximized. Therefore, the cycle time or working rate for these machines is vastly superior to other order picking or bulk, unit-load selection operations.

3. *Improved Height of Activity.* In man-aboard stacker-cranes it is possible to go much higher than with conventional mobile handling equipment with greater operator confidence because this type of stacker-crane is just as stable at elevated heights as it is on lower levels. In an unmanned stacker-crane, of course, operator confidence is not a consideration.

4. *On-Board Work Areas.* With stacker-cranes it is possible to build work platforms where orders may be placed, that can be as large as desirable without having to fear overturning, which would be a concern with mobile equipment.

5. *Elimination of Operator Accidents.* In a manned stacker-crane installation, the man travels with the load and can index it accurately for either placement or retrieval. On an unmanned stacker, this, again, is done automatically. Thus, operator fatigue or the parallax of viewing a load 30 feet in the air from an operator's seat near the ground can cause serious accidents with mobile equipment, whereas this type of problem is eliminated when using stacker-cranes.

6. *Power Requirements.* Stacker-cranes, unlike mobile handling equipment, depend only on feeder-rails (bus bars with collectors) for their power input. There is no wasted time fueling up or changing batteries.

7. *Automation.* The stacker-crane brings us closer to the objective of a completely mechanized warehouse by minimizing the number of personnel it takes to operate a plant. Since a large number of stacker-crane retrieval systems have been placed on complete computer control, we know that this type of automation is both practical and effective, with the result that manpower can be saved in this type of operation to be used more effectively in another part of the plant.

b. Disadvantages

1. *Upgrading Skills.* Since a computer-controlled device is much more complex than simple, manual equipment, we have to upgrade or hire the skills required to service and maintain our S/C system in good working order.

2. *Maintenance.* While stacker-cranes have come of age, and there are hundreds of S/C systems in use, they can be a maintenance nightmare to the plant engineer. One positive aspect is that their reliability is improving every day, and up-time is in many instances far superior to that of mobile equipment. Maintenance personnel will find that there may be new skills needed, such as electronics repair and accompanying or related skills.

3. *Floors and Shims.* Because stacker-cranes must have positive indexing means, they are dependent to a large extent on the precision with which a site floor is poured. A tolerance of plus or minus one-half inch may be asked in order to reduce the requirement for excessive shimming.

II. FIRE PREVENTION ASPECTS OF RACK STORAGE

A. Introduction

Insurance underwriters have been hard pressed to come up with uniform codes that would cover the fire prevention aspects of high-rise, high-density storage rack situations.

During the past few years the National Fire Protection Association has conducted tests that have raised the storage rack heights for which actual data have been established to 25 feet. You can well imagine the difficulty and expense involved in getting these data, as well as the increased cost of trying to obtain test data for pallet storage racks over 25 feet high.

Because of the continuing efforts of the NFPA, however, we have such manuals as the 231-C, which covers storage rack applications. In this manual, which may be obtained by writing to the address given in Appendix B, you will find such items as flue spacings, classes of combustibles, etc.

If your storage racks are over 12 feet high, you should consult this manual and your insurance underwriter. For example, when you are placing racks back-to-back, you must use a row spacer in order to maintain a flue space of at least 6 inches. This may vary depending on the particular application, but most row spacers provide from 6 to 8 inches of flue space. The NFPA also requires an upright post or frame section flue space, again of 6 inches. Normally, this can be readily obtained, since the upright post width or cross section is 3 inches; there is no particular difficulty in obtaining this clearance between pallet storage rack openings that begin and end at the upright post.

B. Sprinkler Systems

Fire protection requirements for rack areas stored with combustible materials, corrugated board containers, wood boxes, and the like, are mainly overhead sprinkler systems when storage racks are 12 feet or lower.

For heights greater than 12 feet, pallet storage racks become more stringently regulated. For example, in some high-rise, high-density storage rack installations, it is necessary to provide standpipes and sprinkler heads in the flue spaces between the racks. In addition, it may be necessary to stagger the sprinkler heads between intermediate levels.

There has been no general policy statement or regulation concerning the storage of shrink-wrapped loads in rack installations. On a local level, underwriters have permitted shrink-wrapped loads to be placed in racks if they are separated at various intervals. The industry is awaiting further clarification on this subject, since, from the layman's standpoint, the plastic film would tend to disperse fire-extinguishing water rather than absorb moisture, which would cause the container to collapse.

C. Rack Decking

Chapter 6 (section IX, B) contains a reference to the fire safety tests conducted by the NFPA at the Natick testing facility. These tests indicated various characteristics of wood decking for pallet storage racks. It was found that fire tends to spread horizontally under decking. In addition, fire may jump from pallet opening to pallet opening when wood decking is used.

To minimize the damage and danger of fire, it is best for the warehouse manager to take as many approaches as possible to fire safety in pallet storage racks.

1. It is advisable to have "smoking areas" at convenient locations and not to permit smoking in rack storage areas.
2. Fire extinguisher stations should be maintained throughout the rack installation at strategic intervals. The fire extinguishers should be of the proper type for the class of materials stored in the rack storage area. This can readily be checked out with the local fire marshal. The fire extinguishers should be painted red and be placed at eye level (of forktruck driver sitting on truck) against a white enamel painted square of plywood as a background.
3. If at all possible, only electric mobile handling equipment should be permitted in this area. Gas and LP trucks, if used, should be equipped with approved safety exhaust mufflers (water exhaust).
4. It is advisable to have periodic safety talks with all mobile handling equipment operators who work in the vulnerable pallet storage rack areas.

III. AIR-SUPPORTED STRUCTURES AND OTHER NONPERMANENT BUILDINGS

A. Introduction

When the military, shortly after World War II, decided to build the DEW-LINE (Defense Early Warning) system, it had a very rigid time frame based upon the objectives of the Defense Department. Some of the difficulties were: the short work season in the Arctic areas where many of the radar outposts were to be located, and the logistic difficulties of transporting the construction materials and the craft skills that are normally required to construct the conventional building. Under these rigorous conditions one type of nonpermanent building, the air-supported structure, received its acid test. This early air-supported structure (called a radome) and other nonpermanent buildings, including metal-framed structures, will be discussed in this section.

B. Air-Supported Structures

The radomes were "temporary" shelters of a vinyl plastic, laminated fabric supported by air blown into the structure, or bubble, at about 5 lb/sq. ft., or about ½ inch of water gauge pressure.

Figure 7-6 shows interior and exterior views of other large (100′ × 500′) air-supported buildings. Figure 7-7 gives some details of the construction features of an air-supported structure. The two structures shown in Fig. 7-6 are used by a large automobile manufacturing company to store sheet metal stampings. Because of the humidity control obtainable in these structures, none of the metal stampings show any signs of rust or corrosion during their storage periods in these buildings. (As this was written, these buildings had just made it through their fourth year of service.)

Needless to say, the automobile manufacturer in the Chicago suburbs has been well satisfied with the two 50,000-square-foot structures.

Some advantages and disadvantages of these structures follow.

1. Advantages

1. With tight capital dollars it has been possible to lease-purchase these structures.
2. The buildings are considerably lower in cost than any other type of structure would be. (Since the automobile manufacturer already had a slab to put the structures on—the parking lot—the total cost of the structures and their instrumentation, etc., came to under $5.00/sq. ft.)
3. The structures may be relocated; for example, they are easily taken down and shipped to another plant for re-erection.
4. They may be taken down, stored, and re-erected during peak loads.
5. They can be erected in less than a week's time.
6. The inside, free-span construction makes excellent storage space.
7. They require a minimum of maintenance.

2. Disadvantages

1. The inflation system requires automatic controls and a standby blower and power source. If there is not strict maintenance—that is, if preventive maintenance practices are not rigorously adhered to—it is possible to lose the structure.
2. During periods of high wind velocities, that is, over 45 mph, the auxiliary

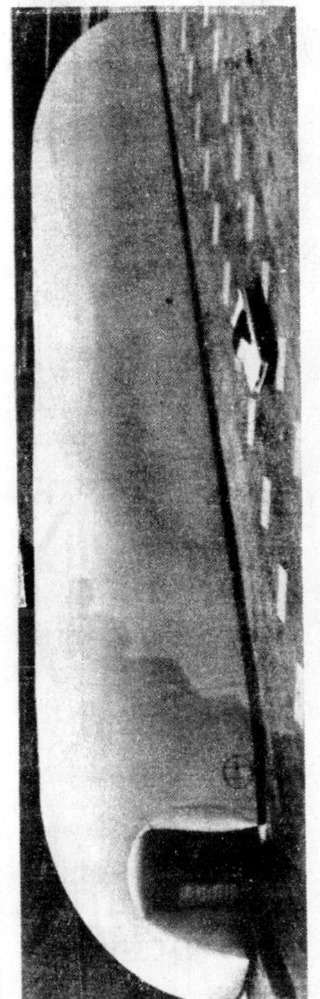

Fig. 7-6. Interior and exterior views of air-supported structures.

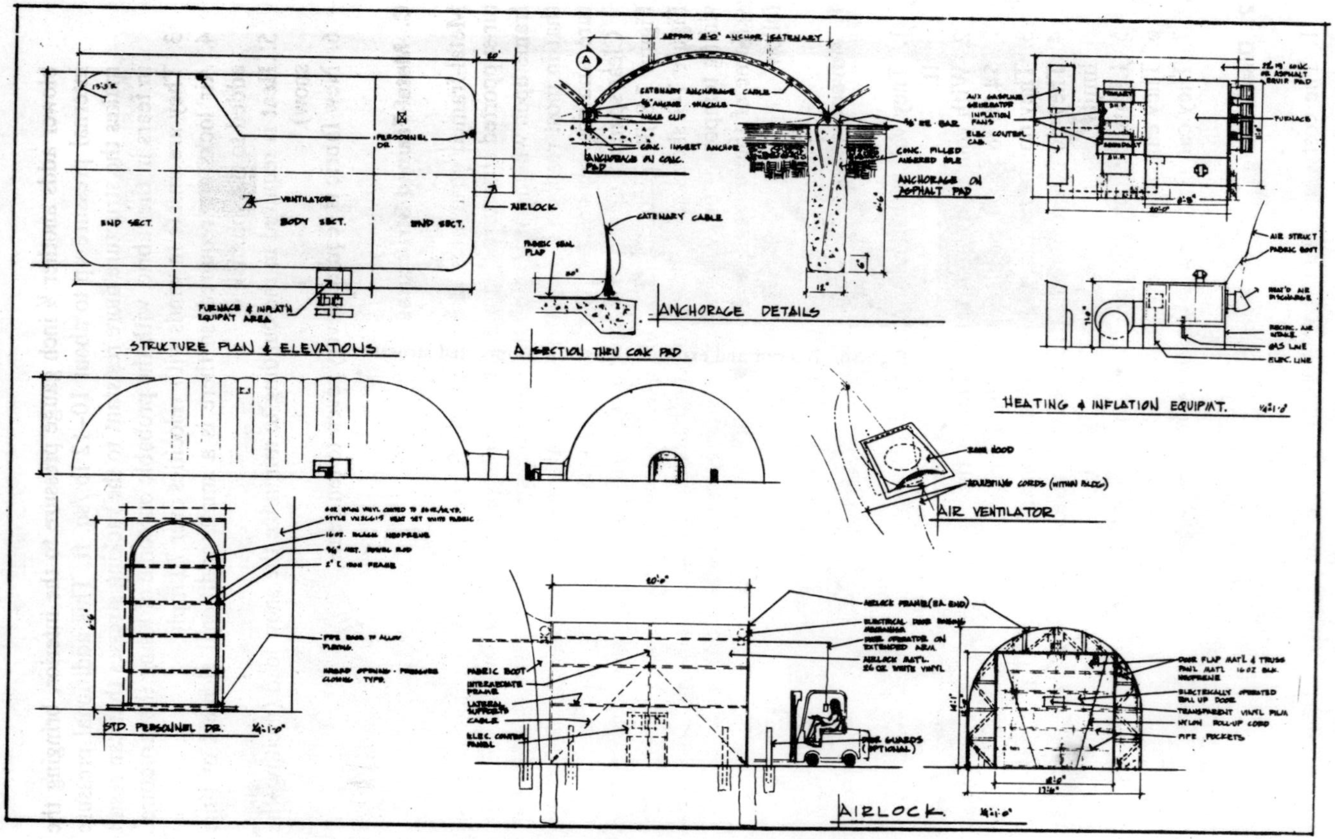

Fig. 7-7. Details of construction of a standard, air-supported structure.

blower adds another ½ inch gauge pressure to the interior, bringing the internal pressure up to about 10–12 lb./sq. ft. This additional pressure makes the structure more resistant to the racking stresses that can result in tears in the fabric, with the probable outcome of losing the structure.
3. They are unsafe in winds with velocities over 70 mph.
4. Air locks are required; so there is a small, additional element of time added to the job task.
5. Heat is required in the building to minimize the snow load (melting the snow).
6. New fabric is required every seven to ten years.

C. Metal-Framed Structures

Metal-framed structures, using a plastic fabric similar to that developed for air-supported structures, have also been built. Imagine if you can a welded steel frame upon which yards of plastic fabric are stretched. The result is a building that in most respects is similar to, but is stronger than an air-supported structure, and possibly costs $1 to $2 more per square foot than the air bubble type.

Clear spans of up to 120 feet are now possible using this type of construction. Figure 7-8 illustrates interior and exterior views of a metal-framed structure. Figure 7-9 shows some details of construction of this unusual method of providing temporary or even long-range storage or manufacturing space.

Some of the advantages and disadvantages of the metal-framed structures follow.

1. Advantages

1. They will withstand wind loads of 110 mph and snow loads of 30 lb./sq. ft.
2. With your own slab to set the unit on, the square-foot cost will range from $4.00 to $6.00, or higher with inflation.
3. They do not require blowers or any control instrumentation.
4. They do not require heat unless snow loads built up beyond the design limits.
5. Lights, heaters, and sprinklers can be hung from the interior steel trusses.
6. They can be rapidly erected in a matter of days.
7. They can be readily taken down and re-erected.

2. Disadvantages

1. The cost per square foot of building is somewhat higher than for air-supported structures.

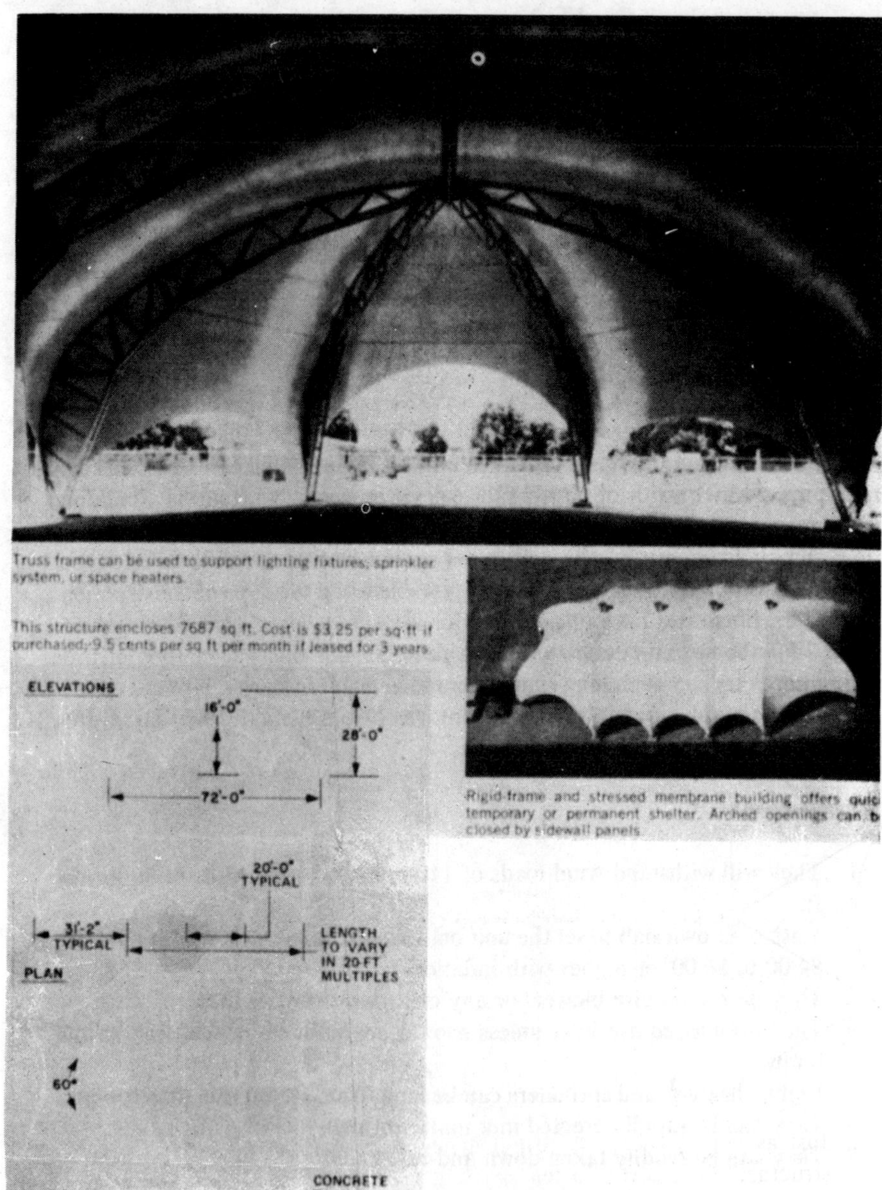

Fig. 7-8. Interior and exterior views of metal-framed structures.

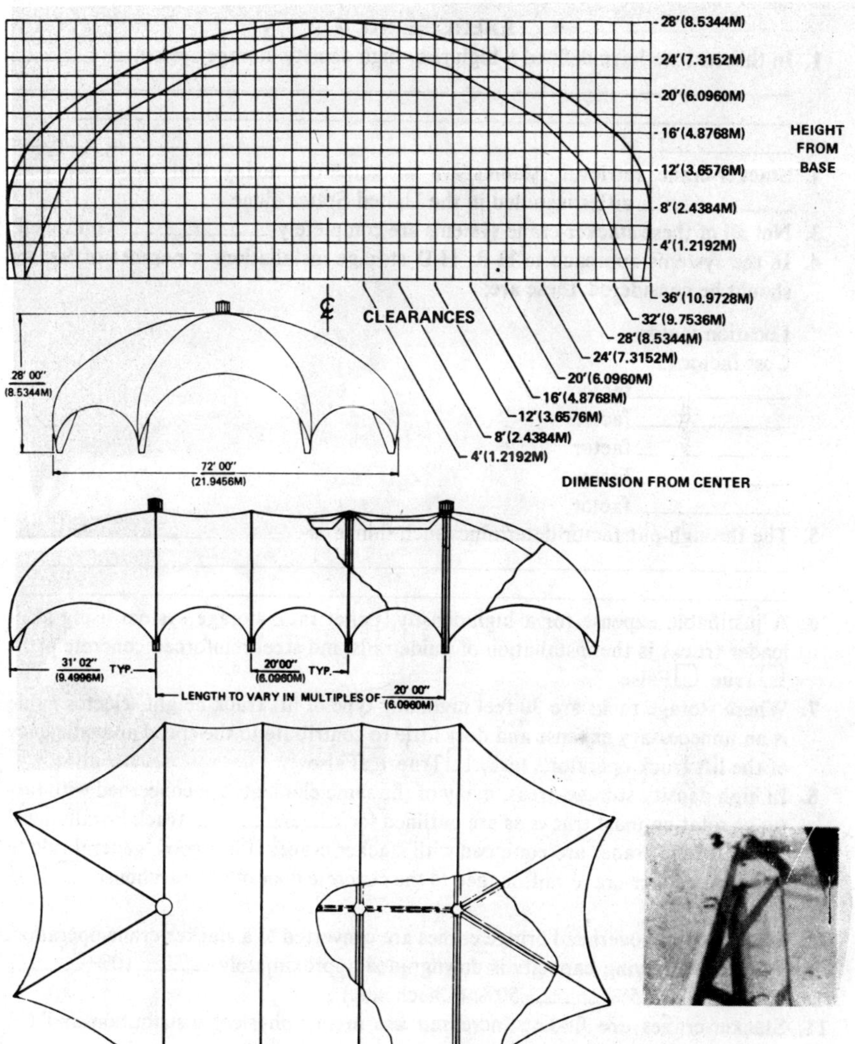

Fig. 7-9. Details of construction of metal-framed structures.

2. Just as is it is necessary to put a new fabric skin on an air-supported structure every seven to ten years, it is necessary to reskin the metal-framed structure, also.

EXERCISE NO. 7

1. In this text we have defined a high-rise, high-density storage system as ____

2. Stacker-crane retrieval systems are so numerous today that there are over __________ aisles installed in the United States alone.

3. Not all of these stacker-crane systems are completely __________-controlled.

4. In the systems approach to H-R, H-D storage installations a number of factors should be considered: these are;

Location factor
Cost factor
__________ factor
__________ factor
__________ factor
__________ factor
__________ factor

5. The through-put factor determines such things as ____

6. A justifiable expense for a high-density, pallet rack storage system using side-loader trucks is the installation of guide rails and steel-reinforced concrete pads. ☐True ☐False

7. Where storage racks are 30 feet high, any type of lift truck height-selector guide is an unnecessary expense and does little to contribute to the speed and efficiency of the lift truck operator's task. ☐True ☐False

8. In high-density storage areas, many of the same elements are concerned with turret or rotating mast trucks as are outlined for __________ truck installations.

9. When bridge cranes are equipped with stacker-cranes it is a good, general rule to keep the stacker-crane rails lagged to the concrete floor of the warehouse. ☐True ☐False

10. When existing overhead bridge cranes are converted to a stacker-crane operation, their load-carrying capacity is downgraded approximately ______10%; ______15%; ______25%; ______50%. (Check one.)

11. Stacker-cranes are finding increased use in (a) physical distribution and (b) ____.

12. Aisles make up at least __________% of a warehouse or plant.

13. Stacker-crane retrieval systems are usually composed of five parts which must be integrated. These are:

1. ________________________________
2. ________________________________
3. ________________________________
4. ________________________________
5. ________________________________

14. In any extensive stacker-crane system, ______________ ______________ account for the largest single item of expenditure; accounting for about ________¾, ________⅓, ________½ of the total amount of the project. (Check one.)

15. One advantage of a stacker-crane retrieval system is in its improved __________ rate (cycle time).

16. Humidity can be controlled in air-supported structures. ☐True ☐False

17. Air-supported structures cannot be relocated very easily. ☐True ☐False

18. What is one of the most important steps to take to prevent collapse of an air-supported structure when wind velocities exceed 45 mph? ______________________________
____
____

19. From your reading of the section on nonpermanent buildings, would you use one of these types of buildings? ☐Yes ☐No If your answer is yes, then which type of building would you prefer? ☐Air-supported ☐Metal-framed

20. If you have selected one of the two types, what are the reasons for your preference? ____
____
____
____

Chapter 8
Packaging Aspects of Receiving and Shipping

I. INTRODUCTION

In Chapter 1 we discussed several reasons why the systems approach to materials handling is extremely important. In addition, we indicated that in the systems approach we must look at the whole picture from raw material source, or supplier, through the production and physical distribution chain and then to the ultimate consumer. Furthermore, we indicated that we must not stop with the user, but instead must determine the last resting place of the item and view its method of disposal. Can the materials of its composition be recycled? Can the item be safely incinerated without producing toxic by-products? And, since incineration is to be avoided at all costs (some communities do not permit this method of disposal), can some further benefit be derived from its chemical and physical properties?

For many manufactured articles, packaging is such an integral part of the product that one of the economic indicators used by federal agencies is the amount of corrugated, kraft, and fiberboard material that is sold and finds its way into the avenues of commerce. The more corrugated sold, the healthier the economy. Thus, there are many facets to the study of packaging.

Another aspect of packaging is its use to promote the sale of soft-goods. In this volume we are not concerned with the retail aspects of packaging, but we shall look at the bulk container that both protects the article to be sold and protects the fancy internal packaging that enhances the attractiveness of the article to the consumer.

In addition to the bulk container used in wholesaling, we are concerned with the bulk containers and the unit loads that production materials require in order to arrive at a particular receiving platform safely, that is, without damage.

This, then, is another link in the chain of the systems approach to materials handling. Why should we be concerned with bulk packaging? No one who has ever watched the way materials arrive at a warehouse or factory will question the need for a coordinated effort in packaging.

Much of the rehandling, repalletizing, picking up of loose pieces, and struggling with broken, torn, or loosely held materials in trucks or railway cars can be avoided if there is a workable packaging program in the company.

The coordinated effort of our systems approach requires the cooperation of the purchasing department, the traffic department, and the warehouse manager and all related personnel when we are talking of the physical distribution network. It might, also, require the sales or marketing departments because they set up the initial mechanism that makes consumers buy certain items in large quantities. These large volumes, then, dictate the need for bulk containers and wholesale quantities of merchandise.

In manufacturing or production operations, we must include not only the above operating groups of the organization, but we may have to obtain the cooperation of the engineering, scheduling, inspection, and quality control departments. In both warehousing and manufacturing we may also need the accounting department to obtain assistance in properly evaluating the cost of packaging, and the effect different methods of handling various types of packages have on departmental costs.

II. RECEIVING—PACKAGING

In order to perform the materials handling function as effectively as possible in the receiving department, it is necessary that incoming materials be packaged in a manner that best conforms to the available (a) space, (b) equipment, and (c) end use.

A. Space

The incoming materials must be placed in some prearranged area, and after all of the receiving functions have been performed (involving the processing of the documents related to the shipment, the checking of packing lists, bills of lading, piece or weight count, inspection, etc.), the material must be put into storage or taken to the first point of use.

If the material does not pass inspection or is part of an O.S. and D. problem (over, short, and damaged), then it is usually placed in a holding area until the problem can be resolved.

In any event, if space is at a premium, as it usually is, we would require that the unit loads be as large as our storage racks or bins will permit—since the larger the loads are, the less the time and space required to handle the total shipment.

If storage racks are not part of our system, then we must design our requirements so that the materials can be block-stored. Block storage requires that the unit loads, containers, or pallets be of a type suitable for stacking. We should try to avoid, as much as possible, packaging that is subject to fatigue and will not stack for reasonable time intervals. The type of cheap packaging that does not hold up well in storage, or that despite its cost has too many void spaces, should be carefully analyzed to determine whether or not it is costing the company more money than necessary. A poorly designed or cheap container may have so many hidden costs that it becomes more expensive than the best possible packaging, from a total cost standpoint.

B. Equipment

If a company, or plant, has the latest in stacker-crane (S/C) retrieval systems, and there are a number of these systems in the United States, then it becomes very necessary that a measure of standardization be incorporated into its packaging program.

This type of standardization should meet certain requirements:

1. The *length, width,* and *height* dimensions should be carefully spelled out because of the very nature of the S/C mechanization. For example, dimensions of incoming conveyors, the S/C shuttle or transfer car dimensions, elevator dimensions, and the storage rack opening sizes would have to accommodate the unit load that crosses the receiving platform. A unit load that did not conform to the above criteria dimensionally would be rejected by the S/C system and would have to be placed in a bulk storage area or some other set-out space. Or, on the other hand, the load would very likely have to be repackaged into an acceptable size to be satisfactorily received by the S/C mechanization complex, and this would involve additional labor and container costs.

2. The *weight* of the unit load is critical, and all of the latest generations of S/C systems are equipped with weigh scales or load cell platforms. Overweight loads would be rejected and handled as indicated above. The reason for the weight limitation is obvious: If a load passed the criterion of size, and its density caused it to weigh more than the design capacity of the shuttle (of the S/C), then it could cause a greater deflection in the shuttle; and if the deflection was larger than the deflection induced by the designed load, the shuttle might not arrive satisfactorily in the allotted space provided in the storage rack. The shuttle might collide with the shelf beam, or cantilevered supports, and damage the S/C mechanism.

3. The packaging must *retain its integrity* through the the entire S/C processing; that is, from the time it enters the system until the time it is outloaded. For example, trailing steel bands, plastic shrouds dangling from the unit load, broken deck boards sticking out during transportation by elements of the S/C system—even corrugated flaps bending over into the path of S/C structural members—can all cause damage or grief that must be relieved, or otherwise resolved.

Other problems that require resolution come about during the order picking cycle with S/C systems. If you have full loads in and full loads out, the situation is fairly simple. On the other hand, if you are order picking and cut the bands in order to remove a carton from a unit load, then care must be exercised with respect to your packaging requirements. A carton may be removed from a shrink-wrapped unit load without, necessarily, destroying its integrity. It has been found helpful where shrink wrapping is not used to strip-glue the cartons making up the unit load with a "high-shear, low-tensile" packaging adhesive. (See Appendix A for a source of palletizing adhesives.)

If your company does not have an S/C retrieval system, you might suppose that a requirement for package size and weight, or unit load size and weight, would be of little concern. This is far from the truth, since the efficiency of the materials handling operation improves in direct relation to the uniformity of package size and weight, as indicated in Chapter 1.

Let us look at the question of size. If containers or unit loads are received that are so large that they will not fit into storage racks or other preassigned spaces, then we have problems which usually result in a great deal of extra handling.

If unit loads are received with densities that are greater than we can handle—for example, a 4,000-pound load when we have only a 2,000-pound lift truck—we have a problem!

C. End Use

Other criteria also cannot be ignored. For example, if the product is packaged in such a manner that unnecessarily large quantities of dunnage are being generated, then it is absolutely certain that we are incurring additional charges for disposal, not to mention the added labor required to remove the dunnage, and so forth.

Also, we mentioned carton fatigue and void spaces as causes of carton failure (in section II, A, above). The characteristics of corrugated materials are no less important in operations that do not use S/C retrieval systems.

Another factor that must be included in our criteria is the necessity for withstanding the rigors of outside storage. In other words, if we are dependent in our storage plan on the use of yard storage, the packaging must be sufficient to provide the proper protection for our product (from the elements).

D. Other Protection

A great deal of money is spent annually on packaging to protect various types of receivables from the effects of sunlight, rain and moisture, corrosive sulfur in the air, and oxidation.

The advent of film plastics signaled a whole new era of packaging. The addition of the expanded polyurethanes, styrofoam, and foamed-in-place types of plastics has meant that innovations in packaging methods are developed every day.

Two of the most commonly used films are polyethylene and polystyrene, with a marked preference being exhibited for the less expensive, though not as transparent, polyethylene.

Clear plastic films that may be heat-sealed can provide a measure of moisture protection for most packaging needs. Desiccants like silica gel may be added to ensure that moisture is trapped before the product is damaged or before rust can form. VCI (vapor controlled inhibitors) may be used to provide a means to coat a part with a film, which is deposited when a VCI chip (paper impregnated with VCI) or VCI granules are placed in a sealed container with the item.

In Chapter 2, we discussed the ultraviolet ray inhibitors used for shrink-wrap and stretch-wrap unitizing. It is interesting to note that protection from sunlight can be built into plastics. Ultraviolet ray inhibitors can be obtained by coloring plastics to opaqueness, black usually being a favorite plastic color for this purpose.

By heat-sealing plastic liners in most packaging, the effects of corrosive fumes and oxidation may be minimized. The strength and exterior characteristics of the package depend, of course, upon such things as the product requirements and the anticipated shelf-life.

1. Product Requirements. When it is necessary to establish guidelines for packaging that is to be received from the suppliers of a company, it is necessary to affirm a policy that will assure specific objectives. These objectives should indicate that it is the company's requirement that all products must be packaged and loaded so that they will arrive at their destinations damage-free and in a package or unit load that is economical to handle. (Recall the discussion of loads in Chapter 2.) Some further considerations are:

1. The incoming packaging should be compatible with your company's materials handling methods and equipment. For example, if the load is too heavy, you may not have sufficient forklift truck capacity to lift the load without renting additional equipment.
2. It should be compatible with your storage facilities; that is, it should fit into prescribed areas, storage racks, bins, etc. If the package or unit is too large, you may not be able to store it in your pallet storage rack openings without repackaging; and, if too small, the package may waste storage rack opening space. Also, if it is too small a load, it will require a number of additional handlings or require consolidation into a satisfactory unit load.

3. It should be compatible with your automatic storage and stacker-crane retrieval system, if you have this type of advanced storage system.
4. The packaging should be planned and thought of in terms of ecological considerations that have to do with the disposal or recycling of dunnage and other packaging materials—as, for example, strapping, corrugated paper, and fiberboard. In other words if kraft paper is to be recycled, instead of having an asphaltic layer as a moisture barrier, an inner wrap, VCI, or other paper should be used, since an asphaltic layer would not permit the kraft fiber to be properly recycled.

III. A PACKAGING MANUAL—THE WHY AND WHEREFORE

In this section we shall discuss the need for a company packaging manual, and relate this to both receiving and shipping functions.

A. The Need for a Manual

Every organization that receives materials or products with any degree of regularity or frequency needs a packaging manual in order to standardize handling methods and equipment, and in order to reduce the cost of operations and increase the effectiveness of the receiving function.

In the systems approach to materials handling we must look at every factor that influences the cost and efficiency of the handling function. Poor packaging requires excessive handling, is unsafe, wastes precious time, and causes many disruptions in the orderly flow of materials through the system.

Therefore, in order to promote the cause of good materials handling it is necessary to attack one of the underlying causes of interrupted work flow and disorganization—poor packaging.

B. Cooperation Essential

A little later in the text we shall discuss the element of communications in packaging. Although much packaging is and can be done without this ingredient, we shall attempt to point out why communications and its related element cooperation are so important to the success of the program.

Another thought: Why reinvent the wheel? And, why not see how others in your company feel about the problem of packaging? It is well worth the effort to get other company management people thoroughly indoctrinated so that they are aware of your program and can offer their support. Also, the packaging manual should reflect the best thinking in the company. Thus, as you develop the various parts of the manual, obtain the cooperation of each department within the company. There are several reasons for involving other departments. A primary one is that their cooperation will make your packaging program function more smoothly. They will have become a part of the undertaking and therefore will give the program their support. Without this kind of support and cooperation your packaging program may never get off the ground.

Another good reason for obtaining departmental cooperation—and by this we mean input from traffic, purchasing, inspection and quality control, etc.—is that their expertise will provide the background and experience to make the program practical and realistic.

Besides the cooperation within the company, cooperation is needed from suppliers. Since the packaging manual will indicate the requirements for identification of items to be supplied, the kinds of packaging, whom the supplier must contact in order to get certain things done, etc., it is necessary that these subjects be spelled out in the manual and achieved in practice.

C. Communications Required

The above comments do not relieve the supplier of his responsibilities for providing adequate protection for the merchandise he is supplying. In addition the supplier must comply with all laws and regulations, including (1) the Railroads' Uniform Freight Classification and (2) the Trucking Industry's National Motor Freight Classification. Within this framework, however, there is a need to establish a line of communication that will permit the supplier to do a good job of packaging for the company. In most companies the purchasing department has the responsibility for communicating with the supplier, and the materials handling engineer and the packaging engineer would do well to observe this protocol.

In a good packaging program, the supplier should work in a climate that permits him as much latitude as possible to make suggestions and recommendations that will help improve packaging and lower the costs involved. The packaging manual should provide guidelines by which each supplier may utilize standard packaging methods and materials; thus, the supplier's constraints will be primarily the packaging and loading requirements of the manual.

Every supplier should be able to indicate how he will package his materials for shipment. To do this properly it is well to use a standard format that will provide all of the necessary information at one time.

A "Packaging & Shipping Data Sheet" can be developed that will contain all of the required packaging elements. A sample data sheet can be seen in Appendix 8-A at the end of this chapter. We shall discuss the elements it contains in the course of the chapter.

Another means of communication with the supplier is a "Packaging Deficiency Notice." For example, if materials are received in less than satisfactory condition, or if they have not been packaged in a manner that conforms to the packaging manual (by virtue of being too large, too small, too heavy, etc.), then the deficiency notice, which is completed by the materials handling or packaging engineer, should be issued to the supplier by the purchasing department. One form of the "Packaging Deficiency Notice" can be seen in Appendix 8-B, also at the end of this chapter.

In order to give the packaging program needed support, it should be a company policy that any deviation from the packaging manual, and the packaging and shipping data sheet, must be approved by both the purchasing department and the plant materials handling engineer. It is, of course, essential that exceptions be made only when emergency shipments are required and then only upon prior notification of the purchasing department.

D. Packaging, An Important Part of Materials Handling and Vice Versa

More and more companies are recognizing that a systems approach to materials handling cuts across departmental lines into other areas of plant operations. One of the important areas, of course, is packaging.

The part that materials handing plays in packaging is varied, especially since it is understood that the excessive handling of a product, whether it is a purchased part or one fabricated in-house, becomes an undesirable and unnecessarily expensive part of plant operations.

In order to reduce the quantity of excessive handling that takes place in a plant, which is costly in terms of both man-hours expended and product damage, we can apply the systems approach to materials handling, which requires a high degree of standardization in packaging.

By determining that the primary objective of packaging is to reduce costs, we are well on the way toward our goal, which is synonymous with decreasing the cost of materials handling.

IV. IMPORTANT ELEMENTS OF A PACKAGING MANUAL

Before we discuss the composition of a packaging manual, here are two reasons why this type of manual is necessary: we have to formalize packaging procedures in order to have them work well, and it is necessary to have a source of reference for all plant personnel and suppliers who are trying to do a good job and save money for the company. The following information is provided as a basis for the manual.

A. Kinds of Packages

Generally speaking, packages, palletized unit loads, and containers should be grouped into two rather broad categories:

1. *Manually handled packages:* Packages that are not suitably or conveniently handled by a forklift, or other industrial truck, and that weigh 50 pounds or less.
2. *Mechanically handled packages:* Unit loads that are palletized, slip-sheeted, skidded, shrink-wrapped, containerized, etc., such that they can be handled, readily, by a forklift, or other industrial truck.

B. Manually Handled Packages

1. Corrugated boxes are the most suitable type of manually handled package, depending on the type of parts to be contained.
2. The package must provide proper and adequate protection for the parts in order that they may arrive safely at their destination.
3. The gross weight of the package should not exceed 50 pounds, and it should be shaped so that it can be easily handled by one individual.
4. The package must be secured in such a fashion that the contents will not spill out, nor should the closure method become a safety hazard; in some instances staples or other metal fasteners should be discouraged. Although gluing may be used, it should be applied in strip or dot form so that it has sufficient strength to withstand shipping and handling, and the container still may be opened without difficulty.
5. The packaging materials may be recycled, but the container should be an expendable or one-way type, unless the form of packaging has been approved by both materials handling and purchasing.
6. Parts that are a meter or so in length should be removable from the end of the package.
7. Try to avoid void spaces when using corrugated cartons. Most damage to packaging of this type is experienced when the voids cause containers to collapse.
8. Bundles may be permitted only when the part configuration or other kinds of packaging become unusually expensive for the part.
9. The use of second-hand corrugated cartons should only be permitted after obtaining approvals from the purchasing department and materials handling.
10. In certain instances containers may have to be tested before shipment. This is especially true when electronic components, ceramics, and other fragile materials are concerned. (Section IV, K of this chapter will go into further detail on this very technical subject.)

C. Mechanically Handled Packages

1. The unitized load must have a reasonably strong pallet base to make certain that the load arrives at its destination safely and may be handled as far as the first point of use within the plant. For this reason it is

important to establish expendable (one-way, or one-use-only) pallet standards, as indicated in Chapter 6. Other types of containers or packaging materials should be expendable, also, unless some understanding or approval is obtained through the purchasing department for a "returnable" container.

2. Drums, barrels, bags, and salvaged containers that are reused should only be used with prior approvals as indicated, above, for returnables. The reason is simply that these items are more difficult and costly to handle from a labor standpoint.
3. The gross weight of palletized or unit loads should be restricted to that of conveniently handled loads. Sometimes materials handling equipment will militate against larger load sizes and weights.
4. Palletized loads should have a minimum underclearance of 3⅝ inches and a minimum width for fork entry of 24 inches.
5. Pallet loads should be stacked properly with materials, generally cartons, placed in an interlocking pattern on the pallet.
6. The palletized load should be securely banded with edge corner protectors where necessary.
7. Strip-gluing should be required for cartons and other materials where the integrity of the load is important.
8. Pallet overhang should be minimized or eliminated. It could cause product damage.
9. The palletized load should be shrink-wrapped whenever possible.
10. Containers that are fabricated from corrugated board are preferred to wire-bound or wood boxes, when practicable. Corrugated materials can be recycled more easily.
11. Palletized loads should consist of only one part number whenever possible, since this minimizes mistakes and makes checking by receiving less difficult.
12. Suitable rust-prevention and anticorrosion guidelines should be included if parts could be adversely affected during shipment and storage.
13. The packaging manual should include definitions for the various types of containers to be received. As an example:
    a. Pallet boxes (corrugated, wire-bound, or wood)
    b. Pallets with loose parts
    c. Boxes on a pallet
    d. Pallet tray pack
    e. Pallet shrink wrap
    f. Crates
14. In addition, instructions should be given so that piece parts may be packaged properly. Individually wrapped parts are not desirable, although some parts may require added protection. Usually descriptions of cellular and die-cut corrugated egg crates are necessary.

D. Fastener and Small Parts Packaging

Small parts such as nuts, bolts, screws, washers, etc., are very dense in weight and should be packaged according to the fastener industry's "Adopted Container Type Standards" as well as applicable carrier regulations.

1. The small parts should be packaged in fiberboard boxes, as indicated below, or in heavy bulk-style expendable, corrugated containers.

CONTAINER STYLE	SIZE IN INCHES
1/16 keg	6¼ × 6¼ × 3⅛
⅛ keg	6¼ × 6¼ × 6¼
¼ keg	9 × 9 × 6½
½ keg	9 × 9 × 13
¾ keg	11 × 11 × 12
Full keg	11 × 11 × 17

2. Palletized containers require sturdily constructed pallets for the dense, small parts indicated above. The pallets, therefore, should conform to the specifications for expendable pallets described for mechanically handled parts, above.
3. It should be a requirement that pre-shipment tests be performed if necessary.
4. Specifications covering corrugated containers using double-wall or triple-wall corrugated board should be included in the manual.

E. Preventing Corrosion

All parts with surfaces that may corrode, rust, or otherwise deteriorate should be protected in some way.

1. The manual should specify the particular type of cleaning method that is desirable for the part. In other words, the part should be cleaned before application of any preservative. Of course, some parts may not require cleaning or preservation, so prior experience may be a satisfactory guide in this regard.
2. The method of application of the preservative should be spelled out; for example, dip, spray, or brush.
3. VCI (volatile corrosion inhibitors) may, also, be specified to minimize deterioration (see section II, D, above). VCI may be used in chip size, or as precut discs of VCI paper, or as paper wrappers. To be most effective the container should be tape-sealed or glued shut. The volatile inhibitor then forms a light film over the metallic part, and although moisture may be present, the part is not affected for a considerable period of time.

F. Returnable Containers versus Nonreturnables

In many companies, the problem of returnable versus expendable, or one-way, nonreturnable containers is never fully resolved. You may see combinations of both types of containers in a large number of styles and shapes in almost any good-size plant.

There being advantages and disadvantages to either type, the materials handling practitioner must carefully weigh the cost of doing business with either of them. For example, it is a general rule of thumb that the point of diminishing returns for most returnable containers is a 300-mile radius of the plant. Beyond this distance the freight rate for over-the-road carriers makes their use rather costly, decreasing the cost benefits that occur when captive or returnable containers are used.

1. Tender Rates. Tender rates or preferred rates may sometimes be obtained from trucking companies, that would in some instances make it possible to achieve cost savings in returning empty containers to the supplier.

A desirable returnable container should have a low tare weight and be capable of being knocked-down, or collpased, or nested. Also, one of the goals when steel containers are used is to obtain maximum truck payloads of up to 40,000 pounds.

2. Railroad Returnables. Railroad returnables are those containers that the railroads will return to a supplier empty, and at no cost to the user. The effective range or radius of this logistic device is much greater than the truck transportation range indicated above.

3. Memo Charges and Accountability. Memo charges and accountability are the primary concerns of the receiving department and the accounting organization, as far as containers are concerned. Usually, when returnable containers are shipped, the invoice will indicate the cost per container. This will be either an actual charge or a memo charge. If the container is destroyed or is used in-house, then the customer must pay the cost. When returnable containers are made of wood, as opposed to steel, it is sometimes difficult to find the container to return it—primarily because it has been thrown in the incinerator or discarded. Constant vigilance and controls are required to plug this leak.

The ordinary difficulties with returnable containers that, more often than not, make them less desirable, are that they require a good deal of storage space; that they are often of such poor quality that they are hardly worth returning; that the containers that are knocked-down, or collapsed, require a good deal of expensive labor to be knocked-down; and that if they can be knocked-down or collapsed, it is only possible to do so with considerable effort, especially after the containers have been in service for a while. The older KD or collapsible containers tend to lose their initial dimensions, and the configuration that permits their easy assembly, etc., no longer exists. In some cases, it becomes virtually impossible to either collapse the containers or assemble them into a useful configuration, and the tendency is to keep them in the assembled configuration.

4. Container Identification. Container identification is important if it is decided to use a captive container purchased either by your company or by the supplier. It is necessary to insist that each returnable container be legibly marked with the following information:

1. The supplier or company name.
2. Return to (location).
3. "Returnable Container" in large letters so that this is clearly visible.

In addition, the supplier should give the same information on all packing lists and invoices. And, as another important facet of this container-returning program, it should be clearly spelled out to each supplier that if the above information is not provided—that is, if the containers are not marked properly—deposits or payments for the containers will not be made.

5. Company-Owned Containers. Company-owned containers are sometimes used in exchange agreements with suppliers, as noted earlier. Where the company wishes to promote this type of program with suppliers, it should make certain that suppliers are informed of the types of containers that are available. It is well to standardize container types also, so that if there is more than one plant involved in the program, storage space and materials handling equipment are compatible with the unit loads being considered.

G. Identification of Incoming Materials

In order to have an effective receiving operation, it is necessary that all incoming merchandise be quickly and easily identified.

1. Methods of Labeling. The company's packaging manual should contain specific instructions as to what is required on all supplier shipping labels and tags, as follows:

1. Ship to: (plant name)
2. Part no.: (give the complete number)
3. Quantity: (number of pieces in each package)

4. P.O. number: (purchase order number)
5. Model or Change No. (if there is an engineering change number give the latest number; if a model number, give the latest model number)
6. Date packed: (show the date by month, day, and year in which the material was packed—this may be necessary for the turnover of inventory and inventory control)
7. Weight: (gross weight in pounds and metric measure)
8. Supplier's name: (the supplier's name and shipping plant address)

Methods of labeling should be standardized as much as possible; so a form should be included in the manual indicating your company's label and tag requirements. To be specific, show the actual dimensions and layout of all identification labels and tags so that the supplier will know what is expected.

In addition, although we are attempting to make identification quick and easy in the receiving department, we should not penalize the supplier by insisting on a *printed* label, but we should make it clear that handwritten labels are acceptable under certain conditions:

1. The labels should be hand-lettered legibly with waterproof ink.
2. Tags, when used, should be of 110-pound card stock, or heavier.

2. Special Instructions. Special instructions should be added to the specific unit load where they are necessary to ensure the safe arrival of the material. However, these instructions should not be a part of the shipping label, but should be clearly marked on the load, as follows:

1. Special handling to prevent damage should be in large letters, either black or other colors, and at least 2 inches high.
2. Tiering instructions, such as "Do Not Bottom Tier," should be given to prevent heavier loads from being placed on top of your materials in transit, especially since LTL (less than truckload) quantities are usually consolidated inside trucking terminals.
3. Direction of travel is sometimes very important, especially for certain types of expendable, block-design pallets that are stronger in one direction than in another at right angles to the first. For example, bottom deck boards of this type of pallet should always run parallel to the direction of travel of the load in transit.

H. Bill of Lading and Packing List

1. Bill of Lading. A bill of lading is a written receipt given by a common carrier for goods accepted for transporation. There are standard or "boilerplate" clauses on this bill; however, the usual information supplied on bills of lading should be supplemented by including the number of units or packages on each pallet or skid.

2. Packing List. A packing list (P.L.) is an essential part of each shipment. Without a packing list it is extremely difficult to check receivables. The P.L. tells you what has been shipped and what should be received. The following remarks pertain to this document:

1. Every shipment should have its own packing list.
2. The P.L. should be easily found in the shipment.
3. The P.L. must be clearly visible on the outside of the container or load.
4. Place the P.L. on the side or end of the load. Never place it on top of the load because if another load is placed on top of it, the P.L. will be lost or destroyed.
5. Whenever possible, place the P.L. on the load that is nearest the loading door.
6. Use a colored, plastic packing list envelope with a pressure-sensitive adhesive backing which will protect the P.L. and is highly visible.

3. P.L. Information. Every P.L. should contain the following information:

1. The supplier's name
2. The part or model number
3. The purchase order number
4. The receiving plant address
5. The number of units or packages per pallet or skid
6. The number of pallets, skids, or bulk containers in the shipment
7. The number of pieces ordered
8. The number of pieces shipped
9. The engineering change number, if applicable
10. A description of the material
11. If returnable containers are included in the shipment, the necessary information indicated in section IV, F4, above ("Container Identification")

I. How to Deal with Hazardous Materials

Hazardous materials can sometimes be quite troublesome for small companies where such material is not handled on a day-to-day basis, but is only infrequently received.

Although it is the responsibility of every supplier of hazardous materials to comply with all federal, state, and local laws or regulations, a certain familiarity with these regulations can be quite helpful. An excellent source for this information is: "Hazardous Materials Regulations of the Department of Transportation, Including Specifications for Shipping Containers" (see Appendix A for source).

By definition, an item may be considered to be hazardous if it is corrosive, explosive, flammable, radioactive, toxic, or packaged in a container that is considered to be hazardous, such as a pressurized, aerosol-type container.

J. The Transportation Mode and Carrier Loading

It is up to your traffic department to specify the method, the type of equipment, and routing for purchased materials. The transportation mode will depend to a great extent on (1) the size of the shipment, (2) the urgency required, and (3) the type of material to be shipped.

1. Carrier Responsibility. The supplier is responsible for the initial loading of merchandise into the load-carrying vehicle. Thereafter, the supplier and carrier are jointly responsible for the method of loading materials into the load-carrying vehicle when the materials are unloaded and then reloaded at transfer terminals or freight consolidation points.

The carrier should report on the B/L (bill of lading) all observations of incorrect loading by the supplier when the merchandise is received at its transfer or consolidation terminals.

K. Pre-Shipment Testing

The "Packaging & Shipping Data Sheet" (Appendix 8-A), discussed above in section III, C, will provide the information needed to determine whether or not most of the packaging will be of sufficient quality to withstand the rigors of the materials handling in both the supplier's and the receiver's plants, the hardship of in-transit shipping, and the bruising and impacts it will take when it has to be unloaded and reloaded at a transfer or consolidation terminal.

In some isolated instances it will not be possible to determine by looking at the information on the "Packaging & Shipping Data Sheet" in what manner the merchandise will arrive at the receiver's plant. For this reason, it may be necessary to require the supplier to certify that his packaging is acceptable and sufficient for the intended protection of the materials to be shipped.

Thus, pre-shipment package testing is a method used to discover potential package design deficiences. Approved testing methods can point out "underpackaging" or "overpackaging" so that these defects may be corrected before the supplier ships his materials.

Certified testing laboratories are located in almost all major cities. They are able to use standardized equipment and procedures to discover deficiencies in packaging that must be corrected prior to shipment. There are (1) vibration, (2) drop, (3) incline-impact, and (4) compression tests that may be employed, together with a number of other material tests that are effective in locating and remedying packaging problems. Appendix 8-C, at the end of this chapter, illustrates the basic components of a "Certification of Pre-Shipment Testing."

V. SHIPPING–PACKAGING

The shipping plant must look at outgoing materials in much the same way that the receiving department views incoming materials. Going through the various sections for receiving–packaging you will note what must be strengthened in the techniques required to improve outbound packaging.

The materials handling practitioner should be aware of a number of aspects of outbound packaging. Unit load and small package shipping generally follows the guidelines, provided in the preceding section, for packaging manual requirements. On the other hand, large structures that are shipped one unit to a carrier require a kind of blocking and bracing that is a science and art unto itself.

The practitioner who is called upon to block and brace a large piece of equipment on a railroad flat car has to know his equipment and materials and thoroughly understand the forces that are stressing the tie-down or blocking points. Railroads and trucking firms have experts who are willing to lend their assistance in providing the kind of know-how required. All outgoing shipments of this type should be inspected by the carrier's representative prior to shipment. Experience then becomes the best teacher on this subject. For example, green cottonwood and gumwood lumber is often used for the blocking and bracing of these large loads. If seasoned wood is used, it is difficult to nail and spike without pre-drilling, but green wood can be spiked to railroad car decks without checking and splitting. Special rail cars can be used with chains and features that permit the load to be properly restrained. These cars are especially easy to ship with, when they are available.

There are a number of military and railroad manuals that cover the finer points of blocking and bracing. The materials handling engineer who is called upon to do this type of work should contact The Department of Defense, Washington, D.C. and the Association of American Railroads, 59 East Van Buren Street, Chicago, Illinois 60605, for further information.

A list of important reference works has been included at the end of this text to help all those who would become more proficient and professional in their endeavors. This listing will be found in Appendix A.

EXERCISE NO. 8

1. Packaging is so integral a part of the product that one of the indicators of economic conditions is the amount of ____________ that is sold.

2. The coordinated effort of a packaging program requires the cooperation of other departments, such as ____________ and ____________.

3. Incoming materials should be packaged in a manner that best conforms to the available (1) ____________, (2) ____________, and (3) ____________ ____________.

4. If storage space is at a premium, we would require that the unit loads be as ____________ as our storage racks will permit, since the larger the loads are, the less the time and space required to handle the total shipment.

5. A poorly designed or cheap container may have so many ____________ that it becomes more expensive than the best possible packaging, from a total cost standpoint.

6. If a company or plant has the latest in S/C retrieval systems, then it becomes very necessary that a measure of ____________ be incorporated into its packaging program.

7. S/C retrieval system standardization, in general, uses the following criteria:

1. Length, width, and height
2. ____________
3. The need for the packaging to retain its ____________

8. A great deal of money is spent annually on packaging in protecting various types of receivables from the effects of: sunlight, ____________, ____________, and oxidation.

9. Two of the most commonly used packaging films are ____________ and polystyrene.

10. Protection from ____________ can be built into plastics.

11. Why does a company need a packaging manual or guide?

____

____

12. A packaging manual does not relieve the supplier of his responsibilities for providing ____________ ____________ for the merchandise he is supplying.

13. One means of communication with the supplier is the "Packaging & Shipping Data Sheet"; the other is the ____________ ____ ____________ ____________.

14. Two broad categories for packages, palletized unit loads, and containers, are:

1. Manually handled packages
2. ____________ ____________ ____________

15. A packaging manual should include definitions for the various types of containers:

1. Pallet boxes
2. ____
3. ____
4. ____
5. ____
6. ____

16. Preferred rates are never obtained from trucking companies for the return of empty containers solely because of their cost of operations. True ☐ False ☐
17. Returnable containers should be identified with the following legible markings:
    1. Supplier/company name
    2. ______________________
    3. ______________________
18. In order to have an effective receiving department operation it is necessary that all incoming merchandise be quickly and easily ____________.
19. What is the definition of a bill of lading?
    ____
    ____
    ____
    ____
20. The packing list tells you what has been shipped and what should be ____________.

APPENDIX 8-A
PACKAGING & SHIPPING DATA SHEET

Supplier Name and Address ______________ Return to: ______________

______________________ ______________________

______________________ ______________________

______________________ ______________________

Date ____________ Part/Model No. ____________ Description ____________

Status: New ☐ Revised ☐ Note: For any changes to be made in Packaging or Shipping Methods, see Plant Purchasing Dept. for prior approvals.

Part or Model	Length	Width	Height	Weight	Materials
					☐Metal ☐Rubber ☐Glass ☐Fiber ☐Plastic ☐Other

Packaging Data

When manually handled packages are unitized with mechanically handled unit loads, complete both sections.

Manually Handled	*Mechanically Handled*	*Closures*	*Banding*
☐Loose	☐Palletized Boxes	☐Glue	☐Metallic
Bundle	Pallet Tray Pack	Tape	Nonmetallic
Bag	Pieces on Pallet	Staple	Wire
Drum	Pallet Box	Wire	Other

Corrugated Box:	Corrugated-Wood	Cord	*Rust Prevention*
Reg. Slotted	Wire-bound	Other	Type:
Telescopic	Crate	________	(Explain)
Full Flap	Returnable Company-Owned	*Interior*	________
Material ________	Returnable Supplier-Owned	Wrapped	________
Bursting Strength ___ lb	Other Type ________	Loose	________
	Send drwgs, specs, photo	Cells	
Other ________	*Load Size:*	Liner	
Load Size:	L ________	Diecut	
L ________	W ________	Nested	
W ________	D ________	Other	
D ________	Gross Wt. ________	________	
Gross Wt. ________	No. of pieces ________		
No. of pieces ________			

Description of Pallet Design:
☐2-way ☐4-way ☐Block ☐Stringer
☐Other ________________________________

Size L ____________ W ____________

Fork Entry: Width ________________ (Min 22 inches)
Height ________________ (Min 3⅝ inches)

Container Charges:
☐Supplier Returnable: Type ________________
Deposit required: $____________
☐Expendable (one-way): Type ________________
Pallet cost: $____________ Packaging Cost $________

Type of Carrier to be used:
☐Rail ☐Truck ☐Other ____________

If part or model cannot be packaged by means of existing container types: (Explain)

____

____

Additional Comments: ________________________________

____

____

Supplier's signature ________ Title ____________ Date ___

For Company Use Only:
Purchasing ________________________________ Date ____________
Matl. Handling Engineering ________________________ Date ____________
Packaging ________________________________ Date ____________

(Note: An instruction sheet should accompany this form, but this can be placed on the back of the form.)

APPENDIX 8-B
PACKAGING & DEFICIENCY NOTICE

Date Rec'd __________ Supplier Name and Address __________ Date of Notice __________

Part or Model No. ______

Gentlemen: The packaging of a recent shipment received from your company resulted in the arrival of the materials in poor condition. Please complete and return two copies of this form indicating the action you have taken to remedy this situation.

Buyer ____________________ Location __________

1. Unit Load:
   - __ Incorrect size for storage L × W × H
     Load size we require L ______ W ______ H ______
   - __ Material loaded in carrier poorly.
   - __ Part numbers mixed. Please consolidate.
   - __ Excessive carton void spaces.
     Pallet too small ______ too large ______.
   - __ Container failed
   - __ Improperly marked
   - __ Banding defective
   - __ Other
2. Identification/Packing List:
   - __ Improper location
   - __ Not available
   - __ Incomplete information
   - __ Other
3. Transportation:
   - __ Unit load failed because of improper loading/handling
   - __ Fragile items not protected
   - __ Dunnage between tiers missing
   - __ Excessive weight on bottom load
4. Pre-shipment Test:
   - __ Container/unit load failed
   - __ Packaging failed
   - __ Pre-shipment test recommended
   - __ Certified pre-shipment test required
5. Comments: ____
   ____
   ____

6. Supplier Action Taken:
   (To be completed by supplier)

   ____

   ____

   ____

   ____

   Packaging/Material Handling Engineer ________________
   Photo Attached ☐

APPENDIX 8-C
CERTIFICATION OF PRE-SHIPMENT TESTING

Part No. or Model No. ________ Date ____________
Name or Description ________________________
Supplier's Name ___________________________
Address ___________________________
Shipped From ___________________________
Packaging
Laboratory Name ___________________________
Address ___________________________
Package Design   Date of Prior Test ________ ☐New ☐Revised

Description

Dimensions

Interior Packaging

No. of Parts/Container   *Gross Weight* ______ lb
______ kg

COMMENTS:

____

____

____

We hereby certify that the package and contents described above have passed the Shipping Container Pre-Shipment Test as prescribed in the "X" (your company) Packaging Manual.

Signature of
Authorized Supplier Official ________________ Title ______________
Date ________________

Chapter 9
Some Mechanization Concepts in Materials Handling

I. AUTOMATION IN MANUFACTURING AND DISTRIBUTION

In earlier chapters we discussed at length the systems approach to materials handling, stating that an absolute essential in applying this approach is an understanding of all of the operations or elements involved in the complete structure and organization of the system. Too often projects fail because of beginning and continuing uncertainties. Unknowns that may seem insignificant and of slight importance become large and formidable obstacles as we get further along in the process of bringing a project on stream.

We may count ourselves fortunate if one or more of the insignificant unknowns do not return to haunt us and destroy the validity of a materials handling mechanization system. As an example, let us suppose that a new warehouse is built with four truck docks. Hardly is the paint dry when it is discovered that because of the average time required to load and unload trucks, two more docks will be required.

Or, let us look at the assembly line where defective products must be sidelined while waiting for either replacement parts or parts that are in short supply (that is, not available at the time), or reworked parts. What will happen if there is insufficient storage space for tbe sidelined product? Can the product be returned to a rework station? If these questions cannot be satisfactorily answered, then clearly the unknowns were not thoroughly anticipated and challenged at the concept stage of the project.

Fortunately, a number of techniques are gaining validity in resolving some of the problems mentioned above. In Chapter 18 we shall discover some useful tools to aid in this type of probelm solving, such as modeling and simulation. For the time being, however, let us consider what can be accomplished in making more automatic (that is, in increasing the mechanization of) the manufacturing and distribution handling functions; and then we'll proceed to describe some of the machines and mechanisms that can be put to good use in these areas.

A. Automation in Manufacturing Materials Handling

Our objectives in mechanizing any operation are several, some of the usual ones being:

1. To increase the productive capacity of the operation, in other words, to produce more.
2. To lower the unit cost of the items produced by taking out labor and overhead costs.
3. To make it possible to meet competition in the marketplace.
4. To conserve plant area by producing larger quantities in less space.

You may be able to think of other reasons why mechanization, or automation, is necessary. Whatever the reasons and the philosophy leading to automation, let us take a look at ways in which it may be applied in manufacturing materials handling.

Raw materials or finished merchandise must be purchased and delivered to our factory. In considering automation let us decide whether the material must be specially packaged or oriented in unit loads for subsequent rehandling. We should ask ourselves some questions, such as, "Can the material be bulk-packaged?" and "Can it be packaged so that it can go directly from the receiving department to the point of first use?"

In large manufacturing operations, questions must be asked such as "Can the material be delivered in hopper cars, or tank cars?" Usually the answers provide cost savings as the bulk handling of the product will eliminate a vast amount of unnecessary labor. Bulk handling of materials is a specialized field that requires a separate section of text; for the time being, we recognize that it plays a significant part in large-scale, automated materials handling.

B. Automation in Distribution Materials Handling

Probably no other single area has exploded technically like the physical distribution aspect of materials handling in the past decade. The computer has taken its place as one of the more important tools in this field as it provides the backup, in terms of data processing, required to handle large volumes of transactions and to provide the bookkeeping that records and stores such information.

The stacker-crane retrieval system, which is guided, instructed, and directed by computer, is another example of mechanizing storage and stock-picking operations. Warehousing in large-scale operations has changed enormously with the advent of these tools. The situation can be likened to that of the telephone system in the thirties before the coming of the dial telephone. For today's number of telephones and calls, there would not be enough operators to handle all of the phone calls using the manual switchboard and operator combination. Mechanization and automation on the part of the telephone company provided the dial and centrex system for handling calls automatically. A similar analogy can be made for the stacker-crane automatic storage and retrieval system. There will not be space enough, or sufficient operators, to handle all of the receipts and disbursements that will have to be made in future decades to fill all of the orders received.

Considerable advances have also been made in the use of cathode ray tube (CRT) displays for transmitting information from the point where it is stored to the point where it is required. The digital type display is also being used in weighing and scale weight counting equipment. Improvements in inventory control are directly related to the speed at which information can be obtained and transmitted. Scale weight counting, for example, can provide precise measurements, or counts, of materials for inventory control purposes. When then transmitted by means of a data terminal on the shop or warehouse floor, the data can make its way directly into a storage mechanism—the computer. The information can be entered into stock records; so an incoming request that would, under any other circumstances, have required back-ordering now represents a viable and profitable transaction.

C. Some New and Improved Methods

When new devices are introduced to improve materials handling effectiveness, the supplier usually leaves no stone unturned to obtain the widest coverage possible. A system that is effective in manufacturing operations may often appear in physical distribution, and vice versa.

In the next three sections we shall review what is happening in important areas of materials handling that will have a great bearing on automation. The equipment and technology are currently on-the-shelf and ready to be installed.

The following sections cover air film handling, in-floor conveyors (compared with tractor-trains), and sortation and dispatching systems. In many instances, these systems are used in both manufacturing and physical distribution, although—because of inherent design characteristics—they may be more suitable in one area than another.

II. AIR FILM HANDLING

A. What Air Film Handling is All About

Most of us have seen air cushion devices in the news media, especially in scenes showing large boats being lifted across the sea on a pillow of air. This type of air handling requires a large volume of air and correspondingly huge pumps and engines to move the large quantity of relatively low-pressure air. Rough-terrain vehicles with skirts around their bases provide the same type of locomotion.

On the other hand, air film handling uses very small quantities of air at relatively high pressures, and is employed primarily in the materials handling industry.

The use of air films was pioneered by technicians in the General Motors Hovair Division during and just after World War II. After the war, GM decided to divest itself of any interest in this novel method for moving materials; therefore, it licensed several firms to develop further applications and do business accordingly.

Fortunately, some of these firms, such as, Airfloat, Rolair, and Aero-Go, have contributed a great deal in the applications area, and in advancing the state-of-the-art by redesigning the air platen itself. So, let us examine the principles of the air bearing (or air platen).

Figure 9-1 illustrates the basic elements of the original GM air bearing. Notice that air enters the bag and then moves out through holes in the bag

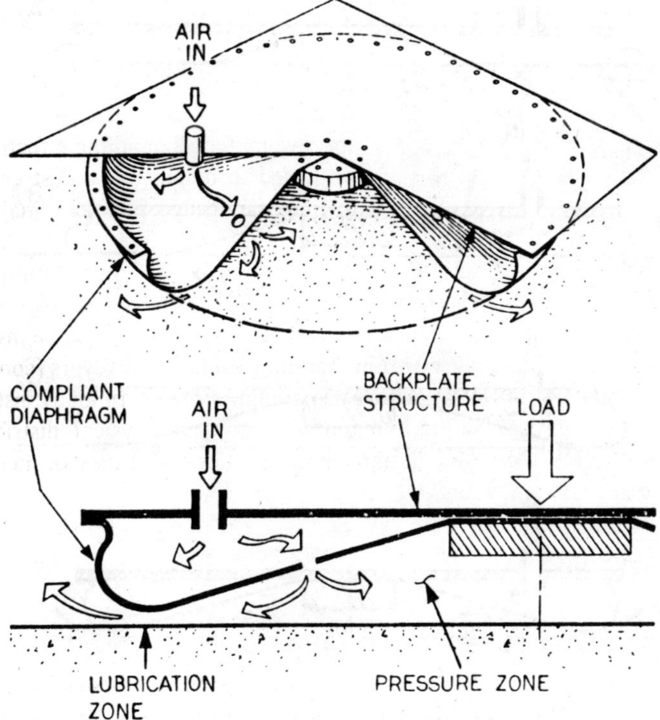

Fig. 9-1. The basic compliant air bearing.

into the larger pressure zone, or plenum chamber. The load is shown acting downward, and the rectangular, shaded area is a pad upon which the load rests when the air pressure is not exerting an upward force. The load does not rest upon the bag, or compliant diaphragm, but upon the pad, which is underneath the backplate structure. This feature is important to the life of the bag because if the load were to rest upon the bag for any length of time, it might crimp it or crush this membrane to the point of rupture.

When air enters the bag and rushes into the plenum chamber, the load is lifted. As air is forced into the plenum chamber, it tends to escape around the perimeter of the bag. This area is called the lubrication zone (see Fig. 9-1). It is this perimeter that floats the load only a few thousandths of an inch above the surface of the ground and permits a load weighing many tens of thousands of pounds to be pushed around by one or two men.

In Fig. 9-2 (A) through (D) we see the operating cycle of an air bearing. In (A) the air bearing rests upon the centrally located pad. The pad, therefore, takes the load from the diaphragm and prevents damage that would occur if

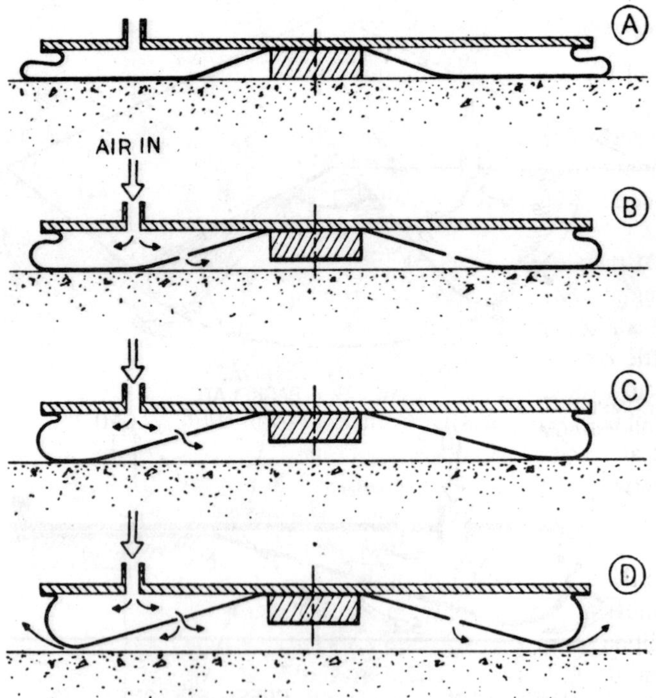

Fig. 9-2. The operating cycle of an air bearing

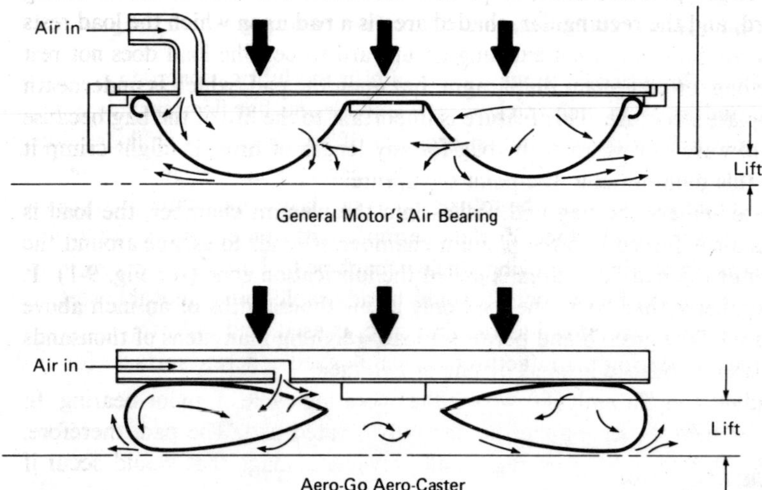

Fig. 9-3. Some fundamental differences between the GM air bearing and the Aero-Caster.

the pressure of the load were to be transmitted directly upon the compliant membrane.

In (B), air is shown entering the bag and being transmitted through the bag into the plenum chamber. As the bag fills up, air escapes into the plenum. In the next view (C) the bag is completely full, and the load has been lifted from the ground.

In view (D) the plenum is full, and air begins to escape from under the air bearing through the lubrication zone. A significant amount of lift has occurred, and the load is now "airborne." When the load is airborne, it is easily moved with very little horizontal effort, because of the lubricating effect of the air escaping through the lubrication zone.

A number of improvements have been made in air bearings since the original development at General Motors Corporation. One of the most effective in terms of general operations is the Aero-Caster developed by Aero-Go. In Fig. 9-3 you can see the principal differences: In the upper sketch (GM air bearing) air enters the diaphragm directly, and then passes on through the plenum chamber into the lubrication zone. In the Aero-Caster, the air enters both the plenum chamber and the diaphragm simultaneously, by means of opposing holes. In addition, since the backplate rests on, or is attached to, the center of the diaphragm donut (torus) in the Aero-Caster, it achieves greater lift than the GM air bearing. Another advantage of this type of construction is that it eliminates flutter or vibration caused by differences or variations in air pressure.

B. Some Required Parameters of Air Film Handling

1. Floor Conditions Since the air film in the lubrication zone is only a few thousandths of an inch thick, a very smooth and flat floor surface is required for the air bearing to function properly, if at all. Cracks or floor joints may cause collapse of the air bearing. A temporary measure, short of sealing the cracks and joints, would be to use sheets of plastic, masonite, or sheet steel to prepare a smooth surface for the intermittent movement of a given load. As an example, in rigging or moving a heavy machine tool over a fairly rough surface, such as a wood block floor, it would be advisable to use movable steel sheets. Lay the next sheet down as the first sheet is used, and so forth.

One air bearing manufacturer has catalogued concrete surfaces for air handling as follows:

SURFACE INDEX	TYPE
No. 2	• Sealed, hand-steel troweled, smooth concrete
No. 7	• Unsealed, hand-steel troweled, smooth concrete
No. 20	• Machine-steel troweled, concrete sidewalk
No. 25	• Wood-float, concrete sidewalk
	• Smooth blacktop with low porosity
No. 50	• Blacktop roadway
No. 60	• Concrete roadway

This Surface Index system was based upon the volume of air required to operate an air bearing on an ideal surface, such as polished glass. This surface is called Index No. 1. Steel plate and vinyl floor tile are examples of surfaces that approach Index No. 1 in effectiveness. The surface identified by No. 7 would require 7 times the air flow that would be required of the ideal surface. As another example, a surface of Index No. 20 would require 20 times the amount of air flow.

When an air bearing handling system is installed, a surface of Index No. 2 is recommended for the best results.

2. Level Surface Another characteristic of the air bearing is that when it has been pressurized and a flow of air is passing through the lubrication zone, it will glide downhill under its own gravitational pull. In other words, if there is a down slope on the floor, the air bearing with its load will slide down this slope; and if the load is fairly massive, it will behave like a runaway locomotive. Therefore, an important consideration is to have the floor as level as possible in order to have effective air bearing results.

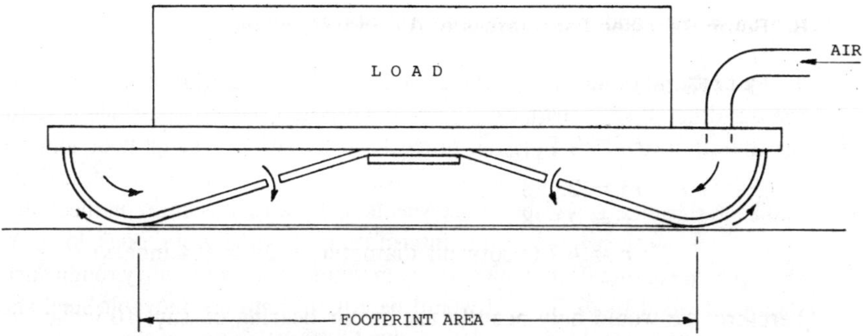

Fig. 9-4. Footprint area. Diameter of circle marks the outer boundary.

C. Simple Air Film Handling Calculations

The load capacity of an air bearing is product of the bearing pressure times the footprint area. The footprint area is measured across the center of the bearing to the point on each side of the bearing that is tangent to the ground when the bearing is fully pressurized. This tangent point is usually about the center of the lubrication zone (see Fig. 9-4).

Example. Suppose we have an air bearing that is 30 inches in footprint diameter. Using the formula for calculating the area of a circle, πr^2, we obtain an area of 706 square inches ($\pi = 3.1416$). This means we have 706 square inches of effective lifting area.

We wish to know how much air pressure we would need to lift a load of 6,000 pounds.

$$\text{Air pressure} = \frac{\text{Load}}{\text{Area}}$$

$$\text{Air pressure} = \frac{6{,}000 \text{ pounds}}{706 \text{ sq. in.}}$$

$$= 8.5 \text{ psi}$$

Shop air, or the pressure supplied by most factory or plant compressor systems, is usually around 90 psi. Therefore, we can say that we have enough air pressure to do the job. In fact, we should be able to use a smaller air bearing to lift the same load. Let us take a look at this calculation:

$$\text{Area} = \frac{\text{Load}}{\text{Air Pressure}}$$

$$= \frac{6{,}000 \text{ pounds}}{90 \text{ psi}}$$

$$\text{Area} = 66.66 \text{ sq. in. (say 70)}$$

Since area $= \pi r^2$, and π is a constant at 3.1416:

$$
\begin{aligned}
3.1416 \times r^2 &= 70 \\
r^2 &= \frac{70}{3.1416} \\
r^2 &= 22.28 \\
r &= 22.28 \\
r &= 4.7 \text{ (Footprint diameter } = 2r = 9.4 \text{ inches)}
\end{aligned}
$$

Therefore, we would only need to use an air bearing of, say, 10 inches in diameter to do the same job, that is, lift the same load. The difference is only in the air pressures used; that is, a 30-inch bearing with 8.5 psi can lift the same 6,000-pound load that a 10-inch bearing can lift using 90 psi.

D. Wear Characteristics of Air Bearings

Almost all air bearings manufactured today use high-strength elastomers for the flexible, compliant diaphragm element—which is really the only point of wear in the air bearing exclusive of the hose line and a few common fittings. The environment in which the air bearing is used will determine the longevity of the diaphragm. Tears in the fabric caused by scrap iron, metal chips, and other hostile elements will shorten the diaphragm life, although it is possible to patch some fabrics using automobile, tire-type patches.

The abrasiveness of the floor surface, especially unsealed concrete, can cause excessive wear and can shorten the useful life of a diaphragm. It is recommended, therefore, that conditions for use of the air bearing be made as perfect as possible, or else the shortened diaphragm life should be determined beforehand and replacement costs introduced into the calculation to determine the net return on the investment of this capital expenditure.

E. How Many and What Shape Bearings to Use

A simple air bearing unit is like a single wheel in that it can support a heavy load only if the load is centered directly above the wheel. Two air bearing units

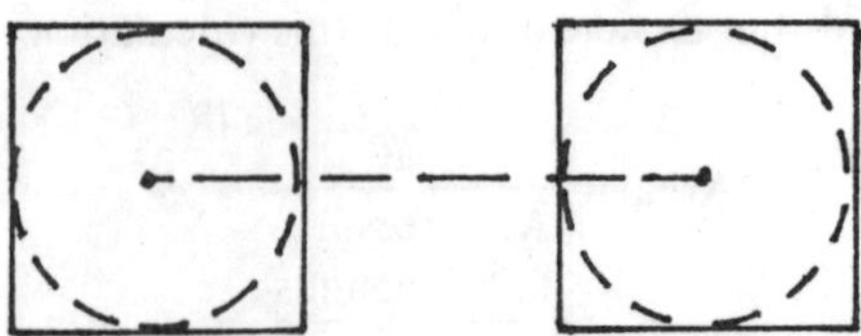

Fig. 9-5. A two-air-bearing combination.

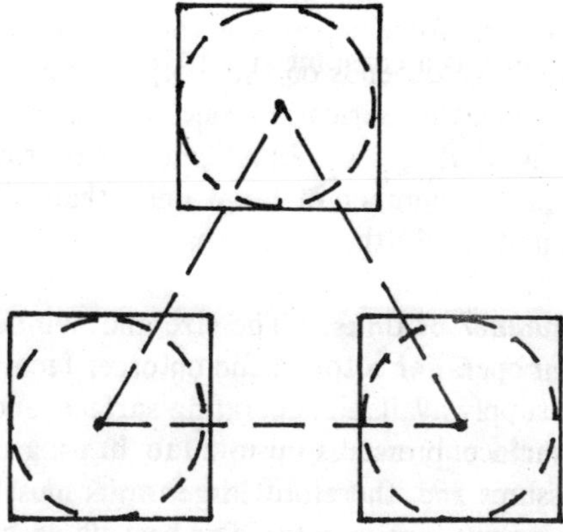

Fig. 9-6. A three-air-bearing combination.

may be used in tandem, but it is important that the center of gravity (C.G.) of the load be directly between the centers of both air bearings (see Fig. 9-5).

Usually, three or more air bearing units are required to provide a stable support for the load (see Fig. 9-6). It is possible, also, to combine air bearing units and caster wheels; for example, one air bearing unit can carry most of the load with two wheels on either side of the load to stabilize it. In general, however, most applications use three or more units for stability and frictionless support.

Where unusually large loads are concerned, it is possible to use many air bearing units, even 10 or 20 units; thus, if each unit is capable of carrying a 10,000-pound load, we would have the capability of sustaining a 100,000- or 200,000-pound load.

Figure 9-7 shows a four-bearing combination. For the combinations shown in Figs. 9-5, 9-6, and 9-7 the C.G. of the load should be as close as possible to the C.G. of the air bearing combination.

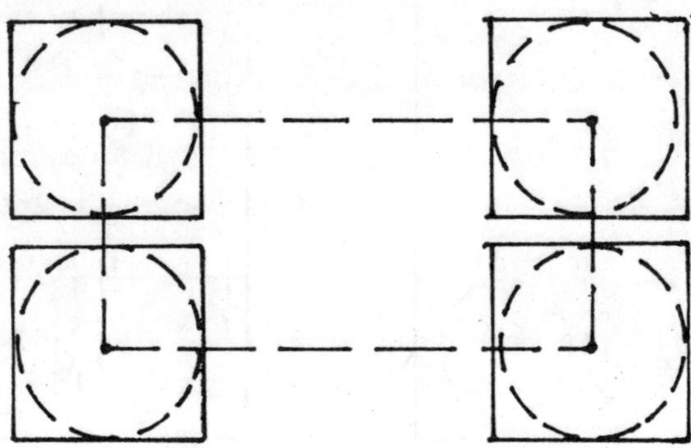

Fig. 9-7. A four-air-bearing combination.

1. Lifting Force. Lifting force depends on the area of the air bearings being employed, and air leakage depends on the footprint perimeter (the perimeter being the distance around the lubrication zone of each air bearing). Therefore, when you are thinking of using a combination of air bearings, it is much more efficient to use a smaller number of large units than a greater number of smaller air bearing units to lift the same capacity.

2. The Size and Number of Units. The size and number of units required for the most efficient operation also depend on other factors, for example, the space available, air supply available, operating surface, and cost.

On a very good surface, pressures up to 20 to 30 psi are practical. On poor surfaces, lower pressures and, therefore, larger units must be used in order to obtain reasonable air consumption rates. The best efficiency is obtained at low operating pressures. Thus, when the air supply is limited, large units should be used.

Size of the units selected may also depend on the air supply that is available. For instance, in the foregoing example, if our 6,000-pound load has to be operated from a blower with a 3-psi output, then the total effective footprint area must measure 2,000 square inches.

3. The Shape of Units to Use. The shape of the air bearing unit is an important consideration. Round, or circular, forms are preferred because they have minimum leakage rates for a given area. Where space is limited, however, racetrack forms are often used. (See Fig. 9-8.)

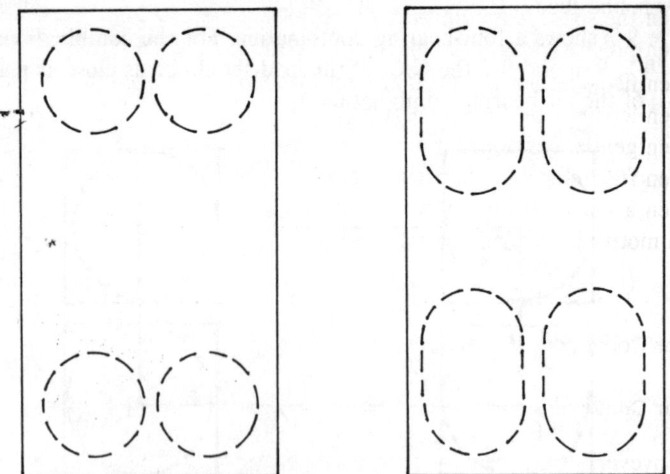

Fig. 9-8. Round and racetrack shapes of air bearing combinations.

F. Practical Applications for Air Bearings

Whenever we think that we have heard of the best application for air bearings, along comes an even more impressive practical solution to a difficult materials handling problem resolved by means of these bearings. A stadium in Hawaii with immense grandstands is moved by the use of air bearings. Dies are placed into machine tools by the use of air bearings. Steel is transferred from bay to bay in a factory using these air handling methods. Pallet storage racks are stowed in a space with only inches between each rack, and they are moved into order selection position on a layer of air.

With the proper design, air bearing units can be sized for any given load capacity, and to work at any air pressure. Untis have been made to work effectively in a range of diameter sizes from 2 inches to 16 feet. In addition, they have operated at pressures of from 1 psi to over 30 psi. Single units have been designed to carry loads up to 70,000 pounds, and multiple, or combination, units have supported loads over 1,000,000 pounds. Their low profile and broad lifting power are their tremendous advantages, as well as their simple construction and maintenance—with the result that their low cost gives them a superb load-bearing capacity per dollar expended.

You should consider air bearings for the solution to materials handling problems under the following circumstances:

1. When there is very little overhead room.
2. When there is very little truss capacity in the building for overhead handling.
3. When the load is too heavy for wheels.
4. When the space is too limited for wheels.
5. When precise spotting, or placement of the load, is required.
6. When floors do not permit high unit loads, or point loading.
7. When low moving force is required.
8. When gentle, cushioned movement is required.
9. When free movement is desired in all horizontal directions.
10. When a hazardous environment precludes the use of internal combustion motive power, or electric motors.

III. In-Floor Conveyors Versus Tractor-Trains

A. In-Floor Conveyors

In-floor conveyors are extremely dependable bulk-handling systems. They are fairly simple to operate depending on the degree of sophistication that is

Warehousing

Freight Handling

Fig. 9-9. A typical towconveyor cart and layout.

Manufacturing

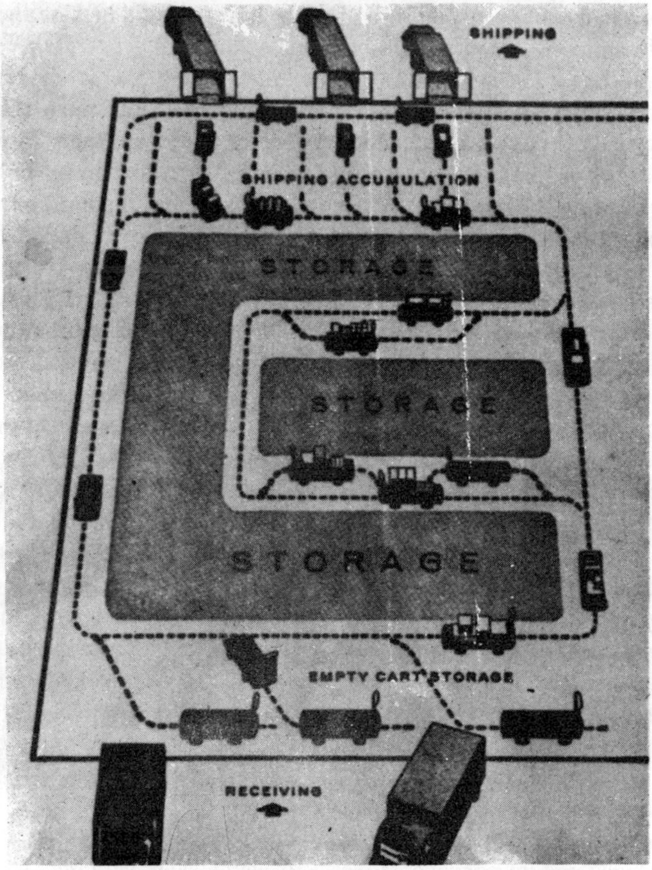

SHIPPING

SHIPPING ACCUMULATION

STORAGE

STORAGE

STORAGE

EMPTY CART STORAGE

RECEIVING

Cart designs and layout variations are virtually unlimited.

designed into the system, and their maintenance cost per ton of material handled is relatively low.

The new, low-profile design of in-floor towconveyors has created additional interest lately because there appears to be an opportunity to interface this type of handling means with the automatic stacker-crane retrieval system. In addition, high-speed sortation systems and conveyorized order-selection operations can be readily integrated into an overall handling system that is computer-controlled, although a computer need not be a part of this integrated system.

In-floor, towline conveyors (towconveyors) have an advantage over fixed-in-place conveyor systems in that they do not block the movement of other types of handling equipment such as forklift trucks, powered carts, and the like.

Towconveyors can also be used for a wide range of assembly-type operations in which the towconveyor cart is hand-pushed through a pallet rack or bin shelving section to fill the material requirements (bill of materials) of a component or the complete assembly, and then the cart is put back on the towline to pass through a whole series of fabrication and assembly operations up to the finished product.

In warehousing operations and in truck or terminal operations, the in-floor towconveyor carts can take incoming materials and route them through the various stages of the plant's processing. For example, incoming merchandise can be placed on the towconveyor cart and be indexed to go to the receiving inspection station or from inspection to a particular storage location.

Order pickers in the storage area can prepare partial or full pallet loads of materials and index the towconveyor cart for packaging, marking, or shipping.

Manufacturers of in-floor towconveyors first used mechanical switching to divert the towconveyor carts. In such a system, a probe is positioned on a bar rack on the front of each cart. A detent on the floor in the path of the cart permits the cart to be diverted to a given spur when the probe strikes the detent to actuate the switch mechanism. Once the cart passes through the switch, the detent returns to its "ready" position, in order to trigger the next diversion. By placing detents in the floor in relation to the cart probe position, it is possible to index each cart for different spurs. These mechanical switching systems are still available, but the main type of cart switching used is electro-mechanical switching, in which magnetic probes are indexed on the cart either manually or automatically (in more sophisticated systems). The magnetic probes actuate reed switches in the floor that, in turn, actuate the switch mechanism. In magnetic systems using reed switches or proximity switches, the advantage is that the devices are flush with the floor surface and do not protrude from the surface as does the mechanical detent.

Most of the in-floor towconveyor systems are on one level, as in trucking terminals and warehouses in single-story buildings. In recent years, however, hospitals have used towconveyors to service several levels, with the towconveyor cart automatically positioned in a specially equipped elevator and programmed to discharge at any given floor and work station by automatic indexing. A few other towconveyor installations have been made in multi-story buildings and operate more or less in the same manner as their hospital counterparts.

B. Towconveyor Carts

Surprisingly, the towconveyor cart may represent the most significant element of cost in this type of handling system. For example, a specially designed cart may cost anywhere from $400 to $1,000 each; so if the system employs 500 carts, the cost is $200,000 to $500,000 for carts alone.

The basic towline cart is an off-the-shelf unit. The various attachments used to make it a towconveyor cart give the designer a chance to put it together. Its elements are: a basic four-wheel cart with a bumper-stop device that picks up the towpin when the towconveyor line, or spur, becomes loaded and the carts queue up; a front end probe or indexing device; and a towpin that can be lifted to disengage the cart from the dog in the in-floor, towconveyor chain (see Fig. 9-9).

There are many variations of carts, from simple steel frameworks to vehicles with elaborate fixtures for assembly, welding, or fabrication. Some carts have fork pockets to permit them to be removed from the towconveyor line and transported to various operations by forktruck. Other carts have shelving or elaborate superstructures including such accessories as product hangers. Even trash containers can be placed on the towconveyor line to improve trash and dunnage disposal and to improve plant housekeeping in general.

C. Towconveyor Tracks—Conventional Versus Low-Profile

As already mentioned, there are two distinctly different types of towconveyor tracks. Both types use forged track links, but there the difference ends because the low-profile track uses the slider principle, whereas the deep track uses a roller type of chain design. The low-profile requires a depth of 3 to 4½ inches, depending on the manufacturer. The deep track requires anywhere from 7 to 13 inches, also depending on which manufacturer's track you intend to use. (See Fig. 9-10).

The manufacturer of the towconveyor will provide such important system features as chain clean-out pits, automatic chain lubricators, and chain take-ups.

Chain clean-out pits are needed because dirt and debris have a tendency to settle into the track groove which is approximately 1 inch wide. A maintenance requirement, therefore, is that the clean-out boxes be emptied periodically.

The chain is lubricated automatically by conventional spray and/or brush applicators. This provision is a must in order to keep the frictional drag of the chain—whether it be the slider or the roller type—to a bare minimum and to

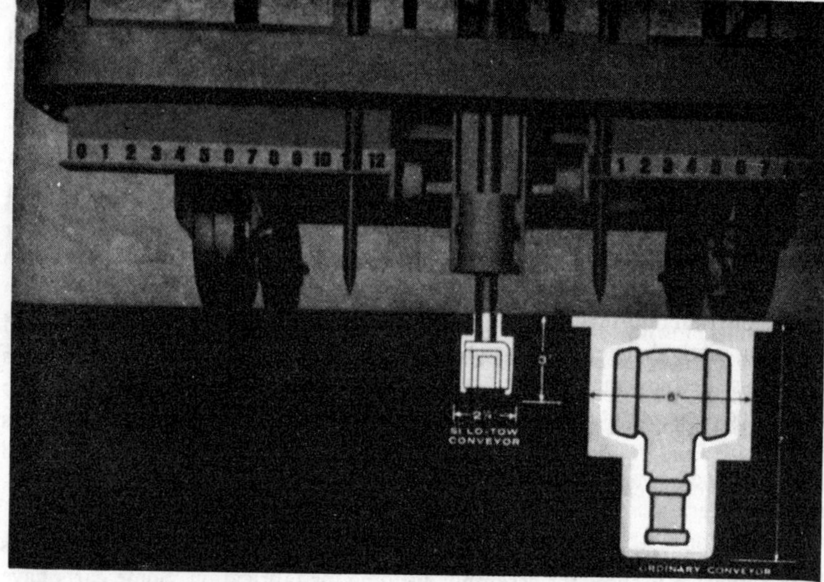

Fig. 9-10. Conventional and low-profile track configurations.

reduce chain wear. Regardless of the lubrication system, there will be chain wear; thus every system will have a take-up mechanism, so that as the chain wears it will be compensated for in the take-up device. During the first few months of the run-in period, a large amount of take-up will be required. Eventually, however, the chain stretch will settle down to a rather small amount requiring less and less take-up.

Motor pits are strategically located by the manufacturer to help balance the chain loading. The user should never attempt to specify the location of the motor pits because all sorts of erratic movements of the conveyor chain will result from poor pit placement. Pulsing and hunting in the chain system sometimes occur when more than one motor drive is used on large installations. This requires the synchronization of motors and should be left strictly to the manufacturer; however, good functional specifications should make it possible to obtain a satisfactory installation.

D. Tractor-Trains (Driverless Tractors and Conventional)

Take one or more four-wheeled warehouse trailers, put couplers on them and hook them up to a forklift truck or a standard tow-tractor, and you have a tractor-train. Almost all forklift truck manufacturers will say that their forklift trucks are not designed for towing; but why are some of these trucks equipped with towing pintles? The answer is obvious: The same operator can thus tow the load to a storage or use point, uncouple the forklift truck from the trailer, and put the load away. This is an effective and efficient use of manpower and equipment.

It is true, of course, that the conventional forklift truck is not designed primarily for towing; but if you have one to four trailers and the loads are within the drawbar pull of the forklift truck, there is certainly nothing to prevent you from utilizing this effective handling method.

Large warehouses and manufacturing plants that move a great number of unit loads daily, whether from incoming receiving or outgoing shipping operations, or from interplant or interbuilding handling, require some form of mass handling method. The tractor-train is an economical way of handling this type of large-scale movement of materials.

It is possible to interface the tractor-train with assembly operations, order picking operations, and the more sophisticated stacker-crane retrieval systems, in all of their many forms up to and including process-control, computer-directed operations.

In addition to the manned tow tractor there is the driverless tractor, which is essentially a battery-powered tow tractor with additional electronic gear on board that permits it to follow a wire emitting a low frequency signal. The wire can be taped to the floor, or it can be buried in a shallow saw cut in the floor. Feedback built into the electronic circuitry keeps it on the wire path; and block signals at various intervals permit it to start and stop automatically, and to wait at each stop for a prescribed length of time, or to wait until it is restarted on its course.

Built-in safety measures stop the vehicle if it strays, or is inadvertently jarred from its path. If the tow tractor encounters an obstacle in its path, it will also stop completely until the obstacle is removed.

Driverless tractors are ideally suited to environments where good housekeeping prevails. If trash and debris accumulate along the drive path, there is usually a great deal of downtime. In addition, if the tractor must traverse an open space between two buildings, the operation is usually very precarious and haphazard, especially if the weather becomes cold, wet, or snow–ice, as in the northern United States during the winter months. If the climate is relatively dry and fairly constant, that is, without sharp temperature variations, then driverless tractors can do very well in performing their particular functions.

In certain types of warehousing, a properly maintained driverless tractor operation can save a company a good deal of money in comparison to the manually operated tow tractor. However, there are other factors that must be regarded in considering a driverless system versus a manned one, not the least of which is the extra skill required on the part of the maintenance department in maintaining the additional electronic components of the driverless vehicle.

Automatic loading and unloading of tow carts can be accomplished with the driverless tractor as well as with the manned tow tractor. Conveyorized platforms on the tow carts and a method for indexing the train through the various stops, plus suitable powerized conveyors or rams at each pick-up and deposit station, are part of the required equipment. This additional mechanization requires computer inputs and remote terminals with which to tie the whole system together.

IV. Sortation and Dispatching Systems

A. High-Speed Sorting

The art of sorting has advanced rapidly in the past 15 to 20 years. Various manufacturers claim sortation speeds of 6,000 to 12,000 peices per hour. In terms of pieces per minute, these cyclic rates amount to an astounding 100 to 200 pieces per minute.

The productivity increases obtainable with high-speed sorting make it possible to return the capital investment in a little over a year in some applications. In addition, the sorting systems that are now available make it practical to convey anything from cantaloupes to steros at a safe, gentle speed. In the Logan Sortation system, for example, the packages slide from belt to chute (see Fig. 9-11). Packages speed along on individual trays on this conveyor. Minicomputers control the tracking and tilting, permitting the merchandise to slide into an unlimited number of sorting positions. In addition to increases in sorting productivity, it is possible to gain up to 50% in floor space.

B. Control Memories

Another innovation provided by the Logan Co., is a solid state memory control for modernizing existing tilt-tray sorters or belt diverter installations. In this system the memory control accepts commodity and destination information from a keyboard, processes it, tracks the merchandise to its destination, and actuates tilting trays or diverters to accomplish the sortation. This memory control unit is compatible with either low- or high-speed sorting; it can be used in automatic or manual loading systems; and it can be interfaced with minicomputers for code translation or the generation of the type of statistics that falls under the heading of management information.

A number of other conveyor controls have been developed in recent years. One of the earliest of the means devised for indexing conveyors was used by the Post Office Department in package sorting in the mid-1950s. It consisted of a rotary wheel with pins in its perimeter. Each pin was analogous to a section of the conveyor, and the rotating motion of the wheel corresponded to the speed of the conveyor in a preset ratio. We have come a long way from the analog computer to the present digital type of correspondence in conveyor indexing.

Fig. 9-11. Example of Tilt-Tray Sorting Conveyor. Courtesy the Logan Company, Louisville, Kentucky.

For example, consider the way in which memory can be implanted in the present-day belt conveyor. There is a conveyor belt impregnated with ferrous metal particles throughout its length. As a carton or piece part passes over a "write" unit, an operator at a keyboard can punch in the "address" of the carton. The carton is transported to its particular destination, passing over a number of "read" stations as it travels. Each "read" station has its own code. The specific "read" station magnetically senses the address in the belt conveyor as it passes this point and closes a circuit that actuates a ram, diverter, gate, or some such device. The reliability of this type of memory control far surpasses any of the less sophisticated methods for indexing a conveyor.

Of course, there are a number of other conveyor memory controls. Some have photo-electric scanners that read retro-reflective tape stuck to each package; others use a multi-colored strip such as Identicon, or Computer Identics. These are similar to the scanning used in railroad freight car identification and classification.

C. Applying Systems Concepts to Sorting Problems

As emphasized repeatedly, our goal should be to apply the systems approach to materials handling. First we must define the problems pertaining to sortation; then we go backward in the chain of handling events in order to obtain the greatest value for the company's materials handling dollar.

For example, the materials handling engineer should be prepared to consult with the purchasing and inventory control departments because purchase quantity, delivery schedules, and the way the material is packaged all have a direct effect on the productivity of materials handling, and thus affect costs. In addition, inventory policies affect the number of times material is handled and the how and where of storage.

The type of packaging used very often determines the type of handling equipment to be employed, as well as the time necessary to unload the carrier and put the material into storage or transport it to the point of use. Whether the package can be handled by conveyor, and how much standardization of packaging can be obtained, are two matters that should be resolved by the materials handling engineer if large-scale mechanization is involved. Also, many double handlings can be avoided if skid heights of vendor packs are compatible with the equipment to be used—that is, when forklift trucks or pallet jacks are employed.

Paraphrasing the definition of industrial engineering: "Materials handling is concerned with the design, improvement, and installation of integrated systems of people, materials, and equipment." To this we should add the phrase "properly controlled," or, more explicitly, "wtih controls built into the system to provide feedbacks to let us know how well the system is working." Therefore, in applying the systems concept to sorting problems, one should try to observe a step-by-step program, as outlined in the following paragraphs.

1. Organize the Objectives. Organize and define the problem so that the objectives of the systems design are clearly in mind. It is helpful to make as precise a statement as possible concerning these objectives.

Studying this statement will permit us to see more clearly the scope of the problem, and it will suggest a tentative array of design specifications.

At this time, also, a schedule of events should be prepared in order to draw up a Pert Chart, or Gantt Chart, of the various steps involved in the systems concept.

2. Get Basic Data—Measure. In reviewing the systems design specifications, basic data will be required. For example, in studying the receiving platform operations as part of the integrated plan, some of the data that would be required would consist of truck arrival and departure times. This information can be obtained from the truck register or log that should be kept in the receiving department. Weights, pieces per hour, total number of units, and so forth, may also be required for a clear definition of the problem. Thus, we can say that an important component of systems design is measurement.

There are several reasons why this is important. Primarily, however, if the operation or function is sufficiently complex, then it may be an important area for cost reduction.

Work standards or elemental time standards are often required in order to obtain a better grasp of what is being accomplished in various departments with the available resources of personnel and equipment.

The measure of work performed before the change takes place is important in justifying the change and in comparing results with the cost of the change.

3. Study the Relationship Among Subsystems. After the problems have been defined (Step No. 1), the various subgroups or subsystems will become apparent.

It is necessary to determine how the departments or functions are related.

Flow charts showing the actual paths of various activities, parts movements, and the like, can be used in an analysis of plant operations.

At this point, a decision is made concerning each of the subsystems on the basis of whether or not it will attain the desired objectives of the program specifications.

If there are conflicts in subsystems, then this is the opportunity to revise or replace a subsystem so that a logical whole is finally derived.

4. Optimize and Obtain the Least Cost. Find the through-put cost of the system, compare this with present costs, and then keep refining the system, if possible, to obtain the least cost.

Some compromising may be necessary, at this stage, in order to accomplish the objective of systems optimization at least cost.

(In Chapter 18 we discuss systems simulation techniques that could be employed at this point in the study. Systems simulation permits us to crank into the systems study a wide range of figures in order to simulate what happens under various conditions of operation.)

5. Coordinate with All Affected Departments. In promoting the most effective program possible, it is necessary to get all of the affected departments into the act at a very early date and to keep them advised of all developments that are pertinent to the project.

Since the total systems approach sometimes cuts across departmental lines, it is absolutely essential to get the cooperation of these departments by doing a good selling job.

6. Install the System. The optimized system is now ready to begin the first step in its installation. It is advisable to prepare bid specifications and obtain a suitable number of quotations (at least three) if equipment is involved. In Step

No. 1, above, it was suggested that Pert or Gantt Charts be used to schedule the various phases of the project. Budget approvals based upon the project costs, design, installation, test, and debug should allow following a prescribed sequence in order to keep the project on its course.

7. Test and Debug. After installation, the system and its equipment must pass acceptance tests, and be debugged, if required.

8. Measure. An accurate indication of the results of the installation will be obtained after the shakedown has been completed. At this final stage measure the performance of the system through work standards, through-put measurement, or work sampling, and determine how closely these results compare with the earlier measurements.

Another advantage of this type of measurement—besides its indicating how well we have accomplished our target objectives—is that if the project is shown to be successful, it will be easier to sell management on future systems applications.

EXERCISE NO. 9

1. Objectives in mechanizing any operation usually include the following:
 1. ____________________
 ____
 2. ____________________
 ____
 3. ____________________
 ____
 4. ____________________
 ____

2. One of the more important tools in the field of physical distribution is the ____________.

3. A cathode ray tube (CRT) display is part of a system for transmitting ____________ from the point where it is stored to the point where it is required.

4. Scale weight counting is used to provide precise measurements or ____________ of materials for inventory control purposes.

5. Air film handling uses very ____________ quantities of air.

6. Air film handling was first developed by ____________ ____________.

7. Three manufacturers of air-film devices are:
 1. ____________________
 2. ____________________
 3. ____________________

8. When air enters the air-film bag and rushes into the plenum chamber, the load is ____________.

9. As air is forced into the plenum chamber it tends to escape around the perimeter of the bag. This area is called the ______ ______.

10. Problem: With a footprint area of 200 square inches and air pressure at 5 psi, what load capacity can an air bearing lift? Answer: ______ pounds.

11. In-floor, towline conveyors have an advantage over fixed-in-place conveyor systems in that they do not ______ the movement of other types of handling equipment.

12. In towconveyor systems one of the major elements of cost is the ______.

13. Dirt and debris are minimized or eliminated in towconveyors installations by the use of ______ ______.

14. What happens when towconveyor chains wear, and how do you compensate for this?

______

______

15. Built into each driverless tractor is a device that ______ the vehicle if it strays from its guidance path.

16. In addition to increases in sorting productivity, it is possible to gain ______ ______ by high-speed sorting.

17. Existing tilt-tray or belt diverter installations may be modernized by adding a ______ ______ ______.

18. The first step in applying the systems concept to sorting problems is to ______.

19. A Gantt or Pert Chart should permit us to ______

______

______.

20. When should you obtain measurements in the design of a system?

______

______

______

Chapter 10
Comparative Physiology, Robotic Versus Human Work Station Arrangement

I. MECHANICAL MANIPULATORS (INDUSTRIAL ROBOTS)

A. Introduction

The 1980s may well be named the decade of the industrial robot because great strides have been made in the past decade that have laid the groundwork for the productive application of the industrial robot. In the eighties, most of the companies making industrial robots will have done all of their pioneering work in the 1970s; the economic climate will be conducive to the application of the robot because wage rates will have advanced to the point where it will be easy to justify the use of robots through a return-on-investment basis; the use of industrial robots in hazardous work areas will be gaining greater acceptance; and many of the installations of the 1960s and 1970s that were poorly conceived will have been largely forgotten.

B. Industrial Robots Defined

You may ask why we have entitled this section "Mechanical Manipulators." We have done this intentionally. The term "robot" seems to imply that a mechanism has replaced a "man" in the performance of a particular job function—an idea suggested by some labor unions in the past. Therefore the manufacturing industry has attempted to substitute the term "mechanical manipulator." There is no reason why management in both manufacturing and physical distribution should not use the "industrial robot" designation once the proper climate within the business location has been established. We shall discuss this idea further in this chapter, since it is vital to the success of an industrial robot application.

A robot is different from a "put-and-take" mechanism in that it can be programmed to perform a large number of repeatable functions for one operation (or a series of operations) and then be reprogrammed for a different operation. The robot has a built-in versatility that ordinary tooling such as a "put-and-take" mechanism designed to load and unload a punch press does not possess.

This, then, is the essential difference between mechanization that increases the productivity of an operation and that which eliminates an operator or operators from a particular job.

There are infintiely more applications for industrial robots in manufacturing than in physical distribution, and it is the imagination of the materials handling engineer, alone, that limits the scope of these applications. In physical distribution the palletizing and packaging operations present rather limited applications for the use of industrial robots; if the volume of these materials is sufficient to justify mechanization, uniform package sizes can best be handled by mechanization that does not need to be programmed by punch cards, tape, or computer.

C. Programming the Robot

There are a number of ways to program a robot. The two generic terms applied to this programming are "continuous path" and "point-to-point."

In understanding these methods it is first necessary to examine the properties of a robot. Essentials of a robot are: a stand or base upon which to rest the mechanism, a trunnion about which the mechanism revolves, an arm that can be extended or retracted telescopically, and a hand with which to grasp an object. The hand can be made to have gripping claws, it can have a vacuum pad or pads, it can be equipped with magnets, and so forth.

In the continuous path (CP) method of programming, the business end of the hand can be made to follow a smooth path or contour, rather than move through a series of coordinates. Programming in the CP method is accomplished by manually leading the hand of the robot through the preferred path. The movements, thus described, are recorded in digital form on magnetic tape. When the machine is set up in this manner, it will repeat the path indefinitely, or until reprogrammed.

The total cycle time in the CP method depends on two factors: (1) the length of the magnetic tape employed; and (2) the speed at which the tape playback is operated.

In the point-to-point programming method the hand moves between precise, three-dimensional points that are coordinates on *X, Y,* and *Z* axes (this is similar to locating an object in gun-fire control). As an example, the hand is moved to the desired position from a point of rest, and a button is pushed to establish the location of the position coordinates on a magnetic drum memory system. When it is time to operate the robot, digital encoders provide feedback that is compared to the information stored on the magnetic drum memory unit. As the correct coordinates are reached, the proper hydraulic valves are blocked off.

D. Robot Tooling

The major tooling effort in robot applications takes place in the area of the hands or gripping area. Manufacturers of robots have been especially ingenious in developing this type of tooling because, essentially, the business end of the robot is the customer's primary concern. Robot hands, fingers, or claws (or whatever else is attached to the working end of the device) are extremely important to the success of the robot application. The amount of tension or grasping pressure sometimes must be regulated and controlled on the basis of the fragility of the object to be picked up. Resistance to heat, and impact, corrosion, and the like, all become parameters that the design engineer must take into consideration; however, it is the tremendous versatility of the robot at the business end—the hand—that makes the game worthwhile. This wide range of tooling gives the robot a vast number of applications in the materials handling industry.

In general, there are three main types of hands: (1) grippers or claws that depend on tensile and compressive forces to grasp and hold (these are the mechanical types); (2) the surface-lift types that include magnets and vacuum cups either singly or in multiple units which can be used to lift and position objects that have flat surfaces like sheets of glass or steel, or rectangular solids, blocks, cartons, etc., or cylindrical objects like bar stock; (3) tools such as impact wrenches, spray-painting guns, welding devices for spot or seam welding, and other machines.

The most generally used hand for robotic applications in materials handling usually has fingerlike levers or cams that are parallel and oppose each other very much in the manner of the human hand, where the thumb and fingers work in opposition to each other in order to grasp an object. While humans are limited to two hands and ten fingers, it is possible to equip a robot with any number of hands and fingers to accomplish extremely complex lifting, grasping, rotating, and positioning operations. The reliability of robots today is such that it is possible to perform hundreds of thousands of repetitive oeprations with a positioning reliability of $\pm 1/64$ inch or better.

An example of a mechanical gripper operation is one that transfers a heat-treated crankshaft from a conveyor into a quenching fixture and then unloads the quench fixture and places the crank onto another conveyor.

An example of a surface-lift operation would be the pick-up and transfer of a glass plate from a cooling conveyor to an edge grinding fixture by means of vacuum cups arranged in series. And, from the grinding operation, the robot would transfer the plate glass into a prepared crate for shipping or storage.

Another application for a surface-lifting hand would entail transferring sheet steel from an incoming conveyor into a stamping press, unloading the blanked piece from the press, and positioning the blank on a pallet for the next operation. Logically, a put-and-take device might be employed in this operation if the stamping press were to produce a very large run of parts of one size. In the case of most stamping operations, however, operations are usually of sufficiently short duration in terms of units produced that short runs are the rule rather than the exception. Thus programmable robots can be profitably employed to handle a large variety of different pieces in relatively short runs where it would not be profitable to design and tool up for each run because of the short duration of the run in terms of the number of parts produced.

Examples of robotic applications include the use of welding guns in the now-famous General Motors Lordstown, Ohio, Vega Division, where a battery of Unimate robots on each side of a long conveyor perform a large number of spot welding operations on a body line. The Unimate robot travels a short distance down the moving conveyor performing its welding task, and then returns to its starting position to repeat its operation on the next car body.

The Gilman Company, which is noted for its complex automatic assembly machines, has recently completed an installation for the Ford Motor Company that combines Unimate and Versatran robots in an automatic car body assembly machine. The unit is over one hundred feet long, and the robots perform spot welding operations on the body to frame, top, and side sections to complete a car body automatically.

The range in price for robot applications may vary from a few thousand dollars for fairly simple operations to millions of dollars for some of the automotive applications described above.

E. Robotic Parameters

In a broad, general sense the work "parameters" is used to indicate the number of *variables* involved in a given distribution. If we were to look at the variables involved in the application of industrial robots, we would find that there are approximately four variables in any given application:

1. The weight of the object or objects to be handled.
2. The rate at which handling is to take place, or the cycle time involved.
3. The orientation or position of the part required to be grasped, or the position of its placement.
4. The quantity of objects to be handled in each complete cycle of the robot.

1. The Weight of the Object, or Objects, to be Handled. At the present time, programmable robots are capable of handling items ranging from parts weighing a few grams (ounces) to objects weighing several hundred kilograms—that is, with weights approaching 1,000 pounds.

One weight-related difficulty that occurs when objects are handled by a robot involves deflection. As the object travels from a position close to the pivotal point of the robot and is extended out over several feet, deflection of the arm of the unit becomes a serious concern if the repeatability of the operation is critical. You may remember that we referred to the reliability of positioning a part within a tolerance of ±1/64 inch (that is, 0.0156 inch, or less than two hundredths of an inch). Thus, as a criterion for stiffness, or minimal deflection in the arm, is made a design characteristic for reliability, certain other relationships are established that affect the operation of the robot. A beefed-up (stiffer) arm involves a greater mass of metal to be moved and consequently a reduced cycle time for the robot, or an increased power input. These considerations then affect costs.

2. The Rate at Which Handling Is to Take Place, or the Cycle Time Involved. As indicated above, the weight of the part may have an influence on the cycle time in which the robot performs its task. A good rule of thumb is that if the number of cycles exceeds 15 complete cycles per minute (that is, one complete cycle every four seconds), high-speed mechanization should be considered.

High-speed mechanization requires a considerable capital investment; so for this type of production equipment to be used, the run of parts to be handled must be large and fairly uniform in configuration. For example, in automotive or similar parts production, a single, unchanged (or very slightly changed) part probably can be profitably tooled up if several hundred thousand parts are to be produced.

3. The Orientation or Position of the Part Required to Be Grasped, or the Position of Its Placement. Almost all of the programmable, industrial robots presently on the market are considered to be second-generation robots in the sense that their reliability (repeatability) of position is fairly consistent, and they can be readily programmed to perform rather intricate tasks.

As an example of the intricacy of operations to be performed, the Unimate Corporation has developed a programmed unit in which the robot picks up a wax pattern and alternately dips it into a ceramic slurry and rotates the part to assure a uniform coating of the ceramic material. After this is accomplished, the robot gently transfers the part and carefully orients it into a drying rack. This is the first step in the investment casting process in which the robot uniformly coats the wax pattern after the manner of an extremely skilled artisan. The repeatability of this delicate task is much more presice that would be possible with a human operator, and the elimination of sheer boredom for the operator assures the high quality necessary for part after part.

Because the robot does not have eyes to see with, the program requires that the tray load of wax patterns be properly oriented on a conveyor within the production cycle of the robot. Also, it is necessary that the patterns be oriented in such a fashion that the robot program can always start and finish a tier in the same position; and built into the program is a dwell time when the first tray can be removed automatically and the next tray positioned to repeat the production cycle.

It is necessary, therefore, that any part to be handled by a programmable industrial robot be properly oriented in its position so that the repeatability of a cycle can be maintained. There are many ways of doing this, some very simple and some requiring a fair amount of ingenuity on the part of the engineer. As an example, a machine operator can place a part on a conveyor face up, or face down, or on its side, etc. The conveyor can have pockets to receive the part in only a certain way. Also, guides, gates, and chutes can be used to orient parts. Or, plastic trays with specifically designed cavities can hold parts in a particular way for the robot fingers or vacuum cups to grasp them.

It follows, then, that there is an analogy here to the first law of automation mechanization, which says, "In automation, never let go of the part." In industrial robotics the saying is, "Keep the part oriented properly."

4. The Quantity of Objects to Be Handled in Each Complete Cycle of the Robot In the machine tool industry one of the most important advantages of the complex machining center (where the cost of the equipment is in the $250,000 to $300,000 range and higher) is that a tape-controlled unit has the versatility to handle a number of very short-run production schedules in rapid succession merely by changing the tape program and the fixture within which the part rests.

Thus it is with programmable robots. As indicated above, high-volume parts production may very well lend itself to specially designed mechanization, provided a satisfactory rate of return may be obtained. On the other hand, with short production runs where the set-up times are not critical, programs can be quickly changed and hands and fingers on the robots can be quickly altered to accommodate the new part.

It is sometimes possible to design a hand mechanism with built-in adaptability to a family of parts that is to be produced and can be sensed by the robot. As an example, a photo-electric cell or switch on a conveyor can actuate a subprogram of the robot to handle the new part with different fingers or to rotate it or position it in a different manner, and so forth.

Hand mechanisms can be designed to grasp one part or a number of parts simultaneously. As indicated above, however, the orientation of the parts becomes extremely critical in this phase of the operating cycle.

F. The General Electric Company Man-Mate

Although the GE CAMS device (Cybernetic Anthropomorphous Machine System) is not in the strictest sense of the term an industrial robot, it deserves mention at this point because of its functions. The CAMS or Man-Mate unit as it is called is a means for amplifying the reach, grasp, and weight-lifting capacity of the human body through electro-hydraulic and mechanical devices. The machine at one time was programmed and run in an automatic mode by computer; therefore, when this model is employed, it can be said to be an industrial robot. Most of the Man-Mate applications, however, are with a man aboard as can be seen below in Figs. 10-9 and 10-10.

The chief advantages of the Man-Mate are that:

1. It can be remotely positioned to remove the operator from a hazardous or hostile environment. In fact, the operator can be completely enclosed in an air-conditioned enclosure, which thus frees him from extremes of temperature or toxic dusts, or other pollutants.
2. It can extend the reach, grasp, and weight-lifting capabilities of the human by many times. Man-Mates are available with 20 to 30 feet of reach, and a grasp and weight-lifting capability thus far of up to 12,000 pounds.
3. It can repeat a production cycle as long as the operator, who is comfortably seated at his console, so desires. The operator's control arm grasps a pistol grip that controls the oepration of the Man-Mate so that any command of the operator can be carried out as required.

The Man-Mate is not in direct competition with industrial robots, as such, but it has a range of activity that adds interest and diminishes the fatigue attendant upon certain tasks when performed by humans unaided by the Man-Mate machine.

For example, at the General Electric, Columbia Park, Maryland, Appliance Division an operator with a CAM-100 Man-Mate unit is centrally located at a point where refrigerators and electric ranges on three assembly conveyors converge. The operator, who controls the Man-Mate, sorts the appliances according to a number code, lifts them from the incoming conveyors, and places them on several warehouse conveyors. The warehouse conveyors transport the appliances from the assembly building over an enclosed conveyor bridge to a warehousing and distribution center building.

Another very successful Man-Mate application was made in a foundry shakeout pit operation. This particular job function was dusty, dirty, and hot because the operators had to stand over the shakeout conveyor as the castings were dumped onto it. Their task was to knock off sprues, gates, and risers, and to separate the castings from the scrap and load the castings onto one monorail carrier and the scrap iron onto another carrier. This obviously difficult job situation created a large amount of employee turnover and absenteeism. Because it was considered such a poor job by the employees, it was always hard to find anyone to assign to this task except the newest employees, and the morale problems it presented were a constant source of irritation to the plant management.

The foundry management spent approximately $150,000 to install a GE Man-Mate with an air-conditioned cab. Fingers were designed for the beefed-up hand so that the operator could knock off sprues, gates, and risers and perform the sorting task with absolutely none of the hardships formerly endured. The GE Man-Mate replaced three operators; whereas the prior operation had required two operators on each of three shifts, now only one operator was required per shift. It eliminated all of the employee absenteeism and turnover, and the job—instead of being difficult to fill—now has a waiting list of employees who want it. The payback on this installation was nearly three years, but with its many intangible benefits it was hailed as an extremely worthwhile investment.

G. Preparing the Climate for the Application of Industrial Robots

1. Displaced Workers, Management, and Unions. It is not enough, when considering the application of industrial robots, simply to prepare a justification that includes a return-on-investment study, although such a course is necessary in any proposal involving the investment of capital. One of the essential ingredients to the successful realization and accomplishment of the objectives of this form of mechanization is that a climate conducive to the application be established on all levels of the enterprise.

You may convince your management that an industrial robot(s) will make money for the company; however, if the departmental foreman in which the robot is to be installed is not in tune with you, you may rest assured that your project will founder on the rocks of his dislike or disinterest.

Also, if the workers in the department feel that ultimately they will be replaced by similar types of industrial robots, you will also have difficulty in gaining acceptance for your brainchild. Sabotage—either willful or through neglect—is one of the silent means by which workers take revenge on the materials handling engineer who is "trying to put one over on them."

It is recommended, then, that the channels of communication be opened as soon as you have received a go-ahead signal from management. If the return-on-investment study clearly shows that workers will be displaced by the industrial robot, it is advisable to find other jobs in the plant that will satisfy the requirements of the displaced workers. As you attempt to increase productivity by greater mechanization (that is, through the use of industrial robots), no worker should lose his job with your company because of this mechanization. With good planning, attrition in various departments will take up the slack of the labor surplus due to the robot application.

By balancing displaced workers with "new hires," the imbalance caused by the introduction of the industrial robot can be corrected. And, the assurance of management that it will be a policy of the company to retain employees will go a long way toward improving the climate between labor and management where technological unemployment is concerned.

There must be good communications with the labor unions and labor officials. Before an order is placed for robotic hardware, it is advisable to communicate your plans to the union officials, and you should keep them well informed. Taking a field trip to the robot manufacturer's plant with some of the union people might be a good way to relieve some of the tensions, concern, and uncertainty caused by the proposed project.

2. Plant Engineering and Maintenance. The selling job that has to be done by the materials handling engineer does not stop at labor's door, or at management's door—unless we include plant engineering and maintenance. What is to be done with the industrial robot after the robot manufacturer's installation crew have gone and you find yourself the proud possessor of a robot? You can start it, and stop it, and even program it to do new tricks, but when it starts to make that funny buzzing sound, and maybe a little red idiot light starts to blink, what then?

The recommended way to forestall emergencies is to tune the plant engineering and maintenance department into your plans just like any other department, and prepare them as members of the team. Factory training prior to the installation of the robot is an excellent way to prepare the climate for this type of mechanization. Also, the purchase price should include a complete set of manuals, wiring diagrams, and other necessary instructions, particularly those concerning the preventive maintenance schedules.

A spare parts provisioning kit may also be in order, depending on the type and complexity of the robot. Usually the best way to learn about the peculiarities of any robot is to visit a plant that uses the manufacturer's robot in a manner that is similar to one's own application. Certainly, the more that is known about the robot before its installation, the more successful the application will become.

Figures 10-1 through 10-10 illustrate some of the characteristics of robots described in the above text. Please study the illustrations carefully in order to be able to answer all questions pertaining to them.

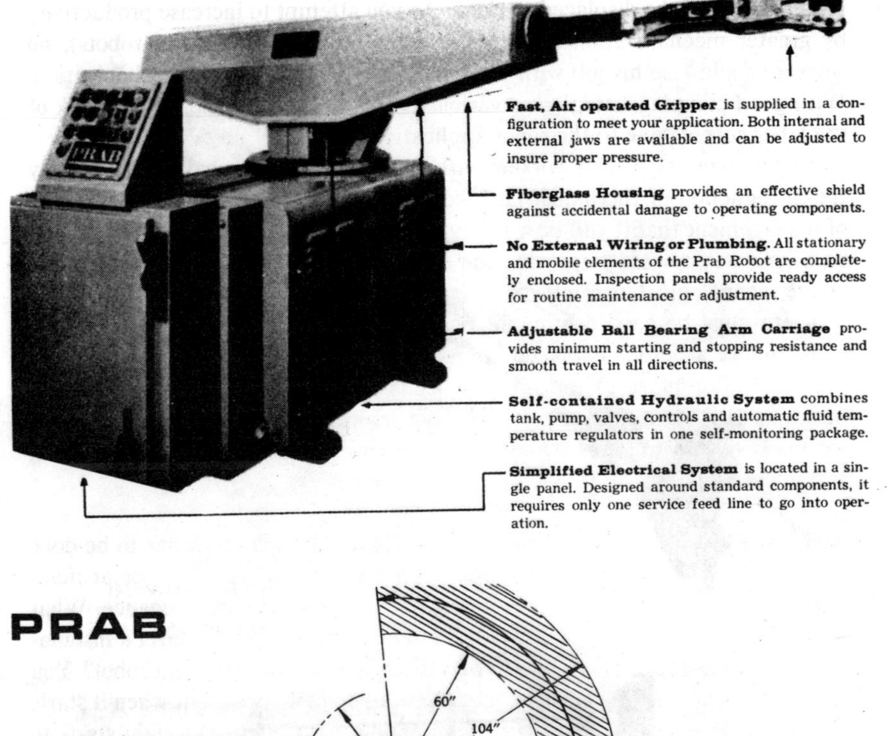

Fig. 10-1. Configuration of a PRAB Industrial Robot.

These controls provide greater flexibility for the Auto-Place units by: (1) coordinating the actions of Auto-Place and other equipment; (2) sequencing Auto-Place actions and (3) monitoring Auto-Place actions by means of air lights which allow for visual detection of any system malfunction. Additional advantages such as ease of programming, minimizing of downtime and resistance to transient or stray electrical signals, all contribute to the overall economy of Auto-Place.

Fig. 10-2. An AUTO-PLACE unit provides up to five actions.

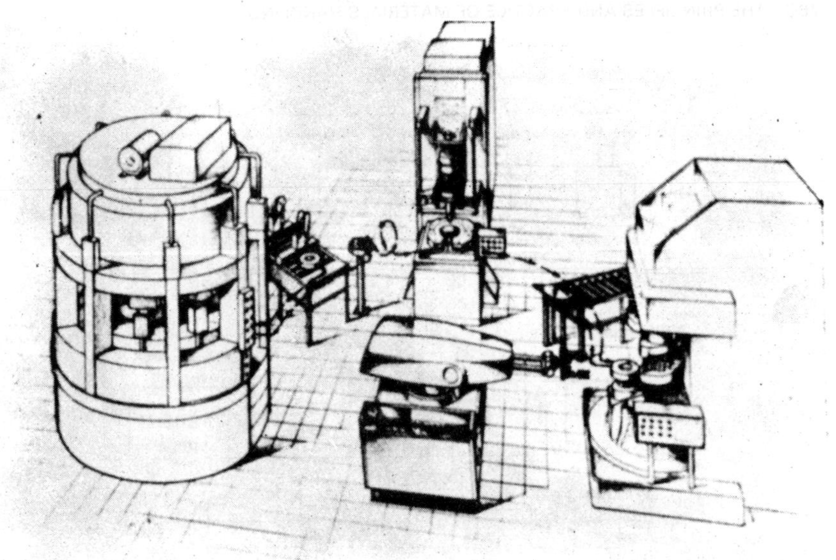

One of the longest-standing applications consists of the 2000 Series Unimate in a machine loading operation for the production of differential ring gears.

APPLICATION DESCRIPTION This operation was originally set up using a model 1900 Unimate industrial robot. When the 2000 Series became available, a 2000 replaced the 1900 in the same operation. A second 2000 Series Unimate was installed in a duplicate operation to handle additional production requirements.

In this operation, several ring gear forgings of different weights and diameters are processed through a Bullard Mult-Au-Matic vertical lathe, then a Colonial broach, and finally through an R & B multi-station, multi-spindle drill. The sequence starts with the Unimate unloading the multi-spindle drill and depositing the finished part on the output conveyor. Unimate rotates to the broach and takes the completed part from there to the multi-spindle drill, then rotates to a hold table and takes a part from there, inverts it, and loads the Colonial broach. The Unimate next positions itself in front of the vertical lathe and processes the ring gear from the Bullard to the hold table.

The last operation in the process is the transfer of forging blanks from the input conveyor, transferring them to the Bullard vertical lathe for the first machining operation. The Unimate is then ready to start the whole sequence again. Sixty pieces per hour are worked through these three machines.

A leading manufacturer of refractories has installed a system for loading refractory bricks into oven cars. This turn-key system, supplied by Unimation Inc., includes a 4000 Series Unimate industrial robot with special tooling, conveyors, and an oven car indexer-positioner.

Fig. 10-3. A Unimate industrial robot work station arrangement.

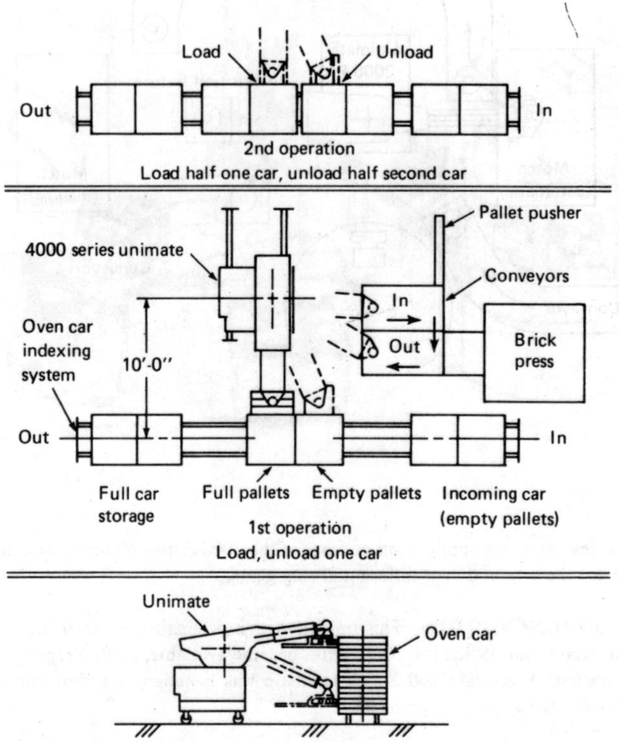

APPLICATION DESCRIPTION Formed bricks are ejected out of a press and pushed onto a metal pallet on a conveyor. A single pallet and brick can weigh up to 75 pounds. Loaded pallets are accumulated in groups of three and picked up by the Unimate with its special tooling for loading into an oven car. The oven cars are divided in half, each of which has twelve shelves for holding six pallets at each level. Since the Unimate robot handles three pallets at a time, it goes to each level twice.

In the first operation one half of the oven car is empty while the other half contains empty pallets. The Unimate picks up three full pallets from the output conveyor and loads them into the proper position in the empty half of the oven car. It then goes to the other half of the oven car, picks up three empty pallets, and deposits them onto the input conveyor. Picking up three more full pallets, the Unimate loads them behind the first three in the oven car. The next set of full pallets will be loaded at the next lower level. This sequence continues until one half of the car is loaded with full pallets while the other half is completely empty. The Unimate robot then proceeds to perform the second operaton.

The oven car indexing system shuttles the half full, half empty car and an oven car filled with only empty pallets, into the proper position. The Unimate robot now loads full pallets into the second half of the first car while removing empty pallets from the first half of the second car. When the second operation is completed, the Unimate robot programs back to the first operation, while the fully loaded car is indexed into position for removal by a forklift truck.

Fig. 10-4. A Unimate industrial robot loading and unloading bricks.

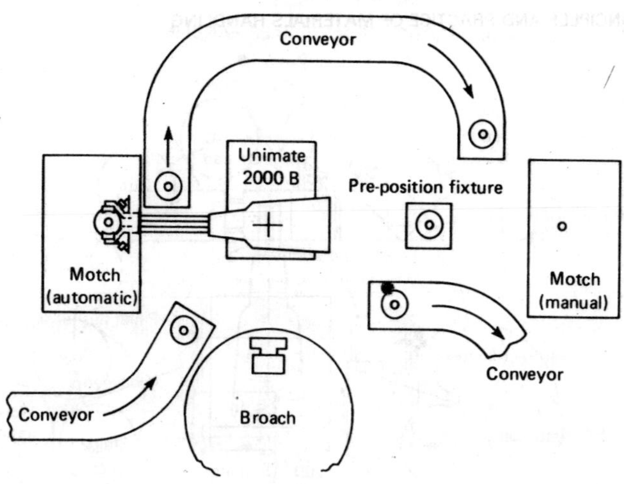

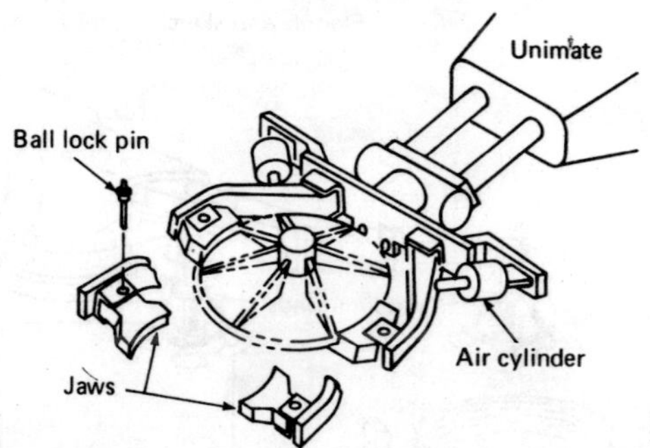

In this machining center a Unimate is used to load and unload an automatic chucking machine and a broaching machine. Differential case castings are transferred to and from conveyors, and from a pre-position fixture.

APPLICATION DESCRIPTION A 2000B, 5 degree Unimate with a special hand is used to load and unload machine tools. The parts being handled are differential case castings which are 12¼″ dia. and 15¼″ dia. weighing 50 to 70#. The special hand picks up a part from a pre-position fixture with the hand gear train wrist and hand straight out. With wrist bent down, the part is loaded into a broaching machine. The Unimate then turns to a Motch and Merryweather vertical chucker and unloads a part from it to a conveyor. Picking up a part from another conveyor, the Unimate loads a Motch, then turns to unload a part from the broaching machine to a conveyor. The part is placed on the pre-position fixture by the oeprator of the manual Motch.

HAND DESCRIPTION For this application the hand is a set of jaws mounted on pivots on a support plate, with carbide tipped inserts for gripping the part. The hand is positioned over the part with the jaws open and the "pancake-type" air cylinders close the jaws, thereby gripping the part. Although the hand is attached to the swivel cylinder of a single acting, hardened hand gear train, it can be readily attached to the housing if swivel motion is not needed.

Fig. 10-5. A Unimate industrial robot used to load and unload machine tools; also, a special "hand" mechanism.

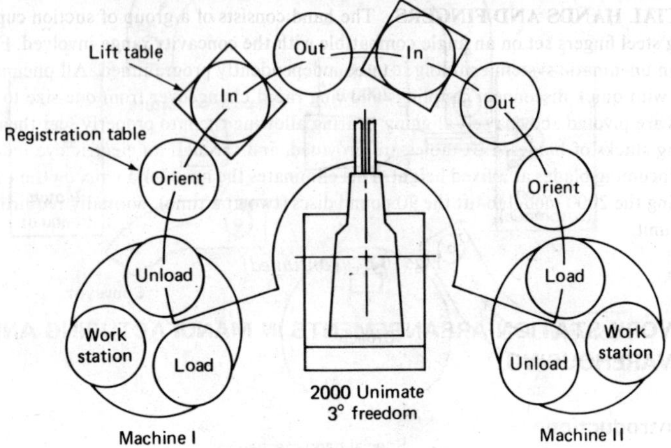

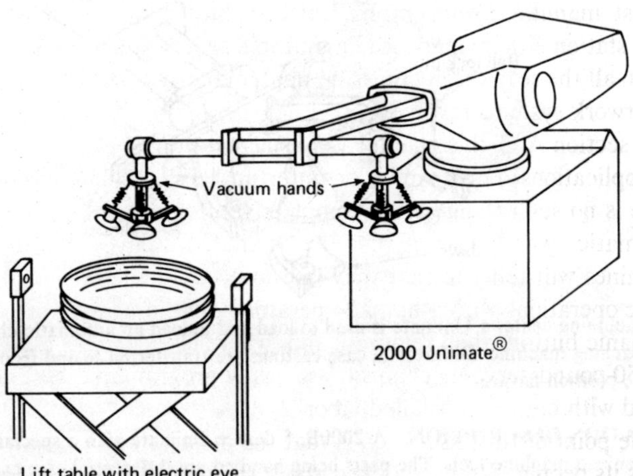

When one of the nation's leading manufacturers decided to automate the grinding of their harrow discs, they contacted Unimation Inc. After careful study of the operation they recommended a Series 2000 Unimate industrial robot with three degrees of freedom, and equipped with a special vacuum air double hand.

APPLICATION DESCRIPTION **In operation, the Unimate robot's hand blows off excess dust from the blade and vacuum lifts it to a registration table where it is oriented, allowing the Unimate robot to regrip in a centered position. This is necessary because incoming stacks of blades can lean as much as 1″ from a centered position. Haivng oriented the blade, the Unimate robot loads Grinder #1 with its left hand, and removes a finished blade with the right hand. The robot then deposits the finished blade at the nearest output station, where it picks up another from the incoming lift table. After orienting this blade and loading Grinder #2, the finished blade is removed and the cycle repeated.**

Fig. 10-6. A Unimate industrial robot 2000 shown in a vacuum lifting application.

SPECIAL HANDS AND FINGERS The hand consists of a group of suction cups attached to spring steel fingers set on an angle compatible with the concavity range involved. Each hand has its own pneumatic system enabling it to be independently programmed. All pneumatic lines are fitted with quick disconnect couplings allowing rapid changeover from one size to another. The hands are pivoted above a self-aligning bearing allowing them to properly seat themselves on the leaning stacks of blades. Lift tables are provided, and through an electric eye indexing system, keep incoming blades at a fixed height. This eliminates the need for a wrist on the Unimate robot, allowing the 2000 model to lift the 90 pound discs (two at a time), normally requiring the heavier 4000 unit.

Fig. 10-6. *(continued)*

II. WORK STATION ARRANGEMENTS IN MANUFACTURING AND WAREHOUSING

A. Introduction

The work station is the place where business profits are generated. From the largest manufacturing or physical distribution facility to the smallest—the work station either singly or in a multiple grouping becomes the complex about which all the service functions, computer controls, hardware and software, and paperwork systems revolve.

In section A of this chapter we discussed the industrial robot and several of its applications. Fortunately, or unfortunately, depending on one's viewpoint, there is no such thing as the completely automatic factory, or the completely automatic warehouse. Even the manufacturers of automatic assembly machines will tell you that they like to break up a series of completely automatic operations with a human operator—that is, someone capable of pushing the panic button when required; and, where else can you obtain as economical a "150-pound servo-mechanism* so easily programmed that can be mass-produced with entirely unskilled labor"?

The point of this discussion is that the most valuable resource any company has is its people. We have talked about the robot and its application, preparing the climate for robot installation, and so forth. In most plants and warehouses we spend more time, usually, in justifying capital dollar expenditures than we do in training workers properly, or in seeing to it that they have the proper tools, place, or environment in which to work.

All too often, an employee who is barely more than five feet tall is working at a conveyor or bench that is almost at (his or her) shoulder level—sometimes more than four feet from the ground. Light levels may be ridiculously low for some types of work. In some activities, workers stand directly on concrete for their entire shift. Anyone who has stood on concrete day after day without

*A human being!

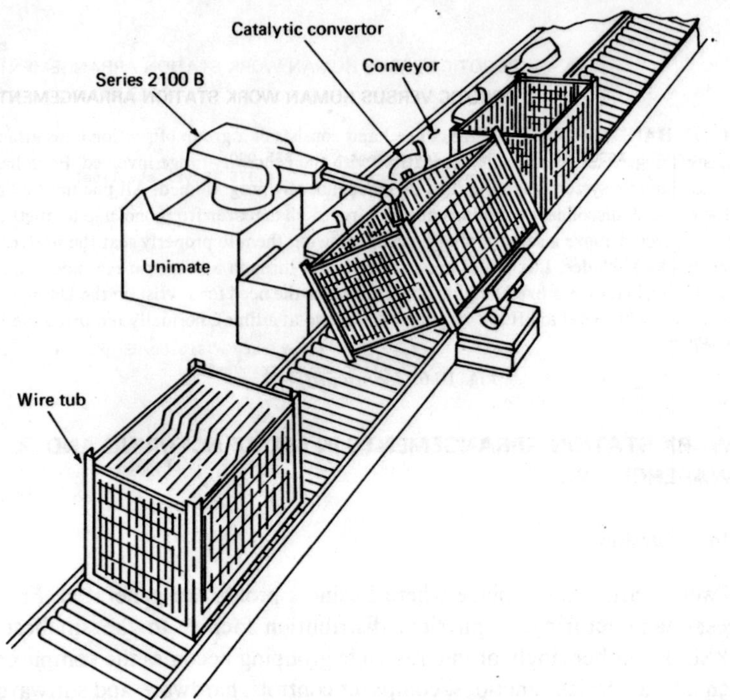

A crash program was needed. Fast delivery—ease of installation—and an automated device to keep pace with the high speed conveyor delivering up to six hundred 45# catalytic convertors per hour—palletizing the convertors into standard industrial wire tubs. Manual loading was impractical. Hard automation and long delivery after design—unprofitable. Solution—the Unimate industrial robot.

APPLICATION DESCRIPTION **A 2100B Series, 5 axis industrial robot with inexpensive hand tooling was used to stack 58 catalytic convertors into wire cage-type transports in proper preprogrammed sequence. These are placed accurately and in the proper position in every tote cage. The convertors are fed from a transport onto a small conveyor which has the capability of tilting the conveyor at a 72° angle for Unimate pick up. It then delivers the convertor to the Unimate, signals the Unimate to pick the convertor up and place it into its proper location. Accuracy of placement must be maintained as convertor surfaces are critical to final finished product. The only difficulty experienced in programming was the odd shape of the convertor having left and right plumbing on its ends. Solution—programming technique combined with alternate end feeding from the input conveyor.**

SPECIAL FEATURES **Due to the quantity of convertors and accuracy of placement required a standard sequence control unit was supplied with the Unimate. The controller allowed the use of a base routine to perform the placement of the convertors in the tilt cage. This reduced the number of steps required and simplified the programming. Since the motions required to pick up the convertor and to move to a point over the tub are the same, the base routine repeats these steps constantly. Then, the subroutine takes over for the individual placement at 58 different positions of the convertor into its proper place in the tub.**

Fig. 10-7. A Unimate industrial robot placing convertors in a wire tub which is tilted during the positioning of the convertor.

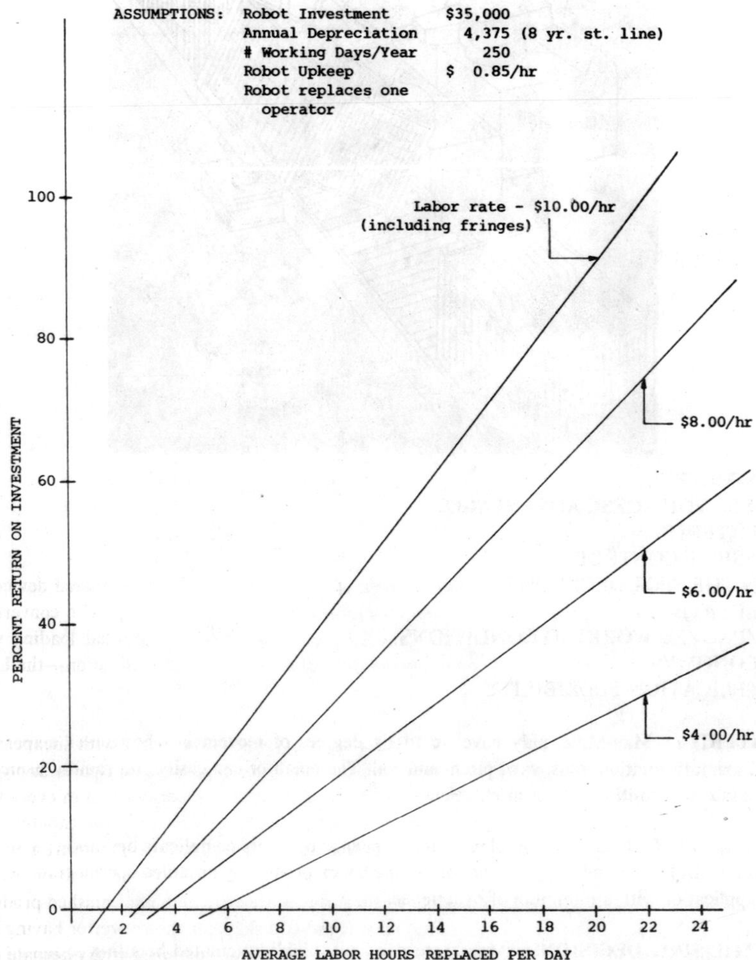

Fig. 10-8. Return on investment for a Unimate industrial robot application.

adequate relief is aware of the direct and indirect suffering that some workers experience, and of the inner rebelliousness engendered by such discomfort and pain. Their attitudes may affect their supervisors, and the situation costs company management dearly in terms of labor conflict, absenteeism, vandalism, and so forth. (If this seems like an exaggeration to you, rest assured that situations of this kind are found time and again in modern industry and commerce.)

A cross section of industry will show a wide variation in the types of work

MAN-MATE™ . . . .
OFFERS YOU THESE ADVANTAGES

- DEXTERITY
- EASE OF CONTROL
- ON THE SPOT DECISIONS
- VERSATILITY
- IMPROVED WORKING CONDITIONS
- ECONOMY
- APPLICATION FLEXIBILITY

DEXTERITY Man-Mate may have up to six degrees of movement—horizontal extension, hoist, azimuth rotation, plus, yaw, pitch, and roll. The operator can easily and rapidly place an object into any position and/or orientation.

EASE OF CONTROL No complex switches, pedals, or levers complicate operation. A single master control commands all gross motions of the boom, permitting unskilled operators to master any application with a minimum of experience.

ON-THE-SPOT DECISIONS Man-Mate can "out-think" automated handling equipment—since the operator can feel, at his hand on the master control, a portion of the forces imposed on the boom by the load, he can instinctively adapt to varying load conditions or unexpected situations.

VERSATILITY Man-Mate can handle a wide range of products, from plate glass which requires delicate handling, to heavy castings requiring superhuman reach and strength.

IMPROVED WORKING CONDITIONS Man-Mate does most of the work, eliminating operator fatigue. Furthermore, operator safety is enhanced by removing him from direct contact with the object handled or from exposure to hostile environments. His interest in his job will increase, he'll derive greater satisfaction from the accomplishment of it, and he'll stay on the job.

ECONOMY Money is saved, manpower efficiently utilized, and productivity increased because Man-Mate has the strength, endurance, and versatility of several men.

APPLICATION FLEXIBILITY

- The *Man-Mate Boom* has three degrees of movement—horizontal extension, hoist, and azimuth rotation. It mimics man's ability to extend, retract, raise, or lower his arm, or even to pivot his entire arm around his shoulder.
- The *terminal positioner* provides the freedom of motion required at the end of the boom to orient the part being handled. Compared to the human anatomy, it performs the equivalent functions of the wrist—yaw, pitch and roll as shown below.
- The *terminal device,* Man-Mate's counterpart to the human hand, may be a vacuum device, mechanical gripper, hook, or other suitable machine-load interface to grasp the load.

Fig. 10-9. The General Electric Co. Man-Mate.

stations and work station arrangements, but basically all work stations must fall into one or more of the following categories:

1. *Transportation and materials control:* The function of changing the storage position and location of materials.
2. *Operation:* The function of changing the shape or configuration of the material.
3. *Storage:* The function of maintaining materials in storage until required.
4. *Inspection:* The function of checking, counting, or testing the quality of the materials produced.
5. *Delay:* The function of holding materials in temporary storage banks or in temporary inactive status until the materials can be processed. The delay may be intentional or unintentional.

(You will notice that five symbols used in "flow-charting" have been ascribed to the work station discussion above. It is understood that at any work station all of the activities described and designated by the symbols could be employed.)

In essence, only one of the five functions adds value to the product, that is, the operation function, which changes the form of a substance. For example, simple bar stock may become a gear shaft with a spline at one end. It can be argued, also, that inspection and testing (quality control) add value by improving the overall quality of the product. Transportation adds a place-value to the product, and storage adds a time-value to the product. These latter concepts

THE TERMINAL DEVICE. . . .

. . .MAN-MATE's counterpart to the human hand is the terminal device—its function is to contact and hold the load. The illustrations below are typical examples of terminal devices that have been designed for specific tasks—custom designed to meet application requirements.

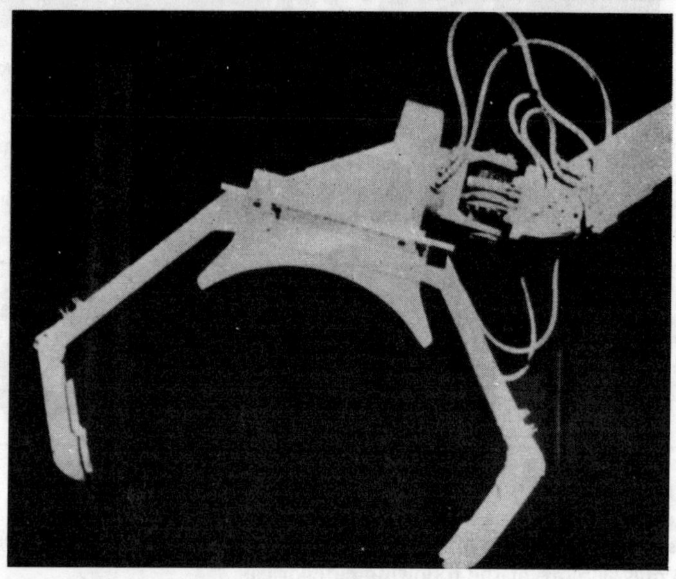

MECHANICAL GRIPPER This "claw" was designed to handle automatic washer drums for a dipping application. Other types of mechanical terminal devices may be a carton-cover lift, a multiple clamp for long objects, or even simple hooks for lifting. The terminal devices may be actuated at the operator's control handle or by a foot switch.

WAREHOUSING—
ELECTRIC RANGE SORTING AND ACCUMULATION

VACUUM TERMINAL DEVICE Vacuum terminal devices are extremely versatile for sheet products such as glass, aluminum or steel, or even loaded corrugated containers, truck platforms, bathtubs, to mention a few. Vacuum cups are available that can handle flat, curved or irregular surfaces—the cup configuration is custom designed for the task.

SHEET PRODUCTS—
PLATE GLASS TRANSFER AND BOXING

Fig. 10-10. GE Man-Mate terminal devices.

are of academic rather than practical interest and are included here to round out the discussion.

B. Planning Used in Work Station Arrangements

The philosophy of the work station was touched upon briefly in the introduction to section II. It can be seen by the materials handling practitioner that the work station is an important aspect of the manufacturing and physical distribution entity.

There are five basic steps in planning the work station in any business enterprise:

1. Exploration
2. Scope planning
3. Subsystem planning
4. Implementation
5. Follow-up

1. Exploration Step 1 is concerned with a survey or exploration of all of the physical factors affecting the work station arrangement: all of the details regarding environmental conditions, the physical location of the area, the type of activities in the area, sizes of parts (if they are involved), quantities, temperature and humidity requirements, light levels, size of the area, ceiling and truss heights, capacity of trusses, and any number of other factors such as electrical service available, drains, the availability of water service and other utilities required, ad infinitum, depending on the nature of the project.

Each work station arrangement may require a new set of parameters; but as the materials handling engineer becomes more adept at this approach, he will have designed his own checklist of items to cover to obtain the optimum design that can be economically justified.

Certain questions should be answered in the exploratory phase of Step 1, and each work station arrangement project should initially specify (1) what is to be accomplished; (2) how it will be accomplished; (3) who will be responsible for each part of the project (that is, the assignment of responsibilities); and (4) the beginning and ending dates of each step of the project.

We have already discussed some elementary phases of scheduling. A Gantt Chart covers the critical time elements of various phases of the project and becomes very important in letting us know where we stand, if we are making progress, it we are falling behind schedule, etc. PERT charts or critical path method charts may be used for more complex projects; however, the materials handling engineer is advised to keep things as simple as possible. Later on we'll cover the rudiments of more complex charting, but in 90% or more of the projects attempted a down-to-earth Gantt Chart will provide all the information required to keep the project on schedule.

Even when complex charting (scheduling) methods are used, it is sometimes helpful to take a subsystem from the program and Gantt-Chart it for easier visualization.

2. Scope Planning. In Step 1 each work station arrangement project requires the collection, compilation, and verification of a number of environmental and numerical data that are the foundation for the project. Basic to obtaining these data, of course, is a *knowledge of the product* or products to be handled *and the quantity of the product to be produced in a given amount of time.*

In addition to the numerical data that are to be collected, a thorough analysis of the product(s) and the materials that are a part of, or comprise, the product should be made. A value analysis study may be required. If you suspect this, or if no V.A. study has been made recently, then it would be helpful to request that one be made, or to analyze the product from a V.A. standpoint yourself. The terms "V.A." and "work simplification" have been used almost synonymously for years, and the intent of each is the same: to try to boil down the nonessentials and come up with the most economical and functional form of the product or method.

Another facet of scope planning is to determine (1) what operations are to be performed and (2) what equipment is to be used and how much of it. In heavy industry the operations to be performed often dictate the work station location and configuration because once a large stamping or forging press has been located, the site does not change, unless some drastic changes are made to the plant, or the equipment is sold or otherwise removed from its expensive foundations. On the other hand, in light industry equipment usually may be moved very readily, so that it is possible to revise, modify, and redo the work station arrangement almost at will. Usually, however, there is a happy middle ground where the decision can be made by the materials handling engineer.

In any event, it is essential that the MHE determine which operations are necessary at the work station; some operations may be combined with others, or perhaps eliminated.

Next, determine what equipment, tooling, and fixtures are required to accomplish the necessary operations.

3. Subsystem Planning. In making work station layouts it is necessary to take into consideration (1) the activity areas, and (2) the space required for each activity. Because space and its relation to the individual are of paramount importance, we must understand the human engineering factors that dictate the work station arrangement. We shall consider a composite individual, there

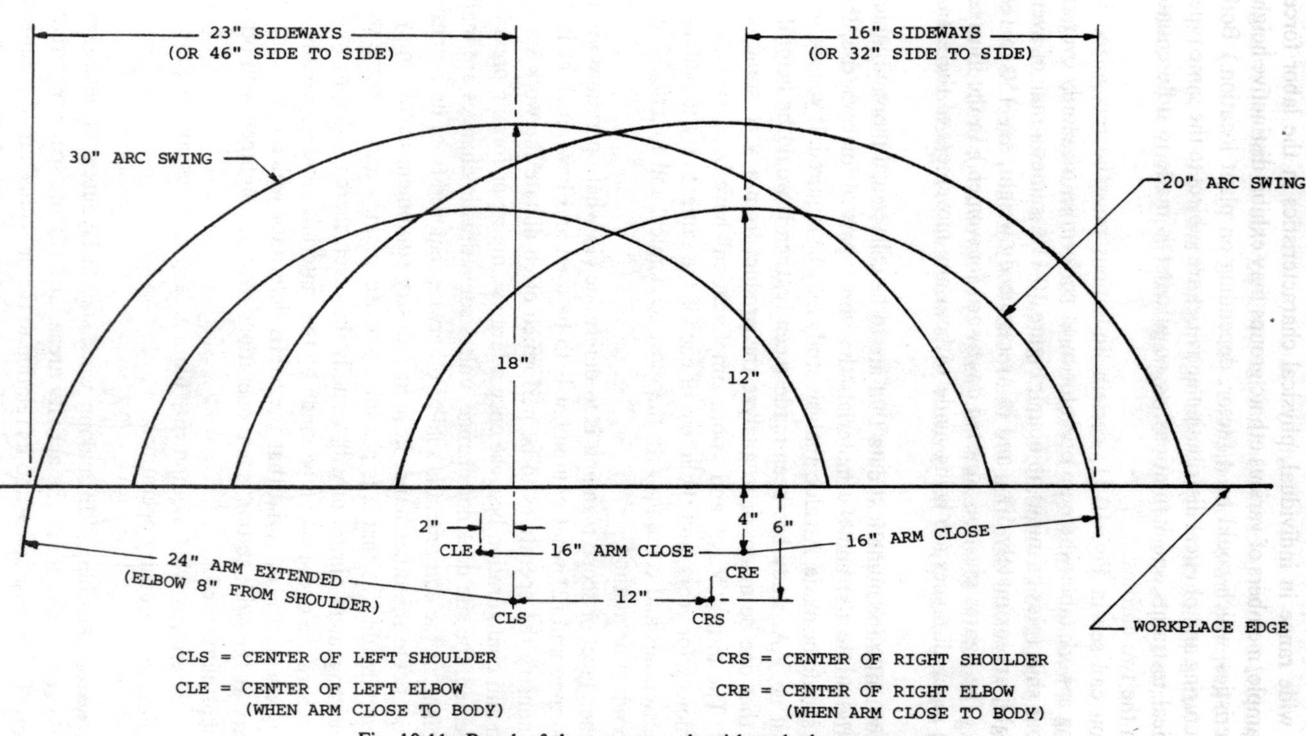

Fig. 10-11. Reach of the average male without body movement.

being a wide range in individual, physical characteristics in the labor force. (For example, members of various ethnic groups may exhibit distinctive height characteristics, which could be a factor, depending on plant location.) Both manufacturing and physical distribution activities are subject to the same types of physical restraints and limitations; so no attempt is made to differentiate between the two entities.

As you can see in Fig. 10-11, certain limitations must be recognized in designing a work table where an operator must perform satisfactorily over an eight-hour shift (plus or minus an hour). Figure 10-11 assumes a man of average height, approximately 5′9″, and of average body weight, say 150 to 160 pounds. (The figures must be adjusted downward for women.) In the illustration the reach distances are being made without any movement of the man's body.

Another aspect of human engineering concerns the vertical plane in which the individual stands. Figure 10-12 indicates some physical relationships that

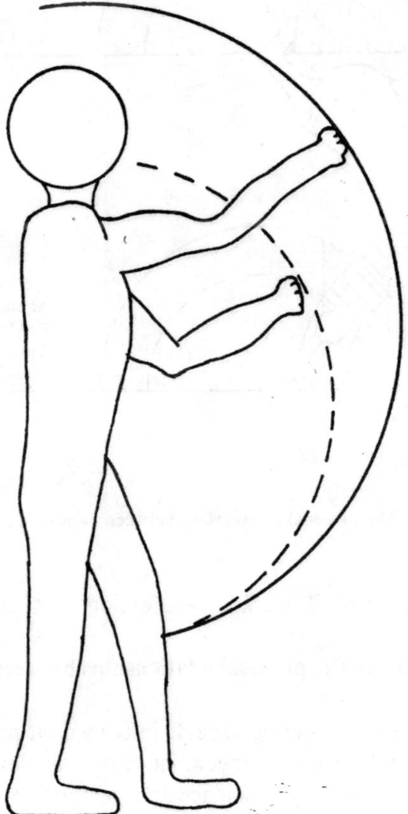

Fig. 10-12. The human body related to the vertical plane.

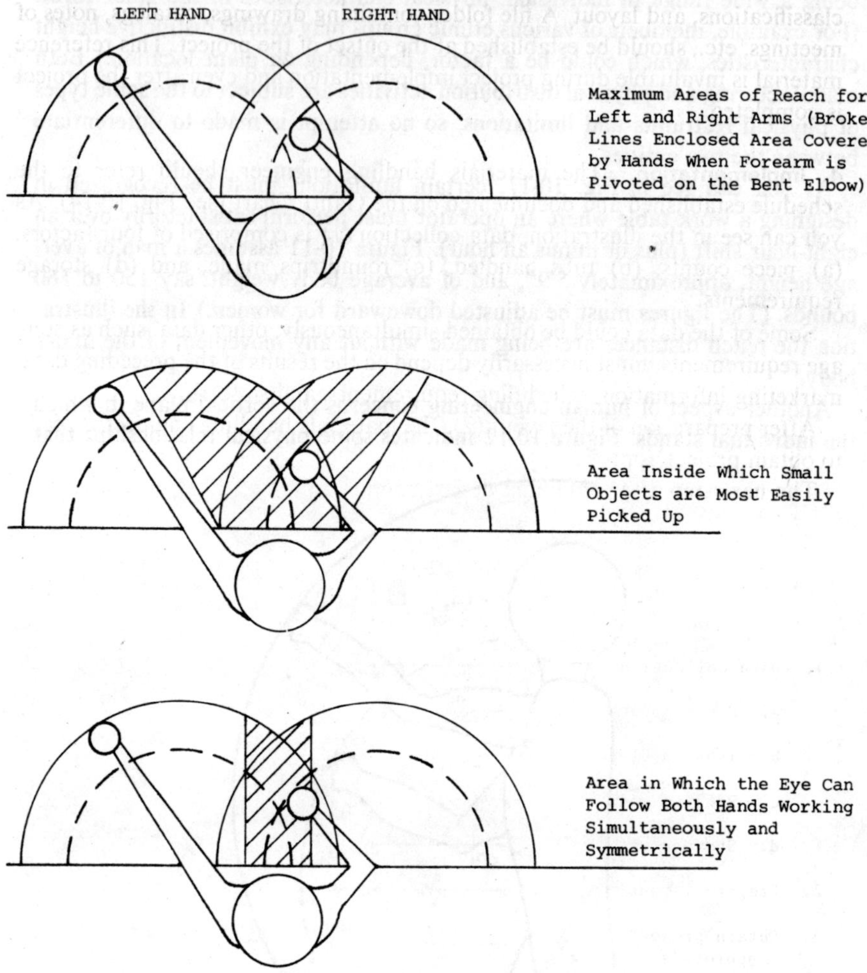

Fig. 10-13. The physical relationship between hand and eye movements.

should not be neglected if worker satisfaction and productivity are to be fostered.

In Fig. 10-13 some of the physical relationships between hand and eye movements are shown.

Taking the human engineering aspects into account provides another building block for the work station arrangement. Since the development of the ideal or optimum work station is part science and part art, it would be well to document the physical arrangement of the product materials, equipment, work classifications, and layout. A file folder containing drawings, catalogs, notes of meetings, etc., should be established at the outset of the project. This reference material is invaluable during project implementation and even after the project is completed.

4. Implementation. The materials handling engineer should refer to the schedule established and documented on the Gantt Chart (see Fig. 10-14). As you can see in the illustration, data collection (1) is comprised of four factors: (a) piece counts, (b) tubs handled, (c) roundtrips made, and (d) storage requirements.

Some of the data could be obtained simultaneously; other data, such as storage requirements, must necessarily depend on the results of the preceding data, marketing information, scheduling requirements, and so forth.

After preparation of the layout (2), the materials handling engineer is ready to obtain project approvals (3).

The next step after obtaining departmental or management approvals is to

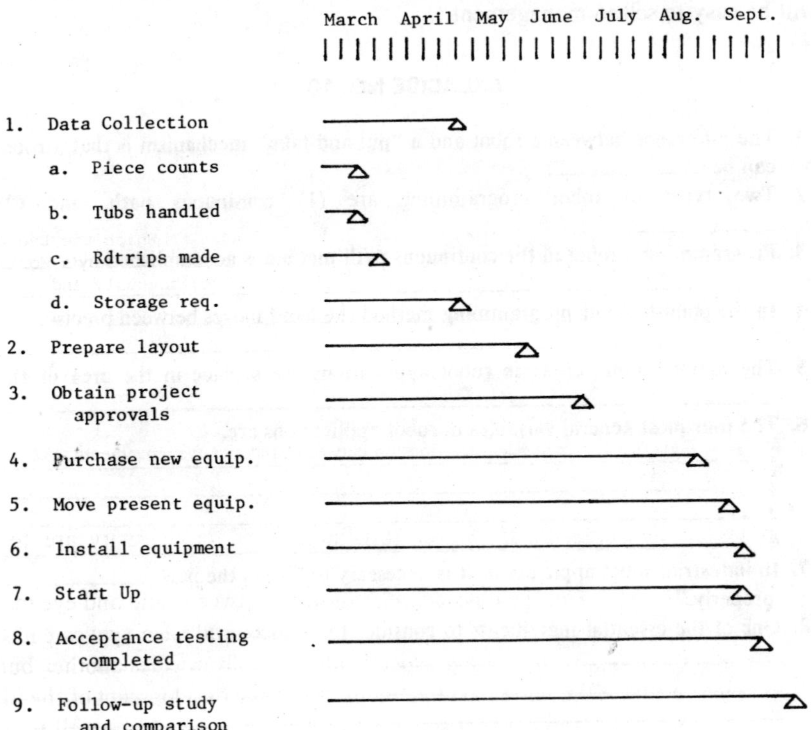

Fig. 10-14. Schedule of events for a work station arrangement project.

purchase new equipment (4). Not all work station arrangement projects require new equipment; so the reader need not feel this is commonplace. When departmental approvals are needed, prices must be obtained so that an R.O.I. (return-on-investment study) may be prepared. After quotations have been received and price comparisons have been made, the equipment may be purchased.

One or two days before the new equipment arrives, the old equipment is removed or transferred to a new location (5).

In this type of project, the disruption in production that occurs when machinery is moved presents a problem. It is necessary to build up a backlog of production parts to use during the disruption, or to make arrangements with a supplier or the parts recipient so that no hardships are suffered or production losses occur.

The equipment is installed (6) and started up (7). After acceptance tests (8) are completed, we have a period of follow-up, in which the operation is watched carefully (9). As part of the follow-up period, data are compiled to provide material for comparison with the former operation.

A successful installation should be properly publicized so that future projects will be easy to sell to management.

EXERCISE NO. 10

1. The difference between a robot and a "put-and-take" mechanism is that a robot can be ____________.
2. Two types of robot programming are (1) continuous path, and (2) ____________.
3. Programming a robot in the continuous path method is accomplished by ____________ ____________.
4. In the point-to-point programming method the hand moves between precise, ____________ ____________.
5. The major tooling effort in robot applications takes place in the area of the ____________.
6. The four most general variables in robot applications are:
   1. ____________
   2. ____________
   3. ____________
   4. ____________
7. In industrial robot applications it is necessary to "Keep the part ____________ properly."
8. One of the essential ingredients to consider for a successful robot application is ____________ ____________ ____________.

9. Why would you advise a visit to a robot manufacturer? ______

10. Why is a robot preventive maintenance program necessary? ______

11. In most plants and warehouses we spend more time, usually, in justifying capital expenditures than we do in training employees.
True ☐ False ☐ Disagree ☐

12. If you disagree, please tell why (optional). ______

13. Give an example of a lack of appreciation of the human engineering aspects of work station layout. ______

14. All work stations usually fall into one or more of the following categories:
1. ______
2. ______
3. ______
4. ______
5. ______

15. Which of the five categories above adds value to the product? ______

16. Five basic steps in planning required to achieve the optimum work station arrangement, are:
1. ______
2. ______
3. ______
4. ______
5. ______

17. Basic to data collection for the work station project is a knowledge of the product and the quantity ______.

18. In making work station layouts it is necessary to take into consideration the (1) acitivity areas, and the (2) space ______.

19. What is the widest arc swing that the average male can make without body movement, 24″ arm extended, elbow 8″ from shoulder? (See Fig. 10-11.) ______ **″ arc swing (Answer)**

20. All work station arrangement projects require new equipment.
True ☐ False ☐

Chapter 11

Equipment Selection: Industrial Powered Trucks and Truck Attachments; Batteries, Chargers, Cables, and Connectors

I. EQUIPMENT SELECTION

Because of the large amounts of money involved in equipment selection, the material handling specialist must take a cautious and conservative approach in the matter. A piece of equipment can be a vital element of the handling process in a plant, or it can be disruptive to plant operations and the focal point of labor problems and other disturbances.

To the extent that it is possible, the materials handling engineer and his associates should get a broad view of the subject, seeing as many different manufacturers' products as necessary in order to have a firm grasp of the type of equipment that is available.

Where equipment systems are concerned, it may be necessary to employ a consultant to obtain the best possible solution to the handling problem.

A. Introduction

This chapter will outline the basic criteria for equipment selection. As in the earlier chapters, we are concerned primarily with a systems approach to materials handling; and nowhere is this approach applied with better results than in the area of equipment selection.

As labor costs continue to increase, the justification for using specialized and even general-purpose equipment in specific applications becomes less difficult—primarily because the cost per hour of labor is often a good deal higher than the cost per hour of the equipment to be selected. However, with labor costs escalating, it also becomes easier to justify operatorless automation, in which the operator has been completely or almost completely eliminated—as in the situation where an operator may oversee several operatorless machines.

There are several beneficial aspects to the proper selection of equipment. For example, there is the high productivity of the operation or process; there is a good working climate with little cause for labor unrest; there is a high rate of return on the investment; labor and equipment downtime are minimized; and maintenance costs may be relatively low, with maintenance easily accomplished.

B. How to Begin to Select Equipment

The materials handling specialist should first obtain data that will enable him to make certain basic assumptions as to the type, size, and quantity of equipment required.

Essentially the data are concerned with: (1) the volume of material to be handled; (2) how far the material must be moved; (3) the way the material is packaged, or not packaged; (4) where and how it is to be stored; and (5) whether or not the volumes to be handled vary from day to day or during the day, week, or month.

Other influences on equipment selection are such physical factors as (1) the type of terrain to be traversed and (2) the load-bearing characteristics of the soil or of the building itself, for an indoor operation.

A good deal of mobile equipment is designed primarily for use on concrete or woodblock floors, which are ideal for industrial powered trucks. The material handling specialist must not feel that because it has relatively wide-tread wheels a vehicle is suitable for muddy yards or steep ramps. The frame of a truck may be so low to the ground, or it may be so underpowered, that its gradability* is somewhat limited.

In Chapter 20 we shall discuss methods for determining the return on investment for capital equipment. In the meantime we shall concentrate on the physical aspects of equipment selection.

II. INDUSTRIAL POWERED TRUCKS

A. Types of Powered Industrial Trucks

In general, industrial powered trucks can be broadly classified into those that are: electric powered (1); and internal combustion (i.c.) engine powered, either gasoline (2) or diesel (3). The gasoline powered trucks can be further broken down into those powered by straight (leaded) gas and those using liquid propane (LP) gas.

The industrial powered truck can be purchased new or used, leased, or obtained on a lease-purchase basis. It is well to note that gas, i.c. trucks have a higher trade-in value than electric trucks of equal capacity, because of the higher demand for the gas trucks, which require neither a battery charger nor

*Gradability—a measure of how steep an incline a forklift truck can climb. This will be discussed further in the chapter.

the installation of heavy-voltage electric lines to supply the charger. Also the battery in a used electric truck may be the deciding factor; since the average life of an electric industrial battery is five to seven years, a battery replacement might be in order—at a cost of $1,200 or more. Usually electric forklift trucks are not traded in at an early age and most "electrics" last through several battery replacements.

Another reason for the popularity of gas trucks is that the small operator likes the lower initial cost; and, he can use the truck almost anywhere that a forklift truck may be used. Most forklift trucks are sold to a market where only two to eight trucks are employed; hence the emphasis on low initial cost, as the operators need cash as well as equipment.

The number of electric trucks in use continues to increase to the extent that about 30% of the forktrucks in use are electric. This slow, upward growth of the electric truck in the total forktruck market is due to several factors: the somewhat lower overall maintenance cost of the electric truck; the lack of smoke, fumes, or toxic emission (present in the i.c. truck exhaust); and lower fuel costs.

In addition to the three general classes of trucks (electric, gas, and diesel), trucks may be characterized by use. There are trucks designed for outdoor, rough-terrain, and towable uses. Trucks used indoors will have solid or cushion tires, of either rubber or polyurethane. The rubber tire is black, and the polyurethane tire a dark amber color.

Polyurethane tires are tough and have excellent wear characteristics with speeds under seven miles per hour. Because of the heat build-up during rotational flexing, they are not used for high-speed yardwork, but are exceptionally good for indoor warehouse or production activities.

1. Trucks with Solid, Cushion, or Semi-Pneumatic Tires. Solid truck tires are used primarily in warehouse or production work where high stacking is required. Cushion tires are similar to solid tires, and the terms are used interchangeably. Semi-pneumatic tires have a hollow core and are used where better riding characteristics are desired, for example, in high-speed dock operations.

Solid tires can be either molded on a rim or molded on a steel sleeve that in turn is pressed onto the truck wheel under high pressure.

2. Trucks with Pneumatic Tires. Pneumatic truck tires can be either tube-type or tubeless, and they are used for outdoor work. They do not allow for very high stacking capabilities because of their lack of stability under heavy loads. However, they do possess a higher degree of flotation, which means that they will spread the load they are carrying over a larger footprint area. They are especially effective in muddy yards, in sandy soils, and over crushed rock.

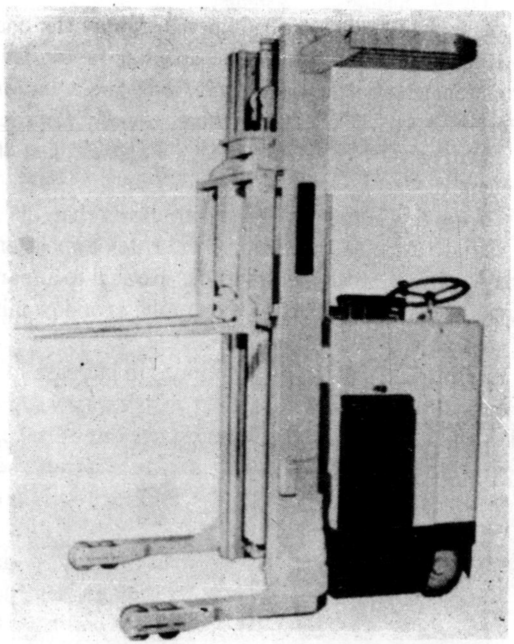

Fig. 11-1. Sit-down straddle truck.

Especially large pneumatic tires are used at construction sites where the terrain is rough and where ordinary pneumatics or solid tires would not have any traction whatsoever.

3. Straddle or Outrigger and Narrow-Aisle Trucks. Under the common grouping of narrow-aisle trucks, we have straddle trucks, sideloaders, and right-angle turn trucks.

Straddle trucks are standup rider types, as shown in Fig. 11-1. They can work in relatively narrow aisles, and their turning radius (Fig. 11-2) is rather sharp.

4. Counterbalanced Forklift Trucks. The counterbalanced forklift truck (Fig. 11-3) is probably the most commonly used type of industrial powered truck. Because it is, we have presented in section I, B, below, a graphic illustration of the various forces at work upon this truck when it is operating under a load.

When specifying this type of truck, one usually decides upon the following characteristics:

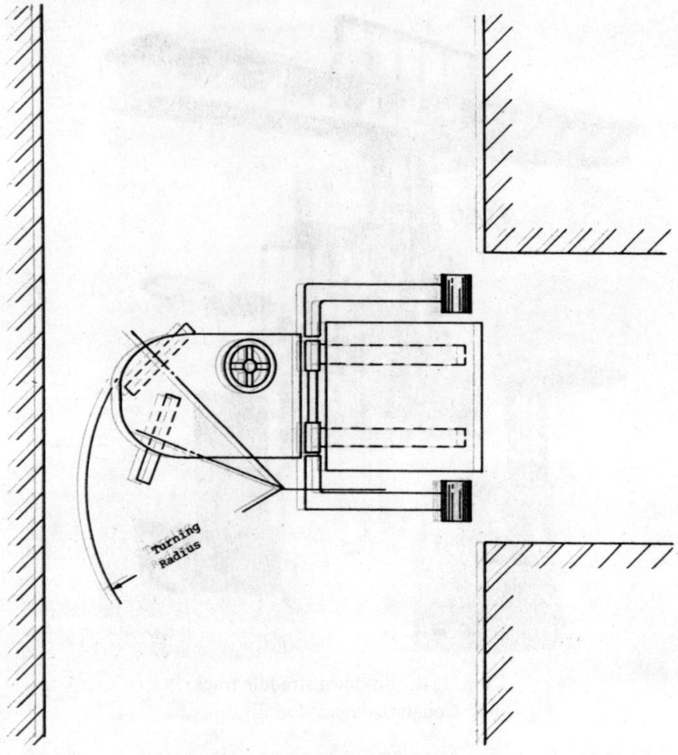

Fig. 11-2. Illustration of turning radius.

a. Capacity in Pounds. If, for example, loads to be lifted, stacked, or transported are 1,500 pounds on the average with no loads greater than 2,000 pounds, we would usually select a 2,000- or 2,500-pound-capacity lift truck. Because almost all counterbalanced trucks are designed for a 25% (approximately) overload, we would be safe in using a 2,000-pound truck. The truck, however, will last longer if it is sized upward from the basic capacity; that is, a 2,500-pound truck or a 3,000-pound truck will last a good deal longer carrying 1,500-pound loads and an occasional 2,000-pound load, than a 2,000-pound truck, which would be working close to its design limits on some occasions.

b. Mast Height. The height and style of the mast depend on how high the loads are to be stacked. Most manufacturers of industrial powered trucks have their own company standards; for example, you may be able to get 72″, 83″, 95″, 107″, 114″, 127″, etc., from a single manufacturer. Settle for a standard mast height, which may be within an inch or two of what you had been think-

Fig. 11-3. Counterbalanced forklift truck.

Fig. 11-4. Straddle carrier.

ing of, or go to the next standard size higher—unless, of course, you wish to pay extra for a "special" size and most likely, live with a longer delivery period because the mast is "special."

c. Fork Size. The length of the fork is very important, usually the forks can be had in 2-inch increments from 36 inches up to 6 feet in length and with a cross-sectional area to suit the weight of the load. Also, the shape and taper of the point of the fork can be specified, such as "chisel" or "blunt."

d. Power Plant. The power plant may be a gas engine, diesel, electric, etc. With gas engines you generally have the choice of a Ford, Chrysler, Continental, or GM engine. With electric trucks the differences rest, generally speaking, with the manufacturer. Here also the controls are sometimes specified; for example, the manufacturer's controls, or G.E. Silicon Rectified Controls, etc.

e. Free Lift. The mast can be a single, double, triple, or quadruple stage. This means one section sliding within the other, or rolling within the other. The free lift is the movement of the forks from the ground up without the movement of any of the other sections. You can see that the free lift is extremely important in covered truck, van, or railcar loading, where without sufficient free lift you would punch a hole in the roof of the carrier with your mast every time you tried to lift a load inside the carrier.

Fig. 11-5. Illustration of a walkie truck. Note the controls in the handle.

f. Standup or Sitdown. Except for narrow-aisle, straddle trucks, which are with few exceptions all standup trucks, you have an option of sitdown or standup counterbalanced trucks, especially in the lower weight capacities.

5. Walkie Trucks. A walkie truck, where the operator guides the truck by means of a handle, is illustrated in Fig. 11-5.

You will have a choice of low-lift or high-lift walkies. These trucks can be counterbalanced by a combination of the batteries and the distance of the load to the center of gravity and by outriggers in high-lift units. In the low-lift models the load wheels in the forks never leave the ground; the wheels are raised and lowered by a cam action in the lifting mechanism.

Since the operator guides the walkie truck by means of a handle, his controls are in this handle. It is important to have included in the handle controls a warning horn button and a safety or "panic" button. The panic button should be of the reversing type; in other words, when the operator strikes the button, or when the button is pressed into any part of the operator's body, the truck will reverse its direction automatically. (See Fig. 11-6.)

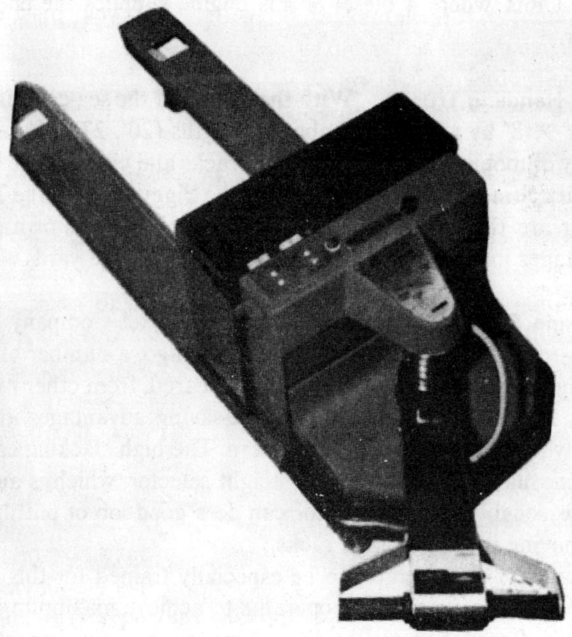

Fig. 11-6. Location of walkie panic button in handle.

6. Towable Trucks. Towable trucks are used, principally, in the cosntruction business. A towable truck is usually counterbalanced with pneumatic tires and a disengageable transmission enabling it to be towed at highway speeds.

7. Low-Profile Trucks. Because of the low overhead height of some carriers (that is, over-the-road trucks in which the truck bed to top door frame distance is only 80 to 87 inches), a driver seated on a counterbalanced forktruck and sticking his head outside the limits of the truck is quite vulnerable to head injuries, as well as decapitation. In addition to the problem of low door height, the load wheels of the truck must climb over the crown of the dock plate to enter the carrier. Putting this all together, several forklift truck manufacturers have developed low-profile forktrucks for which they have lowered the truck seats and overall mast heights.

8. Steel Mill Trucks. Because of the large loads handled in steel mills, coils weighing 60,000 to 70,000 pounds and getting larger, this type of industrial powered truck is in a class by itself. The power plant, gear train, axles, and forks or prongs bear little resemblance to the ordinary forklift truck. Some of these giants of the powered industrial truck family have been equipped with Ready-Power-Units where a diesel or gas engine supplies the energy for an electric motor.

9. Container Handling Trucks. With the advent of the sea-container, an aluminum box 8′ × 8′ by any of a number of lengths (20′, 27′, 35′, or 40′, etc.), a great variety of mobile industrial powered trucks and cranes have been developed. The Clark Straddle Carrier, the Drott, the Piggy-Packer, the Taylor, and the Towmotor are the predominant machines, each with its own advantages and disadvantages in handling the sea-container in storage yards.

10. Right-Angle Stacking Trucks. Since the Drexel Company introduced the first right-angle stacking truck over a decade ago, a number of imitations and improvements of this truck design have appeared, from other manufacturers as well as Drexel. There are many space-saving advantages in using this type of truck where storage space is a concern. The high stacking capability of this truck is unusual. With the use of a height selector, which is automatic in operation, a reasonably skilled operator can do a good job of putting material away and removing it from storage racks.

It is necessary for the operator to be especially trained for this job, and it usually takes a week or two for an operator to achieve maximum proficiency with this vehicle. Because spatial or depth perception is very important in this job, not every forktruck driver can become as proficient with this truck as with the ordinary counterbalanced lift truck.

11. Sideloader and Four-Directional Trucks. The sideloader truck is the only truck capable of stacking material 20 feet or more in height that also can run down aisles that are 6 feet or less in width. Side-loaders are manufactured to transport and stack loads that are 20 feet or more in length (such as pipe, bar stock, sheets, etc.) and weigh anywhere from 2,000 to 10,000 pounds. The exceptional mobility of the sideloader means that it can transport material from stacks or racks directly to the point of use in a production operation or production line, and vice versa.

The four-directional truck is even more versatile than the sideloader in certain operations. It was developed for shipboard use in the U.S. Navy, but it has found application in specific industrial applications where its increased maneuverability makes handling in tight spaces easier.

B. Components and Fundamental Design Considerations

The student of materials handling should be aware of some of the design characteristics that influence the load-carrying and stacking capabilities of the forklift truck—the workhorse of industry.

In Fig. 11-7, a sketch of the counterbalanced truck shows how the front or load wheels serve as the fulcrum or pivot point of the loaded truck. This pivot, like the pivot on the balance beam of a scale, divides the weight evenly. The most common denominator for classifying forklift trucks is based upon a load center (also illustrated), which here is 24 inches out from the heel of the forks. (Forks are measured from the heel.) If the load center shifts outwardly, as in Fig. 11-8, the rated capacity of the truck is reduced; the farther out the center of gravity of the load, the more the truck capacity is reduced.

Figure 11-9 shows a force drawing of a counterbalanced lift truck. The letter *P* represents the weight of the empty truck which acts at its center of gravity,

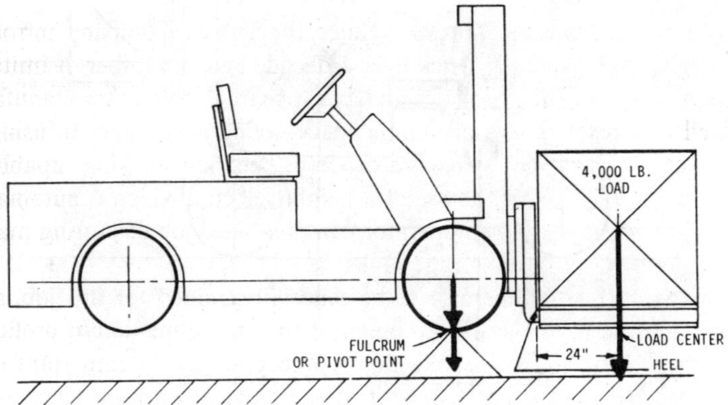

Fig. 11-7. Loaded counterbalanced forklift truck showing the "pivot point" and "load center."

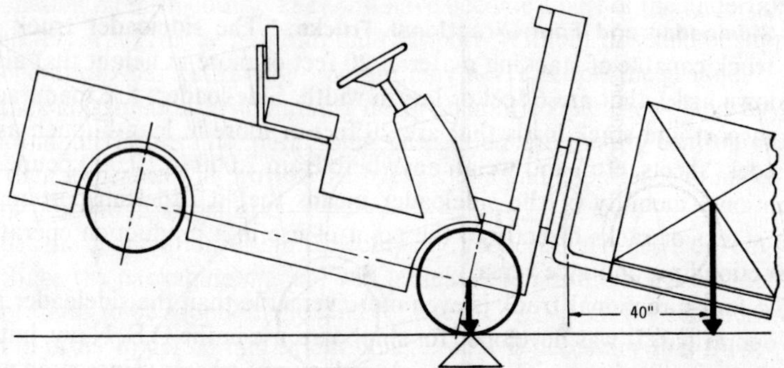

Fig. 11-8. Loaded counterbalanced truck with load center exceeded.

designated *CG*. The load *L* is shown somewhat elevated, but still in its center of gravity at *CG*-2. This load is cantilevered from the front wheels just as in Fig. 11-7. The cantilevering action of the load causes the composite weight of the truck plus the load or *Q* to move forward to the "composite" *CG*-3.

If the mast is tilted backward, the composite *CG*-3 will move backward, thus increasing its stability. If the mast is tilted forward, the center of gravity, that is, the composite *CG*-3, will move forward to a position over the front wheels. The stability of the truck will be endangered, and it may overturn, or the load may slide off the forks. Figure 11-10 illustrates this movement of the composite *CG*-3.

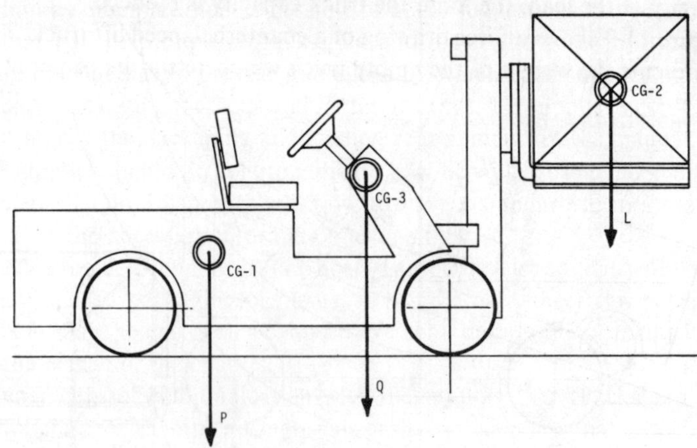

Fig. 11-9. Moment of force diagram for a counterbalanced forklift truck.

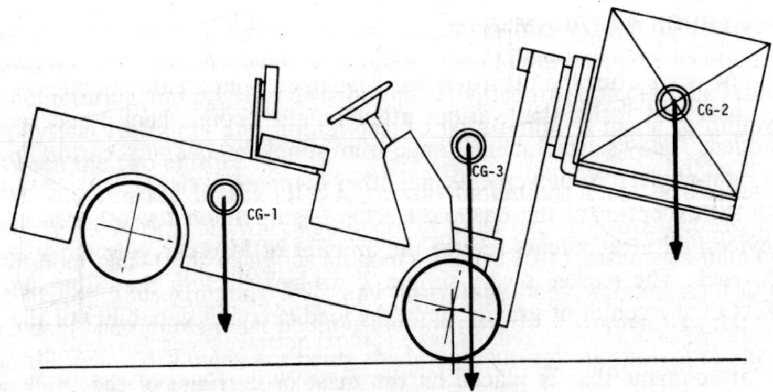

Fig. 11-10. Shift of the composite center of gravity and an overturning moment.

1. Gradability. As indicated earlier in the chapter, gradability is a measure of how steep an incline a forklift truck (or any other piece of mobile materials handling equipment) can climb.

Figure 11-11 describes the way in which gradability is measured. For example, let $X = 200$ feet, and $Y = 10$ feet. Then:

$$\frac{100 \times 10}{200} = 5\% \text{ grade}$$

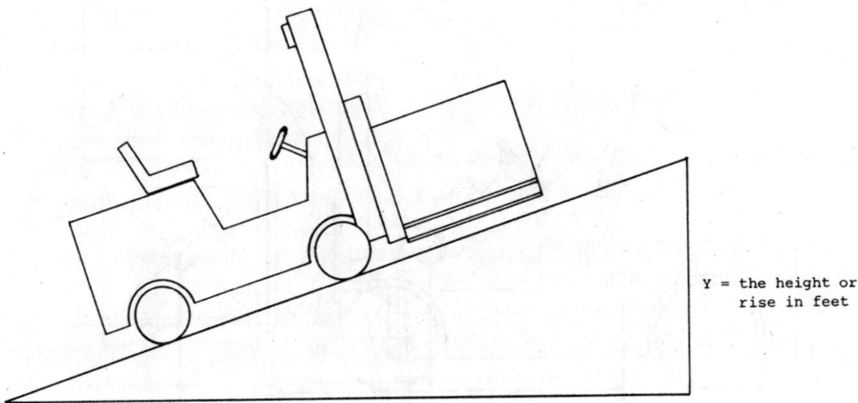

Fig. 11-11. The way to calculate the percentage of grade.

III. LIFT TRUCK ATTACHMENTS

Only a few years after the lift truck was developed from an automobile chassis with a mast and forks, that various attachments, booms, hooks, and scoops were added. Today's attachments range from simple mechanical carton lip lifters to right-angle fork movements and other complex devices.

With the exception of the Basiloid Carton Clamp and a few other mechanical devices, all attachments reduce the amount of load-carrying capacity of the lift truck. The reason is very simple, if we look back at the discussion on the effect of the center of gravity upon the load-carrying capability of the lift truck.

Any attachment that is placed on the mast or carriage of the truck will extend the *CG* outward several inches. As illustrated in Fig. 11-12, this has the effect of decreasing the rated capacity of the truck. The materials handling specialist should ask every supplier of attachments to let him know to what extent his lift truck will be dowrated because of the loss of *CG*. Even a small change in *CG* may mean too great a loss in capacity for your combined truck and load.

A. Sideshifters

The sideshifter attachment is probably one of the most popular and useful of all forklift truck attachments. Quite a few companies today equip each of their forktrucks with this attachment because it saves a great deal of time and eliminates the damage that occurs in positioning loads. A mediocre forklift truck operator can become a competent professional when his truck is equipped with

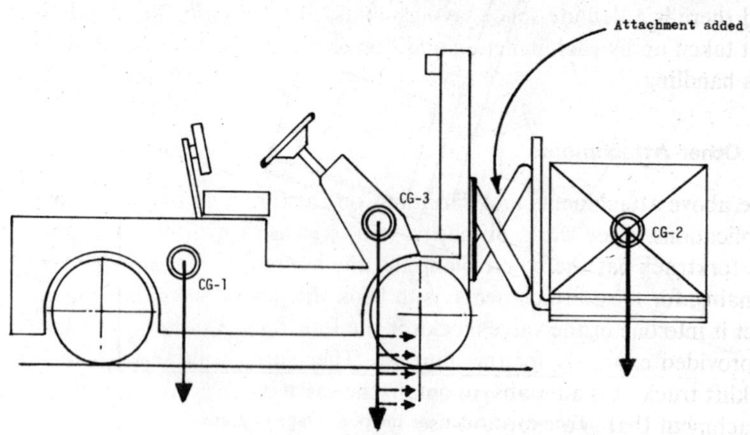

Fig. 11-12. An attachment may shift the *CG* outwardly.

a sideshifting device that can move a load from four to six inches on either side; this saves damage to storage racks and merchandise.

The sideshifter, like most attachments that have a movement independent of the forktruck itself, is actuated by a hydraulic cylinder. Some forktruck manufacturers make their own sideshifters; however, sideshifters, as well as many other attachments, can be obtained from Cascade in Oregon, Long Reach in Texas, Little Giant in Illinois, or HMC in St. Louis, Missouri.

B. Rotators

The rotator is used in industrial applications where a box with fork pockets must be dumped by rotating. The rotator is attached between the truck and the fork carriage. The two most common methods of rotating are a large gear and worm gear arrangement or a chain drive on two sprockets.

With proper maintenance either type of rotator should provide years of service; therefore, in choosing one of these attachments it is advisable to be guided by the loss of load center among several manufacturers' designs. In some instances the chain drive rotator provides a closer fit than the other type of rotator; therefore, it does have the advantage of permitting heavier loads to be carried.

C. Carton Clamps

The carton clamp is a device to stack, destack, and transport cartons without a pallet. Two broad, flat arms squeeze a pallet-load of cartons and lift them without crushing the contents. There are decided advantages in being able to handle cartons without pallets. Pallets cause damage through nail punctures, and there is a definite space savings obtained by eliminating the several cubic feet taken up by each pallet, in addition to the cost savings achieved by palletless handling.

D. Other Attachments

The above attachments and variations on them can be found in thousands of applications. They work, primarily, on the basis of hydraulic actuation. Since the forktruck has the power plant and the hydraulic pumping system, all that remains, for most attachments, is to hook the device on the carriage and connect it into one of the valve blocks of the forktruck. Usually a three-way valve is provided expressly for this purpose. Therefore, in purchasing or leasing a forklift truck, it is advisable to obtain the valve block needed for the particular attachment that you expect to use.

There are a number of simple, mechanical attachments that require no hydraulic hookups; it is sufficient here to mention only the Basiloid carton clamp, booms, and prongs. Booms are used in rigging operations where machinery must be moved from place to place in the plant. Prongs, or some variation of prongs, are used in rug or carpet handling; and another variation of prongs is block forks, which consist of a large number of tines used to stack and load concrete and cinder blocks.

Sometimes the block tines are provided with a sideshifter to improve ease of handling, loading, and stacking.This speeds up the operation and eliminates unnecessary and nonproductive movement of the forktruck.

IV. BATTERIES FOR INDUSTRIAL TRUCKS, CHARGERS, CABLES, AND CONNECTORS

A. Introduction

Storage batteries are a mystery to a great many people. You will see here just how simple a storage battery really is. There is no mystery. The equipment that it operates is often far more complicated than the battery itself.

A storage battery, contrary to the usual belief, does not actually store electricity. It stores chemical energy, which is converted into electrical energy while discharging. On recharging, the electrical energy supplied to the battery is spent in changing the active materials back to their original state, thus restoring the chemical energy necessary for another discharge. These changes (of energy) are made possible by the mechanical design of the cell.

Let's take a look at Figs. 11-13 through 11-16 to consider what actually takes place in a storage battery during discharge and charge.

B. Fully Charged Cell

In a fully charged cell, a positive electrode and a negative electrode are mechanically insulated from one another and immersed in an electrolyte. The active materials of the electrodes are lead peroxide for the positive electrode and sponge lead for the negative, as shown in Fig. 11-13. The electrolyte is a solution of sulfuric acid, varying in specific gravity from 1.200 to 1.280, depending on the type of service for which the cell is built. When fully charged, this combination has a voltage of approximately 2 volts on open circuit, and from 2.12 to 2.70 volts while charging current is flowing through the cell.

C. Discharged Cell

As shown in Fig. 11-14, during discharge the lead peroxide and the sponge lead combine with the sulfuric acid to form lead sulfate on both plates. This explains the changes noticed, namely, the decrease in voltage and the decrease in the electrolyte specific gravity. The decrease in voltage is caused by the two elements or electrodes approaching the same chemical composition, thus decreasing the potential difference between them. The reason for the change in the specific gravity of the electrolyte is that sulfuric acid is removed from the electrolyte, which consequently approaches water's specific gravity of 1.000.

D. Charging the Cell

When a charging current is fed back into a discharged cell, as shown in Fig. 11-15, these reactions are reversed. The lead sulfate is broken up, the active materials are reproduced in the plates, and sulfuric acid is returned to the elecctorlyte. Naturally then, the voltage rises, since the two plates are becoming increasingly different in composition. The electrolyte specific gravity increases as more and more acid returns to the solution.

To sum up, when a cell is fully charged, the positive plates consist of lead peroxide and the negative plates sponge lead. The electrolyte is sulfuric acid. Discharged, the positive plates are lead sulfate, the negative plates are lead sulfate, and the electrolyte is water, as shown in Fig. 11-16.

Thus the most important parts of storage cells are the plates or electrodes. Actually, the power-producing plate is the positive one. In normal oepration, the positive plate is the one that determines the actual life of the battery.

E. Construction of a Battery

A storage battery is an electro-chemical apparatus that accepts electrical energy delivered to it by any electrical charging apparatus, converting this electrical energy into chemical energy, which is gradually accumulated while being charged. A battery is composed of a number of cells, as shown in Fig. 11-17. The cell is the unit part of the battery.

A simple cell, shown in Fig. 11-18, is composed of a container, generally a hard rubber jar, that contains electrolyte into which are placed two electrodes, which are dissimilar in composition and separated electrically from each other. The electrolyte in a lead acid cell is sulfuric acid and water.

Because a single cell does not have sufficient power to handle the usual load requirements, a number of cells are joined together, by connectors, to form a battery, which may be used to power forklift and other types of industrial trucks. These cells have a number of positive plates, sometimes referred to as anodes, and a number of negative plates, sometimes referred to as cathodes.

The capacity of a battery is determined by the work that it is expected to perform. This capacity is expressed in ampere-hours, that is, the number of

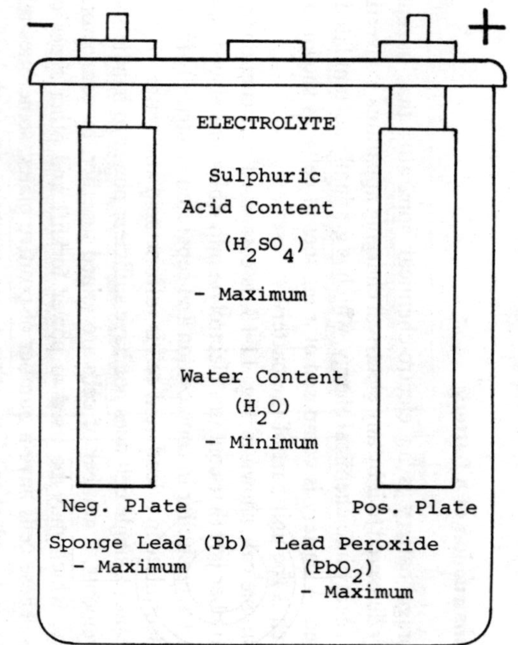

Fig. 11-13. Charged.

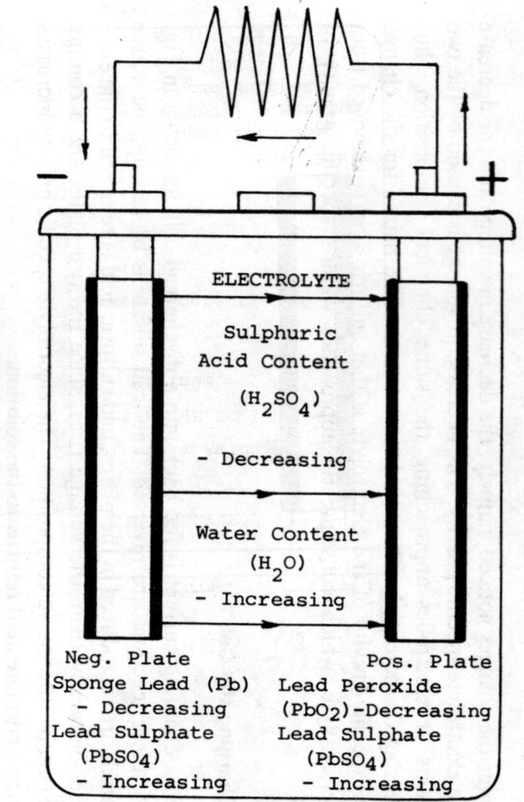

Fig. 1-14. Discharged.

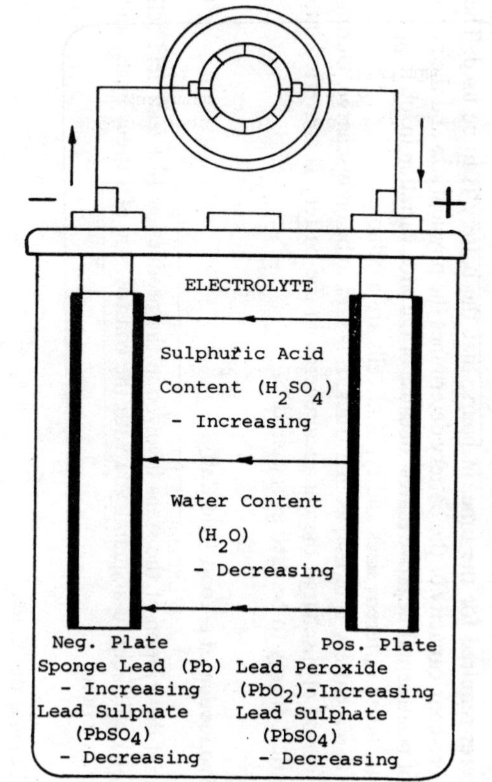

Fig. 11·15. Charging.

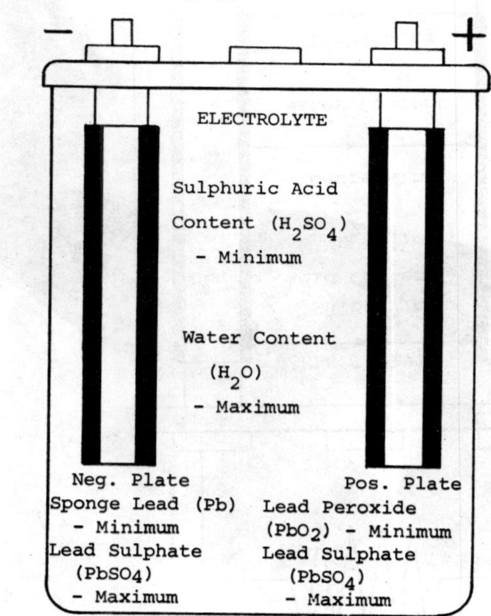

Fig. 11-16. Discharged.

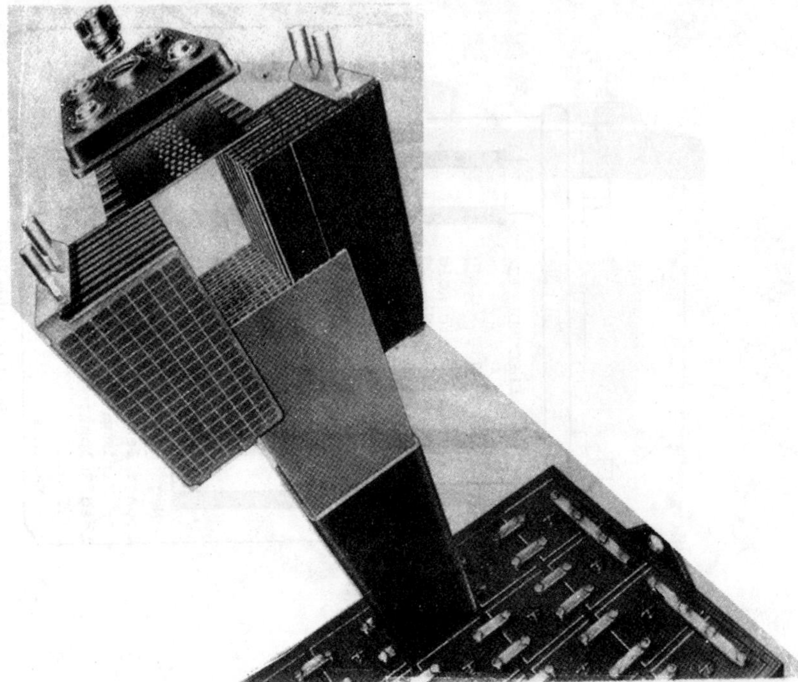

Fig. 11-17. An illustration of a rubber jar battery with the element of one cell exploded to show the positive and negative groups with their posts, plate separators, and cover.

amperes required for the time, in hours, that the battery is to be used. The ampere-hour capacity of the battery determines the physical size and the number of positive and negative plates. Because of the wide variation in job requirements, many different sizes and types of cells are available.

When a battery is in use, as in a truck, it is said to be on discharge. During this period of discharge the chemical energy in the battery is converted into electrical energy to be used as required.

F. Production of a Lead Acid Cell

A brief description of the steps involved in the production of a lead acid cell (below) will help to acquaint you with the construction of various parts, and their functions.

G. Casting the Grids

Basically, a plate is a cast lead grid supporting framework around which certain chemical pastes have been applied (as shown in Fig. 11-19). Because lead

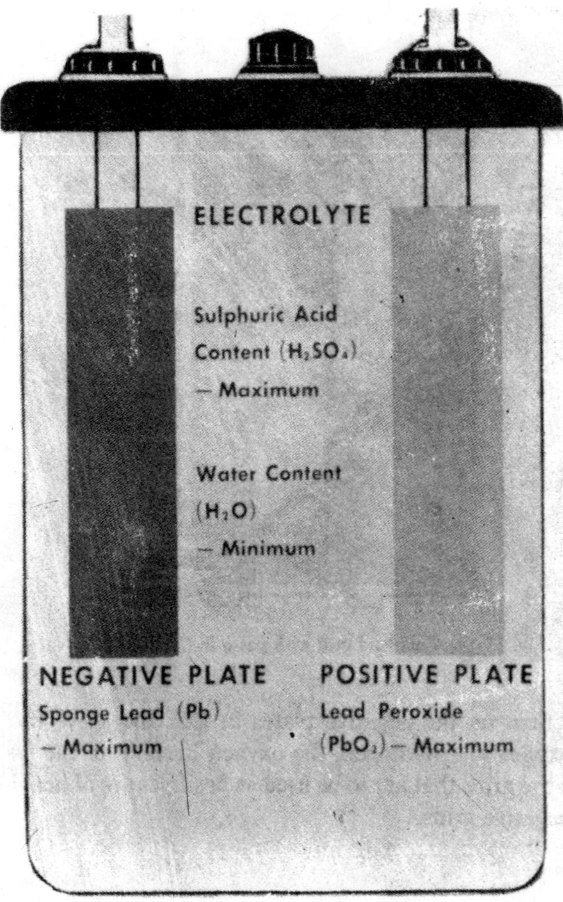

Fig. 11-18. A simple cell.

alone is very soft and is inclined to warp or lose its form, some strengthening or, stiffening agent must be added. Under very rigid control a certain amount of antimony is added to the lead to secure this necessary strengthening feature. This alloy of lead and antimony is heated in melting pots under rigid temperature control, and poured into grid molds. Temperature control at this point is critical because uncontrolled heat would cause the antimony to rise to the surface of the melting pot and then dissipate into the outside air.

The proper casting of a grid is of critical importance because any premature or uneven cooling of the casting can cause fractures or holes, which can reduce the useful life of the battery.

In actual use, the chemical action taking place is more pronounced on the

Fig. 11-19. Cast lead grid with paste in the diamonds.

positive plates than on the negative plates in that the gases formed during charging are oxygen and hydrogen, the oxygen forming in the positive plate. For this reason the grids that are to be used as positives are of heavier construction than the negative grids.

H. Pasting the Grids

After the grids have been cast, chemical pastes are applied, in what is known as a pasting operation. The pastes are the active ingredients. The chemical paste used in a negative plate consists of a spongy lead material with an expander to maintain the spongy condition. The chemical paste used in preparing positive plates is lead oxide, sulfuric acid, and water, and is known as regenerative active material.

The regenerative active material is no named because it grows and replenishes itself as it is used during the life of the plate. Each flake of the oxide has a center of pure metallic lead surrounded by oxide. In service this center gradually, but continuously, oxidizes to form more oxide.

The process of manufacturing the active material consists of reducing pure lead ingots to a molten mass that is poured into a gang mold consisting of many rods about 18 inches in length and about one-half inch in diameter. These rods are cut into slugs and fed into rotary mills. As the mill rotates, the slugs are constantly being rubbed against each other, causing friction, and oxidation takes place. Small, dustlike particles drop to the bottom of the mill where they are drawn off at specified times.

The lead and other chemicals are mixed to a puttylike consistency for pasting on the grids. This operation is done either by hand or by machine. Large grids are pasted by machine. In the machine operation the active materials are automatically applied to the grids, then evenly distributed by a roller. This results in a complete penetration of the paste into the grids.

Small, thin grids are generally pasted by hand. The paster places a predetermined amount of paste on the bare grid and works it into the grid with a special spatula.

After pasting, the grids are known as unformed plates. They are then dried to drive out any moisture in the active ingredients and to secure a solid bonding of the active ingredients with the grid structure.

From the ovens the plates are sent to the forming department. Here the plates are placed in large vats containing low-specific-gravity electrolyte, and given a slow forming charge. They are now formed plates, either positive or negative.

When a battery is charged and discharged in cycle service, some small particles of the active material in the plates become dislodged from the plates and drop down to the sediment space at the bottom of the cell where they can do no useful work (Fig. 11-20). Many methods have been devised to mechanically prevent this destructive action. One of the methods is the use of fiber glass mats for this service.

A fiber glass mat is placed against both sides of the positive plates. This method, over many years of use, has been found to increase the life of the battery substantially. After these mats have been placed on both sides of the

Fig. 11-20. Bottom of a cell showing the sediment that has accumulated.

positive plates, a perforated plastic retainer is wrapped around both the positive plate and the mats, as an additional safeguard. This retainer serves two purposes: (1) it keeps the mat in position; and (2) it prevents "treeing" of active material from positive to negative at the sides.

The long successful service that followed the use of these fiber glass mats brought about a later advance in manufacturing technique. The finding that some exceptionally rugged applications required an even stronger mechanical retainer led to the development of fiber glass tape. The fiber glass tape or ribbon is wrapped, first vertically and then horizontally, over the positive plate, the first wrapping completely covering the plate. This provides even greater positive plate protection. The orientation of the fiber glass tape strands (unlike fiber glass mats) can be controlled during manufacture. In the tape about 85% of the strands are oriented in one direction with about 15% of the strands laid on a bias, to hold the strands together. This results in a very dense and uniform protective coating. (Some manufacturers use a fiber glass mat called a sliver-type mat.)

A perforated plastic envelope is placed over the glass tape. Then a bottom shield is added to complete the positive plate. The positive and negative plates are assembled into positive and negative groups by burning all the positive lead straps together and all the negative straps together at the top or lug end. The groups are then meshed together with separators between each positive and negative plate.

Separators are made of microporous rubber, resistant to both heat and acid. Flat on one side and grooved on the other, they serve as an insulator between the plates but are sufficiently porous to permit the free passage of the electrolyte. The grooved side is placed next to the positive plate to permit free circulation of a large volume of electrolyte to the positive plate. The flat side is placed next to the negative plate because the negative material tends to expand and would fill grooves if they were present. This assembly, now called an element, is placed in a hard rubber jar.

On top of the element is placed a flat plastic splash plate. A special design permits the splash plate to fit snugly under the terminals without any possibility of shifting during operation. This plate serves several purposes; for example:

1. It prevents foreign matter, which might damage the plates, from entering from the top of the cell.
2. It prevents damage to plates or separators through the careless use of a hydrometer or a thermometer.

A hard rubber cover with lead inserts is placed in position on the top. Posts are then burned (or melted) onto the cover inserts. An asphalt-base, hot pliable compound is then applied at the edges of the cover where it meets the sides of the jar.

The cell is now sent to the charging room where acid is added, and it is given its initial charge and discharge. After several cycles of charge and discharge, which are given to assure the proper capacity and quality of product, the cell receives a final inspection.

I. How to Select a Battery of the Proper Size

The proper ampere-hour capacity of a battery is of prime importance because under-capacity causes a battery to run down before the end of the shift. By the same reasoning over-capacity batteries cause unwarranted cost.

Industrial truck manufacturers or battery representatives are glad to help you select a battery of the proper capacity. But, by using the following method, you can check your battery capacity requirements against your own operating conditions.

The Electric Industrial Truck Association in 1950 published the *Handbook of Material Handling* and set up a number of standard procedures that were found necessary through lengthy field operating studies. Figure 11-21 shows the power, in watt hours, necessary to move certain weights over certain distances, over level concrete.

By using this chart, together with other constants given in the *Handbook of Material Handling,* we can arrive at a power requirement figure that will cover not only level concrete hauls, but also such items as grade, lift, and tilt.

We shall use as an example a battery-operated truck that, including the weight of the battery and the weight of the operator, weighs 3,650 pounds or 1.825 tons. We shall also use in our example a load of 2,000 pounds or 1 ton. Average lift is 3 feet. The weight totals 5,650 pounds or 2.825 tons. We shall assume that we wish to move this truck and load a distance of 110 feet, of which 80 feet is along level concrete, and the balance of 30 feet is an up grade of 10%; we discharge the load and then return the unloaded truck over the same route, which now means a down grade for 30 feet and the same 80 feet over level concrete to the starting point.

We desire to calculate watt hours for:

1. Total run with load
2. Extra power for 30 feet of loaded travel up 10% grade
3. Return run unloaded with deduction for down grade
4. Lifting
5. Tilting

To learn the power requirements for item 1 we use the power chart (Fig. 11-21). First, we locate the total distance to be traveled (110 feet) on the left-hand side of the chart. Then we extend a line from the 110-foot point toward the right of the chart until it intersects the standard line; and then we drop the line

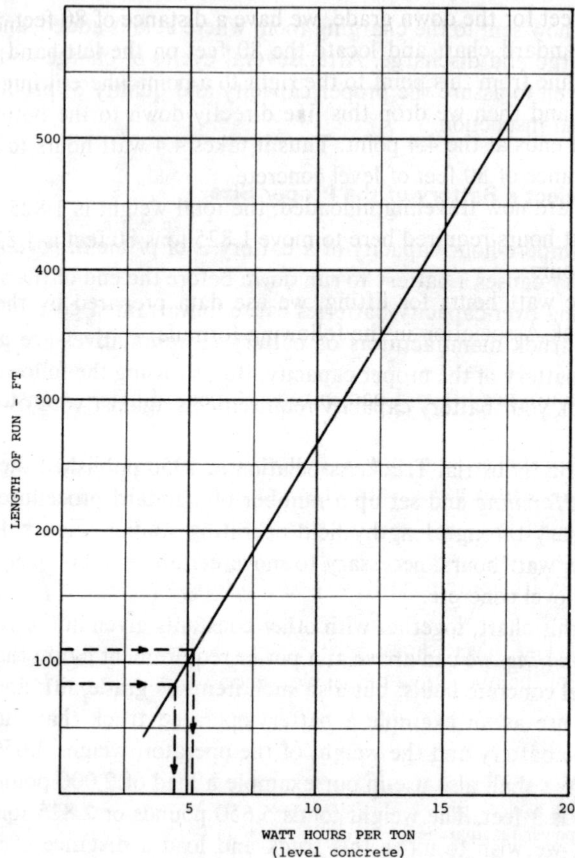

Fig. 11-21. Watt hours per ton required to operate industrial powered trucks over level concrete.

straight down to the bottom of the chart, where it ends at the 5.4 point. Thus it takes 5.4 watt hours to move one ton over a distance of 110 feet of level concrete.

Our loaded truck weighs 2.825 tons, which we multiply by the number of watt hours, 5.4, needed to move one ton. Thus the number of watt hours required here to move 2.825 tons 110 feet is 2.825 × 5.4, or 15.26 watt hours.

To calculate the extra power needed to cover the 30 feet of 10% upgrade, the Electric Industrial Truck Association data are again used as follows: Extra power necessary for grade equals "Tons × Length of grade × Percent of grade × Constant" or 2.825 × 30 × 10 × .013. Thus the power needed is 11.02 watt hours.

For the unloaded return trip, the total distance is the same, 110 feet, and deducting 30 feet for the down grade, we have a distance of 80 feet. Again we refer to the standard chart and locate the 80 feet on the left-hand side, and then extend a line from this point to the right to a point where it intersects the standard line; and then we drop this line directly down to the bottom of the chart, where it ends at the 4.4 point. Thus it takes 4.4 watt hours to move one ton over a distance of 80 feet of level concrete.

Because we are now traveling unloaded, the total weight is 1.825 tons. The number of watt hours required here to move 1.825 tons 80 feet is 1.825 × 4.4, or 8.03 watt hours.

To calculate watt hours for lifting, we use data prepared by the Electric Industrial Truck Association in the following formula:

$$\text{Watt hours per lift} = \text{Load in tons} \times \text{Feet of lift} \times \text{Constant}$$

where 1 ton × 3 feet × 2 = 6 watt hours.

For tilting, we again use Electric Industrial Truck Association data to get our formula, which is:

$$\text{Watt hours per tilt} = \text{Load in tons} \times \text{Constant}$$

where 1 ton × 1 = 1 watt hour.

By addition of the above five items, we obtain the watt hours per round trip. Thus:

1. Run with load	15.26
2. Extra power for upgrade	11.02
3. Empty return, no grade	8.03
4. Lifting	6.00
5. Tilting	1.00
	41.31
For total	Watt hours per round trip

Assuming that the truck makes 250 trips daily, we can obtain the daily watt hours requirement by multiplying this 41.3 watt hours by the number of round trips, 250, for a total of 10,325 watt hours.

Now let us assume that the truck is one that is of the 32-volt type. Use the formula

$$\text{Ampere hours} = \text{Watt hours} \div \text{Volts}$$

Thus, 10,325 watt hours divided by 32 volts is 322.7 ampere hours.

Thus, a battery rated at 323 ampere hours, or the nearest figure above 323, would be the minimum size battery to consider for this duty cycle.

J. How to Determine Battery Condition

There are three general methods of determining the condition of a motive power battery: (1) records, (2) test discharge, and (3) internal inspection.

1. Records. Record keeping provides a day-to-day case history of the battery. Daily forms should indicate: date, battery number, number of truck battery was taken from, specific gravity of battery when put on charge (pilot cell reading), temperature (pilot cell), time put on charge, time taken off charge, specific gravity when taken off charge, and truck number battery is assigned to. Each customer should prepare his own card to suit local conditions.

By comparing specific gravity (corrected for temperature) and time-on-charge data with the previous day's reading, any abnormal battery use or abuse will be indicated, and corrective steps can be taken at once. Through the trend of recent entries, records will indicate when a battery is wearing out and should be replaced.

To present, periodically, a picture of overall battery condition, it is recommended that fully charged specific gravity and voltage readings be taken of each cell every six months, and compared with those of the preceding period. These readings should be taken at the end of an equalizing charge. By such a comparison any marked difference in battery condition, as well as differences between cells, can be noted, and steps can be taken to replace or repair the battery.

2. Test Discharge. If there is a question of whether the battery is delivering its rated capacity, a test discharge may be made. This test is made by discharging a fully charged battery at a constant ampere rate until the battery voltage drops below the accepted discharge-termination value—1.75 volts per cell. The time lapse between the time and the battery is put on discharge and the time its voltage drops below 1.75 volts per cell will indicate whether the battery is delivering rated capacity.

To standardize and simplify test discharging, motive power batteries are generally discharged at the "six-hour rate" cataloged for the particular battery under test. Before making a test, the battery is given an equalizing charge, and the fully charged specific gravity adjusted to normal.

During the test, individual cell voltages and overall battery voltages are recorded at intervals: first, 15 minutes after the test is started, and then hourly until the voltage of any one cell reaches 1.80, and from then on at 15-minute intervals. From this point on, the cell voltages should be under constant observation and the time recorded when each cell voltage goes below 1.75 volts. Terminate the test discharge when the majority of the cell voltages reach 1.75 volts, but stop the test before any single cell goes into reversal.

Record the specific gravity of each cell immediately after terminating the discharge. An examination of these readings will reveal whether the battery is uniform, or if one or more cells are low in capacity.

If the battery is uniform and delivered 80% or more of rated capacity, it may be returned to service.

3. Internal Inspection. If the test discharge indicated that the battery was not capable of delivering more than 80% of rated capacity, and all cells are uniform, an internal inspection should be made of one of the cells.

Failure may be caused by an internal short circuit that can be repaired. The positive plates (which wear out first) should be examined. If it is found that they are falling apart or that the grids (the lead framework supporting the lead peroxide or "active material") have many frame fractures, a replacement battery should be ordered.

If the positive plates are in good condition and the cells contain little sediment, the battery may be sulfated.

a. Causes and Treatment of "Sulfated" Batteries. A sulfated battery is one that has been left standing in a dishcarged condition or undercharged to the point where abnormal lead sulfate has formed on the plates. When this occurs, the chemical reactions within the battery are affected, and loss of capacity results. The main causes of sulfation are:

1. *Undercharging or neglect of equalizing charge.* Repeated partial charges, which do not effect thorough mixing of the electrolyte, also result in sulfation. It is difficult in normal battery operation to determine just when sulfation begins, and only by giving periodic equalizing charges and comparing individual cell specific gravity and voltage readings can it be detected in its early stages and corrected or prevented.
2. *Standing in a partially or completely discharged condition.* Permitting a battery to stand in a partially discharged condition allows the sulfate deposited on the plates to harden and close the pores in the plates. Batteries should be charged as soon as practicable after discharge and never allowed to stand in a completely discharged condition when temperatures are below freezing or for more than 24 hours.
3. *Low electrolyte.* If the level of the electrolyte is permitted to fall below the tops of the plates, the exposed surfaces will harden and become sulfated.

4. *Adding acid.* If acid is added to a cell in which sulfation exists, the condition will be aggravated.
5. *High specific gravity.* In general, the higher the fully charged specific gravity of a cell, the more likely sulfation is to occur, and the more difficult it is to reduce. If in any battery there exist cells having specific gravity more than 0.015 above the average, the possibility of sulfation in these cells will be enhanced.
6. *High temperature.* High temperatures accelerate sulfation, particularly of an idle, partially discharged battery.

All cells of a sulfated battery will give low specific gravity and voltage readings. They will not become fully charged after normal charging. An internal inspection will disclose negative plates with a slatelike feeling, sulfated negative-plate material being hard and gritty and feeling sandy when rubbed between the thumb and forefinger. The internal inspection should be made after a normal charge because a discharged plate is always somewhat sulfated. A good fully charged negative plate is spongy and springy to the touch and has a metallic sheen when stroked with a fingernail or knife. A sulfated positive plate is a lighter brown color than a normal plate.

Thorough and careful attention to the following steps often will restore a sulfated battery to good operating condition:

1. Clean the battery.
2. Bring the electrolyte level to the proper height by adding water.
3. Put the battery on charge at the prescribed finishing rate until full ampere-hour capacity has been put into the battery, based on the eight-hour rate. If at any time during these procedures the temperature of the battery exceeds 110°F, reduce the charge rate to maintain the temperature at or below this point. If any cell gives low readings (0.20 volt less than the average cell voltage of the battery), pull and repair the cell before continuing with the procedure.
4. After full ampere-hour capacity has been put into the battery, continue the charge at the finishing rate until the specific gravity shows no change for a four-hour period with readings taken hourly. Record voltage and specific gravity readings. Correct specific gravity readings for temperature. These readings indicate the state of charge of the battery.
5. Place the battery on discharge at the six-hour rate, and during the test record individual cell voltages and overall battery voltage at intervals: 15 minutes after the test is started, then hourly until voltage on any one cell reaches 1.80, and from then on at 15-minute intervals. From this point on, the cell voltages should be under constant observation and the time recorded when each cell voltage goes below 1.75 volts. Terminate

the test discharge when the majority of the cell voltages reach 1.75 volts, but stop the test before any single cell goes into reversal.

6. If the battery gives rated capacity, no further treatment is required other than normal recharge and equalization of gravity.
7. If the battery does not deliver near-rated capacity, continue the discharge without adjusting the discharge rate until one or more cells reach 1.0 volts.
8. Recharge the battery at the finishing rate, again charging until there is no further rise in specific gravity over a four-hour period, with readings taken hourly.
9. Discharge again at the six-hour rate, and if the battery gives full capacity, recharge it and put it into service.
10. If this procedure does not result in at least 80% capacity, perform it once more.
11. If the battery does not respond to this treatment, it is sulfated to the point where it is impractical to attempt further treatment, and it should be replaced.

K. Equalizing Charge

One way to prolong battery life is to give the battery an equalizing charge.

The equalizing charge is a low-rate charge given to restore all cells in the battery to a fully charged condition. In motive power work, it is recommended periodically, at least once a month but no more often than once a week, depending upon the duty cycle. On a heavy duty cycle, where batteries are discharged to a major extent one or more times a day, the equalizing charge should be given weekly. On a light duty cycle, where a battery may be charged once every two or three days, the equalizing charge may be given once a month.

In motive power work it is customary to use a center cell in the battery as the pilot cell for the equalizing charge.

L. Connectors—Charging Plugs and Receptacles

Every industrial battery is equipped with a device for connecting it to the machine it drives and to the charging equipment. Known as charging plugs and receptacles, these devices are made in several sizes in five or more types (Fig. 11-22) and are designed to be disconnected easily and quickly. Although these devices are locked together as a unit in use or on charge, they consist of two separate parts: the plug (male half) and the receptacle (female half). One half is shipped with the battery, and the other is shipped with the machine (for example, a forklift truck). The battery charging equipment also has leads furnished with either a receptacle or a plug. Obviously, the purchaser of battery-

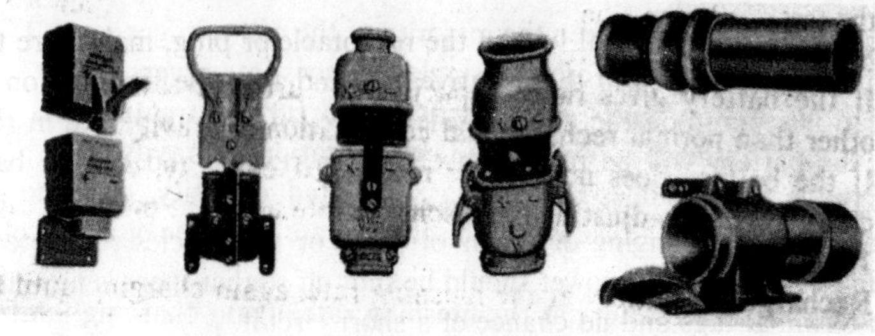

Fig. 11-22. Types of terminal connectors.

powered equipment must make certain that the same type and size of charging plugs and receptacles are supplied with the truck, battery, and charger. He should also be specific about what units the plugs and receptacles should be attached to. Usually, the receptacle is attached to the battery unit, and the plugs are assembled to the truck and the charger.

Although plugs and receptacles are of rugged design, they are not indestructible and can be damaged by misuse. Foreign material such as water, grease, oil, dirt, etc., in the receptacle will make it useless unless it is repaired. It may also be necessary to change the size or type of plug.

In repairing a damaged or dirty plug or receptacle connected to a battery, the user must not forget that the leads that terminate in the receptacle are live or "hot" with the total voltage of the battery existing across the terminals. In other words, one lead is secured to the positive post on the battery and the other to the negative. When the terminal lugs are enclosed in the receptacle, they are held apart with little danger of short-circuiting. Before the terminal lugs are removed from the receptacle, the battery circuit must be opened or broken. If this is not done and the terminal lugs are accidentally touched together, a short circuit and arcing will occur that can injure personnel and equipment. The strength of the arc will depend on the size of the battery. The amperage carried may reach 10,000 amperes and may exceed the current-carrying capacity of the leads. The short-circuit rate will equal three times the one-minute discharge rate of the battery.

To open the circuit, either disconnect one lead from the battery post or sever one of the cell connectors.

The terminal lugs are held in the plug or receptacle by a bolt or screw that, when loosened, will permit the lugs to be withdrawn for cleaning or replacement.

After the broken or damaged terminal lug is severed from the cable, the proper length of wire to fit the terminal must be bared, cleaned, and tinned. Some terminal lugs have short or shallow recesses into which the wire must be soldered, and it is doubly important to clean and tin the wire to obtain a secure bond.

In reassembling the terminal lugs in the receptacle or plug, make sure that the negative wire is placed in the negative side and that the terminal on the positive lead is secured on the positive side. If the leads are reversed in reassembling, the battery will be placed on charge in reverse and will be badly damaged.

Obviously, during changing or repair of plugs or receptacles connected to the charging equipment, the power should be shut off so that there is no voltage across the terminal lugs and no chance of a short circuit.

M. Cables

Select cables for batteries that are as large as possible to lower charging resistance. This same advice applies to wiring in battery chargers.

N. Chargers

Battery chargers have been part of a very competitive market ever since the shift from the motor generator set to the silicon-controlled rectifier type of charging machine. Motor generators were reliable, and with proper maintenance, brush replacement, armature truing, etc., they lasted for 20 to 30 years or longer; but they are not as efficient as the SCR units.

Manufacturers of extremely reliable SCR units are KW, Westinghouse, Gould, and Exide.

EXERCISE NO. 11

1. The justification of specialized equipment continues to become less difficult as ____________ ____________ rises higher than ____________ ____________

2. The materials handling specialist requires data to make some basic assumptions in equipment selection, such as:
1. ____________
2. ____________
3. ____________
4. ____________
5. ____________

3. In general, industrial powered trucks can be classified into three broad groupings:
1. ____________
2. ____________
3. ____________

4. There are more electric trucks today than there are gas and diesel. True ☐ False ☐

5. Indoor forklift trucks have pneumatic tires and disc brakes. True ☐ False ☐

6. What is the most commonly used type of industrial powered truck? ____________

7. Why use standard mast heights when selecting fork trucks? ____________
____

8. What is meant by free lift? ______________________________

____

9. Load wheels in a walkie truck are free to ride with the load. True ☐ False ☐

10. Towable trucks are used, primarily, in what industry? ____________

11. Describe what happens when a load is elevated on the forks of a lift truck and the mast is tilted forward.

____

____

____

____

____

12. What happens when the mast in Question 11 is tilted as far back as it will go?

____

____

____

____

____

13. What is meant by gradability? ______________________________

____

____

____

14. What is the percentage grade of a ramp that is 25 feet long and 4 feet in height? __________%. (Show your calculations.)

15. Name three types of hydraulic, forklift truck attachments:
(1) ______________, (2) ______________, and
(3) ______________

16. A battery is composed of a number of ______________.

17. Basically, a plate is a cast ______________ ______________ supporting framework, around which certain chemical ______________ have been applied.

18. There are three general methods of determining the condition of a motive power battery. These are:
1. ______________________________
2. ______________________________
3. ______________________________

19. If there is a question as to whether the battery is delivering its rated capacity, a ______________ may be made.

20. A sulfated battery is one that has been left standing in a ______________ condition or undercharged to the point where abnormal ______________ ______________ has formed on the plates.

Chapter 12
Conveyors, Cranes, Lifting Rigs, Chains, and Slings

I. CONVEYORS

A. Introduction

Conveyors of diverse types and sizes are found in many industrial plants, with the exception of the oil and chemical industries. In many instances, conveyors are used to pace production operations, in addition to providing the feed rates upon which many production processes depend. Thus we should become familiar with some of the terms of conveyorization and with conveyor applications.

1. Where and Why Use Conveyors? Conveyors are usually used where the flow of work is more or less continuous and can be directed along a fixed path. Batch processing can be accomplished by means of forktrucks and pallets where the product is required sporadically. Also, batch processing can use the pallet system where delays in delivery will not interrupt production. But if a steady and sufficient stream of material is required, some type of conveyor is usually employed.

Conveyors are very versatile in that it is possible to start and stop them, interrupting the flow of materials to suit given conditions. Materials can be diverted, transferred, raised or lowered, as well as loaded upon the conveyor or unloaded. All of these functions can be accomplished by means of conveyors, at one or more locations and in virtually any quantity to suit a large variety of processing requirements.

Many types of conveyors can be obtained, both portable and fixed. One serious drawback to the fixed or stationary conveyor is that, once installed, it is fairly inflexible regarding alterations in location, shape, capacity, or type of materials to be handled.

This inflexibility or rigidity means that the equipment is best suited for installations with operations that are fairly permanent and not likely to be changed for a considerable length of time.

Conveyors usually carry material along fairly direct routes and at extremely high capacity rates. They can be placed at floor level, at worker (work station) heights, or elevated above the workers' heads or other operational levels. Therefore, conveyors do not necessarily have to occupy valuable floor space; they can utilize the air-rights of the plant to excellent advantage.

Conveyors, like some cranes or mobile, industrial powered trucks, do not necessarily have to have an operator. Moreover, work performed by an operator can be carried out while material is actually being moved by the conveyor, and material can be accumulated and stored upon the conveyor.

When properly designed and installed, conveyors are very reliable in operation, requiring a minimum amount of downtime for routine preventive maintenance. Thus, they are particularly desirable for manufacturing or commercial operations that must be performed on a continuous basis.

Preventive maintenance is important with conveyors as it is with all machinery, scheduled PM being especially important for conveyors in order that they run continuously, without stopping for long periods of time. Scheduled PM can be very important for conveyors that are used in heat-treating and annealing operations; for example, a stoppage while expensive ferrous metal parts are undergoing a timed travel through a furnace might destroy the part and the conveyor, if the stoppage were due to neglect or poor maintenance. Also, if a package conveyor were to break down in a post office plant, a mail order house, or a warehouse during peak periods, it could cause numerous delays throughout the system, as well as idle a large number of employees.

2. Types of Materials That Can be Handled. Conveyors can be used to handle many different types of materials, but these materials usually fall into the following three broad classifications.

a. Packages. The packages can be corrugated cartons, wood boxes, drums, bagged materials, and the like.

Package specifications are concerned with the shape, dimensions, and weight of the package. While it is not always so, the contents of the package may have an important bearing on the type of conveyor to be employed; so any special characteristics should be spelled out, such as whether or not the contents are toxic or nontoxic, whether the contents will be affected by temperature or humidity changes, whether the contents are flammable or nonflammable, what kind of exterior package is to be encountered, and so forth. (For examples of package conveyors see Fig. 12-1.)

b. Loose Materials. This type of conveyorized material usually takes the form of in-process parts, such as metal stampings, nuts, bolts, castings, forgings, plastic parts, and the like.

Loose materials can be specified by description of the items, by weight per foot of conveyor space or per cubic foot, and by their dimensions and compo-

Powdered belt and roller conveyors

Belt on rollers

Gravity

Fig. 12-1. Examples of package conveyors.

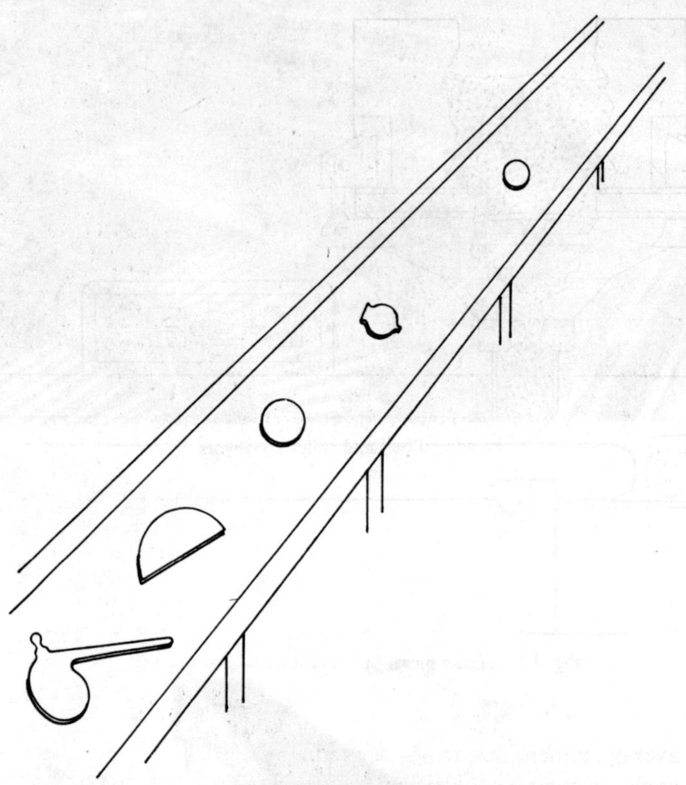

Fig. 12-2. Examples of loose material on a conveyor.

sition. Where there are special characteristics, such as temperature, as in the handling of hot forgings or annealed parts, or where fragile or hygienic parts or items are concerned, as in the handling of food, fruit, or bakery products, this information should be noted. (See Fig. 12-2 for examples of loose materials on conveyors.)

c. Bulk Materials. This type of material can take the form of granulated substances, crushed rock, powdered materials such as flours, sand, and cement, or slurries and liquids.

Bulk materials may have widely varying characteristics, and it is necessary to have complete detailed specifications because of the customized design requirements. A bulk conveyor carrying an abrasive, granular material like ceramic chips requires a different approach from one carrying soap powder.

In addition, bulk materials are described in the following manner:

1. By density, or weight per cubic foot

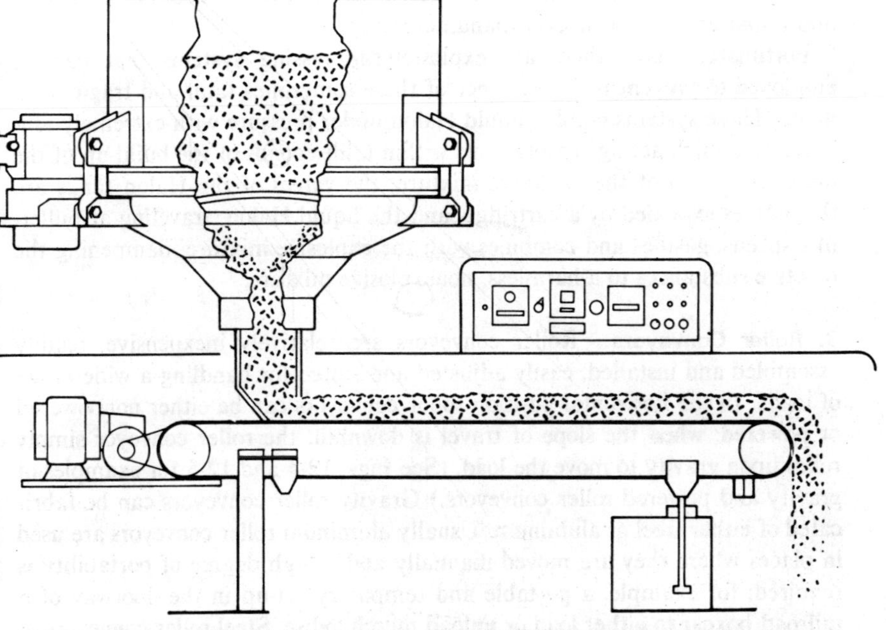

Fig. 12-3. Example of bulk material on a conveyor.

2. By average dimensions, mesh, or grade
3. By angles of repose or cohesion
4. By other characteristics such as the shape or nature of the particles

Bulk density is usually measured by the amount of material that can be poured into a cubic foot of space.

The angle of repose is the angle formed by the horizontal with the side of the conical pile made by the product when it falls freely from a small height. This angle varies from approximately 20° to about 70° and depends largely on the size and shape of the individual particles or granules.

The subject of bulk handling is a very specialized one, which we shall discuss separately in Chapter 13. (See Fig. 12-3 for an example of bulk material on a conveyor.)

d. Hazardous Materials. Somewhat neglected and just beginning to be understood is the subject of dust from a wide variety of materials that, in themselves, are not explosive but when airborne can form exceedingly explosive mixtures. In some cases, grain elevators and other large, reinforced concrete structures have been literally blown apart by dust explosions.

Because of such potential hazards, when the type of material to be conveyorized is being specified, as much information as possible should be developed and imparted to the conveyor manufacturer.

Fortunately, now there are explosion-suppressing systems that can be employed to prevent the occurrence of these sometimes fatal and tragic accidents. These systems employ liquid Halon under pressure with extremely sensitive and quick-acting sensors; thus within milliseconds of the build-up of the ion composition of the explosive mixture, the valves of the Halon tanks are themselves exploded by a cartridge, and the liquid Halon, traveling at bullet-like speeds, gasifies and combines with the explosive mixture, dampening the reactive substances to a harmless, nonexplosive mixture.

3. Roller Conveyors. Roller conveyors are relatively inexpensive, readily assembled and installed, easily adjusted and suited for handling a wide range of loads. In the horizontal position roller conveyors can be either nonpowered or powered; when the slope of travel is downhill, the roller conveyor simply relies upon gravity to move the load. (See Figs. 12-4 and 12-5 for examples of gravity and powered roller conveyors.) Gravity roller conveyors can be fabricated of either steel or aluminum. Usually aluminum roller conveyors are used in places where they are moved manually and a high degree of portability is required; for example, a portable and temporary set-up in the doorway of a railroad boxcar to either load or unload merchandise. Steel roller conveyors of the gravity type are considerably heavier and can usually be moved by means

Fig. 12-4. A gravity roller conveyor.

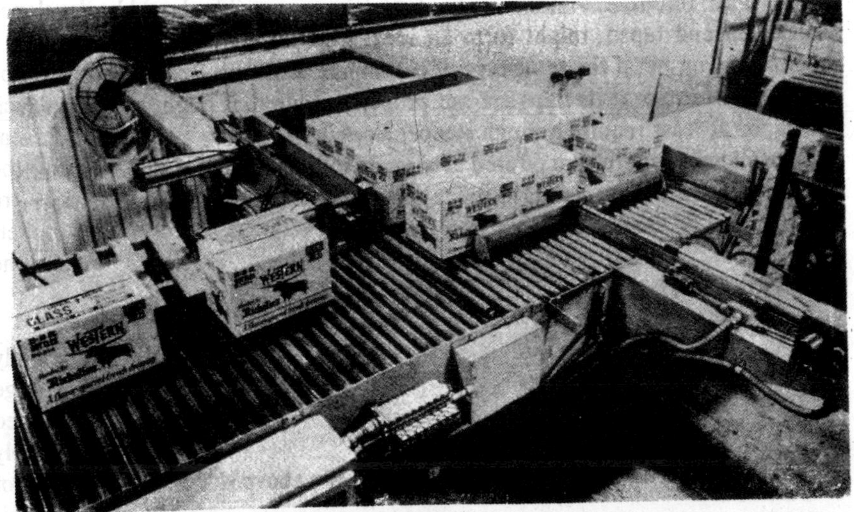

Fig. 12-5. A powered roller conveyor.

of a forklift truck, but they are more permanent in nature with respect to installation. All powered roller conveyors are made of steel and can range from the relatively simple chain-driven or snubbing belt-driven conveyor to the accumulation type. (See Fig. 12-6.)

Within limits, any load having a rigid, smooth base can be moved on roller conveyors, but quite small irregularities on the base can prevent free movement. For instance, a wood box with steel strapping, set at right angles to the rollers of the conveyor, might be entirely satisfactory for gravity movement; but if the nail heads protrude from the strapping, the load movement, if any,

Fig. 12-6. An example of an accumulation-type, powered, roller conveyor.

can be quite different. Again, a carton composed of good corrugated board, well-sealed and taped, might form an ideal load for conveying by a gravity roller conveyor; but if the same type of carton has become softened by repeated use, or moisture, or if its flaps are not properly secured, it might present difficulties, or at least require a much steeper slope.

The following figures are offered as a guide to the amount of slope that may be required when using standard roller conveyors. Wherever possible, however, *trials should be made with the actual loads.*

Weight, pounds	Inches of fall in 10 feet
9–15	6–7
15–50	4–5
50–120	3–4
120–250	2–3

Curves require an increase of about 75% on the above slopes.

If a change of slope between sections of the conveyor is to take place, then care must be taken to ensure that a situation does not arise in which the load can wedge itself against the next roller.

When items have to be moved that would not normally travel on a roller conveyor, flat boards are frequently used, with the items placed on them; but obviously the boards must eventually be returned to the top of the slope.

Gravity roller conveyors are usually manufactured in 10-foot lengths, which can be linked together to form a continuous track.

The carrying capacity is related to the diameter of the roller; usually rollers vary from one to three inches in diameter. It should be noted, also, that the pitch of the rollers should be such that three rollers are always under the load.

4. Troughed Belt Conveyors. Troughed belt conveyors are composed of a pair of pulleys, or end drums, with one of them driven to impart motion to the belt, the carrying strand of which is carried on idlers. The return strand of the belt is supported on flat rollers, the whole assembly being supported on a suitable framework.

The capacity of the conveyor is governed by the speed, width, and depth of troughing of the belt. The strength of the belt is chosen to suit the above conditions.

The belts, which are generally rubber-covered, can also be obtained in solid woven fabric. These relatively long belts can be manufactured endless, or vulcanized on the site, or joined on the site by means of belt fasteners.

Up to a few years ago, the great majority of conveyor belts were composed of a combination of India rubber and canvas. The strength of the belt was in the body or carcass, which was composed of layers or plies of cotton fabric known as duck. These plies were vulcanized together, and the whole was covered with a coating of rubber. The thickness of the rubber varied from ⅓₂ to ¼ of an inch on the carrying face, and from nothing to, say, ⅛ inch on the under face. The thickness of the top cover was chosen to suit the type of material being carried. If a heavy or rugged material such as rock or coal was involved, a thick top cover of up to ¼ inch was applied, whereas with a more gentle material such as cement a top cover of ⅓₂ inch would be ample. Obviously, the thicker the rubber covers, the more expensive the belt.

During the past 15 years, rayon, nylon, and other synthetic fiber yarns have been widely used to form the body fabric of conveyor belts. These yarns are stronger than cotton, and their use can make it possible to adopt a lighter (lesser number of plies) belt for the same duty. The diameter of the end drums of a conveyor is governed by the stiffness (number of plies) of the belt; so the use of the more flexible nylon or synthetic fiber yarn permits smaller end drums, with overall reduction of the weight and possibly the cost of the conveyor.

The trough is imparted to the belt by means of the idler rollers that carry the belt. These are generally of the three- or five-roller pattern, the length and diameter of the rollers being increased from 4 to 6 inches as the width and weight of the conveyor belt increase. The wing rollers of the standard three-roller carrying idler sets for use with rubber and canvas conveyor belts are set at 20° to 30° to the horizontal (Fig. 12-7). The use of nylon and polyester conveyor belts, which are more flexible than cotton, has made it possible to increase the depth of the trough; and "deep troughed" carrying idlers, with the wing rollers set at 50° to 70° to the horizontal, are now available (Fig. 12-8). This deeper troughing of the belt enables a greater volume of material to be carried for the same width of belt, and in many cases can cheapen the installation.

Belt conveyors require little maintenance once they are "run in," but they do require very careful attention when first installed. Conveyor belts stretch (it is normal to allow for 1% stretch when first installing a belt), and if this slack is not taken up, the driving drums will start to slip, heat will be generated, and

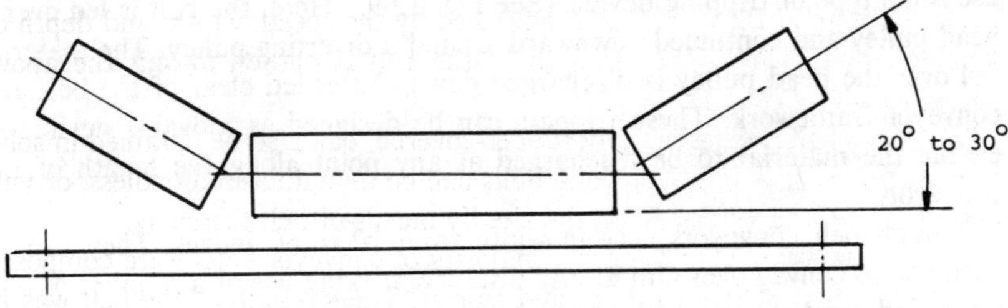

Fig. 12-7. Roll carrying idler.

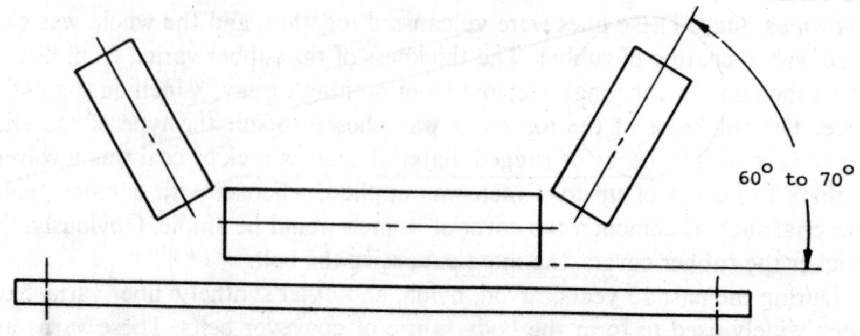

Fig. 12-8. Roll carrying idler, deep trough type.

the belt can rapidly deteriorate. A take-up device for easy adjustment of the tension in the conveyor belt and to take up the slack in the belt is an essential feature of every well-designed conveyor.

Again, if belts are allowed to become misaligned and wander, the edges can come into contact with the conveyor frame, and very expensive damage can be cuased in a short time.

Considerable damage can be caused to conveyor belts by material getting onto and adhering to the underside of the belt. This material is carried onto the head and tail pulleys, and can rapidly cause the belt to wander. Decking plates should be fitted between the carrying and return strand of the belt, and scrapers or brushes should be applied to the belt, close to the head pulley. Tramp metal can cause belt problems and processing difficulties; however, there are permanent magnets and electro-magnetic traps that can be installed to remove this type of debris.

Trough belt conveyors can carry material up slopes of 16° to the horizontal, depending on the shape and characteristics of the material. Obviously, damp sand will travel up a steeper slope than pebbles. Slopes steeper than 16° can be achieved when the conveyor belts are fitted with special surfaces, cleats, or flights.

Material is readily delivered over the head pulley of trough belt conveyors. Where it is essential to deliver at intermediate points, the usual method is to use some type of tripping device. (See Fig. 12-9.) Here, the belt is led over a head pulley and continued downward around a diverting pulley. The material fed over the head pulley is discharged down chutes led clear of the belt and conveyor framework. These trippers can be designed as movable devices to enable the material to be discharged at any point along the length of the conveyor.

Trough belt conveyors vary in width from 10 to 60 inches. They can be designed to convey over almost any distance, making use of a number of sections, and can have capacities up to thousands of tons per hour, depending on the type of material to be conveyed.

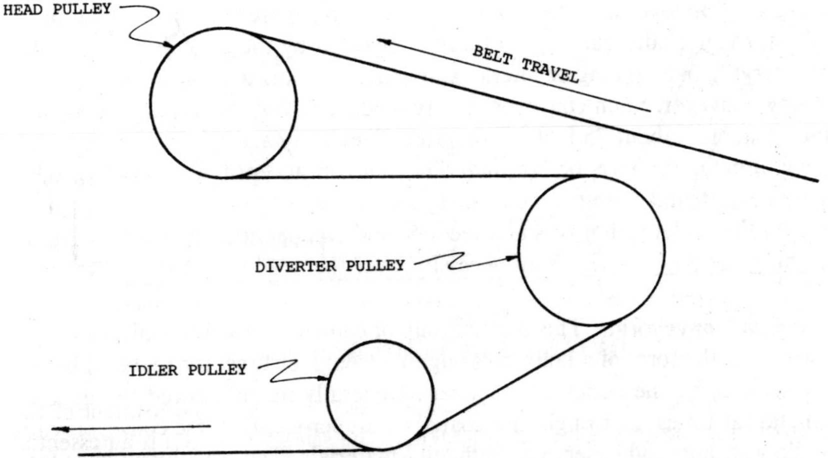

Fig. 12-9. Trip path of conveyor belt.

5. Flat Belts and Slider Belts. Flat belts can be used to handle bulk materials also. These belts either run on flat tables (and then are called slider belts) or on rollers, or on a combination of both. The belts may be fitted with side flanges to retain material.

Discharge of material from a flat belt can sometimes be achieved by the use of plows that sweep the material off the belt. These plows can be made movable or removable so that the discharge of the material can be arranged at any point along the conveyor.

6. Steel Slat Conveyors. Steel slat conveyors, manufactured in carbon or stainless steel, are particularly suitable for certain high-temperature applications. The slats can be manufactured in very wide widths (12-foot-wide slats are in operation) and are particularly advantageous when very hot, acidic, sticky, or wet materials have to be conveyed, or when cleanliness is of paramount importance. The slats can operate in temperatures of 500°F and above, and are widely used in the food, chemical, and metal-fabricating industries. The minimum diameter of the end pulleys on steel slat conveyors is normally much greater than it is for rubber belt conveyors.

7. Woven Wire Belts. Many conveyors are fitted with mesh belts, woven from stainless steel, mild steel, monel metal, and other metals. They are used for carrying materials through ovens and quenching baths; and because hot air can be readily passed through the mesh, they can be applied to washing and drying plants.

8. Apron Conveyors. The apron conveyor is composed of a pair of parallel, endless, roller chains running on tracks supported by the conveyor framework and carrying overlapping or interlocking plates or pans to form a continuously moving conveyor. Such conveyors are rugged, relatively heavy, and slow-running (generally about 75 feet per minute). They can handle large quantities of heavy, lumpy, abrasive, or hot materials and can accept impact loading that would be quite unsuitable to belt conveyors. This type of conveyor is frequently used on the outlet of hoppers and feeders, and can operate up or down slopes. Discharge of the material is, of necessity, over the head end of the conveyor.

9. Screw Conveyors. This useful group of conveyors is composed of a screw or worm, in the form of a helix, rotating in a trough or tube, the material being moved along by the action of the screw. Generally manufactured throughout of metal (at times the troughs are coated or rubber-lined), these conveyors can handle wet, hot, and otherwise "difficult" materials. The trough can have top covers to form a seal and retain the material or prevent ingress of moisture or contamination. The screws can be full-bladed for maximum conveying capacity, a ribbon type suitable for materials that tend to adhere to the screw or screw shaft, or specially designed to agitate or mix the material during conveying.

Screw conveyors can operate in the horizontal, on a slope or even vertically, although the carrying capacity is reduced as the slope increases. A great variety of materials—from fine powder to animal feeds, coal to slurries, etc.—can be handled in screw conveyors, but the materials must be of a type that will readily drop out of the discharge apertures; otherwise, the action of the screw will soon cause them to pack solid, with serious trouble resulting. Stringy material is not suitable for handling by screw conveyors.

If hot materials are to be handled, special care must be taken to accommodate the expansion that will occur in both screw and conveyor casing; and if abrasive materials are involved, extra seals should be fitted to the screw shaft bearings, which, of necessity, are frequently immersed in the material.

The screws of the traditional type of screw conveyor run at speeds of 40 to 160 rpm. High-speed screw conveyors, also known as auger conveyors, have been designed that will handle a variety of materials if they are of a free-flowing and nonabrasive nature. These conveyors will operate at a very steep angle, but in general, are more suitable for use in intermittent or light-duty applications, or in handling grain such as shelled corn, and silage for placement into storage bins and silos.

10. En Masse Conveyors. This type of equipment is composed of an endless chain carrying a series of flights, at pitched intervals, the whole moving through the enclosed duct. The flights, which may be in skeletal or solid form, slide along the metal duct (or over a layer of the material lying in the duct) and propel the mass of the material along. The ducts can go around bends and follow slopes when changing plane, and can be designed to follow either horizontal or vertical paths.

The material, which is fed into the duct through feed chutes, is drawn along the duct and discharged through an aperture in the floor of the duct. Obviously, then, for satisfactory operation the material must be of a type that will fall freely from the conveyor when it reaches the discharge aperture.

The mass movement of the material, causing a minimum of relative movement between the particles, is gentle and reduces degradation and breakage. The ducts can be made dust-proof and gas-tight, thus controlling the dust hazard.

11. Vibrating Conveyors. Vibrating conveyors can be classed in two broad groups, as follows:

1. Vibrating conveyors with a high-frequency wave form, usually imparted by electro-magnets or unbalanced pulleys.
2. Oscillating conveyors operating at slow speeds, with the pulsations imparted by an eccentric or crank shaft.

These types of conveyors can be fitted with a metal or plastic trough, which may have a top cover or may be in the form of a tube.

The action of vibrating conveyors is gentle, only the trough being in contact with the material. This trough can be quite smooth and clean and thus may be used for handling food items or material that must be kept from contamination. If the material consists of fragments of varying size, down to dust, some separation is likely to occur, and the larger particles may travel at a different speed from the smaller.

It is essential that the nature of the material to be handled be accurately specified, as any change in its bulk density, grain size, or other characteristics may seriously affect the efficiency of conveying.

Vibrating conveyors are generally made up in sections of 10-foot lengths, which can be fastened together to form one conveyor. It is possible to cause material to travel up slopes of about 10° maximum; and spiral vibratory conveyors are also available to elevate particular types of materials.

12. Gravity Bucket Conveyor. In the gravity bucket conveyor, freely swinging buckets are carried between a pair of parallel, endless chains, which can follow any path from vertical to horizontal. (See Fig. 12-10.) The buckets are loaded by a specially designed feeder and are tipped or inverted to discharge. The device that causes the bucket to discharge can be set at any point along a

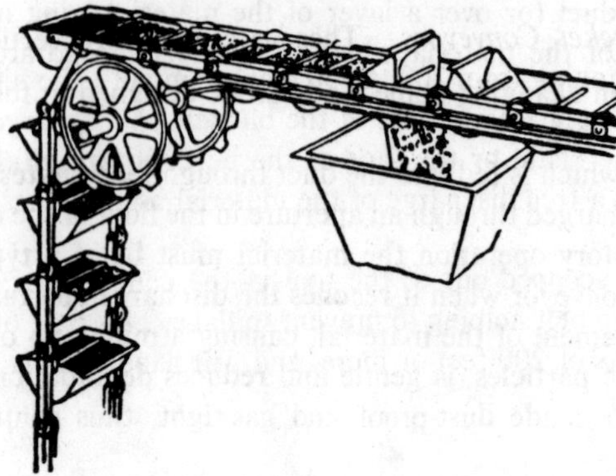

Fig. 12-10. Gravity bucket conveyor.

horizontal run of the conveyor and can be remotely controlled. By this means, material can be delivered into any one of a number of bunkers, and as materials of different types can be fed into the buckets, controlled mixing can be achieved.

This type of conveyor is slow-running (usually about 50 feet per minute), rugged, and capable of giving fairly trouble-free service. The buckets, being made of steel, can carry hot, abrasive materials, or materials that tend to compact or cling together. These conveyors are widely used in coal-fired power stations for feeding coal into each of a number of bunkers and for handling hot ashes.

In addition to the gravity bucket conveyor, there are a number of variations of this type of conveyor, primarily consisting of an endless chain (or chains) or an endless belt, to which buckets are attached, either at pitched distances or adjoining or overlapping one another to form a "continuous bucket." Generally, the conveyors are totally enclosed by means of a metal casing which can be made dust- or even gas-tight.

Material is fed in or near the bottom or foot of the conveyor, and is either scooped from the foot or caught by the buckets passing the inlet chute. Discharge is either by gravity or by centrifugal action as the buckets invert after passing over the head of the elevator.

There are a number of different types of bucket conveyors, each having features to make it especially suitable for the handling of certain types of material:

a. Chain and Bucket Conveyors. These conveyors are arranged to operate either vertically or inclined, with the buckets set at regular intervals or pitch. The speed of the chain is usually about 150 feet per minute, with capacities from 10 to 100 tons per hour, depending on the size of the material and the weight per cubic foot.

b. Centrifugal Bucket Conveyors. These are generally vertical conveyors, with the buckets running from 200 to 500 feet per minute, the high speed being necessary to fling the material clear of the buckets on discharge. The buckets are attached to the chain or the face of the belt and are pitched at regular intervals to permit a free discharge of the material as they pass over the head sprockets or pulley.

The material is scooped out of the foot of the conveyor or caught by the passing buckets, the belt helping to prevent spillage. This type of conveyor can discharge at heights of 200 feet or more, and will handle many materials of a free-flowing nature.

c. Other Types of Bucket Conveyors. These include positive discharge, internal discharge, and super-capacity conveyors. The positive discharge type is a pitched bucket conveyor running at about 150 feet per minute, the buckets being completely inverted when passing over the head of the conveyor. The internal discharge type is a continuous chain or bucket conveyor, operating at relatively slow speeds and arranged to discharge "internally" between the chains. The super-capacity conveyor is composed of chains and buckets, making use of buckets specially shaped to provide maximum capacity.

13. Skip Hoists. When very large quantities of material have to be elevated, or when the material is composed of large lumps, then a skip hoist may be the most suitable and, in fact, the only choice.

A skip hoist is composed of a wheeled car or skip, running up and down rails and made to tip at the discharge point. Skip hoists have bucket capacities up to 150 or more cubic feet and can lift material 200 or more feet. They can be made automatic in operation, and when well designed are fairly maintenance-free. A common application is in foundries and steel mills, where they hoist raw materials into cupolas and furnaces.

14. Gravity Chutes. We can't leave this topic without some discussion of gravity conveyor chutes, which have long been known simply as "chutes." Everyone is familiar with the coal chute—a simple, straight section of cold rolled steel with the edges turned up several inches. Every ready-mix concrete truck has a concrete chute to deliver its mix to the site.

Chutes can be large or small, curved or straight. The chutes, either in the form of flat-bottomed troughs or with troughs curved to conform to loads (bagged materials or sacks, etc.), can be manufactured of steel, wood, or plastic, or lined with various materials, and can handle packages or loose items. While gravity chutes are of a simple nature, the behavior of packages traveling down the chutes can vary greatly; so except in instances of very small installations, it is desirable to obtain the advice of one of the manufacturers of this

Fig. 12-11. Illustration of a spiral chute conveyor.

type of materials handling equipment. Satisfactory application depends on controlling the speed of travel and delivery. The packages should always be fed and discharged from a straight section of the chute.

It is desirable to restrict the number of different configurations and weights of packages; otherwise, the heavier packages will travel very rapidly, and the lighter ones tend to come to rest. Again, the center of gravity of the package must be sufficiently low to prevent the possibility of its toppling over while descending the chute, as this could lead to very troublesome delays. (See Fig. 12-11.)

15. Drag Chains. In-floor towconveyors (discussed in Chapter 9) may be compared with in-floor drag chain conveyors that can pull or drag parts, assemblies, chassis, or massive components from fixed point to fixed point in a plant—usually in a manufacturing environment, usually indoors under a roof, but not necessarily confined to these areas.

Drag chains are usually steel forgings that can pull loads measured in pounds or hundreds of tons. Pits are placed in the floor for motor drives at the head sprocket drive end which pulls the load. (See Fig. 12-12.)

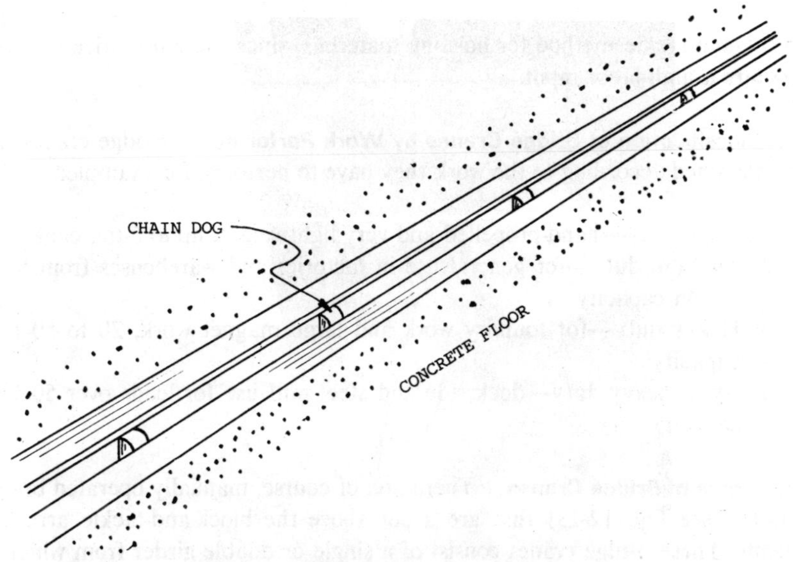

Fig. 12-12. Drag chain conveyor showing pulling chain dog.

II. CRANES

A. Introduction

Cranes, except for certain types of very small, column cranes, are very much like powered conveyors, in that once installed they are somewhat inflexible and cannot be inexpensively moved or relocated.

Also, cranes of sufficient capacity should be installed initially with generous tolerances; it is better to err on the side of a larger capacity than to install an expensive crane and then find out five years down the road that the steel coils it has to handle are 5 to 20 tons heavier than its handling capacity.

Roof truss capacity and column load-bearing capacity are other important factors that must be considered during installation of overhead cranes. A number of other factors sometimes cause problems with crane systems of the super-heavy type. Alluvial soils with very low shear strengths can make building plans and site planning expensive and difficult where new plant construction or plant expansion is concerned, since deep piling for foundations may be required, especially when the new building is to be equipped with overhead handling devices, such as cranes, in order to handle heavy tonnages.

With today's high labor costs, the mechanization of many operations is becoming more feasible; and, we must look beyond the simple chain fall or block-and-tackle method for hoisting materials, since these primitive methods require a high labor input.

1. Classification of Bridge Cranes by Work Performed. Bridge cranes can be classified according to the work they have to perform; for example:

1. Light duty—hand-propelled and very lightweight, up to 5-ton capacities
2. Medium duty—for general use in factories and warehouses from 5- to 20-ton capacity
3. Heavy duty—for foundry work and large magnet work, 20 to 50 tons capacity
4. Extra heavy duty—dock side and steel mill use for loads over 50 tons capacity

2. Types of Bridge Cranes. There are, of course, manually operated bridge cranes (see Fig. 12-13) that are a cut above the block-and-tackle arrangements. These bridge cranes consist of a single or double girder from which is suspended an electric hoist. The main purpose of this type of bridge crane is to serve a work station or other small area of the plant. As shown in Fig. 12-13, the operator simply pulls the hoist to the place where the lifting is required, and then uses a pendant control box to control the hoist movement. It is very rare for this type of bridge crane hoist to have more than a 5-ton capacity. For larger, heavy duty hoists we have to move up to one of the two major types of overhead traveling cranes:

1. Top running (Fig. 12-14)
2. Bottom running (Fig. 12-15)

The cross girders of the top running bridge crane are carried on top of the end trolleys. The cross girders of the bottom running bridge crane are suspended from the end trolleys; that is, the crane is suspended by the end trolleys. It should be noted that the main dimensions of an overhead traveling crane (span, headroom, end space, and hook lift) are critical figures in designing a building. It is therefore highly desirable that the type of crane to be used be

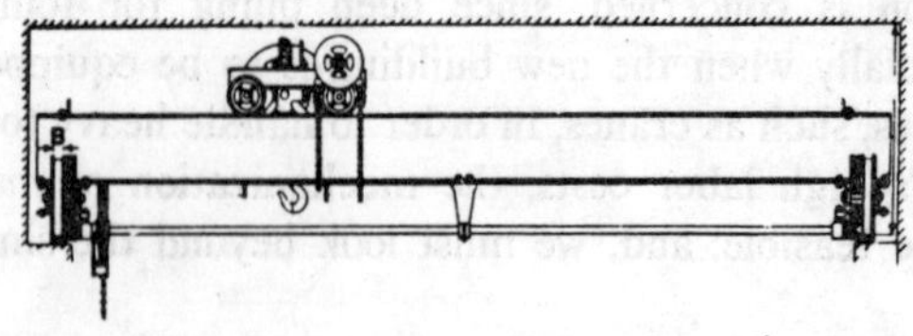

Fig. 12-13. Manually operated, double girder bridge crane.

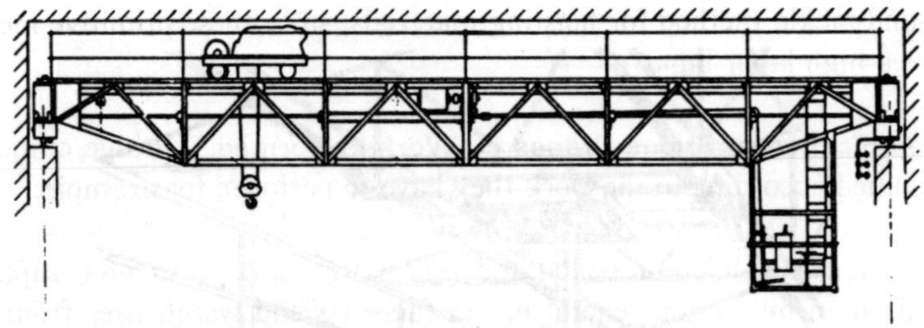

Fig. 12-14. Top running bridge crane.

decided upon before work on the design of the building has progressed beyond the point of no return.

When deciding the height of lift of the crane hook, one should remember that in the highest position the hook can be above the bottom of the crane girders; thus, if the load is a large one, it can smash into the girders. Also, provision must be made for the height taken up by the slings used to hold the load.

a. Speeds, Controls, and Interlocking. The speeds of hoisting, cross travel, and longitudinal (downshop) travel vary widely and are fixed to suit the conditions of the work or shop processes involved. For a typical 5-ton overhead electric traveling crane, the speeds might be as follows: hoisting, 40 feet per minute and traveling 10 feet per minute; cross travel, 100 feet per minute; longitudinal travel for cage control, 300 feet per minute, and if floor-controlled, 150 feet per minute.

Slow or creeping speeds can be provided, particularly for the hoisting motion, and are most desirable where precise positioning of the loads is required.

Other types of traveling cranes are available, and while they may have been designed originally for specialized work, they have many applications.

All electric cranes can be controlled from the floor, that is, with a pendant-type control box. They can also be controlled by remote radio control with a transmitter in the hands of the operator and a receiver on the crane. This type of radio operation is usually reserved for the large, heavy duty, double girder

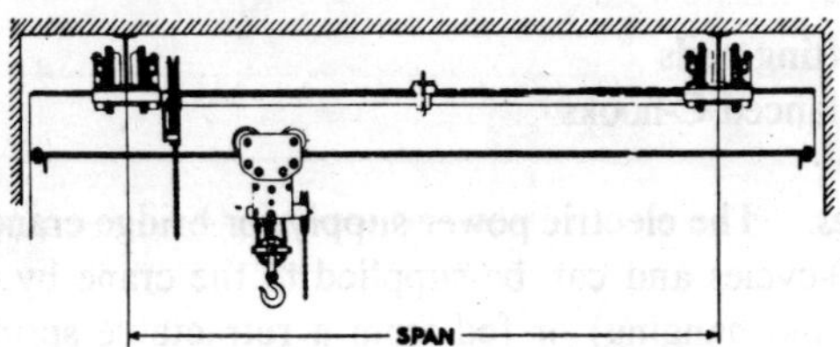

Fig. 12-15. Bottom running bridge crane.

Fig. 12-16. Use of interlocking craneways to transfer hoist between bays.

cranes used in steel fabricating operations, although other applications may be noted for remote control systems.

Sometimes, the large double girder cranes have a cab with an operator who travels suspended from this cage between the two strands of the girder and can follow the hook very closely. A number of companies have converted this type of cab-operated crane to a remote, radio-controlled crane with substantial savings in operating cost.

In some operations where overhead traveling cranes are normally confined to each bay, a method has been developed to interlock cranes so that the same hoist and trolley arrangement can be used in more than one bay. (See Fig. 12-16.)

b. Lifting Attachments. Overhead, traveling bridge cranes can be fitted with a wide variety of attachments to perform the job of lifting and transporting materials. Among the more common attachments (see Fig. 12-17) will be found the following:

1. Grabs and hooks
2. Magnets
3. Vacuum lifting pads
4. Counterbalanced C-hooks

c. Power Sources. The electric power supply for bridge cranes is usually 440 AC, 3-phase, 60-cycles and can be supplied to the crane by cable, festooned (that is, looped and hanging) or fed from a retractable spring-loaded drum. Many of the large, heavy duty cranes use bare wires, bus bars, or feedrails with collector shoes.

Digital crane scale

Pallet lifter attachments

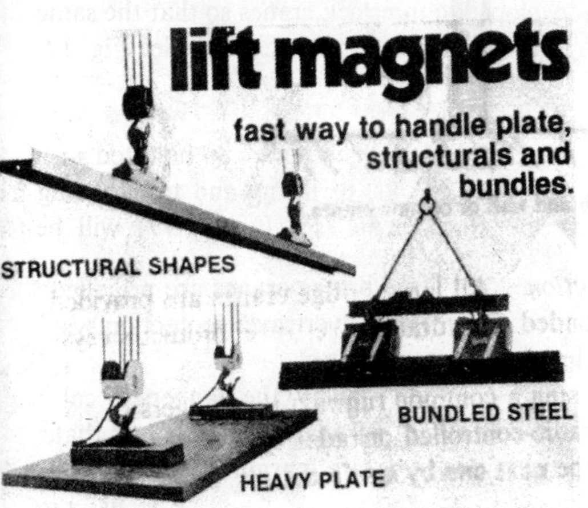

Applications range from single magnet installations lifting 1,000 to 10,000 lbs., to multi-magnet systems lifting 100,000 lbs. and more.

Vacuum Lifter

Fig. 12-17. Common bridge crane attachments.

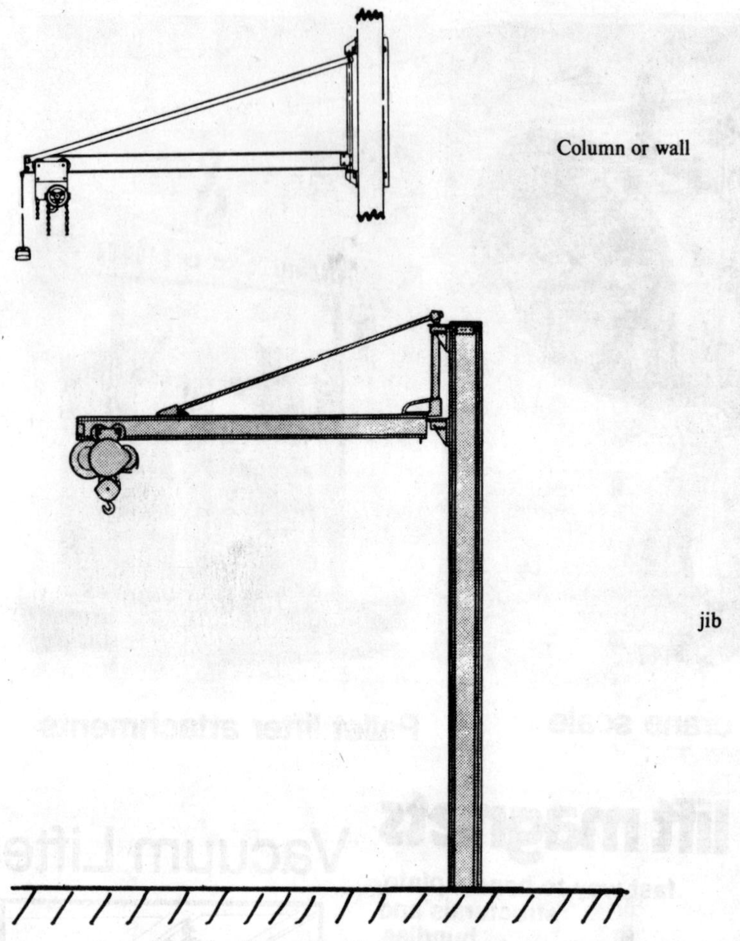

Fig. 12-18. Jib and wall or column cranes.

d. Overtravel and Collision Protection. All large bridge cranes are provided with overtravel stops and spring-loaded or hydraulic overtravel protection systems like the bumpers used on railroad, team track stops.

When two or more cranes are using a common runway, the dangers of collision can be avoided by using a radio-controlled or radar type of sensor that limits the travel of each crane to the next one by a safe margin.

3. Jib Cranes, Wall or Column Cranes. Jib and wall or column cranes can be seen in Fig. 12-18. These cranes are extremely useful for the work station arrangement and in small shops.

Rail-mounted gantry

Fig. 12-19. Types of gantry cranes.

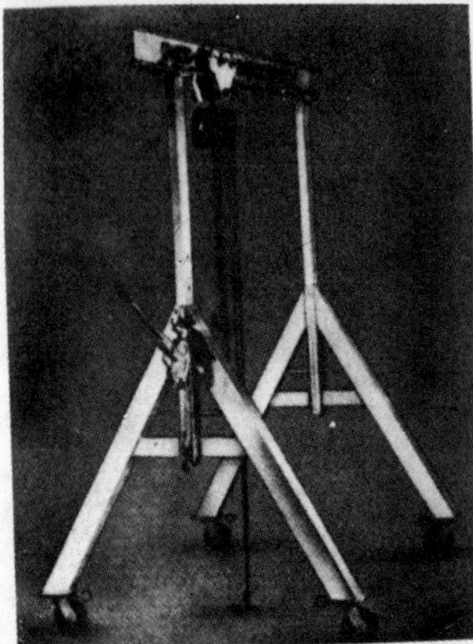

Lightweight gantry

Fig. 12-19. *(continued)*

4. Gantry Cranes. A few types of gantries are illustrated in Fig. 12-19, which shows clearly how these cranes are constructed. This type of crane is used both indoors and outdoors, with a wide variety of applications including manufacturing, service, and dockside use.

III. LIFTING RIGS, CHAINS, AND SLINGS

OSHA has done a great deal to safeguard operators who work with hoisting equipment. Mainly, this emphasis has been concentrated in the area of the chains and slings used to grab and attach to the material or item being lifted.

Hooks and chains must be inspected at specific intervals, and certain records must be kept.

A. Pallet Sling

Figure 12-20 shows merchandise loaded on an open wing-type or stevedore pallet. Usually this type of pallet is fairly large, measuring 4′ × 6′. It is used principally for ship loading and unloading onto the dock.

B. Drum-Handling Sling

The drum-handling sling is a device for picking up drums or barrels. (See Fig. 12-21.) It was designed for shipboard loading, but can be used with a crane

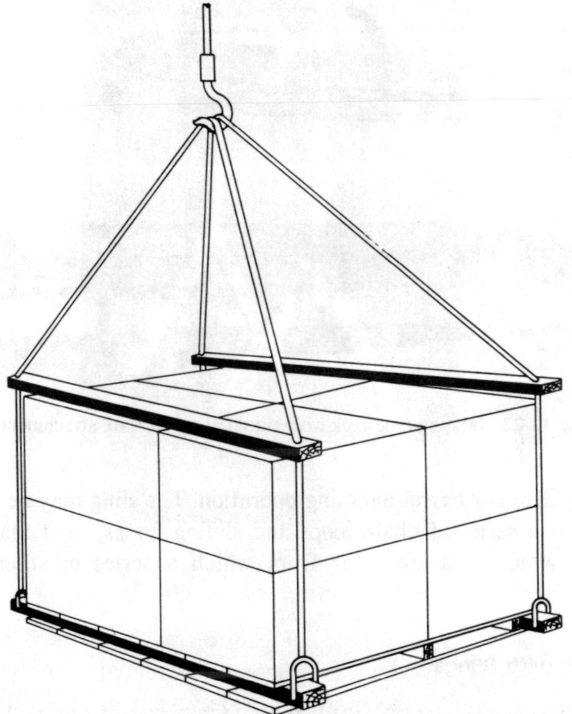

Fig. 12-20. "Wing-type" or stevedore pallet.

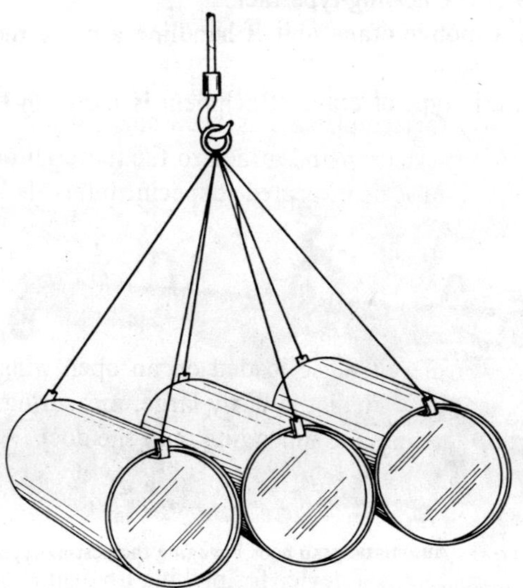

Fig. 12-21. Example of drum-handling sling.

Fig. 12-22. Nesting-type rack with automatic grab hook attachment.

truck for any drum or barrel-handling operation. The sling may be of the chain type, which is a series of chain loops and sliding hooks; or it may be of the frame type, which is a steel bar from which a series of sling hooks are suspended.

C. Spreader with Slings

In Fig. 12-22, an automatic grab hook attachment is shown placing a load of steel bars into a nesting-type rack. In Fig. 12-23, the automatic grab hook has engaged the ears of the nesting-type rack.

In Fig. 12-24, a mobile crane unit is handling a cable reel by means of a spreader bar.

Another automatic type of crane attachment is shown in Fig. 12-25, lifting a load of pipe.

Fig. 12-23. Automatic grab hook engaging the nesting-type rack.

Fig. 12-24. Handling cable reel by crane using a spreader bar.

Fig. 12-25. Crane handling loaded rack.

EXERCISE NO. 12

1. Give two advantages of conveyor installations:
   1. ______
   2. ______
2. What is the principal disadvantage of a conveyor installation? ______
3. Why is preventive maintenance of conveyors so important? ______
4. A rubber-covered belt conveyor can be used to carry hot forgings. True ☐ False ☐
5. Bulk density is usually measured by the amount of material that can be poured into ______.
6. The angle of repose (for bulk materials) is the angle formed by ______
7. Give one method for suppressing a dust explosion. ______
8. What happens to the carrying capacity of a screw conveyor as the slope increases?
9. Why should you limit the different configurations and weights of packages, and keep the center of gravity of packages low when using chute conveyors? ______
10. What are two methods used to control electric bridge cranes?
    1. ______
    2. ______
11. What are four types of lifting attachments?
    1. ______
    2. ______
    3. ______
    4. ______
12. A single-phase, 110V, AC, 60-cycle, power supply is sufficient for most bridge cranes. True ☐ False ☐
13. Why use an overtravel stop on a bridge crane? ______

14. What has OSHA done to improve the safety of crane operations?

15. Why is a stevedore pallet necessary when loading a ship?

Chapter 13
Bulk Handling Equipment and Methods, Including Pneumatic Systems

I. BULK HANDLING EQUIPMENT AND METHODS

A. Introduction

Two decades ago it was said that in order to justify a pneumatic, bulk handling system, a company should be handling over 1,000,000 pounds of a substance every year. With today's high labor costs, this quantity has shrunk to less than half that amount, or approximately 400,000 pounds.

It is also true that 1½% of all bagged material is wasted, and that most bags are handled five times, as follows:

1. At delivery
2. During storage
3. During a transfer from storage
4. At processing
5. At disposal of the empty bag

With a through-put of 1,000,000 pounds of a substance annually, it costs from $175.00 to $275.00 per week to dispose of the empty bags.

Not all bulk materials are powdered or granular, of course, and we have to differentiate between dry and liquid materials. In general, it is much easier to handle liquids than dry materials, although about the same amount of knowledge, both theoretical and practical, is required to handle either type of substance efficiently and economically, as well as safely.

In this chapter we shall try to cover both dry and liquid materials, as far as it is practical to do so.

1. Tote Bins. Sometimes it is important to think small, before advancing to the next larger step in automation or mechanization. Thus, it is with the use of tote bins. For example, if your plant is using pallet loads of bagged materials that are granular, or similarly flowable, then you should be considering the use of tote bins. (See Fig. 13-1).

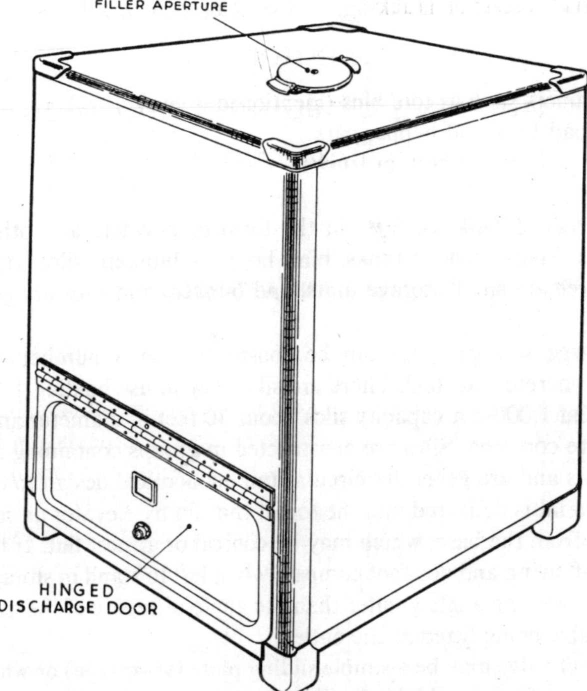

Fig. 13-1. The basic bulk handling unit—the tote bin.

Some tote bins can be used for both liquid and dry materials. Hopper bottoms can be used for dry materials, and spigots or taps can be used for free-flowing liquids. With heavier or viscous fluids, such as lubricating oils, pumps can be immersed in the bins, and they can be metered if necessary. A standard-sized tote bin (from 60 to 80 cubic feet in volume) used for liquids can replace 8 barrels of 52 gallons each. Thus, a savings in handling costs usually results from obtaining liquids in bulk from tank cars or trucks.

2. Movement and Storage in Bulk Modes. Most industries producing powdered or granular material find it necessary to ship a considerable part of their output in some type of package suitable for manual handling (sacks, drums, etc.), but these packages are costly to provide, fill, and handle. With the development of fork trucks and the use of the unit load system, many packages holding powdered or granular material have been palletized, and this method of movement and storage is likely to continue where users' demands are relatively small, and where site conditions rule out more sophisticated methods. Where materials are used in large quantities, however, industry looks for more advantageous means of handling, and development has followed three main lines:

1. Containers such as tote bins (mentioned above)
2. Railroad tank and hopper cars
3. Tank and hopper-bottom trucks

The storage of bulk material in the form of powders and other granular materials is usually done in tanks, bins, hoppers, bunkers, silos, etc. Generally the first three are small storage units, and bunkers and silos are large storage units.

These large storage units can be constructed of a number of materials including concrete and steel. There are silos now in use holding 10,000 tons of material; and 1,000-ton capacity silos about 30 feet in diameter and 80 to 100 feet high are common. Silos are constructed in groups containing any number of such units and are generally circular (an economical design to construct).

The material is delivered into the top of the silo by elevator or conveyor and is removed from the base, which may be conical or almost flat. If the material is very free-flowing and does not compact when left to stand in storage, a simple conical base with an angle greater than the angle of repose of the material may suffice, a valve being fitted at the outlet.

The type of valve may be a simple sliding plate (visor type) or what is known as a diaphragm type, in which a flexible sleeve is twisted to throttle the material flow. This type of valve has the advantages of being truly "full bore," is easily controlled from fully open to closed, and contains no moving parts that can become blocked with the material.

If the material is not free-flowing enough for a 100% discharge, it is still possible to use a hopper-bottomed storage unit and fit a device to agitate the material, in the vicinity of the outlet, to assist discharge. In one such device a rotating arm travels through the stored material. Alternately, pneumatic pads may be caused to inflate and deflate, or electric or pneumatic vibrators may be fitted near the outlet.

Fluidizing techniques can be applied to the discharge of powders from hopper-bottomed units. Often fine-powdered materials tend to bridge or arch when directed toward the base by the sloping walls of the hopper bottom, and local fluidization of the material can greatly ease the situation. (See Fig., 13-2.) This fluidization can take the form of feeding a small quantity of dry air (at, say, 2 to 5 psi) into the base of the unit, in the vicinity of the outlet, through fluidizing pads set into the hopper base.

Another way to improve the flowability of the stored materials is to provide "air lances" at various points in the silo to locally disturb the material and break down any bridging. (See Fig. 13-3.)

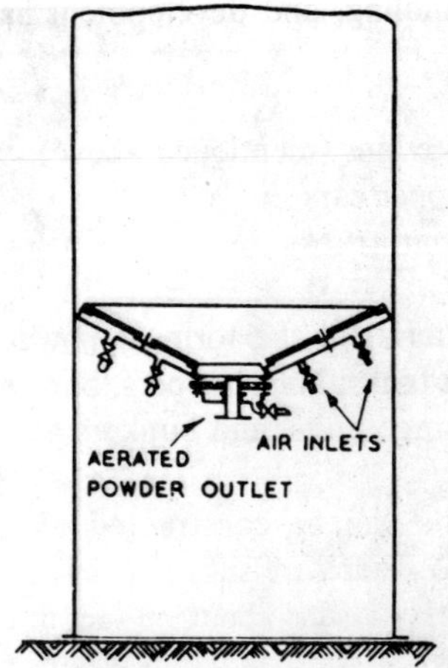

Fig. 13-2. Fluidizing applied to hopper bases.

More elaborate uses of fluidization to facilitate the emptying of material from hoppers and silos can be achieved by fitting fluidizing tiles to cover the whole of the base of the hopper and causing sections to be fluidized in a cycle. Air pressure can be from 2 to 15 psi, depending on the type of material being handled.

Some powdered materials tend to settle and compact so rapidly that they are very difficult to store in hoppers or silos. One technique is to keep the whole mass of material in a constant state of fluidization.

As shown in Fig. 13-4, a group of storage silos has been constructed using a

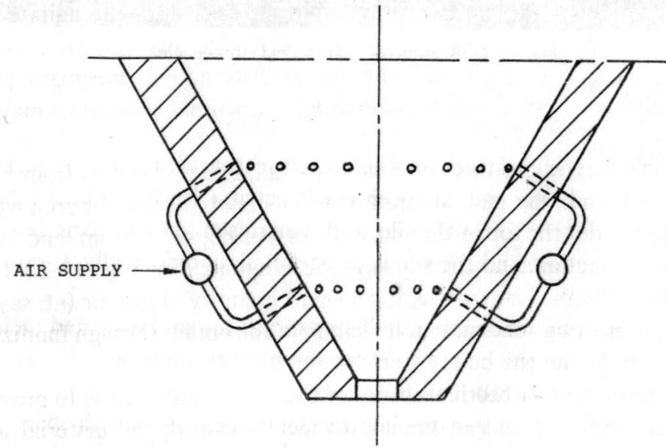

Fig. 13-3. Hopper base with air lances.

Fig. 13-4. A group of bolted steel storage silos.

modular, bolted-type construction where each section is raised upon jacks after the concrete foundation pad has been constructed. (See Fig. 13-5.) Each section is bolted under the top of the silo, and then raised to make room for bolting the next lower section, and the silo is constructed, paradoxically, from the top down to the bottom.

There is a growing tendency in industry to use the prefabricated method of silo construction, and the bolted steel section has certain economic advantages over the welded type of fabrication.

The interior surfaces of storage silos are sometimes coated with epoxy paints. One such type, known as the EFP or electro-fused polymer coating, is very abrasion-resistant as well as rust-proof.

Fig. 13-5. View showing concrete pad in place, and lifting jacks used to bolt up one section after another starting with the top section.

II. PNEUMATIC HANDLING SYSTEMS

The economies of scale certainly apply to bulk handling of dry materials. Once the economic justification in terms of volumes of materials handled has indicated the need for this type of mechanization, a satisfactory pneumatic handling system is made according to the following guidelines.

A. Requirements of a Satisfactory System

A satisfactory pneumatic handling system:

1. Must receive and store.
2. Must distribute to using points.
3. Must be able to reclaim dusts that are generated, if any.
4. Must operate economically.

B. Specific Design Requirements

In addition to the above requirements, specific systems design requirements should be recognized when considering bulk handling systems:

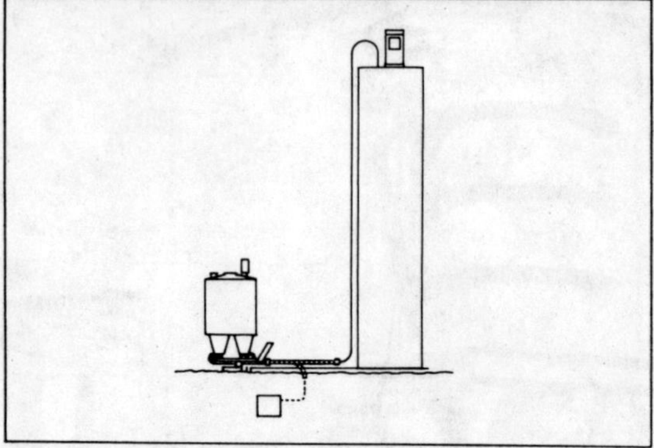

Typical unloading system for GATX airslide car.

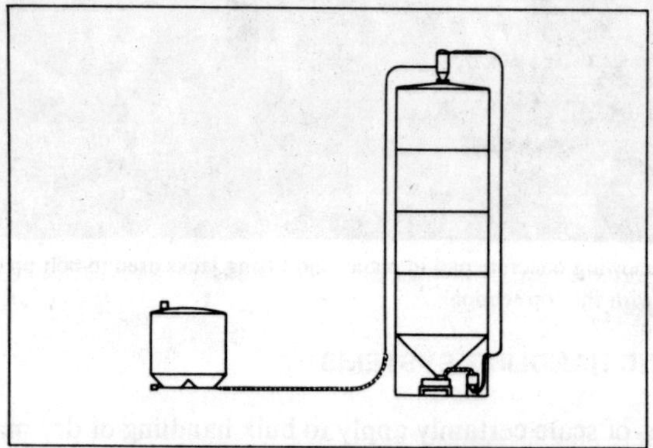

Typical vacuum unloader system.

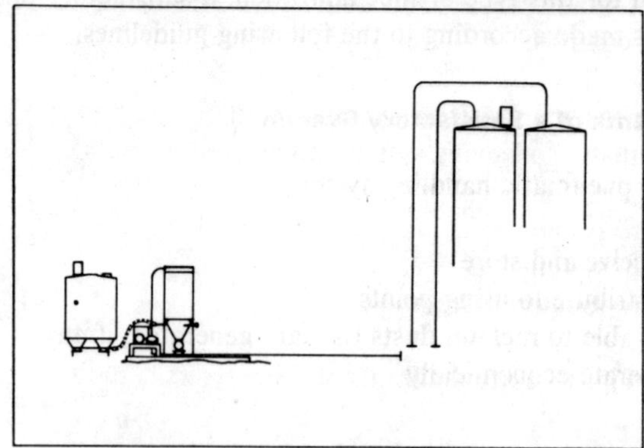

Typical vacuum-pressure unloading system.

Fig. 13-6. Typical unloading systems.

Fig. 13-7. A portable unit supplying both vacuum and pressure for unloading material from railcar to storage.

1. Adequate size of system
2. Correct feeds
3. Correct separation
4. Proper controls

Observing the more or less specific requirements (above), there are three typical pneumatic conveying systems to be considered:

1. Pressure system
2. Vacuum system
3. Pressure-vacuum system

Shown in Fig. 13-6 are diagrams of three typical unloading systems for bulk handling.

Portable units are available that can provide both vacuum and pressure for unloading material from railcars into storage silos. (See Fig. 13-7.)

We next discuss the essential components of a pressure system.

C. Components of a Pressure System for Bulk Handling

The system components include:

1. Blower package (positive displacement type) plus silencers, such as an OSHA-required sound shield
   a. High-pressure, safety, differential switch
   b. High-temperature switch
2. Feeder group (regulates the amount of material going into the system)
   a. Light duty unit—3 psi pressure with dust collection
   b. Heavy duty unit—8 to 10 psi pressure with 8 to 10 hours of daily operation; chrome plate on all wear, iron, parts
   c. Maximum duty unit—operating 24 hours a day, continuously (uses outboard bearings and packing glands)
3. Feeder unit (uses slider gates)
4. Airlock-type vent assembly
5. Hopper adapter (high-velocity air stream)
6. Reclaim unit (a surge bin with a continuous-type filter; or, use a cyclone-type receiver)
7. Control panel (use J.I.C. electrical standards and N.E.M.A. specs)
   a. Relay logic
   b. Starters
   c. Time delay components

D. Pneumatic Movement of Materials

Pneumatic conveying of bulk solids has many advantages when powdered or granular materials are moved.

Every pneumatic system makes use of ducts or pipes called transport lines that carry a mixture of the material and air (or any other gas), and these lines can follow very winding paths, passing through floors and walls, under roads, etc., changing from vertical to horizontal in a manner that would be quite impossible for mechanical types of equipment. Also, the systems can be dust-proof and even totally enclosed; and, a number of operators required for normal operation can be kept to a minimum. Fine, free-flowing powders or granules are the easiest material to convey pneumatically. Materials that tend to stick or compact or are abrasive are not suitable. In all instances actual samples of the material in the state in which it has to be conveyed should be supplied to the equipment manufacturers.

Materials can be conveyed by pneumatic conveyors over many hundreds of yards and in very considerable quantities, as the rate of conveying is maintained as long as material is fed into the system.

It should be stated that expert knowledge of conveying of solids by pneumatic means is still largely in the hands of the established manufacturers. The theory available from textbooks is more useful as a guide than as a complete answer to a problem.

The power consumption of pneumatic conveyors is higher per unit of material conveyed than that of mechanical conveyors and elevators. The wearing of the transport lines, particularly at the bends, due to abrasion, can be troublesome, and the possibility of the generation of static electricity with consequent explosion must be guarded against constantly. With certain materials where there is a serious explosion hazard, it may be necessary to use an inert gas for conveying, together with other safeguards.

The most common forms of pneumatic conveying systems are:

1. Negative pressure, or vacuum system (see Fig. 13-8)
2. Positive pressure, or blowing system (see Fig. 13-9)

In both systems, the solid material has to be: (a) fed into the air stream, (b) conveyed by the air stream, and (c) separated from the air stream and discharged from the system; and (d) the conveying air has to be disposed of either by discharge to the atmosphere, usually after passing through a filter, or by recirculation.

In the case of the most simple *negative pressure* system, the material is fed into a hopper to be sucked to a cyclone (see Fig. 13-10). (The material can be sucked into the open end of the conveying pipe.) Because the air expands in the cyclone and loses velocity, it can no longer hold the solid material in suspension, so this material drops to the base of the cyclone, and from there, by gravity, through a power-driven rotary vane valve. (See Fig. 13-11.) The conveying air continues through a filter (to take out very fine dust that may have carried through the cyclone) and so to the pump, fan, or compressor.

In the most simple *positive pressure* system, the conveying air is blown along the transport line and picks up material that has been fed through a power-driven rotary vane valve or other type of feeder. The air and solids are carried through a cyclone where the solids drop out of the air stream, because of reduced velocity, and fall, by gravity, into another power-driven rotary vane valve or other type of seal. The conveying air continues to the atmosphere, via an air filter or a dust collector.

More elaborate pneumatic systems are available, with other methods for feeding material into and discharging material from the system.

When the dust from the material is in very small particles, the final filtering of the air may require special attention; otherwise dust can build up over a considerable area adjacent to the final air discharging point.

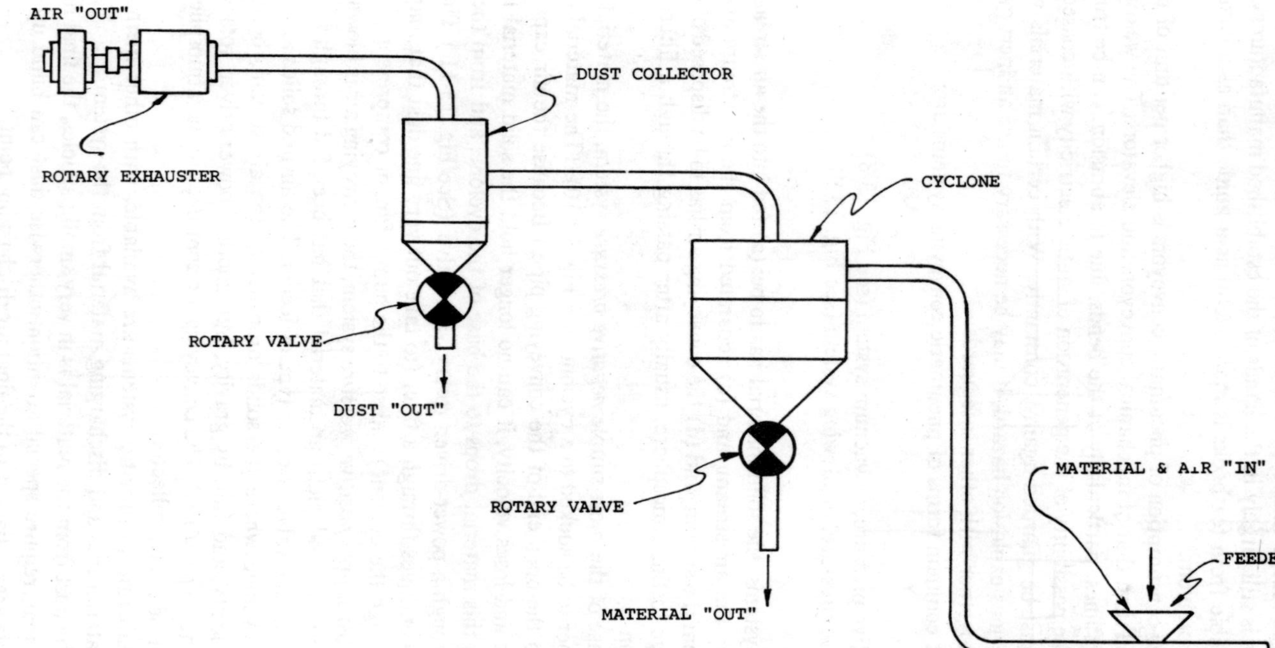

Fig. 13-8. A simple negative or vacuum pressure system.

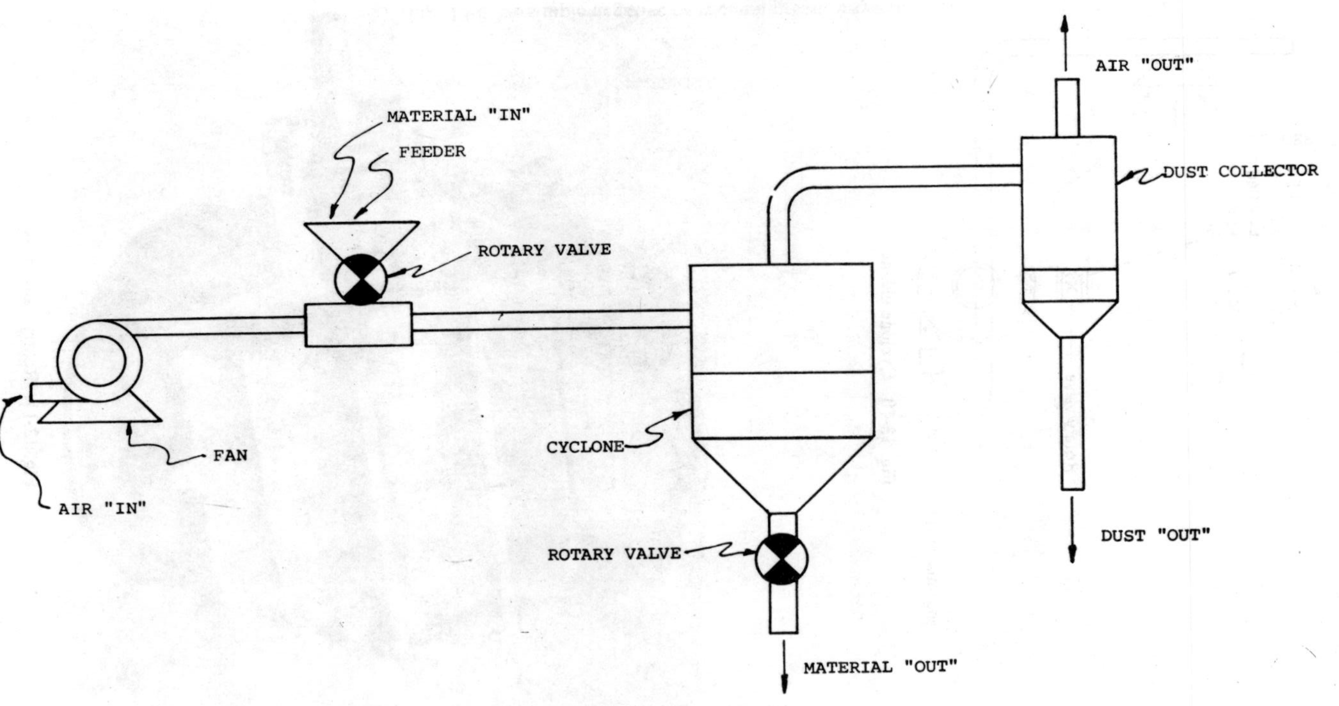

Fig. 13-9. A simple positive or pressure system.

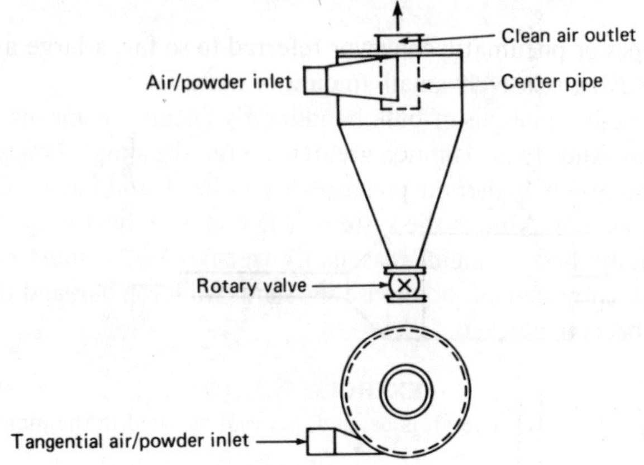

Fig. 13-10. Cyclone cleaner.

Fig. 13-11. Rotary vane valve.

In the types of pneumatic conveyor referred to so far, a large amount of air is used to move a relatively small amount of material.

There are other systems of bulk handling by pneumatic means in which the proportion of solids to air is much greater than in the simple systems described above. Considerably higher air pressures are utilized, and the material is mixed with the air before it enters the system. The material must be such that it will fluidize readily, and although reasonably free-flowing, it must be capable of retaining the entrained air; otherwise the solids will drop out, and the conveying ducts may become blocked.

EXERCISE NO. 13

1. How many times, in general, is bagged material handled in the plant? ________

2. One tote bin can replace how many barrels? ________

3. What are the requirements of a satisfactory system for pneumatic handling?

1. ________
2. ________
3. ________
4. ________

4. Name some specific design requirements for a pneumatic system:

1. ________
2. ________
3. ________
4. ________

5. What are three typical pneumatic systems called?

1. ________
2. ________
3. ________

Chapter 14
OSHA Safety Requirements Applied to Practical Materials Handling

I. THE WILLIAMS-STEIGER ACT

A. OSHA

1. Introduction. The Williams-Steiger Act of 1970, which created OSHA, affects every employer of more than seven workers throughout the United States. The Occupational Safety and Health Administration (OSHA) oversees a wide range of activities throughout industry and agriculture. As often happens when new governmental bureaus are formed, during the early years of its formation there was undue haste to issue regulations and to hire personnel to assist in the inspections required to police the hastily made regulations.

The general tenor of the law has been good, but certain aspects of the establishment and enforcement of the regulations have caused some resentment on the part of employers—especially in cases where hardnosed inspectors have "thrown the book" at them with little regard to cost. In one instance a handrail on a long, little-used mezzanine was an inch and a half higher than the code. The entire balustrade, costing several hundred dollars, had to be replaced because of an arbitrary inspection. Happily, there have not been too many such occurrences, but this simple illustration indicates the way in which an arbitrary decision, made by a poorly trained and poorly disciplined bureaucrat, can turn an otherwise good and necessary law into a nightmare.

The purpose of this chapter is to examine how the public law affects materials handling practitioners and their areas of responsibility.

2. Subpart N—Materials Handling and Storage

Paragraph 1910.176 Handling Materials—General. The above heading is shown exactly as it appears in the *Federal Register,* which records the OSHA regulations. Although I cannot interpret the regulations in a strict legal sense, I shall try to illustrate how much of the substance of Subpart N makes good sense from the standpoint of practical materials handling. The reader should be aware, also, that a good many of the regulations contained in the OSHA law have been obtained from standards developed by the professional and trade associations in each of the respective fields—for example, the Industrial Truck Association, American National Standards Institute, National Fire Protection Association, and so forth (ITA, ANSI, NFPA, etc.). (Please note: Each reference letter, number, and heading is exactly as it is in the OSHA regulations.)

a. Use of Mechanical Equipment
Where mechanical handling equipment is used, sufficient safe clearances shall be allowed for aisles, at loading docks, through doorways, and wherever turns or passage must be made. Aisles and passageways shall be kept clear and in good repair, with no obstruction across or in aisles that could create a hazard. Permanent aisles and passageways shall be appropriately marked.

(It is both necessary by law and advisable from the standpoint of efficiency to clearly mark aisles in factories or warehouses wherever mechanical equipment such as forklift trucks, towconveyors, tractor-trains, pallet jacks, and other similar moving equipment is used. The primary reason, of course, is safety to personnel. There are other intangible and psychological reasons to do so, also. The more orderly and organized a plant appears to be, the more conducive this appearance of orderliness is to the promotion of improved morale and productivity. On January 31, 1978, the author was granted United States Patent No. 4,071,302, for "Aisle Designators." The abstract of the invention reads, in part, "This invention relates to the designation of aisles by providing a visual device for separating horizontal, vertical, or inclined spaces. In warehouse set-out areas merchandise or traffic patterns can more nearly be controlled by the use of this invention in designating these set-out spaces. In factories, safety aisles for pedestrian or vehicular traffic may, also, be more readily controlled by the use of the aisle designators described in these specifications. . . .")

b. Secure Storage
Storage of material shall not create a hazard. Bags, containers, bundles, etc., stored in tiers shall be stacked, blocked, interlocked, and limited in height so that they are stable and secure against sliding or collapse.

c. Housekeeping
Storage areas shall be kept free from accumulation of materials that constitute hazards from tripping, fire, explosion, or pest harborage. Vegetation control will be exercised when necessary.

d. Drainage
Proper drainage shall be provided.

e. Clearance Limits
Clearance signs to warn of clearance limits shall be provided.

f. Rolling Railroad Cars

Derail and/or bumper blocks shall be provided on spur railroad tracks where a rolling car could contact other cars being worked, or enter a building, work or traffic area.

g. Guarding

Covers and/or guardrails shall be provided to protect personnel from the hazards of open pits, tanks, vats, ditches, etc.

3. Para. 1910.178 Powered Industrial Trucks.

a. General Requirements (1) This section applies to all of the mobile equipment used by materials handling practitioners. (2) All new, powered industrial trucks acquired after February 15, 1972 shall meet the design and construction requirements of ANSI-B56.1-1969. (3) Approved trucks must have identifying labels as indicated in ANSI-B56.1. (4) A very important note concerns the modifications to industrial powered trucks—any modification that may affect capacity or safety *cannot be performed by the user without the truck manufacturer's prior written approval.* When modifications are made—for example, when a rotator attachment is added to the truck—a new label has to be added indicating the attachment and change in capacity of the truck. (5) If the truck is equipped with front-end attachments other than factory-installed attachments, the user must request that the truck be marked to identify the attachments and show the weight of the truck and attachment combination and to indicate the capacity of the truck with the attachment as maximum elevation with a load that is centered on the attachment. (6) The user must ensure that all truck nameplates and markings are in place and maintained in a legible condition. This is one of the most abused of the regulations dealing with industrial powered trucks. The author has found it almost impossible to comply totally with this regulation. Periodic truck inspections (which we shall discuss later) may shed some light on this subject.

b. Designations

The truck user should be able to recognize the following symbols for powered industrial *trucks:*

D—diesel
DS—diesel with exhaust, fuel, electrical safeguards
DY—all DS features including temperature limitation features; and, no electrical or ignition equipment
E—electric
ES—electric with spark arrestors and surface temperature limitations

EE—electric with completely enclosed electrical systems
EX—electric, explosion-proof
G—gas
GS—gas with exhaust, fuel, and electrical safeguards
LP—liquefied petroleum (propane)
LPS—liquefied petroleum with exhaust, fuel, and electrical safeguards

c. (2)(i) Power-Operated Industrial Trucks Shall not be Used in Atmospheres Containing Hazardous Concentrations of Acetylene, Butadiene, Ethylene Oxide, Hydrogen, and so Forth.
(12)(2)(ii) Power-operated industrial trucks shall not be used in atmospheres containing hazardous concentrations of metal dust, including aluminum, magnesium, carbon black, coal or coke dust except approved EX-rated trucks.

Note: If the user has any doubt as to what trucks may be used in certain locations, he should refer to the *Federal Register,* Chapter XVII, Occupational Safety and Health Administration, Subpart N, 1910.178, Table N-1 "Summary Table on Use of Industrial Trucks in Various Locations."

d. Converted Industrial Trucks
Trucks that were originally approved for the use of gasoline for fuel, when converted to LP gas may be used in those locations where G, GS, or LP and LPS trucks have been designated for use provided that the truck conforms to the GS and LPS requirements.

e. Safety Guards
(1) Overhead guards and (2) load backrest extensions must be provided on all trucks where *lifts higher than six feet are made.*

f. Fuel Handling and Storage
(1) The storage and handling of liquid fuels such as gasoline and diesel fuel shall be in accordance with NFPA Flammable and Combustible Liquids Code (NFPA No. 30-1969). (2) The storage and handling of LP gas fuel shall be in accordance with NFPA Storage and Handling of Liquified Petroleum Gases (NFPA No. 58-1969). (In Appendix C you will find the sources of the standards used throughout this text.)

g. Changing and Charging Storage Batteries
(1) Battery charging installations shall be located in areas designated for that purpose. (2) Facilities shall be provided for flushing and neutralizing spilled electrolyte, for fire protection, for protecting charging apparatus from damage by trucks, and for adequate ventilation for the dispersal of fumes from gassing batteries. (3) Battery racks shall be nonsparking. (4) A conveyor or hoist for

changing batteries should be provided depending on the type of battery and truck. (5) Reinstalled batteries shall be properly positioned and secured in the truck. (6) A carboy tilter or siphon shall be provided for handling the electrolyte. (7) When charging batteries (or mixing electrolyte), acid shall be poured into water, *never the reverse.* (8) Trucks shall be properly positioned with their brakes applied before attempting to change or charge batteries. (9) Keep vent caps in place when charging batteries. Make sure the vent caps work. Open the battery compartment cover to dissipate the heat. (10) No smoking in the charging area. Post the area, accordingly. (11) No welding in charging area—precautions should be taken to prevent open flames, sparks, or electric arcs in the battery charging areas. (12) Tools, wrenches, etc., should be kept away from the tops of uncovered batteries—otherwise serious, or fatal, short circuits may result.

h. Lighting for Operating Areas

(1) Controlled lighting of adequate intensity should be provided in operating areas. [See American National Standard Practice for Industrial Light, A11.1-1965 (R 1970), which can be obtained at many public libraries.] (2) Where light levels are less than two lumens per square foot, auxiliary directional lighting shall be provided on the truck.

i. Control of Noxious Gases and Fumes

(1) Concentration levels of carbon monoxide (CO) gas created by powered industrial truck operations shall not exceed the levels specified in Para. 1910.1000 (Subpart Z) of OSHA. From (Subpart Z) 1910.1000:

Table Z-1

$$\text{CO} = \text{PPM } 50^{(a)}\ 55\ \text{mg/M}^{3(b)}$$

where (a) is parts of vapor or gas per million parts of contaminated air by volume at 25°C and 760 mm Hg pressure, and (b) is approximate milligrams of particulate per cubic meter of air.

Any qualified industrial hygienist can measure the above concentrations if you have any doubt as to whether or not you can comply with OSHA standards in particular areas of your plant.

j. Dockboards (Bridge Plates) (from 1910.30(a))

Portable and powered dockboards shall be strong enough to carry the load imposed on them. They must have some means to anchor them to keep them from slipping; and, portable dockboards must have handholds to lift them so they can be safely handled manually. Usually dockboards are positioned and placed at a car or truck spot by forklift truck. Dockboards of 20,000 pounds or larger capacity cannot be handled manually because of their weight.

Powered dockboards have to be designed and constructed according to Commercial Standard CS 202-56 (1961) "Industrial Lifts and Hinged Loading Ramps," published by the U.S. Department of Commerce.

k. Trucks and Railroad Cars

Positive protection must be provided to prevent railroad cars from being moved while dockboards or bridge plates are in position.

The same is true of truck loading and unloading operations with dockboards, since air lines and wheel chocks have to be in place and brakes set in order to prevent the truck from moving. In addition, if a semi has only the van trailer at the truck spot, that is, the tractor has been removed and the box is sitting on front landing wheels, then two jacks have to be placed under the nose of the van trailer to prevent overturning.

l. Operator Training

Only trained and authorized operators shall be permitted to operate a powered industrial truck. Methods shall be developed to train operators in the safe operation of powered industrial trucks.

m. Truck Operations

OSHA requires that operators of powered industrial trucks be knowledgeable concerning the safe operation of their equipment. It would be well for a plant that uses powered industrial trucks on a continuous basis to invest in a packaged training program if it does not have one of its own. The International Materials Management Society with headquarters at 3900 Capital City Blvd., Lansing, Michigan 48906 [phone (517)321-6713] can provide the location of the nearest chapter offering training sessions, or can send you manuals on forklift truck operator training.

1. Trucks shall not be driven up to anyone standing in front of a bench or other fixed object.
2. No person shall be allowed to stand or pass under the elevated portion of any truck, whether loaded or empty.
3. Unauthorized personnel shall not be permitted to ride on powered industrial trucks. A safe place to ride shall be provided where riding of trucks is authorized.
4. The employer shall prohibit arms or legs from being placed between the uprights of the mast or outside the running lines of the truck.
5. (i) When a powered industrial truck is left unattended, load engaging means shall be fully lowered, controls shall be neutralized, power shall be shut off, and brakes set. Wheels shall be blocked if the truck is parked on an incline.

   (ii) A powered industrial truck is unattended when the operator is 25 feet or more away from a vehicle that remains in his view, or whenever the operator leaves the vehicle and it is not in his view.

(iii) When the operator of an industrial truck is dismounted and within 25 feet of the truck still in his view, the load engaging means shall be fully lowered, controls neutralized, and the brakes set to prevent movement.

6. A safe distance shall be maintained from the edge of ramps or platforms while on any elevated dock, or platform or freight car. Trucks shall not be used for opening or closing freight doors.
7. Brakes shall be set and wheel blocks shall be in place to prevent movement of trucks, trailers, or railroad cars while loading or unloading. Fixed jacks may be necessary to support a semitrailer during loading or unloading when the trailer is not coupled to a tractor. The flooring of trucks, trailers, and railroad cars shall be checked for breaks and weakness before they are driven onto.
8. There shall be sufficient headroom under overhead installations, lights, pipes, sprinkler system, etc.
9. An overhead guard shall be used as protection against falling objects. It should be noted that an overhead guard is intended to offer protection from the impact of small packages, boxes, bagged material, etc., representative of the job application, but not to withstand the impact of a falling capacity load.
10. A load backrest extension shall be used whenever necessary to minimize the possibility that the load or part of it will fall rearward.
11. Only approved industrial trucks shall be used in hazardous locations.
12. Whenever a truck is equipped with vertical only, or vertical and horizontal controls elevatable with the lifting carriage or forks for lifting personnel, the following additional precautions shall be taken for protection of personnel being elevated.

    (i) A safety platform firmly secured to the lifting carriage and/or forks will be used.

    (ii) Means shall be provided whereby personnel on the platform can shut off power to the truck.

    (iii) Such protection from falling objects as indicated necessary by the operating conditions shall be provided.
13. Reserved. (To date nothing further has been added to section 13, but it would be advisable to request the plant safety officer to check this out. If there is no plant safety officer in your organization, then a call to the local OSHA office listed in your telephone directory should bring you current information on this subject. You do not have to give your company name in order to get this information.)
14. Fire aisles, access to stairways, and fire equipment shall be kept clear.

n. Traveling

1. All traffic regulations shall be observed, including authorized plant speed limits. (The author established the following rules for manufacturing operations: 5 mph on main aisles with two-way traffic and 3 mph on side aisles and other aisles.) A safe distance shall be maintained approximately three truck lengths from the truck ahead, and the truck shall be kept under control at all times.
2. The right of way shall be yielded to ambulances, fire trucks, or other vehicles in emergency situations.
3. Other trucks traveling in the same direction at intersections, blind spots, or other dangerous locations shall not be passed.
4. The driver shall be required to slow down and sound the horn at cross aisles and other locations where vision is obstructed. If the load being carried obstructs the forward view, the driver shall be required to travel with the load trailing.
5. Railroad tracks shall be crossed diagonally wherever possible. Parking closer than eight feet from the center of railroad tracks is prohibited.
6. The driver shall be required to look in the direction of, and keep a clear view of the path of travel.
7. Grades shall be ascended or decended slowly.
   (i) When ascending or descending grades in excess of 10%, loaded trucks shall be driven with the load upgrade.
   (ii) Unloaded trucks should be operated on all grades with the load engaging means downgrade.
   (iii) On all grades the load and load engaging means shall be tilted back if applicable, and raised only as far as necessary to clear the road surface.
8. Under all travel conditions the truck shall be operated at a speed that will permit it to be brought to a stop in a safe manner.
9. Stunt driving and horseplay shall not be permitted.
10. The driver shall be required to slow down for wet and slippery floors.
11. Dockboards or bridgeplates, shall be properly secured before they are driven over. Dockboards or bridgeplates shall be driven over carefully and slowly and their rated capacity never exceeded.
12. Elevators shall be approached slowly, and then entered squarely after the elevator car is properly leveled. Once on the elevator, the controls shall be neutralized, power shut off, and the brakes set.
13. Motorized hand trucks must enter elevator or other confined areas with the load end forward.
14. Running over loose objects on the roadway surface shall be avoided.
15. While turns are being negotiated, speed shall be reduced to a safe level

by means of turning the hand steering wheel in a smooth, sweeping motion. Except when maneuvering at a very low speed, the hand steering wheel shall be turned at a moderate, even rate.

o. Loading

1. Only stable or safely arranged loads shall be handled. Caution shall be exercised when handling off-center loads that cannot be centered.
2. Only loads within the rated capacity of the truck shall be handled.
3. The long or high (including multiple-tiered) loads that may affect capacity shall be adjusted.
4. When attachments are used, particular care should be taken in securing, manipulating, positioning, and transporting the load. Trucks equipped with attachments shall be operated as partially loaded trucks when not handling a load.
5. A load engaging means shall be placed under the load as far as possible; the mast shall be carefully tilted backward to stabilize the load.
6. Extreme care shall be used when tilting the load forward or backward, particularly when high tiering. Tilting forward with load engaging means elevated shall be prohibited except to pick up a load. An elevated load shall not be tilted forward except when the load is in a deposit position over a rack or stack. When stacking or tiering, only enough backward tilt to stabilize the load shall be used.

p. Operation of the Truck

1. If at any time a powered industrial truck is found to be in need of repair, defective, or in any way unsafe, the truck shall be taken out of service until it has been restored to safe operating condition.
2. Fuel tanks shall not be filled while the engine is running. Spillage shall be avoided.
3. Spillage of oil or fuel shall be carefully washed away or completely evaporated and the fuel tank cap replaced before the engine is restarted.
4. No truck shall be operated with a leak in the fuel system; the leak must be corrected.
5. Open flames shall not be used for checking the electrolyte level in storage batteries or the gasoline level in fuel tanks.

q. Maintenance of Industrial Trucks

1. Any power-operated industrial truck not in safe operating condition shall be removed from service. All repairs shall be made by authorized personnel.

2. No repairs shall be made in Class I, II, and III locations. (The classes indicate the degree of hazard.)
3. Those repairs to the fuel and ignition systems of industrial trucks that involve fire hazards shall be conducted only in locations designated for such repairs.
4. Trucks in need of repairs to the electrical system shall have the battery disconnected prior to such repairs.
5. All parts of any such industrial truck requiring replacement shall be replaced only by parts as safe as those used in the original design.
6. Industrial trucks shall not be altered so that the relative positions of the various parts are different from what they were when originally received from the manufacturer, nor shall they be altered either by the addition of extra parts not provided by the manufacturer or by the elimination of any parts, except as provided in item (12) of this list. Additional counterweighting of fork trucks shall not be done unless approved by the truck manufacturer.
7. Industrial trucks shall be examined before being placed in service, and shall not be placed in service if the examination shows any condition adversely affecting the safety of the vehicle. Such examination shall be made at least daily. Where industrial trucks are used on a round-the-clock basis, they shall be examined after each shift. Defects when found shall be immediately reported and corrected.
8. Water mufflers shall be filled daily or as frequently as necessary to prevent depletion of the supply of water below 75% of the filled capacity. Vehicles with mufflers having screens or other parts that may become clogged shall not be operated while such screens or parts are clogged. Any vehicle that emits hazardous sparks or flames from the exhaust system shall immediately be removed from service, and not returned to service until the cause for the emission of such sparks and flames has been eliminated.
9. When the temperature of any part of any truck is found to be in excess of its normal operating temperature, thus creating a hazardous condition, the vehicle shall be removed from service and not returned to service until the cause for such overheating has been elminated.
10. Industrial trucks shall be kept in a clean condition, free of lint, excess oil, and grease. Noncombustible agents should be used for cleaning trucks. Low-flash-point (below 100° F) solvents shall not be used. High-flash-point (at or above 100° F) solvents may be used. Precautions regarding toxicity, ventilation, and fire hazard shall be consonant with the agent or solvent used.
11. Where it is necessary to use antifreeze in the engine cooling system, only those products having a glycol base shall be used.
12. Industrial trucks originally approved for the use of gasoline for fuel may

be converted to liquefied petroleum gas fuel provided the complete conversion results in a truck that embodies the features specified for LP or LPS designated trucks. Such conversion equipment shall be approved. The description of the component parts of this conversion system and the recommended method of installation on specific trucks are contained in the "Listed by Report" (39 FR 23502, June 27, 1974, as amended at 40 FR 23073, May 28, 1975).

4. Para. 1910.179—Overhead and Gantry Cranes. By definition, a crane is a machine for lifting and lowering a load and moving it horizontally, with the hoisting mechanism an integral part of the machine. Cranes whether fixed or mobile are driven manually or by power. OSHA thus has defined the type of crane that is most often used for yard work and indoors for manufacturing and storage operations.

5. Para. 1910.180—Crawler Locomotive and Truck Cranes. A crawler crane consists of a rotating superstructure with power plant, operating machinery, and boom, mounted on a base, equipped with crawler treads for travel. Its function is to hoist and swing loads at various radii.

The materials handling practitioner who has the above types of mobile, materials handling equipment in his fleet (that is, overhead and gantry cranes, crawler locomotives, etc.) would do well to obtain the OSHA regulations in the *Federal Register* (obtained at any public library) in order to study the regulations that apply to these vehicles and their use.

6. Para. 1910.184—Slings.

a. Scope

This section applies to slings used in conjunction with other material handling equipment for the movement of material by hoisting, in employments covered by this paragraph. The types of slings covered are those made from alloy steel chain, wire rope, metal mesh, natural or synthetic fiber rope (conventional three-strand construction), and synthetic webs (nylon, polyester, and polypropylene).

b. Definitions

Angle of loading is the inclination of a leg or branch of a sling measured from the horizontal or vertical plane as shown below in Fig. 14-5 (N-184-5), provided that an angle of loading of five degrees or less from the vertical may be considered a vertical angle of loading.

Basket hitch is a sling configuration whereby the sling is passed under the load and has both ends, end attachments, eyes, or handles on the hook or a single master link.

Braided wire rope is a wire rope formed by plaiting component wire ropes.

Bridle wire rope sling is a sling composed of multiple wire rope legs with the top ends gathered in a fitting that goes over the lifting hook.

Cable laid endless sling—mechanical joint is a wire rope sling made endless by joining the ends of a single length of cable laid rope with one or more metallic fittings.

Cable laid grommet—hand tucked is an endless wire rope sling made from one length of rope wrapped six times around a core formed by hand tucking the ends of the rope inside the six wraps.

Cable laid rope is a wire rope composed of six wire ropes wrapped around a fiber or wire rope core.

Cable laid rope sling—mechanical joint is a wire rope sling made from a cable laid rope with eyes fabricated by pressing or swaging one or more metal sleeves over the rope of junction.

Choker hitch is a sling configuration with one end of the sling passing under the load and through an end attachment, handle, or eye on the other end of the sling.

Coating is an elastomer or other suitable material applied to a sling or to a sling component to impart desirable properties.

Cross rod is a wire used to join spirals of metal mesh to form a complete fabric. [See Fig. 14-2 (N-184-2).]

Designated means selected or assigned by the employer or the employer's representative as being qualified to perform specific duties.

Equivalent entity is a person or organization (including an employer) that, by possession of equipment, technical knowledge, and skills, can perform with equal competence the same repairs and tests as the person or organization with which it is equated.

Fabric (metal mesh) is the flexible portion of a metal mesh sling consisting of a series of transverse coils and cross rods.

Female handle (choker) is a handle with a handle eye and a slot of such dimension as to permit passage of a male handle, thereby allowing the use of a metal mesh sling in a choker hitch. [See Fig. 14-1 (N-184-1).]

Handle is a terminal fitting to which metal mesh fabric is attached. [See Fig. 14-1 (N-184-1).]

Handle eye is an opening in a handle of a metal mesh sling shaped to accept a hook, shackle, or other lifting device. [See Fig. 14-1 (N-184-1).]

Hitch is a sling configuration whereby the sling is fastened to an object or load, either directly to it or around it.

Link is a single ring of a chain.

Male handle (triangle) is a handle with a handle eye.

Master coupling link is an alloy steel welded coupling link used as an intermediate link to join alloy steel chain to master links. [See Fig. 14-3 (N-184-3).]

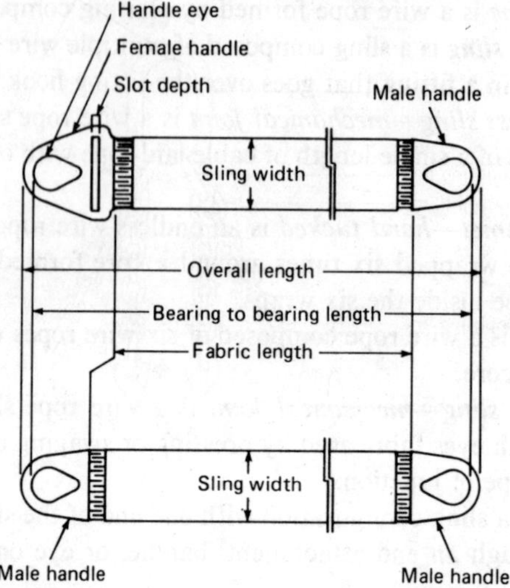

Fig. 14-1 (Fig. N-184-1). Metal mesh sling (typical).

Master link or *gathering ring* is a forged or welded steel link used to support all members (legs) of an alloy steel chain sling or wire rope sling. [See Fig. 14-3 (N-184-3).]

Mechanical coupling link is a nonwelded, mechanically closed steel link used to attach master links, hooks, etc., to alloy steel chain.

Proof load is the load applied in performance of a proof test.

Proof test is a nondestructive tension test performed by the sling manufacturer or an equivalent entity to verify construction and workmanship of a sling.

Rated capacity or *working load limit* is the maximum working load permitted by the provisions of this section of the regulations and as shown in the charts that accompany the text.

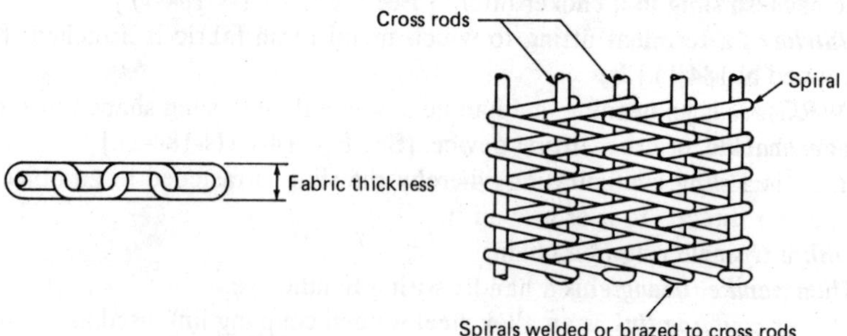

Fig. 14-2 (Fig. N-184-2). Metal mesh construction.

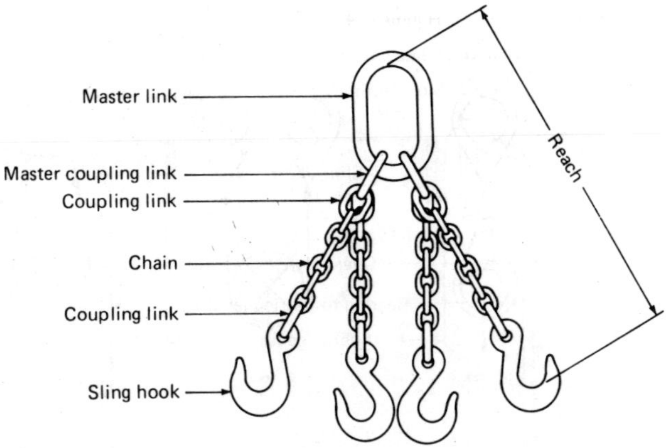

Fig. 14-3 (Fig. N-184-3). Major components of a quadruple sling.

Reach is the effective length of an alloy steel chain sling measured from the top bearing surface of the upper terminal component to the bottom bearing surface of the lower terminal component.

Selvage edge is the finished edge of synthetic webbing designed to prevent unraveling.

Sling is an assembly that connects the load to the material handling equipment.

Sling manufacturer is a person or organization that assembles sling components into their final form for sale to users.

Spiral is a single transverse coil that is the basic element from which metal mesh is fabricated. [See Fig. 14-2 (N-184-2).]

Strand laid endless sling—mechanical joint is a wire rope sling made endless from one length of rope with the ends joined by one or more metallic fittings.

Strand laid grommet—hand tucked is an endless wire rope sling made from one length of strand wrapped six times around a core formed by hand-tucking the ends of the strand inside the six wraps.

Strand laid rope is a wire rope made with strands (usually six or eight) wrapped around a fiber core, wire strand core, or independent wire rope core (IWRC).

Vertical hitch is a method of supporting a load by a single, vertical part or leg of the sling. [See below Fig 14-4 (N-184-4).]

c. Safe Operating Practices

Whenever any sling is used, the following practices shall be observed:

1. Slings that are damaged or defective shall not be used.

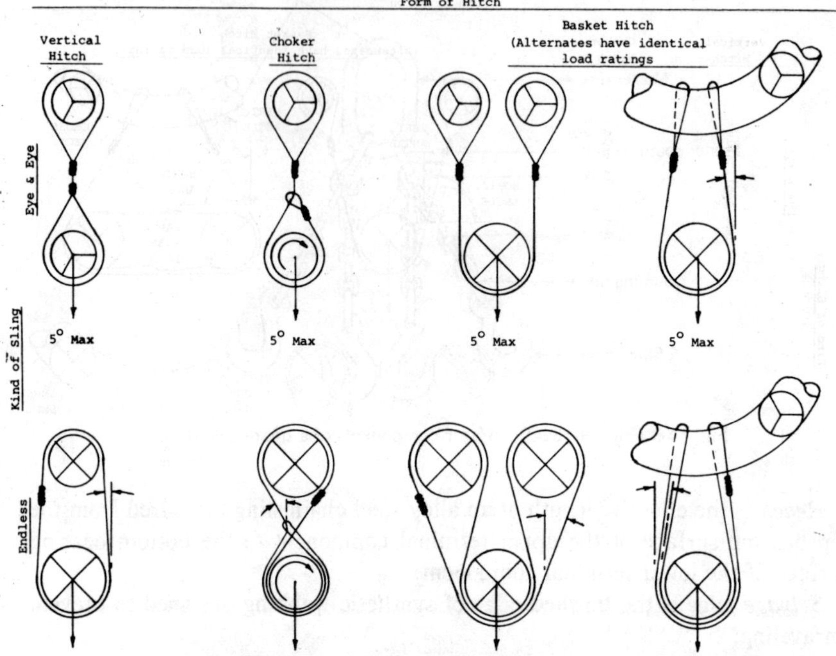

NOTES: Angles 5° or less from the vertical may be considered vertical angles. For slings with legs more than 5° off vertical, the actual angle as shown in Fig. 14-5 (N-184-5) must be considered.

Fig. 14-4 (N-184-4). Basic sling configurations with vertical legs.

2. Slings shall not be shortened with knots or bolts or other makeshift devices.
3. Sling legs shall not be kinked.
4. Slings shall not be loaded in excess of their rated capacities.
5. Slings used in a basket hitch shall have the loads balanced to prevent slippage.
6. Slings shall be securely attached to their loads.
7. Slings shall be padded or protected from the sharp edges of their loads.
8. Suspended loads shall be kept clear of all obstructions.
9. All employees shall be kept clear of loads about to be lifted and of suspended loads.
10. Hands or fingers shall not be placed between the sling and its load while the sling is being tightened around the load.
11. Shock loading is prohibited.
12. A sling shall not be pulled from under a load when the load is resting on the sling.

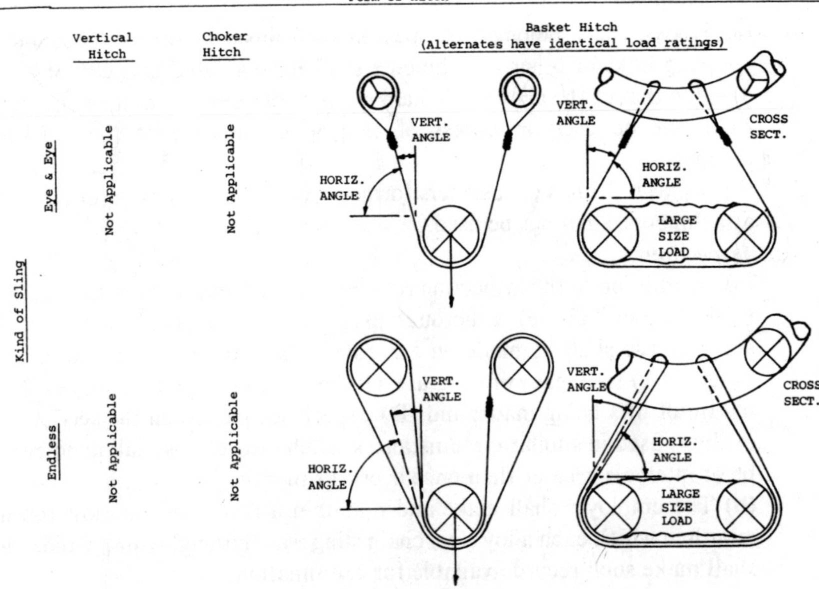

NOTES: For vertical angles of 5° or less, refer to Fig. 14-4 (N-184-4), "Basic Sling Configurations with Vertical Legs."
See Fig. 14-4 (N-184-4) for explanation of symbols.

Fig. 14-5 (N-184-5). Sling configurations with angled legs.

d. Inspections

Each day before being used, the sling and all fastenings and attachments shall be inspected for damage or defects by a competent person designated by the employer. Additional inspections shall be performed during sling use, where service conditions warrant. Damaged or defective slings shall be immediately removed from service.

e. Alloy Steel Chain Slings

1. *Sling identification.* Alloy steel chain slings shall have permanently affixed durable identification stating size, grade, rated capacity, and reach. (A metal tag should be stamped and wired to the chain sling in much the same manner that a tag is attached to a key for identification. Where large numbers of slings of different sizes and capacities are used, it is advisable to have a clean, well-lighted central location where the slings can be hung in an orderly fashion with each chain location clearly painted in its hanging place. This is very much like a key rack where tagged keys are hung with their own designated place.)

2. *Attachments.*
   (a) Hooks, rings, oblong links, pear-shaped links, welded or mechanical coupling links or other attachments shall have a rated capacity at least equal to that of the alloy steel chain with which they are used, or the sling shall not be used in excess of the rated capacity of the weakest component.
   (b) Makeshift links or fasteners formed from bolts or rods, or other such attachments, shall not be used.
3. *Inspections.*
   (a) In addition to the inspection required by paragraph (d) of this section ("Inspections," above), a thorough periodic inspection of alloy steel chain slings in use shall be made on a regular basis, to be determined on the basis of (A) frequency of sling use; (B) severity of service conditions; (C) nature of lifts being made; and (D) experience gained on the service lift of slings used in similar circumstances. Such inspections shall in no event be at intervals greater than once every 12 months.
   (b) The employer shall make and maintain a record of the most recent month in which each alloy steel chain sling was thoroughly inspected, and shall make such record available for examination.
   (c) The thorough examination of alloy steel chain slings shall be performed by a competent person designated by the employer, and shall include a thorough inspection for wear, defective welds, deformation, and increase in length. Where such defects or deterioration are present, the sling shall be immediately removed from service.
4. *Proof testing.* The employer shall ensure that before use, each new, repaired, or reconditioned alloy steel chain sling, including all welded components in the sling assembly, shall be proof-tested by the sling manufacturer or equivalent entity, in accordance with paragraph 5.2 of the American Society of Testing and Materials Specification A391-65 (ANSI G61.1-1968). The employer shall retain a certificate of the proof test and shall make it available for examination.
5. *Sling use.* Alloy steel chain slings shall not be used with loads in excess of the rated capacities prescribed in Table 14-1 (N-184-1). Slings not included in this table shall be used only in accordance with the manufacturer's recommendations.
6. *Safe operating temperatures.* Alloy steel chain slings shall be permanently removed from service if they are heated above 1000°F. When exposed to service temperatures in excess of 600°F, maximum working load limits permitted in Table 14-1 (N-184-1) shall be reduced in accordance with the chain or sling manufacturer's recommendations.
7. *Repairing and reconditioning alloy steel chain slings.*
   (a) Worn or damaged alloy steel chain slings or attachments shall not be

Table 14-1. Rated Capacity (Working Load Limit), for Alloy Steel Chain Slings (Table N-184-1).

Chain Size, Inches	Single Branch Sling - 90 degree Loading	Double Sling Vertical Angle (1) / Horizontal Angle (2)			Triple and Quadruple Sling (3) Vertical Angle (1) / Horizontal Angle (2)		
		30 degree / 60 degree	45 degree / 45 degree	60 degree / 30 degree	30 degree / 60 degree	45 degree / 45 degree	60 degree / 30 degree
1/4	3,250	5,650	4,550	3,250	8,400	6,800	4,900
3/8	6,600	11,400	9,300	6,600	17,000	14,000	9,900
1/2	11,250	19,500	15,900	11,250	29,000	24,000	17,000
5/8	16,500	28,500	23,300	16,500	43,000	35,000	24,500
3/4	23,000	39,800	32,500	23,000	59,500	48,500	34,500
7/8	28,750	49,800	40,600	28,750	74,500	61,000	43,000
1	38,750	67,100	54,800	38,750	101,000	82,000	58,000
1-1/8	44,500	77,000	63,000	44,500	115,500	94,500	66,500
1-1/4	57,500	99,500	81,000	57,500	149,000	121,500	86,000
1-3/8	67,000	116,000	94,000	67,000	174,000	141,000	100,500
1-1/2	80,000	138,000	112,900	80,000	207,000	169,000	119,500
1-3/4	100,000	172,000	140,000	100,000	258,000	210,000	150,000

(1) Rating of multileg slings adjusted for angle of loading measured as the included angle between the inclined leg and the vertical as shown in Figure 14-5 (N-184-5).

(2) Rating of multileg slings adjusted for angle of loading between the inclined leg and the horizontal plane of the load, as shown in Figure 14-5 (N-184-5).

(3) Quadruple sling rating is same as triple sling because normal lifting practice may not distribute load uniformly to all 4 legs.

Table 14-2. Minimum allowable chain size at any point of Link

Chain Size, Inches	Minimum Allowable Chain Size, Inches
1/4	13/64
3/8	19/64
1/2	25/64
5/8	31/64
3/4	19/32
7/8	45/64
1	13/16
1-1/8	29/32
1-1/4	1
1-3/8	1-3/32
1-1/2	1-3/16
1-3/4	1-13/32

used until repaired. When welding or heat testing is performed, slings shall not be used unless repaired, reconditioned, and proof-tested by the sling manufacturer or an equivalent entity.

(b) Mechanical coupling links or low carbon steel repair links shall not be used to repair broken lengths of chain.

8. *Effects of wear.* If the chain size at any point of any link is less than that stated in Table 14-2 (N-184-2), the sling shall be removed from service.
9. *Deformed attachments.*

   (a) Alloy steel chain slings with cracked or deformed master links, coupling links or other components shall be removed from service.

   (b) Slings shall be removed from service if hooks are cracked, have been opened more than 15% of the normal throat opening measured at the narrowest point, or twisted more than ten degrees from the plane of the unbent hook.

f. Wire Rope Slings

1. *Sling use.* Wire rope slings shall not be used with loads in excess of the rated capacities shown in Tables N-184-3 (Table 14-3) through N-184-14. Slings not included in these tables shall be used only in accordance with the manufacturer's recommendations.
2. *Minimum sling lengths.*

   (a) Cable laid and 6 × 19 and 6 × 37 slings shall have a minimum clear length of wire rope 10 times the component rope diameter between splices, sleeves, or end fittings.

Table 14-3. Rated Capacities For Single Leg Slings 6 × 19 and 6 × 37 Classification Improved Plow Steel Grade Rope with Fiber core (FC) (Table N-184-3).

Rope		Rated Capacities, Tons (2,000 lb)								
		Vertical			Choker			Vertical Basket*		
Dia (Inches)	Constr	HT	MS	S	HT	MS	S	HT	MS	S
1/4	6 x 19	0.49	0.51	0.55	0.37	0.38	0.41	0.99	1.0	1.1
5/16	6 x 19	0.76	0.79	0.85	0.57	0.59	0.64	1.5	1.6	1.7
3/8	6 x 19	1.1	1.1	1.2	0.80	0.85	0.91	2.1	2.2	2.4
7/16	6 x 19	1.4	1.5	1.6	1.1	1.1	1.2	2.9	3.0	3.3
1/2	6 x 19	1.8	2.0	2.1	1.4	1.5	1.6	3.7	3.9	4.3
9/16	6 x 19	2.3	2.5	2.7	1.7	1.9	2.0	4.6	5.0	5.4
5/8	6 x 19	2.8	3.1	3.3	2.1	2.3	2.5	5.6	6.2	6.7
3/4	6 x 19	3.9	4.4	4.8	2.9	3.3	3.6	7.8	8.8	9.5
7/8	6 x 19	5.1	5.9	6.4	3.9	4.5	4.8	10.0	12.0	13.0
1	6 x 19	6.7	7.7	8.4	5.0	5.8	6.3	13.0	15.0	17.0
1-1/8	6 x 19	8.4	9.5	10.0	6.3	7.1	7.9	17.0	19.0	21.0
1-1/4	6 x 37	9.8	11.0	12.0	7.4	8.3	9.2	20.0	22.0	25.0
1-3/8	6 x 37	12.0	13.0	15.0	8.9	10.0	11.0	24.0	27.0	30.0
1-1/2	6 x 37	14.0	16.0	17.0	10.0	12.0	13.0	28.0	32.0	35.0
1-5/8	6 x 37	16.0	18.0	21.0	12.0	14.0	15.0	33.0	37.0	41.0
1-3/4	6 x 37	19.0	21.0	24.0	14.0	16.0	18.0	38.0	43.0	48.0
2	6 x 37	25.0	28.0	31.0	18.0	21.0	23.0	49.0	55.0	62.0

HT = Hand Tucked Splice and Hidden Tuck Splice
For hidden tuck splice (IWRC) use values in HT columns.
MS = Mechanical Splice
S = Swaged or Zinc Poured Socket

* These values only apply when the D/d ratio for HT slings is 10 or greater, and for MS and S slings is 20 or greater where: D = Diameter of curvature around which the body of the sling is bent.
d = Diameter of rope.

(b) Braided slings shall have a minimum clear length of wire rope 40 times the component rope diameter between the loops or end fittings.
(c) Cable laid grommets, strand laid grommets, and endless slings shall have a minimum circumferential length of 96 times their body diameter.

3. *Safe operating temperatures.* Fiber core wire rope slings of all grades shall be permanently removed from service if they are exposed to temperatures in excess of 200°F. When nonfiber core wire rope slings of any grade are used at temperatures above 400°F or below minus 60°F, recommendations of the sling manufacturer regarding use at that temperature shall be followed.
4. *End attachments.*
(a) Welding of end attachments, except covers to thimbles, shall be performed prior to the assembly of the sling.
(b) All welded-end attachments shall not be used unless proof-tested by the manufacturer or equivalent entity at twice their rated capacity prior to initial use. The employer shall retain a certificate of the proof test, and make it available for examination.
5. *Removal from service.* Wire rope slings shall be immediately removed from service if any of the following conditions are present:
(a) Ten randomly distributed broken wires in one rope lay, or five broken wires in one strand in one rope lay.
(b) Wear or scraping of one-third the original diameter of outside individual wires.
(c) Kinking, crushing, bird caging, or any other damage resulting in distortion of the wire rope structure.
(d) Evidence of heat damage.
(e) End attachments that are cracked, deformed, or worn.
(f) Hooks that have been opened more than 15% of the normal throat opening measured at the narrowest point or twisted more than ten degrees from the plane of the unbent hook.
(g) Corrosion of the rope or end attachments.

g. Metal Mesh Slings

1. *Sling marking.* Each metal mesh sling shall have permanently affixed to it a durable marking that states the rated capacity for vertical basket hitch and choker hitch loadings.
2. *Handles.* Handles shall have a rated capacity at least equal to the metal fabric and exhibit no deformation after proof testing.
3. *Attachments of handles to fabric.* The fabric and handles shall be joined so that:
(a) The rated capacity of the sling is not reduced.

(b) The load is evenly distributed across the width of the fabric.
(c) Sharp edges will not damage the fabric.

4. *Sling coatings.* Coatings that diminish the rated capacity of a sling shall not be applied.
5. *Sling testing.* All new and repaired metal mesh slings, including handles, shall not be used unless proof-tested by the manufacturer or equivalent entity at a minimum of 1½ times their rated capacity. Elastomer-impregnated slings shall be proof-tested before coating.
6. *Proper use of metal mesh slings.* Metal mesh slings shall not be used to lift loads in excess of their rated capacities as prescribed in Table N-184-15. Slings not included in this table shall be used only in accordance with the manufacturer's recommendations.
7. *Safe operating temperatures.* Metal mesh slings that are not impregnated with elastomers may be used in a temperature range from minus 20°F to plus 550°F without decreasing the working load limit. Metal mesh slings impregnated with polyvinyl chloride or neoprene may be used only in a temperature range from zero degrees to plus 200°F. For operations outside these temperature ranges or for metal mesh slings impregnated with other materials, the sling manufacturer's recommendations shall be followed.
8. *Repairs.*
(a) Metal mesh slings that are repaired shall not be used unless repaired by a metal mesh sling manufacturer or an equivalent entity.
(b) Once repaired, each sling shall be permanently marked or tagged, or a written record maintained, to indicate the date and nature of the repairs and the person or organization that performed the repairs. Records of repairs shall be made available for examination.
9. *Removal from service.* Metal mesh slings shall be immediately removed from service if any of the following conditions are present:
(a) A broken weld or broken brazed joint along the sling edge.
(b) Reduction in wire diameter of 25% due to abrasion or 15% due to corrosion.
(c) Lack of flexibility due to distortion of the fabric.
(d) Distortion of the female handle so that the depth of the slot is increased more than 10%.
(e) Distortion of either handle so that the width of the eye is decreased more than 10%.
(f) A 15% reduction of the original cross-sectional area of metal at any point around the handle eye.
(g) Distortion of either handle out of its plane.

(Please Note: Any materials handling practitioner who must make use of

Tables N-184-4 through F-184-15 mentioned in the above text, please consult the OSHA regulations as published in the *Federal Register*.)

h. Natural and Synthetic Fiber Rope Slings

1. *Sling use.*
   (a) Fiber rope slings made from conventional three-strand-construction fiber rope shall not be used with loads in excess of the rated capacities prescribed in Tables N-184-16 through N-184-19.
   (b) Fiber rope slings shall have a diameter of curvature meeting at least the minimums specified in Figs. 14-4 (N-184-4) and 15-4 (N-184-5).
   (c) Slings not included in these tables shall be used only in accordance with the manufacturer's recommendations.
2. *Safe operating temperatures.* Natural and synthetic fiber rope slings, except for wet frozen slings, may be used in a temperature range from minus 20°F to plus 180°F without decreasing the working load limit. For operations outside this temperature range and for wet frozen slings, the sling manufacturer's recommendations shall be followed.
3. *Splicing.* Spliced fiber rope slings shall not be used unless they have been spliced in accordance with the following minimum requirements and in accordance with any additional recommendations of the manufacturer:
   (a) In manila rope, eye splices shall consist of at least three full tucks, and short splices shall consist of at least six full tucks, three on each side of the splice center line.
   (b) In synthetic fiber rope, eye splices shall consist of at least four full tucks, and short splices shall consist of at least eight full tucks, four on each side of the center line.
   (c) Strand end tails shall not be trimmed flush with the surface of the rope immediately adjacent to the full tucks. This applies to all types of fiber rope and both eye and short splices. For fiber rope under one inch in diameter, the tail shall project at least six rope diameters beyond the last full tuck. For fiber rope one inch in diameter and larger, the tail shall project at least six inches beyond the last full tuck. Where a projecting tail interferes with the use of the sling, the tail shall be tapered and spliced into the body of the rope using at least two additional tucks (which will require a tail length of approximately six rope diameters beyond the last full tuck).
   (d) Fiber rope slings shall have a minimum clear length of rope between eye splices equal to ten times the rope diameter.
   (e) Knots shall not be used in lieu of splices.
   (f) Clamps not designed specifically for fiber ropes shall not be used for splicing.

(g) For all eye splices, the eye shall be of such size to provide an included angle of not greater than 60 degrees at the splice when the eye is placed over the load or support.

4. *End attachments.* Fiber rope slings shall not be used if end attachments in contact with the rope have sharp edges or projections.
5. *Removal from service.* Natural and synthetic fiber rope slings shall be immediately removed from service if any of the following conditions are present:
   (a) Abnormal wear.
   (b) Powdered fiber between strands.
   (c) Broken or cut fibers.
   (d) Variations in the size or roundness of strands.
   (e) Discoloration or rotting.
   (f) Distortion of hardware in the sling.
6. *Repairs.* Only fiber rope slings made from new rope shall be used. Use of repaired or reconditioned fiber rope slings is prohibited.

i. Synthetic Web Slings

1. *Sling identification.* Each sling shall be marked or coded to show the rated capacities for each type of hitch and type of synthetic web material.
2. *Webbing.* Synthetic webbing shall be of uniform thickness and width and selvage edges shall not be split from the webbing's width.
3. *Fittings.* Fittings shall be:
   (a) Of a minimum breaking strength equal to that of the sling.
   (b) Free of all sharp edges that could in any way damage the webbing.
4. *Attachment of end fittings to webbing and formation of eyes.* Stitching shall be the only method used to attach end fittings to webbing and to form eyes. The thread shall be in an even pattern and contain a sufficient number of stitches to develop the full breaking strength of the sling.
5. *Sling use.* Synthetic web slings illustrated in Fig. 14-6 (N-184-6) shall not be used with loads in excess of the rated capacities specified in Tables N-184-20 through N-184-22. Slings not included in these tables shall be used only in accordance with the manufacturer's recommedations.
6. *Environmental conditions.* When synthetic web slings are used, the following precautions shall be taken:
   (a) Nylon web slings shall not be used where fumes, vapors, sprays, mists, or liquids of acids or phenolics are present.
   (b) Polyester and polypropylene web slings shall not be used where fumes, vapors, sprays, mists, or liquids of caustics are present.
   (c) Web slings with aluminum fittings shall not be used where fumes, vapors, sprays, mists, or liquids of caustics are present.

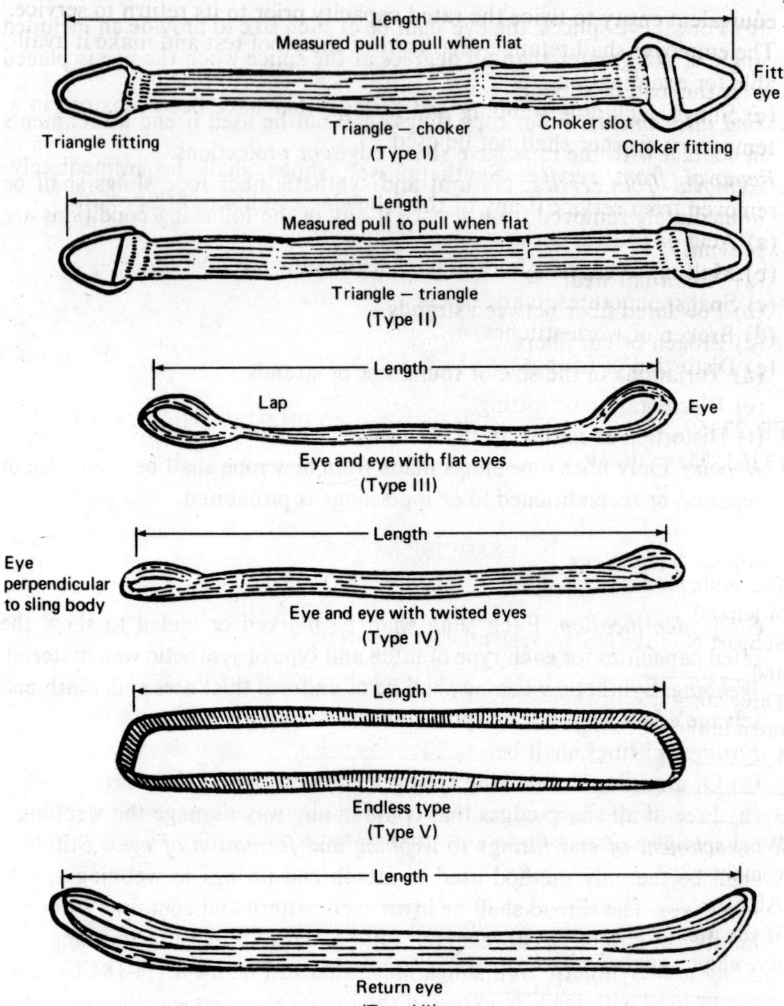

Fig. 14-6 (Fig. N-184-6). Basic synthetic web sling constructions.

7. *Safe operating temperatures.* Synthetic web slings of polyester and nylon shall not be used at temperatures in excess of 180°F. Polypropylene web slings shall not be used at temperatures in excess of 200°F.
8. *Repairs.*
   (a) Synthetic web slings that are repaired shall not be used unless repaired by a sling manufacturer or an equivalent entity.
   (b) Each repaired sling shall be proof-tested by the manufacturer or

equivalent entity to twice the rated capacity prior to its return to service. The employer shall retain a certificate of the proof test and make it available for examination.

(c) Slings, including webbing and fittings, that have been repaired in a temporary manner shall not be used.

9. *Removal from service.* Synthetic web slings shall be immediately removed from service if any of the following conditions are present:
   (a) Acid or caustic burns.
   (b) Melting or charring of any part of the sling surface.
   (c) Snags, punctures, tears, or cuts.
   (d) Broken or worn stitches.
   (e) Distortion of fittings.

(40 FR 27369, June 27, 1975, as amended at 40 FR 31598, July 28, 1975; 41 FR 13353, Mar. 30, 1976.)

EXERCISE NO. 14

1. The Williams-Steiger Act of 1970 is known as ____________. (4 letters)
2. Subpart N of the OSHA regulations concerns the subject of materials ________ and ____________.
3. Three standards organizations that have provided regulations that are incorporated in the OSHA rules are:
   1. ____________________
   2. ____________________
   3. ____________________
4. What specifications must a forklift truck manufactured after February 15, 1972 comply with?
   ANSI—____________________
5. If you wanted to modify a forklift truck in a manner that would change its capacity, whose approval would you have to obtain?
   ____
6. When must a truck nameplate be changed? ____________________
   ____
   ____
7. What does the designation EX mean when applied to forklift trucks?
   ____
   ____
   ____
8. Can you convert a straight gas truck to LP gas? ____________
9. When must you provide an overhead guard on a forklift truck?
   ____
   ____

10. It is not good practice to smoke in the battery charging room.
True ☐ False ☐

11. Why is it dangerous to place a steel wrench on top of a battery?
____
____

12. Concentrations of __________ parts per million, or higher are harmful.

13. What forklift truck traveling speeds would you recommend for your plant? ____
____
____

14. A forklift truck battery should not be disconnected before attempting repairs on its electrical system. True ☐ False ☐

15. According to OSHA you can increase the counterweight on a forklift truck.
True ☐ False ☐

16. According to OSHA does a sling have to be inspected more than once a week?
____
____

17. Give three wire rope defects or causes that would warrant removing the rope from service.
1. _______________
2. _______________
3. _______________

Chapter 15
Materials Handling Safety and Training

I. THE NEED FOR SAFETY AND TRAINING

A. Introduction

When discussing safety problems we like to cite statistics that back up our remarks. Unfortunately, there is no central data collection point for these very complex problems. Many smaller companies do not report accidents, and there is a lack of uniformity in describing the accidents themselves.

OSHA, as a branch of the U.S. Labor Department, and the Labor Department, itself, have collected data; but because plants with seven or fewer employees do not report accident data except in connection with workmen's compensation claims, it is very difficult to derive anything but approximations from the information that is collected.

Some assumptions can be made, however, For example, although forklift truck injuries may represent only 1% of the medical cases, they comprise about 10% of the disabling or serious injuries—an indication that while the number of forklift truck injury accidents is small, they are more severe than many other types of industrial injury accidents.

Statistics, also, are not available in another important area: damage to property caused by forklift trucks. Ask any plant employee, and you will find numerous examples of such damage, indicating how very costly this aspect of forklift truck operations is. In the author's opinion, if operators can be trained properly, to regard employee safety as of primary importance, then secondary benefits will occur that will minimuze property damage.

By studying the ten most common forklift truck accidents, we shall be better able to cope with other plant safety problems as well.

B. Ten Common Forklift Truck Accidents

1. Employee Struck by Forklift Truck. This type of accident which is potentially fatal, is one of the most common types. A moving forklift truck, even one traveling slowly, cannot stop "on a dime." A two-ton-capacity gas-powered forklift weighs about 6,800 pounds without a load. A pedestrian stepping in front of it is certain to be injured, sometimes fatally.

Examples of this type of accident include:

1. Employees not paying attention to their surroundings, and stepping out into the vehicle aisle in front of a moving forklift truck, or into its side. Walking into the side of the truck and receiving a glancing blow may not, in itself, cause serious injury; but if, for example, employee bounces off the truck and lands on a load of sharp sheet metal parts, then a very serious injury can occur.
2. Employees walking alongside a moving truck as the vehicle turns a corner. The leading rear steering wheels can run over the employees' feet.

2. Forklift Shoves a Container or Part into an Employee. The operator must always be aware of developing situations, such as driving up to an employee who is standing between the forklift truck and a fixed object. Three typical examples follow:

1. An operator is driving down an aisle with a load. Extending into the aisle is a part or a container. The operator may see the obstruction in the aisle, and think that there is enough room to pass it, or he may be distracted for a moment and not see the obstruction. He proceeds, and shoves the object into an employee standing behind it. But behind the employee is a fixed object—a wall, bench, or machine—and the employee is crushed.
2. The operator is servicing a work station with a load of parts. In the station is an employee, working attentively, and he does not observe the vehicle. The operator decides simply to move the load close to the employee, set it down, and move out quickly without distracting the employee from his detailed work. As the operator does this, the employee suddenly turns around and steps in front of the load as it is being set down. The worker is crushed between the load and the fixed object behind him.
3. A forklift operator is putting material away in storage racks that are back-to-back. As the operator of the forklift truck pushes a load into an empty space on a rack on the second or third level, or higher, a clerk taking inventory in the opposite aisle is struck or crushed by material that has been pushed off the higher level by the forklift truck driver, the driver not having realized that the load he was putting away was pushing an oversized load out of position. (In a manufacturing plant located in the Midwest, such an accident actually happened a few years ago. Only instead of one clerk in the aisle opposite the forklift driver, there were two clerks, one counting inventory and the other recording and tagging the merchandise. A pallet load of materials was dumped upon them from a height of approximately 20 feet. Both were injured severely, and one of them was left crippled for life—an unfortunate accident that should

never have occurred.) Dividers or safety backstops down the center portion of back-to-back storage racks can prevent this type of accident.

3. Operator Struck by Falling Parts While Manually Handling Materials. This occurs when the operator is off the truck and is manually "jockeying" a load or part into position. The load or object may be on the forks, or on the floor. Either the load shifts on the forks and falls off, or parts fall out of the container, striking the operator's legs or feet.

5. Operator or Other Employee is Injured While Boarding or Stepping Down from the Forklift. This seemingly simple act results in many knee or ankle sprains, but the cause is not clear. In many such injuries it appears the cause may be the sudden transfer of body weight onto one leg, when the person either steps up onto the truck, or steps down and puts all his weight on the leg. Sometimes the operator or another individual working with him steps on a fabricated part or dunnage lying on the floor, severely twisting his ankle or knee.

6. Operator Fails to Recognize a Potentially Serious Hazard Ahead, and Fails to Slow Down. Although tip-over type accidents are relatively rare, most operators have had some close calls. This is another serious type of accident that can result in a fatality. In every case, the accident can be prevented if the operator sizes up the situation and reduces the truck's speed. Going around a corner or down a ramp can be particularly dangerous if the forklift is traveling too fast. Three-wheeled trucks have less stability than four-wheeled vehicles; too much speed can overturn either of them. Carrying a load too high raises a truck's center of gravity. Add too much speed, plus a corner, and you have the ingredients for a forklift to tip over.

7. Vehicle Runs into Other Moving Vehicles. This type of accident can occur any time, with disastrous results, particularly if the other vehicle is smaller than the forklift truck. In many of our units, small personnel carriers, carts, scooters, and bicycles are in frequent use. When they are driven carelessly and at too high a speed, they become potential accident-makers, particularly at intersections.

8. Vehicle Backs or Runs off the Edge of the Loading Dock. This is another area with high potential for fatalities. Any time a forklift runs off a dock, either by backing or by the operator's getting too close to an unguarded edge, there is a strong chance of severe injury or death. A common reason for a truck to run off a dock while loading or unloading a truck trailer is failure to chock or block the trailer wheels *on both sides*.

It is an OSHA violation to load or unload a truck without blocking its wheels to prevent truck movement. However, this rule is commonly violated by forklift truck operators.

Sometimes it is not clear who has the responsibility for seeing that an over-the-road carrier has its wheels properly chocked. In any event, it is the forklift truck operator's supervisor who has this responsibility—and he should be so informed. He may not necessarily place the chocks under the trailer wheels, but he should see that this gets done before any forklift truck driver enters the trailer.

Another potentially dangerous area is the loading or unloading of flat-bed trailers. In some instances forklift operators have misjudged the distance to the edge of a flat-bed trailer and then backed over it. The same can be said of flat-bed railroad cars.

9. Part of Operator's Body Protruding outside the Running Lines of the Truck Is Injured. Too often the operator of a forklift truck lets his feet or hands rest outside the vehicle. The result is usually severe bumping, scraping, twisting, or other injury to that part of the body.

Unusual? Not at all. In one incident a forklift operator driving an electric stand-up truck stuck his head outside the running lines on the left side of the truck to look ahead. He struck his head on a building column as he passed it. The odd thing about that accident was that the operator was not carrying any loads, had excellent forward visibility—but was going down the wrong side of a 16-foot-wide aisle.

10. Parts Fall on the Operator. All forklift operators should have overhead canopy guards when any loads are lifted or carried above the truck's mast. These guards protect the driver from falling objects.

However, there is still an area of vulnerability where a driver needs to use additional caution: the area between the mast and the canopy guard.

While a driver is stacking a load, he raises the forks and inches into position, but perhaps the container he is stacking is overloaded with parts, or is otherwise unbalanced. As he inches forward, he runs over a rough spot in the concrete, or some object. It's enough to shake the truck; the loose parts suddenly fall back behind the mast and onto the operator.

Sometimes just raising the forks and tilting the mast back is enough to start an unstable load sliding back into the operator's lap.

High back rests and stable loads that do not extend above the back rest will prevent many of these types of accidents.

While the author was setting up a warehouse system in the Boston area, this freak accident occured: A forklift operator was entering a railroad car and driving over the dock plate into the car. The jostling over the plate dislodged and loosened the load of cartons; so the driver reached through the mast as he was elevating the forks, and his hand was mangled between the chain and the load backrest.

11. A Summary. We have discussed some of the common forklift truck accidents, and the injuries and fatalities that may result. To these direct effects must be added the indirect costs of the possibly damaged forklift truck, replacement of employees, damaged materials, and related expenses.

In a small company, the repeated occurrence of this type of injury accident can be disastrous. Worker's compensation premium rates are tremendously expensive, and a serious industrial injury could explode such rates for a smaller company.

Perhaps the small firm has only one forklift truck; it could be put out of service because of the accident. Quite possibly, another person would have to be temporarily added to the payroll. Thus, an accident of such magnitude for a small firm can be the difference between showing a year-end profit or a loss because the indirect costs of a personal injury accident can be many times higher than those directly related to the individual.

Mechanical problems or conditions—such as mechanical malfunction—do not seem to be a major factor. Less than 1% (only 0.7%) of forklift accidents are caused by or involve mechanical failure.

In general, accidents usually have multiple causes. But the other causes are relatively minor compared to operator and fellow-employee error.

12. The Causes of Accidents. Assuming that no one would intentionally cause an accident, these forklift truck accidents are unintentional. When, then, do they occur? There are three main causes:

1. Lack of knowledge or skill
2. Operator being inattentive to the job at hand
3. Operator taking chances, with full knowledge of the possible consequences

In the first case, lack of skill or knowledge is a contributing factor in many forklift truck accidents, and it's also a reason why OSHA regulations state that forklift operators must be trained before operating such vehicles.

The second factor involved in such accidents is that operators are not concentrating on what they are doing. This can happen to even the best-trained person, but usually when his defenses are down, and he is most vulnerable to an accident.

A recent study of over-the-road truck drivers indicated that the safest drivers had one thing in common: *an intense concentration on what they were doing while driving.* These same top drivers did not do any better than any other driver in the various other tests, such as knowledge of rules of the road, but they did excel in one major area, and that was *keeping their minds on what they were doing when they were driving.*

The third factor, taking chances, is the most difficult one to change. All of us take certain chances every day. We take a chance every time we walk across a busy intersection; there is no guarantee that a car will not strike us. But we must draw the line at taking chances that are likely to result in injury.

13. An Accident Reduction Program. Having examined the types and causes of accidents, it is fitting that we now develop a program with the goal of reducing (or, hopefully, eliminating) these accidents. Three basic elements of such a program are discussed in the following paragraphs.

a. Provide Quality Training

A good forklift truck operator training program starts with the employee selection process. For example, an employee who has lost his automobile driver's license certainly does not give any indication that he will be any safer or more responsible operating a forklift. A physical examination is recommended in which certain valid medical criteria applicable to forklift truck driving are used. For example, using visual criteria developed for airline pilots is needlessly restrictive for forklift truck operators; but employees who have a medical problem such as a heart condition or epilepsy and require medication to keep the problem under control, should not be considered as forklift operators because of the potential hazard to themselves and to others.

All operators need quality training to operate their vehicles, whether they are part-time or full-time drivers. OSHA requires that they be trained, and with good reason. Training means more than hustling a group of potential operators through a classroom training program, and then assigning them a truck and letting them drive it. In addition to teaching the rules, practical hands-on training is needed.

There are side benefits to a good training program. Although the basic objective of training is not safety, the fact that it is definitely covered—in the text, in the instructional manual, and through driving practice—does have a bearing on the performance and maintenance of forklift trucks.

Maintenance costs on trucks drop dramatically for a period of up to six months after such a training program is presented. This indicates that:

1. The quality of the training can be such that the operators are motivated to take better care of their trucks.
2. Periodic refresher training is needed, not only for review of operating procedures, but also as a motivational reinforcement tool.

b. Incorporate "Follow-up" into Every Program
Monitoring a new forklift truck operator's performance after training is a necessity to make sure that poor work practices aren't learned and used. Psychologists say it takes seven years to break a bad habit. Operating people don't have that long to change an employee's behavior. Immediate follow-up is needed—not a day later, not a week later, but within hours. Don't wait for a bad habit to develop before trying to correct it. Correct it immediately—before an accident occurs; and if any habits are going to be formed, make sure that they are good work habits.

c. Control Safe Work Practices
Enforcement of safe work practices by supervision is necessary to control forklift truck operation.

Control should be exercised through a blend of both positive and negative means. Negative control incorporates the use of consistently applied disciplinary measures that will have to be used, hopefully infrequently. If discipline is thought of in terms of what it would take to rehabilitate an individual, then the measures used may be more effective.

Positive control using safe behavioral reinforcement techniques focuses and builds on pleasurable rewards, such as immediately complimenting an operator who stops and sounds his horn at a busy intersection. This, if repeated, will act as a positive reinforcement to that employee, so that the desired performance will be repeated.

II. AREAS TO COVER IN VEHICULAR TRAINING

A. Introduction

One of the objects of this book is to combine the theoretical aspects of materials handling and materials management with practical information that can be used on the job. For this reason, then, the following text will assume that you have the responsibility for establishing a mobile equipment operators' training program.

1. Scope. The course is designed to instruct *new* operators (and the operators' supervisor) in the safe, efficient, and economical operation of forklift trucks and other special industrial trucks powered by electric motors or internal combustion engines.

This training will conducted in three phases:

Phase I uses a seven-hour programmed learning course developed by DuPont's Education & Applied Technology Division, consisting of five units designed to teach safe, accident-free, efficient operation (each of which will take about 1¼ hours to complete), plus a sixth unit, a 45-minute written qualifying exam. Details for conducting this course are covered in the Administrator's Guide, which is part of the DuPont program.

Phase II uses the Towmotor color film "Color of Danger," which is available on loan from The Towmotor Co. (but depending on anticipated usage, you may wish to order a copy for your facility's use). Suggestions on how to use this with the trainee are discussed later in this section. There are also excellent films available from the Hyster Company.

Phase III is on-the-truck training. Suggestions on how to conduct this phase are given later in this section.

After the training has been given (all three phases), line supervision must maintain the newly established performance levels, set a good example through personal actions, establish a climate conducive to maintaining proper attitudes, enforce rules in a fair and consistent manner, and provide and maintain a safe working environment.

The rules and regulations specified are in accordance with the Occupational Safety and Health Administration (OSHA) standards dated May 29, 1971.

Special note: Upon request from the line orgaization to train a potential new vehicle operator, two very important steps should be mandatory before any classroom or on-the-truck training is given:

1. Determine acceptable safety consciousness of the employee through a review of his previous safety record.
2. Determine the acceptable physical capability of the employee. This will mean a medical examination for hearing, eyesight, and depth perception and a review of prior health records.

2. Phase I—Beginning Instruction. *Administrator's Guide from DuPont.* The guide explains the function of the administrator, schedule of presentation, training record, and review of concepts, and includes answers to operator tests. (Note: Included with this guide is a supervisory information booklet, to familiarize supervision with the concepts and objectives of the program. The booklet describes the problem of an increasing accident rate, points to the programmed instruction course as a partial solution to the problem, and explains to the supervisor how the course will be conducted.)

Operator Training. The material in this packet consists of the operator training booklet (Units 1 through 5 in the programmed learning course, including the answer sheets), review questions for each unit, and the qualifying written exam. The exam should be removed from the packet before the rest of the material is given to the trainee.

When administering the units, inform the trainee that the answers are provided for each question in the back of the workbook. Tell the trainee to tear the answer sheet section from the back of the workbook and place it beside the operator training booklet for easy reference.

The last unit of the course is the *qualifying written exam,* which should not be administered to the trainee until he has successfully completed the first five units.

3. Phase II—Training Films. *Material/Aids.* Show the film "Color of Danger" (or a Hyster film) after supplying the trainee with pencil and paper.

A suggested introduction to the film is: "This is a safety film made by Towmotor [Hyster] showing examples of how carelessness in operating a fork truck creates problems on the job. Although a few of the examples are extreme, they can or do happen every day. This film calls your attention to *danger* points by coloring them *red,* the color of danger. Look for these danger signs and make a note of them as they occur because we'll be discussing them after the film."

After showing the film, review danger points as recalled by the trainee, and list them on the blackboard. Be sure to cover all of the following danger points:

1. Traveling with forks high
2. Carrying improperly secured loads
3. Lack of preventive maintenance
4. Carrying passengers
5. Ignoring principles of leverage, counterbalance, and steering
6. Improper handling of loads

Suggested concluding comments are: "As the film attempts to point out, it's important to recognize *danger before* accidents happen. People who take things for granted will almost always *miss* the signs of danger until it's too late to prevent accidents and injury."

4. Phase III—On-the-Truck Training. This training should be administered by a qualified person (instructor, supervisor, or experienced operator) in a remote area of the storeroom.

Two to four hours are recommended for on-the-truck training. This training should include:

1. *Inspection.* Have the trainee walk around the truck completely, checking for irregularities. Ask him to inspect the general condition (forks, tires, motor) and cleanliness *before* getting on the lift truck. Point out weight limitations of the truck and load center as shown on the truck.

2. *Start-up.* Stress the importance of a safe start-up. First, ask him to neutralize all controls and set the brake. Show him how to start the motor, and then have him do it. Instruct him in how to test/operate all parts (horn, steer-

ing, hoist, tilt, lights, brakes, motor operation), and then give him a chance to do it.

Concerning the tilt operation, first show him how to raise the lift mechanism and operate the tilt both forward and back as far as it will travel.

Stress that a complete pre-use inspection of the lift truck should be made by the operator each day before he begins his day's work, and observe him as he conducts such an inspection as part of his training, and later, on a workday as he begins work.

3. *Steering.* Point out that the weight of the load is carried by the front wheels on a counterbalanced type lift truck and that turning is done with the rear wheels.

Have him get the feel of the steering wheel. Stress that rear wheels bouncing up and down indicate that too much weight is being carried on the forks. This can impair steering or cause an operator to lose control.

4. *Operation.* Stress that forks should be positioned to within two inches of the floor before moving. Have him practice smooth operation of the lift truck, avoiding jerky starts. Have him test the brakes for positive stopping power. Point out the need to plan ahead to avert panic stops. Have him practice staying clear of racks, tubs, walls, and other areas. Stress that the lift truck should *not* be stopped by putting the drive control in reverse (since the abrupt strain on the motor and gear drives can result in untimely breakdowns). Have him practice approaching main aisles and blind corners. Have him practice steering by going in and out of aisles (no load initially). Stress proper use of the horn (at intersections, when people/machines are in an aisle). Instruct him in the right-of-way rules at your facility. Stress that error-free operation can only be achieved by facing the direction of travel and keeping alert.

Stress that particular attention should be paid to the way the lift truck functions mechanically during the shift.

5. *Emergencies:*

Truck (Electric) Catching on Fire. Explain the emergency procedure, and then have him practice it. Have the trainee immediately stop the unit, turn off the switch, get off, disconnect the battery, remove the fire extinguisher from the truck, or secure one nearby. Explain that, in the case of an actual fire, he should extinguish the blaze and then notify his supervisor and safety personnel.

Truck (Gas) Catching on Fire. Have the trainee simultaneously turn off the ignition switch, stop the unit, and dismount. Explain that he should clear the area of bystanders and try to get assistance to procure a fire extenguisher if one is not on the unit, and then notify his supervisor and safety personnel.

Run Away (throttle stuck or accelerator device won't release). Explain that the brake should be applied and the battery cable disconnected. Have him practice disconnecting the battery cable. Tell him that his supervisor and maintenance personnel should then be notified.

Vertical Run Away (hydraulic lift fails to shut off, and forks continue to rise). Explain that the operator should immediately step off the unit and either disconnect the emergency battery lever or pull the external battery cable. Have him practice disconnections. Specify that his supervisor and maintenance personnel should then be notified.

6. *Load Handling.* Have him practice adjusting forks to most spread, and keeping the top of the forks level. The lift truck should approach the load *slowly and squarely*.

Have him practice inserting the forks into the tub or pallet opening until the load is positioned all the way back to the mast.

Have him practice picking up the load by adjusting the lift control.

Have him practice backing out to a clear position, tilting the load back to the limit, and adjusting the height to the carrying position.

Stress the importance of making sure that loads are free of obstructions and in a safe condition before they are picked up. Take the driver to a series of loads, some stable and some not. Ask him which ones should be picked up, and which ones shouldn't. Point out that unsafe loads should *not* be moved until the hazard is corrected.

Have him practice carrying loads where his vision is obscured by the size of the load by having him turn the truck around and drive in reverse (looking in the direction of travel).

Have him practice crossing railroad tracks or other uneven surfaces with a load. Point out that he should approach at an angle so that only one wheel crosses the rough spot at a time.

Have him practice on ramps at shipping/receiving docks. When driving with a load on a ramp, he should practice driving with the load uphill to keep the load from falling off. Also, he should practice driving a lift truck down a ramp by driving backward with the load uphill.

He should have practice unloading an on-highway truck. Stress that he must chock the wheels of the truck, secure the dock board, and inspect the floor of the truck. Point out the danger of oily dock boards. Have him look for obstructions on the dock. Have him check the entrance door on the vehicle to clear the lift truck mast by at least two inches. Wheels on railroad cars should be blocked to prevent movement in either direction.

7. *Parking.* Have him practice parking in approved locations at your facility. Caution him to be sure to set brakes, lower the forks, place the forks flat on the floor, neutralize the controls, and turn off the electrical switch. Blocking of wheels is recommended on a slope.

8. *General.* Point out that the "professional" operator considers all of the aforementioned skills as his responsibilities as an operator.

Job-Oriented Work Performance. Anywhere from two hours to two days of work performance is recommended (under the occasional observation of an administrator but under the actual control of the immediate supervisor).

Closing Comments. The overall course objective should be kept clearly in mind—that the operator be skilled in handling the lift truck, that he use preventive driving techniques and safe operating procedures, and that he have a "professional" viewpoint and desire for error-free operation on the job.

5. Follow-up. The operator's physical qualifications should be checked yearly.

Licensing. Consider issuing a temporary license after classroom and on-the-truck training is completed. During the following four weeks, the new operator should be carefully observed by his supervisor. After observation of acceptable work/safe operation, a permanent license should be given to the operator.

6. Conclusion. To a large extent, the success of this program depends on the manner in which it is administered by the supervisor.

The supervisor's responsibilities are: (1) to select qualified operators for training and licensing, (2) to make certain that only licensed operators are permitted to handle the equipment, and (3) to revoke an operator's license if that operator no longer performs his duties in a safe and acceptable manner.

III. SAFETY ENGINEERING

A. Introduction

We have, in sections I and II of this chapter, developed a strong point of view on the problems of vehicular traffic and movement within the plant. A larger overview of the whole matter of safety, however, is the province of safety engineering, which is the study of the causes and prevention of accidental deaths and injuries wherever they may occur.

For those materials handling and materials management practitioners who would like to delve deeper into the intricacies of safety engineering, it is suggested that you explore what the National Safety Council has to offer. The Council is a cooperative, nonprofit organization that was founded in 1913. Its main purpose is to reduce the number and severity of industrial, traffic, transportation, home, school, and farm accidents. It is a central gathering place and distribution point for all information about the causes of accidents and ways to prevent them. Information is collected from the more than 11,000 members of the Council, from the large staff of technicians within the Council, and from the U.S. government.

The Council maintains a Safety Training Institute where classes are held. In addition, it offers a series of home study courses for supervisors and maintains the largest safety library in the world. The Council publishes the *National Safety News* and a host of other magazines and periodicals that cover current items on safety. The main office of the Council is in Chicago; however, regional offices are located in New York and San Francisco.

This section of the chapter contains a history of the industrial safety movement and an overview of industrial safety programs which the reader should find of value in developing a healthy perspective on plant safety operations.

1. Background and Perspective. In the industrialized communities of the world, accidents are responsible for more deaths than all infectious diseases, and cause more deaths than does any single illness with the exception of heart disease and cancer. According to recent World Health Organization statistics, approximately 38% of accidental deaths occur in motor vehicle accidents. On a worldwide basis, motor vehicle accidents are the primary cause of accidental deaths, followed closely by those in industry and in the home.

Nonfatal injuries are far more numerous than deaths, but the types of injuries fluctuate from year to year without, seemingly, any definite trend. Suffice it to say that motor vehicle and home accidents are much more frequent than accidents in industrial settings. One of the main reasons for the lower number of industrial accidents may well be industry's emphasis on safety, spurred by the realization on the part of management that industrial accidents are costly in terms of both lost production and higher rates for workmen's compensation insurance.

Insurance companies have collaborated with industrial management in developing highly structured accident-prevention programs, in developing methods of evaluating risks, and in assisting employers in taking preventive measures. In these programs safety engineering, industrial hygiene, and industrial medicine are a three-pronged approach to preventing injury to the worker and eliminating some of the high costs of accidents.

The first measures in safety engineering were directed toward providing guards and protective devices on machines, floor gratings, and the like. Industrial hygiene and medicine have concentrated on controlling environmental factors, noise levels (measured in decibels), exposures to toxic gases and fumes (measured in parts per million), and other harmful exposures. An increasingly sophisticated approach has emphasized personal factors such as the role mental and emotional adjustment have on the worker, and the part these factors play in causing accidents. Despite the contributions of safety engineers, industrial hygienists, and others in this field of endeavor, the primary responsibility for the application of safety engineering principles, employee education for safety, and the enforcement of safety rules within the plant rests with the individual employer, and this responsibility is delegated to the lowest supervisory level of management.

2. Accident Frequency and Severity Rates. Statistical analyses of accidents are based on frequency and severity. The American National Standards Institute (ANSI) has provided a substantial degree of standardization by developing the standard frequency rate, which represents the number of disabling injuries per 1,000,000 man-hours of exposure. The standard severity rate is the total time charged as a result of lost-time injuries per 1,000,000 man-hours of exposure. The time charges include both the actual days lost and standardized charges for permanent disabilities and deaths. Death or permanent total disability charges are arbitrarily set at 6,000 days per occurrence. Permanent, partial disabilities have charges that vary from 35 to 4,500 days.

Frequency and severity rates vary widely from one industry to another. Communications and insurance industries have low frequency and severity rates. On the opposite end of the spectrum are mining, lumbering, and farming. These differences reflect not only the inherent dangers within the industries, but also other factors such as the effectiveness of safety programs and safety education.

In mining, lumbering, and farming, the employees work more or less independently, spread out over large areas where direct supervision is often impossible. Also, permanent safeguards are not widely used because the work environment or location is constantly changing. The worker is left more or less to his own devices and has to protect himself from mining equipment, explosives, saws, axes, etc.

3. Evaluating the Effectiveness of Safety Programs. It is possible to determine how effective a plant's safety program is above and beyond the indexes established by the accident frequency and severity rates. Three ways to do this are as follows:

1. Obtain estimates of the total direct and indirect costs of accidents.
2. Obtain the loss ratio, an index based upon the amount paid for insurance compensation in terms of what might be expected on the basis of industry averages.
3. Apply statistical quality control to the accident record. The index obtained will indicate whether the frequency of accidents is becoming excessive, or improving in relation to past experience.

These three methods should serve to alert management and the plant safety director as to the direction of the safety program. Another good barometer, of course, is the total cost of work injuries and accidents as the sum of "insured" and "uninsured" costs. Insured costs are the amounts paid for compensation and medical insurance premiums. The uninsured costs are those costs attributable to lost-time accidents; injuries requiring medical attention, but with no day's work lost; first-aid injuries; and accidents that cause property damage and work disruptions.

An evaluation of the effectiveness of the plant safety program should include a review of the following areas:

1. Plant layout
2. Housekeeping
3. Maintenance
4. Protective equipment required
5. Safety program organization
6. Medical facilities available
7. Employee training programs
8. Firefighting organization and equipment

To sum up this section, the degree of communication achieved between the director of the safety program and other department heads has an important bearing on the overall effectiveness of the plant's safety program. In the final analysis the education of the employee in the areas of safety will reflect the attitude of plant management and top management, and full support on all levels of management is required.

4. Identifying Critical Areas. The plant safety engineer should constantly review accident reports in order to improve safety conditions within the plant. In addition to the post-accident review, however, is the more important accident-prevention identification of critical areas. This method of analysis is called the *critical-incident technique*. The plant safety director selects a random sample of workers from various locations within the plant where the worker is exposed to various hazardous conditions. The workers are interviewed and asked to describe incidents that might have become accidents. An attempt is made to get the workers to describe safety errors they have made that would have resulted in accidents. A rapport must be established between the worker and the interviewer in order for any meaningful data to be obtained. Ordinarily, most workers are not reluctant to discuss safety matters inasmuch as this is being done on company time. This method is usually a better source of accident prevention than an examination of company records.

a. Work Station Layout

Reference was made in Chapter 10 to the design of work stations from the standpoint of productive efficiency. It is usually a truism that an effective work station layout is also a safe one. This is so because almost all of today's equipment is designed with safety in mind. Machine tools, for example, are well guarded, have dual, two-handed operating controls so that fingers and hands are not in the way of moving parts, and so forth.

b. Environmental Factors

It has long been known that environmental factors influence safety. For example, extremes of heat and cold, humidity, noise, ventilation, and vibration result in worker discomfort or fatigue, lower worker effectiveness, and increase the accident rate. OSHA has been extremely effective in emphasizing these factors in recent years, although good plant safety programs have always taken these variables into consideration. Table 15-1 gives values of these variables that should be found acceptable and conducive to improved working conditions; it is not always possible to establish these ideal conditions, but serious attempts should be made to arrive at them.

B. Failsafe Machinery and Work Areas

1. General Concepts. Although automation has greatly reduced industrial safety hazards where it is used, there are many areas where automation still has not had an appreciable impact. The basic principle of providing guards for machinery continues to be a primary, physical feature of plant safety programs—examples being found in metal removal, chemical tank splashbacks, footing areas around greasy machinery, or shot-blast machine areas where gratings should be installed so that the spherical shot does not make the ground an ice-skating rink. (The author was reponsible for gratings used to capture shot on more than one wheelabrator machine, so that today gratings are standard equipment in such installations.)

In one tragic accident, an overzealous degreasing tank operator climbed over the tank to free a blockage on an overhead conveyor, lost his footing, and was killed instantly when he plunged into the tank of hot solvent. Because gruesome

Table 15-1. Variables affecting the working environment.

ITEM	CONDITION DESIRED MAXIMUM/MINIMUM VALUE
Temperature	63–71°F (20–22°C) winter; 66–75°F (21–24°C) summer.
Humidity	25–50 percent relative humidity.
Noise	Conversations to be carried on at distance of 3 feet without extra effort: 80–85 decibels overall, and 50–60 decibels in the 1200–2400 hertz band.
Ventilation	Sufficient added fresh air to remove odors; 20 cubic feet (0.6 cubic meters) per minute of fresh air.
Vibration	Reduced below threshold of perception; 0.002 inch (0.05 mm) at 20 hertz or more.

incidents such as these are not unknown in the annals of industrial accidents, most safety programs have certain inflexible rules: no rings will be worn in machine shop areas, there will be no loose clothing or long hair around rotating machinery, safety glasses will be issued to all workers and visitors to plant manufacturing areas, etc. It simply is not enough to warn workers not to climb over certain areas of machines, dip tanks, and so forth; the rules must be rigidly followed.

The days of the old line shaft and pulley belt machine operations are almost all gone; modern machinery for the most part is totally enclosed. Nevertheless, pinch points where fingers and hands can be mangled are much in evidence throughout the world of manufacturing, and these areas must be made as fail-safe as possible. Railings and toe guards are still very much a part of plant safety, as well as the color coding of pipes, steam lines, etc. In our consideration of human synergistics (section III, C), we shall discuss how to make the plant safety program more effective.

a. Lifting

Despite the fact that mechanization is very much in evidence in the manufacturing, maintenance, and service industries, there is still a vast amount of manual handling done in industry. Many union contracts still have provisons that men cannot be required to lift more than 50 pounds and women 35 pounds without a hoist (United Auto Workers). Unfortunately, however, if you are lifting only 5 or 10 pounds out of a steel tote tub and you are not lifting in a proper position (that is, if you are largely bent over and off-center), then immense strains are placed on the spine and back muscles that may result in injury, especially for the older worker. One of the most commonly reported accidental injuries is to the spinal column and lower back. Thus, it is that the manual handling of materials is the cause of the largest number of all fatal, permanent, and temporary disabilities.

In manual lifting the most important vector of the force is the distance of the feet from the point at which the object is grasped. The lifting vector or force is greatest when the weight is lifted in the same vertical plane as the body and decreases rapidly as the weight moves away from the plane of the body. The best height for lifting is at or slightly above the level of the middle fingertip of a person standing with arms hanging at the sides. Above this height, lifting power decreases very rapidly; below this height, more slowly. As an example, for a load on the floor, the lifting force is about three-fourths to four-fifths of that force with the load at the best height.

In general terms. lifting with the back vertical and the legs bent affords a slightly stronger vertical pull than lifting with the back bent and the legs straight, and is less conducive to back injury.

It has been found that the average male can move about 220 tons (200 metric tons) per eight-hour shift through a horizontal distance of 3.3 feet (1 meter); or 55 tons (50 metric tons) through a vertical distance of 3.3 feet (1 meter).

For loads of 20 to 60 pounds (9 to 27 kilograms) a yoke has been found to be effective. The hand-carry method with one load in each hand is the next best method; and, for heavy loads, it has been found physically less tiring to carry one load a given distance than to divide the load in half and make two carries.

Physiologically speaking, it has been found that women demonstrate about 55 to 65% as much strength as do men in equivalent tasks.

b. Robotics Safety

One area of mechanization that requires attention to safety is the location of working robots. The swing clearance of moving robot arms was given in Chapter 10. This area requires guarding, by safety railings, or better still, by an enclosure. The robot arm usually moves very swiftly, and it moves in virtual silence, so that it is possible for an unwary human employee or visitor to be hit unless the proper safeguards are provided. Also, it is necessary that interlocks be available in the controls of most robots so that maintenance workers can safely service the areas or the mechanisms without unwarned start-ups occurring. Other safety precautions are usually obtained from the robot installers. These safety measures should be given to the plant safety director for review, concurrence, and implementation.

c. Electrical Safety

Electrical safety hazards are less familiar than those for steam or radiation, for which many safety standards have been published, Almost all accidents involving electricity are preventable.

Electric shock is a function of the rate of current flow through the body. The higher the current, the greater the damage. A 60-cycle, alternating current of 100 milliamperes (0.1 ampere) may result in fatal injury if it passes through the vital organs. A person may still free himself from an object if the current ranges from 8 to 16 milliamperes, depending on a number of factors. The body's resistance to electrical current is chiefly supplied by the skin. Wet skin is 100 to 600 times less resistant than dry skin. The longer the current continues to flow through the body, the greater the severity of damage. With high voltage only short exposures can be survived. Electric currents may cause inteference with breathing by contracting chest muscles or paralyzing the respiratory nerve centers. The current may block the rhythm and muscular action of the heart, or it may destroy tissue, nerves, or muscles from heat due to the heavy current. It should be noted that burns from electrical flashing or arcing are deep and slow to heal.

Electrical accidents are mainly caused by switches and systems improperly selected for the task, or without interlocks and failsafe features. Circuit breakers and groundfault systems are important safety precautions. Groundfault systems cut off the current if a machine is improperly grounded or if a short circuit occurs. Explosion-proof electrical systems are also necessary where some types of hazardous materials are stored or used.

d. Chemical Safety

Chemicals in solid, gaseous, or liquid forms are used in a number of manufacturing and processing industries. Hazardous chemicals are chiefly known for their toxicity and such physical properties as flash points below 100°F, their reactions when mixed with other chemicals, and their decomposition under heat.

There are recommended safety practices for the receipt, storage, handling, and disposal of chemicals and hazardous materials. The Defense Logistics Agency, in Richmond, Virginia, has established a data base composed of the various characteristics of industrial chemicals and hazardous materials. Computer printouts and microfiche describing these characteristics may be obtained from this agency at a reasonable cost.

The use of exhaust hoods, air-filtering, and air-monitoring systems to provide protection from gases and airborne hazards is a subject onto itself. Suffice it to say that respiratory devices, protective clothing, safety showers, and eyewash stands should be carefully used, and located, as needed, by the plant safety engineer. OSHA regulations provide the best guide available in this area.

e. Radiation Safety

The measurement of radiation is indirect, by means of ionization in which electrically charged atoms are produced in the passage of the radiation through a medium. The plant safety engineer is concerned with the alteration of human body cells by exposure to radioactive substances. Protection programs include radiation detection, measurement, and shielding, and monitoring personnel exposure levels in order to limit personnel exposure to the minimum accepted levels.

The use of radioactive sources in manufacturing processes is increasing. Irradiated tools can measure the wear on cutting surfaces and on dies; gauges can measure and control the thickness of layers of paint; radioactive isotopes follow fluid flow in process lines, in lubrication, and in the wear on internal parts of engines and fabricating machinery, etc.

A number of instruments have been developed to make surveys of radiation, and it is recommended that intensive training be undertaken in this area by the materials handling or materials management practioner who does not have a plant safety engineer in charge of radiation safety.

f. Safety Equipment

While it is true that safety that is engineered or designed into equipment is generally more reliable than the safety practices of human beings, the need remains for personal safety equipment. For example, hard hats are required for construction workers, safety goggles for factory workers, shields for welders, and so forth. Most factory workers are required to wear safety shoes with steel toe parts. Firefighters have a variety of complex respiratory and protective clothing that has been designed to offer maximum protection in a hostile environment. Since local, state, and federal laws do require that certain, specific items of protective equipment be used, it would be well for plant management to assign the responsibility for compliance with these regulations to one person. This individual is usually the plant safety director.

c. Human Synergistics

Plant safety programs in which workers are herded into one location for periodic talks on safety are among the most boring, and generally unproductive—or, we should say, counterproductive—ways to lower plant accident rates. Thus most companies try to obtain personnel for this task who are properly and reasonably dedicated to the promotion of safety principles.

Recently, consultants in the behaviorial sciences devised a method of promoting safety that uses the latest theories in the psychology of human behavior. Their recommendations were to stop *telling* the employees to work safely—that was a sure-fire way of putting them to sleep. The best safety method they found was to get the employee involved in thinking his way out of hypothetical safety hazards. They call this the "You are there" safety method. In the manuals used for this instruction, life-threatening hazardous situations have been developed. Through group (small-group) interaction, the workers have to visualize themselves in the given situation, then give the best solution, the next best, and so forth. At the end of the session the group discusses the reasons for certain choices and a consensus is derived. No one falls asleep at these meetings because every one of the participants is actively taking part in the proceedings. This smacks of role-playing, and it may possibly be considered in this vein; apparently it works.

EXERCISE NO. 15

1. What are ten common forklift truck accidents?
   1. Employee struck by forklift truck.
   2. __________
   3. __________
   4. __________
   5. __________

6. ______
7. ______
8. ______
9. ______
10. Parts fall on operator.

2. What happens to workmen's compensation premium rates when there are many accidents at a plant? ______

3. What are the causes of accidents?
1. ______
2. ______
3. ______

4. What are three elements of an accident reduction program?
1. ______
2. ______
3. ______

5. What are the danger points illustrated in Phase II of the vehicular training program?
1. Traveling with forks high.
2. ______
3. ______
4. ______
5. ______
6. Improper handling of loads.

6. Name or list four emergency situations that should be reviewed in a training program.
1. Electric truck catching on fire.
2. ______
3. ______
4. ______

7. When one is driving with a load on a ramp, the load should be (uphill) (downhill). (Cross out incorrect one.)

8. When the load is wider than the truck, thus blocking the driver's forward view, what should the driver do? ______

9. The operator's physical condition (qualifications) should be checked at least (a) once a month; (b) annually; (c) twice yearly.
(______) Answer, a, b, or c.

10. In vehicular training it is the supervisor's responsibility to:
1. Select qualified operators for licensing and training.
2. ______
3. ______

11. A definition of safety engineering is: ______________________________
____
____
____

12. In the industrialized world, accidents are responsible for more deaths than all the infectious diseases. True ☐ False ☐

13. According to recent World Health Organization statistics, approximately _____ % of accidental deaths occur in motor vehicle accidents.

14. The first measures in safety engineering were directed toward providing _______ and _____________ devices on machines, floor gratings, and the like.

15. The standard frequency rate represents the number of disabling injuries per ☐ 100,000 man-hours, ☐ 1,000,000 man-hours, ☐ 10,000,000 man-hours of exposure. (Select one.)

Chapter 16

Equipment Maintenance, Replacement, and Justification

I. EQUIPMENT MAINTENANCE

A. Introduction

The importance of a good equipment maintenance program cannot be overemphasized. In many tangible and intangible ways good operating equipment helps companies function well and profitably; and morale-building factors are tied directly to a good preventive maintenance program.

B. In-House versus Contract Maintenance

To be assured of reasonable maintenance cost and satifactory reliability, plant management can select either of two main alternatives:

1. In-house maintenance using the regular plant maintenance workforce.
2. Contract maintenance services provided at a guaranteed rate.

In the following pages, we shall try to evaluate the two methods so that you, as a materials handling practitioner, can apply the concepts to your own plant situation. The two factors upon which the evaluation is based are *cost* and *reliability*.

C. Maintenance Evaluation

In-house maintenance can, under some circumstances, provide immediate service because it is close at hand. This alone creates a sense of security; but closer examination shows that immediate service alone is not a maintenance program—it is strictly firefighting.

The maintenance program for materials handling equipment requires a systems approach. Its elements are:

1. Routine servicing and lubrication

2. Periodic inspection and tune-up
3. Minor repairs, replacement of parts, etc.
4. Major actions

The performance of major planned actions includes component changes, rebuilds, overhauls, and so forth.

The ability of in-house maintenance and contract service organizations to meet desired reliability levels should be tested against each of these elements of the maintenance program. Let us compare the two methods:

	IN-HOUSE MAINTENANCE	CONTRACT MAINTENANCE
Routine servicing	Satisfactory if schedule is adhered to.	Specializes in this.
Periodic inspection	Satisfactory if mechanics have proper skills	Specializes in this.
Minor repairs	Usually satisfactory if done on time. Compete with other maintenance activities.	Special call needed.
Major actions	Work competes with other maintenance needs and other uses of maintenance facilities. Downtime accrued unless replacements are leased.	Can provide replacement equipment during conduct of overhauls, etc.

The comparison indicates that, of the two, the contract approach meets reliability needs more directly. The in-house approach has many "ifs"; however, these "ifs" may well be canceled out under certain circumstances, as indicated below.

1. Personnel Who Are Qualified and Facilities That are Suitable. Large industrial plants have the best chance to provide in-house service equal to contract service because they often have maintenance facilities and specialists devoted to materials handling equipment only. If so, this moves the considerations into a cost-oriented comparison.

Smaller organizations often maintain materials handling equipment alongside all their other mobile equipment. Regular vehicular mechanics do the work, and they are not always proficient on materials handling equipment repairs specifically. Special tools, parts, and facilities are not oriented toward the maintenance of materials handling equipment.

Competency of supervision and competency of the mechanics who perform the work is a large issue in the reliability of maintenance performed, regardless of who performs it. No matter how well-conceived the overall program of maintenance may be, it is the mechanics who perform the work that makes it successful, especially if they have good supervision.

The resident maintenance workforce establishes a reputation. If it is good, plant management may not even consider the alternative of contract maintenance of material handling equipment. However, if a plant does not have competency in this area of maintenance, its first alternative is to seek contract support. On the other hand, there must be competency in the mechanics provided by the contractor.

2. Spare Parts Supply. Even large organizations have trouble stocking or obtaining all of the spare parts necessary for the maintenance of a mobile equipment fleet. Although stanardization of equipment will help reduce this problem, many organizations are stuck with maintaining the equipment they already have. To a large degree the organization that has a mixed fleet of materials handling equipment has a parts problem—regardless of whether the plant is large or small. As a result, plant managers must weight the availability of repair and replacement parts as they consider the in-house approach to meeting maintenance requirements.

Contract maintenance service organizations may have the same problem with parts, but it is a problem they must resolve satisfactorily before they can offer services to an industrial plant.

While it's easy to say that contract maintenance organizations couldn't stay in business if they weren't competitive, it is a good idea for plant management to inquire how well other plants were serviced by the contractor before making a commitment.

3. Checklist for Reliability. In general, the larger companies may be better able than the smaller ones to support a satisfactory maintenance program for materials handling equipment, but this does not eliminate their consideration of contract maintenance under guaranteed conditions.

Where reliability is concerned, the criterion to be applied is the degree of availability of the equipment for use in the plant.

While service contracts may be able to guarantee a specific level of maintenance service, they may not be able to guarantee a certain level of equipment availability. Many factors make an availability guarantee extremely difficult, among them the state of operator proficiency, operating environment (a clean warehouse versus a foundry), age of equipment, training of operators, and so forth. Yet, with the satisfactory provisions of maintenance services by either in-house or contract organizations, there should be reasonable assurance that availability of equipment will be satisfactory.

Materials handling practitioners, therefore, consider the reliability of maintenance service in terms of a satisfactory maintenance program with the availability of equipment. The decision to consider the use of contract maintenance services versus in-house maintenance should be evaluated in terms of the satisfactory provision of all the elements of the maintenance program.

The following questions are suggested checkpoints in considering maintenance contract services:

1. Do the servicing requirements meet minimum needs or standards?
2. Are servicing requirements flexible in meeting different environmental conditions in which the equipment must operate?
3. Is there an adequate inspection program in which problems can be discovered in time to avoid untimely or unnecessary downtime?
4. What alternates are provided to ensure that parts shortages will not result in unnecessary downtime? Are replacement units provided?
5. Are all of the other plants using the contract maintenance service satisfied with the work being performed?
6. Does service offered include a total maintenance program? If so, how flexible is the provision for unplanned or unscheduled problems? Are premium costs charged for work of this nature?
7. Are rebuilds and overhauls an integral part of the contract? Is replacement equipment provided during prolonged absence of equipment?

In considering the use of in-house maintenance, the following questions should be raised by the materials handling practitioner:

1. Can the regular maintenance workforce support the program required to adequately maintain materials handling equipment?
2. Are facilities adequate? If not, will they be later? If so, can adequate maintenance be performed during the interim period?
3. Are the mechanics competent? If not, can they be trained? Are there other demands on these mechanics that may interfere with satisfactory maintenance work?
4. Is the mobile equipment fleet a mixed bag with unusual parts needs? Is equipment obsolete or overage? Can resident mechanics and purchasing agents cope with the problems adequately?
5. What is the probability of meeting a certain minimum level of availability when using in-house maintenance services for materials handling equipment?

If, in considering these reliability aspects of maintenance, the materials handling engineer does not come up with a clear decision between contract maintenance and in-house maintenance, then he must consider cost as well as reliability.

4. Cost of Maintenance. The major problem facing materials handling engineers in evaluating the cost aspects of maintaining materials handling equipment is the availability of cost data. We shall try here to establish what cost data are needed in order to make a realistic evaluation.

Materials handling equipment should be considered as key equipment, critical to an operation. Since each piece of equipment represents a capital investment, its subsequent repair and upkeep will have some effect on the total economic picture of the entire fleet. Consequently, cost analysis should be approached on two levels:

1. Repair costs per unit
2. Total cost of fleet ownership and use

On an individual basis, units of equipment should have cost records kept regarding monthly use of labor and materials in their maintenance. Such monthly data and year-to-date or purchase-to date cost data are helpful in spotting the "bad actors"; however, they do not provide a complete picture. A consistently higher labor cost may indicate that planned component change-outs, rebuilds, etc., are missing from the maintenance program. Excessive material costs at irregular intervals may indicate that the planned maintenance approach is being replaced by breakdown maintenance (the firefighting approach).

Essentially, the repair costs for particular units of equipment can provide clues to certain problems:

1. Vastly different costs for equipment of the same model and year can help pinpoint a possible equipment abuse problem resulting in higher maintenance costs.
2. Differing costs for equipment used in about the same way may point out an unsatisfactory unit of equipment.
3. Progressively higher maintenance costs for equivalent units can point out the need for an overhaul or unit replacement.

While the data thus obtained can help formulate a picture of what in-house costs of maintenance are, they must still be contrasted with guaranteed costs for contract maintenance services. There must be a common measurement at the time the decision is made to consider contract mainetnance and a running measure thereafter to ensure that satisfactory performance continues.

If the materials handling engineer is aware of in-house maintenance costs for each unit of equipment, he can develop some broad estimates of the comparative value of contract work. Costs for each unit expressed on an annual basis will provide a basis of comparison with the contract price.

Subsequently, continuing the collection of maintenance costs per operating hour will help to determine the effectiveness of the maintenance services during the contract period.

5. The Total Systems Approach. The materials handling department—which, it is assumed, has responsibility for the plant's materials handling equipment—is concerned with a problem of greater magnitude than simply maintaining a materials handling fleet.

The total systems approach involves the economics of ownership, including the following items:

1. Capital investiment
2. Depreciation
3. Maintenance
4. The cost of downtime
5. Availability of equipment
6. The cost of equipment obsolescence

When these aspects are contrasted for in-house maintenance and contract maintenance, they not only provide a basis for evaluation but provide a means for formulating decisions concerning each unit of the fleet and the management of the fleet as a whole.

II. Replacement and Justification

A. Introduction

In the following discussion, the cost of two 4,000-pound-capacity, cushion-tired trucks, one gasoline, the other electric-powered, is compared. LP gas is not considered in the example. Generally speaking, the difference in total cost between LP-gas and gasoline truck operation is minimal. LP operation does extend engine life because it uses a cleaner-buring fuel; however, LP use involves additional componentry such as converters, which add to routine repair costs. These costs offset the economics of extended life, and whether or not savings can be realized through the use of LP gas instead of gasoline depends largely upon fuel costs, which vary widely from one locale to another.

The data presented in the accompanying tables are based on a computerized study of the life cycles of over 96,000 forklift trucks and their components, compiled over an eight-year period beginning in 1965.

The electric truck detailed in Table 16-1, has a higher acquisition cost ($10,176 versus $8,732) than the gas truck. In addition, the electric-power truck has a higher ownership cost, because it is worth less at the time of trade-in. For instance, at an operating level of 1,000 hours per year and an economic life of 10 years, the 4,000-pound electric truck is worth only $600 at trade-in time ($10,176 acquisition minus $9,576 ownership). A similarly equipped gas truck is worth $1,300 ($8,732 acquisition minus $7,432 ownership).

On the other hand, electric trucks offer the advantages of greater reliability and lower maintenance requirements. Cost of maintenance for an electric truck is less than for a gas-powered truck (see table 16-1).

The key element in the analysis, however, is the total cost of operation per hour. This cost is influenced by a number of factors, the most important of which are the number of running hours and labor rates, and their effect on maintenance costs and downtime costs. Operating environment and fuel costs are also significant.

Running hours are critical to the gas versus electric truck decision. Consider a clean plant environment in which a truck must operate 1,000 hours per year. The gas truck is more economical (Table 16-1) because the higher ownership cost of the electric truck, $2,144, is only partly offset by savings of $1,128 in the maintenance cost and $564 in downtime cost with the economic life for each truck 10 years. At the end of this period, the total cost per hour to operate the gas truck is $1.60, as compared to $1,64 for the electric truck.

The 1,000-running-hour level is common in many operations. One thousand hours per year would be 50% utilization of a truck in an eight-hour-day, five-day-a-week operation. However, there are many heavy-duty, high-running-hour applications in which a lift truck must run 2,000, 2,500, or even 3,000 hours a year. For these applications, a different set of economics applies.

Consider the 3,000-running-hour situation (Table 16-2). Because of greater equipment usage, the economic life of each truck is shortened to six years for the electric truck and five years for the gas truck. During the sixth year, the cost per hour to operate the electric truck reaches its lowest leve, $1.35. The gas truck reaches its lowest cost per hour, $1.44, during the fifth year. Thus, in this case, the electric truck's higher ownership cost has been offset by lower maintenance costs and resulting lower downtime costs.

It might be concluded from these data alone that electric-powered trucks should be used when high-running-hour operations are required, and gas-powered equipment should be used for lowrunning-hour operations, or intermittent use.

Other factors, however, could make electric-powered equipment the more economical choice for even a light-duty operation. Such factors include a shortage of mechanics, high labor costs, or severe environments.

Another consideration is whether downtime is critical to an operation. If an idle truck has a direct impact on production, then the truck that is more reliable and requires less maintenance may be a better choice, even if it has a higher cost of ownership.

Table 16-1. Lift truck cost factors when running hours are low*

GAS POWERED TRUCK
TOTAL PRICE $8,732

Year	Running Time (hr)	Maintenance Amount (dollars)	Maintenance Cost/hr (dollars)	Ownership Amount (dollars)	Ownership Cost/hr (dollars)	Down Time Cost (dollars)	Obsolescence Cost (dollars)	Total Cost Amount (dollars)	Total Cost Cost/hr (dollars)	Replacement Savings (dollars)
1	1,000	312	0.31	4,532	4.53	156	1	5,001	5.00	
2	2,000	698	0.34	5,413	2.70	349	1	6,462	3.23	
3	3,000	1,220	0.40	6,082	2.02	610	1	7,912	2.64	
4	4,000	1,606	0.40	6,463	1.61	803	1	8,874	2.22	
5	5,000	2,200	0.44	6,782	1.35	1,100	1	10,084	2.02	
6	6,000	3,517	0.58	6,912	1.15	1,758	1	12,188	2.03	
7	7,000	4,049	0.57	7,042	1.00	2,024	1	13,116	1.87	
8	8,000	4,571	0.57	7,172	0.89	2,286	1	14,030	1.75	
9	9,000	5,176	0.57	7,302	0.81	2,588	1	15,067	1.67	
10	10,000	5,699	0.56	7,432	0.74	2,849	1	15,981	1.60	

ELECTRIC TRUCK

TOTAL PRICE $10,176

Year	Running Time (hr)	Maintenance Amount (dollars)	Maintenance Cost/hr (dollars)	Ownership Amount (dollars)	Ownership Cost/hr (dollars)	Down Time Cost (dollars)	Obsolescence Cost (dollars)	Total Cost Amount (dollars)	Total Cost Cost/hr (dollars)	Replacement Savings (dollars)
1	1,000	245	0.24	5,326	5.32	122	1	5,694	5.69	
2	2,000	627	0.31	6,370	3.18	314	1	7,311	3.66	
3	3,000	1,223	0.40	7,276	2.42	612	1	9,112	3.04	
4	4,000	1,468	0.36	8,050	2.01	734	1	10,253	2.56	
5	5,000	2,088	0.41	8,676	1.73	1,044	1	11,809	2.36	
6	6,000	2,542	0.42	8,856	1.47	1,271	1	12,670	2.11	
7	7,000	2,907	0.41	9,036	1.29	1,453	1	13,397	1.91	
8	8,000	3,455	0.43	9,216	1.15	1,727	1	14,399	1.80	
9	9,000	3.981	0.44	9,396	1.04	1,990	1	15,368	1.71	
10	10,000	4,571	0.45	9,576	0.95	2,285	1	16,433	1.64	

* 4000-lb. capacity trucks operating one shift per day on good floors in a clean plant.

Table 16-2. Lift truck cost factors when running hours are high*

GAS POWERED TRUCK

TOTAL PRICE $8,732

Year	Running Time (hr)	Maintenance Amount (dollars)	Maintenance Cost/hr (dollars)	Ownership Amount (dollars)	Ownership Cost/hr (dollars)	Downtime Cost (dollars)	Obsolescence Cost (dollars)	Total Cost Amount (dollars)	Total Cost Cost/hr (dollars)	Replacement Savings (dollars)
1	3,000	1,220	0.40	4,532	1.51	610	1	6,362	2.12	
2	6,000	3,517	0.58	5,413	0.90	1,758	1	10,690	1.78	
3	9,000	5,176	0.57	6,082	0.67	2,588	1	13,847	1.54	
4	12,000	7,693	0.64	6,463	0.53	3,847	1	18,004	1.50	
5	15,000	9,885	0.65	6,782	0.45	4,943	1	21,611	1.44	******
6	18,000	12,765	0.70	6,912	0.38	6,383	1	26,061	1.45	126
7	21,000	15,707	0.74	7,042	0.33	7,854	1	30,604	1.46	336
8	24,000	19,278	0.80	7,172	0.29	9,639	1	36,090	1.50	1,512
9	27,000	22,875	0.84	7,302	0.27	11,437	1	41,615	1.54	2,700
10	30,000	27,022	0.90	7,432	0.24	13,511	1	47,966	1.60	4,740

ELECTRIC TRUCK

TOTAL PRICE $10,176

Year	Running Time (hr)	Maintenance		Ownership		Downtime Cost (dollars)	Obsolescence Cost (dollars)	Total Cost		Replacement Savings (dollars)
		Amount (dollars)	Cost/hr (dollars)	Amount (dollars)	Cost/hr (dollars)			Amount (dollars)	Cost/hr (dollars)	
1	3,000	1,223	0.40	5,326	1.77	612	1	7,162	2.38	
2	6,000	2,542	0.42	6,370	1.06	1,271	1	10,184	1.70	
3	9,000	3,981	0.44	7,276	0.80	1,990	1	13,248	1.47	
4	12,000	5,591	0.46	8,050	0.67	2,796	1	16,438	1.37	
5	15,000	8,056	0.53	8,676	0.57	4,028	1	20,761	1.38	
6	18,000	10,322	0.57	8,856	0.49	5,161	1	24,340	1.35	******
7	21,000	12,987	0.61	9,036	0.43	6,494	1	28,518	1.36	126
8	24,000	16,301	0.67	9,216	0.38	8,151	1	33,669	1.40	1,224
9	27,000	20,727	0.76	9,396	0.34	10,364	1	40,488	1.50	3,996
10	30,000	25,757	0.85	9,576	0.31	12,878	1	48,212	1.61	7,650

* 4000-lb capacity trucks operating two shifts per day on good floors in a clean plant.

Labor requirements have a dramatic effect on maintenance cost, total cost, and economic life of a lift truck. There is now a critical shortage of qualified mechanics, which is due at least in part, to the technological advances that have made the design of both gas and electric trucks more sophisticated. Most general plant mechanics are not fully qualified to handle the repairs necessary to keep a truck in top operating condition. Several lift truck manufacturers have taken steps to overcome this problem. Mechanic-training centers have been established to train lift truck service personnel. Test equipment has also been developed that will permit a relatively unskilled worker to troubleshoot and repair the truck.

A higher degree of maintenance skills has generally been considered necessary for electric trucks than for gas-powered units; however, the difference has been narrowed with the advent of electronic controls and plug-in componentry for electric trucks. At the same time, gas trucks have become more complicated with the introduction of high-performance automatic transmissions and electronic ignition systems.

Maximum fork truck availability and performance, at minimum total cost, cannot be attained with unskilled, jack-of-all-trades maintenance people. And, as the skill requirements rise, the cost of labor also goes up. Maintenance requirements for gas trucks are generally considered higher than for electric units in many plants. However, the computerized data bank has added another dimension to this consideration—maintenance cost consists of a higher percentage of labor for gas-powered trucks than for electric trucks.

On an average, maintenance cost on a gas truck is 60% labor and 40% parts. Electric trucks, however, with their more expensive components that can be installed quickly, have maintenance cost that are more likely 50% labor and 50% parts.

Thus, as labor rates rise, electric trucks, with lower maintenance requirements, should provide an increasing cost advantage over their gas counterparts.

Downtime costs vary from operation to operation. Usually, they are represented by the cost of extra equipment, or at least the cost of an operator. These costs are usually a minimum of $5 per hour. However, in many operations where the constant availability of forklift equipment is required to keep production moving, an idle truck may cost as much as $10, $15, or even $20 per hour.

In Table 16-2, the average annual downtime for a gas truck is 198 hours, determined by its relationship to maintenance cost. Industry studies show that for every $10 of maintenance cost incurred, the truck will be out of service for a minimum of one hour. At $9885 maintenance bill for a five-year period would result in a total downtime of 989 hours. The electric truck's average downtime, similarly calculated, is 172 hours over its six-year economic life, which would incur approximately 1,032 downtime hours. Comparing cumulative costs, the gas truck costs $1222 more to operate than an electric truck over a six-year period.

The operating environment can have a significant effect on maintenance costs and downttime costs, and, therefore, on the gas versus electric decision. Dirty, dusty, or corrosive environments have a drastic effect on maintenance cost. As the cost of maintenance increases per operating hour, the higher acquisition cost of electric trucks is offset more quickly. This would be true even if the cost of maintenance of a gas truck and an electric truck both increased proportionately in severe applications. However, this is not the case. Internal combution engines are seriously affected by foreign particles and dust. Carburetors suck in dirty air causing throttles to stick. Dirty air is drawn into combustion chambers, and blowby forces grit and abrasives into the lower end of the engine causing excessive wear of bearings and rings.

Electric drive motors can be effectively sealed against such problems. On electric trucks the sealing of controls is a relatively simple matter. On gas trucks there are a number of minor problems created by dusty, dirty atmospheres, which are time-consuming and expensive from a maintenance standpoint. For example, radiators become clogged, and engines overheat. All of these things affect maintenance cost, downtime cost, economic life, and the relative economics of using gas trucks and electric trucks.

Fuel cost may be the most important single cost factor in the gas versus electric decision, regardless of how other considerations stack up. Fuel costs have taken on new importance since the energy crisis with its rising costs became a part of our everyday life. A few years ago, the difference in cost of power between a gas and an electric truck was considered insignificant. Today, however, it is the basis for possible significant industry shifts in the type of equipment to be used.

Table 16-3 provides projected total costs for both gas and electric trucks, at two different fuel cost levels, and at an annual operating rate of 1,500 hours. All other costs are held constant. At a 1970 gasoline price* of 30 cents per gallon, the gas truck would have accumulated a total fuel cost of $3,870 over ten years, and a total cost of $27,479, or $1.83 per hour. At an electric power cost of 2 cents per kilowatt hour, the electric truck would have incurred a total charging cost of $1,281 over a ten-year-period, and a total cost of $28,484 or $1.90 an hour. At this point, with all else being equal, the gas truck would have been more economical to operate than an electric truck.

Assume now that fuel costs doubled during this time. (In fact, gasoline costs have more than tripled since the energy crisis started, but the cost of electricity has gone up far less.) The gas truck now would have incurred a total fuel cost

*Energy prices having escalated since these figures were derived, it is important to realize that the exercise shows the *methodology* and the *relative* values of the various costs involved.

Table 16-3. Effect of fuel costs on total lift truck costs

Case No. 1.

GAS OPERATED TRUCK

Gasoline price = 30 cents/gal

Year	Running Time (hr)	Fuel Cost (dollars)	Total Cost Amount (dollars)	Total Cost Cost/hr (dollars)
1	1,500	387	5,601	3.73
2	3,000	774	7,916	2.64
3	4,500	1,161	9,993	2.22
4	6,000	1,548	14,276	2.38
5	7,500	1,935	15,792	2.11
6	9,000	2,322	17,833	1.98
7	10,500	2,709	19,348	1.84
8	12,000	3,096	23,601	1.97
9	13,500	3,483	25,071	1.86
10	15,000	3,870	27,479	1.83

ELECTRIC TRUCK

Electricity Cost = 2 cents/kwh

Year	Running Time (hr)	Cost of Charging (dollars)	Total Cost Amount (dollars)	Total Cost Cost/hr (dollars)
1	1,500	128	7,806	5.20
2	3,000	256	10,873	3.62
3	4,500	384	12,866	2.86
4	6,000	512	15,505	2.58
5	7,500	640	17,523	2.34
6	9,000	768	19,345	2.15
7	10,500	897	21,446	2.04
8	12,000	1,025	24,052	2.00
9	13,500	1,153	26,555	1.97
10	15,000	1,281	28,484	1.90

Case No. 2: Fuel Costs Doubled

GAS OPERATED TRUCK

Gasoline price = 60 cents/gal

Year	Running Time (hr)	Fuel Cost (dollars)	Total Cost Amount (dollars)	Total Cost Cost/hr (dollars)
1	1,500	774	5,988	3.99
2	3,000	1,548	8,690	2.90
3	4,500	2,322	11,154	2.48
4	6,000	3,096	15,824	2.64
5	7,500	3,870	17,727	2.36
6	9,000	4,644	20,155	2.24
7	10,500	5,418	22,057	2.10
8	12,000	6,192	26,697	2.22
9	13,500	6,966	28,554	2.12
10	15,000	7,740	31,349	2.09

ELECTRIC TRUCK

Electricity Cost = 4 cents/kwh

Year	Running Time (hr)	Cost of Charging (dollars)	Total Cost Amount (dollars)	Total Cost Cost/hr (dollars)
1	1,500	256	7,934	5.29
2	3,000	512	11,129	3.71
3	4,500	768	13,251	2.94
4	6,000	1,025	16,017	2.67
5	7,500	1,281	18,164	2.42
6	9,000	1,537	20,113	2.23
7	10,500	1.793	22,343	2.13
8	12,000	2,049	25,077	2.09
9	13,500	2,305	27,708	2.05
10	15,000	2,562	29,765	1.98

of $7,740 over 10 years, and a total cost of $31,349 or $2.09 per hour. At 4 cents per kilowatt hour, the truck's charging cost over those 10 years would have been $2,562, with a total cost of $29,765, or $1.98 an hour. Thus, as fuel prices increased, the cost advantage shifts to electric trucks.

The cost reflected in Table 16-3 include the cost of buying the necessary batteries and chargers and maintaining those batteries and chargers over the life of the equipment.

All of these factors—running hours, labor rate, downtime cost, operating environment, and fuel cost—affect the gas versus electric purchase decision. Because of the complexity of the many variables that control total costs, a computerized cost analysis system can greatly facilitate the decision-making process by displaying all of the operating costs.

2. Signaling Equipment Replacement. The replacement of mobile equipment is not subject to hard and fast rules. Some people have ideas about the best method to use in determining when to replace equipment, while many others have no definite opinion.

One method to justifying replacement of equipment involves using job assignment, utilization, and life cost per hour of equipment; rotating equipment to other jobs; installing new equipment on the highest-utilized job, applying cost-per-hour figures at which the new unit should operate; and consequently phasing out a high-cost unit. Savings are generated in this manner, and replacement of the unit of equipment is approved. Figure 16-1 represents a typical example of this type of justification.

In Figure 16-1, Unit 0375 is to be replaced, owing to high cost and overall condition. Two other units are to be rotated—Unit 0280, a comparably new

THE LAST 4 QUARTERS							
UNIT NO.	TOTAL HOURS	AVERAGE COST PER HOUR	REPAIR & MAINTENANCE COST	UNIT NO.	ASSIGNED HOURS	COST PER HOUR	4 QUARTERS REPAIR & MAINT. COST
0190	3702	$.24	$816	New Unit	3702	$.06*	$185*
0280	1475	.18	210	0190	1475	.24	310
0375	2535	.35	885	0280	2535	18	467
			$1911				$962*

Note: Unit 0375 is to be removed from the fleet.
*Estimated

Cost before replacement and reassignment	$1911
Cost after changes	962
Potential Savings in Repair & Maintenance	$ 949

Fig. 16-1. An example of equipment replacement justification.

unit with low utilization and low cost, and Unit 0190, a unit with high utilization and an average maintenance cost.

The next three columns represent the last four quarters of operation of each unit, expressed in total hours, average cost per hour, and repair and maintenance cost. Total repair and maintenance costs of the three units is $1,911.

On the rotating method, a new unit will be put in the place of Unit 0190. Unit 0190 is moved to replace Unit 0280, and Unit 0280 replaces Unit 0375, which will be removed from the fleet.

Inasmuch as Unit 0190 has utilized 3,702 hours in the last four quarters, it is assumed that the new unit will be placed on the same job. Thus the 3,702 hours will be applicable to the new unit. The new unit is given a maintenance cost of $.06 per operating hour.

Unit 0190 now has a new operating utilization of 1,375 hours and retains its life cost. Unit 0280, which replaced Unit 0375, increased its utilization to 2,535 hours and retained its life cost; therefore, with the new unit and the rotating of Units 0190 and 0280, there is a total maintenance cost of $962.

Subtracting the $962 from the $1,911, there is a potential repair and maintenance saving of $949.

This method looks good on paper, but in actual practice it is not always practical, one reason being that operating departments do not like to receive used equipment. And, by the reassignment method, department lines could be crossed.

Another reason is that by placing Unit 0190 in a lower-utilized job, repairs have been delayed that would normally have occurred on its original job and thus delayed its replacement. In essence some repair costs have been delayed, but eventually the unit will have to be repaired and replaced, even on the lower-utilized job.

The second way to justify replacement is by using the increased cost per hour (see Fig. 16-2). By this method, a justification is written stating that for the past 1,000 hours of operation the maintenance cost was increased from $.50 to $.56 an hour. Therefore, owing to the high maintenance cost increase, the unit should be replaced. In reality, the unit cost $1.04 an hour for the additional 1,000 hours.

At 8,000 hours the unit was operating at $.50 an hour, or $4,000 in maintenance costs. At 9,000 hours, the unit operated at $.56 an hour, or $5,040 in maintenance costs. The difference, $1.040 divided by 1,000 hours, equals $1.04 an hour.

In each of the above examples replacement came after money had been spent to repair the equipment.

The lowest total cost point, or LTCP concept, was developed by an engineer, who knew that each unit has its own individual cost curve. (see Fig. 16-3). This total cost curve is reached by marrying the cumulative maintenance cost per

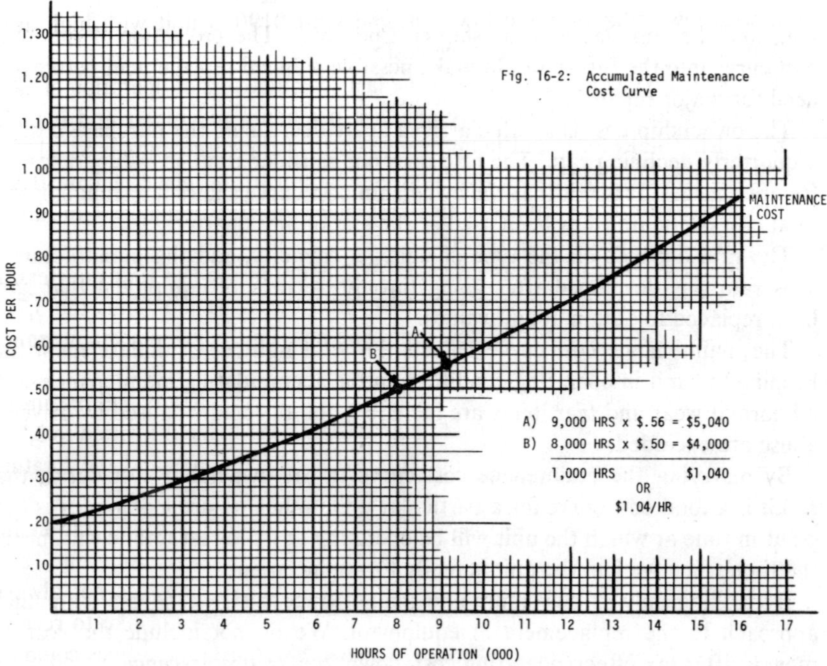

Fig. 16-2. Accumulated maintenance cost curve

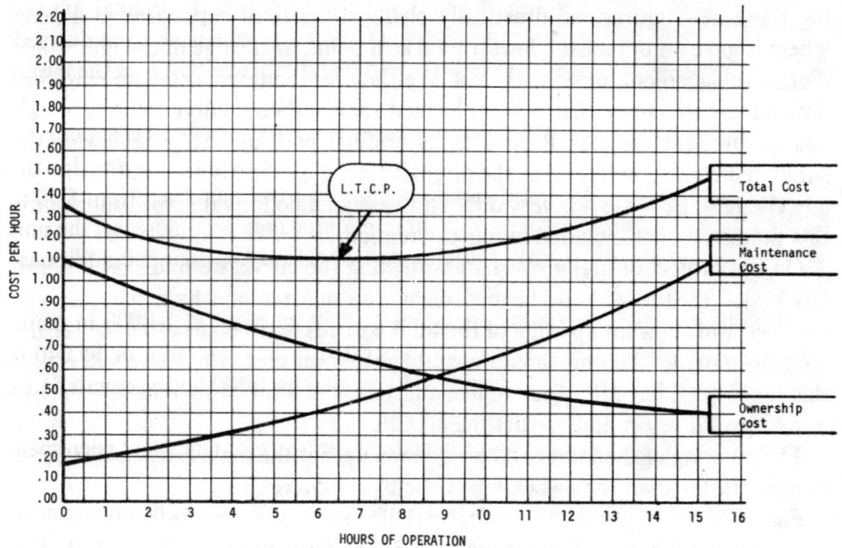

Fig. 16-3. L.T.C.P. Concept, The least total cost point.

hour and the cumulative ownership cost per hour. The projection of the total cost curve into the future would make possible planned replacement before the need for major repairs.

The ownership cost is a value arrived at by decreasing the purchase cost at a quarterly declining rate. The rate does not consider trade-in value, taxes, or freight charges. It is felt that the ownership cost curve shows how much of the total cost of the unit has been used at the end of any quarter.

The rate depends on the type of unit, its capacity, and the manufacturer. This rate was developed after going through records of equipment that had been replaced to obtain actual values.

The maintenance cost curve reflects the total number of dollars spent for keeping the unit in operating condition. In the accumulating maintenance cost all normal wear and tear items are included, but all repairs caused by drivers' abuse are excluded.

By marrying the maintenace cost curve to the ownership cost curve, the result is a total cost curve for a particular unit. What we are looking for is the point in time at which the unit will be operating at its lowest total cost. This is the time when we feel the unit is ready for replacement.

By looking only at onwership and maintenance cost, we have a simplified approach to the replacement of equipment. We do not include the cost of money, after-tax effect, operating cost, downtime, or obsolescence.

We have simulated graphs using known maintenance and ownership cost, and then applied cost of money, the after-tax effect, and operating cost. Installing these new figures, we drastically changed the total cost curve to a point where it gave an unrealistic lowest total cost point, as the age of the unit would dictate replacement, more than cost. We then recalculated, using an empirical downtime cost factor that again changed the total cost curve. However, this change brought the LTCP back to its original position. After reviewing the simulated curves, we feel that the original LTCP method is acceptable without any changes. Because it is very difficult to assign a dollar value to obsolescence, this factor was not included in our calculations.

On the subject of major overhauls affecting the curve, we find that if a unit has major repair work performed on it, the quarter in which the cost was incurred will show an upswing of the total cost curve, whereas after the repairs have been made, the unit should operate at a lower cost. The curve will reflect this lower cost; but after four to five quarters, the total cost curve will start to move upward again and predict the LTCP.

The upswing of the total cost curve shows us that the maintenance cost curve is rising faster than the ownership cost curve is decreasing.

Figure 16-4 is a graph of a typical forklift that was in a manufacturing plant "X." It is a 5,000-pound unit operating 3,400 hours per year. Note the maintenance cost curve, the ownership cost curve, and the total cost curve. The

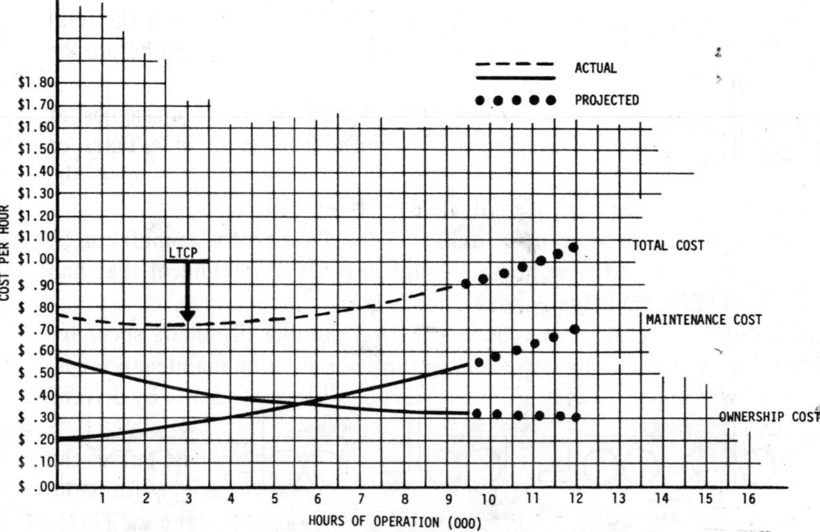

Fig. 16-4. Unit #0004—Plant "X," 5000# Unit, 3400 hrs/year

LTCP of this particular unit was at 3,000 hours of operation. This unit was in place before the conception of the LTCP program. The dotted lines at the end of each curve are projected cost per hour figures.

Figure 16-5 depicts the former concept of replacement versus the LTCP concept.

In the figure, the former concept states that a new unit is justified, operated for 12,000 hours, and then replaced. During that period $8,640 is spent in maintenance. When it is time for replacement $3,270 of new money needs to be added to the trade-in value to purchase the new unit. Addition of the $8,640 in maintenance cost and the $3,270 of new money gives $12,360.

New Money is considered to be the amount of capital needed to make up the difference between the purchase price of the new unit and the trade-in value of the old unit.

The LTCP concept is simply the justification of a new unit, its operation until it reaches its LTCP (which according to the previous graph was at 3,000 hours), and then its replacement.

The first 3,000 hours cost $840 in maintenance, and to replace the unit, $1,350 in new money would be needed. A second unit is purchased, which again will be operated for 3,000 hours. Here we are assuming that the unit will be placed on the same job; so all conditions being equal, the same maintenance cost and the same trade-in value should be experienced.

After 3,000 hours, the second unit is replaced, and again there is the $840 in maintenance cost and the $1,350 in new money. And at the end of 9,000

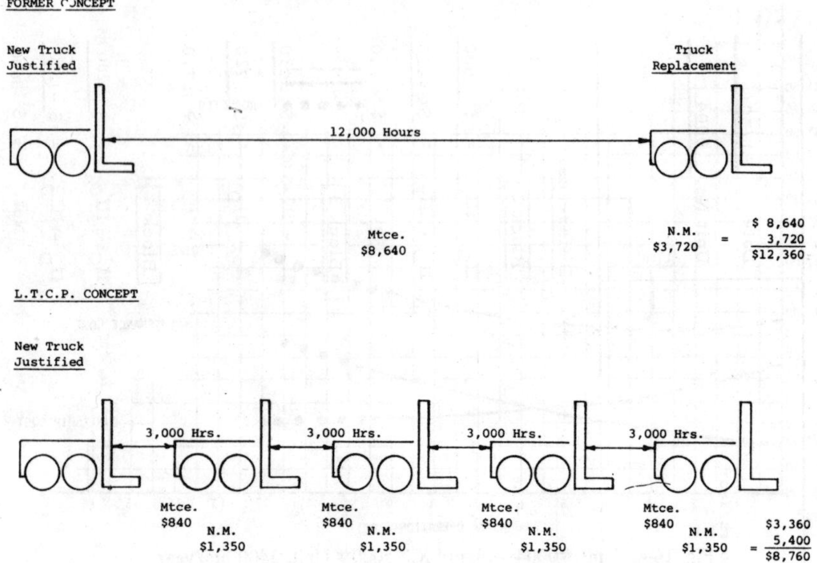

Fig. 16-5. Former versus L.T.C.P. concept

hours there is a third replacement, again with the $840 in maintenance cost and the $1,350 is new money.

At 12,000 hours the unit is replaced once more, again with the $840 in maintenance cost and the $1,350 in new money.

Therefore, according to the LTCP concept $3,360 will have been spent in maintenance costs, and $5,400 in new money, for a total cost of $8,760. with a potential savings of $3,600.

Figure 16-6 shows the computation of Figure 16-5.

Item I is concerned with the LTCP. Block 1 points out the LTCP was at 3,000 hours, at which point the maintenace cost per hour was $.28. We have spent a total of $840 on maintenance, and the new money required was $1,350. The ownership cost at 3,000 hours was $.45 an hour.

Item II is additional justification for replacement. Block 2 shows the unit was operated until 6,000 hours; at that time the maintenance cost was $.38 an hour, the total maintenance being $2,280, and new money required was $2,280. At this point the ownership and maintenance cost curves crossed.

Item III is multiples of Item 1, Block 1. In Block 1 the maintenance cost is $840 for operating one unit. By operating the second unit to the same point, with the same cost, you would have a maintenance cost of $1,680. New money to replace at 3,000 hours was $1,350; to operate a second unit the same length of time would be $2,700.

In comparing the maintenace cost of one unit operating 6,000 hours, and

I. Lowest Total Cost Point

Block 1

A.	L. T. C. P.	3000 Hrs.	
B.	Cost/Hr. Mtce.	$ .28	
C_1	Total (AxB)	$ 840	
D_1	New $ Reqd.	$ 1350	3000 x $.45

Comments: 3400 Hours/Year

Date 1/30/

Unit No. 0004

II. Additional Blocks

Block 2

A.	Next Block	6000 Hrs.	
B.	Cost/Hr. Mtce.	$ .38	
C.	Total (AxB)	$ 2280	
D.	New $ Reqd.	$ 2280	6000 X $.38

Block 3

A.	Next Block	9000 Hrs.	
B.	Cost/Hr. Mtce.	$ .55	
C.	Total (AxB)	$ 4950	
D.	New $ Reqd.	$ 3330	9000 x $.37

Block 4

A.	Next Block	12,000 Hrs.	
B.	Cost/Hr. Mtce.	$ .72	
C.	Total (AxB)	$ 8640	
D.	New $ Reqd.	$ 3720	12,000 x $.31

III. Multiples of Block 1 L. T. C. P.

Block 2

C_1	Total Cost	$ 840 x 2 = $1680
D_1	New Money	$1350 x 2 = $2700

Block 3

C_1	Total Cost	$ 840 x 3 = $ 2520
D_1	New Money	$1350 x 3 = $ 4050

Block 4

C_1	Total Cost	$ 840 x 4 = $ 3360
D_1	New Money	$1350 x 4 = $ 5400

IV. Difference

Block 2

$II_C - III_{C1}$	= $ 600
$II_D - III_{D1}$	= $ -420
Net	= $ 180

Block 3

$II_C - III_{C1}$	= $ 2430
$II_D - III_{D1}$	= $ -720
Net	= $ 1710

Block 4

$II_C - III_{C1}$	= $ 5280
$II_D - III_{D1}$	= $ -1680
Net	= $ 3600

Fig. 16-6. Replacement Savings Analysis

two units operating at 3,000 hours each, you subtract the $1,680 from the $2,280 for a maintenance cost difference of $600.

To compare the capital cost and the new money cost, subtract the $2,280, cost of one unit, from the $2,700, cost of two units, to arrive at $420.

Therefore, comparing the former concept to the LTCP concept, at this point, there is a potential savings of $180.

In Block 3, after 9,000 hours of operation, the maintenance cost of the unit is $.55 an hour, the total maintenance cost is $4,950, and the new money is $3,330. At this point the ownership cost is down to $.37 an operating hour. The total maintenance cost is now $2,520 ($840 times three units); and the new money required in $4,050 ($1,350 times three units). When we subtract the maintenance cost of three units from the cost of one unit, operating at 9,000 hours, the difference is $2,430.

Capital required for three units is $4,050. For one unit operating at 9,000 hours, additional money required at this time would be $3,330. The difference ($4,050 minus $3,330) is $720, for a net potential savings of $1,710.

To operate one unit 12,000 hours, the maintenance cost would be $.72 an hour, or a total of $8,640. To replace at 12,000 hours, $3,720 of new money is needed.

To replace a unit every 3,000 hours would require four units each with a maintenance cost of $840, or a total of $3,360. The new money would be $1,350 times the four units, or $5,400. For the comparison of the maintenance cost between one unit and four units, subtract $3,360 from $8,640, for a difference of $5,280. In regard to the new money, $5,400 would be spent for four units as compared to spending $3,720 for one unit, a difference of $1,680.

Thus the net difference in replacing four units in lieu of operating one unit for 12,000 hours is $3,600.

Continuing our study of equipment replacement let's take a look at the information supplied from the using locations.

Figure 16-7 is a preprinted form that is mailed to all using locations at the end of each quarter. Constant information, such as unit numbers, location, division, and quarter date, is preprinted on this sheet. Personnel at each location are required to fill in the work code, hours/miles utilized during the past quarter, the maintenance cost charged to the unit during the past quarter, and any comments they wish to make, preferably if they have spent money in a certain way that they wish to record for future reference.

Figure 16-8 represents a typical unit sheet, sent out after receipt of the input information. In the top upper left-hand corner, the unit number appears. This is the identification number given to the unit at the time the purchase order is submitted to the dealer. The dealer stencils the number on the unit, thus giving the complete identification of a particular unit from date of delivery.

The next line shows where the unit is used, and in what division of the company. Next is the classification of the unit, which tells us that this unit is a

XYZ Company
Materials Handling Usage Report
Quarter of 4/82

Date 1/83
Completed by JOHN DOE

GROUP: STAMPING PLANT DIVISION: OPERATIONS SUB-DIV: F/P: LOC: RALEIGH

UNIT NO	C C	QTR YR	WORK CODE	USAGE	MAINT COST	COST 2	COST 3	COMMENT
1 - 5	6	8-9	10 11	12 17	18 22	23 27	28 32	49 77
60005	9	824	AS	210	51			PM
60006	9	824	AS	159	267			TUNE-UP - VALVE REPLACE
60007	9	824	AS	308	32			PM
60008	9	824	AS	98	265			TIRES/TUNE-UP/OIL CHANGE
60009	9	824	AS	189	83			
60010	9	824	AS	231	52			
60012	9	824	AS	274	148			
60020	9	824	AS	103	157			
60021	9	824	AS	311	32			PM
62500	9	824	AS	3507	389			RPR AIRLINE-BRAKES-LEAK
62501	9	824	AS	4692	0			NO COST
62502	9	824	AS	6566	208			TUNE-UP
62503	9	824	AS	8221	346			WATER LEAK + Oil Change
62504	9	824	AS	10390	372			Reline BRAKES
62505	9	824	AS	5468	230			RPL PWR STRING PUMP
62506	9	824	AS	11109	385			RPL WHeel Bearings
62507	9	824	AS	13413	95			
62508	9	824	AS	7641	76			
62510	9	824	AS	5903	83			
62511	9	824	AS	8713	107			
63100	9	824	AS	9482	0			NO COSTS
63101	9	824	AS	4986	53			
63102	9	824	AS	3729	856			RPL TANDEM WHEEL

Fig. 16-7. Materials handling usage report.

combustion engine forklift, cushion tire, LPG; the manufacturer is Hyster; the transmission is automatic; and the capacity is 5,000 pounds.

Reading on, we find the model number, serial number, and purchase price, from which we calculate the ownership cost. Next is the decline rate—7%. This is the percentage by which the purchase price is reduced quarterly.

The next section is the configuration of the unit, mast size, overhead guard, hour meter, loadback rest, and other pertinent information.

The fourth line shows the P.O. under which the unit was purchased, what unit was traded, the value received, and the capital identification number.

In the left-hand column is the quarterly cost history, under which are listed the quarters, beginning with the first quarter in which the company began receiving reports. Shown next are the hours used, percent utilization, maintenance cost, and cost per hour. This is the information supplied to the materials handling department from all of the locations.

The center section shows the cumulative cost history. First listed are the

REPORT ON EQUIPMENT USAGE

**UNIT # 0143 ** CCDE 1001010 3512   MATERIALS HANDLING

DEPT: MOBILE EQUIPMENT

GROUP: STAMPING PLANT   DIVISION: OPERATIONS   SUB-DIV: MANUFACTURING   LOCATION: RALEIGH

--CLASS A-BBB COMB ENG FORK TRUCKS CUSHION   TIRE LPG   MFG HYSTER   TRANS AUTOMATIC   CAPACITY 5000

MODEL NUM S50CP   SERIAL NUM -2178X   PRICE 16,208   OWNERSHIP COST 7.0   RECEIVED 12/15/76   STARTS 4-76

FEATURES, SPECIAL EQUIPMENT & COMMENTS - 1 - MAST 77/174/ 48 FORKS 48   HM X OHG X LBR " PS X ACCUM

2 -

3 -   HM 099

4 - PC#23547 TRADEIN -0056 - VALUE $1500   ARA#9389

COST HISTORY

	QUARTERLY				CUMULATIVE							
									COST PER HOUR			
QTR	HOURS USED	PERC UTIL	MAINT COST	COST/ HOUR	HOURS USED	MAINT COST	DEPREC COST	TOTAL COST	MAINT	DEPREC	TOTAL	COMMENTS
4- 76	11	0.5	12	1.091	11	12	435	447	1.091	36.55	40.64	
1- 77	1,245	57.0	96	.077	1,256	108	839	947	.086	.67	.75	
2- 77	934	42.8	112	.120	2,190	220	1,215	1,435	.100	.55	.66	
3- 77	926	42.4	172	.186	3,116	392	1.565	1,937	.128	.50	.63	
4- 77	833	38.1	626	.752	3,949	1,018	1,890	2,908	.258	.46	.74	HOIST REPAIR
1- 78	678	31.0	924	1.363	4,627	1,942	2,192	4,134	.420	.47	.89	HOIST CYL CONTROL VALVE
2- 78	771	35.3	238	.309	5,398	2,180	2,473	4,653	.404	.46	.86	
3- 78	1,209	55.4	248	.205	6,607	2,428	2,734	5,162	.367	.41	.78	
4- 78	1,111	50.5	343	.309	7,718	2,771	2,977	5,748	.399	.39	.74	
1- 79	1,005	46.0	257	.256	8,723	3,026	3,203	6,231	.347	.37	.71	$97.12 MALTREAT
2- 79	1,071	49.0	547	.511	9,794	3,575	3,413	6,988	.389	.36	.71	
3- 79	762	34.9	547	.718	10,556	4,122	3,609	7,731	.390	.34	.73	208 MALTREAT FRAME CRACKED
4- 79	725	58.1	852	1.175	11,281	4,974	3,791	8,765	.441	.34	.78	$28 ENGINE REPAIR
1- 80	726	58.4	595	.816	12,010	5,569	3,960	9,529	.484	.33	.79	
2- 80	750	60.1	691	.921	12,760	6,260	4,117	10,377	.491	.32	.81	ENGINE REPAIR
3- 80	683	54.7	315	.461	13,443	6,575	4,.63	10,836	.489	.32	.81	
4- 80	706	32.3	547	.775	14,149	7,122	4,399	11,521	.503	.30	.81	ENGINE REPAIR
1- 81	764	61.2	379	.496	14,913	7,501	4,526	12,027	.503	.30	.81	
3- 81	773	61.9	414	.536	16,373	8,119	4,753	12,872	.496	.29	.79	$145 DAMAGE TO FORKS
4- 81	734	58.8	408	.556	17,107	8,527	4,855	13,382	.499	.28	.78	$245 BROKEN CARRIAGE
1- 82	799	64.0	909	1.138	17,906	9,436	4,950	14,382	.527	.28	.80	
2- 82	474	38.0	878	1.852	18,380	10,314	5,083	15,352	.561	.27	.84	REPLACED ENGINE

RESIDUAL VALUE OF UNIT   1,170   **UNIT # 0143 **

Fig 16-8 XYZ company report on equipment usage

hours used, maintenance cost, depreciation cost, and total cost. The last three columns are the life maintenance cost per hour, depreciation cost per hour, and total cost per hour. These are the figures from which the LTCP curve is constructed.

In reviewing this unit's history, we see that the LTCP was reached in the second quarter of 1969. At that time the total cost was $.71 an hour. Owing to a capital restraint, the decision was made to retain this unit. And you can readily see how the maintenance cost rose: from $3,575, second quarter 1969, to $10,314, second quarter 1972.

Using the LTCP concept of replacing at the lowest total cost per hour, let's briefly go through the calculations to see what would have happened had we replaced the unit at the second quarter of 1969, with another unit operated for the same number of hours.

At the end of the second quarter 1969, this unit had 9,794 hours, $3,575 in maintenance costs, and $3,413 in depreciation, with a total cost of $6,988. Taking this unit and operating it for the 9,794 hours, at $.71 an hour, and purchasing another unit and operating it the same number of hours, the combination of the two would be 19,588 hours, $7,150 maintenance costs, and $6,826 in depreciation, for a total cost of $13,976. Then subtracting the $13,976 from $15,352 (cost for running one unit 18,380 hours), we would have a difference of $1,376. Therefore by operating two units for a total of 19,588 hours (9,794 hours each), we could have saved $1,376 in total cost, compared to running one unit for the shorter time of 18,380 hours.

Look now at Fig. 16-9, which is the graph that our computer prints from information supplied by the using locations. The M's indicate maintenance, the D's depreciation, while the T's stand for total cost.

After logging six quarters of information, the computer will take all known data and forecast a trend for the next eight quarters. If the LTCP will be reached in the eight quarters projected, the computer will indicate the quarter in which this will occur. Therefore, we have an eight-quarter lead time to make a decision to repair or to replace a unit.

Figure 16-10 is a summary report of all units forecast for replacement decision at a given location. This gives the operations people a capsule view of which units are nearing or have reached the replacement quarter.

The units with an asterisk next to them that are listed under the third quarter 1984, are units whose replacement the computer had prediced at least eight quarters earlier, and a decision should already have been made about their replacement. However, management makes such decisions, and not all units are replaced at their predicted time.

If you look at the third unit, Unit 0160, you will see that it is flagged for replacement in the fourth quarter 1985. Local operations management at the time of this report has six quarters in which to review the condition of the unit and decide whether to repair or replace it. If the decision is to replace it, then

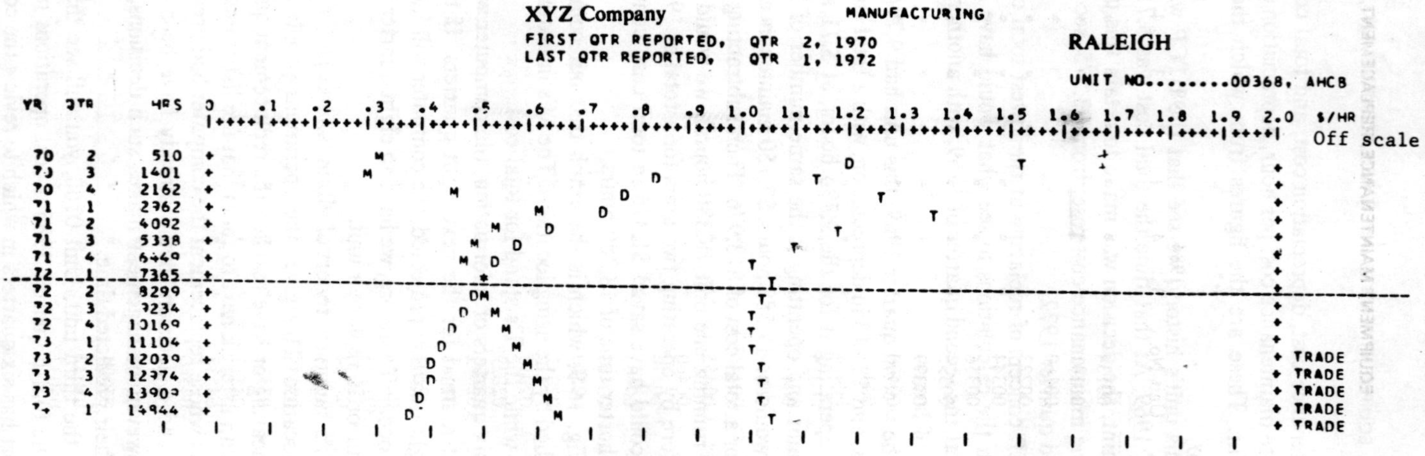

XYZ Company MANUFACTURING **RALEIGH**

FIRST QTR REPORTED, QTR 2, 1970

LAST QTR REPORTED, QTR 1, 1972

UNIT NO........00368, AHCB

```
YR  QTR    HRS  0    .1   .2   .3   .4   .5   .6   .7   .8   .9   1.0  1.1  1.2  1.3  1.4  1.5  1.6  1.7  1.8  1.9  2.0  $/HR
                |++++|++++|++++|++++|++++|++++|++++|++++|++++|++++|++++|++++|++++|++++|++++|++++|++++|++++|++++|++++|  Off scale
70   2     510
70   3    1401
70   4    2162
71   1    2362
71   2    4092
71   3    5338
71   4    6449
72   1    7365
72   2    8299
72   3    9234
72   4   10169
73   1   11104
73   2   12039                                                                                                    TRADE
73   3   12974                                                                                                    TRADE
73   4   13909                                                                                                    TRADE
74   1   14944                                                                                                    TRADE
                                                                                                                  TRADE
```

Fig. 16-9. A typical plant report.

XYZ Company								Manufacturing	
		1984		1985				1986	
Location	Unit No.	3	4	1	2	3	4	1	2
PLANT RALEIGH	00134	*	*	*	*	*	*	*	*
	00141	*	*	*	*	*	*	*	*
	00160						*	*	*
	00223				*	*	*	*	*
	00344	*	*	*	*	*	*	*	*
	00356		*	*	*	*	*	*	*
	00395	*	*	*	*	*	*	*	*
	00399		*	*	*	*	*	*	*
	00400	*	*	*	*	*	*	*	*
	00401				*	*	*	*	*
	00414	*	*	*	*	*	*	*	*
	00416		*	*	*	*	*	*	*
	00417	*	*	*	*	*	*	*	*
	00418				*	*	*	*	*
	00446	*	*	*	*	*	*	*	*
	00455	*	*	*	*	*	*	*	*
	00460	*	*	*	*	*	*	*	*
	00474						*	*	*
	00487	*	*	*	*	*	*	*	*
	00488							*	*
	00500		*	*	*	*	*	*	*
	02012	*	*	*	*	*	*	*	*
	02013	*	*	*	*	*	*	*	*
	02039	*	*	*	*	*	*	*	*
	02042	*	*	*	*	*	*	*	*
	02043								*
	02104	*	*	*	*	*	*	*	*
	02132			*	*	*	*	*	*
	02136					*	*	*	*
	02344		*	*	*	*	*	*	*
	03047	*	*	*	*	*	*	*	*
	03076				*	*	*	*	*
	03333	*	*	*	*	*	*	*	*
	04517	*	*	*	*	*	*	*	*
	04538	*	*	*	*	*	*	*	*
	04540							*	*
	05001	*	*	*	*	*	*	*	*
	05002	*	*	*	*	*	*	*	*
	05004	*	*	*	*	*	*	*	*
	05032								*
	05037			*	*	*	*	*	*

Fig. 16-10. Summary report of all units forecast for replacement decision, XYZ company.

steps should be taken immediately to start the paperwork so that in the fourth quarter of 1985 the new unit will be delivered.

C. What the Lowest Total Cost Point Concept Yields

Let us summarize what the LTCP method offers:

1. *A consistent approach for determining the trade-in point of equipment.* This method eliminates the hit-or-miss approach of replacing equipment. Rather, it gives definite guidelines to follow.

2. *A tool to eliminate costly overhauls and rebuilds.* With the LTCP graph, trends can be predicted and forecasts made, enabling us to see what a unit will look like eight quarters in advance. If the unit is nearing the LTCP, then naturally we would not spend large amounts for overhauls. If the LTCP is not forecast within the next eight quarters, then the decision could be made to rebuild instead of waiting for replacement.

3. *A tool to minimize general maintenance.* With the LTCP system you get quarterly reports on maintenance and utilization, with the ability to spot high-maintenance-cost units. Thus, there is an opportunity to review the equipment, the specifications, and the operating conditions, and to learn why the cost is high on a certain unit or in a certain department.

4. *A tool to assist in the preparation of requests for capital funds.* Use of the LTCP method gives more credibility to the justification written for replacement of equipment.

5. *A tool to assist in the forecast of equipment purchases.* Because we can forecast which units are going to be replaced, a decision can be made to allow the equipment to be placed in the manufacturer's build schedule, thus reducing a long delivery time and in some cases avoiding higher prices. It also gives management a guide as to the need for capital dollars for mobile equipment replacement.

III. RETURN ON INVESTMENT (R.O.I.) USING THE DISCOUNTED CASH FLOW METHOD

A. Introduction

In this section we shall discuss the method for presenting materials handling projects to top management because at that level specific justification is required for large expenditures of company funds.

For example, if the company has established a capital expenditure limit of, say, $2,500 for division managers' approval, then any expenditure below this amount will require only a one-page summary of benefits or advantages that may accrue to the company. On the other hand, expeditures of over $2,500 may require more elaborate explanations and supporting data, especially if hundreds of thousands, or millions, of dollars are involved in the project. For example, it may take a staff of ten working from 6 to 18 months (full-time) to provide the necessary back-up and supporting data to justify the expenditure of $15 million for a new warehouse and an automatic storage and retrieval (S/R) system with computerized co⌃trols.

The situation, in short, is this: (a) Management needs to establish the proper priorities for the allocation of funds; (b) the money must be made available by borrowing or other means; and (c) the return on investment must be capable of satisfying the stockholders of the company. Then (d) a management decision must be made as to the adequacy of the return based on the cost of the money to be invested with a specific margin for error.

There are many ways of determing return on investiment. Here we shall outline two of the most commonly used methods, and then concentrate on explaining the most widely accepted method, which is used in virtually all major project justifications.

1. The first commonly used method may be expressed mathematically in this way (with sample figures included):

$$\text{Annual return} = \frac{\text{Yearly savings}}{\text{Investment}} = \frac{\$\,2{,}000}{\$10{,}000} = 20\%$$

or a 20% per year return for this example.

2. The second, most widely accepted method is called the discounted cash flow (DCF), which is summarized as follows: Savings less depreciation times tax rate plus depreciation equals cash flow (DCF).

B. Determining the R.O.I. by means of the Discounted Cash Flow Method

There are usually many demands on a company for capital investment from many departments. It is locigal to assume that you will choose the investment that will result in the largest return.

1. Rate of Return Suppose you have a choice of two injection molding machines (or two types of lathes, etc.): Machine A can be purchased for $10,000 and will result in a savings of $10,000 per year for the next seven years, whereas Machine B can be purchased for $20,000 and will save $15,000 per year for the next seven years.

As you can see, Machine A will return 100% per year, and Machine B will return 75% per year, or:

$$\text{Savings minus cost} = \text{Return}$$

Based on the above returns it looks like Machine A is the better choice; however, we may be too hasty. Let us examine Machine B again.

Machine B costs $20,000. If we take $10,000 (or the cost of Machine A) from Machine B and say that it will return 100% in the first year, we can say that the additional $10,000 will return $5,000, or 50% in the first year. If you cannot make an additional or alternate investment with the second $10,000 increment that will return the same amount, 50%, in the first year, then the second, Machine B, wiould be more logical investment of capital.

From the simple example above, it is evident that there are a number of things to evaluate when considering the investment of capital. In essence, we have shown that the *rate of return* may vary according to the choice of investment; in addition to this, however, there are other considerations.

2. Pay-back Period Another element to consider in capital investment is the pay-back period, which is the amount of time required for the return to equal the investment.

As an example, let us say you are going to invest $100,000 in plant expansion and new equipment, and your projections for this investment indicate the annual return to be $10,000. Your company pays a tax rate of 48%, but you assume 50%, to be conservative (and for easier calculation). Your pay-back period, before taxes are removed, equals 10 years ($100,000 ÷ $10,000). If you figure the pay-back period after taxes, then the pay-back period is 20 years (or $100,000 ÷ $5,000).

It is important to remember when comparing different investment possibilities that you must use the same ground rules for each investment; otherwise you are comparing apples to oranges and getting a biased result. For example, if the pay-back period is after taxes for one investment, it should be on this same basis for the other investment opportunities that are under consideration.

In another example, Investment (X), consider buying a piece of equipment costing $20,000 with a life expectancy of ten years. The gross savings in the first year will be $38,000, but there will be no further savings after that year.

Let us perform the calculation, as follows:

1. Gross savings	$38,000
2. Less depreciation	2,000
3. Savings before taxes	36,000
4. Taxes @ 50%	18,000
5. Net savings	18,000
6. Add back depreciation	2,000
7. Cash Flow	$20,000
8. Pay-back period = 1 year	

In Investment (X) we can invest $20,000 in a piece of equipment and obtain a $20,000 return in one year; thereafter there are no further returns.

You will note in 6, above, that the depreciation was added back to the savings to arrive at a cash flow amount. Therefore, it is our *cash flow* that we are considering as our *savings* each year.

Since we are putting in $20,000 and taking out $20,000, we have not made any progress—we haven't gained anything, therefore, we would consider this a poor investment, since we actually lost the use of $20,000 for one year, although it may be possible to sell the piece of equipment at the end of the year for $15,000 to $18,000 and receive some return.

Investment (Y) also demands the purchase of a $20,000 machine, again with a life of ten years. This alternate investment will produce a gross savings of $8,000 for several years; so let's examine it

1. Gross savings	$8,000
2. Less depreciation	2,000
3. Savings before taxes	6,000
4. Taxes @ 50%	3,000
5. Net savings	3,000
6. Add back depreciation	2,000
7. Cast flow	5,000
8. Pay-back period = 4 years	

In Investment (Y), our gross savings of $8,000 is decreased to a cash flow of only $5,000. It will take four years before we start making a profit on the capital we have invested.

Investment (Z) indicates an expenditure of $20,000, also, with a ten-year life for the equipment. This piece of equipment will produce the following savings:

1st year	=	$ 2,000
2nd year	=	$ 6,000
3rd year	=	$10,000
Each additional year	=	$16,000

In evaluating the pay-back period, let's see what will happen

	1ST YR.	2ND YR.	3RD YR.	EVERY ADDITIONAL YEAR
1. Gross savings	$2,000	$6,000	$10,000	$16,000
2. Less 10% depreciation	2,000	2,000	2,000	2,000
3. Savings before taxes	0	4,000	8,000	14,000
4. Taxes @ 50%	0	2,000	4,000	7,000
5. Net savings	0	2,000	4,000	7,000
6. Add back depreciation	2,000	2,000	2,000	2,000
7. Cash flow	2,000	4,000	6,000	9,000
8. Pay-back period = 4 years				

The $20,000 investment will be returned in four years.

Let's compare Investments X, Y, and Z.

	PAY-BACK PERIOD	CASH FLOW EACH ADDITIONAL YEAR
Investment X	1	$0
Investment Y	4	$5,000
Investment Z	4	$9,000

Each of the above investiments require an amount of $20,000. So, let's calculate the percent of return on each investment after the pay-back period:

$$X = 0 \quad \text{or,} \quad \frac{0}{20{,}000} = 0$$

$$Y = 25\% \quad \text{or,} \quad \frac{5{,}000}{20{,}000} = 25\%$$

$$Z = 45\% \quad \text{or,} \quad \frac{9{,}000}{20{,}000} = 45\%$$

It appears that Investment Z is the best choice.

Unfortunately, a difficulty with using only pay-back period calculations is that the length of the return is not factored in. For example, if the 25% return for Investment Y was for the next five years, but the 45% return after pay-back of Investment Z was only for one more year, then we would have to admit that Investment Y is the best choice—because the *total return* for Investment Y is $45,000, figured in this manner:

Cash flow of $5,000/year for 9 years = $45,000

And, the *total return* for Investment Z is $30,000, figured thus: cash flow in pay-back period = $21,000 plus $9,000 in the fifth year $30,000.

The *rate-of-return* method of evaluating investments attempts to correct one of the problems of the pay-back period. It does this by taking into consideration the length of return on the investment.

For example, a company requires replacement of a critical piece of equipment on its production line, and it has the choice of two alternate machines, each costing $20,000.

MachineA:

Cost		$20,000
Return/year		$5,000
Pay-back period	=	4 years

By using the rate-of-return method, we factor in the length of the return. Both machines have a life of ten years. The return per year of Machine A is $5,000. Therefore, the total return will be $50,000 ($5,000 × 10-year life).

$$\text{The total return in \%} = \frac{\text{Total return}}{\text{Original investment}}, \text{ or:}$$

$$\frac{\$50{,}000}{\$20{,}000} = 250\%$$

Machine A will return 250% over its ten-year life. The average yearly rate then for Machine A is:

$$\frac{250\%}{10 \text{ years}} = 25\% \text{ per year}$$

Machine B also costs $20,000 but its yearly return is as follows:

1st year return	=	0
2nd year return	=	$1,000
3rd year return	=	$3,000
Each additional year	=	$8,000

The pay-back period for Machine B is five years.

If we add the sum of the returns for ten years of the Machine B's life, we obtain the following:

YEAR		
1		$ 0
2		1,000
3		3,000
4		8,000
5		8,000
6		8,000
7		8,000
8		8,000
9		8,000
10		8,000
Total Return	=	$60,000

Then,

$$\frac{\text{Total Return}}{\text{Original Investment}} = \frac{\$60{,}000}{\$20{,}000} = 300\%$$

and the average yearly return for Machine B is equal to 30%:

$$300\% \div 10 \text{ years}$$

We can summarize the investments for the two machines as follows:

	MACHINE A	MACHINE B
Investment	$20,000	$20,000
Pay-back period	4 years	5 years
Total return (%)	250%	300%
Average return (%)	25%	30%

It is now possible to make the decision to purchase Machine B.

It is obvious, therefore,that the advantage of the rate-of-return method rests in the fact that it takes into consideration the length of time over which a return can be expected. If we had used only the pay-back method, Machine A would have seemed the better investment of the two, since it showed a shorter pay-back period.

3. Present Value Concept. In the discussion above, we assumed that the dollars used will remain at a fixed value from year to year. But, let us look at this in another way. Let us suppose that we have to choose between receiving $1,000 now or $1,000 one year from now. Wouldn't we choose the $1,000 now? Of course, we would. We could invest the $1,000 we receive now and have more than $1,000 a year from now.

Let us look at another example: Just suppose we are able to invest $10,000 in one of two investments, X and Y. The investments are shown below:

	RETURNS		
	1st year	2nd year	3rd year
X $10,000	$500	$300	$200
Y $10,000	200	300	500

The Total return in each of the two investments is the same; however, wouldn't we choose Investment X as the better one to make? Of course, we would! Investment X is the better choice because it has a larger first-year return of $500, which we can invest for a larger gain. This is a lot better than having only $200 to invest, as in the case of Investment Y.

It stands to reason that the money we recieve in the future is not worth as much as the money we receive now. Therefore, in evaluating investment projects, we should discount, by a certain amount, money to be received in the future.

Let us consider investing one dollar for one year. At the end of the year that dollar placed in a bank at an interest rate of 5% would return to us $1.05. Or, we could invest $0.952 now and, at 5%, draw out $1.00 one year from now.

Therefore, the *present value* of the dollar we will receive one year from now is $.952, if discounted at the rate of 5%.

In order to minimize the amount of calculations that must be made, we find it very convenient to use Table 16-4. The left column indicates the number of periods during which interest is compounded on the investment.

Table 16-4. Present value of $1.00.

n	6%	7%	8%	9%	10%	11%
1	0.9434	0.9346	0.9259	0.9174	0.9091	0.9009
2	0.8900	0.8734	0.8573	0.8417	0.8264	0.8116
3	0.8396	0.8163	0.7938	0.7722	0.7513	0.7312
4	0.7921	0.7629	0.7350	0.7084	0.6830	0.6587
5	0.7473	0.7130	0.6806	0.6499	0.6209	0.5935
6	0.7050	0.6663	0.6302	0.5963	0.5645	0.5346
7	0.6651	0.6227	0.5835	0.5470	0.5132	0.4817
8	0.6274	0.5820	0.5403	0.5019	0.4665	0.4339
9	0.5919	0.5439	0.5002	0.4604	0.4241	0.3909
10	0.5584	0.5083	0.4632	0.4224	0.3855	0.3522
11	0.5268	0.4751	0.4289	0.3875	0.3505	0.3173
12	0.4970	0.4440	0.3971	0.3555	0.3186	0.2858
13	0.4688	0.4150	0.3677	0.3262	0.2897	0.2575
14	0.4423	0.3878	0.3405	0.2992	0.2633	0.2320
15	0.4173	0.3624	0.3521	0.2745	0.2394	0.2090
16	0.3936	0.3387	0.2919	0.2519	0.2176	0.1883
17	0.3714	0.3166	0.2703	0.2311	0.1978	0.1696
18	0.3503	0.3959	0.2502	0.2120	0.1799	0.1528
19	0.3305	0.2765	0.2317	0.1945	0.1635	0.1377
20	0.3118	0.2584	0.2145	0.1784	0.1486	0.1240
21	0.2942	0.2415	0.1987	0.1637	0.1351	0.1117
22	0.2775	0.2257	0.1839	0.1502	0.1228	0.1007
23	0.2618	0.2109	0.1703	0.1378	0.1117	0.0907
24	0.2470	0.1971	0.1577	0.1264	0.1015	0.0817
25	0.2330	0.1842	0.1460	0.1160	0.0923	0.0736
26	0.2198	0.1722	0.1352	0.1064	0.0839	0.0663
27	0.2074	0.1609	0.1252	0.0976	0.0763	0.0597
28	0.1956	0.1504	0.1159	0.0895	0.0693	0.0538
29	0.1846	0.1406	0.1073	0.0822	0.0630	0.0485
30	0.1741	0.1314	0.0994	0.0754	0.0573	0.0437
35	0.1301	0.0937	0.0676	0.0490	0.0356	0.0259
40	0.0972	0.0668	0.0460	0.0318	0.0221	0.0154
45	0.0727	0.0476	0.0313	0.0207	0.0137	0.0091
50	0.0543	0.0339	0.0213	0.0134	0.0085	0.0054

From the table we can determine the value of one dollar for different investment periods and interest rates; for example:

6 years @ 7% = 0.6663
15 years @ 8% = 0.3152
20 years @ 9% = 0.1784
25 years @ 10% = 0.0923

1. Let us use an example to apply the above knowledge to two investment projects requiring the same initial amount of capital:
(a) Investment X returns $300 in two years.
(b) Investment Y returns $400 in four years.
Say, for example, that we discount both at 8%.

Investment X = 8% for 2 years = 0.8573
$300 × 0.8573 = $257.19
Investment Y = 8% for 4 years = 0.7350
$400 × 0.7350 = $294.00

Investment Y has the larger *present value;* therefore, it is the better of the two investments.

2. In another example, let us suppose that a company has to decide between two expansion projects:

(a) With Project A it can invest $100,000 to expand its plant with certain high-production equipment. The company is very conservative and feels that this is a relatively safe investment that will return $30,000 the first year, $60,000 in the second year, and $60,000 in the third year. Because this is a relatively safe investment, the company decides to discount the investment at 6%, which is exactly the cost of acquiring the money to finance this expansion program.

The *present value* of the return on investment, if calculated, is, as follows:

$30,000 for one year @ 6% discount =	
$30,000 × 0.9434 =	$ 28,302
$60,000 for two years @ 6% discount =	
$60,000 × 0.8900 =	53,400
$60,000 for three years @ 6% discount =	
$60,000 × 0.8396 =	50,376
Present value =	$132,078

(b) With Project B the company can install a new production line that will increase a certain product's share of the market; but since it is a fairly new product and not so well established, there is a high degree of risk involved for the investment in launching this product.

The company, therefore, sets the discount at 30% or five times the cost of obtaining the money. In other words, the risk is high, but the gain could be high also. Let's calculate the returns, as follows:

$40,000 for one year × 0.7692	=	$ 30,768
$80,000 for two years × 0.5917	=	47,336
$140,000 for three years × 0.4552	=	63,738
Present value	=	$141,832

Project A has a present value of $132,078, whereas Project B has a present value of $141,832.

3. Taking another example, let us suppose that a company will invest in a project and receive the following returns:

INVESTMENT	RETURN 1ST YEAR	RETURN 2ND YEAR	RETURN 3RD YEAR
$20,351	$6,000	$8,000	$10,000

Let us calculate the yield, or rate of return, on the above investment. In the first place, we need to find the rate of discount that causes the sum of the present values to equal the investment. This is done on a trial-and-error basis; so, let's start by applying a discount rate of 6% to the returns and see what the sum of the present values turns out to be.

$ 6,000 × 0.9434	=	$ 5,660
8,000 × 0.8900	=	7,120
10,000 × 0.8396	=	8,396
Present value	=	$21,176

The present value of $21,176 is more than the original investment of $20,351; therefore, the discount wasn't large enough. Now, we'll try 10% and see what happens:

$ 6,000 × 0.9091	=	$ 5,455
8,000 × 0.8264	=	6,611
10,000 × 0.7513	=	7,513
Present value	=	$19,579

As we can see, the discounted rate of 10% gave us too low a figure, $19,579 versus the $20,351 of our investment. So, we try 8%.

$$\begin{aligned} \$\ 6{,}000 \times 0.9259 &= \$\ 5{,}555 \\ 8{,}000 \times 0.8573 &= 6{,}858 \\ 10{,}000 \times 0.7938 &= 7{,}938 \\ \text{Present value} &= \$20{,}351 \end{aligned}$$

Our computations indicate, therefore, that the present values of the return at 8% are equivalent to our original investment. This investment bears the same return as if the investment had been deposited in a bank bearing an interest rate of 8%.

EXERCISE NO. 16

1. To obtain assurance of reasonable maintenance cost and satisfactory reliability, plant management can turn to two principal methods of getting maintenance done:
   1. ______
   2. ______
2. The maintenance program for materials handling equipment requires a systems approach. Its elements are:
   1. ______
   2. ______
   3. ______
   4. ______
3. Name at least three checkpoint items in considering maintenance contract services:
   1. ______
   2. ______
   3. ______
4. Name at least three questions that should be raised when considering in-house maintenance:
   1. ______
   2. ______
   3. ______
5. In considering the cost of maintenance, the cost analysis should be approached on two levels:
   1. Repair cost per ______.
   2. Total cost of ______
6. The total systems approach involves the economics of ownership including the following items:
   1. Capital investment
   2. Depreciation
   3. ______
   4. ______

5. ______________________________
6. ______________________________

7. Labor requirements have a dramatic effect on maintenance cost, total cost, and economic life of a lift truck. The shortage of __________ is presently at a critical level.

8. A higher degree of __________ __________ has generally been considered necessary for electric trucks than for gas-powered units; however, the difference has been narrowed with the advent of __________ and plug-in__________ for electric trucks.

9. One method of justifying replacement of equipment involves using job assignment, utilization, and __________; rotating equipment to other jobs; installing new equipment on the highest-utilized job; applying cost __________ __________ figures at which the new unit should operate; and consequently phasing-out a high cost unit.

10. The LTCP concept yields:
1. A consistent approach for determining trade-in point of equipment.
2. A tool to eliminate costly overhauls and rebuilds.
3. ______________________________
4. ______________________________
5. ______________________________

11. Using this formula:

$$\frac{\text{Yearly savings}}{\text{Investment}} = \text{Annual return in \%}$$

if an investment of $20,000 brings yearly savings of $2,000, what is the annual return?

12. If the annual return of an investment of $50,000 is 10%, what are the savings?

13. One element to consider in capital investment is the pay-back period, which is the amount of time required for ______________________________
______________________________.

14. It is important to remember when comparing different investment possibilities that you must use the same ground rules ______________________________
______________________________.

15. Perform the following calculations to determine the pay-back period of a piece of equipment whose original cost is $42,000:

1. Gross savings	$40,000
2. Less depreciation	2,000
3. Savings before taxes	
4. Taxes at 50%	
5. Net savings	
6. Add back depreciation	
7. Cash flow	
8. Pay back period = ________	

16. A company wants to know what the pay-back period will be for a piece of equipment costing $30,000 with a ten-year life. The machine will generate savings of $2,500 the first year, $5,500 the second year, $8,000 the third year, and $12,000 each additional year.

	1st year	2nd year	3rd year	Each additional year
1. Gross Savings				
2. Less 10% depreciation				
3. Savings before taxes				
4. Taxes at 50%				
5. Net savings				
6. Add back depreciation				
7. Cash flow				
8. Pay-back period = ________				

17. There are three solutions to an investment problem, as follows:

	PAY-BACK PERIOD	CASH FLOW EACH ADDITIONAL YEAR
Solution (a)	1	$ 0
Solution (b)	4	$4,000
Solution (c)	4	$5,000

Each solution required an investment of $20,000. What is the percent return on each after the pay-back period?

1. ____________
2. ____________
3. ____________

18. Which of the above solutions in No. 17 (a, b, c) is the best one?

____________.

19. Total % return $= \dfrac{\text{Total return}}{\text{Original investment}}$

The return per year of Machine A is $6,000, and its life is 10 years. Therefore, the total return in $60,000. Since the machine costs $15,000, what is the total return as a percent of the original investment for Machine A? ____________

20. What is the average yearly rate of return for Machine A ____________

Chapter 17
Work Measurement Applied to Materials Handling; The Need For, And How To Collect Different Types Of Data To Support Materials Handling Projects

I. Work Measurement Applied to Materials Handling

A. The Need for Data

Every organization, whether large or small, has the problem of planning, scheduling, and otherwise controlling production. The reliability of decisions made by management in this area—and in many other related areas and for different purposes—depends to a great extent upon the accuracy or precision with which human work can be measured.

Past experience, which is used as a basis for forecasting work effort, is only a very crude and often unreliable way of predicting the amount of work to be expected from an individual or group of individuals.

Work measurement, as the name implies, can provide plant management with a means for measuring the amount of time to be expended in the performance of a task, regardless of its complexity, and thereby provide a yardstick to compare or measure human effort.

B. How to Collect Different Types of Data

1. Time and Methods Studies in General. While the materials handling engineer may be very much concerned about the time it takes to do a task, he is also concerned about the method employed to perform it. A methods study attempts to improve the methods used to achieve a desirable end by eliminating, combining, or changing motions, the aim being to eliminate wasted motions.

For many years, the industrial engineer spoke of time and motion study. The motions concerned mainly methods, and, of course, the time to accomplish a task followed as a result of study of the motions involved. It is logical to assume that by investigating motions and/or methods, ineffective times will be eliminated or reduced substantially.

Since methods and time are so closely interrelated, we must not lock them up in separate boxes and study them separately. If we did, we might wind up with the time to perform very unsatisfactorily. Work effort, therefore, should be timed only after the method for performing the work has been improved.

2. Work Measurement Techniques. In many companies, the term "work measurement" still stands for "time study using a stopwatch." Stopwatch time studies have acquired a somewhat dirty name, especially among labor union workers, primarily because of abuses, which although carried out under the guise of scientific management, were nothing more nor less than "speedup." It would be well, however, to understand how pure "time study" works, because it is a basic tool and a building block of many other work measurement systems.

The engineer first studies the job, and then breaks the job down into its various measurable elements. Of course, if the job content varied considerably during the course of a work shift, the results would be very unsatisfactory. Therefore, the task to be studied must be highly repetitive; for example, a laborer digging a trench, a telephone operator at a switchboard, a worker putting candies into a box, and so forth. In order to illustrate what we have been discussing, let us take a relatively simple task in a frozen-food plant, putting chopped spinach from a conveyor line into 10-ounce, wax-coated boxes.

The methods study sheet that is used would contain a diagram of the work station arrangement, a breakdown of the elements, and a description of the task and equipment (see Fig. 17-1).

The sketch shows in a very simplistic manner the general arrangement of the work place layout and work station. The operator fills empty boxes on conveyor A by taking chopped spinach from conveyor B and putting the spinach into the box. The operator slides the box onto a scale across conveyor line A, filling it until the 10-ounce weight is reached as he/she fills the box. The correct weight having been reached, the box is pushed from the scale to continue to a wrapping station, from which it proceeds into the freezer.

In Fig. 17-1 a detailed explanation relays information concerning the work methods used. It is advisable to use your own judgement in selecting a qualified operator to study. After the methods study then, if a stopwatch time study is desirable, the observer will transfer the elements of the job onto a time study sheet. The observer will record the starting and ending times of each element for a fairly large number of repetitions of the operator. The observer will rate the effectiveness level of the operator against a judgment factor of what normal work effort consists of. In our example, if a qualified operator is moving somewhat faster than expected, this rating factor may be as much as 125%. (That

Date: **Engineer:** **SKETCH**

Location:

Task:

Equipment:

Job Elements

1.
2.
3.
4.
5.
6.
7.
8.
9.
10.
11.
12.
13.
14.
15.

Fig. 17-1. Typical methods study sheet

is, the observer feels that the operator is working 25% harder than can normally be expected.)

After reducing the elemental times to normalcy (for the 125% rating factor, deducting 25% from the elemental times), the observer introduces an added factor for fatigue allowances. Fatigue allowances are rest periods which are usually combined with "delay" allowances. Delays are contingency allowances in which the conveyor line might be stopped from time to time for servicing of one sort or another. For example, the line may run out of food products (spinach, for instance), or it may run out of boxes. If these stoppages are customary in the operation, then they must be taken care of, statistically, in the work measurement study.

An excellent treatment of work measurement is given in the *Industrial Engineering Handbook* by Maynard. It is advisable that any serious practitioner have as a handy reference either the Maynard book or "Motion and Time Study" by Ralph M. Barnes. In Maynard's book the predetermined time standards and work sampling are also covered in detail. A practical knowledge of these work measurement techniques, which are briefly discussed in this chapter, can be very helpful in understanding the nature of work, the worker, and the work effort.

After many different time studies are carried out in a plant, it is possible to assemble a library of standards from the compilation of the time studies. This library of standards is called a *standard data file.* It becomes possible, then, to put together a work standard from this data file of standard elements. It is even possible to computerize standard data and to feed into the computer a request for a standard.

A number of computer programs can be obtained to accomplish the objectives of standards preparation. These systems have their proponents and critics; therefore, we should let each system stand on its own merit.

Predetermined time standards are used primarily by companies that do not want to be accused of using the stopwatch for measuring work. Since most of the elemental times have been developed by the stopwatch, this is merely a subterfuge that fools almost no one. Predetermined time standards such as MTM (methods time measurement) or BMT (basic motion times) are useful and relatively more inexpensive to develop than stopwatch standards. Their fundamental principle is that all motions of the human body are capable of having assigned to them time values; for example, a reach at arm's length, a short reach, a grasping with the fingers, etc. Since this is so, it is possible to combine all of the motions required to perform a given task and thereby develop a standard.

Another, quite popular, work measurement technique is called "work sampling" or "ratio-delay." It was developed originally by the British management expert L. H. C. Tippett during his work studies in textile mills in England. In this method observations are made of a worker at random time intervals throughout a period of time. By using a chart of random numbers, randomness for the time intervals can be obtained. Statistically speaking, it is a perfectly logical method for determining and measuring human effort. The random observations indicate solely whether the laborer is either "working" or "not working." By taking a large enough sample of observations, and by coding the elements of the laborers' task, a perfectly valid work standard may be developed. The author prefers to use this method rather than a stopwatch and in the past has used it to establish work standards for a number of occupations, including the following:

1. Frozen food packaging
2. Order picking
3. Forklift truck operations
4. Equipment maintenance operations
5. Manufacturing production operations

C. Data to Support Materials Handling Projects

In the folloiwng section we shall describe ways to collect data that will support the need for materials handling equipment or facilities.

For example, we shall try to show how self-leveling docks can be justified, how warehouses and their additions can be shown to be necessary, and so forth.

Earlier in the text (in Chapter 6), we discussed briefly a concept of order picking work measurement, and indicated the range of order picking in a conventional layout of bin shelving to be on the order of 20 to 35 line items per man-hour.

The above measurement can be obtained more precisely for your establishment by applying any of the above techniques for developing a work standard: stopwatch time study, MTM, or work sampling.

1. Dock Space. Let us assume that you have simple, nonpowered dock plates in your receiving department. You are convinced that the department requires more dock space and powered dockplates, but you are not exactly certain how many may be required. All you know is that some truckers have griped about not being unloaded and having to remain overnight with a load.

It would be possible to decide upon the number of dock spaces and powered dockplates after certain facts are known concerning the operation. We should gather as much information as possible, as follows:

1. Examine the incoming truck register to determine the arrival times of the truckers.
2. Find out how long it takes each trucker to get unloaded.
3. Make a chart showing arrival times, and see what the peak hours are.
4. See if staggering your receiving department working hours will improve the situation. In other words, it might be advisable to start unloading two hours earlier and extend the work day one or two hours in that particular department.
5. Perform a methods study to see whether or not there are any ineffective operations being performed on the receiving dock that cause delays. Sometimes paper shuffling, examining documents, and routine clerical tasks are mistakenly being performed by the productive workers instead of by clerical help.
6. Perform a simple simulation study of the operation by taking present work standards and projecting future work standards with specific numbers of truck dock spaces and powered dockplates.

The above data should indicate where the needs exist and should help make a valid presentation to management possible.

2. Additional Warehouse Space. Prepare information as follows:

1. We are assuming that this is a pharmaceutical warehouse and we are trying to prepare for a 25% increase in order picking business volume. One of the first things to decide is what the types and sizes are of the items that will be added to the inventory.
2. We have decided to depart from historical (past experience) standards, and by using work sampling techniques we are establishing valid work standards. The work standards will indicate, approximately, the number of additional employees required in the order picking function, as well as indicate the number of additional order picking carts and other equipment required to outfit each order picker.
3. Since we know, from (1) above, what the quantity, type, and size of the materials are to be, we can estimate the number of additional bin shelves, storage racks, and the like, that will be required.
4. From a layout of the additional bin shelving plan, we can determine the size of the plant expansion required.

3. In-Depth Analysis of Projected Plant Expansion with Types of Data Compiled. At present a plant is operating three lines for medium and heavy duty models and must consider them individually. (See Fig. 17-2) There is little opportunity to move models from one line to another, and thus capacities cannot be considered on a total basis.

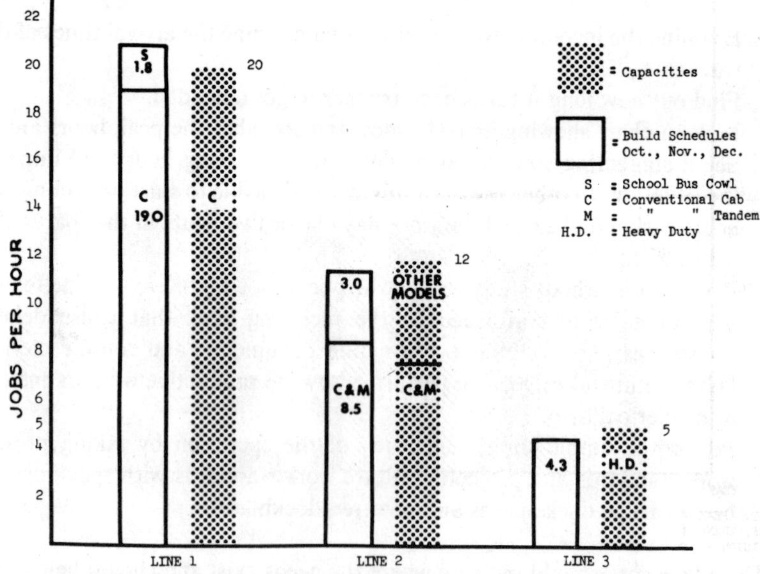

Fig. 17-2. October, November, and December 1979 build schedules of 1980 models.

Line #1: This line assembles the simpler C models at a 20/hr. rate. Present schedules reflect a requirement of 20.8/hr. Plant X requested 800 added models for October, November, and December, which we cannot supply.
Line #2: The 1980 model assignment for this line requires an average rate of 11.5/hr. (8.5 "heavy" C and M models and 3/hr. of Z's and steel widgets). Current production schedules require close to the 11.5/hr. rate.
Line #3: This line currently assembles only heavy duty models. Its maximum capacity is 5/hr., with current schedules of 4.3/hr. Plant X is marketing the PZ models in 1980; so it is assumed that the demands on this line will be substantially increased in the months ahead.

Comparison of current market demands with current capacities shows that we shall have difficulty keeping up without substantial overtime. (See Fig. 17-3.)

Future Capacity Needs, C and M Models. Increased volume requirements, beyond the 1980 needs just discussed, amount to about 4% per year for C and M models. On an annual trend basis, this is an increase of well over one model per hour each year. This is more than current schedules of these models (27.5/hr.) and would require major overtime hours.

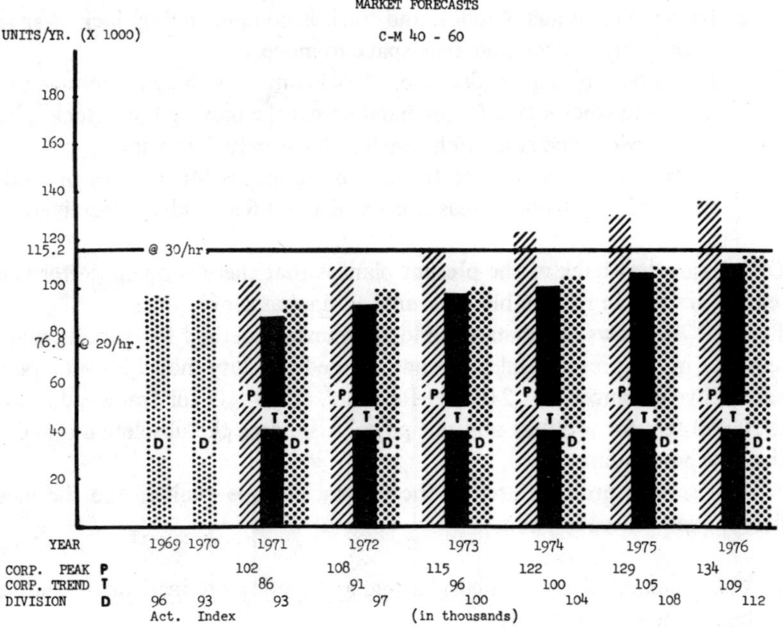

Fig. 17-3. Market forecasts.

A new assembly plant at 30/hr. capacity would meet the forecast trend needs for C and M models in 1986.

With modernization of the older plant, sufficient capacity for school models and "P" jobs on line #1 will be available to meet market forecasts through 1984. Capacity will also be available in this plant to meet market forecast trend needs for all heavy duty models through 1984.

In comparing the older plant to the proposed new plant, we stress the following considerations:

1. Worn-out facilities result in high maintenance costs and excessive downtime. Facilities in the present model plant are over 80% depreciated.
2. The floor space of the existing plant is inadequate:
   a. Line lengths are inadequate
   b. Repair is made in stalls versus conditioning lines because of the space lack. Quality and costs suffer.
   c. There is insufficient storage space; so 265,000 sq. ft. of outside space is used for storage of components. This creates problems with respect to snow, ice, and cold weather as well as rain and darkness.
   d. There is no space for banking as required for schedule changes, both planned and emergency.
   e. Disposal of dunnage, offal, and trash is complicated by lack of space to properly collect, and aisle space to move.
   f. Line stock space is inadequate. Model trim lines share a common five-foot-wide stock space fed by hand across the moving line. Stock space that services one side of chassis line #1 is only 7′4″ wide.
   g. Narrow aisles contribute to material damage. Main aisles in model trim and chassis line areas are six feet and 6′8″ wide, respectively.

One major drawback of the present plant is that there is no space for sub-assembly activity in reasonable proximity to final assembly lines.

Figure 17-4 shows the distance and the moving method for various major assemblies in the present and the proposed medium duty model layouts. Note the excessive distances of 1,210 feet for axles, 1,250 feet for frame-side rails, and 10,000 feet for mufflers and tail pipes. Also, note the obsolete method of delivery of some items.

A most serious problem area in the present plant is quality, and the most deficient quality area is paint:

1. The pre-paint cleaning, phosphating, and sealing are inadequate and far below present standards.

	PRESENT		PROPOSED	
COMPONENT	TRAVEL DISTANCE FROM PRIME STORAGE TO PRODUCTION (FEET)	METHOD OF DELIVERY	TRAVEL DISTANCE FROM PRIME STORAGE TO PRODUCTION (FEET)	METHOD OF DELIVERY
Axles	1,210	Train*	540	Power & free conveyor
Engines	420 +1900 to assy. line	Fork truck	855	Power & free conveyor
Transmissions	715 (Bldg. 65)	Fork truck	585	Fork truck
Frame-side rails	1,250	Train	(On-line)**	
Propshafts	150	Dolly	180	Power & free conveyor
Sheet metal	4400 (Bldg. 25)	Trailer—fork truck	315	Train
Tires	120	Fork truck	315	Powered conveyor
Chassis springs	500	Fork truck	540	Train
Cab glass	1,225	Fork truck	585	Fork truck
Mufflers	10,000 (Plt. Y)	Trailer—fork truck	810	Train
Tail pipes	10,000 (Plt. Y)	Trailer—fork truck	810	Train
Unitized loads	1,770 (Bldg. 65) (Misc. material)	Train	1,255	Train

*Three dollies pulled by tractor.
**80% of usage will be stored directly on line.

Fig. 17-4. Medium duty subassembly material movement, comparison of present and proposed facility.

2. Very poor quality is obtained in prime facilities. Nonstandard materials must be used owing to inadequate baking time and temperature.
3. Very poor quality is obtained in color facilities, which cannot provide standard bakes for the super enamels now used. There is also a lack of booth time for good coverage.
4. The present facility cannot apply current acrylic enamels.
5. The present facility cannot apply the requested number of metallic colors, this plant being restricted to three metallics in 1980 versus ten standard metallic colors used at all light duty assembly plants.

In the above examples, we have shown some of the types of data needed to support materials handling projects. As you will have noticed, some of the data are readily available, whereas some must be extrapolated and are relatively subjective. The above data (shown here with only minor changes) were used by the author in actual projects, some involving millions of dollars.

EXERCISE NO. 17

1. Past experience, which is used as a basis for forecasting work effort, is only a very ____________ and often ____________ way of predicting the amount of work from an individual or group of individuals.
2. A methods study attempts to improve the methods used to achieve a desirable end by eliminating, combining, or changing motions. True ☐ False ☐
3. Work effort should be timed only after the method for performing the work has been ____________.
4. In many companies, work measurement still stands for only: ____.
5. In a stopwatch time study, the task to be studied should be highly ____________.
6. Two predetermined time standards are MTM and ____________.
7. The fundamental principle of predetermined time standards is that all motions of the human body are capable of having assigned to them ____________ ____________.
8. Ratio-delay is another name for ____________ ____________.
9. In work sampling, by using a chart of random numbers, ____________ for the time intervals can be obtained.
10. What could you learn from the plant incoming truck register? ____ ____

Chapter 18
Stochastic Simulation and Mathematical Modeling for the Layman and Engineer; Industrial Engineering Aspects of Handling

I. STOCHASTIC SIMULATION

A. Definition

Stochastic simulation, systems simulation, or just plain simulation has come to mean the technique of preparing a model of a real-life situation and then performing a series of sampling experiments upon the model. The engineer or modeler then observes the behavior of the model while changing certain variables, asking "what if?" types of questions. Observing the behavior of the model then forms the basis for predicting the behavior of the real-life situation—and subsequently is useful in controlling the real situation.

When we talk about a "model" we mean a representation of a real situation, as, for example, a process or system.

Models may be classified in several different ways according to how closely they appear to typify the real situation. Models that include all the characteristics of the real situation, which could, in effect, replace the real situation, we call *isomorphic*. If we could structure and observe the operation of a perfectly isomorphic model, we could make accurate predictions concerning the behavior of the real situation. Of course, when the subject of inquiry is exceedingly complex, an isomorphic model is impossible to structure, and from a practical sense, it is unnecessary to do so.

In various situations in which systems simulation is normally applied, we often find it both necessary and convenient to group seemingly related variables in our models. This is done in order to allow some more or less broad assumptions to be made, and to try to reproduce the gross effects of interactions in the real system rather than the detailed effects, all in order to ease the task of structuring the model and interpreting the results. Systems simulation models of this type we call homorphic.

In any systems simulation problem it is of primary importance to establish the degree of homorphism that is adequate to achieve the desired results. Variations in the different systems being studied demand specialized knowledge on the part of the modeler and the people he is working with. In other words, a computer programmer who is setting up the model has to know as much as possible about the present situation, for example, the operation of the manufacturing plant, or the paint line, or the warehouse, in order for him to ask intelligent questions and to properly develop the model to be simulated.

B. Classifying Simulation Models

Classifying simulation models can be done by delineating their characteristics. When we do this, we can derive three different types of models, as follows:

1. Iconic Models. Iconic models appear similar to the subject of inquiry, and are characterized by the use of some metric transformation or scaling. They are of use in describing static things, or dynamic things at a point in time. Examples of this general type of simulation model include a globe, still photos, and so forth.

2. Analog Models. Analog models are characterized by the use of a convenient transformation of one set of properties for another set of properties in accordance with certain specified rules. They are used to describe most dynamic systems or processes. Examples include flow charts, schedule boards, plant layouts, and so forth.

3. Symbolic Models. Symbolic models are characterized by the fact that the components of the subject of inquiry, and the interrelationship among them, are represented by symbols, both mathematical and logical. This class is the substance of systems simulation.

C. Identifying Homorphic Models

In order to identify the particular homorphic, symbolic model used in systems simulation, one more stratification is required. This is by the solution mode, as follows:

1. *Solution by analytic methods*: This is the straightforward application of mathematical techniques to the solution of the model, with a resultant explicit answer that may be tested for acceptance.
2. *Solution by numerical methods*: This normally involves iterative procedures to test all conceivable states of a model to isolate the optimum state.
3. *Solution by "Monte Carlo" methods* (also called unrestricted random sampling, or stochastic sampling): This normally involves testing states

of the model to determine some probabilistic property of the system by the use of random sampling applied to the system elements, and applying the statistics of parametric testing to isolate desirable responses.

II. INDUSTRIAL ENGINEERING ASPECTS OF HANDLING

A. Solution of Symbolic Models

In general, in the solution of symbolic models, an analytic method is desirable so that the exact answer is derived; a numerical method is acceptable when no analytic method exists; and a Monte Carlo solution is applied only if the other modes are either impossible or impractical. This last is by no means a rare condition. For example, let us take a familiar problem, factory scheduling.

Consider a factory having five machines. Six different orders must be scheduled through these machines, each order starting at machine 1, going to machine 2, and so forth through machine 5, at which point the order is considered to have been completed. Since each order requires a varying amount of processing time at each machine, it is obvious that different sequences will yield different amounts of idle time at the downstream machines. The scheduler's problem is to assign a sequence that yields a minimum of idle time.

There is no known analytic solution to this problem. A numerical solution might seem feasible until one recognizes that the number of possible sequences is equal to six factorial raised to the fifth power—somewhat greater than 190 trillion. Even for so small a problem, an exhaustive solution is rarely possible. Yet the potential for savings in this area practically demands solution; so we apply systems simulation.

Systems simulation, in this case, duplicates, on paper, the operation of a real system in time, using homorphic symbolic models of that operation in which each element in turn executes a sequence of actions that depends upon and affects the execution of the various other elements. It is particularly suitable to the investigation of those systems having stochastic characteristics, that is, characteristics that permit different variables to be inserted in the equations of the problem, and different values for each of the variables, so that we can test the different parameters and examine the results.

Systems simulation employs a mathematical and logical model that is "run," not "solved." That is, it is not inherently optimizing, but rather is descriptive of the processing of work elements through service channels, of the impact of this processing on the service channels, and the performance of the total system. Each simulation "pass" constitutes an observation of the performance of a single configuration of the system. Optimization is approached by varying this configuration and comparing the alternate results.

B. Three Stages of Exploration

Applying the technique of systems simulation to the investigation of a real system, three stages of exploration may be differentiated as follows:

1. Collection of the necessary data for the problem and reduction to an appropriate form.
2. Structuring of a model of the real system that neither oversimplifies the system to the point that the model becomes trivial, nor retains so many details of the real system that the model becomes prohibitively clumsy.
3. Combining the data and the model in a sampling experiment designed to discover how the real system tends to behave under a variety of prescribed conditions and restraints.

C. Typical Statistics for Manufacturing and Warehousing

Different types of statistics have been processed for manufacturing and warehousing area simulation studies. These include, but are not limited to, the following:

1. Process operating statistics (a complete set for each process-machine group—or subprocess designation)
   a. Observation of the ratio of actual to planned hours of performance
   b. Observation of scrap occurrence
   c. Observation of maintenance downtime
2. Job statistics
   a. Jobs received per day by type of job
   b. Number of items per job (component parts comprising the job)
   c. Quantity of pieces per item
   d. Number of operations per item
3. Routing statistics
   a. Cumulative frequency distributions of "first operations"
   b. Cumulative frequency distributions of "last operations"
   c. Cumulative frequency distributions of "following operation relationships"
4. Promise date statistics by job type by estimated order size
5. Validating statistics (typical)
   a. Gross statistics such as number of orders, items, etc., per period of time
   b. Shop cycle time statistics
   c. Promise date performance statistics
   d. Overall maintenance and scrap occurrence statistics

This outline suggests the variety of data to be collected and analyzed. The computer programmer can provide for updating and for the elimination of data so that the simulation model will fairly represent the real situation.

III. CONCLUSIONS AND RECOMMENDATIONS

Simulation has become increasingly popular because its use does not require a knowledge of abstruse mathematics. It is, however, an extremely complex computer science, certainly not for amateurs. The use of the computer language GPSS (General Purpose Systems Simulation) itself evolved from Geoffrey Gordon's original program for the IBM 7090 written in 1960, and proliferated into other computer languages and equipment. For example, existing versions of GPSS are:

Computer	*Program*
Burroughs 550	GPSS 5500
Control Data 3600	GPSS III
General Electric 600 (series)	GESIM
Honeywell 200 (series)	GPS-K
IBM System/360	GPSS/360
RCA Spectra 70	Flow Simulator
UNIVAC 1100 (series)	GPSS/1100
Xerox Data Systems Sigma Series	GPDS

Since this list was compiled, probably new programs and even new computers have been introduced.

SIMSCRIPT, originally written by the RAND Corporation, is a more conventional programming language when compared with GPSS; also its output is not automatic like that of GPSS. In addition to GPSS and SIMSCRIPT, there are many other discrete-event simulation languages, for example, SIMULA, CSL, and GASP. Space does not permit a detailed analysis of the differences and complexities of the computer languages and the programming techniques required for successful systems simulation.

Despite the fact that simulation is a powerful and widely used computer technique, there are certain disadvantages that must be considered whenever its use is contemplated:

In the first place, simulation studies are rather expensive. They require both high-priced talent for programming, and a good deal of computer time because they are statistical techniques that require fairly substantial computer runs. Also, because they require a good deal of data collection before use of the computer, they can involve more time and money than originally estimated. Sometimes, the analyst becomes carried away by the use of "what if?" questions, and the program becomes unnecessarily complex and too all-encompassing.

In addition, every simulation model contains a good many assumptions about the composition of the system, the nature of the input, and the operating rules to be used. These assumptions are necessary in order to keep the model as orderly as possible. The problem arises, however, that if the assumptions made are not factored into the final results by the user, or if these assumptions are not known to him, the outcome, or the computer output, may be erroneous or misleading.

The materials handling practitioner who would like to use the systems simulation approach to the solution of his handling problems would do well to contact any local representatives of IBM and ask for their GPSS program, and to consult with them on its application and validity for the type of problem at hand.

Other computer companies, also, can offer assistance in this area. If your plant uses a computer, you are at least capable of discussing the problem with your computer department and seeking its assistance.

If your plant does not have a computer, and the problem is of some significance in terms of scale (size or cost), then a local computer services company that offers a time-sharing service or computer time may be the logical place to get assistance.

EXERCISE NO. 18

1. Explain what you believe stochastic simulation means:
____
____
____
____
____
____
____
____
____

2. When we talk about a "model" we mean a representation of a ____________ situation, as, for example, a process or system.
3. In various situations in which systems simulation is normally applied, we often find it both necessary and convenient to group seemingly ____________.
4. Variations in the different systems being studied demand ____________ knowledge on the part of the modeler and the people his is working with.
5. Three different types of model classification are as follows:
   1. Iconic models
   2. Analog models
   3. ____________ ____________
6. In order to identify the particular homorphic, symbolic model used in systems

simulation, one more stratification is required. This is by the solution mode, as follows:

1. **Solution by analytical methods**
2. **Solution by numerical methods**
3. **____________________**

7. Another name for solution by Monte Carlo methods is unrestricted random sampling, or __________ __________.

8. In general, in the solution of symbolic models, an analytic method is desirable so that the __________ __________ is derived.

9. The Monte Carlo solution is applied only if the other modes are either __________ or __________.

10. Applying the technique of systems simulation to the investigation of a real system, three stages of investigation may be distinguished, as follows:

1. **Collection of the necessary data for the problem and reduction to __________ __________ __________.**
2. **Structuring of a model of the real system that neither oversimplifies the system to the point that the model becomes trivial, nor retains so many details of the real system that the model becomes __________ __________.**
3. **Combining the data and the model in a sampling experiment designed to discover how the real system tends to behave under a variety of __________ __________ and __________.**

Chapter 19
Relationship of Materials Handling to Materials Management; Engineering Versus Administration

I. RELATIONSHIP OF MATERIALS HANDLING TO MATERIALS MANAGEMENT

A. Introduction

There has been, in the past two decades, an increasing realization that the practitioner in the materials handling field requires a broader view than the restrictive aspect of transporting materials—the lifting, lowering, placing into storage, and removing from storage point of view.

To this end the concept of materials management has developed, which says, in effect, that there is a systems approach that must be applied to materials handling because of the impact of so many other factors in the world of business, such as purchasing, traffic, inspection, and so forth. We discussed these factors in Chapter I.

Since we are concerned with the need for a larger piece of the pie, the author has included some views on this subject that provide a wider horizon for materials handling.

B. Organizing for Materials Handling Engineering*

We shall talk about organizing for materials handling engineering and related subjects; but first, by way of illustration, here is a little story to emphasize an important aspect of materials handling organization.

It was the occasion of a testimonial dinner for the town's leading citizen. He told his story in a quiet, shaking voice. "Friends and neighbors," he said, "when I first came here 47 years ago I came in no limousine. I walked into your town on a muddy, dirty road. I had only one suit on my back, one pair of shoes on

*The remainder of this chapter is based on the author's remarks at the Region V Seminar of the International Materials Management Society in April 1972 at the McCormick Place Convention Hall in Chicago, Illinois.

my feet, and all my earthly possessions were wrapped in a red handkerchief I carried over my shoulder. Now, 47 years later, I am on the Board of Directors of your leading bank. I own apartment buildings and office buildings. I am on the boards of your leading clubs, and I own three concerns with branches in 39 cities.

"Yes, friends, your town has been good to me, and I have come a long way since I first walked down your muddy, dirty road."

After the banquet, an awed youngster approached the great man, and asked timidly, "Tell me, sir, what did you have in the red handkerchief you carried over your shoulder when you walked into our town 47 years ago?"

"Let me think, son. If I recall rightly, I was carrying about $300,000 in cash and $750,000 in negotiable securities."

I think you can see the point I am trying to illustrate by this little story. I would say, first, that to have a successful materials handling program you have to have something in the bank before you can borrow. And, if I can stretch the analogy—that little something is top management support. Without top management support even a fine, excellently conceived organizational plan will have very tough sledding, and that is why you have to concentrate on obtaining success in at least one area and capitalize upon it so that you can command management interest and attention for the larger plan.

Now, I would like to begin the subject of organizing for materials handling engineering by stating that it will be somewhat futile, also, to try to organize a structure without attempting to define its scope and purpose. To put it in another way, we have to develop a systems approach to materials handling so that we can give purpose to the larger plan for organizing the materials handling effort.

During the course of the last decade, worldwide momentum has been building based on higher wage rates and fringe benefits for labor that has resulted in propelling materials handling mechanization forward at a faster pace than ever before.

In the United States, materials handling in the smaller and medium-sized plants has felt the impetus of higher wage rates and a newer phenomenon on the horizon—the Williams-Steiger Act, or OSHA as it is commonly called. Thus it is that the new compilation of federal standards for occupational safety and health has also added its impetus to the already burgeoning pressures of increased wage rates, and the profit squeeze that has resulted from this and other cost increases. The large plants, naturally, find these same pressures forcing them to approach materials handling on a more systematic basis to the extent that they have increased the degree of sophistication of present systems, up to and including the use of computers for processing and control.

1. Ratio of MHE's to Plant Size Most large corporation maintain materials handling departments on a corporate level in order to supplement the materials handling function at the plant level. Corporate guidelines are usually developed or finalized in the central office with special assignments delegated to the plants on occasion. While some companies subscribe to this concept, other multiplant companies are dependent, for their materials handling impetus, upon a cadre of MH engineers in each plant.

If it is at all possible, regardless of the basic method of organization, a ratio of materials handling engineering personnel to total plant employment should be established. As a gauge, I would suggest at least one MHE to every 850 plant employees, based upon total employment.

Nevertheless, it is extremely practical, regardless of any distinctions that may be drawn between large and small companies, that each plant should have the prerogative of deciding the identity and priority of specific projects to be accomplished with minimal guidance from the corporate office. The principal effort or endeavor of the corporate office is to provide suggestions and recommendations for the study of specific problem areas and to supply technical source materials and information. Another area in which the corporate materials handling effort should be exerted is that of maintaining communications between plants so that repetition of past failures either in or out of the company is not common, and reviewing special projects that may be the result of top management planning.

2. Communications and the Systems Viewpoint Since the major aspects or principles of materials handling are common to all plants, regardless of size, the results of work done in one plant, or in one company usually, are readily transferable to other plants or companies. So, realistically speaking, cost savings, methods improvements, mechanization, consulting work between departments or functional areas, and training are important phases of all materials handling group efforts. Properly utilized, each materials handling group should form a valuable adjunct to plant management to ensure the continued profitability of the enterprise.

The key word in the above discussion, then, is "profitability." Let us examine this in somewhat greater detail. If we say that we are concerned with profitability, then we should be examining the *least total cost* of materials handling in our plants regardless of whether we are talking about manufacturing operations or distribution operations. Therefore, if we are talking about total cost, we must look at the entire system, or to phrase this more adequately, we have to approach materials handling from the systems viewpoint.

Let us look at the symptoms that propel us toward the systems approach to materials handling in these days of the profit squeeze.

a. Declining Profits and Higher Manufacturing or Distribution Costs. Symptoms to watch for are higher indirect labor costs and all of the concomitant waste inherent in either manufacturing or distributive operations that have not been periodically scrutinized with a total materials handling planning approach in mind.

b. Inventory Control Problems. Symptoms of inventory problems are either too much inventory, too little inventory, or not enough of the right inventory.

c. Continuing Need to Improve Customer Service. Customer service can be improved by decreasing the response time between the customer's order and the delivery of the product. Shortening response time is dependent on good materials handling practices.

d. Increasingly High Maintenance Costs. When materials handling equipment is poorly maintained, or when it is overworked, maintenance costs will increase. Also, equipment costs will rise when too much equipment, that is, underutilized equipment, is on hand. These weak points cannot be determined without a comprehensive program of preventive maintenance and consistently good record-keeping. Record-keeping alone, however, is not sufficient without frequent analysis of the records and an action program to accompany the review and thus put teeth into the program.

e. Excessive Processing Time. Excessive processing time often throws schedules out of line, results in overtime, results in late deliveries, and creates both customer and supplier problems that in turn wind the spiral even tighter to thrust costs higher than budgets will allow. The systems approach to materials handling will effectively encompass the MRP II methodology (discussed in section C of this chapter).

f. Inefficient Materials Flow. Inefficient materials flow may or may not be obvious, but will show up, nevertheless, on the bottom line in reduced profits. A plant materials handling survey will quickly reveal the weak spots in the system.

g. Integration of Functions. The need for integrating other functions with mater' 's handling, such as equipment allocation and specification, capital equipment investment justification, return on investment feasibility studies, and the like, will show up in the fine tuning of the total systems approach.

C. MRP II

A brief mention of MRP II is given here in order that the materials handling practitioner be familiar with the concept. It is not intended that substantive information or a formulation be presented to make the reader an expert in this area, since it is relatively complex and would itself be the subject for an entire text.

Closed-loop material requirements planning gives management the tools for scheduling manufacturing operations effectively. MRP II was the natural outcome of the material requirements planning concept, since the recent computer explosion has resulted in a computer-based production and inventory management system.

The fundamental manufacturing equation that supplies answers to the following questions will give the reader some understanding of the essential process of MRP II:

What have we got? (That is, what have we in inventory, or in backlog?)
What are we going to sell?
What are we going to make?
What do we have to get?

The answers to the above questions result in the formulation of a master production schedule, and in a material and capacity requirements plan. Software (computer programs) exists that is off-the-shelf because the fundamental manufacturing equation mentioned above has become relatively standardized.

D. Bar Coding in Manufacturing and Physical Distribution

It is useful to the materials handling practitioner to have an understanding of bar code methodology. In my view, the control of inventory throughout the distribution cycle from manufacturing to the ultimate consumer will be materially assisted by the use of this concept, or by similar concepts, where the item and its component parts will be tracked expeditiously and cost-effectively.

Many individuals will recognize the bar code used on supermarket or grocery shelves and products as the UPC or Uniform Product Code. This is known to the initiated as a "2 of 5" bar code. All bar codes, of which there are several varieties, are composed of a narrow bar, a narrow space, a wide bar, and a wide space. If the code is printed horizontally, it is called a "picket fence"; if it is vertical, it is called a "ladder."

A brief history of the development of bar coding is as follows:

1949—A patent for a circular bar code was filed by N. J. Woodland et al.

1960—Rail car identification symbology was developed by Sylvania.
1963—Bar code techniques were described in *Control Engineering,* October 1963.
1970—U.S. Supermarket Ad Hoc Committee on Universal Product Coding was formed.
1971—Plessey code was used in European libraries.
1972—Codabar patent was filed. The interleaved 2 of 5 was proposed.
1973—UPC symbol was adopted.
1974—Code 39 was developed.
1977—EAN (European Article Numbering) symbol was adopted. American Blood Commission Standard became Codabar. Code 11 developed, and the Department of Defense LOGMARS study effort was started.
1981—Distribution Symbol Study Group was originally commissioned by the Uniform Product Code Council to study the feasibility of printing bar codes directly on corrugated fiberboard cartons. Code 39 was recommended.
1982—Department of Defense, MIL-STD-1189, "Standard Symbology for Marking Unit Packs, Outer Containers and Selected Documents" was published. (LOGMARS Program of the DoD is the acronym for "Logistics Applications for Marking and Reading Symbols.")

Bar coding is essentially a data entry system. It was the necessity for compiling and digesting or manipulating data quickly and accurately that propelled the concept to the relative importance it now enjoys.

I shall stress the Code 39 or 3 of 9 bar code here because it has been adopted by the Department of Defense as the basic bar code of its logistics systems. (See MIL-STD-1189 for a detailed description of the code structure.)

The Code 39 bar code was developed in 1974 by Intermec to meet the requirements for a fully alphanumeric bar code system. The structure of the code enables it to be printed by a wide variety of techniques including offset, letterpress, fully formed impact printers, dot matrix printers, and non-impact printing devices.

Bar code data input should be used by all organizations that require that item movement information be obtained. Bar coding is used for inventory control, manufacturing work-in-process tracking, wholesale and retail distribution, property accountability, and automotive parts assembly and repair facilities. New applications for bar coding are found every day, only a few of the more obvious uses having been indicated here.

Bar codes may be read by the use of pen-wand scanners, or by the much more rapid and more accurate laser scanners. In studies conducted by the DoD, first-read error rates were in the neighborhood of one error for several million characters read. This is a far cry from the one to three errors per hundred of the human readable type of data entry capability.

(The appendix of this text contains a bibliography of literature for the reader who would like to become more proficient with this fascinating and extremely useful tool.)

II. WHAT TO EXPECT FROM CHANGING MATERIALS HANDLING METHODS AND FUNCTIONAL ORGANIZATION

All materials handling groups should have as a goal progress within one or more of the following categories: cost savings, methods improvement, consulting, and training. First, let us take cost savings: the primary result of the materials handling effort is in the savings produced. These savings may result from the modification of present methods, the introduction of new handling methods or equipment, or the elimination of unnecessary operations. Ideas for cost savings projects come from many directions; however, the most fruitful source is usually the materials handling engineer himself. If properly selected, this individual should be sufficiently industrious and creative to generate a constant stream of projects of his own undertaking. If these are bona fide cost savings efforts, they will provide a sense of accomplishment within the individual and be pursued even more diligently because of their pride of origin.

Suggestions for cost savings projects are frequently obtained from the materials handling engineer's immediate chain of command. Having broader experience, these supervisors can often pinpoint areas for savings without having expended preliminary investigative effort. Nevertheless, the materials handling group should have contacts in all other departments, and in turn, should be readily approachable by these other departments.

Some of the more substantial cost savings may be realized in departments other than manufacturing or distribution, but can only be implemented within the manufacturing or distribution departments. Therefore, the MH group should serve as a sounding board to the other departments, in order to develop the least total cost of materials handling.

Furthermore, the plant manager should find the materials handling group an invaluable source for experimentation and validation of new materials handling concepts. Often the plant manager alone must weigh the merits of several cost savings projects, and he must decide where to exert the most influence so that the largest savings will be realized in the shortest time.

Next, let us take methods improvement. In the press of the daily routine, the line processor is often forced or pressured into duplicating the same processing utilized on a previously processed part, instead of being innovative and initiating a new method of handling in manufacturing. This is a normal and not unusual circumstance. The line processor seldom concerns himself with: the materials handling equipment to be used; the kind of container or lifting equipment to be used; the location of one machine with respect to another; or the flow path of parts being processed.

New methods of materials handling can seldom be installed without diligent application of prior experimentation, or study, or both. Obviously, the line processor cannot cover this field of endeavor and still get his daily work done. Therefore, the processor should work with the MHE, and vice versa. In order to be most effective, the materials handling engineer must keep pace with the changing world of technology. By reading technical literature and by attending seminars and technical conferences, the materials handling engineer should, generally, be aware of the capabilities and limitations of new methods and equipment as they are exposed to his understanding and capabilities. Thus, in working together with the line processor, he can be productive and help generate cost savings in the application of new techniques. Also, he must have a certain amount of experience in the manufacturing areas that he serves; and, above all, he must have the capability of using his powers of observation. Properly dedicated to the task, the materials handling engineer working with the line processors can install materials handling improvements as rapidly as the various projects can be assimilated by the departments concerned, provided he has the backing and full support of the plant management staff.

A properly selected materials handling group is a storehouse of materials handling experience and technical knowledge. The members of the group should be available to all departments and to all plants for their exploitation.

The processing and layout planning departments should be able to make extremely advantageous use of members of such a group. Also, the purchasing and inspection departments should call on the materials handling engineer to supply packaging information and inspection procedures for packing whenever a new, purchased-finished part is to be received.

In the areas of physical distribution, the materials handling engineer who specializes in packaging, or the packaging engineer assigned to this group, would have the responsibility of establishing standards.

III. TRAINING

The optimum materials handling group is comprised of a mixture of experienced materials handling practitioners and young, college-trained, industrial engineers. An equitable promotion ladder should be the incentive within the organizational structure for a maximum exchange of information, with all of the individual strengths focused on problem areas, each forte supplementing the others.

A high turnover rate in a group of this type is normal. It should be considered from two aspects, however. Personnel moving from such a group into other activities within the plant carry with them knowledge and experience that can be gained in no other way. It gives them a valuable advantage in their new jobs, especially in the manufacturing area.

On the other hand, excessive turnover in the materials handling group will render the group impotent and incapable of showing significant cost savings or other achievements. Depending on the size of the group, a turnover rate of 10 to 25% annually should be practiced. A higher turnover is an indication of a bleeding of the group and may well defeat its purpose, from the standpoint of both future training and other materials handling functions.

IV. MAINTENANCE

The maintenance of mobile materials handling equipment and the allocation and control of handling equipment throughout the plant should also be a functional responsibility of the materials handling department.

In the above paragraphs, the logic of this management strategem is based upon an integration of related functions; in some plants, however, functional responsibilities are sometimes divided, and usually there is a redundancy between operations and operators that contributes to a high cost of manufacturing and distribution.

Also, automotive or mobile equipment maintenance in most plants comes under the aegis of plant engineering. Often the wheel that squeaks the loudest receives the grease, and the department that makes the loudest outcry or carries the most weight has its equipment serviced more promptly than another, sometimes at a disadvantage in cost or schedules. Even when maintenance costs continue to rise, as in most companies, the maintenance function doesn't have as much trouble obtaining funding as other departments—only because nobody takes the time to analyze maintenance costs properly.

V. PLANT ORGANIZATIONAL STRUCTURE

A. General Approach to Organization

Now, let us discuss briefly the subject of organizing the plant or warehouse structure to obtain the most value from a systems approach to materials handling. In order to achieve the most effective materials handling performance within the broad limits of the company complex, it is necessary, as we have already said, that an organizational structure be developed.

As to the type of organizational structure, materials handling work can be carried out under a number of organizational plans. For example, at one company in which I worked, all materials handling engineers were under the planning manager, with one exception: in one plant, the materials handling man reported directly to the plant engineer. Actually, it is not too important to whom the materials handling engineer reports, but the greatest and most substantial progress can be made, in terms of cost savings, when the materials handling engineer in each plant is on the same level as the planning manager, or the material control manager. What is extremely important, however, is to have the complete responsibility for the flow of materials and in-process parts from the source to the customer. This total responsibility makes it possible to achieve the systems efficiency needed to obtain the least total cost of materials handling in the company.

The greatest danger to the materials handling program occurs when the materials handling engineers are utilized as "handy" people to fill in busy areas and to put out fires. This type of interruption generally hampers the MH program and results in relative ineffectiveness.

Therefore, in order to perform effectively, the materials handling group has to work closely with other planning and material control activities. In fact, there are very few areas or activities within a company that do not in some way impinge on the materials handling area, or vice versa. Ideally, a materials handling engineer should be assigned specific areas and departments within the plant. For example, one MHE or group should handle shipping, receiving, yard storage, packaging functions, and export shipping. Another MHE or group should handle work-in-process, finished worked material, assembly storage, purchased-finished movement, containers, and work station arrangements. Another MHE or group could handle steel storage and weld stores functions, reclamation, mobile equipment allocation, maintenance and selection, interplant transportation, debris removal, and ecological factors. Another MHE or group could handle all crating and shipping of prime product, paint systems, prime product painting, tote and container maintenance (that is, cleaning and painting), and container accountability.

The above assignment of responsibilities would permit the MHE to become intimately aware of the problems and potential for cost improvement in his area, especially since each of the manufacturing superintendents, layout planners, and line processors would recognize the individual MHE as a source of information.

Furthermore, if all plants had this type of materials handling organization, a breed of specialists would be developed who would soon become the backbone of a "systems-oriented" materials handling program. This type of intensively trained individual could be of great value in planning new plants and plant modifications. We should not leave this subject without saying that when the size of the plant warrants at least two or more people in the materials handling program, it is best to appoint a working supervisor who has specific MH assignments in addition to the task of supervising other MHE's. In the smaller companies, of course, one materials handling engineer may wear many hats, and his task becomes a very challenging one in which priorities may dictate every move he makes. Nevertheless, a systems approach is absolutely necessary regardless of plant size.

B. Perpetuation of the MH Program

Now, let us discuss the perpetuation of the materials handling program, looking at the larger picture and projecting the image of materials handling five to ten years into the future. The supervisory materials handling engineer in the larger manufacturing plants will have the same status as is presently accorded the planning and tooling manager, if he does not already enjoy this status. The possibility also exists that as the importance of materials handling increases in the profit squeezes of the future, the focus of materials handling will be on a truly integrated system of materials management. Present material control functions probably will have been integrated into the materials handling department, and the flow of material from source to customer will come under intensive scrutiny and surveillance to obtain the least total cost of handling.

As the materials handling group make better and more extensive use of computers and new techniques like MRP II, their stature and credibility in the manufacturing or distribution environment will continue to increase. In conjunction with the use of the new tools and the applications of the principles of materials handling and management developed in this text, periodic reports should be transmitted to top management. These reports should show the savings and cost avoidance that the materials handling practitioner has accomplished. A quarterly or semiannual report of real accomplishment will serve to perpetuate the MH group and will establish the viability of the program.

First, how are savings measured? There should be an established procedure for doing this—for example, an R.O.I. (a return on investment analysis), or a comparable accounting device such as the Machinery and Allied Products Institute (MAPI) formula, or the like—that standardizes the procedure. The mechanism for measuring savings would proceed in this manner:

Each materials handling engineer justifies the initiation of a project based upon expected savings. As a follow-up, he then prepares measurement data after the project has been installed and is producing savings. These data are screened by each plant's accounting department for the validity of the claims. Because standard accounting principles are used to determine cost benefits, there is definite comparability between plants, that is, the measure of cost savings effectiveness due to improvements in materials handling. Even more important is the capability each plant develops for gauging its own effectiveness against a very reliable yardstick, and that is the amount of cost savings it can generate from period to period.

Let us recapitulate the standard. In the beginning of this chapter it was suggested that it should be reasonable to expect to employ one MHE for every 850 persons in total plant employment. I shall go somewhat further and say that materials handling engineers who are employed solely in cost savings projects could readily return $70,000 annually before taxes, or an after-tax savings of approximately $35,000 per man in most companies.

Using the above cost savings measure, we indicate that we intend to save a certain sum each year through materials handling improvements. This then places a relative numerical control on the staffing pattern, and we thus allocate men for the several specific functional responsibilities within the company.

VI. SUMMARY

We are now off and running, but the important question is how do we keep the train on the track, and, more important, how do we keep up the head of steam we need for the proper momentum of the materials handling program?

I have found the following general plan to be useful, and within its very broad limits, it can be varied considerably. For example, the activity or "action" within the total program can be shifted from time to time to concentrate on different areas where work is most urgently needed—keeping in mind that the work that is receiving the new emphasis was part of the overall system-oriented program, but has been time-phased somewhat differently from the way it was originally scheduled.

Basically, the major mechanisms of any systems-oriented materials handling program are materials handling equipment and standardization. These two large areas are tied together by means of centralized coordination; that is, it is necessary to focus or concentrate coordination in one individual who is corporately responsible for the direction and guidance of the total materials handling program. As President Truman said, "The buck stops here."

Within each of the two major areas there are subgroups with the following composition. Under materials handling equipment we would have: accounting liaison and data processing; parts distribution and supply liaison; equipment maintenance; equipment selection; equipment replacement; training; safety; and equipment utilization. Under the heading of standardization, we would have the following subgroups: supplier load sizes; manufacturing material handling containers; suppliers' captive containers; pallets; and storage aids.

By setting up the two functional areas so that they are operating committees, you can keep the momentum of the program fairly well under control. These two major committees, then, provide the kind of interfunctional participation that the systems approach demands, and, in addition, provide the planning background that must be obtained to forecast materials handling projects and progress one, two, three, or five years into the future.

Since the basis of the systems approach is to consider all of the factors that affect the system, it is important to focus all of the company's in-house strength on those functions whose work affects and is affected by materials handling.

In each of the two committees you can have two different groups of people. One group in each committee should be composed of the materials handling engineers from the functional areas within the plant. The other group in each committee should include a number of corporate staff people who represent such functions as: purchasing; manufacturing development; accounting; factory planning; and so forth. The contacts made during the committee meetings and in working on special assignments and projects bring people with diverse interests and functional responsibilities together, and permit the materials handling engineers to obtain a better knowledge of the way other departments operate, and vice versa. In addition, this makes it a lot easier for the materials handling engineer to cut across departmental lines and thus to get a better grasp of the concept of least total cost through systems engineering techniques.

The committees should meet regularly to review project progress and to study proposals for new areas of work, to assign projects to subgroups, and to recommend action required by specific departments. They should review new procedures, standards, and projects upon which the subcommittees have reached agreement.

It must be realized that because this is essentially a materials handling program, the materials handling engineers should, or ordinarily would, do most of the work. This may not always be the case, however, because in some projects data processing programming, or the like, may be the larger part of the task, and the materials handling engineer would, in these instances, act as advisor and counselor. For the most part, however, you will find that the representatives from the other essentially non-material-handling departments will act as the advisors, consultants, and coordinators with and for their departments.

Materials handling know-how and understanding thus can be diffused to the parts of the company where this sympathetic understanding will do the most good. The materials handling engineer then acquires "a friend in court" when it comes time to enlist the assistance of these other departments.

As another means of promoting this understanding, department heads should be asked to select individuals from their departments to serve on the materials handling committees.

An additional feature of the committee method which seems to work fairly well is to group the committee work into three phases:

Phase I: There is a general discussion of the problem when it is first proposed.

Phase II: The members of the committee supply progress reports on the problem at each meeting until it is completed. Also, during Phase II, they may make individual contributions, offer suggestions and criticisms, and so forth.

Phase III: The committee members help prepare and review the final recommendations.

There you have a basic plan for organizing materials handiing based on a systems-oriented philosophy. We have divided the plant or company into functional areas, and we have placed responsibilities for these areas under a materials handling engineer or a group of materials handling engineers. Then, we have organized the essentially non-materials-handling groups in such a fashion that within the two major areas of materials handling there are both materials handling engineers and non-materials-handling engineers, who, in total, represent all of the materials management subgroups of the plant or company.

You may ask at this point, what about the tools used in systems engineering? Where do they come in? Well, in shooting for the objective of the least total cost of materials handling, you have to use, on occasion, all of the tools and techniques that are currently available and pertinent—such tools as systems simulation, MRP II, and the like—and hope that you can budget for enough computer programming and machine time to give you the information you are trying to obtain. But, on the other hand, it is not always necessary to require computer assistance on some small-scale simulation problems; many other methods and means are available today.

EXERCISE NO. 19

1. Do you feel that you can have and maintain a good materials handling department effort without management support? Please explain, briefly, why you can (or cannot). ____________________

2. If you were in charge of materials handling in a corporate office, upon what areas of MH would you concentrate? (Explain why you would establish these priorities, if possible.) ____________________

3. Do you maintain a record of MH savings accomplishments? (If yes, explain why, if possible.) ____________________

4. Does your materials handling effort encompass the packaging area? (If no, please explain, if possible, the reasons for this.)

5. Have you done any training in the MH area? (If yes, please explain what you have done in this area, if possible.)

6. Do you feel that a high turnover rate in the materials handling department is reasonable? (If yes, please explain what you mean, if possible.)

7. In what department should the MH people be located?
Can you explain why you think so?

8. Do you feel that the functional responsibility for the maintenance of mobile MH equipment should be in the MH department? (Please explain, if possible.)

9. Would you establish goals or quotas for savings if you had the opportunity?
Yes ☐ No ☐ (Please explain your answer.)

____

____

10. Would you establish priorities for MH projects and time schedules for accomplishment if you had the opportunity to do so? Yes ☐ No ☐ (Please explain your answer if possible.)

____

____

____

____

____

____

____

____

____

Chapter 20
Presenting Materials Handling Projects to Management

A. Introduction

It is not sufficient for the materials handling practitioner to say, "Here, I have solved my problem and put this project together—this is the solution." Would management buy this solution? Is the solution, of and by itself, sufficient reason to obtain management's approval? You and I know the answer is no. We know that we have to prepare a presentation properly and then hope it gets the desired results.

Similarly, I wish I could tell you a single concise way to organize your presentation; what to include; how to present your report; and how to secure management's approval. I cannot, because there are so many factors that determine the best approach.

The very fact that you and I, and your management staff, are people capable of responding to many different stimuli makes *one absolutely certain approach* extremely difficult to derive.

You are in the business of problem solving. And you're darned good at it, too. But, to identify and solve problems is not enough. If we believe in our assignment and our recommendations, then we have a further responsibility—to find a way to communicate our findings and motivate management to *act* on our recommendations. If we are not smart enough to help our management buy our recommendations, we have failed them. We must share the responsibility of a negative answer, or the pleasures of an affirmative one.

We all want our plans to be accepted; so in the next few pages we'll try to put it all together. These thoughts are based on experiences gained in years of making presentations to management. Not all of the presentations were successful, but many were. The ones that failed to survive failed, not so much by virtue of content, but by conflicts of management personalities that doomed a very small number of presentations from their beginning.

B. How to Organize Your Presentation

1. Establish your objectives for the presentation.
   - Be practical in your expectations.
2. Know your audience.

- Know how they think!
- Who will attend?
- What are their interests?
- What motivates them?
- Who is the key individual?
- Does he have any special interests?
- Who will have the greatest influence on the decisions?
- Do not embarrass anyone!

3. Don't be so presumptuous as to believe that everything important to you will be enthusiastically received by your audience. People (management) buy ideas for many reasons. We would like to believe that we can make all purchasing decisions on good facts and sound judgment. No so. Decisions may be based on:
   a. Past experience.
   b. Romance.
   c. What competition is doing—"they can't be completely foolish."
   d. Desire to impress stockholders.
   e. Desire to impress customers with an image of progress—a forward-looking company.
   f. "Too many people problems."
   g. "Must gear up for next boom."
   h. Need to reduce costs.
   i. Need to increase capacity.
   j. Expectation that government will demand major plant safety improvements.
   k. Poor labor market.
   l. Difficult labor/management relationship.
   m. Safety.
   n. Desire to improve profit potential.
   o. Need for increased flexibility, to remove a bottleneck.
4. Develop a presentation control plan—to control your audience.
   - Chart your presentation to end on a high note.
   - Determine highs and plan around them.
5. Consider time and timing.
   - How much time do you have?
   - Can you influence the selection of time of day and day of week? What is best at your company?
   - Are there any other major decisions developing at this time? If so, try to avoid them.
6. Decide how complete the presentation should be.
   - Overprepare.
   - Anticipate.

- Put yourself in management's shoes. What would you be looking for?
- Be concise.

7. Develop a management overview:
   - Objectives.
   - Recommendations.
   - Action plan.
8. Distribute reports a few days prior to the meeting. Give management a chance to say yes!!
9. Consider how long you have been working on this project. Have you left behind someone who isn't updated?

C. What to Include

1. Project objectives—priority list.
2. Parameters.
3. Needs (developed).
4. Opportunities the project offers.
5. Hard and soft benefits:
   - Economic/R.O.I.
   - Other.
6. Pro and con considerations.
7. Development of ideas.
8. Recommendations.
   - Allow a way out.
   - Do not trap yourself into getting a "no" answer. Allow room for possible alternatives.
9. Results and benefits as a range, rather than specific. Be conservative by not claiming immediate results.
10. Master plan with modular expansion.
11. List of existing problems.
12. Similar installations.
13. Your preferred vendor's reputation, resources, people, and experience to assist in selling.
14. Preparation for everything—anticipate; do *not* assume.
15. Description of system features and characteristics:
    a. Operating capacity.
    b. Initial cost and operating costs.
    c. Space savings.
    d. System availability.
    e. Manageability.
    f. Flexibility.

g. Responsiveness.
h. Expandability.
i. Labor force—numbers and skills required.
j. Economic justification.
k. Avoidance of capital investment—if applicable.

16. Statement that you can continue to operate well during installation.

D. How to Present the Report

1. Prepare a professional presentation—no matter how small the project. Let your management know that you respect them and appreciate their valuable time.
2. As briefly as possible, give the management overview. Consider the following (giving good news first):
   a. Objectives.
   b. Findings/conclusions.
   c. Recommendations—$.
   d. Questions and answers.
   e. Commitment required.
   f. Action plan/schedule.
3. Use ample graphics. Minimize or eliminate the use of engineering drawings or prints. Use perspectives or pictures. Consider the use of movies, video tape, or slides or similar systems or functions, to add credibility to your ideas.
4. Present the big picture. Stay above details (you must know them) unless and until management wants to get into this kind of discussion.
5. Stay in control.
6. Use a minimum of written communication in the presentation.
7. What does management want? Put yourself in their shoes.

E. How to Get Management Approval

1. *Pre-sell*—before the presentation, with personal visits, etc.
2. Be convinced of your recommendations.
3. Give management a chance to approve.
   - Do not ask management to do the impossible, and do not expect them to do your work.
   - Place them in a position of making decisions—not solving problems.
4. Relate the pending decision to time, cost, and results.
5. Tell why we should make this decision, and what happens if we don't.
6. Ask for the commitment and involvement of management.

7. *If possible, do not let the meeting disband without specific dates, people, etc., to continue.*

As a last word of advice, the name of the game is to sell yourself and your ideas, but sell the ideas in such a manner that they are developed in consort with management, as though they were management ideas. In short: *Sell!*

Appendices

Appendices

Appendix A
Source Materials for Packaging, Carrier Regulations, and Materials Handling

PUBLICATION	APPROXIMATE PRICE
Uniform Freight Classification (UFC) "Ratings, Rules and Regulations" J. D. Sherson, Tariff Publishing Officer Room 1106, 222 South Riverside Plaza Chicago, Illinois 60606	$15.00
National Motor Freight Classification (NMFC) "Classes and Rules" H. J. Sonnenberg, Issuing Officer 1616 P Street, N.W. Washington, D.C. 20036	$15.00
Hazardous Materials Regulation of the Department of Transportation including "Specifications for Shipping Containers" Issued by: R. M. Graziano, Agent 1920 L Street, N.W. Washington, D.C. 20036	$15.00
Material Handling Engineering Handbook and Directory Published by: Industrial Publishing Co. 614 Superior Avenue West Cleveland, Ohio 44113	$20.00
Motor Carriers' Explosives and Dangerous Articles Issued by: American Trucking Association, Inc. 1616 P Street, N.W. Washington, D.C. 20036	$11.00
Official Air Transport Restricted Articles Issued by: Airline Tariff Publishers, Inc. 1825 K Street, N.W. Washington, D.C. 20006	$ 2.50
Modern Packaging Encyclopedia Published by: McGraw-Hill, Inc. 330 West 42nd Street New York, New York 10036	$10.00

(Annual encyclopedia is included free with one-year subscription to the regular monthly publication *Modern Packaging Magazine.*)

Federal specifications on the following containers can be obtained at no charge* through local U.S. government (General Services Administration) offices, or from:

Superintendent of Documents
U.S. Government Printing Office
Washington, D.C. 20402

CONTAINER TITLE	FEDERAL SPECIFICATION NUMBER	
Box, Fiberboard	PPP-B-636	No charge
Boxes, Fiberboard Corrugated, Triple-Wall	PPP-B-640	No charge
Boxes, Wood, Nailed	PPP-B-621	No charge
Boxes, Wood, Wirebound	PPP-B-585	No charge
Boxes, Wood, Wirebound Pallet Type	PPP-B-587	No charge
Crates, Wood, Open and Covered	PPP-C-650	No charge

Several prominent and widely read monthly publications on packaging and materials handling are listed below for information and reference:

Publication	Approximate Price
Package Engineering 5 South Wabash Avenue Chicago, Illinois 60606	$10.00
Modern Packaging (Includes *Modern Packaging Annual Encyclopedia*) 1221 Avenue of the Americas New York, New York 10020	$10.00
Package Development 169 Scarborough Road Briarcliff Manor, New York 10510	$10.00
Handling & Shipping The Industrial Publishing Co. 614 Superior Avenue West Cleveland, Ohio 44113	$12.00
Material Handling Engineering The Industrial Publishing Co. 614 Superior Avenue West Cleveland, Ohio 44113	$12.00
Modern Material Handling Cahners Publishing Co. 221 Columbus Avenue Boston, Massachusetts 02116	Controlled circulation or available at $18.00 annually

**Index of Federal Specification and Standards* (including most basic types of containers and component packaging materials) is $7.50 from the Superintendent of Documents.

Each member of the International Materials Management Society automatically receives a regular subscription to the *Modern Materials Handling* magazine as a membership benefit.)

PUBLICATION	APPROXIMATE PRICE
ASTM Standards: Part 15 (Packaging Materials & Container Testing Methods) American Society for Testing and Materials 1916 Race Street Philadelphia, Pennsylvania 19103	$36.50
Fibre Box Handbook Published by: Fibre Box Association 224 S. Michigan Ave. Chicago, Illinois 60604 (Available only through local-member fibre box suppliers) Contents: Box styles, interior packaging forms, closures, etc., are illustrated and described Carrier regulations, motor, rail, air, express, parcel post, and miscellaneous important requirements are extracted from the various carrier publications and listed in this *excellent handbook*.	No charge
Pallets and Palletization (a handbook on wooden pallet construction and usage) and *Wooden Pallet Containers & Container Systems* (a handbook on pallet container construction and usage) National Wooden Pallet & Container Association 1619 Massachusetts Avenue, N.W. Washington, D.C. 20036	$ 3.40
Wirebound Boxes, Crates and Pallet Boxes and *Wirebound Pallet Boxes* Wirebound Box Manufacturers Association 1211 West 22nd Street Oak Brook, Illinois 60525	No charge
A Guide to Good Construction of Nailed Wooden Boxes, Bulletin No. 102, and *The A-B-C of Good Crating,* Bulletin No. 101 Issued by: Association of American Railroads Freight Loss and Damage Prevention Section Freight Loading and Container Bureau 59 East Van Buren Street Chicago, Illinois 60605	No charge

Appendix B
National Organizations for the Issuing of Standards

American National Standards Institute (ANSI)
1430 Broadway
New York, New York 10018

National Fire Protection Association (NFPA)
470 Atlantic Avenue
Boston, Mass. 02210

American Society of Mechanical Engineers, Inc. (ASME)
United Engineering Center
345 East 47th Street
New York, New York 10017

Underwriters' Laboratories, Inc.
207 East Ohio Street
Chicago, Illinois 60611

American Society for Testing & Materials (ASTM)
1916 Race Street
Philadelphia, Pennsylvania 19103

Appendix C
OSHA, Sources of Standards

SEC.	SOURCE
1910.176	41 CFR 50-204.3
1910.177	NFPA No. 231-1970, General Indoor Storage
1910.178 (a) (1)	NFPA No. 505-1969, Powered Industrial Trucks
1910.178 (a) (2)	ANSI B56.1-1969, Standard for Powered Industrial Trucks, Part II
1910.178 (a) (3)	NFPA No. 505-1969, Powered Industrial Trucks
1910.178 (a) (4)–(7)	ANSI B56.1-1969, Standard for Powered Industrial Trucks
1910.178 (b)–(d)	NFPA No. 505-1969, Powered Industrial Trucks
1910.178 (e)–(p)	ANSI B56.1-1969, Powered Industrial Trucks
1910.178 (q)	NFPA No. 505-1969, Powered Industrial Trucks
1910.179	ANSI B30.2.0-1967, Safety Code for Overhead and Gantry Cranes
1910.180	ANSI B30.5-1968, Safety Code for Crawler, Locomotive and Truck Cranes
1910.181	ANSI B30.6-1969, Safety Code for Derricks

(39FR 23502, June 27, 1974. Redesignated as 40 FR 13441, March 26, 1975.)

Appendix D
Storage Rack Design Standards

Rack Manufacturers' Institute
1326 Freeport Road
Pittsburgh, Pennsylvania 15238
"Interim Specification for the Design, Testing and Utilization of Steel Storage Racks"
(single copies free)

International Conference of Building Officials
5360 South Mills Road
Whittier, California 90695
"Uniform Building Code"
($12.50 each copy)

National Fire Protection Association
470 Atlantic Avenue
Boston, Massachusetts 02110
"Standard for Rack Storage of Materials, NFPA-231C-1973"
($1.75 each copy)

American National Standards Institute, Inc.
1430 Broadway
New York, New York 10018
"ANSI MH16.1" ($6.00 each copy)
"Specifications for the Design, Testing, and Utilization of Storage Racks"

American Iron and Steel Institute (AISI)
150 E. 42nd Street
New York, New York 10017
"Design of Cold-Formed Steel Structural Members"

American Institute of Steel Construction (AISC)
101 Park Avenue
New York, New York 10017
"Specification for the Design, Fabrication and Erection of Structural Steel for Buildings"

Appendix E
Members of the Rack Manufacturers' Institute

American Steel Building Co., Inc.
American Steel Products Div.
12218 Robin Blvd., P.O. Box 14244
Houston, TX 77221
(713) 433-5661

Artco Corporation
Penn Avenue
Hatfield, PA 19440
(215) 723-6041

Broad Corporation
7445 Allen Road
Allen Park, Michigan 48101
(313) 388-5800

Buckhorn, Inc.
Materials Handling Group
Storage Products Div.
10605 Chester Road
Cincinnati, OH 45215
(513) 772-1313

Buckley Corporation
175 Union Street
Rockland, Massachusetts 02370
(617) 871-0700

Burtman Iron Works, Inc.
59 Sprague Street
Readville, MA 02137
(617) 364-1200

D'Altrui Industries
685 U.S. Highway #1
P.O. Box 902
Elizabeth, NJ 07207
(201) 351-8900

Engineered Products
P.O. Box 6767
Greenville, SC 29606
(803) 967-7951

Frazier Industrial Company
P.O. Box F, Fairview Ave.
Long Valley, NJ 07853
(201) 876-3001

The Frick-Gallagher Mfg. Co.
201 S. Michigan Ave.
Wellston, OH 45692
(614) 384-2121

Frontier Manufacturing Company
9910 Monroe Drive
Dallas, TX 75220
(214) 350-1313

Hartman Material Handling Systems
P.O. Box 231
Waterloo, NY 13165
(315) 539-9256

Husky Storage Systems, Inc.
9111 Nevada Ave.
Cleveland, OH 44104
(216) 368-0301

Inca Metal Products Corporation
P.O. Box 897, One Inca Place
Lewisville, TX 75067
(214) 436-5581

Interlake, Inc.
100 Tower Drive
Burr Ridge, IL 60521
(312) 789-0333

Keneco, Inc.
660 N. Michigan Ave.
Kenilworth, NJ 07033
(201) 241-3700

The Kingston-Warren Corporation
Route 85
Newfields, NH 03856
(603) 772-3771

Lok-Rak Corporation of America
P.O. Box 8267, 71 George St.
East Hartford, Connecticut 06108
(203) 289-4391

Nestaway, A Bliss & Laughlin Industry
9501 Granger Road
Cleveland, OH 44125
(216) 587-1500

Paltier Division/Lyon Metal
Products, Inc.
1701 Kentucky St.
Michigan City, IN 46360
(219) 872-7238

Penco Products, Inc.
Brower Avenue
Oaks, PA 19456
(215) 666-0500

Rack Engineering Company
Sixth Street
Connellsville, PA 15425
(412) 628-8400

Republic Steel Corporation
Storage Rack Division
1315 Albert Street
Youngstown, OH 44505
(216) 742-6005

Ridg-U-Rak, Inc.
120 South Lake Street
North East, PA 16428
(814) 725-8751

Sammons & Sons
2911 Norton Avenue
P.O. Box 309
Lynwood, CA 90262
(213) 636-2488

Sempco, Inc.
201 N. 8th Street
P.O. Box 7
West Branch, Michigan 48661
(517) 345-2750

Speedrack Incorporated
5300 Golf Road
P.O. Box 163
Skokie, IL 60077
(312) 966-5100

SPS Technologies, Automated Systems Div.
Township Line Road
Hatfield, PA 19440
(215) 721-2100

Steel King Industries, Inc.
2700 Chamber Street
Stevens Point, WI 54481
(715) 341-3120

Stor-Dynamics Corporation
99 Main Avenue
Elmwood Park, NJ 07407
(201) 791-1800

Teilhaber Manufacturing Corporation
2685 Industrial Lane
Broomfield, Colorado 80020
(303) 466-2323

Tier-Rack Corporation
706 Chestnut Street
St. Louis, Missouri 63101
(314) 241-5451

Unarco Materials Storage/
A UNR Company
332 S. Michigan Avenue
Chicago, IL 60604
(312) 341-1234

United Steel Products Company
10 Park Avenue
East Orange, NJ 07019
(201) 482-2086

Jervis B. Webb Company
Storage Products Division
Webb Drive
Farmington Hills, Michigan 48018
(313) 553-1000

Warehouse Storage Systems Company
Hi-Line Drive & Ridge Road
Perkasie, PA 18944
(215) 257-3601

Wisconsin Bridge & Iron Company
5023 North 35th Street
Milwaukee, Wisconsin 53209
(414) 466-2100

Appendix F
The Material Handling Institute

The Material Handling Institute, Inc. (MHI) is composed of a membership of over 350 firms in the materials handling equipment industry. The MHI promotes the education and training of materials handling practitioners through literature, trade shows, conferences, and financial grants for the conduct of institutes and seminars for materials handling teachers.

To receive a free copy of the most recent MHI literature catalog, contact:

Literature Department
The Material Handling Institute, Inc.
1326 Freeport Road
Pittsburgh, Pennsylvania 15238

Appendix G
Supplier Information

For your convenience in obtaining further information the names, phone numbers, and addresses of suppliers of some of the items mentioned in the text are listed below:

Air-Film Pallets

Aero-Go, Incorporated
1170 Andover Park West
Seattle, Washington 98188
(206) 575-3344

Airfloat Corporation
1550 McBride Avenue
Decatur, Illinois 62526
(217) 422-8365

Rolair Systems, Incorporated
P.O. Box 30363
Santa Barbara, California 93105
(805) 968-1536

Bar Coding Equipment and Labels

Avery Label
An Avery International Company
777 East Foothill Boulevard
Azusa, California 91702
(213) 969-3311

Compucon, Incorporated
P.O. Box 401229
Dallas, Texas 75240
(214) 233-4380

Computer Identics Corporation
31 Dartmouth Street
Westwood, Massachusetts 02090
(617) 329-1980

Dennison Manufacturing Company
300 Howard Street
Framingham, Massachusetts 01701
(617) 879-0511

Identicon Corporation
Subsidiary of Ferranti-Packard Limited
1 Kenwood Circle
Franklin, Massachusetts 02038
(617) 528-6500

Intermec Corporation
4405 Russell Road
Lynnwood, Washington 98036
(206) 743-7036

Logisticon, Incorporated
350 Potrero Avenue
Sunnyvale, California 94086
(408) 732-0441

Markem Corporation
Scanmark Division
150 Congress
Keene, New Hampshire 03431
(603) 352-1130

SPS Technologies Automated Systems
Township Line Road
Hatfield, Pennsylvania 19440
(918) 664-2200

Skan-A-Matic Corporation
P.O. Box S
Elbridge, New York 13060
(315) 689-3961

Bin Flow Racks

Frick-Gallagher Manufacturing Company
201 South Michigan Avenue
Wellston, Ohio 45692
(614) 384-2121

Hytrol Conveyor Company, Incorporated
2020 Hytrol Street
Jonesboro, Arkansas 72401
(501) 935-3700

The Kingston-Warren Corporation
Kingway Division
100 Foundry Street
Newfields, New Hampshire 03856
(603) 772-3771

Kornylak Corporation
400 Heaton Street
Hamilton, Ohio 45011
(513) 863-1277

Penco Products, Incorporated
Subsidiary of Vesper Corporation
Brower Avenue
Oaks, Pennsylvania 19456
(215) 666-0500

Teilhaber Manufacturing Corporation
P.O. Box 366
Broomfield, Colorado 80020
(303) 466-2323

Bin Shelving and Mezzanines

Equipto Company
225 South Highland Avenue
Aurora, Illinois 60507
(312) 859-1000
(800) 323-0801

Lyon Metal Products, Incorporated
101 Montgomery Street
Aurora, Illinois 60507
(312) 892-8941

Stanley-Vidmar Company
Division of the Stanley Works
11 Grammes Road
Allentown, Pennsylvania 18103
(215) 797-6600

Teilhaber Manufacturing Corporation
P.O. Box 366
Broomfield, Colorado 80020
(303) 466-2323

Bulk Handling Equipment

Butler Manufacturing Company
Bolted Tank Group
7400 East 13th Street
Kansas City, Missouri 64126
(816) 968-6205

A. O. Smith Harvestore Products, Incorporated
Industrial Sales Department
550 West Algonquin Road
Arlington Heights, Illinois 60005
(312) 439-1530

Computers and Controls

Ann Arbor Computer Company
Division of Jervis B. Webb Company
1201 East Ellsworth Street
Ann Arbor, Michigan 48104
(313) 761-2151

Containers

Cargotainer Division
Tri-State Engineering Company
1480 Jefferson Street
P.O. Box 509
Washington, Pennsylvania 15301
(412) 222-3300

Morton Metalcraft Company
Route 98W
Morton, Illinois 61550
(309) 267-7176

NVF Company
Container Division
Box 160
Kennett Square, Pennsylvania 19348
(215) 444-2800

Nestier Corporation
10605 Chester Road
Cincinnati, Ohio 45215
(513) 772-1313

Portage Industries Corporation
1325 Adams Street
Portage, Wisconsin 53901
(608) 742-7123

Powell Pressed Steel Company
500 Erie Street
Hubbard, Ohio 44425
(216) 534-1133

Rubbermaid Commercial Products, Incorporated
3124 Valley Avenue
Winchester, Virginia 22601
(703) 667-8700

Steel King Industries, Incorporated
2700 Chamber Street
Stevens Point, Wisconsin 54481
(715) 341-3120

Streator Dependable Company
410 W. Broadway Street
Streator, Illinois 61364
(815) 672-0551

Conveyors

Alvey, Incorporated
9297 Olive Boulevard
St. Louis, Missouri 63132
(314) 993-4700

A. J. Bayer Company
Subsidiary of Interlake, Incorporated
Material Handling & Storage Products Division
P.O. Box 276
Shepherdsville, Kentucky 40165
(502) 957-6521

The E. W. Buschman Company
4429 Clifton Avenue
Cincinnati, Ohio 45232
(513) 681-1600

CM Chain
Division of Columbus McKinnon Corporation
Audubon and Sylvan Parkways
Amherst, New York 14228
(716) 696-3500

Economy Engineering Company
484 Thomas Drive
Bennsenville, Illinois 60106
(312) 860-3460

Kornylak Corporation
400 Heaton Street
Hamilton, Ohio 45011
(513) 863-1277

Logan Company
A Figgie International Company
P.O. Box 6107
Louisville, Kentucky 40206
(502) 587-1361

Materials Handling Equipment Division
Jervis B. Webb Company
2619 N. Normandy Avenue
Chicago, Illinois 60635
(312) 889-1670

Mayfran International
A Division of Fischer Industries
P.O. Box 43038
Cleveland, Ohio 44143
(216) 461-4100

Metzgar Conveyor Company, Incorporated
901 Metzgar Drive N.W.
Comstock Park, Michigan 49321
(616) 784-0930

Norfolk Conveyor Division
Jervis B. Webb Company
155 King Street, Route 3A
Cohasset, Massachusetts 02025
(617) 383-9400

Prab Conveyors, Inc.
5944 E. Kilgore Road
Kalamazoo, Michigan 49003
(616) 349-8761

Rapistan Division
Lear Siegler, Incorporated
825 Rapistan Building
Grand Rapids, Michigan 49505
(616) 451-6525

Rexnord, Incorporated
P.O. Box 2022
Milwaukee, Wisconsin 53201
(414) 643-3000

Richards Wilcox Manufacturing Company
430 Third Street
Aurora, Illinois 60507
(312) 897-6951

SI Handling Systems, Incorporated
Easton, Pennsylvania 18042
(215) 252-7321

Taylor & Gaskin, Incorporated
Conveyor Systems Division
6440 Mack Avenue
Detroit, Michigan 48207
(313) 925-9550

Jervis B. Webb Company
Webb Drive
Farmington Hills, Michigan 48018
(313) 553-1220

Z-Loda Corporation
Harp Road
P.O. Box 503
Canastota, New York 13032
(315) 697-3911

Corrugated Steel Tote Boxes

Powell Pressed Steel Company
500 Erie Street
Hubbard, Ohio 44425
(216) 534-1133

Streator Dependable Manufacturing Company
410 W. Broadway Street
Streator, Illinois 61364
(815) 672-0551

Crane Controls

Telemotive Product Group
Dynascan Corporation
6460 W. Cortland Street
Chicago, Illinois 60635
(312) 889-9035

Dock Boards (Portable)

Aero Industries
3014 W. Morris Street
Indianapolis, Indiana 46241
(317) 244-2434

Copperloy Corporation
8903 E. Pleasant Valley Road
Cleveland, Ohio 44131
(216) 524-7420

Langsenkamp Company
P.O. Box 1106
Indianapolis, Indiana 46206
(317) 636-4321

MAGCOA
P.O. Box 1227
Aberdeen, North Carolina 28315
(919) 944-2167

Magline, Incorporated
500 Maple Road
Pinconning, Michigan 48650
(517) 879-2411

Dock Levelers

Beacon Machinery, Incorporated
8025 South Broadway Street
St. Louis, Missouri 63111
(314) 631-5000

Globe Wayne Products
Dresser Crane Hoist & Tower Division
Dresser Industries, Incorporated
Muskegon, Michigan 49443
(616) 733-0821

Kelley Company, Incorporated
6720 N. Teutonia Avenue
Milwaukee, Wisconsin 53209
(414) 352-1000

The McGuire Company, Incorporated
P.O. Box 636
Hudson, New York 12534
(518) 828-7652

Rite Hite Corporation
9019 N. Deerwood Drive
Milwaukee, Wisconsin 53223
(414) 355-2600

Dock Lights

The McGuire Company Incorporated
P.O. Box 636
Hudson, New York 12534
(518) 828-7652

Phoenix Products Company, Incorporated
4705 N. 27th Street
Milwaukee, Wisconsin 53209
(414) 871-1680

Dock Shelters

Airlocke Dock Seal
Division of O'Neal Tarpaulin Company
549 W. Indianola Avenue
Youngstown, Ohio 44511
(216) 788-6504

Frommelt Industries, Incorporated
465 Huff Street
P.O. Box 1200
Dubuque, Iowa 52001
(800) 553-4834

The McGuire Company, Incorporated
P.O. Box 636
Hudson, New York 12534
(518) 828-7652

Rite-Hite Corporation
9019 N. Deerwood Drive
Milwaukee, Wisconsin 53223
(414) 355-2600

Forklift Tires

Bearcat Tire Company
5201 West 65th Street
Chicago, Illinois 60638
(312) 458-7100

Firestone Tire & Rubber Company
1200 Firestone Parkway
Akron, Ohio 44317
(216) 379-6614

Forklift Truck Attachments

Basiloid Products Corporation
312 N. East Street
Elnora, Indiana 47529
(812) 692-5511

Cascade Corporation
P.O. Box 25240
Portland, Oregon 97225
(503) 666-1511

HMC Attachments Company
Division of Missouri Research Labs, Incorporated
3800 Highway 40, P.O. Box 876
St. Charles, Missouri 63301
(800) 325-8086

Little Giant Products, Incorporated
1600 N.E. Adams Street
Peoria, Illinois 61601
(309) 673-9091
(800) 477-2266
(800) 322-2285

Long Reach Manufacturing Company
Division of Anderson, Clayton & Company Incorporated
P.O. Box 45069
Houston, Texas 77245
(713) 433-9861

Forklift Truck Hour Meters

Engler Instrument Company
250 Culver Avenue
Jersey City, New Jersey 07305
(201) 332-5353

The Service Recorder Company
Division of Sycon Corporation
P.O. Box 491
Marion, Ohio 43302
(614) 382-5771

Guided Vehicles

Barrett Electronics Corporation
Industrial Truck Division
630 Dundee Road
Northbrook, Illinois 60062
(312) 272-2300

Portec, Incorporated
Pathfinder Division
47520 Westinghouse Drive
Fremont, California 94538
(415) 490-3700

Industrial Robots

Auto-Place Incorporated
1401 E. 14 Mile Road
Troy, Michigan 48084
(313) 585-5972

General Electric Company
1 River Road Building 23
Room 210
Schenectady, New York 12345
(518) 385-2355

Unimation Incorporated
Shelter Rock Lane
Danbury, Connecticut 06810
(203) 744-1800

Industrial Truck Batteries, Chargers and Connectors

Anderson Power Products, Incorporated
145 Newton Street
Boston, Massachusetts 02135
(617) 787-5880

C & D Batteries, An Allied Company
3043 Walton Road
Plymouth Meeting, Pennsylvania 19462
(215) 828-9000

Exide Company

101 Gilbralter Road
Horsham, Pennsylvania 19044
(215) 674-9500

General Battery Corporation
P.O. Box 1262
Reading, Pennsylvania 19603
(215) 378-0500

Gould, Incorporated
Industrial Battery Division
2050 Cabot Boulevard West
Landhorne, Pennsylvania 19047
(215) 752-0555

Hobart Brothers Company
Power Systems Division
1177 Trade Road East
Troy, Ohio 45373
(513) 339-6011

KW Battery Company
3555 Howard Street
Skokie, Illinois 60076
(312) 982-8346

LaMarche Manufacturing Company
106 Bradrock Drive
Des Plaines, Illinois 60018
(312) 299-1188

Industrial Trucks and Related Equipment

Allis-Chalmers Corporation
Industrial Truck Division
21800 S. Cicero Avenue
Matteson, Illinois 60443
(312) 747-5151

Baker Material Handling Corporation
5000 Tiedeman Road
Cleveland, Ohio 44144
(216) 433-7000

Caterpillar Tractor Company
100 N.E. Adams Street
Peoria, Illinois 61629
(309) 675-5175

Clark Equipment Company
Industrial Truck Division
525 N. 24th Street
Battle Creek, Michigan 49016
(616) 966-4200

Crown Lift Trucks Company
New Bremen, Ohio 45869
(419) 629-2311

Datsun Forklift Division
Nissan Industrial Equipment Company
2900 Datsun Drive
P.O. Box 161404
Memphis, Tennessee 38116
(901) 396-5170

Drott Manufacturing Company
Division of J. I. Case Company
Wassau, Wisconsin 54401
(715) 359-6511

Drexel Industries, Incorporated
P.O. Box 248
Horsham, Pennsylvania 19044
(215) 672-2200

Eaton Corporation
Industrial Truck Division
11000 Roosevelt Boulevard
Philadelphia, Pennsylvania 19115
(215) 698-6000

The Elwell-Parker Electric Company
4205 St. Clair Avenue
Cleveland, Ohio 44103
(216) 881-6200

Gerlinger Industries Corporation
2690 Blossom Drive N.E.
P.O. Box 2008
Salem, Oregon 97308
(503) 399-2634

Grove Manufacturing Company Incorporated
Division of Kidde, Incorporated
P.O. Box 21
Shady Grove, Pennsylvania 17256
(717) 597-8121

Hyster Company
P.O. Box 2902
Portland, Oregon 97208
(503) 280-7288

Komatsu Forklifts (USA), Incorporated
14815 Firestone Boulevard
La Mirada, California 90637
(714) 994-4913

Lull Engineering Company, Incorporated
3045 Highway 13
St. Paul, Minnesota 55121
(612) 454-4300

Massey-Ferguson Industrial & Construction Machinery Company
Massey-Ferguson, Incorporated
1901 Bell Avenue
Des Moines, Iowa 50315
(515) 247-2011

Mitsubishi International Corporation
Fork Lift Truck Group
1000 West Thorndale Avenue
Elk Grove Village, Illinois 60007
(312) 595-9400

Pettibone Mercury Corporation
Division of Pettibone Corporation
4700 W. Division Street
Chicago, Illinois 60651
(312) 772-9300

The Raymond Corporation
40 Madison Street
Green, New York 13778
(607) 656-2311

Schreck Industries, Incorporated
14675 Foltz Parkway
P.O. Box 36008
Strongsville, Ohio 44136
(216) 238-8500

Taylor Machine Works, Incorporated
P.O. Box 150
Louisville, Mississippi 39339
(601) 773-3421

Towmotor Corporation
Subsidiary of Caterpillar Tractor Company
7800 Tyler Boulevard
Mentor, Ohio 44060
(800) 528-6050

Intraplant Vehicles

Cushman/OMC Lincoln
Division of Outboard Marine Corporation
900 N. 21st Street
P.O. Box 82409
Lincoln, Nebraska 68501
(402) 435-7208

Taylor-Dunn Manufacturing Company
P.O. Box 4240-M
Anaheim, California 92803
(714) 956-4040

Knock-Down Tiering Racks

Cerco Stak-Pal Corporation
1051 Old Lindale Road
P.O. Box 1026
Rome, Georgia 30161
(404) 232-6533

Jarke Corporation
6333 W. Howard Street
Niles, Illinois 60648
(312) 647-9633

Tier-Rack Corporation
706 Chestnut Street
St. Louis, Missouri 63101
(314) 231-5553

Lifters, Scales, Grabs, and Hoists

Anver Corporation
73 Pond Street
Waltham, Massachusetts 02154
(617) 899-7272

Bunting Magnetics Company
500 South Spencer Avenue
Newton, Kansas 67114
(316) 284-2020

The Caldwell Company
5045 26th Avenue
Rockford, Illinois 61125
(815) 226-5667

Crane Hoist Engineering Corporation
Subsidiary of Acco Industries, Incorporated
12140 Bellflower Boulevard
Downey, California 90241
(213) 773-2404

Detroit Hoist & Crane Company
P.O. Box 686
Warren, Michigan 48090
(313) 268-2600

Eriez Magnetics Company
467 Magnet Drive
Erie, Pennsylvania 16514
(814) 833-9881

Harnischfeger Corporation
P.O. Box 310
Milwaukee, Wisconsin 53201
(414) 671-4400

Ingersoll-Rand Company
Woodcliff Lake, New Jersey 07675
(201) 573-0123

MAGCOA
P.O. Box 1227
Aberdeen, North Carolina 28315
(919) 944-2167

Mannesmann Demag
P.O. Box 39245
Solon, Ohio 44139
(216) 248-2400

Morse Manufacturing Company, Incorporated
771 W. Manlius Street
P.O. Box 518 MMH
East Syracuse, New York 13057
(315) 437-8475

Weigh-Tronix, Incorporated
1000 N. Armstrong Drive
Fairmont, Minnesota 56031
(507) 238-4461

Materials Handling Equipment and Systems

Airfloat Corporation
1550 McBride Avenue
Decatur, Illinois 62526
(217) 422-8365

Logan Company
A Figgie International Company
P.O. Box 6107
Louisville, Kentucky 40206
(502) 587-1361

Mannesmann Demag
Material Handling Division
P.O. Box 39245
Cleveland (Solon), Ohio 44139
(216) 248-2400

Materials Handling Equipment Division
Jervis B. Webb Company
2619 N. Normandy Avenue
Chicago, Illinois 60635
(312) 889-1670

Mayfran International Company
A Division of Fischer Industries
P.O. Box 43038
Cleveland, Ohio 44143
(216) 461-4100

Munck Systems, Inc.
P.O. Box 9287
Hampton, Virginia 23369
(804) 838-6010

Rapistan Division
Lear Siegler, Incorporated
825 Rapistan Building
Grand Rapids, Michigan 49505
(616) 451-6525

Rexnord, Incorporated
P.O. Box 2022
Milwaukee, Wisconsin 53201
(414) 643-3000

Richards Wilcox Manufacturing Company
430 Third Street
Aurora, Illinois 60507
(312) 897-6951

SI Handling Systems, Incorporated
Easton, Pennsylvania 18042
(215) 252-7321

Stanley-Vidmar
Division of the Stanley Works
11 Grammes Road
Allentown, Pennsylvania 18103
(215) 797-6600

Taylor & Gaskin Incorporated
Conveyor Systems Division
6440 Mack Avenue
Detroit, Michigan 48207
(313) 925-9550

The Triax Company
Subsidiary of Webb-Triax Company
1361 Chardon Road
Cleveland, Ohio 44117
(313) 553-1220

Jervis B. Webb Company
Webb Drive
Farmington Hills, Michigan 48018
(313) 553-1220

Z-Loda Corporation
Harp Road
P.O. Box 503
Canastota, New York 13032
(315) 697-3911

Mezzanines and Decking

Borden Metal Products Company
P.O. Box 172
Elizabeth, New Jersey 07207
(201) 352-6410

The Frick-Gallagher Manufacturing Company
201 S. Michigan Avenue
Wellston, Ohio 45692
(614) 384-2121

Hef-T Products Corporation
720-740 Park Avenue
Peoria, Illinois 61603
(800) 447-0875
(309) 685-5777

Packaging Materials

Blocksom & Company
406 Center Street
Michigan City, Indiana 46360
(219) 874-3231

Insta-Foam Products Division
An Indian Head Company
1500 Cedarwood Drive
Joliet, Illinois 60435
(815) 741-6800

Jiffy Packaging Corporation
360 Florence Avenue
Hillside, New Jersey 07205
(201) 688-9200

Marsh Stencil Machine Company
707 E. "B" Street
Belleville, Illinois 62222
(618) 234-1122

Mead Paperboard Products Company
Division of the Mead Corporation
801 Main Street, Suite 912
Lynchburg, Virginia 24504
(804) 847-5521

Mobil Plastics Company
Route 31
Macedon, New York 14502
(716) 248-5700

Monarch Marking Systems, Incorporated
Subsidiary of Pitney Bowes Corporation
P.O. Box 608
Dayton, Ohio 45401
(800) 543-6650

Nashua Corporation
Industrial Tape Division
44 Franklin Street
Nashua, New Hampshire 03061
(603) 880-2323

The Orchard Corporation of America
1154 Reco Avenue
St. Louis, Missouri 63126
(314) 822-3880

Paslode Company
Division of Signode Corporation
8080 McCormick Boulevard
Skokie, Illinois 60076
(312) 679-1200

Pitney Bowes Corporation
Wheeler Drive
Stamford, Connecticut 06926
(203) 356-5088

St. Regis Flexible Packaging Company
P.O. Box 225325
Dallas, Texas 75265
(214) 421-4161

Signode Corporation
3610 W. Lake Avenue
Glenview, Illinois 60025
(312) 724-6100

3M Company
3M Center
St. Paul, Minnesota 55144
(612) 733-1110

Toledo Scale Company
Division of Reliance Electric Company
5225 Telegraph Road
Toledo, Ohio 43612
(419) 470-6200

Tri-Wall Containers, Incorporated
7600 Jericho Turnpike
Woodbury, New York 11797
(516) 364-2800

Veeder-Root Company
70 Sargeant Street
Hartford, Connecticut 06102
(203) 527-7201

Weber Marking Systems, Incorporated
711 W. Algonquin Road
Arlington Heights, Illinois 60005
(312) 364-8500

Weigh-Tronix, Incorporated
1000 N. Armstrong Drive
Fairmont, Minnesota 56031
(507) 238-4461

Weldotron Corporation
1532 S. Washington Avenue
Piscataway, New Jersey 08854
(201) 752-6700

Palletizing Adhesives

H. B. Fuller Company
2400 Kasota Avenue
St. Paul, Minnesota 55108
(612) 645-3401

Pallets

Hinchcliff Products Company
20784 Westwood Drive
Cleveland, Ohio 44136
(216) 238-5200

Pallet Storage Racks

Equipment Manufacturing Incorporated (EMI)
21554 Hoover Road
Detroit, Michigan 48205
(313) 536-5070

Frazier Industrial Company
Long Valley, New Jersey 07853
(201) 876-3001

Interlake, Incorporated
Material Handling Storage Products Division
100 Tower Drive
Burr Ridge, Illinois 60521
(312) 789-0333

Palmer-Shile Company
16000 Fullerton Street
Detroit, Michigan 48227
(313) 836-4400

Paltier Corporation
c/o Lyon Metal Products, Incorporated
P.O. Box 671
Aurora, Illinois 60507
(219) 872-7238

Ridg-U-Rak, Incorporated
120 S. Lake Street
North East, Pennsylvania 16428
(814) 725-8751

Sturdi-Bilt
Division of Unarco Industries, Incorporated
332 S. Michigan Avenue
Chicago, Illinois 60604
(312) 341-1234

The Triax Company
Subsidiary of Webb-Triax Company
1361 Chardon Road
Cleveland, Ohio 44117
(313) 553-1220

Unarco Materials Storage Company
Division of Unarco Industries, Incorporated
332 S. Michigan Avenue
Chicago, Illinois 60604
(312) 341-1234

Plastics Pallets

Amoco Chemicals Corporation
Plastics Division
200 E. Randolph Street
Chicago, Illinois 60601
(312) 856-3200

Portable Shrink Guns

Gloucester Engineering Company
Shrinkfast Division
P.O. Box 900
Gloucester, Massachusetts 01930
(617) 281-1800

Shrink and Stretch Wrap Packaging Equipment and Supplies

E. I. du Pont de Nemours & Company
1007 Market Street
Wilmington, Delaware 19898
(302) 774-2421

Lantech, Incorporated
11000 Bluegrass Parkway
Louisville, Kentucky 40299
(502) 267-4200

Oven Systems, Incorporated
New Berlin, Wisconsin 53151
(414) 786-2000

Signode Corporation
3610 W. Lake Avenue
Glenview, Illinois 60025
(312) 724-6100

Weldotron Company
1532 So. Washington Avenue
Piscataway, New Jersey 08854
(201) 752-6700

Tiering Racks

Jarke Corporation
6333 W. Howard Street
Niles, Illinois 60648
(312) 647-9633

Paltier Corporation
c/o Lyon Metal Products, Incorporated
P.O. Box 671
Aurora, Illinois 60507
(219) 872-7238

Tier-Rack Corporation
706 Chestnut Street
St. Louis, Missouri 63101
(314) 231-5553

Trash Handling

Dempster Systems, Incorporated
Subsidiary of Technology Incorporated
Springdale Avenue
P.O. Box 3127
Knoxville, Tennessee 37917
(615) 637-3711

Warehousing Equipment

Morse Manufacturing Company, Incorporated
771 W. Manlius Street
P.O. Box 518 MMH
East Syracuse, New York 13057
(315) 437-8475

Nutting Truck & Caster Company
1201 W. Division Street
Faribault, Minnesota 55021
(507) 334-4333

Otis Elevator Company
1 Farm Springs Road
Farmington, Connecticut 06032
(203) 677-6000

Overhead Door Corporation
6750 LBJ Freeway
P.O. Box 400150
Dallas, Texas 75240
(214) 233-6611

Stokvis Multiton Corporation
520 W. John Street
Hicksville, New York 11801
(516) 822-7400

Tennant Company
701 N. Lilac Drive
Minneapolis, Minnesota 55440
(612) 540-1200

Toledo Scale Company
Division of Reliance Electric Corporation
5225 Telegraph Road
Toledo, Ohio 43612
(419) 470-6200

Weight-Tronix, Incorporated
1000 N. Armstrong Drive
Fairmont, Minnesota 56031
(507) 238-4461

Weighing Equipment

Howe Richardson Scale Company
680 Van Houten Avenue
Clifton, New Jersey 07015
(201) 471-3400

Wheel Chocks and Standards

Copperloy Corporation
8903 E. Pleasant Valley Road
Cleveland, Ohio 44131
(216) 524-7420

McQuire Company, Incorporated
P.O. Box 636
Hudson, New York 12534
(518) 828-7653

Rowe-Bumpers, Incorporated
2534 Detroit Avenue
Cleveland, Ohio 44113
(216) 621-9847

Appendix H
Manufacturers and Suppliers of Models and Layout/Materials

Chartpak
Avery Products Corporation
One River Road
Leeds, Massachusetts 01053
(413) 584-5446

Creative Industries of Detroit
3080 E. Outer Drive
Detroit, Michigan 48234
(313) 366-3020

Design Engineering Company
600 Stokes Avenue
Trenton, New Jersey 08638
(609) 882-8800

Industrial Pattern Works, Inc.
3170 Roosevelt Avenue
York, Pennsylvania 17404
(717) 764-4920

Model Planning Company, Inc.
Box A264
Blairstown, New Jersey 07825
(201) 362-8112

Planprint Company, Inc.
68 King Road
Chalfont, Pennsylvania 18914
(215) 249-3501

Index